Microsoft Office 97
Visual Basic® Language Reference

Microsoft® Visual Basic® for Applications and Shared Libraries References

Microsoft® Press

PUBLISHED BY
Microsoft Press
A Division of Microsoft Corporation
One Microsoft Way
Redmond, Washington 98052-6399

Library of Congress Cataloging-in-Publication Data
Microsoft Office 97/Visual Basic language reference / Microsoft Corporation.
p. cm.
ISBN 1-57231-339-0
1. Integrated software. 2. Microsoft Office. 3. Microsoft Visual Basic. I. Microsoft Corporation.
QA76.76.I57M455 1997
005.369--dc21 97-3521
CIP

Printed and bound in the United States of America.

1 2 3 4 5 6 7 8 9 Rand-T 2 1 0 9 8 7

Distributed to the book trade in Canada by Macmillan of Canada, a division of Canada Publishing Corporation.

A CIP catalogue record for this book is available from the British Library.

Microsoft Press books are available through booksellers and distributors worldwide. For further information about international editions, contact your local Microsoft Corporation office. Or contact Microsoft Press International directly at fax (206) 936-7329.

Part Number: 097-0001685

Acquisitions Editor: Casey D. Doyle
Project Editor: Maureen Williams Zimmerman

Contents

Volume 5: Microsoft Visual Basic for Applications and Shared Libraries Reference

Microsoft Visual Basic for Applications Language Reference

– Operator

Description

Used to find the difference between two numbers or to indicate the negative value of a numeric expression.

Syntax 1

result = *number1*–*number2*

Syntax 2

–*number*

The – operator syntax has these parts

Part	Description
result	Required; any numeric variable.
number	Required; any numeric expression.
number1	Required; any numeric expression.
number2	Required; any numeric expression.

Remarks

In Syntax 1, the – operator is the arithmetic subtraction operator used to find the difference between two numbers. In Syntax 2, the – operator is used as the unary negation operator to indicate the negative value of an expression.

The data type of *result* is usually the same as that of the most precise expression. The order of precision, from least to most precise, is **Byte**, **Integer**, **Long**, **Single**, **Double**, **Currency**, and **Decimal**. The following are exceptions to this order

If	Then *result* is
Subtraction involves a **Single** and a **Long**,	converted to a **Double**.
The data type of *result* is a **Long**, **Single**, or **Date** variant that overflows its legal range,	converted to a **Variant** containing a **Double**.
The data type of *result* is a **Byte** variant that overflows its legal range,	converted to an **Integer** variant.
The data type of *result* is an **Integer** variant that overflows its legal range,	converted to a **Long** variant.
Subtraction involves a **Date** and any other data type,	a **Date**.
Subtraction involves two **Date** expressions,	a **Double**.

One or both expressions are **Null** expressions, *result* is **Null**. If an expression is **Empty**, it is treated as 0.

Note The order of precision used by addition and subtraction is not the same as the order of precision used by multiplication.

See Also

Operator precedence.

Example

This example uses the – operator to calculate the difference between two numbers.

```
Dim MyResult
MyResult = 4 - 2                        ' Returns 2.
MyResult = 459.35 - 334.90              ' Returns 124.45.
```

#Const Directive

Description

Used to define conditional compiler constants for Visual Basic.

Syntax

#Const *constname* = *expression*

The **#Const** compiler directive syntax has these parts

Part	Description
constname	Required; **Variant** (**String**). Name of the constant; follows standard variable naming conventions.
expression	Required. Literal, other conditional compiler constant, or any combination that includes any or all arithmetic or logical operators except **Is**.

Remarks

Conditional compiler constants are always **Private** to the module in which they appear. It is not possible to create **Public** compiler constants using the **#Const** directive. **Public** compiler constants can only be created in the user interface.

Only conditional compiler constants and literals can be used in *expression*. Using a standard constant defined with **Const**, or using a constant that is undefined, causes an error to occur. Conversely, constants defined using the **#Const** keyword can only be used for conditional compilation.

Conditional compiler constants are always evaluated at the module level, regardless of their placement in code.

See Also

#If...Then...#Else directive, **Const** statement.

Specifics (Microsoft Access)

In Microsoft Access, you can define a public conditional compiler constant in the Declarations section of a module. A public compiler constant is applicable to all modules in the current database, but not in any other database.

You can also declare a public compiler constant by clicking **Options** on the **Tools** menu, then clicking the **Advanced** tab. Enter the constant in the **Conditional Compilation Arguments** box.

For example, you might enter the following expression into the **Conditional Compilation Arguments** box.

```
conDebug = 1
```

You can use a public compiler constant in code in any module. For example, you can create an **#If...Then...#Else** construct to optionally run debug code.

```
#If conDebug = 1 Then
    .       ' Run debug code.
    .
    .
#Else
    .       ' Run streamlined code.
    .
    .
#End If
```

To create multiple public conditional compilation constants, declare them on separate lines in the Declaration section. In the **Conditional Compilation Arguments** box, separate them with colons. For example, you can enter the following conditional compilation constants in the **Conditional Compilation Arguments** box.

```
conActiveLanguage = 1 : conDebug = 1
```

You can use a logical operator to include both constants in an **#If...Then...#Else** construct. In the following example, the first segment of code runs only if both constants are currently equal to 1, so that the expression containing the constants is true.

```
#If (conActiveLanguage = 1 And conDebug = 1) Then
    .       ' Run debug code for the active language version.
    .
    .
#Else
    .       ' Run another code segment.
    .
    .
#End If
```

If either or both constants have a different value, then the code in the **#Else** portion of the construct runs. To change which block of code runs, you can simply change the values of the constants.

Notes

- A conditional compilation constant is always evaluated with a text-based string comparison method. This evaluation is equivalent to having an **Option Compare Text** statement in the module and occurs even if the module contains an **Option Compare Database** statement.

- When writing code for conditional compilation, it may be less confusing to view one procedure at a time rather than all procedures in the module. To change how you view your code, click **Options** on the **Tools** menu, then click the **Module** tab. Under **Code View**, clear the **Full Module View** check box.

Example

This example uses the **#Const** directive to declare conditional compiler constants for use in **#If...#Else...#End If** constructs.

```
#Const DebugVersion = 1        ' Will evaluate true in #If block.
```

#If...Then...#Else Directive

Description

Conditionally compiles selected blocks of Visual Basic code.

Syntax

#If *expression* **Then**
    statements
[**#ElseIf** *expression-n* **Then**
    [*elseifstatements*]]
[**#Else**
    [*elsestatements*]]
#End If

The **#If...Then...#Else** directive syntax has these parts

Part	Description
expression	Required. Any expression, consisting exclusively of one or more conditional compiler constants, literals, and operators, that evaluates to **True** or **False**.
statements	Required. Visual Basic program lines or compiler directives that are evaluated if the associated expression is **True**.
expression-n	Optional. Any expression, consisting exclusively of one or more conditional compiler constants, literals, and operators, that evaluates to **True** or **False**.
elseifstatements	Optional. One or more program lines or compiler directives that are evaluated if *expression-n* is **True**.
elsestatements	Optional. One or more program lines or compiler directives that are evaluated if no previous *expression* or *expression-n* is **True**.

Remarks

The behavior of the **#If...Then...#Else** directive is the same as the **If...Then...Else** statement, except that there is no single-line form of the **#If**, **#Else**, **#ElseIf**, and **#End If** directives; that is, no other code can appear on the same line as any of the directives. Conditional compilation is typically used to compile the same program for different platforms. It is also used to prevent debugging code from appearing in an executable file. Code excluded during conditional compilation is completely omitted from the final executable file, so it has no size or performance effect.

Regardless of the outcome of any evaluation, all expressions are evaluated. Therefore, all constants used in expressions must be defined—any undefined constant evaluates as **Empty**.

Note The **Option Compare** statement does not affect expressions in **#If** and **#ElseIf** statements. Expressions in a conditional-compiler directive are always evaluated with **Option Compare Text**.

See Also

#Const directive, **If...Then...Else** statement.

Example

This example references conditional compiler constants in an **#If...Then...#Else** construct to determine whether to compile certain statements.

```
' If Mac evaluates as true, do the statements following the #If.
#If Mac Then
    '. Place exclusively Mac  statements here.
    '.
    '.
' Otherwise, if it is a 32-bit Windows program, do this:
#ElseIf Win32 Then
    '. Place exclusively 32-bit Windows statements here.
    '.
    '.
' Otherwise, if it is neither, do this:
#Else
    '. Place other platform statements here.
    '.
    '.
#End If
```

& Operator

Description

Used to force string concatenation of two expressions.

Syntax

result = *expression1* **&** *expression2*

The **&** operator syntax has these parts

Part	Description
result	Required; any **String** or **Variant** variable.
expression1	Required; any expression.
expression2	Required; any expression.

Remarks

If an *expression* is not a string, it is converted to a **String** variant. The data type of *result* is **String** if both expressions are string expressions; otherwise, *result* is a **String** variant. If both expressions are **Null**, *result* is **Null**. However, if only one *expression* is **Null**, that expression is treated as a zero-length string (" ") when concatenated with the other expression. Any expression that is **Empty** is also treated as a zero-length string.

See Also

Operator precedence.

Example

This example uses the **&** operator to force string concatenation.

```
Dim MyStr
MyStr = "Hello" & " World"              ' Returns "Hello World".
MyStr = "Check " & 123 & " Check"       ' Returns "Check 123 Check".
```

* Operator

Description

Used to multiply two numbers.

Syntax

result = *number1***number2*

The * operator syntax has these parts

Part	Description
result	Required; any numeric variable.
number1	Required; any numeric expression.
number2	Required; any numeric expression.

Remarks

The data type of *result* is usually the same as that of the most precise expression. The order of precision, from least to most precise, is **Byte**, **Integer**, **Long**, **Single**, **Currency**, **Double**, and **Decimal**. The following are exceptions to this order

If	Then *result* is
Multiplication involves a **Single** and a **Long**,	converted to a **Double**.
The data type of *result* is a **Long**, **Single**, or **Date** variant that overflows its legal range,	converted to a **Variant** containing a **Double**.
The data type of *result* is a **Byte** variant that overflows its legal range,	converted to an **Integer** variant.
the data type of *result* is an **Integer** variant that overflows its legal range,	converted to a **Long** variant.

If one or both expressions are **Null** expressions, *result* is **Null**. If an expression is **Empty**, it is treated as 0.

Note The order of precision used by multiplication is not the same as the order of precision used by addition and subtraction.

See Also

Operator precedence.

Example

This example uses the * operator to multiply two numbers.

```
Dim MyValue
MyValue = 2 * 2                       ' Returns 4.
MyValue = 459.35 * 334.90             ' Returns 153836.315.
```

/ Operator

Description

Used to divide two numbers and return a floating-point result.

Syntax

result = *number1*/*number2*

The / operator syntax has these parts

Part	Description
result	Required; any numeric variable.
number1	Required; any numeric expression.
number2	Required; any numeric expression.

Remarks

The data type of *result* is usually a **Double** or a **Double** variant. The following are exceptions to this rule

If	Then *result* is
Both expressions are **Byte**, **Integer**, or **Single** expressions,	a **Single** unless it overflows its legal range; in which case, an error occurs.
Both expressions are **Byte**, **Integer**, or **Single** variants,	a **Single** variant unless it overflows its legal range; in which case, *result* is a **Variant** containing a **Double**.
Division involves a **Decimal** and any other data type,	a **Decimal** data type.

One or both expressions are **Null** expressions, *result* is **Null**. Any expression that is **Empty** is treated as 0.

See Also

Operator precedence.

Example

This example uses the **/** operator to perform floating-point division.

```
Dim MyValue
MyValue = 10 / 4          ' Returns 2.5.
MyValue = 10 / 3          ' Returns 3.333333.
```

\ Operator

Description

Used to divide two numbers and return an integer result.

Syntax

result = *number1******number2*

The **** operator syntax has these parts

Part	Description
result	Required; any numeric variable.
number1	Required; any numeric expression.
number2	Required; any numeric expression.

Remarks

Before division is performed, the numeric expressions are rounded to **Byte**, **Integer**, or **Long** expressions.

Usually, the data type of *result* is a **Byte**, **Byte** variant, **Integer**, **Integer** variant, **Long**, or **Long** variant, regardless of whether *result* is a whole number. Any fractional portion is truncated. However, if any expression is **Null**, *result* is **Null**. Any expression that is **Empty** is treated as 0.

See Also

Operator precedence.

Example

This example uses the **** operator to perform integer division.

```
Dim MyValue
MyValue = 11 \ 4          ' Returns 2.
MyValue = 9 \ 3           ' Returns 3.
MyValue = 100 \ 3         ' Returns 33.
```

^ Operator

Description

Used to raise a number to the power of an exponent.

Syntax

result = *number*^*exponent*

The ^ operator syntax has these parts

Part	Description
result	Required; any numeric variable.
number	Required; any numeric expression.
exponent	Required; any numeric expression.

Remarks

A *number* can be negative only if *exponent* is an integer value. When more than one exponentiation is performed in a single expression, the ^ operator is evaluated as it is encountered from left to right.

Usually, the data type of *result* is a **Double** or a **Variant** containing a **Double**. However, if either *number* or *exponent* is a **Null** expression, *result* is **Null**.

See Also

Operator precedence.

Example

This example uses the ^ operator to raise a number to the power of an exponent.

```
Dim MyValue
MyValue = 2 ^ 2            ' Returns 4.
MyValue = 3 ^ 3 ^ 3        ' Returns 19683.
MyValue = (-5) ^ 3         ' Returns -125.
```

+ Operator

Description

Used to sum two numbers.

Syntax

result = *expression1*+*expression2*

The + operator syntax has these parts

Part	Description
result	Required; any numeric variable.
expression1	Required; any expression.
expression2	Required; any expression.

Remarks

When you use the + operator, you may not be able to determine whether addition or string concatenation will occur. Use the **&** operator for concatenation to eliminate ambiguity and provide self-documenting code.

If at least one expression is not a **Variant**, the following rules apply

If	Then
Both expressions are numeric data types (**Byte**, **Boolean**, **Integer**, **Long**, **Single**, **Double**, **Date**, **Currency**, or **Decimal**),	Add.
Both expressions are **String**,	Concatenate.
One expression is a numeric data type and the other is any **Variant** except **Null**,	Add.
One expression is a **String** and the other is any **Variant** except **Null**,	Concatenate.
One expression is an **Empty Variant**,	Return the remaining expression unchanged as *result*.
One expression is a numeric data type and the other is a **String**,	A `Type mismatch` error occurs.
Either expression is **Null**,	*result* is **Null**.

If both expressions are **Variant** expressions, the following rules apply

If	Then
Both **Variant** expressions are numeric,	Add.
Both **Variant** expressions are strings,	Concatenate.
One **Variant** expression is numeric and the other is a string,	Add.

For simple arithmetic addition involving only expressions of numeric data types, the data type of *result* is usually the same as that of the most precise expression. The order of precision, from least to most precise, is **Byte**, **Integer**, **Long**, **Single**, **Double**, **Currency**, and **Decimal**. The following are exceptions to this order

If	Then *result* is
A **Single** and a **Long** are added,	a **Double**.
The data type of *result* is a **Long**, **Single**, or **Date** variant that overflows its legal range,	converted to a **Double** variant.

(continued)

The data type of *result* is a **Byte** variant that overflows its legal range,	converted to an **Integer** variant.
The data type of *result* is an **Integer** variant that overflows its legal range,	converted to a **Long** variant.
A **Date** is added to any data type,	a **Date**.

If one or both expressions are **Null** expressions, *result* is **Null**. If both expressions are **Empty**, *result* is an **Integer**. However, if only one expression is **Empty**, the other expression is returned unchanged as *result*.

Note The order of precision used by addition and subtraction is not the same as the order of precision used by multiplication.

See Also

Operator precedence.

Example

This example uses the **+** operator to sum numbers. The **+** operator can also be used to concatenate strings. However, to eliminate ambiguity, you should use the **&** operator instead. If the components of an expression created with the **+** operator include both strings and numerics, the arithmetic result is assigned. If the components are exclusively strings, the strings are concatenated.

```
Dim MyNumber, Var1, Var2
MyNumber = 2 + 2  ' Returns 4.
MyNumber = 4257.04 + 98112     ' Returns 102369.04.

Var1 = "34": Var2 = 6          ' Initialize mixed variables.
MyNumber = Var1 + Var2         ' Returns 40.

Var1 = "34": Var2 = "6"        ' Initialize variables with strings.
MyNumber = Var1 + Var2         ' Returns "346" (string concatenation).
```

Abs Function

Description

Returns a value of the same type that is passed to it specifying the absolute value of a number.

Syntax

Abs(*number*)

The required *number* argument can be any valid numeric expression. If *number* contains **Null**, **Null** is returned; if it is an uninitialized variable, zero is returned.

Remarks

The absolute value of a number is its unsigned magnitude. For example, `ABS(-1)` and `ABS(1)` both return 1.

See Also

Sgn function.

Example

This example uses the **Abs** function to compute the absolute value of a number.

```
Dim MyNumber
MyNumber = Abs(50.3)        ' Returns 50.3.
MyNumber = Abs(-50.3)       ' Returns 50.3.
```

Activate, Deactivate Events

Applies To

UserForm object.

Description

The Activate event occurs when an object becomes the active window. The Deactivate event occurs when an object is no longer the active window.

Syntax

Private Sub *object*_**Activate( )**
Private Sub *object*_**Deactivate( )**

The *object* placeholder represents an object expression that evaluates to an object in the Applies To list.

Remarks

An object can become active by using the **Show** method in code.

The Activate event can occur only when an object is visible. A **UserForm** loaded with **Load** isn't visible unless you use the **Show** method.

The Activate and Deactivate events occur only when you move the focus within an application. Moving the focus to or from an object in another application doesn't trigger either event.

The Deactivate event doesn't occur when unloading an object.

Example

The following code uses two **UserForm** objects: UserForm1 and UserForm2. Copy these procedures into the UserForm1 module, then add UserForm2. UserForm1's caption is created in its Activate event procedure. When the user clicks the client area of UserForm1, UserForm2 is loaded, and shown, triggering UserForm1's Deactivate event, changing their captions.

```
' Activate event for UserForm1.
Private Sub UserForm_Activate()
   UserForm1.Caption = "Click my client area"
End Sub

' Click event for UserForm1.
Private Sub UserForm_Click()
   Load UserForm2
   UserForm2.StartUpPosition = 3
   UserForm2.Show
End Sub

' Deactivate event for UserForm1.
Private Sub UserForm_Deactivate()
   UserForm1.Caption = "I just lost the focus!"
   UserForm2.Caption = "Focus just left UserForm1 and came to me"
End Sub
```

Add Method

Applies To

Collection object.

Description

Adds a member to a **Collection** object.

Syntax

object.**Add** ***item***, ***key***, ***before***, ***after***

The **Add** method syntax has the following object qualifier and named arguments

Part	Description
object	Required. An object expression that evaluates to an object in the Applies To list.
item	Required. An expression of any type that specifies the member to add to the collection.
key	Optional. A unique string expression that specifies a key string that can be used, instead of a positional index, to access a member of the collection.
before	Optional. An expression that specifies a relative position in the collection. The member to be added is placed in the collection ***before*** the member identified by the ***before*** argument. If a numeric expression, ***before*** must be a number from 1 to the value of the collection's **Count** property. If a string expression, ***before*** must correspond to the ***key*** specified when the member being referred to was added to the collection. You can specify a ***before*** position or an ***after*** position, but not both.

(continued)

Part	Description
after	Optional. An expression that specifies a relative position in the collection. The member to be added is placed in the collection after the member identified by the ***after*** argument. If numeric, ***after*** must be a number from 1 to the value of the collection's **Count** property. If a string, ***after*** must correspond to the ***key*** specified when the member referred to was added to the collection. You can specify a ***before*** position or an ***after*** position, but not both.

Remarks

Whether the ***before*** or ***after*** argument is a string expression or numeric expression, it must refer to an existing member of the collection, or an error occurs.

An error also occurs if a specified ***key*** duplicates the ***key*** for an existing member of the collection.

See Also

Item method, **Remove** method.

Specifics (Microsoft Access)

Items added to a user-defined collection are automatically indexed. You can refer to an individual item by this index. For example, if you have a collection `colThings` that contains four objects, you can refer to the third item in the collection with the expression `colThings(3)`.

Note When you add items to a **Collection** object, they are automatically indexed beginning with the number 1. Therefore, when you enumerate a **Collection** object, keep in mind that the index begins at 1. This may be different from built-in collections, which usually are indexed beginning with 0.

When you add an object to a user-defined collection, you can also specify a custom key for that object in addition to the automatic index. In subsequent references to the object, you can refer to the custom key. For example, you can add an object `objMine` with the following key.

```
colThings.Add Item := objMine, key := ("A")
```

Subsequently you can refer to this particular object in the collection either as `colThings(A)`, or by its numeric index.

Example

This example uses the **Add** method to add `Inst` objects (instances of a class called `Class1` containing a **Public** variable `InstanceName`) to a collection called `MyClasses`. To see how this works, insert a class module and declare a public variable called `InstanceName` at module level of `Class1` (type **Public** `InstanceName`) to hold the names of each instance. Leave the default name as `Class1`. Copy and paste the following code into the Form_Load event procedure of a form module.

```
Dim MyClasses As New Collection        ' Create a Collection object.
Dim Num As Integer                     ' Counter for individualizing keys.
Dim Msg
Dim TheName                            ' Holder for names user enters.
Do
   Dim Inst As New Class1              ' Create a new instance of Class1.
   Num = Num + 1                       ' Increment Num, then get a name.
   Msg = "Please enter a name for this object." & Chr(13) _
      & "Press Cancel to see names in collection."
   TheName = InputBox(Msg, "Name the Collection Items")
   Inst.InstanceName = TheName         ' Put name in object instance.
   ' If user entered name, add it to the collection.
   If Inst.InstanceName <> "" Then
      ' Add the named object to the collection.
      MyClasses.Add item := Inst, key := CStr(Num)
   End If
   ' Clear the current reference in preparation for next one.
   Set Inst = Nothing
Loop Until TheName = ""
For Each x In MyClasses
   MsgBox x.instancename, , "Instance Name"
Next
```

Example (Extensibility Object Model)

The following example uses the **Add** method to add one standard module to the **VBComponents** collection.

```
Application.VBE.VBProjects(1).VBComponents.Add(vbext_ct_StdModule)
```

And Operator

Description

Used to perform a logical conjunction on two expressions.

Syntax

result = *expression1* **And** *expression2*

The **And** operator syntax has these parts

Part	Description
result	Required; any numeric variable.
expression1	Required; any expression.
expression2	Required; any expression.

Remarks

If both expressions evaluate to **True**, *result* is **True**. If either expression evaluates to **False**, *result* is **False.** The following table illustrates how *result* is determined

If *expression1* is	And *expression2* is	The *result* is
True	**True**	**True**

(continued)

If *expression1* is	And *expression2* is	The *result* is
True	**False**	**False**
True	**Null**	**Null**
False	**True**	**False**
False	**False**	**False**
False	**Null**	**False**
Null	**True**	**Null**
Null	**False**	**False**
Null	**Null**	**Null**

The **And** operator also performs a bitwise comparison of identically positioned bits in two numeric expressions and sets the corresponding bit in *result* according to the following table

If bit in *expression1* is	And bit in *expression2* is	The *result* is
0	0	0
0	1	0
1	0	0
1	1	1

See Also

Operator precedence.

Example

This example uses the **And** operator to perform a logical conjunction on two expressions.

```
Dim A, B, C, D, MyCheck
A = 10: B = 8: C = 6: D = Null           ' Initialize variables.
MyCheck = A > B And B > C                ' Returns True.
MyCheck = B > A And B > C                ' Returns False.
MyCheck = A > B And B > D                ' Returns Null.
MyCheck = A And B                        ' Returns 8 (bitwise comparison).
```

AppActivate Statement

Description

Activates an application window.

Syntax

AppActivate *title*[, *wait*]

The **AppActivate** statement syntax has these named arguments

Part	Description
title	Required. String expression specifying the title in the title bar of the application window you want to activate. The task ID returned by the **Shell** function can be used in place of ***title*** to activate an application.
wait	Optional. **Boolean** value specifying whether the calling application has the focus before activating another. If **False** (default), the specified application is immediately activated, even if the calling application does not have the focus. If **True**, the calling application waits until it has the focus, then activates the specified application.

Remarks

The **AppActivate** statement changes the focus to the named application or window but does not affect whether it is maximized or minimized. Focus moves from the activated application window when the user takes some action to change the focus or close the window. Use the **Shell** function to start an application and set the window style.

In determining which application to activate, ***title*** is compared to the title string of each running application. If there is no exact match, any application whose title string begins with ***title*** is activated. If there is more than one instance of the application named by ***title***, one instance is arbitrarily activated.

See Also

SendKeys statement, **Shell** function.

Example

This example illustrates various uses of the **AppActivate** statement to activate an application window. The **Shell** statements assume the applications are in the paths specified. On the Macintosh, you can use the **MacID** function to specify the application's signature instead of the application's name. The **AppActivate** statement is available with Macintosh System 7.0 or later.

```
Dim MyAppID, ReturnValue
' In Microsoft Windows:
AppActivate "Microsoft Word"                 ' Activate Microsoft
                                             ' Word.

' AppActivate can also use the return value of the Shell function.
MyAppID = Shell("C:\WORD\WINWORD.EXE", 1)    ' Run Microsoft Word.
AppActivate MyAppID                          ' Activate Microsoft
                                             ' Word.

' You can also use the return value of the Shell function.
ReturnValue = Shell("c:\EXCEL\EXCEL.EXE",1)  ' Run Microsoft Excel.
AppActivate ReturnValue                      ' Activate Microsoft
                                             ' Excel.
```

Array Function

Description

Returns a **Variant** containing an array.

Syntax

Array(*arglist*)

The required *arglist* argument is a comma-delimited list of values that are assigned to the elements of the array contained within the **Variant**. If no arguments are specified, an array of zero length is created.

Remarks

The notation used to refer to an element of an array consists of the variable name followed by parentheses containing an index number indicating the desired element. In the following example, the first statement creates a variable named A as a **Variant**. The second statement assigns an array to variable A. The last statement assigns the value contained in the second array element to another variable.

```
Dim A As Variant
A = Array(10,20,30)
B = A(2)
```

The lower bound of an array created using the **Array** function is always zero. Unlike other types of arrays, it is not affected by the lower bound specified with the **Option Base** statement.

Note A **Variant** that is not declared as an array can still contain an array. A **Variant** variable can contain an array of any type, except fixed-length strings and user-defined types. Although a **Variant** containing an array is conceptually different from an array whose elements are of type **Variant**, the array elements are accessed in the same way.

See Also

Def*type* statements, **Dim** statement, **Let** statement, **Option Base** statement, **Variant** data type.

Example

This example uses the **Array** function to return a **Variant** containing an array.

```
Dim MyWeek, MyDay
MyWeek = Array("Mon", "Tue", "Wed", "Thu", "Fri", "Sat", "Sun")
' Return values assume lower bound set to 1 (using Option Base
' statement).
MyDay = MyWeek(2)                    ' MyDay contains "Tue".
MyDay = MyWeek(4)                    ' MyDay contains "Thu".
```

Example (Microsoft Excel)

This example fills the range A1:C5 on Sheet1, Sheet5, and Sheet7 with the contents of the same range on Sheet1.

```
x = Array("Sheet1", "Sheet5", "Sheet7")
Sheets(x).FillAcrossSheets _
   Worksheets("Sheet1").Range("A1:C5")
```

This example consolidates data from Sheet2 and Sheet3 onto Sheet1, using the SUM function.

```
Worksheets("Sheet1").Range("A1").Consolidate _
   sources:=Array("Sheet2!R1C1:R37C6", "Sheet3!R1C1:R37C6"), _
   Function:=xlSum
```

This example adds an array of strings as a custom list.

```
Application.AddCustomList Array("cogs", "sprockets", _
   "widgets", "gizmos")
```

This example hides Chart1, Chart3, and Chart5. Note that in this example, the **Charts** property returns a **Sheets** object instead of a **Charts** object.

```
Charts(Array("Chart1", "Chart3", "Chart5")).Visible = False
```

This example sets the entries in list box one on Dialog1.

```
DialogSheets("Dialog1").ListBoxes(1).List = _
   Array("cogs", "widgets", "sprockets", "gizmos")
```

This example creates a group that includes drawing objects one, three, and five on Sheet1.

```
Set myGroup = Worksheets("Sheet1").DrawingObjects(Array(1, 3, 5)).Group
Worksheets("Sheet1").Activate
myGroup.Select
```

Asc Function

Description

Returns an **Integer** representing the character code corresponding to the first letter in a string.

Syntax

Asc(*string***)**

The required *string* argument is any valid string expression. If the *string* contains no characters, a run-time error occurs.

Remarks

The range for returns is 0–255 on non-DBCS systems, but –32768–32767 on DBCS systems.

Note The **AscB** function is used with byte data contained in a string. Instead of returning the character code for the first character, **AscB** returns the first byte. The **AscW** function returns the Unicode character code except on platforms where Unicode is not supported, in which case, the behavior is identical to the **Asc** function.

See Also

Chr function, Type conversion functions.

Example

This example uses the **Asc** function to return a character code corresponding to the first letter in the string.

```
Dim MyNumber
MyNumber = Asc("A")                          ' Returns 65.
MyNumber = Asc("a")                          ' Returns 97.
MyNumber = Asc("Apple")                      ' Returns 65.
```

Atn Function

Description

Returns a **Double** specifying the arctangent of a number.

Syntax

Atn(*number***)**

The required *number* argument is a **Double** or any valid numeric expression.

Remarks

The **Atn** function takes the ratio of two sides of a right triangle (*number*) and returns the corresponding angle in radians. The ratio is the length of the side opposite the angle divided by the length of the side adjacent to the angle.

The range of the result is –pi/2 to pi/2 radians.

To convert degrees to radians, multiply degrees by pi/180. To convert radians to degrees, multiply radians by 180/pi.

Note **Atn** is the inverse trigonometric function of **Tan**, which takes an angle as its argument and returns the ratio of two sides of a right triangle. Do not confuse **Atn** with the cotangent, which is the simple inverse of a tangent (1/tangent).

See Also

Cos function, **Sin** function, **Tan** function.

Example

This example uses the **Atn** function to calculate the value of pi.

```
Dim pi
pi = 4 * Atn(1)                  ' Calculate the value of pi.
```

Beep Statement

Description

Sounds a tone through the computer's speaker.

Syntax

Beep

Remarks

The frequency and duration of the beep depend on your hardware and system software, and vary among computers.

Example

This example uses the **Beep** statement to sound three consecutive tones through the computer's speaker.

```
Dim I
For I = 1 To 3                        ' Loop 3 times.
   Beep                               ' Sound a tone.
Next I
```

Boolean Data Type

Description

Boolean variables are stored as 16-bit (2-byte) numbers, but they can only be **True** or **False**. **Boolean** variables display as either `True` or `False` (when **Print** is used) or `#TRUE#` or `#FALSE#` (when **Write #** is used). Use the keywords **True** and **False** to assign one of the two states to **Boolean** variables.

When other numeric types are converted to **Boolean** values, 0 becomes **False** and all other values become **True**. When **Boolean** values are converted to other data types, **False** becomes 0 and **True** becomes –1.

See Also

Data type summary, **Def***type* statements, **Integer** data type.

Byte Data Type

Description

Byte variables are stored as single, unsigned, 8-bit (1-byte) numbers ranging in value from 0 to 255.

The **Byte** data type is useful for containing binary data.

See Also

Data type summary, **Def***type* statements, **Integer** data type.

Calendar Property

Description

Returns or sets a value specifying the type of calendar to use with your project.

You can use one of two settings for Calendar

Setting	Value	Description
vbCalGreg	0	Use Gregorian calendar (default).
vbCalHijri	1	Use Hijri calendar.

Remarks

You can only set the Calendar property programmatically. For example, to use the Hijri calendar, use:

```
Calendar = vbCalHijri
```

Call Statement

Description

Transfers control to a **Sub** procedure, **Function** procedure, or dynamic-link library (DLL) procedure.

Syntax

[**Call**] *name* [*argumentlist*]

The **Call** statement syntax has these parts

Part	Description
Call	Optional; keyword. If specified, you must enclose *argumentlist* in parentheses. For example: `Call MyProc(0)`
name	Required. Name of the procedure to call.
argumentlist	Optional. Comma-delimited list of variables, arrays, or expressions to pass to the procedure. Components of *argumentlist* may include the keywords **ByVal** or **ByRef** to describe how the arguments are treated by the called procedure. However, **ByVal** and **ByRef** can be used with **Call** only when calling a DLL procedure.

Remarks

You are not required to use the **Call** keyword when calling a procedure. However, if you use the **Call** keyword to call a procedure that requires arguments, *argumentlist* must be enclosed in parentheses. If you omit the **Call** keyword, you also must omit the parentheses around *argumentlist*. If you use either **Call** syntax to call any intrinsic or user-defined function, the function's return value is discarded.

To pass a whole array to a procedure, use the array name followed by empty parentheses.

See Also

Declare statement, **Function** statement, **Sub** statement.

Specifics (Macintosh)

ByVal and **ByRef** can be used with **Call** when making a call to a Macintosh code resource.

Example

This example illustrates how the **Call** statement is used to transfer control to a **Sub** procedure, an intrinsic function, a dynamic-link library (DLL) procedure, and a procedure in a Macintosh code resource.

```
' Call a Sub procedure.
Call PrintToDebugWindow("Hello World")
' The above statement causes control to be passed to the following
' Sub procedure.
Sub PrintToDebugWindow(AnyString)
   Debug.Print AnyString              ' Print to Debug window.
End Sub

' Call an intrinsic function. The return value of the function is
' discarded.
Call Shell(AppName, 1)                ' AppName contains the path of the
                                      ' executable file.

' Call a Microsoft Windows DLL procedure. The Declare statement must be
' Private in a Class Module, but not in a standard Module.
Private Declare Sub MessageBeep Lib "User" (ByVal N As Integer)
Sub CallMyDll()
   Call MessageBeep(0)                ' Call Windows DLL procedure.
   MessageBeep 0                      ' Call again without Call keyword.
End Sub

' Call a Macintosh code resource.
Declare Sub MessageAlert Lib "MyHd:MyAlert" Alias "MyAlert" (ByVal N _
   As Integer)
Sub CallMyCodeResource()
   Call MessageAlert(0)               ' Call Macintosh code resource.
   MessageAlert 0                     ' Call again without Call keyword.
End Sub
```

ChDir Statement

Description

Changes the current directory or folder.

Syntax

ChDir *path*

The required *path* argument is a string expression that identifies which directory or folder becomes the new default directory or folder. The *path* may include the drive. If no drive is specified, **ChDir** changes the default directory or folder on the current drive.

Remarks

The **ChDir** statement changes the default directory but not the default drive. For example, if the default drive is C, the following statement changes the default directory on drive D, but C remains the default drive:

```
ChDir "D:\TMP"
```

See Also

ChDrive statement, **CurDir** function, **Dir** function, **MkDir** statement, **RmDir** statement.

Specifics (Macintosh)

On the Power Macintosh, the default drive always changes to the drive specified in *path*. Full path specifications begin with the volume name, and relative paths begin with a colon (**:**). **ChDir** resolves any aliases specified in the path:

```
ChDir "MacDrive:Tmp"        ' On the Macintosh.
```

Note that when making relative directory changes, different symbols are used in Microsoft Windows and on the Macintosh:

```
ChDir ".."                  ' Moves up one directory in Microsoft Windows.
ChDir "::"                  ' Moves up one directory on the Macintosh.
```

Example

This example uses the **ChDir** statement to change the current directory or folder.

```
' Change current directory or folder to "MYDIR".
ChDir "MYDIR"

' In Microsoft Windows:
' Assume "C:" is the current drive. The following statement changes
' the default directory on drive "D:". "C:" remains the current drive.
ChDir "D:\WINDOWS\SYSTEM"

' On the Macintosh:
' Changes default folder and default drive.
ChDir "HD:MY FOLDER"
```

ChDrive Statement

Description

Changes the current drive.

Syntax

ChDrive *drive*

The required *drive* argument is a string expression that specifies an existing drive. If you supply a zero-length string (""), the current drive doesn't change. If the *drive* argument is a multiple-character string, **ChDrive** uses only the first letter.

See Also

ChDir statement, **CurDir** function, **MkDir** statement, **RmDir** statement.

Specifics (Macintosh)

On the Macintosh, **ChDrive** changes the current folder to the root folder of the specified drive.

Example

This example uses the **ChDrive** statement to change the current drive.

```
' In Microsoft Windows:
ChDrive "D"                          ' Make "D" the current drive.

' On the Macintosh:
' Make "MY DRIVE" the current drive.
ChDrive "MY DRIVE:"
' Make "MY DRIVE" the current drive and current folder because
' it's the root.
ChDrive "MY DRIVE:MY FOLDER"
```

Choose Function

Description

Selects and returns a value from a list of arguments.

Syntax

Choose(*index***,** *choice-1*[**,** *choice-2*, ... [**,** *choice-n*]]**)**

The **Choose** function syntax has these parts

Part	Description
index	Required. Numeric expression or field that results in a value between 1 and the number of available choices.
choice	Required. **Variant** expression containing one of the possible choices.

Remarks

Choose returns a value from the list of choices based on the value of *index*. If *index* is 1, **Choose** returns the first choice in the list; if *index* is 2, it returns the second choice, and so on.

You can use **Choose** to look up a value in a list of possibilities. For example, if *index* evaluates to 3 and *choice-1* = "one", *choice-2* = "two", and *choice-3* = "three", **Choose** returns "three". This capability is particularly useful if *index* represents the value in an option group.

Choose evaluates every choice in the list, even though it returns only one. For this reason, you should watch for undesirable side effects. For example, if you use the **MsgBox** function as part of an expression in all the choices, a message box will be displayed for each choice as it is evaluated, even though **Choose** returns the value of only one of them.

The **Choose** function returns a **Null** if *index* is less than 1 or greater than the number of choices listed.

If *index* is not a whole number, it is rounded to the nearest whole number before being evaluated.

See Also

IIf function, **Select Case** statement, **Switch** function.

Specifics (Microsoft Access)

You can also use the **Choose** function in a calculated control on a Microsoft Access form or report. For example, you can use the **Choose** function to set the value of a control based on the value of another field. Set the **ControlSource** property of the control to an expression containing the **Choose** function. The expression in the following example can be used to set the **ControlSource** property of a control based on the value of a field called ShipVia in an Orders table.

```
=Choose([ShipVia], "Speedy", "United", "Federal")
```

In the preceding example, if ShipVia contains 1, the **Choose** function returns the first string, "Speedy." If it contains 2, the function returns the second string, "United," and so on. If ShipVia contains 0, the **Choose** function returns a **Null**.

The next example shows how you can ensure that a string is returned even if the field contains 0.

```
=Choose([ShipVia] + 1, "none", "Speedy", "United", "Federal")
```

Note In a Visual Basic module, you can use the more full-featured **Select Case** statement to return a value from a set of several choices.

Example

This example uses the **Choose** function to display a name in response to an index passed into the procedure in the `Ind` parameter.

```
Function GetChoice(Ind As Integer)
   GetChoice = Choose(Ind, "Speedy", "United", "Federal")
End Function
```

Example (Microsoft Access)

You can use the **Choose** function to create a calculated control whose value is determined by the value of a field in a table in your database. For example, suppose you have a Shippers table that contains a field called ShipperID. You could create a calculated control on a form to display a text name for the shipper based on the value of the ShipperID field.

```
=Choose([ShipperID], "Speedy", "United", "Federal")
```

Chr Function

Description

Returns a **String** containing the character associated with the specified character code.

Syntax

Chr(*charcode*)

The required *charcode* argument is a **Long** that identifies a character.

Remarks

Numbers from 0 to 31 are the same as standard, nonprintable ASCII codes. For example, **Chr**(10) returns a linefeed character. The normal range for *charcode* is 0–255. However, on DBCS systems, the actual range for *charcode* is –32768 to 65536.

Note The **ChrB** function is used with byte data contained in a **String**. Instead of returning a character, which may be one or two bytes, **ChrB** always returns a single byte. The **ChrW** function returns a **String** containing the Unicode character except on platforms where Unicode is not supported, in which case, the behavior is identical to the **Chr** function.

See Also

Asc function, **Str** function.

Example

This example uses the **Chr** function to return the character associated with the specified character code.

```
Dim MyChar
MyChar = Chr(65)                        ' Returns A.
MyChar = Chr(97)                        ' Returns a.
MyChar = Chr(62)                        ' Returns >.
MyChar = Chr(37)                        ' Returns %.
```

Example (Microsoft Excel)

This example fills list box one on Dialog1 with the letters A through Z.

```
For i = 65 To 90
   DialogSheets("Dialog1").ListBoxes(1).AddItem Text:=Chr(i)
Next i
```

This example creates a line break in a message box by using the **Chr** function.

```
msgText = "The current folder is:" & Chr(13) & CurDir()
MsgBox msgText
```

Clear Method

Applies To

Err object.

Description

Clears all property settings of the **Err** object.

Syntax

object.**Clear**

The *object* is always the **Err** object.

Remarks

Use **Clear** to explicitly clear the **Err** object after an error has been handled, for example, when you use deferred error handling with **On Error Resume Next**. The **Clear** method is called automatically whenever any of the following statements is executed:

- Any type of **Resume** statement.
- **Exit Sub**, **Exit Function**, **Exit Property**.
- Any **On Error** statement.

Note The **On Error Resume Next** construct may be preferable to **On Error GoTo** when handling errors generated during access to other objects. Checking **Err** after each interaction with an object removes ambiguity about which object was accessed by the code. You can be sure which object placed the error code in **Err.Number**, as well as which object originally generated the error (the object specified in **Err.Source**).

See Also

Description property, **Err** object, **HelpContext** property, **HelpContextID** property ("Extensibility Object Model Language Reference"), **HelpFile** property, **LastDLLError** property, **Number** property, **On Error** statement, **Raise** method, **Source** property.

Example

This example uses the **Err** objects **Clear** method to reset the numeric properties of the **Err** object to zero and its string properties to zero-length strings. If **Clear** were omitted from the following code, the error message dialog box would be displayed on every iteration of the loop (after an error occurs) whether or not a successive calculation generated an error. You can single-step through the code to see the effect.

```
Dim Result(10) As Integer               ' Declare array whose elements
                                        ' will overflow easily.
Dim indx
On Error Resume Next                    ' Defer error trapping.
Do Until indx = 10
   ' Generate an occasional error or store result if no error.
   Result(indx) = Rnd * indx * 20000
   If Err.Number <> 0 Then
      MsgBox Err, , "Error Generated: ", Err.HelpFile, Err.HelpContext
      Err.Clear               ' Clear Err object properties.
   End If
   indx = indx + 1
Loop
```

Close Statement

Description

Concludes input/output (I/O) to a file opened using the **Open** statement.

Syntax

Close [*filenumberlist*]

The optional *filenumberlist* argument can be one or more file numbers using the following syntax, where *filenumber* is any valid file number:

[[#]*filenumber*] [, [#]*filenumber*] **. . .**

Remarks

If you omit *filenumberlist*, all active files opened by the **Open** statement are closed.

When you close files that were opened for **Output** or **Append**, the final buffer of output is written to the operating system buffer for that file. All buffer space associated with the closed file is released.

When the **Close** statement is executed, the association of a file with its file number ends.

See Also

End statement, **Open** statement, **Reset** statement, **Stop** statement.

Example

This example uses the **Close** statement to close all three files opened for **Output**.

```
Dim I, FileName
For I = 1 To 3                          ' Loop 3 times.
   FileName = "TEST" & I                ' Create file name.
   Open FileName For Output As #I       ' Open file.
   Print #I, "This is a test."          ' Write string to file.
Next I
Close                                   ' Close all 3 open files.
```

Collection Object

Description

A **Collection** object is an ordered set of items that can be referred to as a unit.

Remarks

The **Collection** object provides a convenient way to refer to a related group of items as a single object. The items, or members, in a collection need only be related by the fact that they exist in the collection. Members of a collection don't have to share the same data type.

A collection can be created the same way other objects are created. For example:

```
Dim X As New Collection
```

Once a collection is created, members can be added using the **Add** method and removed using the **Remove** method. Specific members can be returned from the collection using the **Item** method, while the entire collection can be iterated using the **For Each...Next** statement.

Properties

Count property.

Methods

Add method, **Item** method, **Remove** method.

See Also

Add method, **For Each…Next** statement, **Item** method, **Remove** method.

Specifics (Microsoft Access)

In Microsoft Access, a **Collection** object can consist of a set of objects of any type. You can create a **Collection** object that consists of several objects of the same type or objects of different types.

The collection defined by a **Collection** object can contain any combination of Microsoft Access objects, Data Access Objects (DAO), and objects from any other application that exposes its objects to Microsoft Access. You can also add a **Collection** object to a collection defined by a **Collection** object.

The collection can also contain user-defined objects that you create in Microsoft Access. For example, you can create user-defined objects with custom methods and properties from a form module or report module. Then you can add these objects to a collection defined by a **Collection** object, and manipulate them as a set.

Example

This example creates a **Collection** object (`MyClasses`), and then creates a dialog box in which users can add objects to the collection. To see how this works, choose the **Class Module** command from the **Insert** menu and declare a public variable called `InstanceName` at module level of Class1 (type **Public** `InstanceName`) to hold the names of each instance. Leave the default name as Class1. Copy and paste the following code into the General section of another module, and then start it with the statement `ClassNamer` in another procedure. (This example only works with host applications that support classes.)

```
Sub ClassNamer()
   Dim MyClasses As New Collection    ' Create a Collection object.
   Dim Num                            ' Counter for individualizing keys.
   Dim Msg As String ' Variable to hold prompt string.
   Dim TheName, MyObject, NameList    ' Variants to hold information.
   Do
      Dim Inst As New Class1          ' Create a new instance of Class1.
      Num = Num + 1                   ' Increment Num, then get a name.
      Msg = "Please enter a name for this object." & Chr(13) _
         & "Press Cancel to see names in collection."
      TheName = InputBox(Msg, "Name the Collection Items")
      Inst.InstanceName = TheName     ' Put name in object instance.
      ' If user entered name, add it to the collection.
      If Inst.InstanceName <> "" Then
         ' Add the named object to the collection.
         MyClasses.Add item := Inst, key := CStr(Num)
      End If
      ' Clear the current reference in preparation for next one.
      Set Inst = Nothing
   Loop Until TheName = ""
   For Each MyObject In MyClasses     ' Create list of names.
      NameList = NameList & MyObject.InstanceName & Chr(13)
   Next MyObject
   ' Display the list of names in a message box.
   MsgBox NameList, , "Instance Names In MyClasses Collection"

   For Num = 1 To MyClasses.Count     ' Remove name from the collection.
      MyClasses.Remove 1              ' Since collections are reindexed
                                      ' automatically, remove the first
   Next                               ' member on each iteration.
End Sub
```

Command Function

Description

Returns the argument portion of the command line used to launch Microsoft Visual Basic or an executable program developed with Visual Basic.

Syntax

Command

Remarks

When Visual Basic is launched from the command line, any portion of the command line that follows `/cmd` is passed to the program as the command-line argument. In the following example, `cmdlineargs` represents the argument information returned by the **Command** function.

```
VB /cmd cmdlineargs
```

For applications developed with Visual Basic and compiled to an .exe file, **Command** returns any arguments that appear after the name of the application on the command line. For example:

```
MyApp cmdlineargs
```

To find how command line arguments can be changed in the user interface of the application you're using, search Help for "command line arguments."

Specifics (Microsoft Access)

To change a command-line argument once a database has been opened, click **Options** on the **Tools** menu. On the **Advanced** tab of the **Options** dialog box, enter a new argument in the **Command-Line Arguments** box. The **Command** function will now return the new argument you've entered.

When the **Command** function is used anywhere other than in Visual Basic code in a module, you must include empty parentheses after the function. For example, to use the **Command** function in a text box on a form, you would set the **ControlSource** property of the text box to an expression like the following:

```
=Command()
```

Example

This example uses the **Command** function to get the command line arguments in a function that returns them in a **Variant** containing an array.

```
Function GetCommandLine(Optional MaxArgs)
   'Declare variables.
   Dim C, CmdLine, CmdLnLen, InArg, I, NumArgs
   'See if MaxArgs was provided.
   If IsMissing(MaxArgs) Then MaxArgs = 10
   'Make array of the correct size.
   ReDim ArgArray(MaxArgs)
```

```
    NumArgs = 0: InArg = False
    'Get command line arguments.
    CmdLine = Command()
    CmdLnLen = Len(CmdLine)
    'Go thru command line one character
    'at a time.
    For I = 1 To CmdLnLen
       C = Mid(CmdLine, I, 1)
       'Test for space or tab.
       If (C <> " " And C <> vbTab) Then
          'Neither space nor tab.
          'Test if already in argument.
          If Not InArg Then
          'New argument begins.
          'Test for too many arguments.
             If NumArgs = MaxArgs Then Exit For
                NumArgs = NumArgs + 1
                InArg = True
             End If
          'Add character to current argument.
          ArgArray(NumArgs) = ArgArray(NumArgs) + C
       Else
          'Found a space or tab.
          'Set InArg flag to False.
          InArg = False
       End If
    Next I
    'Resize array just enough to hold arguments.
    ReDim Preserve ArgArray(NumArgs)
    'Return Array in Function name.
    GetCommandLine = ArgArray()
End Function
```

Comparison Operators

Description

Used to compare expressions.

Syntax

result = *expression1 comparisonoperator expression2*
result = *object1* **Is** *object2*
result = *string* **Like** *pattern*

Comparison operators have these parts

Part	Description
result	Required; any numeric variable.
expression	Required; any expression.
comparisonoperator	Required; any comparison operator.

(continued)

Part	Description
object	Required; any object name.
string	Required; any string expression.
pattern	Required; any string expression or range of characters.

Remarks

The following table contains a list of the comparison operators and the conditions that determine whether *result* is **True**, **False**, or **Null**

Operator	True if	False if	Null if
< (Less than)	*expression1* < *expression2*	*expression1* >= *expression2*	*expression1* or *expression2* = **Null**
<= (Less than or equal to)	*expression1* <= *expression2*	*expression1* > *expression2*	*expression1* or *expression2* = **Null**
> (Greater than)	*expression1* > *expression2*	*expression1* <= *expression2*	*expression1* or *expression2* = **Null**
>= (Greater than or equal to)	*expression1* >= *expression2*	*expression1* < *expression2*	*expression1* or *expression2* = **Null**
= (Equal to)	*expression1* = *expression2*	*expression1* <> *expression2*	*expression1* or *expression2* = **Null**
<> (Not equal to)	*expression1* <> *expression2*	*expression1* = *expression2*	*expression1* or *expression2* = **Null**

Note The **Is** and **Like** operators have specific comparison functionality that differs from the operators in the table.

When comparing two expressions, you may not be able to easily determine whether the expressions are being compared as numbers or as strings. The following table shows how the expressions are compared or the result when either expression is not a **Variant**

If	Then
Both expressions are numeric data types (**Byte**, **Boolean**, **Integer**, **Long**, **Single**, **Double**, **Date**, **Currency**, or **Decimal**)	Perform a numeric comparison.
Both expressions are **String**	Perform a string comparison.
One expression is a numeric data type and the other is a **Variant** that is, or can be, a number	Perform a numeric comparison.
One expression is a numeric data type and the other is a string **Variant** that can't be converted to a number	A `Type Mismatch` error occurs.
One expression is a **String** and the other is any **Variant** except a **Null**	Perform a string comparison.

(continued)

One expression is **Empty** and the other is a numeric data type	Perform a numeric comparison, using 0 as the **Empty** expression.
One expression is **Empty** and the other is a **String**	Perform a string comparison, using a zero-length string ("") as the **Empty** expression.

If *expression1* and *expression2* are both **Variant** expressions, their underlying type determines how they are compared. The following table shows how the expressions are compared or the result from the comparison, depending on the underlying type of the **Variant**

If	Then
Both **Variant** expressions are numeric	Perform a numeric comparison.
Both **Variant** expressions are strings	Perform a string comparison.
One **Variant** expression is numeric and the other is a string	The numeric expression is less than the string expression.
One **Variant** expression is **Empty** and the other is numeric	Perform a numeric comparison, using 0 as the **Empty** expression.
One **Variant** expression is **Empty** and the other is a string	Perform a string comparison, using a zero-length string ("") as the **Empty** expression.
Both **Variant** expressions are **Empty**	The expressions are equal.

When a **Single** is compared to a **Double**, the **Double** is rounded to the precision of the **Single**.

If a **Currency** is compared with a **Single** or **Double**, the **Single** or **Double** is converted to a **Currency**. Similarly, when a **Decimal** is compared with a **Single** or **Double**, the **Single** or **Double** is converted to a **Decimal**. For **Currency**, any fractional value less than .0001 may be lost; for **Decimal**, any fractional value less than 1E-28 may be lost, or an overflow error can occur. Such fractional value loss may cause two values to compare as equal when they are not.

See Also

Is operator, **Like** operator, Operator precedence, **Option Compare** statement.

Example

This example shows various uses of comparison operators, which you use to compare expressions.

```
Dim MyResult, Var1, Var2
MyResult = (45 < 35)                      ' Returns False.
MyResult = (45 = 45)                      ' Returns True.
MyResult = (4 <> 3)                       ' Returns True.
MyResult = ("5" > "4")                    ' Returns True.

Var1 = "5": Var2 = 4                      ' Initialize variables.
MyResult = (Var1 > Var2)                  ' Returns True.
```

```
Var1 = 5: Var2 = Empty
MyResult = (Var1 > Var2)                    ' Returns True.

Var1 = 0: Var2 = Empty
MyResult = (Var1 = Var2)                    ' Returns True.
```

Const Statement

Description

Declares constants for use in place of literal values.

Syntax

[**Public** | **Private**] **Const** *constname* [**As** *type*] = *expression*

The **Const** statement syntax has these parts

Part	Description
Public	Optional. Keyword used at module level to declare constants that are available to all procedures in all modules. Not allowed in procedures.
Private	Optional. Keyword used at module level to declare constants that are available only within the module where the declaration is made. Not allowed in procedures.
constname	Required. Name of the constant; follows standard variable naming conventions.
type	Optional. Data type of the constant; may be **Byte**, **Boolean**, **Integer**, **Long**, **Currency**, **Single**, **Double**, **Decimal** (not currently supported), **Date**, **String**, or **Variant**. Use a separate **As** *type* clause for each constant being declared.
expression	Required. Literal, other constant, or any combination that includes all arithmetic or logical operators except **Is**.

Remarks

Constants are private by default. Within procedures, constants are always private; their visibility can't be changed. In standard modules, the default visibility of module-level constants can be changed using the **Public** keyword. In class modules, however, constants can only be private and their visibility can't be changed using the **Public** keyword.

To combine several constant declarations on the same line, separate each constant assignment with a comma. When constant declarations are combined in this way, the **Public** or **Private** keyword, if used, applies to all of them.

You can't use variables, user-defined functions, or intrinsic Visual Basic functions (such as **Chr**) in expressions assigned to constants.

Note Constants can make your programs self-documenting and easy to modify. Unlike variables, constants can't be inadvertently changed while your program is running.

If you don't explicitly declare the constant type using **As** *type*, the constant has the data type that is most appropriate for *expression*.

Constants declared in a **Sub**, **Function**, or **Property** procedure are local to that procedure. A constant declared outside a procedure is defined throughout the module in which it is declared. You can use constants anywhere you can use an expression.

See Also

#Const directive, **Def***type* statements, **Function** statement, **Let** statement, **Property Get** statement, **Property Let** statement, **Property Set** statement, **Sub** statement.

Specifics (Microsoft Access)

A constant in a Microsoft Access standard module is private by default. If you precede a constant with the keyword **Public**, however, it is then available to other modules in the current database. It is also available to modules that reference the current database.

A constant defined in a class module is always private to that module, and can't be made public by using the **Public** keyword.

Example

This example uses the **Const** statement to declare constants for use in place of literal values. **Public** constants occur in the General section of a standard module, rather than a class module. **Private** constants can go in the General section of any type of module.

```
' Constants are Private by default.
Const MyVar = 459

' Declare Public constant.
Public Const MyString = "HELP"

' Declare Private Integer constant.
Private Const MyInt As Integer = 5

' Declare multiple constants on same line.
Const MyStr = "Hello", MyDouble As Double = 3.4567
```

Example (Microsoft Access)

In Microsoft Access, you cannot declare public constants in the Declarations section of a class module. Constants in a class module must be private. You can declare both public and private constants in the Declarations section of a standard module.

```
' In class module.
Const conCommission As Single = .08

' In standard module.
Const conErrorNumber As Integer = 91
Public Const conAddress As String = "8421 58th Avenue, College Park, MD"
```

Cos Function

Description

Returns a **Double** specifying the cosine of an angle.

Syntax

Cos(*number***)**

The required *number* argument is a **Double** or any valid numeric expression that expresses an angle in radians.

Remarks

The **Cos** function takes an angle and returns the ratio of two sides of a right triangle. The ratio is the length of the side adjacent to the angle divided by the length of the hypotenuse.

The result lies in the range –1 to 1.

To convert degrees to radians, multiply degrees by pi/180. To convert radians to degrees, multiply radians by 180/pi.

See Also

Atn function, **Sin** function, **Tan** function.

Example

This example uses the **Cos** function to return the cosine of an angle.

```
Dim MyAngle, MySecant
MyAngle = 1.3                          ' Define angle in radians.
MySecant = 1 / Cos(MyAngle)            ' Calculate secant.
```

Count Property

Applies To

Collection object, **LinkedWindows** collection, **Windows** collection.

Description

Returns a **Long** (**Long Integer**) containing the number of objects in a collection. Read-only.

See Also

Add method, **Item** method, **Item** method ("Extensibility Object Model Language Reference"), **Remove** method.

Example

This example uses the **Collection** object's **Count** property to specify how many iterations are required to remove all the elements of the collection called `MyClasses`. When collections are numerically indexed, the base is 1 by default. Since collections are reindexed automatically when a removal is made, the following code removes the first member on each iteration.

```
Dim Num, MyClasses
For Num = 1 To MyClasses.Count          ' Remove name from the collection.
   MyClasses.Remove 1                   ' Default collection numeric indexes
Next                                    ' begin at 1.
```

CreateObject Function

Description

Creates and returns a reference to an ActiveX object.

Syntax

CreateObject(*class***)**

The *class* argument uses the syntax *appname***.***objecttype* and has these parts

Part	Description
appname	Required; **Variant** (**String**). The name of the application providing the object.
objecttype	Required; **Variant** (**String**). The type or class of object to create.

Remarks

Every application that supports Automation provides at least one type of object. For example, a word processing application may provide an **Application** object, a **Document** object, and a **Toolbar** object.

To create an ActiveX object, assign the object returned by **CreateObject** to an object variable:

```
' Declare an object variable to hold the object
' reference. Dim as Object causes late binding.
Dim ExcelSheet As Object
Set ExcelSheet = CreateObject("Excel.Sheet")
```

This code starts the application creating the object, in this case, a Microsoft Excel spreadsheet. Once an object is created, you reference it in code using the object variable you defined. In the following example, you access properties and methods of the new object using the object variable, `ExcelSheet`, and other Microsoft Excel objects, including the `Application` object and the `Cells` collection.

```
' Make Excel visible through the Application object.
ExcelSheet.Application.Visible = True
' Place some text in the first cell of the sheet.
ExcelSheet.Cells(1, 1).Value = "This is column A, row 1"
' Save the sheet to C:\test.doc directory.
ExcelSheet.SaveAs "C:\ TEST.DOC"
' Close Excel with the Quit method on the Application object.
ExcelSheet.Application.Quit
' Release the object variable.
Set ExcelSheet = Nothing
```

Declaring an object variable with the `As Object` clause creates a variable that can contain a reference to any type of object. However, access to the object through that variable is late bound; that is, the binding occurs when your program is run. To create an object variable that results in early binding; that is, binding when the program is compiled, declare the object variable with a specific class ID. For example, you can declare and create the following Microsoft Excel references:

```
Dim xlApp As Excel.Application

Dim xlBook As Excel.Workbook

Dim xlSheet As Excel.WorkSheet

Set xlApp = CreateObject("Excel.Application")

Set xlBook = xlApp.Workbooks.Add

Set xlSheet = xlBook.Worksheets(1)
```

The reference through an early-bound variable can give better performance, but can only contain a reference to the class specified in the declaration.

You can pass an object returned by the **CreateObject** function to a function expecting an object as an argument. For example, the following code creates and passes a reference to an Excel.Application object:

```
Call MySub (CreateObject("Excel.Application"))
```

Note Use **CreateObject** when there is no current instance of the object. If an instance of the object is already running, a new instance is started, and an object of the specified type is created. To use the current instance, or to start the application and have it load a file, use the **GetObject** function.

If an object has registered itself as a single-instance object, only one instance of the object is created, no matter how many times **CreateObject** is executed.

See Also

GetObject function, **Set** statement.

Example

This example uses the **CreateObject** function to set a reference (`xlApp`) to Microsoft Excel. It uses the reference to access the **Visible** property of Microsoft Excel, and then uses the Microsoft Excel **Quit** method to close it. Finally, the reference itself is released.

```
Dim xlApp As Object      ' Declare variable to hold the reference.

Set xlApp = CreateObject("excel.application")
' You may have to set Visible property to True
' if you want to see the application.
xlApp.Visible = True
   ' Use xlApp to access Microsoft Excel's
   ' other objects.
xlApp.Quit               ' When you finish, use the Quit method to close
Set xlApp = Nothing      ' the application, then release the reference.
```

CurDir Function

Description

Returns a **Variant** (**String**) representing the current path.

Syntax

CurDir[(*drive*)]

The optional *drive* argument is a string expression that specifies an existing drive. If no drive is specified or if *drive* is a zero-length string (""), **CurDir** returns the path for the current drive.

See Also

ChDir statement, **ChDrive** statement, **MkDir** statement, **RmDir** statement.

Specifics (Macintosh)

The optional *drive* argument is a string expression that specifies an existing drive. **CurDir** ignores any *drive* specified and simply returns the path for the current drive.

Example

This example uses the **CurDir** function to return the current path.

```
' In Microsoft Windows:
' Assume current path on C drive is "C:\WINDOWS\SYSTEM".
' Assume current path on D drive is "D:\EXCEL".
' Assume C is the current drive.
Dim MyPath
MyPath = CurDir' Returns "C:\WINDOWS\SYSTEM".
MyPath = CurDir("C")                   ' Returns "C:\WINDOWS\SYSTEM".
MyPath = CurDir("D")                   ' Returns "D:\EXCEL".

' On the Macintosh:
' Drive letters are ignored. Path for current drive is returned.
' Assume current path on HD Drive is "HD:MY FOLDER".
' Assume HD is the current drive. Drive MD also exists on the machine.
Dim MyPath
MyPath = CurDir                        ' Returns "HD:MY FOLDER".
MyPath = CurDir("HD")                  ' Returns "HD:MY FOLDER".
MyPath = CurDir("MD")                  ' Returns "HD:MY FOLDER".
```

Currency Data Type

Description

Currency variables are stored as 64-bit (8-byte) numbers in an integer format, scaled by 10,000 to give a fixed-point number with 15 digits to the left of the decimal point and 4 digits to the right. This representation provides a range of –922,337,203,685,477.5808 to 922,337,203,685,477.5807. The type-declaration character for **Currency** is the at sign (@).

The **Currency** data type is useful for calculations involving money and for fixed-point calculations in which accuracy is particularly important.

See Also

Data type summary, **Def*type*** statements, **Long** data type.

CVErr Function

Description

Returns a **Variant** of subtype **Error** containing an error number specified by the user.

Syntax

CVErr(*errornumber***)**

The required *errornumber* argument is any valid error number.

Remarks

Use the **CVErr** function to create user-defined errors in user-created procedures. For example, if you create a function that accepts several arguments and normally returns a string, you can have your function evaluate the input arguments to ensure they are within acceptable range. If they are not, it is likely your function will not return what you expect. In this event, **CVErr** allows you to return an error number that tells you what action to take.

Note that implicit conversion of an **Error** is not allowed. For example, you can't directly assign the return value of **CVErr** to a variable that is not a **Variant**. However, you can perform an explicit conversion (using **CInt**, **CDbl**, and so on) of the value returned by **CVErr** and assign that to a variable of the appropriate data type.

See Also

Data type summary, **IsError** function.

Example

This example uses the **CVErr** function to return a **Variant** whose **VarType** is **vbError** (10). The user-defined function `CalculateDouble` returns an error if the argument passed to it isn't a number. You can use **CVErr** to return user-defined errors from user-defined procedures or to defer handling of a run-time error. Use the **IsError** function to test if the value represents an error.

```
' Call CalculateDouble with an error-producing argument.
Sub Test()
   Debug.Print CalculateDouble("345.45robert")
End Sub
' Define CalculateDouble Function procedure.
Function CalculateDouble(Number)
```

```
   If IsNumeric(Number) Then
      CalculateDouble = Number * 2    ' Return result.
   Else
      CalculateDouble = CVErr(2001)   ' Return a user-defined error
   End If' number.
End Function
```

Example (Microsoft Excel)

This example inserts the seven cell error values into cells A1:A7 on Sheet1.

```
myArray = Array(xlErrDiv0, xlErrNA, xlErrName, xlErrNull, _
   xlErrNum, xlErrRef, xlErrValue)
For i = 1 To 7
   Worksheets("Sheet1").Cells(i, 1).Value = CVErr(myArray(i - 1))
Next i
```

This example displays a message if the active cell on Sheet1 contains a cell error value. You can use this example as a framework for a cell-error-value error handler.

```
Worksheets("Sheet1").Activate
If IsError(ActiveCell.Value) Then
   errval = ActiveCell.Value
   Select Case errval
      Case CVErr(xlErrDiv0)
         MsgBox "#DIV/0! error"
      Case CVErr(xlErrNA)
         MsgBox "#N/A error"
      Case CVErr(xlErrName)
         MsgBox "#NAME? error"
      Case CVErr(xlErrNull)
         MsgBox "#NULL! error"
      Case CVErr(xlErrNum)
         MsgBox "#NUM! error"
      Case CVErr(xlErrRef)
         MsgBox "#REF! error"
      Case CVErr(xlErrValue)
         MsgBox "#VALUE! error"
      Case Else
         MsgBox "This should never happen!!"
   End Select
End If
```

Data Type Summary

Description

The following table shows the supported data types, including storage sizes and ranges.

Data type	Storage size	Range
Byte	1 byte	0 to 255
Boolean	2 bytes	**True** or **False**

(continued)

Data type	Storage size	Range
Integer	2 bytes	–32,768 to 32,767
Long (**Long Integer**)	4 bytes	–2,147,483,648 to 2,147,483,647
Single (single-precision floating-point)	4 bytes	–3.402823E38 to –1.401298E–45 for negative values; 1.401298E–45 to 3.402823E38 for positive values
Double (double-precision floating-point)	8 bytes	–1.79769313486232E308 to –4.94065645841247E–324 for negative values; 4.94065645841247E–324 to 1.79769313486232E308 for positive values
Currency (scaled integer)	8 bytes	–922,337,203,685,477.5808 to 922,337,203,685,477.5807
Decimal	14 bytes	+/-79,228,162,514,264,337,593,543,950,335 with no decimal point; +/-7.9228162514264337593543950335 with 28 places to the right of the decimal; smallest non-zero number is +/-0.0000000000000000000000000001
Date	8 bytes	January 1, 100 to December 31, 9999
Object	4 bytes	Any **Object** reference
String (variable-length)	10 bytes + string length	0 to approximately 2 billion
String (fixed-length)	Length of string	1 to approximately 65,400
Variant (with numbers)	16 bytes	Any numeric value up to the range of a **Double**
Variant (with characters)	22 bytes + string length	Same range as for variable-length **String**
User-defined (using **Type**)	Number required by elements	The range of each element is the same as the range of its data type.

Note Arrays of any data type require 20 bytes of memory plus 4 bytes for each array dimension plus the number of bytes occupied by the data itself. The memory occupied by the data can be calculated by multiplying the number of data elements by the size of each element. For example, the data in a single-dimension array consisting of 4 **Integer** data elements of 2 bytes each occupies 8 bytes. The 8 bytes required for the data plus the 24 bytes of overhead brings the total memory requirement for the array to 32 bytes.

A **Variant** containing an array requires 12 bytes more than the array alone.

See Also

Boolean data type, **Byte** data type, **Currency** data type, **Date** data type, **Decimal** data type, **Def***type* statements, **Double** data type, **Int**, **Fix** functions, **Integer** data type, **Long** data type, **Object** data type, **Single** data type, **String** data type, **Type** statement, User-defined data type, **Variant** data type.

Date Data Type

Description

Date variables are stored as IEEE 64-bit (8-byte) floating-point numbers that represent dates ranging from 1 January 100 to 31 December 9999 and times from 0:00:00 to 23:59:59. Any recognizable literal date values can be assigned to **Date** variables. Date literals must be enclosed within number signs (#), for example, `#January 1, 1993#` or `#1 Jan 93#`.

Date variables display dates according to the short date format recognized by your computer. Times display according to the time format (either 12-hour or 24-hour) recognized by your computer.

When other numeric types are converted to **Date**, values to the left of the decimal represent date information while values to the right of the decimal represent time. Midnight is 0 and midday is 0.5. Negative whole numbers represent dates before 30 December 1899.

See Also

Data type summary, **Def***type* statements, **Double** data type, **Variant** data type.

Date Function

Description

Returns a **Variant** (**Date**) containing the current system date.

Syntax

Date

Remarks

To set the system date, use the **Date** statement.

See Also

Date statement, **Format** function, **Now** function, **Time** function, **Time** statement.

Specifics (Microsoft Access)

You can insert the current date on a form or report by clicking **Date and Time** on the **Insert** menu. This command creates a text box on a form or report and sets the **ControlSource** property of the text box to an expression containing the **Date** function. This expression will vary according to the format you have chosen to display the date. This command is available only in form Design view and report Design view.

You can also use the **Date** function in a query expression or in a macro. However, you must include the parentheses after the function when you use it anywhere other than a Visual Basic module, as in the expression `Date()`.

Example

This example uses the **Date** function to return the current system date.

```
Dim MyDate
MyDate = Date   ' MyDate contains the current system date.
```

Example (Microsoft Access)

You can use the **Date** function in a calculated control by setting the **ControlSource** property of the control as in the following example.

```
=Date()
```

You can also use the **Date** function to set criteria for a query. For example, if you have an Orders table that contains an OrderDate field, you can create a query on the Orders table to return all records that have an OrderDate between 4-1-95 and today's date. Enter the following in the Criteria cell under the OrderDate field.

```
Between #4-1-95# and Date()
```

Date Statement

Description

Sets the current system date.

Syntax

Date = *date*

For systems running Microsoft Windows 95, the required *date* specification must be a date from January 1, 1980 through December 31, 2099. For systems running Microsoft Windows NT, *date* must be a date from January 1, 1980 through December 31, 2079.

See Also

Date function, **Time** function, **Time** statement.

Specifics (Macintosh)

For the Macintosh, *date* must be a date from January 1, 1904 through February 5, 2040.

Example

This example uses the **Date** statement to set the computer system date. In the development environment, the date literal is displayed in short date format using the locale settings of your code.

```
Dim MyDate
MyDate = #February 12, 1985#          ' Assign a date.
Date = MyDate                         ' Change system date.
```

DateAdd Function

Description

Returns a **Variant** (**Date**) containing a date to which a specified time interval has been added.

Syntax

DateAdd(*interval, number, date*)

The **DateAdd** function syntax has these named arguments

Part	Description
interval	Required. String expression that is the interval of time you want to add.
number	Required. Numeric expression that is the number of intervals you want to add. It can be positive (to get dates in the future) or negative (to get dates in the past).
date	Required. **Variant** (**Date**) or literal representing date to which the interval is added.

Settings

The ***interval*** argument has these settings

Setting	Description
yyyy	Year
q	Quarter
m	Month
y	Day of year
d	Day
w	Weekday
ww	Week
h	Hour
n	Minute
s	Second

Remarks

You can use the **DateAdd** function to add or subtract a specified time interval from a date. For example, you can use **DateAdd** to calculate a date 30 days from today or a time 45 minutes from now.

To add days to ***date***, you can use Day of Year ("y"), Day ("d"), or Weekday ("w").

The **DateAdd** function won't return an invalid date. The following example adds one month to January 31:

```
DateAdd("m", 1, "31-Jan-95")
```

In this case, **DateAdd** returns 28-Feb-95, not 31-Feb-95. If ***date*** is 31-Jan-96, it returns 29-Feb-96 because 1996 is a leap year.

If the calculated date would precede the year 100 (that is, you subtract more years than are in ***date***), an error occurs.

If ***number*** isn't a **Long** value, it is rounded to the nearest whole number before being evaluated.

See Also

DateDiff function, **DatePart** function, **Day** function, **Format** function, **Now** function, **Weekday** function, **Year** function.

Example

This example takes a date and, using the **DateAdd** function, displays a corresponding date a specified number of months in the future.

```
Dim FirstDate As Date          ' Declare variables.
Dim IntervalType As String
Dim Number As Integer
Dim Msg
IntervalType = "m"             ' "m" specifies months as interval.
FirstDate = InputBox("Enter a date")
Number = InputBox("Enter number of months to add")
Msg = "New date: " & DateAdd(IntervalType, Number, FirstDate)
MsgBox Msg
```

Example (Microsoft Access)

The following example shows how you can create a calculated control by using the **DateAdd** function to display the date by which a particular order must be shipped—in this case, thirty days after the OrderDate. Suppose you have a form based on an Orders table, with a field called OrderDate. You can create another text box on the form to display the shipping date by setting the **ControlSource** property of this text box as in the following example.

```
=DateAdd("d", 30, [OrderDate])
```

DateDiff Function

Description

Returns a **Variant** (**Long**) specifying the number of time intervals between two specified dates.

Syntax

DateDiff(*interval, date1, date2*[*, firstdayofweek*[*, firstweekofyear*]])

The **DateDiff** function syntax has these named arguments

Part	Description
interval	Required. String expression that is the interval of time you use to calculate the difference between ***date1*** and ***date2***.
date1*, *date2	Required; **Variant** (**Date**). Two dates you want to use in the calculation.
firstdayofweek	Optional. A constant that specifies the first day of the week. If not specified, Sunday is assumed.
firstweekofyear	Optional. A constant that specifies the first week of the year. If not specified, the first week is assumed to be the week in which January 1 occurs.

Settings

The ***interval*** argument has these settings

Setting	Description
yyyy	Year
q	Quarter
m	Month
y	Day of year
d	Day
w	Weekday
ww	Week
h	Hour
n	Minute
s	Second

The ***firstdayofweek*** argument has these settings

Constant	Value	Description
vbUseSystem	0	Use the NLS API setting.
vbSunday	1	Sunday (default)
vbMonday	2	Monday
vbTuesday	3	Tuesday
vbWednesday	4	Wednesday
vbThursday	5	Thursday
vbFriday	6	Friday
vbSaturday	7	Saturday

The ***firstweekofyear*** argument has these settings

Constant	Value	Description
vbUseSystem	0	Use the NLS API setting.
vbFirstJan1	1	Start with week in which January 1 occurs (default).
vbFirstFourDays	2	Start with the first week that has at least four days in the new year.
vbFirstFullWeek	3	Start with first full week of the year.

Remarks

You can use the **DateDiff** function to determine how many specified time intervals exist between two dates. For example, you might use **DateDiff** to calculate the number of days between two dates, or the number of weeks between today and the end of the year.

To calculate the number of days between ***date1*** and ***date2***, you can use either Day of year ("y") or Day ("d"). When ***interval*** is Weekday ("w"), **DateDiff** returns the number of weeks between the two dates. If ***date1*** falls on a Monday, **DateDiff** counts the number of Mondays until ***date2***. It counts ***date2*** but not ***date1***. If ***interval*** is Week ("ww"), however, the **DateDiff** function returns the number of calendar weeks between the two dates. It counts the number of Sundays between ***date1*** and ***date2***. **DateDiff** counts ***date2*** if it falls on a Sunday; but it doesn't count ***date1***, even if it does fall on a Sunday.

If ***date1*** refers to a later point in time than ***date2***, the **DateDiff** function returns a negative number.

The ***firstdayofweek*** argument affects calculations that use the "w" and "ww" interval symbols.

If *date1* or *date2* is a date literal, the specified year becomes a permanent part of that date. However, if *date1* or *date2* is enclosed in double quotation marks (" "), and you omit the year, the current year is inserted in your code each time the *date1* or *date2* expression is evaluated. This makes it possible to write code that can be used in different years.

When comparing December 31 to January 1 of the immediately succeeding year, **DateDiff** for Year ("yyyy") returns 1 even though only a day has elapsed.

See Also

DateAdd function, **DatePart** function, **Day** function, **Format** function, **Now** function, **Weekday** function, **Year** function.

Example

This example uses the **DateDiff** function to display the number of days between a given date and today.

```
Dim TheDate As Date     ' Declare variables.
Dim Msg
TheDate = InputBox("Enter a date")
Msg = "Days from today: " & DateDiff("d", Now, TheDate)
MsgBox Msg
```

Example (Microsoft Access)

The following examples use the **DateDiff** function to calculate the number of calendar weeks between the first of the year and today, and the number of days since February 1, 1995 respectively.

```
Debug.Print DateDiff("ww", "1-1", Now())
Debug.Print DateDiff("y", #1-Feb-1995#, Now())
```

The next example shows how to use the **DateDiff** function in a query expression. Suppose you have an Orders table that contains an OrderDate field and a ShippedDate field. You can create a calculated field in a query to display the time elapsed between an order date and a shipped date for each order. In the Query window, create a new query by adding the Orders table and dragging the OrderID field to the query design grid. In an empty **Field** cell, enter the following to create a calculated field.

```
DaysElapsed: DateDiff("y", [OrderDate], [ShippedDate])
```

DatePart Function

Description

Returns a **Variant** (**Integer**) containing the specified part of a given date.

Syntax

DatePart(*interval, date*[*,firstdayofweek*[*, firstweekofyear*]])

The **DatePart** function syntax has these named arguments

Part	Description
interval	Required. String expression that is the interval of time you want to return.
date	Required. **Variant** (**Date**) value that you want to evaluate.
firstdayofweek	Optional. A constant that specifies the first day of the week. If not specified, Sunday is assumed.
firstweekofyear	Optional. A constant that specifies the first week of the year. If not specified, the first week is assumed to be the week in which January 1 occurs.

Settings

The ***interval*** argument has these settings

Setting	Description
yyyy	Year
q	Quarter
m	Month
y	Day of year
d	Day
w	Weekday
ww	Week
h	Hour
n	Minute
s	Second

The ***firstdayofweek*** argument has these settings

Constant	Value	Description
vbUseSystem	0	Use the NLS API setting.
vbSunday	1	Sunday (default)
vbMonday	2	Monday
vbTuesday	3	Tuesday
vbWednesday	4	Wednesday
vbThursday	5	Thursday
vbFriday	6	Friday
vbSaturday	7	Saturday

The *firstweekofyear* argument has these settings

Constant	Value	Description
vbUseSystem	0	Use the NLS API setting.
vbFirstJan1	1	Start with week in which January 1 occurs (default).
vbFirstFourDays	2	Start with the first week that has at least four days in the new year.
vbFirstFullWeek	3	Start with first full week of the year.

Remarks

You can use the **DatePart** function to evaluate a date and return a specific interval of time. For example, you might use **DatePart** to calculate the day of the week or the current hour.

The *firstdayofweek* argument affects calculations that use the "w" and "ww" interval symbols.

If *date* is a date literal, the specified year becomes a permanent part of that date. However, if *date* is enclosed in double quotation marks (" "), and you omit the year, the current year is inserted in your code each time the *date* expression is evaluated. This makes it possible to write code that can be used in different years.

See Also

DateAdd function, **DateDiff** function, **Day** function, **Format** function, **Now** function, **Weekday** function, **Year** function.

Example

This example takes a date and, using the **DatePart** function, displays the quarter of the year in which it occurs.

```
Dim TheDate As Date   ' Declare variables.
Dim Msg
TheDate = InputBox("Enter a date:")
Msg = "Quarter: " & DatePart("q", TheDate)
MsgBox Msg
```

Example (Microsoft Access)

The following example uses the **DatePart** function to specify criteria for a select query. For example, suppose you want to create a query based on an Orders table to list all orders placed in the first quarter of 1996. Assuming your Orders table has a OrderID field and an OrderDate field, you can drag the OrderID field to the first cell in the query design grid, and enter the following in the **Criteria** cell beneath it.

```
(DatePart("q", [OrderDate]) = 1) and (DatePart("yyyy", [OrderDate]) = 1996)
```

DateSerial Function

Description

Returns a **Variant** (**Date**) for a specified year, month, and day.

Syntax

DateSerial(*year*, *month*, *day*)

The **DateSerial** function syntax has these named arguments

Part	Description
year	Required; **Integer**. Number between 100 and 9999, inclusive, or a numeric expression.
month	Required; **Integer**. Any numeric expression.
day	Required; **Integer**. Any numeric expression.

Remarks

To specify a date, such as December 31, 1991, the range of numbers for each **DateSerial** argument should be in the accepted range for the unit; that is, 1–31 for days and 1–12 for months. However, you can also specify relative dates for each argument using any numeric expression that represents some number of days, months, or years before or after a certain date.

The following example uses numeric expressions instead of absolute date numbers. Here the **DateSerial** function returns a date that is the day before the first day (`1 - 1`), two months before August (`8 - 2`), 10 years before 1990 (`1990 - 10`); in other words, May 31, 1980.

```
DateSerial(1990 - 10, 8 - 2, 1 - 1)
```

For the ***year*** argument, values between 0 and 99, inclusive, are interpreted as the years 1900–1999. For all other ***year*** arguments, use a four-digit year (for example, 1800).

When any argument exceeds the accepted range for that argument, it increments to the next larger unit as appropriate. For example, if you specify 35 days, it is evaluated as one month and some number of days, depending on where in the year it is applied. If any single argument is outside the range –32,768 to 32,767, an error occurs. If the date specified by the three arguments falls outside the acceptable range of dates, an error occurs.

See Also

Date function, **Date** statement, **DateValue** function, **Day** function, **Month** function, **Now** function, **TimeSerial** function, **TimeValue** function, **Weekday** function, **Year** function.

Example

This example uses the **DateSerial** function to return the date for the specified year, month, and day.

```
Dim MyDate
' MyDate contains the date for February 12, 1969.
MyDate = DateSerial(1969, 2, 12)      ' Return a date.
```

Example (Microsoft Access)

The following example uses the **DateSerial** function together with the **Year**, **Month**, and **Day** functions to return the number of days in a month. You can pass either a date or a string to the DaysInMonth function.

```
Function DaysInMonth(dteInput As Date) As Integer
   Dim intDays As Integer

   ' Add one month, subtract dates to find difference.
   intDays = DateSerial(Year(dteInput), Month(dteInput) + 1, Day(dteInput)) _
      - DateSerial(Year(dteInput), Month(dteInput), Day(dteInput))
   DaysInMonth = intDays
   Debug.Print intDays
End Function
```

The following **Sub** procedure shows several different ways that you might call the DaysInMonth function.

```
Sub CallDaysInMonth()
   Dim intDays As Integer
   intDays = DaysInMonth(#4/1/96#)
   intDays = DaysInMonth("4-1-96")
   intDays = DaysInMonth("April 1, 1996")
End Sub
```

DateValue Function

Description

Returns a **Variant** (**Date**).

Syntax

DateValue(*date***)**

The required *date* argument is normally a string expression representing a date from January 1, 100 through December 31, 9999. However, *date* can also be any expression that can represent a date, a time, or both a date and time, in that range.

Remarks

If *date* is a string that includes only numbers separated by valid date separators, **DateValue** recognizes the order for month, day, and year according to the Short Date format you specified for your system. **DateValue** also recognizes unambiguous dates that contain month names, either in long or abbreviated form. For example, in addition to recognizing 12/30/1991 and 12/30/91, **DateValue** also recognizes December 30, 1991 and Dec 30, 1991.

If the year part of *date* is omitted, **DateValue** uses the current year from your computer's system date.

If the *date* argument includes time information, **DateValue** doesn't return it. However, if *date* includes invalid time information (such as "89:98"), an error occurs.

See Also

Date function, **Date** statement, **DateSerial** function, **Day** function, **Month** function, **Now** function, **TimeSerial** function, **TimeValue** function, **Weekday** function, **Year** function.

Example

This example uses the **DateValue** function to convert a string to a date. You can also use date literals to directly assign a date to a **Variant** or **Date** variable, for example, MyDate = #2/12/69#.

```
Dim MyDate
MyDate = DateValue("February 12, 1969")      ' Return a date.
```

Day Function

Description

Returns a **Variant** (**Integer**) specifying a whole number between 1 and 31, inclusive, representing the day of the month.

Syntax

Day(*date*)

The required *date* argument is any **Variant**, numeric expression, string expression, or any combination, that can represent a date. If *date* contains **Null**, **Null** is returned.

See Also

Date function, **Date** statement, **Hour** function, **Minute** function, **Month** function, **Now** function, **Second** function, **Weekday** function, **Year** function.

Example

This example uses the **Day** function to obtain the day of the month from a specified date. In the development environment, the date literal is displayed in short format using the locale settings of your code.

```
Dim MyDate, MyDay
MyDate = #February 12, 1969#          ' Assign a date.
MyDay = Day(MyDate)                   ' MyDay contains 12.
```

Example (Microsoft Access)

See the **DateSerial** function example (Microsoft Access).

DDB Function

Description

Returns a **Double** specifying the depreciation of an asset for a specific time period using the double-declining balance method or some other method you specify.

Syntax

DDB(*cost, salvage, life, period*[, *factor*])

The **DDB** function has these named arguments

Part	Description
cost	Required. **Double** specifying initial cost of the asset.
salvage	Required. **Double** specifying value of the asset at the end of its useful life.
life	Required. **Double** specifying length of useful life of the asset.
period	Required. **Double** specifying period for which asset depreciation is calculated.
factor	Optional. **Variant** specifying rate at which the balance declines. If omitted, 2 (double-declining method) is assumed.

Remarks

The double-declining balance method computes depreciation at an accelerated rate. Depreciation is highest in the first period and decreases in successive periods.

The ***life*** and ***period*** arguments must be expressed in the same units. For example, if ***life*** is given in months, ***period*** must also be given in months. All arguments must be positive numbers.

The **DDB** function uses the following formula to calculate depreciation for a given period:

Depreciation / ***period*** = ((***cost*** – ***salvage***) * ***factor***) / ***life***

See Also

FV function, **IPmt** function, **IRR** function, **MIRR** function, **NPer** function, **NPV** function, **Pmt** function, **PPmt** function, **PV** function, **Rate** function, **SLN** function, **SYD** function.

Example

This example uses the **DDB** function to return the depreciation of an asset for a specified period given the initial cost (`InitCost`), the salvage value at the end of the asset's useful life (`SalvageVal`), the total life of the asset in years (`LifeTime`), and the period in years for which the depreciation is calculated (`Depr`).

```
Dim Fmt, InitCost, SalvageVal, MonthLife, LifeTime, DepYear, Depr
Const YRMOS = 12                    ' Number of months in a year.
Fmt = "###,##0.00"
InitCost = InputBox("What's the initial cost of the asset?")
SalvageVal = InputBox("Enter the asset's value at end of its life.")
```

```
MonthLife = InputBox("What's the asset's useful life in months?")
Do While MonthLife < YRMOS ' Ensure period is >= 1 year.
   MsgBox "Asset life must be a year or more."
   MonthLife = InputBox("What's the asset's useful life in months?")
Loop
LifeTime = MonthLife / YRMOS         ' Convert months to years.
If LifeTime <> Int(MonthLife / YRMOS) Then
   LifeTime = Int(LifeTime + 1)      ' Round up to nearest year.
End If
DepYear = CInt(InputBox("Enter year for depreciation calculation."))
Do While DepYear < 1 Or DepYear > LifeTime
   MsgBox "You must enter at least 1 but not more than " & LifeTime
   DepYear = InputBox("Enter year for depreciation calculation.")
Loop
Depr = DDB(InitCost, SalvageVal, LifeTime, DepYear)
MsgBox "The depreciation for year " & DepYear & " is " & _
   Format(Depr, Fmt) & "."
```

Deactivate Event

See Activate, Deactivate Events.

Debug Object

Description

The **Debug** object sends output to the **Immediate** window at run time.

Methods

Print method.

Decimal Data Type

Description

Decimal variables are stored as 96-bit (12-byte) unsigned integers scaled by a variable power of 10. The power of 10 scaling factor specifies the number of digits to the right of the decimal point, and ranges from 0 to 28. With a scale of 0 (no decimal places), the largest possible value is +/-79,228,162,514,264,337,593,543,950,335. With a 28 decimal places, the largest value is +/-7.9228162514264337593543950335 and the smallest, non-zero value is +/-0.0000000000000000000000000001.

Note At this time the **Decimal** data type can only be used within a Variant, that is, you cannot declare a variable to be of type **Decimal**. You can, however, create a **Variant** whose subtype is **Decimal** using the **CDec** function.

See Also

Data type summary.

Declare Statement

Description

Used at module level to declare references to external procedures in a dynamic-link library (DLL).

Syntax 1

[**Public** | **Private**] **Declare Sub** *name* **Lib** "*libname*" [**Alias** "*aliasname*"] [([*arglist*])]

Syntax 2

[**Public** | **Private**] **Declare Function** *name* **Lib** "*libname*" [**Alias** "*aliasname*"]
↪ [([*arglist*])] [**As** *type*]

The **Declare** statement syntax has these parts

Part	Description
Public	Optional. Used to declare procedures that are available to all other procedures in all modules.
Private	Optional. Used to declare procedures that are available only within the module where the declaration is made.
Sub	Optional (either **Sub** or **Function** must appear). Indicates that the procedure doesn't return a value.
Function	Optional (either **Sub** or **Function** must appear). Indicates that the procedure returns a value that can be used in an expression.
name	Required. Any valid procedure name. Note that DLL entry points are case sensitive.
Lib	Required. Indicates that a DLL or code resource contains the procedure being declared. The **Lib** clause is required for all declarations.
libname	Required. Name of the DLL or code resource that contains the declared procedure.
Alias	Optional. Indicates that the procedure being called has another name in the DLL. This is useful when the external procedure name is the same as a keyword. You can also use **Alias** when a DLL procedure has the same name as a public variable, constant, or any other procedure in the same scope. **Alias** is also useful if any characters in the DLL procedure name aren't allowed by the DLL naming convention.
aliasname	Optional. Name of the procedure in the DLL or code resource. If the first character is not a number sign (#), *aliasname* is the name of the procedure's entry point in the DLL. If (#) is the first character, all characters that follow must indicate the ordinal number of the procedure's entry point.
arglist	Optional. List of variables representing arguments that are passed to the procedure when it is called.

(continue)

Part	Description
type	Optional. Data type of the value returned by a **Function** procedure; may be **Byte**, **Boolean**, **Integer**, **Long**, **Currency**, **Single**, **Double**, **Decimal** (not currently supported), **Date**, **String** (variable length only), or **Variant**, a user-defined type, or an object type.

The *arglist* argument has the following syntax and parts:

[Optional] [ByVal | ByRef] [ParamArray] *varname*[( )] **[As** *type*]

Part	Description
Optional	Optional. Indicates that an argument is not required. If used, all subsequent arguments in *arglist* must also be optional and declared using the **Optional** keyword. **Optional** can't be used for any argument if **ParamArray** is used.
ByVal	Optional. Indicates that the argument is passed by value.
ByRef	Indicates that the argument is passed by reference. **ByRef** is the default in Visual Basic.
ParamArray	Optional. Used only as the last argument in *arglist* to indicate that the final argument is an **Optional** array of **Variant** elements. The **ParamArray** keyword allows you to provide an arbitrary number of arguments. The **ParamArray** keyword can't be used with **ByVal**, **ByRef**, or **Optional**.
varname	Required. Name of the variable representing the argument being passed to the procedure; follows standard variable naming conventions.
( )	Required for array variables. Indicates that *varname* is an array.
type	Optional. Data type of the argument passed to the procedure; may be **Byte**, **Boolean**, **Integer**, **Long**, **Currency**, **Single**, **Double**, **Decimal** (not currently supported), **Date**, **String** (variable length only), **Object**, **Variant**, a user-defined type, or an object type.

Remarks

For **Function** procedures, the data type of the procedure determines the data type it returns. You can use an **As** clause following *arglist* to specify the return type of the function. Within *arglist*, you can use an **As** clause to specify the data type of any of the arguments passed to the procedure. In addition to specifying any of the standard data types, you can specify **As Any** in *arglist* to inhibit type checking and allow any data type to be passed to the procedure.

Empty parentheses indicate that the **Sub** or **Function** procedure has no arguments and that Visual Basic should ensure that none are passed. In the following example, `First` takes no arguments. If you use arguments in a call to `First`, an error occurs:

```
Declare Sub First Lib "MyLib" ()
```

If you include an argument list, the number and type of arguments are checked each time the procedure is called. In the following example, `First` takes one **Long** argument:

```
Declare Sub First Lib "MyLib" (X As Long)
```

Note You can't have fixed-length strings in the argument list of a **Declare** statement; only variable-length strings can be passed to procedures. Fixed-length strings can appear as procedure arguments, but they are converted to variable-length strings before being passed.

Note The **vbNullString** constant is used when calling external procedures, where the external procedure requires a string whose value is zero. This is not the same thing as a zero-length string ("").

See Also

Call statement, **Function** statement, **LastDLLError** property, **Sub** statement.

Specifics (Macintosh)

On the Power, the **Declare** syntax is the same as in Windows, except that the **CDecl** keyword can be used to indicate that the procedure uses C language argument order, naming conventions, and calling conventions:

[**Public** | **Private**] **Declare Function** *name* [**CDecl**] **Lib** "*libname*"
↪ [**Alias** "*aliasname*"] [([*arglist*])] [**As** *type*]

The **Alias** keyword indicates that the procedure being called is in a Macintosh code resource. This is useful when the external procedure name is the same as a keyword.

Use the *aliasname* to specify the code resource type as follows:

"[*resourcetype*]$[*resourcename*]"

The *resourcetype* is any valid 4-character constant. If omitted, the default *resourcetype* is CODE. The *resourcename* is the procedure name in the code resource. If *resourcename* is omitted, it is assumed to be the same as *name*.

On the Power Macintosh, the **Declare** statement supports calls into native code for code fragments only. Calling into code resources is also supported, but only in 68000 emulation mode.

When used on the Power Macintosh, the **Declare** statement syntax is as follows:

```
Declare Function MyFunction Lib "hd:system folder:extensions: _
   MyCodeFragment" Alias "MyFunction" () As Long
```

For both code fragments and code resources, a full or partial path name may be specified for the **Lib** clause. If the specified **Lib** clause is ambiguous, it is resolved as follows:

- If the file contains a 'cfrg' resource, it's treated as a code fragment.
- If it doesn't contain a 'cfrg' resource, it is treated as a file containing code resources.

This allows the creation of "fat" code fragments, that is, files that contain both code fragments and 68000 code resources. When running Visual Basic for Applications on a 68000 Macintosh, the code resource is used. When running it on a Power Macintosh, the native code fragment is used.

The Macintosh toolbox can be accessed on the Power Macintosh using a declaration into the system code fragment.

Specifics (Microsoft Access)

In Microsoft Access, **Declare** statements are public by default. In a standard module, a public **Declare** statement is available to all procedures in the current database and in any referencing databases. You can preface a **Declare** statement with the **Private** keyword to ensure that it is not available outside of the current module.

To use a **Declare** statement in a class module, you must precede the statement with the **Private** keyword. If you fail to include the **Private** keyword, Microsoft Access generates a compile-time error.

Example

This example shows how the **Declare** statement is used at the module level of a standard module to declare a reference to an external procedure in a dynamic-link library (DLL) or Macintosh code resource. You can place the **Declare** statements in class modules if the **Declare** statements are **Private**.

```
' In Microsoft Windows (16-bit):
Declare Sub MessageBeep Lib "User" (ByVal N As Integer)
' Assume SomeBeep is an alias for the procedure name.
Declare Sub MessageBeep Lib "User" Alias "SomeBeep"(ByVal N As Integer)
' Use an ordinal in the Alias clause to call GetWinFlags.
Declare Function GetWinFlags Lib "Kernel" Alias "#132"() As Long

' In 32-bit Microsoft Windows systems, specify the library USER32.DLL,
' rather than USER.DLL. You can use conditional compilation to write
' code that can run on either Win32 or Win16.
#If Win32 Then
   Declare Sub MessageBeep Lib "User32" (ByVal N As Long)
#Else
   Declare Sub MessageBeep Lib "User" (ByVal N As Integer)
#End If

' On the Macintosh:
Declare Sub MessageAlert Lib "MyHd:MyAlert" Alias "MyAlert" (ByVal N _
   As Integer)
' Use a code resource in the Alias clause.
Declare Sub MessageAlert Lib "MyHd:MyAlert" Alias "XTST$MyAlert" _
   (ByVal N As Integer)
```

```
' If the code-resource type specifier has only 3 characters, be sure to
' leave a blank space where the final character would normally be.
Declare Sub MessageAlert Lib "MyHd:AnAlert" Alias "COD $AnAlert" _
   (ByVal N As Integer)
```

Example (Microsoft Access)

In Microsoft Access, you can use the **Declare** statement at the module level of a standard module to declare a reference to an external procedure in a dynamic-link library (DLL). A **Declare** statement is public by default. In order to include a **Declare** statement in a class module, precede it with the **Private** keyword.

The following example references a procedure in a DLL, then calls that procedure from Visual Basic.

```
' In standard module.
Declare Sub MessageBeep Lib "User32" (ByVal intN As Integer)

' In class module.
Private Declare Sub MessageBeep Lib "User32" (ByVal intN As Integer)

' Once you have referenced procedure in DLL with Declare
' statement, you can call that procedure normally from code.
Sub SystemBeep(intBeeps As Integer, sngPause As Single)
   Dim intI As Integer
   Dim sngStart As Single

   For intI = 1 To intBeeps
      ' Call system function.
      Call MessageBeep(intBeeps)
      ' Get start time.
      sngStart = Timer
      ' Pause between beeps.
      Do While Timer < sngStart + sngPause
         ' Return control to operating system.
         DoEvents
      Loop
   Next intI
End Sub
```

Deftype Statements

Description

Used at module level to set the default data type for variables, arguments passed to procedures, and the return type for **Function** and **Property Get** procedures whose names start with the specified characters.

Syntax

DefBool *letterrange*[, *letterrange*] . . .
DefByte *letterrange*[, *letterrange*] . . .
DefInt *letterrange*[, *letterrange*] . . .

DefLng *letterrange*[, *letterrange*] . . .
DefCur *letterrange*[, *letterrange*] . . .
DefSng *letterrange*[, *letterrange*] . . .
DefDbl *letterrange*[, *letterrange*] . . .
DefDec *letterrange*[, *letterrange*] . . .
DefDate *letterrange*[, *letterrange*] . . .
DefStr *letterrange*[, *letterrange*] . . .
DefObj *letterrange*[, *letterrange*] . . .
DefVar *letterrange*[, *letterrange*] . . .

The required *letterrange* argument has the following syntax:

letter1[-*letter2*]

The *letter1* and *letter2* arguments specify the name range for which you can set a default data type. Each argument represents the first letter of the variable, argument, **Function** procedure, or **Property Get** procedure name and can be any letter of the alphabet. The case of letters in *letterrange* isn't significant.

Remarks

The statement name determines the data type

Statement	Data Type
DefBool	**Boolean**
DefByte	**Byte**
DefInt	**Integer**
DefLng	**Long**
DefCur	**Currency**
DefSng	**Single**
DefDbl	**Double**
DefDec	**Decimal** (not currently supported)
DefDate	**Date**
DefStr	**String**
DefObj	**Object**
DefVar	**Variant**

For example, in the following program fragment, `Message` is a string variable:

```
DefStr A-Q
. . .
Message = "Out of stack space."
```

A **Def***type* statement affects only the module where it is used. For example, a **DefInt** statement in one module affects only the default data type of variables, arguments passed to procedures, and the return type for **Function** and **Property Get** procedures declared in that module; the default data type of variables, arguments, and return types in other modules is unaffected. If not explicitly declared with a **Def***type* statement, the default data type for all variables, all arguments, all **Function** procedures, and all **Property Get** procedures is **Variant**.

When you specify a letter range, it usually defines the data type for variables that begin with letters in the first 128 characters of the character set. However, when you specify the letter range A–Z, you set the default to the specified data type for all variables, including variables that begin with international characters from the extended part of the character set (128–255).

Once the range A–Z has been specified, you can't further redefine any subranges of variables using **Def***type* statements. Once a range has been specified, if you include a previously defined letter in another **Def***type* statement, an error occurs. However, you can explicitly specify the data type of any variable, defined or not, using a **Dim** statement with an **As** *type* clause. For example, you can use the following code at module level to define a variable as a **Double** even though the default data type is **Integer**:

```
DefInt A-Z
Dim TaxRate As Double
```

Def*type* statements don't affect elements of user-defined types because the elements must be explicitly declared.

See Also

Function statement, **Let** statement, **Property Get** statement.

Example

This example shows various uses of the **Def***type* statements to set default data types of variables and function procedures whose names start with specified characters. The default data type can be overridden only by explicit assignment using the **Dim** statement. **Def***type* statements can only be used at the module level, that is, not within procedures.

```
' Variable names beginning with A through K default to Integer.
DefInt A-K
' Variable names beginning with L through Z default to String.
DefStr L-Z
CalcVar = 4                             ' Initialize Integer.
StringVar = "Hello there"               ' Initialize String.
AnyVar = "Hello"                        ' Causes "Type mismatch" error.
Dim Calc As Double                      ' Explicitly set the type to Double.
Calc = 2.3455                           ' Assign a Double.

' Deftype statements also apply to function procedures.
CalcNum = ATestFunction(4)  ' Call user-defined function.
' ATestFunction function procedure definition.
Function ATestFunction(INumber)
   ATestFunction = INumber * 2          ' Return value is an integer.
End Function
```

DeleteSetting Statement

Description

Deletes a section or key setting from an application's entry in the Windows registry.

Syntax

DeleteSetting ***appname*****,** ***section***[**,** ***key***]

The **DeleteSetting** statement syntax has these named arguments

Part	Description
appname	Required. String expression containing the name of the application or project to which the section or key setting applies.
section	Required. String expression containing the name of the section where the key setting is being deleted. If only ***appname*** and ***section*** are provided, the specified section is deleted along with all related key settings.
key	Optional. String expression containing the name of the key setting being deleted.

Remarks

If all arguments are provided, the specified key setting is deleted. However, the **DeleteSetting** statement does nothing if the specified section or key setting does not exist.

See Also

GetAllSettings function, **GetSetting** function, **SaveSetting** statement.

Example

The following example first uses the **SaveSetting** statement to make entries in the Windows registry (or .ini file on 16-bit Windows platforms) for the `MyApp` application, and then uses the **DeleteSetting** statement to remove them. Because no ***key*** argument is specified, the whole section is deleted, including the section name and all its keys.

```
' Place some settings in the registry.
SaveSetting appname := "MyApp", section := "Startup", _
   key := "Top", setting := 75
SaveSetting "MyApp","Startup", "Left", 50
' Remove section and all its settings from registry.
DeleteSetting "MyApp", "Startup"
```

Description Property

Applies To

Err object, **Reference** object ("Extensibility Object Model Language Reference").

Description

Returns or sets a string expression containing a descriptive string associated with an object. Read/write.

For the **Err** object, returns or sets a descriptive string associated with an error.

Remarks

The **Description** property setting consists of a short description of the error. Use this property to alert the user to an error that you either can't or don't want to handle. When generating a user-defined error, assign a short description of your error to the **Description** property. If **Description** isn't filled in, and the value of **Number** corresponds to a Visual Basic run-time error, the string returned by the **Error** function is placed in **Description** when the error is generated.

See Also

Err object, **Error** function, **HelpContext** property, **HelpFile** property, **LastDLLError** property, **Number** property, **Source** property.

Example

This example assigns a user-defined message to the **Description** property of the **Err** object.

```
Err.Description = "It was not possible to access an object necessary " _
   & "for this operation."
```

Dim Statement

Description

Declares variables and allocates storage space.

Syntax

Dim [**WithEvents**] *varname*[([*subscripts*])] [**As** [**New**] *type*] [**,** [**WithEvents**]
➥ *varname*[([*subscripts*])] [**As** [**New**] *type*]] **. . .**

The **Dim** statement syntax has these parts

Part	Description
WithEvents	Optional. Keyword that specifies that *varname* is an object variable used to respond to events triggered by an ActiveX object. Valid only in class modules. You can declare as many individual variables as you like using **WithEvents**, but you can't create arrays with **WithEvents**. You can't use **New** with **WithEvents**.
varname	Required. Name of the variable; follows standard variable naming conventions.

(continue)

Part	Description
subscripts	Optional. Dimensions of an array variable; up to 60 multiple dimensions may be declared. The *subscripts* argument uses the following syntax: [*lower* **To**] *upper* [**,** [*lower* **To**] *upper*] **. . .** When not explicitly stated in *lower*, the lower bound of an array is controlled by the **Option Base** statement. The lower bound is zero if no **Option Base** statement is present.
New	Optional. Keyword that enables implicit creation of an object. If you use **New** when declaring the object variable, a new instance of the object is created on first reference to it, so you don't have to use the **Set** statement to assign the object reference. The **New** keyword can't be used to declare variables of any intrinsic data type, can't be used to declare instances of dependent objects, and can't be used with **WithEvents**.
type	Optional. Data type of the variable; may be **Byte**, **Boolean**, **Integer**, **Long**, **Currency**, **Single**, **Double**, **Decimal** (not currently supported), **Date**, **String** (for variable-length strings), **String** * *length* (for fixed-length strings), **Object**, **Variant**, a user-defined type, or an object type. Use a separate **As** *type* clause for each variable you declare.

Remarks

Variables declared with **Dim** at the module level are available to all procedures within the module. At the procedure level, variables are available only within the procedure.

Use the **Dim** statement at module or procedure level to declare the data type of a variable. For example, the following statement declares a variable as an **Integer**.

```
Dim NumberOfEmployees As Integer
```

Also use a **Dim** statement to declare the object type of a variable. The following declares a variable for a new instance of a worksheet.

```
Dim X As New Worksheet
```

If the **New** keyword is not used when declaring an object variable, the variable that refers to the object must be assigned an existing object using the **Set** statement before it can be used. Until it is assigned an object, the declared object variable has the special value **Nothing**, which indicates that it doesn't refer to any particular instance of an object.

You can also use the **Dim** statement with empty parentheses to declare a dynamic array. After declaring a dynamic array, use the **ReDim** statement within a procedure to define the number of dimensions and elements in the array. If you try to redeclare a dimension for an array variable whose size was explicitly specified in a **Private**, **Public**, or **Dim** statement, an error occurs.

If you don't specify a data type or object type, and there is no **Def***type* statement in the module, the variable is **Variant** by default.

When variables are initialized, a numeric variable is initialized to 0, a variable-length string is initialized to a zero-length string (""), and a fixed-length string is filled with zeros. **Variant** variables are initialized to **Empty**. Each element of a user-defined type variable is initialized as if it were a separate variable.

Note When you use the **Dim** statement in a procedure, you generally put the **Dim** statement at the beginning of the procedure.

See Also

Array function, **Option Base** statement, **Private** statement, **Public** statement, **ReDim** statement, **Set** statement, **Static** statement, **Type** statement.

Specifics (Microsoft Access)

You can use the **New** keyword with the **Dim** statement to declare an object variable of a specific type. If you include the **New** keyword in your variable declaration, you automatically create a new object and point the object variable to it. If you declare an object variable by using the **New** keyword, you don't need to use the **Set** statement.

By using the **New** keyword, you can create an object variable to point to any type of object. The **New** keyword is used most frequently to create a new instance of a class or to create a new **Collection** object, as shown in the following example.

```
' Create object variable and point it to new object.
Dim colInstances As New Collection
```

The following example shows how to use the **New** keyword to create a new instance of a class.

```
' Create new instance of class module.
Dim obj As New Class1
```

You can use the **New** keyword to create a new Microsoft Access object from some components that support Automation. Check the component's documentation to determine whether or not it supports this syntax.

For example, from another component, assuming you have established a reference to the Microsoft Access type library, you can create a new Microsoft Access **Application** object with the following code.

```
Dim appAccess As New Access.Application
```

Example

This example shows various uses of the **Dim** statement to declare variables. It also shows the **Dim** statement being used to declare arrays. The default lower bound for array subscripts is 0 and can be overridden at the module level using the **Option Base** statement.

```
' AnyValue and MyValue are declared as Variant by default with values
' set to Empty.
Dim AnyValue, MyValue
```

```
' Explicitly declare a variable of type Integer.
Dim Number As Integer

' Multiple declarations on a single line. AnotherVar is of type Variant
' because its type is omitted.
Dim AnotherVar, Choice As Boolean, BirthDate As Date

' DayArray is an array of Variants with 51 elements indexed, from
' 0 thru 50, assuming Option Base is set to 0 (default) for
' the current module.
Dim DayArray(50)

' Matrix is a two-dimensional array of integers.
Dim Matrix(3, 4) As Integer

' MyMatrix is a three-dimensional array of doubles with explicit
' bounds.
Dim MyMatrix(1 To 5,  4 To 9,  3 To 5) As Double

' BirthDay is an array of dates with indexes from 1 to 10.
Dim BirthDay(1 To 10) As Date

' MyArray is a dynamic array of variants.
Dim MyArray()
```

Dir Function

Description

Returns a **String** representing the name of a file, directory, or folder that matches a specified pattern or file attribute, or the volume label of a drive.

Syntax

Dir[(*pathname*[, *attributes*])]

The **Dir** function syntax has these parts

Part	Description
pathname	Optional. String expression that specifies a file name—may include directory or folder, and drive. A zero-length string ("") is returned if *pathname* is not found.
attributes	Optional. Constant or numeric expression, whose sum specifies file attributes. If omitted, all files are returned that match *pathname*.

Settings

The *attributes* argument settings are

Constant	Value	Description
vbNormal	0	Normal.
vbHidden	2	Hidden.

(continue)

vbSystem	4	System file.
vbVolume	8	Volume label; if specified, all other attributes are ignored.
vbDirectory	16	Directory or folder.

Note These constants are specified by Visual Basic for Applications and can be used anywhere in your code in place of the actual values.

Remarks

Dir supports the use of multiple-character (*) and single-character (**?**) wildcards to specify multiple files.

You must specify *pathname* the first time you call the **Dir** function, or an error occurs. If you also specify file attributes, *pathname* must be included.

Dir returns the first file name that matches *pathname*. To get any additional file names that match *pathname*, call **Dir** again with no arguments. When no more file names match, **Dir** returns a zero-length string (""). Once a zero-length string is returned, you must specify *pathname* in subsequent calls or an error occurs. You can change to a new *pathname* without retrieving all of the file names that match the current *pathname*. However, you can't call the **Dir** function recursively. Calling **Dir** with the **vbDirectory** attribute does not continually return subdirectories.

Tip Because file names are retrieved in no particular order, you may want to store returned file names in an array and then sort the array.

See Also

ChDir statement, **CurDir** function, **MacID** function.

Specifics (Macintosh)

In Microsoft Windows, **Dir** supports the use of multiple character (*) and single character (**?**) wildcards to specify multiple files. On the Macintosh, these characters are treated as valid file name characters and can't be used as wildcards to specify multiple files.

Since the Macintosh doesn't support the wildcards, use the file type to identify groups of files. You can use the **MacID** function to specify file type instead of using the file names. For example, the following statement returns the name of the first TEXT file in the current folder:

```
Dir("SomePath", MacID("TEXT"))
```

To iterate over all files in a folder, specify an empty string:

```
Dir("")
```

If you use the **MacID** function with **Dir** in Microsoft Windows, an error occurs.

Any *attribute* value greater than 256 is considered a **MacID** value.

The following constants aren't available on the Macintosh

Constant	Value	Description
vbSystem	4	System file
vbVolume	8	Volume label

The following constant is available only on the Macintosh

Constant	Value	Description
vbAlias	64	Specified file name is an alias.

Example

This example uses the **Dir** function to check if certain files and directories exist. The **MacID** function may be used on the Macintosh to specify the file type.

```
Dim MyFile, MyPath, MyName
' In Microsoft Windows:
' Returns "WIN.INI" if it exists.
MyFile = Dir("C:\WINDOWS\WIN.INI")

' Returns filename with specified extension. If more than one *.ini
' file exists, the first file found is returned.
MyFile = Dir("C:\WINDOWS\*.INI")

' Call Dir again without arguments to return the next *.INI file in the
' same directory.
MyFile = Dir

' Return first *.TXT file with a set hidden attribute.
MyFile = Dir("*.TXT", vbHidden)

' Display the names in C:\ that represent directories.
MyPath = "c:\"                          ' Set the path.
MyName = Dir(MyPath, vbDirectory)       ' Retrieve the first entry.
Do While MyName <> ""                   ' Start the loop.
   ' Ignore the current directory and the encompassing directory.
   If MyName <> "." And MyName <> ".." Then
      ' Use bitwise comparison to make sure MyName is a directory.
      If (GetAttr(MyPath & MyName) And vbDirectory) = vbDirectory Then
         Debug.Print MyName             ' Display entry only if it
      End If                    ' it represents a directory.
   End If
   MyName = Dir                         ' Get next entry.
Loop

' On the Macintosh:
' Use the MacID function to specify file type.
' The following statement returns the first "TEXT" file found in the
' specified directory or folder.
MyFile = Dir("HD:MY FOLDER:", MacID("TEXT"))
```

Do...Loop Statement

Description

Repeats a block of statements while a condition is **True** or until a condition becomes **True**.

Syntax

Do [{**While** | **Until**} *condition*]
  [*statements*]
  [**Exit Do**]
  [*statements*]
Loop

Or, you can use this syntax:

Do
  [*statements*]
  [**Exit Do**]
  [*statements*]
Loop [{**While** | **Until**} *condition*]

The **Do Loop** statement syntax has these parts

Part	Description
condition	Optional. Numeric expression or string expression that is **True** or **False**. If *condition* is **Null**, *condition* is treated as **False**.
statements	One or more statements that are repeated while, or until, *condition* is **True**.

Remarks

Any number of **Exit Do** statements may be placed anywhere in the **Do...Loop** as an alternate way to exit a **Do...Loop**. **Exit Do** is often used after evaluating some condition, for example, **If...Then**, in which case the **Exit Do** statement transfers control to the statement immediately following the **Loop**.

When used within nested **Do...Loop** statements, **Exit Do** transfers control to the loop that is one nested level above the loop where **Exit Do** occurs.

See Also

Exit statement, **For...Next** statement, **While...Wend** statement.

Example

This example shows how **Do...Loop** statements can be used. The inner **Do...Loop** statement loops 10 times, sets the value of the flag to **False**, and exits prematurely using the **Exit Do** statement. The outer loop exits immediately upon checking the value of the flag.

```
Dim Check, Counter
Check = True: Counter = 0              ' Initialize variables.
Do ' Outer loop.
   Do While Counter < 20               ' Inner loop.
      Counter = Counter + 1            ' Increment Counter.
      If Counter = 10 Then             ' If condition is True.
         Check = False                 ' Set value of flag to False.
         Exit Do                       ' Exit inner loop.
      End If
   Loop
Loop Until Check = False               ' Exit outer loop immediately.
```

Example (Microsoft Excel)

This example sorts the data in the first column on Sheet1 and then deletes any rows that contain duplicate data.

```
Worksheets("Sheet1").Range("A1").Sort _
   key1:=Worksheets("Sheet1").Range("A1")
Set currentCell = Worksheets("Sheet1").Range("A1")
Do While Not IsEmpty(currentCell)
   Set nextCell = currentCell.Offset(1, 0)
   If nextCell.Value = currentCell.Value Then
      currentCell.EntireRow.Delete
   End If
   Set currentCell = nextCell
Loop
```

DoEvents Function

Description

Yields execution so that the operating system can process other events.

Syntax

DoEvents( )

Remarks

The **DoEvents** function returns an **Integer** representing the number of open forms in stand-alone versions of Visual Basic, such as Visual Basic, Standard Edition. **DoEvents** returns zero in all other applications.

DoEvents passes control to the operating system. Control is returned after the operating system has finished processing the events in its queue and all keys in the **SendKeys** queue have been sent.

DoEvents is most useful for simple things like allowing a user to cancel a process after it has started, for example a search for a file. For long-running processes, yielding the processor is better accomplished by using a Timer or delegating the task to an ActiveX EXE component. In the latter case, the task can continue completely independent of your application, and the operating system takes case of multitasking and time slicing.

Caution Any time you temporarily yield the processor within an event procedure, make sure the procedure is not executed again from a different part of your code before the first call returns; this could cause unpredictable results. In addition, do not use **DoEvents** if other applications could possibly interact with your procedure in unforeseen ways during the time you have yielded control.

See Also

SendKeys statement.

Specifics (Microsoft Access)

In Microsoft Access, the **DoEvents** function is ignored if you use it in:

- A user-defined function or a procedure that calculates a field in a query, form, or report.
- A user-defined function that creates a list to fill a combo box, a list box, or an OLE object.

If you include the **DoEvents** function in any of these, Microsoft Access will not relinquish control to the operating system.

Example

This example uses the **DoEvents** function to cause execution to yield to the operating system once every 1000 iterations of the loop. **DoEvents** returns the number of open Visual Basic forms, but only when the host application is Visual Basic.

```
' Create a variable to hold number of Visual Basic forms loaded
' and visible.
Dim I, OpenForms
For I = 1 To 150000                   ' Start loop.
   If I Mod 1000 = 0 Then             ' If loop has repeated 1000 times.
      OpenForms = DoEvents            ' Yield to operating system.
   End If
Next I' Increment loop counter.
```

Example (Microsoft Access)

The following example uses the **DoEvents** function to return control to the operating system while a loop is executing. The **DoEvents** function always returns 0.

```
Sub LongLoop()
   Dim intI As Integer

   For intI = 1 To 1500               ' Start loop.
      If intI Mod 100 = 0 Then        ' If loop has repeated 100 times.
         DoEvents                     ' Yield to operating system.
         Debug.Print intI
      End If
   Next intI                          ' Increment loop counter.
End Sub
```

Double Data Type

Description

Double (double-precision floating-point) variables are stored as IEEE 64-bit (8-byte) floating-point numbers ranging in value from –1.79769313486232E308 to –4.94065645841247E–324 for negative values and from 4.94065645841247E–324 to 1.79769313486232E308 for positive values. The type-declaration character for **Double** is the number sign (#).

See Also

Data type summary, **Def***type* statements, **Single** data type.

End Statement

Description

Ends a procedure or block.

Syntax

End
End Function
End If
End Property
End Select
End Sub
End Type
End With

The **End** statement syntax has these forms

Statement	Description
End	Terminates execution immediately. Never required by itself but may be placed anywhere in a procedure to end code execution, close files opened with the **Open** statement and to clear variables.
End Function	Required to end a **Function** statement.
End If	Required to end a block **If...Then...Else** statement.
End Property	Required to end a **Property Let**, **Property Get**, or **Property Set** procedure.
End Select	Required to end a **Select Case** statement.
End Sub	Required to end a **Sub** statement.
End Type	Required to end a user-defined type definition (**Type** statement).
End With	Required to end a **With** statement.

Remarks

When executed, the **End** statement resets all module-level variables and all static local variables in all modules. To preserve the value of these variables, use the **Stop** statement instead. You can then resume execution while preserving the value of those variables.

Note The **End** statement stops code execution abruptly, without invoking the Unload, QueryUnload, or Terminate event, or any other Visual Basic code. Code you have placed in the Unload, QueryUnload, and Terminate events of forms and class modules is not executed. Objects created from class modules are destroyed, files opened using the **Open** statement are closed, and memory used by your program is freed. Object references held by other programs are invalidated.

The **End** statement provides a way to force your program to halt. For normal termination of a Visual Basic program, you should unload all forms. Your program closes as soon as there are no other programs holding references to objects created from your public class modules and no code executing.

See Also

Exit statement, **Function** statement, **If...Then...Else** statement, **Property Get** statement, **Property Let** statement, **Property Set** statement, **Select Case** statement, **Stop** statement, **Sub** statement, **Type** statement, **With** statement.

Example

This example uses the **End** Statement to end code execution if the user enters an invalid password.

```
Sub Form_Load
   Dim Password, Pword
   PassWord = "Swordfish"
   Pword = InputBox("Type in your password")
   If Pword <> PassWord Then
      MsgBox "Sorry, incorrect password"
      End
   End If
End Sub
```

Environ Function

Description

Returns the **String** associated with an operating system environment variable.

Syntax

Environ({***envstring*** | ***number***}**)**

The **Environ** function syntax has these named arguments

Part	Description
envstring	Optional. String expression containing the name of an environment variable.
number	Optional. Numeric expression corresponding to the numeric order of the environment string in the environment-string table. The ***number*** argument can be any numeric expression, but is rounded to a whole number before it is evaluated.

Remarks

If ***envstring*** can't be found in the environment-string table, a zero-length string ("") is returned. Otherwise, **Environ** returns the text assigned to the specified ***envstring***; that is, the text following the equal sign (=) in the environment-string table for that environment variable.

If you specify ***number***, the string occupying that numeric position in the environment-string table is returned. In this case, **Environ** returns all of the text, including ***envstring***. If there is no environment string in the specified position, **Environ** returns a zero-length string.

Example

This example uses the **Environ** function to supply the entry number and length of the PATH statement from the environment-string table.

```
Dim EnvString, Indx, Msg, PathLen              ' Declare variables.
Indx = 1                                       ' Initialize index to 1.
Do
   EnvString = Environ(Indx)                   ' Get environment
                                               ' variable.
   If Left(EnvString, 5) = "PATH=" Then        ' Check PATH entry.
      PathLen = Len(Environ("PATH"))           ' Get length.
      Msg = "PATH entry = " & Indx & " and length = " & PathLen
      Exit Do
   Else
      Indx = Indx + 1                          ' Not PATH entry,
   End If                                 ' so increment.
Loop Until EnvString = ""
If PathLen > 0 Then
   MsgBox Msg                                  ' Display message.
Else
   MsgBox "No PATH environment variable exists."
End If
```

EOF Function

Description

Returns an **Integer** containing the **Boolean** value **True** when the end of a file opened for **Random** or sequential **Input** has been reached.

Syntax

EOF(*filenumber*)

The required *filenumber* argument is an **Integer** containing any valid file number.

Remarks

Use **EOF** to avoid the error generated by attempting to get input past the end of a file.

The **EOF** function returns **False** until the end of the file has been reached. With files opened for **Random** or **Binary** access, **EOF** returns **False** until the last executed **Get** statement is unable to read an entire record.

With files opened for **Binary** access, an attempt to read through the file using the **Input** function until **EOF** returns **True** generates an error. Use the **LOF** and **Loc** functions instead of **EOF** when reading binary files with **Input**, or use **Get** when using the **EOF** function. With files opened for **Output**, **EOF** always returns **True**.

See Also

Get statement, **Loc** function, **LOF** function, **Open** statement.

Example

This example uses the **EOF** function to detect the end of a file. This example assumes that MYFILE is a text file with a few lines of text.

```
Dim InputData
Open "MYFILE" For Input As #1                ' Open file for input.
Do While Not EOF(1)                          ' Check for end of file.
   Line Input #1, InputData                  ' Read line of data.
   Debug.Print InputData                     ' Print to Debug window.
Loop
Close #1                                     ' Close file.
```

Eqv Operator

Description

Used to perform a logical equivalence on two expressions.

Syntax

result = *expression1* **Eqv** *expression2*

The **Eqv** operator syntax has these parts

Part	Description
result	Required; any numeric variable.
expression1	Required; any expression.
expression2	Required; any expression.

Remarks

If either expression is **Null**, *result* is also **Null**. When neither expression is **Null**, *result* is determined according to the following table

If *expression1* is	And *expression2* is	The *result* is
True	**True**	**True**
True	**False**	**False**
False	**True**	**False**
False	**False**	**True**

The **Eqv** operator performs a bitwise comparison of identically positioned bits in two numeric expressions and sets the corresponding bit in *result* according to the following table

If bit in *expression1* is	And bit in *expression2* is	The *result* is
0	0	1
0	1	0
1	0	0
1	1	1

See Also

Operator precedence.

Example

This example uses the **Eqv** operator to perform logical equivalence on two expressions.

```
Dim A, B, C, D, MyCheck
A = 10: B = 8: C = 6: D = Null          ' Initialize variables.
MyCheck = A > B Eqv B > C               ' Returns True.
MyCheck = B > A Eqv B > C               ' Returns False.
MyCheck = A > B Eqv B > D               ' Returns Null.
MyCheck = A Eqv B                       ' Returns -3 (bitwise comparison).
```

Erase Statement

Description

Reinitializes the elements of fixed-size arrays and releases dynamic-array storage space.

Syntax

Erase *arraylist*

The required *arraylist* argument is one or more comma-delimited array variables to be erased.

Remarks

Erase behaves differently depending on whether an array is fixed-size (ordinary) or dynamic. **Erase** recovers no memory for fixed-size arrays. **Erase** sets the elements of a fixed array as follows

Type of array	Effect of Erase on fixed-array elements
Fixed numeric array	Sets each element to zero.
Fixed string array (variable length)	Sets each element to a zero-length string ("").
Fixed string array (fixed length)	Sets each element to zero.
Fixed **Variant** array	Sets each element to **Empty**.
Array of user-defined types	Sets each element as if it were a separate variable.
Array of objects	Sets each element to the special value **Nothing**.

Erase frees the memory used by dynamic arrays. Before your program can refer to the dynamic array again, it must redeclare the array variable's dimensions using a **ReDim** statement.

See Also

Array function, **Dim** statement, **Private** statement, **Public** statement, **ReDim** statement, **Static** statement.

Example

This example uses the **Erase** statement to reinitialize the elements of fixed-size arrays and deallocate dynamic-array storage space.

```
' Declare array variables.
Dim NumArray(10) As Integer              ' Integer array.
Dim StrVarArray(10) As String            ' Variable-string array.
Dim StrFixArray(10) As String * 10       ' Fixed-string array.
Dim VarArray(10) As Variant              ' Variant array.
Dim DynamicArray() As Integer            ' Dynamic array.
ReDim DynamicArray(10)                   ' Allocate storage space.
Erase NumArray                           ' Each element set to 0.
Erase StrVarArray                        ' Each element set to zero-length
                                         ' string ("").
Erase StrFixArray                        ' Each element set to 0.
Erase VarArray                           ' Each element set to Empty.
Erase DynamicArray                       ' Free memory used by array.
```

Err Object

Description

Contains information about run-time errors.

Remarks

The properties of the **Err** object are set by the generator of an error—Visual Basic, an object, or the Visual Basic programmer.

The default property of the **Err** object is **Number**. Because the default property can be represented by the object name **Err**, earlier code written using the **Err** function or **Err** statement doesn't have to be modified.

When a run-time error occurs, the properties of the **Err** object are filled with information that uniquely identifies the error and information that can be used to handle it. To generate a run-time error in your code, use the **Raise** method.

The **Err** object's properties are reset to zero or zero-length strings ("") after any form of the **Resume** or **On Error** statement and after an **Exit Sub**, **Exit Function**, or **Exit Property** statement within an error-handling routine. The **Clear** method can be used to explicitly reset **Err**.

Use the **Raise** method, rather than the **Error** statement, to generate run-time errors for a class module. Using the **Raise** method in other code depends on the richness of the information you want to return. In code that uses **Error** statements instead of the **Raise** method to generate errors, the properties of the **Err** object are assigned the following default values when **Error** is executed

Property	Value
Number	Value specified as argument to **Error** statement. Can be any valid error number.
Source	Name of the current Visual Basic project.
Description	A string corresponding to the return of the **Error** function for the specified **Number**, if this string exists. If the string doesn't exist, **Description** contains "Application-defined or object-defined error".
HelpFile	The fully qualified drive, path, and file name of the Visual Basic Help file.
HelpContext	The Visual Basic Help file context ID for the error corresponding to the **Number** property.
LastDLLError	On 32-bit Microsoft Windows operating systems only, contains the system error code for the last call to a dynamic-link library (DLL). The **LastDLLError** property is read-only.

You don't have to change existing code that uses the **Err** object and the **Error** statement. However, using both the **Err** object and the **Error** statement can result in unintended consequences. For example, even if you fill in properties for the **Err** object, they are reset to the default values indicated in the preceding table as soon as the **Error** statement is executed. Although you can still use the **Error** statement to generate Visual Basic run-time errors, it is retained principally for compatibility with existing code. Use the **Err** object, the **Raise** method, and the **Clear** method for system errors and in new code, especially for class modules.

The **Err** object is an intrinsic object with global scope. There is no need to create an instance of it in your code.

Properties

Description property, **HelpContext** property, **HelpContextID** property, **HelpFile** property, **LastDLLError** property, **Number** property, **Source** property.

Methods

Clear method, **Raise** method.

See Also

Error function, **Error** object ("DAO Language Reference" in Volume 1), **Error** statement, **On Error** statement, **Resume** statement.

Example

This example uses the properties of the **Err** object in constructing an error-message dialog box. Note that if you use the **Clear** method first, when you generate a Visual Basic error with the **Raise** method, Visual Basic's default values become the properties of the **Err** object.

```
Dim Msg
' If an error occurs, construct an error message
On Error Resume Next                    ' Defer error handling.
Err.Clear
Err.Raise 6                             ' Generate an "Overflow" error.
' Check for error, then show message.
If Err.Number <> 0 Then
   Msg = "Error # " & Str(Err.Number) & " was generated by " _
      & Err.Source & Chr(13) & Err.Description
   MsgBox Msg, , "Error", Err.Helpfile, Err.HelpContext
End If
```

Error Function

Description

Returns the error message that corresponds to a given error number.

Syntax

Error[(*errornumber*)]

The optional *errornumber* argument can be any valid error number. If *errornumber* is a valid error number, but is not defined, **Error** returns the string "Application-defined or object-defined error." If *errornumber* is not valid, an error occurs. If *errornumber* is omitted, the message corresponding to the most recent run-time error is returned. If no run-time error has occurred, or *errornumber* is 0, **Error** returns a zero-length string ("").

Remarks

Examine the property settings of the **Err** object to identify the most recent run-time error. The return value of the **Error** function corresponds to the **Description** property of the **Err** object.

See Also

Err object.

Example

This example uses the **Error** function to print error messages that correspond to the specified error numbers.

```
Dim ErrorNumber
For ErrorNumber = 61 To 64              ' Loop through values 61 - 64.
   Debug.Print Error(ErrorNumber)       ' Print error to Debug window.
Next ErrorNumber
```

Error Statement

Description

Simulates the occurrence of an error.

Syntax

Error *errornumber*

The required *errornumber* can be any valid error number.

Remarks

The **Error** statement is supported for backward compatibility. In new code, especially when creating objects, use the **Err** object's **Raise** method to generate run-time errors.

If *errornumber* is defined, the **Error** statement calls the error handler after the properties of **Err** object are assigned the following default values

Property	Value
Number	Value specified as argument to **Error** statement. Can be any valid error number.
Source	Name of the current Visual Basic project.
Description	String expression corresponding to the return value of the **Error** function for the specified **Number**, if this string exists. If the string doesn't exist, **Description** contains a zero-length string ("").
HelpFile	The fully qualified drive, path, and file name of the appropriate Visual Basic Help file.
HelpContext	The appropriate Visual Basic Help file context ID for the error corresponding to the **Number** property.
LastDLLError	Zero.

If no error handler exists or if none is enabled, an error message is created and displayed from the **Err** object properties.

Note Not all Visual Basic host applications can create objects. See your host application's documentation to determine whether it can create classes and objects.

See Also

Clear method, **Err** object, **Error** function, **On Error** statement, **Raise** method, **Resume** statement.

Example

This example uses the **Error** statement to simulate error number 11.

```
On Error Resume Next          ' Defer error handling.
Error 11                      ' Simulate the "Division by zero" error.
```

Exit Statement

Description

Exits a block of **Do…Loop**, **For...Next**, **Function**, **Sub**, or **Property** code.

Syntax

Exit Do
Exit For
Exit Function
Exit Property
Exit Sub

The **Exit** statement syntax has these forms

Statement	Description
Exit Do	Provides a way to exit a **Do...Loop** statement. It can be used only inside a **Do...Loop** statement. **Exit Do** transfers control to the statement following the **Loop** statement. When used within nested **Do...Loop** statements, **Exit Do** transfers control to the loop that is one nested level above the loop where **Exit Do** occurs.
Exit For	Provides a way to exit a **For** loop. It can be used only in a **For...Next** or **For Each...Next** loop. **Exit For** transfers control to the statement following the **Next** statement. When used within nested **For** loops, **Exit For** transfers control to the loop that is one nested level above the loop where **Exit For** occurs.
Exit Function	Immediately exits the **Function** procedure in which it appears. Execution continues with the statement following the statement that called the **Function**.
Exit Property	Immediately exits the **Property** procedure in which it appears. Execution continues with the statement following the statement that called the **Property** procedure.
Exit Sub	Immediately exits the **Sub** procedure in which it appears. Execution continues with the statement following the statement that called the **Sub** procedure.

Remarks

Do not confuse **Exit** statements with **End** statements. **Exit** does not define the end of a structure.

See Also

Do...Loop statement, **End** statement, **For Each...Next** statement, **For...Next** statement, **Function** statement, **Property Get** statement, **Property Let** statement, **Property Set** statement, **Stop** statement, **Sub** statement.

Example

This example uses the **Exit** statement to exit a **For...Next** loop, a **Do...Loop**, and a **Sub** procedure.

```
Sub ExitStatementDemo()
Dim I, MyNum
   Do                                        ' Set up infinite loop.
      For I = 1 To 1000                      ' Loop 1000 times.
         MyNum = Int(Rnd * 1000)             ' Generate random numbers.
         Select Case MyNum                   ' Evaluate random number.
            Case 7: Exit For                 ' If 7, exit For...Next.
            Case 29: Exit Do                 ' If 29, exit Do...Loop.
            Case 54: Exit Sub                ' If 54, exit Sub procedure.
         End Select
      Next I
   Loop
End Sub
```

Exp Function

Description

Returns a **Double** specifying *e* (the base of natural logarithms) raised to a power.

Syntax

Exp(*number***)**

The required *number* argument is a **Double** or any valid numeric expression.

Remarks

If the value of *number* exceeds 709.782712893, an error occurs. The constant *e* is approximately 2.718282.

Note The **Exp** function complements the action of the **Log** function and is sometimes referred to as the antilogarithm.

See Also

Log function.

Example

This example uses the **Exp** function to return *e* raised to a power.

```
Dim MyAngle, MyHSin
' Define angle in radians.
MyAngle = 1.3
' Calculate hyperbolic sine.
MyHSin = (Exp(MyAngle) - Exp(-1 * MyAngle)) / 2
```

FileAttr Function

Description

Returns a **Long** representing the file mode for files opened using the **Open** statement.

Syntax

FileAttr(*filenumber*, *returntype*)

The **FileAttr** function syntax has these named arguments

Part	Description
filenumber	Required; **Integer**. Any valid file number.
returntype	Required; **Integer**. Number indicating the type of information to return. Specify 1 to return a value indicating the file mode. On 16-bit systems only, specify 2 to retrieve an operating system file handle. ***Returntype*** 2 is not supported in 32-bit systems and causes an error.

Return Values

When the ***returntype*** argument is 1, the following return values indicate the file access mode

Mode	Value
Input	1
Output	2
Random	4
Append	8
Binary	32

See Also

GetAttr function, **Open** statement, **SetAttr** statement.

Example

This example uses the **FileAttr** function to return the file mode and file handle of an open file.

```
Dim FileNum, Mode, Handle
FileNum = 1                                  ' Assign file number.
Open "TESTFILE" For Append As FileNum        ' Open file.
Mode = FileAttr(FileNum, 1)                  ' Returns 8 (Append file mode).
Handle = FileAttr(FileNum, 2)                ' Returns file handle.
Close FileNum                                ' Close file.
```

FileCopy Statement

Description

Copies a file.

Syntax

FileCopy ***source*****,** ***destination***

The **FileCopy** statement syntax has these named arguments

Part	Description
source	Required. String expression that specifies the name of the file to be copied. The ***source*** may include directory or folder, and drive.
destination	Required. String expression that specifies the target file name. The ***destination*** may include directory or folder, and drive.

Remarks

If you try to use the **FileCopy** statement on a currently open file, an error occurs.

See Also

Kill statement, **Name** statement.

Example

This example uses the **FileCopy** statement to copy one file to another. For purposes of this example, assume that `SRCFILE` is a file containing some data.

```
Dim SourceFile, DestinationFile
SourceFile = "SRCFILE"                       ' Define source file name.
DestinationFile = "DESTFILE"                 ' Define target file name.
FileCopy SourceFile, DestinationFile         ' Copy source to target.
```

FileDateTime Function

Description

Returns a **Variant** (**Date**) that indicates the date and time when a file was created or last modified.

Syntax

FileDateTime(*pathname*)

The required *pathname* argument is a string expression that specifies a file name. The *pathname* may include the directory or folder, and the drive.

See Also

FileLen function, **GetAttr** function, **VarType** function.

Example

This example uses the **FileDateTime** function to determine the date and time a file was created or last modified. The format of the date and time displayed is based on the locale settings of your system.

```
Dim MyStamp
' Assume TESTFILE was last modified on February 12, 1993 at 4:35:47 PM.
' Assume English/U.S. locale settings.
MyStamp = FileDateTime("TESTFILE")    ' Returns "2/12/93 4:35:47 PM".
```

FileLen Function

Description

Returns a **Long** specifying the length of a file in bytes.

Syntax

FileLen(*pathname*)

The required *pathname* argument is a string expression that specifies a file. The *pathname* may include the directory or folder, and the drive.

Remarks

If the specified file is open when the **FileLen** function is called, the value returned represents the size of the file immediately before it was opened.

Note To obtain the length of an open file, use the **LOF** function.

See Also

FileDateTime function, **GetAttr** function, **LOF** function.

Example

This example uses the **FileLen** function to return the length of a file in bytes. For purposes of this example, assume that `TESTFILE` is a file containing some data.

```
Dim MySize
MySize = FileLen("TESTFILE")          ' Returns file length (bytes).
```

Fix Function

See Int, Fix Functions.

For Each...Next Statement

Description

Repeats a group of statements for each element in an array or collection.

Syntax

For Each *element* **In** *group*
  [*statements*]
  [**Exit For**]
  [*statements*]
Next [*element*]

The **For...Each...Next** statement syntax has these parts

Part	Description
element	Required. Variable used to iterate through the elements of the collection or array. For collections, *element* can only be a **Variant** variable, a generic object variable, or any specific object variable. For arrays, *element* can only be a **Variant** variable.
group	Required. Name of an object collection or array (except an array of user-defined types).
statements	Optional. One or more statements that are executed on each item in *group*.

Remarks

The **For...Each** block is entered if there is at least one element in *group*. Once the loop has been entered, all the statements in the loop are executed for the first element in *group*. If there are more elements in *group*, the statements in the loop continue to execute for each element. When there are no more elements in *group*, the loop is exited and execution continues with the statement following the **Next** statement.

Any number of **Exit For** statements may be placed anywhere in the loop as an alternative way to exit. **Exit For** is often used after evaluating some condition, for example **If...Then**, and transfers control to the statement immediately following **Next**.

You can nest **For...Each...Next** loops by placing one **For...Each...Next** loop within another. However, each loop *element* must be unique.

Note If you omit *element* in a **Next** statement, execution continues as if *element* is included. If a **Next** statement is encountered before its corresponding **For** statement, an error occurs.

You can't use the **For...Each...Next** statement with an array of user-defined types because a **Variant** can't contain a user-defined type.

See Also

Do...Loop statement, **Exit** statement, **For...Next** statement, **While...Wend** statement.

Example

This example uses the **For Each...Next** statement to search the **Text** property of all elements in a collection for the existence of the string "Hello." In the example, `MyObject` is a text-related object and is an element of the collection `MyCollection`. Both are generic names used for illustration purposes only.

```
Dim Found, MyObject, MyCollection
Found = False                              ' Initialize variable.
For Each MyObject In MyCollection          ' Iterate through each element.
   If MyObject.Text = "Hello" Then         ' If Text equals "Hello".
      Found = True                         ' Set Found to True.
      Exit For                             ' Exit loop.
   End If
Next
```

Example (Microsoft Excel)

This example loops on cells A1:D10 on Sheet1. If one of the cells has a value less than 0.001, the code replaces the value with 0 (zero).

```
For Each c in Worksheets("Sheet1").Range("A1:D10")
   If c.Value < .001 Then
      c.Value = 0
   End If
Next c
```

This example loops on the range named "TestRange" and then displays the number of empty cells in the range.

```
numBlanks = 0
For Each c In Range("TestRange")
   If c.Value = "" Then
      numBlanks = numBlanks + 1
   End If
Next c
MsgBox "There are " & numBlanks & " empty cells in this range."
```

This example closes and saves changes to all workbooks except the one that's running the example.

```
For Each w In Workbooks
   If w.Name <> ThisWorkbook.Name Then
      w.Close savechanges:=True
   End If
Next w
```

This example deletes every worksheet in the active workbook without displaying the confirmation dialog box. There must be at least one other visible sheet in the workbook.

```
Application.DisplayAlerts = False
For Each w In Worksheets
   w.Delete
Next w
Application.DisplayAlerts = True
```

This example creates a new worksheet and then inserts into it a list of all the names in the active workbook, including their formulas in A1-style notation in the language of the user.

```
Set newSheet = ActiveWorkbook.Worksheets.Add
i = 1
For Each nm In ActiveWorkbook.Names
   newSheet.Cells(i, 1).Value = nm.NameLocal
   newSheet.Cells(i, 2).Value = "'" & nm.RefersToLocal
   i = i + 1
Next nm
```

For...Next Statement

Description

Repeats a group of statements a specified number of times.

Syntax

For *counter* = *start* **To** *end* [**Step** *step*]
  [*statements*]
  [**Exit For**]
  [*statements*]
Next [*counter*]

The **For...Next** statement syntax has these parts

Part	Description
counter	Required. Numeric variable used as a loop counter. The variable can't be a **Boolean** or an array element.
start	Required. Initial value of *counter*.
end	Required. Final value of *counter*.
step	Optional. Amount *counter* is changed each time through the loop. If not specified, *step* defaults to one.
statements	Optional. One or more statements between **For** and **Next** that are executed the specified number of times.

Remarks

The *step* argument can be either positive or negative. The value of the *step* argument determines loop processing as follows

Value	Loop executes if
Positive or 0	*counter* <= *end*
Negative	*counter* >= *end*

After all statements in the loop have executed, *step* is added to *counter*. At this point, either the statements in the loop execute again (based on the same test that caused the loop to execute initially), or the loop is exited and execution continues with the statement following the **Next** statement.

Tip Changing the value of *counter* while inside a loop can make it more difficult to read and debug your code.

Any number of **Exit For** statements may be placed anywhere in the loop as an alternate way to exit. **Exit For** is often used after evaluating of some condition, for example **If...Then**, and transfers control to the statement immediately following **Next**.

You can nest **For...Next** loops by placing one **For...Next** loop within another. Give each loop a unique variable name as its *counter*. The following construction is correct:

```
For I = 1 To 10
   For J = 1 To 10
      For K = 1 To 10
         ...
      Next K
   Next J
Next I
```

Note If you omit *counter* in a **Next** statement, execution continues as if *counter* is included. If a **Next** statement is encountered before its corresponding **For** statement, an error occurs.

See Also

Do...Loop statement, **Exit** statement, **For Each...Next** statement, **While...Wend** statement.

Example

This example uses the **For...Next** statement to create a string that contains 10 instances of the numbers 0 through 9, each string separated from the other by a single space. The outer loop uses a loop counter variable that is decremented each time through the loop.

```
Dim Words, Chars, MyString
For Words = 10 To 1 Step -1                ' Set up 10 repetitions.
   For Chars = 0 To 9                      ' Set up 10 repetitions.
      MyString = MyString & Chars          ' Append number to string.
   Next Chars                              ' Increment counter
   MyString = MyString & " "               ' Append a space.
Next Words
```

Example (Microsoft Excel)

This example displays the number of columns in the selection on Sheet1. The code also tests for a multiple-area selection; if one exists, the code loops on the areas of the selection.

```
Worksheets("Sheet1").Activate
areaCount = Selection.Areas.Count
If areaCount <= 1 Then
   MsgBox "The selection contains " & _
      Selection.Columns.Count & " columns."
Else
   For i = 1 To areaCount
      MsgBox "Area " & i & " of the selection contains " & _
         Selection.Areas(i).Columns.Count & " columns."
   Next i
End If
```

This example creates a new worksheet and then inserts a list of the active workbook's sheet names into the first column of the worksheet.

```
Set newSheet = Sheets.Add(Type:=xlWorksheet)
For i = 1 To Sheets.Count
   newSheet.Cells(i, 1).Value = Sheets(i).Name
Next i
```

This example selects every other item in list box one on Sheet1.

```
Dim items() As Boolean
Set lbox = Worksheets("Sheet1").ListBoxes(1)
ReDim items(1 To lbox.ListCount)
For i = 1 To lbox.ListCount
   If i Mod 2 = 1 Then
      items(i) = True
   Else
      items(i) = False
   End If
Next
lbox.MultiSelect = xlExtended
lbox.Selected = items
```

Format Function

Description

Returns a **Variant** (**String**) containing an expression formatted according to instructions contained in a format expression.

Syntax

Format(*expression*[, *format*[, *firstdayofweek*[, *firstweekofyear*]]]**)**

The **Format** function syntax has these parts

Part	Description
expression	Required. Any valid expression.
format	Optional. A valid named or user-defined format expression.
firstdayofweek	Optional. A constant that specifies the first day of the week.
firstweekofyear	Optional. A constant that specifies the first week of the year.

Settings

The *firstdayofweek* argument has these settings

Constant	Value	Description
vbUseSystem	0	Use NLS API setting.
VbSunday	1	Sunday (default).
vbMonday	2	Monday.
vbTuesday	3	Tuesday.
vbWednesday	4	Wednesday.
vbThursday	5	Thursday.
vbFriday	6	Friday.
vbSaturday	7	Saturday.

The *firstweekofyear* argument has these settings

Constant	Value	Description
vbUseSystem	0	Use NLS API setting.
vbFirstJan1	1	Start with week in which January 1 occurs (default).
vbFirstFourDays	2	Start with the first week that has at least four days in the year.
vbFirstFullWeek	3	Start with the first full week of the year.

Remarks

To Format	Do This
Numbers	Use predefined named numeric formats or create user-defined numeric formats.
Dates and times	Use predefined named date/time formats or create user-defined date/time formats.
Date and time serial numbers	Use date and time formats or numeric formats.
Strings	Create your own user-defined string formats.

If you try to format a number without specifying *format*, **Format** provides functionality similar to the **Str** function, although it is internationally aware. However, positive numbers formatted as strings using **Format** don't include a leading space reserved for the sign of the value; those converted using **Str** retain the leading space.

See Also

Format function—different formats for different numeric values, **Format** function—different formats for different string values, **Format** function—named date/time formats, **Format** function—named numeric formats, **Format** function—user-defined date/time formats, **Format** function—user-defined numeric formats, **Format** function—user-defined string formats, **Str** function.

Specifics (Microsoft Access)

In Microsoft Access versions 1.*x* and 2.0, you could use the **Format** function to return one value for a zero-length string and another for a **Null** value. For example, you could use a format expression such as the following with the **Format** function to return the appropriate string value from code:

```
Dim varX As Variant, varStrX As Variant
' Assign some value to varStrX and pass to Format function.
varX = Format(varStrX, "@;ZLS;Null")
```

In Microsoft Access 97, you must test separately for the **Null** case, then return the appropriate value based on the result. For example, you could use the **IIf** function in an expression with the **Format** function such as the following:

```
varX = IIf(IsNull(varStrX),"Null", Format(varStrX, "@;ZLS"))
```

This change applies only when you use the **Format** function to format a string dependent on whether it's a zero-length string or a **Null** value. Other format expressions used with the **Format** function continue to work as they did in previous versions.

If you convert a database from Microsoft Access version 1.*x* or 2.0 to Microsoft Access 97, you'll need to change code to test separately for the **Null** case.

Example

This example shows various uses of the **Format** function to format values using both named formats and user-defined formats. For the date separator (**/**), time separator (**:**), and AM/PM literal, the actual formatted output displayed by your system depends on the locale settings on which the code is running. When times and dates are displayed in the development environment, the short time format and short date format of the code locale are used. When displayed by running code, the short time format and short date format of the system locale are used, which may differ from the code locale. For this example, English/U.S. is assumed.

`MyTime` and `MyDate` are displayed in the development environment using current system short time setting and short date setting.

```
Dim MyTime, MyDate, MyStr
MyTime = #17:04:23#
MyDate = #January 27, 1993#

' Returns current system time in the system-defined long time format.
MyStr = Format(Time, "Long Time")
```

```
' Returns current system date in the system-defined long date format.
MyStr = Format(Date, "Long Date")

MyStr = Format(MyTime, "h:m:s")                ' Returns "17:4:23".
MyStr = Format(MyTime, "hh:mm:ss AMPM")        ' Returns "05:04:23 PM".
MyStr = Format(MyDate, "dddd, mmm d yyyy")     ' Returns "Wednesday,
    ' Jan 27 1993".
' If format is not supplied, a string is returned.
MyStr = Format(23)                             ' Returns "23".

' User-defined formats.
MyStr = Format(5459.4, "##,##0.00")            ' Returns "5,459.40".
MyStr = Format(334.9, "###0.00")               ' Returns "334.90".
MyStr = Format(5, "0.00%")                     ' Returns "500.00%".
MyStr = Format("HELLO", "<")                   ' Returns "hello".
MyStr = Format("This is it", ">")              ' Returns "THIS IS IT".
```

Format Function — Different Formats for Different Numeric Values

Description

A user-defined format expression for numbers can have from one to four sections separated by semicolons. If the *format* argument contains one of the named numeric formats, only one section is allowed.

If you use	The result is
One section only	The format expression applies to all values.
Two sections	The first section applies to positive values and zeros, the second to negative values.
Three sections	The first section applies to positive values, the second to negative values, and the third to zeros.
Four sections	The first section applies to positive values, the second to negative values, the third to zeros, and the fourth to **Null** values.

The following example has two sections: the first defines the format for positive values and zeros; the second section defines the format for negative values.

```
"$#,##0;($#,##0)"
```

If you include semicolons with nothing between them, the missing section is printed using the format of the positive value. For example, the following format displays positive and negative values using the format in the first section and displays “Zero” if the value is zero.

```
"$#,##0;;\Z\e\r\o"
```

See Also

Format function, **Format** function—different formats for different string values.

Format Function — Different Formats for Different String Values

Description

A format expression for strings can have one section or two sections separated by a semicolon (;).

If you use	The result is
One section only	The format applies to all string data.
Two sections	The first section applies to string data, the second to **Null** values and zero-length strings ("").

See Also

Format function, **Format** function—different formats for different numeric values.

Specifics (Microsoft Access)

See the **Format** property specifics (Microsoft Access).

Format Function — Named Date/Time Formats

Description

The following table identifies the predefined date and time format names

Format Name	Description
General Date	Display a date and/or time. For real numbers, display a date and time, for example, 4/3/93 05:34 PM. If there is no fractional part, display only a date, for example, 4/3/93. If there is no integer part, display time only, for example, 05:34 PM. Date display is determined by your system settings.
Long Date	Display a date according to your system's long date format.

(continued)

Medium Date	Display a date using the medium date format appropriate for the language version of the host application.
Short Date	Display a date using your system's short date format.
Long Time	Display a time using your system's long time format; includes hours, minutes, seconds.
Medium Time	Display time in 12-hour format using hours and minutes and the AM/PM designator.
Short Time	Display a time using the 24-hour format, for example, 17:45.

See Also

Format function, **Format** function—named numeric formats, **Format** function—user-defined date/time formats.

Format Function — Named Numeric Formats

Description

The following table identifies the predefined numeric format names:

Format name	Description
General Number	Display number with no thousand separator.
Currency	Display number with thousand separator, if appropriate; display two digits to the right of the decimal separator. Output is based on system locale settings.
Fixed	Display at least one digit to the left and two digits to the right of the decimal separator.
Standard	Display number with thousand separator, at least one digit to the left and two digits to the right of the decimal separator.
Percent	Display number multiplied by 100 with a percent sign (%) appended to the right; always display two digits to the right of the decimal separator.
Scientific	Use standard scientific notation.
Yes/No	Display No if number is 0; otherwise, display Yes.
True/False	Display **False** if number is 0; otherwise, display **True**.
On/Off	Display Off if number is 0; otherwise, display On.

See Also

Format function, **Format** function—named date/time formats, **Format** function—user-defined numeric formats.

Format Function — User-Defined Date/Time Formats

Description

The following table identifies characters you can use to create user-defined date/time formats:

Character	Description
(:)	Time separator. In some locales, other characters may be used to represent the time separator. The time separator separates hours, minutes, and seconds when time values are formatted. The actual character used as the time separator in formatted output is determined by your system settings.
(/)	Date separator. In some locales, other characters may be used to represent the date separator. The date separator separates the day, month, and year when date values are formatted. The actual character used as the date separator in formatted output is determined by your system settings.
c	Display the date as `ddddd` and display the time as `ttttt`, in that order. Display only date information if there is no fractional part to the date serial number; display only time information if there is no integer portion.
d	Display the day as a number without a leading zero (1–31).
dd	Display the day as a number with a leading zero (01–31).
ddd	Display the day as an abbreviation (Sun–Sat).
dddd	Display the day as a full name (Sunday–Saturday).
ddddd	Display the date as a complete date (including day, month, and year), formatted according to your system's short date format setting. For Microsoft Windows, the default short date format is `m/d/yy`.
dddddd	Display a date serial number as a complete date (including day, month, and year) formatted according to the long date setting recognized by your system. For Microsoft Windows, the default long date format is `mmmm dd, yyyy`.
w	Display the day of the week as a number (1 for Sunday through 7 for Saturday).
ww	Display the week of the year as a number (1–54).
m	Display the month as a number without a leading zero (1–12). If `m` immediately follows `h` or `hh`, the minute rather than the month is displayed.
mm	Display the month as a number with a leading zero (01–12). If `m` immediately follows `h` or `hh`, the minute rather than the month is displayed.
mmm	Display the month as an abbreviation (Jan–Dec).
mmmm	Display the month as a full month name (January–December).
q	Display the quarter of the year as a number (1–4).

(continued)

Character	Description
y	Display the day of the year as a number (1–366).
yy	Display the year as a 2-digit number (00–99).
yyyy	Display the year as a 4-digit number (100–9999).
h	Display the hour as a number without leading zeros (0–23).
hh	Display the hour as a number with leading zeros (00–23).
n	Display the minute as a number without leading zeros (0–59).
nn	Display the minute as a number with leading zeros (00–59).
s	Display the second as a number without leading zeros (0–59).
ss	Display the second as a number with leading zeros (00–59).
t t t t t	Display a time as a complete time (including hour, minute, and second), formatted using the time separator defined by the time format recognized by your system. A leading zero is displayed if the leading zero option is selected and the time is before 10:00 A.M. or P.M. For Microsoft Windows, the default time format is `h:mm:ss`.
AM/PM	Use the 12-hour clock and display an uppercase AM with any hour before noon; display an uppercase PM with any hour between noon and 11:59 P.M.
am/pm	Use the 12-hour clock and display a lowercase AM with any hour before noon; display a lowercase PM with any hour between noon and 11:59 P.M.
A/P	Use the 12-hour clock and display an uppercase A with any hour before noon; display an uppercase P with any hour between noon and 11:59 P.M.
a/p	Use the 12-hour clock and display a lowercase A with any hour before noon; display a lowercase P with any hour between noon and 11:59 P.M.
AMPM	Use the 12-hour clock and display the AM string literal as defined by your system with any hour before noon; display the PM string literal as defined by your system with any hour between noon and 11:59 P.M. AMPM can be either uppercase or lowercase, but the case of the string displayed matches the string as defined by your system settings. For Microsoft Windows, the default format is AM/PM.

See Also

Format function.

Example

The following are examples of user-defined date and time formats for December 7, 1958:

Format	Display
`m/d/yy`	12/7/58
`d-mmm`	7-Dec
`d-mmmm-yy`	7-December-58
`d mmmm`	7 December

(continued)

Format	Display
`mmmm yy`	December 58
`hh:mm AM/PM`	08:50 PM
`h:mm:ss a/p`	8:50:35 p
`h:mm`	20:50
`h:mm:ss`	20:50:35
`m/d/yy h:mm`	12/7/58 20:50

Format Function — User-Defined Numeric Formats

Description

The following table identifies characters you can use to create user-defined number formats:

Character	Description
None	Display the number with no formatting.
(**0**)	Digit placeholder. Display a digit or a zero. If the expression has a digit in the position where the 0 appears in the format string, display it; otherwise, display a zero in that position. If the number has fewer digits than there are zeros (on either side of the decimal) in the format expression, display leading or trailing zeros. If the number has more digits to the right of the decimal separator than there are zeros to the right of the decimal separator in the format expression, round the number to as many decimal places as there are zeros. If the number has more digits to the left of the decimal separator than there are zeros to the left of the decimal separator in the format expression, display the extra digits without modification.
(#)	Digit placeholder. Display a digit or nothing. If the expression has a digit in the position where the # appears in the format string, display it; otherwise, display nothing in that position. This symbol works like the 0 digit placeholder, except that leading and trailing zeros aren't displayed if the number has the same or fewer digits than there are # characters on either side of the decimal separator in the format expression.

(continued)

Character	Description
(.)	Decimal placeholder. In some locales, a comma is used as the decimal separator. The decimal placeholder determines how many digits are displayed to the left and right of the decimal separator. If the format expression contains only number signs to the left of this symbol, numbers smaller than 1 begin with a decimal separator. To display a leading zero displayed with fractional numbers, use 0 as the first digit placeholder to the left of the decimal separator. The actual character used as a decimal placeholder in the formatted output depends on the Number Format recognized by your system.
(%)	Percentage placeholder. The expression is multiplied by 100. The percent character (%) is inserted in the position where it appears in the format string.
(,)	Thousand separator. In some locales, a period is used as a thousand separator. The thousand separator separates thousands from hundreds within a number that has four or more places to the left of the decimal separator. Standard use of the thousand separator is specified if the format contains a thousand separator surrounded by digit placeholders (**0** or **#**). Two adjacent thousand separators or a thousand separator immediately to the left of the decimal separator (whether or not a decimal is specified) means "scale the number by dividing it by 1000, rounding as needed." For example, you can use the format string "##0,," to represent 100 million as 100. Numbers smaller than 1 million are displayed as 0. Two adjacent thousand separators in any position other than immediately to the left of the decimal separator are treated simply as specifying the use of a thousand separator. The actual character used as the thousand separator in the formatted output depends on the Number Format recognized by your system.
(:)	Time separator. In some locales, other characters may be used to represent the time separator. The time separator separates hours, minutes, and seconds when time values are formatted. The actual character used as the time separator in formatted output is determined by your system settings.
(/)	Date separator. In some locales, other characters may be used to represent the date separator. The date separator separates the day, month, and year when date values are formatted. The actual character used as the date separator in formatted output is determined by your system settings.
(**E- E+ e- e+**)	Scientific format. If the format expression contains at least one digit placeholder (**0** or **#**) to the right of E-, E+, e-, or e+, the number is displayed in scientific format and E or e is inserted between the number and its exponent. The number of digit placeholders to the right determines the number of digits in the exponent. Use E- or e- to place a minus sign next to negative exponents. Use E+ or e+ to place a minus sign next to negative exponents and a plus sign next to positive exponents.
- + $ ( )	Display a literal character. To display a character other than one of those listed, precede it with a backslash (\) or enclose it in double quotation marks (" ").

(continued)

Character	Description
(\)	Display the next character in the format string. To display a character that has special meaning as a literal character, precede it with a backslash (\). The backslash itself isn't displayed. Using a backslash is the same as enclosing the next character in double quotation marks. To display a backslash, use two backslashes (\\). Examples of characters that can't be displayed as literal characters are the date-formatting and time-formatting characters (a, c, d, h, m, n, p, q, s, t, w, y, / and :), the numeric-formatting characters (#, 0, %, E, e, comma, and period), and the string-formatting characters (@, &, <, >, and !).
("ABC")	Display the string inside the double quotation marks (" "). To include a string in ***format*** from within code, you must use **Chr**(34) to enclose the text (34 is the character code for a quotation mark (")).

See Also

Format function.

Example

The following table contains some sample format expressions for numbers. (These examples all assume that your system's locale setting is English-U.S.) The first column contains the format strings; the other columns contain the resulting output if the formatted data has the value given in the column headings.

Format (*format*)	Positive 5	Negative 5	Decimal .5	Null
`Zero-length string ("")`	`5`	`-5`	`0.5`	
`0`	`5`	`-5`	`1`	
`0.00`	`5.00`	`-5.00`	`0.50`	
`#,##0`	`5`	`-5`	`1`	
`#,##0.00;;;Nil`	`5.00`	`-5.00`	`0.50`	`Nil`
`$#,##0;($#,##0)`	`$5`	`($5)`	`$1`	
`$#,##0.00;($#,##0.00)`	`$5.00`	`($5.00)`	`$0.50`	
`0%`	`500%`	`-500%`	`50%`	
`0.00%`	`500.00%`	`-500.00%`	`50.00%`	
`0.00E+00`	`5.00E+00`	`-5.00E+00`	`5.00E-01`	
`0.00E-00`	`5.00E00`	`-5.00E00`	`5.00E-01`	

Format Function — User-Defined String Formats

Description

You can use any of the following characters to create a format expression for strings:

Character	Description
@	Character placeholder. Display a character or a space. If the string has a character in the position where the at symbol (@) appears in the format string, display it; otherwise, display a space in that position. Placeholders are filled from right to left unless there is an exclamation point character (!) in the format string.
&	Character placeholder. Display a character or nothing. If the string has a character in the position where the ampersand (&) appears, display it; otherwise, display nothing. Placeholders are filled from right to left unless there is an exclamation point character (!) in the format string.
<	Force lowercase. Display all characters in lowercase format.
>	Force uppercase. Display all characters in uppercase format.
!	Force left to right fill of placeholders. The default is to fill placeholders from right to left.

See Also

Format function, **Format** function—different formats for different string values, **Format** function—user-defined date/time formats, **Format** function—user-defined numeric formats.

FreeFile Function

Description

Returns an **Integer** representing the next file number available for use by the **Open** statement.

Syntax

FreeFile[(*rangenumber*)]

The optional *rangenumber* argument is a **Variant** that specifies the range from which the next free file number is to be returned. Specify a 0 (default) to return a file number in the range 1–255, inclusive. Specify a 1 to return a file number in the range 256–511.

Remarks

Use **FreeFile** to supply a file number that is not already in use.

See Also

Open statement.

Example

This example uses the **FreeFile** function to return the next available file number. Five files are opened for output within the loop, and some sample data is written to each.

```
Dim MyIndex, FileNumber
For MyIndex = 1 To 5                                      ' Loop 5 times.
   FileNumber = FreeFile                                  ' Get unused file
                                                          ' number.
   Open "TEST" & MyIndex For Output As #FileNumber        ' Create filename.
   Write #FileNumber, "This is a sample."                 ' Output text.
   Close #FileNumber                                      ' Close file.
Next MyIndex
```

Function Statement

Description

Declares the name, arguments, and code that form the body of a **Function** procedure.

Syntax

[**Public** | **Private**] [**Static**] **Function** *name* [(*arglist*)] [**As** *type*]
  [*statements*]
  [*name* = *expression*]
  [**Exit Function**]
  [*statements*]
  [*name* = *expression*]
End Function

The **Function** statement syntax has these parts:

Part	Description
Public	Optional. Indicates that the **Function** procedure is accessible to all other procedures in all modules. If used in a module that contains an **Option Private**, the procedure is not available outside the project.
Private	Optional. Indicates that the **Function** procedure is accessible only to other procedures in the module where it is declared.
Static	Optional. Indicates that the **Function** procedure's local variables are preserved between calls. The **Static** attribute doesn't affect variables that are declared outside the **Function**, even if they are used in the procedure.
name	Required. Name of the **Function**; follows standard variable naming conventions.
arglist	Optional. List of variables representing arguments that are passed to the **Function** procedure when it is called. Multiple variables are separated by commas.

(continued)

type	Optional. Data type of the value returned by the **Function** procedure; may be **Byte**, **Boolean**, **Integer**, **Long**, **Currency**, **Single**, **Double**, **Decimal** (not currently supported), **Date**, **String**, or (except fixed length), **Object**, **Variant**, or any user-defined type. Arrays of any type can't be returned, but a **Variant** containing an array can.
statements	Optional. Any group of statements to be executed within the **Function** procedure.
expression	Optional. Return value of the **Function**.

The *arglist* argument has the following syntax and parts:

[Optional] [ByVal | ByRef] [ParamArray] *varname*[( )] [**As** *type*] [= *defaultvalue*]

Part	Description
Optional	Optional. Indicates that an argument is not required. If used, all subsequent arguments in *arglist* must also be optional and declared using the **Optional** keyword. **Optional** can't be used for any argument if **ParamArray** is used.
ByVal	Optional. Indicates that the argument is passed by value.
ByRef	Optional. Indicates that the argument is passed by reference. **ByRef** is the default in Visual Basic.
ParamArray	Optional. Used only as the last argument in *arglist* to indicate that the final argument is an **Optional** array of **Variant** elements. The **ParamArray** keyword allows you to provide an arbitrary number of arguments. It may not be used with **ByVal**, **ByRef**, or **Optional**.
varname	Required. Name of the variable representing the argument; follows standard variable naming conventions.
type	Optional. Data type of the argument passed to the procedure; may be **Byte**, **Boolean**, **Integer**, **Long**, **Currency**, **Single**, **Double**, **Decimal** (not currently supported) **Date**, **String** (variable length only), **Object**, **Variant**. If the parameter is not **Optional**, a user-defined type or an object type may also be specified.
defaultvalue	Optional. Any constant or constant expression. Valid for **Optional** parameters only. If the type is an **Object**, an explicit default value can only be **Nothing**.

Remarks

If not explicitly specified using either **Public** or **Private**, **Function** procedures are public by default. If **Static** is not used, the value of local variables is not preserved between calls.

Caution **Function** procedures can be recursive; that is, they can call themselves to perform a given task. However, recursion can lead to stack overflow. The **Static** keyword is usually not used with recursive **Function** procedures.

All executable code must be in procedures. You can't define a **Function** procedure inside another **Function**, **Sub**, or **Property** procedure.

The **Exit Function** statement causes an immediate exit from a **Function** procedure. Program execution continues with the statement following the statement that called the **Function** procedure. Any number of **Exit Function** statements can appear anywhere in a **Function** procedure.

Like a **Sub** procedure, a **Function** procedure is a separate procedure that can take arguments, perform a series of statements, and change the values of its arguments. However, unlike a **Sub** procedure, you can use a **Function** procedure on the right side of an expression in the same way you use any intrinsic function, such as **Sqr**, **Cos**, or **Chr**, when you want to use the value returned by the function.

You call a **Function** procedure using the function name, followed by the argument list in parentheses, in an expression. See the **Call** statement for specific information on how to call **Function** procedures.

To return a value from a function, assign the value to the function name. Any number of such assignments can appear anywhere within the procedure. If no value is assigned to *name*, the procedure returns a default value: a numeric function returns 0, a string function returns a zero-length string (" "), and a **Variant** function returns **Empty**. A function that returns an object reference returns **Nothing** if no object reference is assigned to *name* (using **Set**) within the **Function**.

The following example shows how to assign a return value to a function named `BinarySearch`. In this case, **False** is assigned to the name to indicate that some value was not found.

```
Function BinarySearch(. . .) As Boolean
. . .
   ' Value not found. Return a value of False.
   If lower > upper Then
      BinarySearch = False
      Exit Function
   End If
. . .
End Function
```

Variables used in **Function** procedures fall into two categories: those that are explicitly declared within the procedure and those that are not. Variables that are explicitly declared in a procedure (using **Dim** or the equivalent) are always local to the procedure. Variables that are used but not explicitly declared in a procedure are also local unless they are explicitly declared at some higher level outside the procedure.

Caution A procedure can use a variable that is not explicitly declared in the procedure, but a naming conflict can occur if anything you defined at the module level has the same name. If your procedure refers to an undeclared variable that has the same name as another procedure, constant, or variable, it is assumed that your procedure refers to that module-level name. Explicitly declare variables to avoid this kind of conflict. You can use an **Option Explicit** statement to force explicit declaration of variables.

Caution Visual Basic may rearrange arithmetic expressions to increase internal efficiency. Avoid using a **Function** procedure in an arithmetic expression when the function changes the value of variables in the same expression.

See Also

Call statement, **Dim** statement, **Option Explicit** statement, **Property Get** statement, **Property Let** statement, **Property Set** statement, **Sub** statement.

Specifics (Microsoft Access)

In Microsoft Access, a public **Function** procedure is available to all other procedures in the current database and in referencing Microsoft Access databases. However, it is not available to any other applications.

If you declare a **Function** procedure as private in any module by preceding it with the **Private** keyword, that procedure is available only to other procedures in the same module.

If a **Function** procedure is declared as public within a private module, such as a class module, then the procedure is available to all other procedures in that database, but is not available to other Microsoft Access databases.

Example

This example uses the **Function** statement to declare the name, arguments, and code that form the body of a **Function** procedure. The last example uses hard-typed, initialized **Optional** arguments.

```
' The following user-defined function returns the square root of the
' argument passed to it.
Function CalculateSquareRoot(NumberArg As Double) As Double
   If NumberArg < 0 Then                       ' Evaluate argument.
      Exit Function                            ' Exit to calling procedure.
   Else
      CalculateSquareRoot = Sqr(NumberArg)     ' Return square root.
   End If
End Function
```

Using the **ParamArray** keyword enables a function to accept a variable number of arguments. In the following definition, `FirstArg` is passed by value.

```
Function CalcSum(ByVal FirstArg As Integer, ParamArray OtherArgs())
Dim ReturnValue
' If the function is invoked as follows:
ReturnValue = CalcSum(4, 3 ,2 ,1)
' Local variables are assigned the following values: FirstArg = 4,
' OtherArgs(1) = 3, OtherArgs(2) = 2, and so on, assuming default
' lowerbound for arrays = 1.
```

Optional arguments can now have default values and types other than **Variant**.

```
' If a function's arguments are defined as follows:
Function MyFunc(MyStr As String, Optional MyArg1 As _ Integer = 5, _
   Optional MyArg2 = "Dolly")
Dim RetVal
' The function can be invoked as follows:
RetVal = MyFunc("Hello", 2, "World")        ' All 3 arguments supplied.
RetVal = MyFunc("Test", , 5)                ' Second argument omitted.
' Arguments one and three using named-arguments.
RetVal = MyFunc(MyStr:="Hello ", MyArg1:=7)
```

FV Function

Description

Returns a **Double** specifying the future value of an annuity based on periodic, fixed payments and a fixed interest rate.

Syntax

FV(*rate*, *nper*, *pmt*[, *pv*[, *type*]])

The **FV** function has these named arguments:

Part	Description
rate	Required. **Double** specifying interest rate per period. For example, if you get a car loan at an annual percentage rate (APR) of 10 percent and make monthly payments, the rate per period is 0.1/12, or 0.0083.
nper	Required. **Integer** specifying total number of payment periods in the annuity. For example, if you make monthly payments on a four-year car loan, your loan has a total of 4 * 12 (or 48) payment periods.
pmt	Required. **Double** specifying payment to be made each period. Payments usually contain principal and interest that doesn't change over the life of the annuity.

(continued)

pv Optional. **Variant** specifying present value (or lump sum) of a series of future payments. For example, when you borrow money to buy a car, the loan amount is the present value to the lender of the monthly car payments you will make. If omitted, 0 is assumed.

type Optional. **Variant** specifying when payments are due. Use 0 if payments are due at the end of the payment period, or use 1 if payments are due at the beginning of the period. If omitted, 0 is assumed.

Remarks

An annuity is a series of fixed cash payments made over a period of time. An annuity can be a loan (such as a home mortgage) or an investment (such as a monthly savings plan).

The ***rate*** and ***nper*** arguments must be calculated using payment periods expressed in the same units. For example, if ***rate*** is calculated using months, ***nper*** must also be calculated using months.

For all arguments, cash paid out (such as deposits to savings) is represented by negative numbers; cash received (such as dividend checks) is represented by positive numbers.

See Also

DDB function, **IPmt** function, **IRR** function, **MIRR** function, **NPer** function, **NPV** function, **Pmt** function, **PPmt** function, **PV** function, **Rate** function, **SLN** function, **SYD** function.

Example

This example uses the **FV** function to return the future value of an investment given the percentage rate that accrues per period (`APR / 12`), the total number of payments (`TotPmts`), the payment (`Payment`), the current value of the investment (`PVal`), and a number that indicates whether the payment is made at the beginning or end of the payment period (`PayType`). Note that because `Payment` represents cash paid out, it's a negative number.

```
Dim Fmt, Payment, APR, TotPmts, PayType, PVal, FVal
Const ENDPERIOD = 0, BEGINPERIOD = 1          ' When payments are made.
Fmt = "###,###,##0.00"                        ' Define money format.
Payment = InputBox("How much do you plan to save each month?")
APR = InputBox("Enter the expected interest annual percentage rate.")
If APR > 1 Then APR = APR / 100               ' Ensure proper form.
TotPmts = InputBox("For how many months do you expect to save?")
PayType = MsgBox("Do you make payments at the end of month?", vbYesNo)
If PayType = vbNo Then PayType = BEGINPERIOD Else PayType = ENDPERIOD
PVal = InputBox("How much is in this savings account now?")
FVal = FV(APR / 12, TotPmts, -Payment, -PVal, PayType)
MsgBox "Your savings will be worth " & Format(FVal, Fmt) & "."
```

Get Statement

Description

Reads data from an open disk file into a variable.

Syntax

Get [#]*filenumber*, [*recnumber*], *varname*

The **Get** statement syntax has these parts

Part	Description
filenumber	Required. Any valid file number.
recnumber	Optional. **Variant** (**Long**). Record number (**Random** mode files) or byte number (**Binary** mode files) at which reading begins.
varname	Required. Valid variable name into which data is read.

Remarks

Data read with **Get** is usually written to a file with **Put**.

The first record or byte in a file is at position 1, the second record or byte is at position 2, and so on. If you omit *recnumber*, the next record or byte following the last **Get** or **Put** statement (or pointed to by the last **Seek** function) is read. You must include delimiting commas, for example:

```
Get #4,,FileBuffer
```

For files opened in **Random** mode, the following rules apply:

- If the length of the data being read is less than the length specified in the **Len** clause of the **Open** statement, **Get** reads subsequent records on record-length boundaries. The space between the end of one record and the beginning of the next record is padded with the existing contents of the file buffer. Because the amount of padding data can't be determined with any certainty, it is generally a good idea to have the record length match the length of the data being read.
- If the variable being read into is a variable-length string, **Get** reads a 2-byte descriptor containing the string length and then reads the data that goes into the variable. Therefore, the record length specified by the **Len** clause in the **Open** statement must be at least 2 bytes greater than the actual length of the string.

- If the variable being read into is a **Variant** of numeric type, **Get** reads 2 bytes identifying the **VarType** of the **Variant** and then the data that goes into the variable. For example, when reading a **Variant** of **VarType** 3, **Get** reads 6 bytes: 2 bytes identifying the **Variant** as **VarType** 3 (**Long**) and 4 bytes containing the **Long** data. The record length specified by the **Len** clause in the **Open** statement must be at least 2 bytes greater than the actual number of bytes required to store the variable.

  Note You can use the **Get** statement to read a **Variant** array from disk, but you can't use **Get** to read a scalar **Variant** containing an array. You also can't use **Get** to read objects from disk.

- If the variable being read into is a **Variant** of **VarType** 8 (**String**), **Get** reads 2 bytes identifying the **VarType**, 2 bytes indicating the length of the string, and then reads the string data. The record length specified by the **Len** clause in the **Open** statement must be at least 4 bytes greater than the actual length of the string.
- If the variable being read into is a dynamic array, **Get** reads a descriptor whose length equals 2 plus 8 times the number of dimensions, that is, 2 + 8 * *NumberOfDimensions*. The record length specified by the **Len** clause in the **Open** statement must be greater than or equal to the sum of all the bytes required to read the array data and the array descriptor. For example, the following array declaration requires 118 bytes when the array is written to disk.

  ```
  Dim MyArray(1 To 5,1 To 10) As Integer
  ```

  The 118 bytes are distributed as follows: 18 bytes for the descriptor (2 + 8 * 2), and 100 bytes for the data (5 * 10 * 2).
- If the variable being read into is a fixed-size array, **Get** reads only the data. No descriptor is read.
- If the variable being read into is any other type of variable (not a variable-length string or a **Variant**), **Get** reads only the variable data. The record length specified by the **Len** clause in the **Open** statement must be greater than or equal to the length of the data being read.
- **Get** reads elements of user-defined types as if each were being read individually, except that there is no padding between elements. On disk, a dynamic array in a user-defined type (written with **Put**) is prefixed by a descriptor whose length equals 2 plus 8 times the number of dimensions, that is, 2 + 8 * *NumberOfDimensions*. The record length specified by the **Len** clause in the **Open** statement must be greater than or equal to the sum of all the bytes required to read the individual elements, including any arrays and their descriptors.

For files opened in **Binary** mode, all of the **Random** rules apply, except:

- The **Len** clause in the **Open** statement has no effect. **Get** reads all variables from disk contiguously; that is, with no padding between records.
- For any array other than an array in a user-defined type, **Get** reads only the data. No descriptor is read.

- **Get** reads variable-length strings that aren't elements of user-defined types without expecting the 2-byte length descriptor. The number of bytes read equals the number of characters already in the string. For example, the following statements read 10 bytes from file number 1:

  ```
  VarString = String(10," ")
  Get #1,,VarString
  ```

See Also

Open statement, **Put** statement, **Seek** function, **Type** statement, **VarType** function.

Example

This example uses the **Get** statement to read data from a file into a variable. This example assumes that `TESTFILE` is a file containing five records of the user-defined type `Record`.

```
Type Record                                    ' Define user-defined type.
   ID As Integer
   Name As String * 20
End Type

Dim MyRecord As Record, Position               ' Declare variables.
' Open sample file for random access.
Open "TESTFILE" For Random As #1 Len = Len(MyRecord)
' Read the sample file using the Get statement.
Position = 3                                   ' Define record number.
Get #1, Position, MyRecord                     ' Read third record.
Close #1                                       ' Close file.
```

GetAllSettings Function

Description

Returns a list of key settings and their respective values (originally created with **SaveSetting**) from an application's entry in the Windows registry.

Syntax

GetAllSettings(*appname, section*)

The **GetAllSettings** function syntax has these named arguments

Part	Description
appname	Required. String expression containing the name of the application or project whose key settings are requested.
section	Required. String expression containing the name of the section whose key settings are requested. **GetAllSettings** returns a **Variant** whose contents is a two-dimensional array of strings containing all the key settings in the specified section and their corresponding values.

Remarks

GetAllSettings returns an uninitialized **Variant** if either ***appname*** or ***section*** does not exist.

See Also

DeleteSetting statement, **GetSetting** function, **SaveSetting** statement.

Example

This example first uses the **SaveSetting** statement to make entries in the Windows registry (or .ini file on 16-bit Windows platforms) for the application specified as ***appname***, then uses the **GetAllSettings** function to display the settings. Note that application names and ***section*** names can't be retrieved with **GetAllSettings**. Finally, the **DeleteSetting** statement removes the application's entries.

```
' Variant to hold 2-dimensional array returned by GetAllSettings
' Integer to hold counter.
Dim MySettings As Variant, intSettings As Integer
' Place some settings in the registry.
SaveSetting appname := "MyApp", section := "Startup", _
   key := "Top", setting := 75
SaveSetting "MyApp","Startup", "Left", 50
' Retrieve the settings.
MySettings = GetAllSettings(appname := "MyApp", section := "Startup")
   For intSettings = LBound(MySettings, 1) To UBound(MySettings, 1)
      Debug.Print MySettings(intSettings, 0), MySettings(intSettings, 1)
   Next intSettings
DeleteSetting "MyApp", "Startup"
```

GetAttr Function

Description

Returns an **Integer** representing the attributes of a file, directory, or folder.

Syntax

GetAttr(*pathname*)

The required *pathname* argument is a string expression that specifies a file name. The *pathname* may include the directory or folder, and the drive.

Return Values

The value returned by **GetAttr** is the sum of the following attribute values

Constant	Value	Description
vbNormal	0	Normal
vbReadOnly	1	Read-only
vbHidden	2	Hidden
vbSystem	4	System
vbDirectory	16	Directory or folder
vbArchive	32	File has changed since last backup

Note These constants are specified by Visual Basic for Applications. The names can be used anywhere in your code in place of the actual values.

Remarks

To determine which attributes are set, use the **And** operator to perform a bitwise comparison of the value returned by the **GetAttr** function and the value of the individual file attribute you want. If the result is not zero, that attribute is set for the named file. For example, the return value of the following **And** expression is zero if the Archive attribute is not set:

```
Result = GetAttr(FName) And vbArchive
```

A nonzero value is returned if the Archive attribute is set.

See Also

And operator, **FileAttr** function, **SetAttr** statement.

Specifics (Macintosh)

The following constants aren't available on the Macintosh

Constant	Value	Description
vbSystem	4	System file.
vbArchive	32	File has changed since last backup.

The following constant is available only on the Macintosh

Constant	Value	Description
vbAlias	64	Specified file name is an alias.

Example

This example uses the **GetAttr** function to determine the attributes of a file and directory or folder.

```
Dim MyAttr
' Assume file TESTFILE has hidden attribute set.
MyAttr = GetAttr("TESTFILE")                         ' Returns 2.

' Returns nonzero if hidden attribute is set on TESTFILE.
Debug.Print MyAttr And vbHidden
```

```
' Assume file TESTFILE has hidden and read-only attributes set.
MyAttr = GetAttr("TESTFILE")                              ' Returns 3.

' Returns nonzero if hidden attribute is set on TESTFILE.
Debug.Print MyAttr And (vbHidden + vbReadOnly)

' Assume MYDIR is a directory or folder.
MyAttr = GetAttr("MYDIR")                                 ' Returns 16.
```

GetObject Function

Description

Returns a reference to an ActiveX object from a file.

Syntax

GetObject([*pathname*] [**,** *class*]**)**

The **GetObject** function syntax has these named arguments

Part	Description
pathname	Optional; **Variant** (**String**). The full path and name of the file containing the object to retrieve. If *pathname* is omitted, *class* is required.
class	Optional; **Variant** (**String**). A string representing the class of the object.

The *class* argument uses the syntax *appname***.***objecttype* and has these parts

Part	Description
appname	Required; **Variant** (**String**). The name of the application providing the object.
objecttype	Required; **Variant** (**String**). The type or class of object to create.

Remarks

Use the **GetObject** function to access an ActiveX object from a file and assign the object to an object variable. Use the **Set** statement to assign the object returned by **GetObject** to the object variable. For example:

```
Dim CADObject As Object
Set CADObject = GetObject("C:\CAD\SCHEMA.CAD")
```

When this code is executed, the application associated with the specified *pathname* is started and the object in the specified file is activated.

If *pathname* is a zero-length string (""), **GetObject** returns a new object instance of the specified type. If the *pathname* argument is omitted, **GetObject** returns a currently active object of the specified type. If no object of the specified type exists, an error occurs.

Some applications allow you to activate part of a file. Add an exclamation point (!) to the end of the file name and follow it with a string that identifies the part of the file you want to activate. For information on how to create this string, see the documentation for the application that created the object.

For example, in a drawing application you might have multiple layers to a drawing stored in a file. You could use the following code to activate a layer within a drawing called `SCHEMA.CAD`:

```
Set LayerObject = GetObject("C:\CAD\SCHEMA.CAD!Layer3")
```

If you don't specify the object's ***class***, Automation determines the application to start and the object to activate, based on the file name you provide. Some files, however, may support more than one class of object. For example, a drawing might support three different types of objects: an **Application** object, a **Drawing** object, and a **Toolbar** object, all of which are part of the same file. To specify which object in a file you want to activate, use the optional ***class*** argument. For example:

```
Dim MyObject As Object
Set MyObject = GetObject("C:\DRAWINGS\SAMPLE.DRW", "FIGMENT.DRAWING")
```

In the above example, `FIGMENT` is the name of a drawing application and `DRAWING` is one of the object types it supports.

Once an object is activated, you reference it in code using the object variable you defined. In the preceding example, you access properties and methods of the new object using the object variable `MyObject`. For example:

```
MyObject.Line 9, 90
MyObject.InsertText 9, 100, "Hello, world."
MyObject.SaveAs "C:\DRAWINGS\SAMPLE.DRW"
```

Note Use the **GetObject** function when there is a current instance of the object or if you want to create the object with a file already loaded. If there is no current instance, and you don't want the object started with a file loaded, use the **CreateObject** function.

If an object has registered itself as a single-instance object, only one instance of the object is created, no matter how many times **CreateObject** is executed. With a single-instance object, **GetObject** always returns the same instance when called with the zero-length string ("") syntax, and it causes an error if the ***pathname*** argument is omitted. You can't use **GetObject** to obtain a reference to a class created with Visual Basic.

See Also

CreateObject function, **Set** statement.

Example

This example uses the **GetObject** function to get a reference to a specific Microsoft Excel worksheet (`MyXL`). It uses the worksheet's **Application** property to make Microsoft Excel visible, to close it, and so on. Using two API calls, the DetectExcel **Sub** procedure looks for Microsoft Excel, and if it is running, enters it in the Running Object Table. The first call to **GetObject** causes an error if Microsoft Excel is not running. In the example, the error causes the ExcelWasNotRunning flag to be set to **True**. The second call to **GetObject** specifies a file to open. If Microsoft Excel is not already running, this second call starts it and returns a reference to the worksheet represented by the specified file. The file in the example, `mytest.xls`, must exist in the specified location; otherwise the Visual Basic error "Automation error" is generated. Next the example code makes both Microsoft Excel and the window containing the specified worksheet visible. Finally, if no previous version of Microsoft Excel was running, the code uses the **Application** object's **Quit** method to close Microsoft Excel. If the application was already running, no attempt is made to close it. The reference itself is released by setting it to **Nothing**.

```
' Declare necessary API routines:
Declare Function FindWindow Lib "user32" Alias _
   "FindWindowA" (ByVal lpClassName as String, _
   ByVal lpWindowName As Long) As Long

Declare Function SendMessage Lib "user32" Alias _
   "SendMessageA" (ByVal hWnd as Long,ByVal wMsg as Long _
   ByVal wParam as Long _
   ByVal lParam As Long) As Long

Sub GetExcel()
   Dim MyXL As Object                  ' Variable to hold reference
   ' to Microsoft Excel.
   Dim ExcelWasNotRunning As Boolean   ' Flag for final release.

   ' Test to see if there is a copy of Microsoft Excel already running.
   On Error Resume Next                ' Defer error trapping.
   ' Getobject function called without the first argument returns a
   ' reference to an instance of the application. If the application isn't
   ' running, an error occurs. Note the comma used as the first argument
   ' placeholder.
   Set MyXL = Getobject(, "Excel.Application")
   If Err.Number <> 0 Then ExcelWasNotRunning = True
   Err.Clear                           ' Clear Err object in case error occurred.

   ' Check for Excel. If Excel is running,
   ' enter it into the Running Object table.
   DetectExcel

Set the object variable to reference the file you want to see.
   Set MyXL = Getobject("c:\vb4\MYTEST.XLS")

   ' Show Microsoft Excel through its Application property. Then
   ' show the actual window containing the file using the Windows
   ' collection of the MyXL object reference.
   MyXL.Application.Visible = True
   MyXL.Parent.Windows(1).Visible = True
   ' Do manipulations of your
   ' file here.
   ' ...
```

```
    ' If this copy of Microsoft Excel was not already running when you
    ' started, close it using the Application property's Quit method.
    ' Note that when you try to quit Microsoft Excel, the Microsoft Excel
    ' title bar blinks and Microsoft Excel displays a message asking if you
    ' want to save any loaded files.
    If ExcelWasNotRunning = True Then
        MyXL.Application.Quit
    End IF

    Set MyXL = Nothing                  ' Release reference to the
                                        ' application and spreadsheet.
End Sub

Sub DetectExcel()
    ' Procedure dectects a running Excel and registers it.
    Const WM_USER = 1024
    Dim hWnd As Long
    ' If Excel is running this API call returns its handle.
    hWnd = FindWindow("XLMAIN", 0)
    If hWnd = 0 Then                    ' 0 means Excel not running.
        Exit Sub
    Else
        ' Excel is running so use the SendMessage API
        ' function to enter it in the Running Object Table.
        SendMessage hWnd, WM_USER + 18, 0, 0
    End If
End Sub
```

GetSetting Function

Description

Returns a key setting value from an application's entry in the Windows registry.

Syntax

GetSetting(*appname*, *section*, *key*[, *default*])

The **GetSetting** function syntax has these named arguments

Part	Description
appname	Required. String expression containing the name of the application or project whose key setting is requested.
section	Required. String expression containing the name of the section where the key setting is found.
key	Required. String expression containing the name of the key setting to return.
default	Optional. Expression containing the value to return if no value is set in the key setting. If omitted, ***default*** is assumed to be a zero-length string (" ").

Remarks

If any of the items named in the **GetSetting** arguments do not exist, **GetSetting** returns the value of ***default***.

See Also

DeleteSetting statement, **GetAllSettings** function, **SaveSetting** statement.

Example

This example first uses the **SaveSetting** statement to make entries in the Windows registry (or .ini file on 16-bit Windows platforms) for the application specified as ***appname***, and then uses the **GetSetting** function to display one of the settings. Because the ***default*** argument is specified, some value is guaranteed to be returned. Note that ***section*** names can't be retrieved with **GetSetting**. Finally, the **DeleteSetting** statement removes all the application's entries.

```
' Variant to hold 2-dimensional array returned by GetSetting.
Dim MySettings As Variant
' Place some settings in the registry.
SaveSetting "MyApp","Startup", "Top", 75
SaveSetting "MyApp","Startup", "Left", 50

Debug.Print GetSetting(appname := "MyApp", section := "Startup", _
   key := "Left", default := "25")

DeleteSetting "MyApp", "Startup"
```

GoSub...Return Statement

Description

Branches to and returns from a subroutine within a procedure.

Syntax

GoSub *line*

. . .

line

. . .

Return

The *line* argument can be any line label or line number.

Remarks

You can use **GoSub** and **Return** anywhere in a procedure, but **GoSub** and the corresponding **Return** statement must be in the same procedure. A subroutine can contain more than one **Return** statement, but the first **Return** statement encountered causes the flow of execution to branch back to the statement immediately following the most recently executed **GoSub** statement.

Note You can't enter or exit **Sub** procedures with **GoSub...Return**.

Tip Creating separate procedures that you can call may provide a more structured alternative to using **GoSub...Return**.

See Also

GoTo statement, **On...GoSub**, **On...GoTo** statements, **Sub** statement.

Example

This example uses **GoSub** to call a subroutine within a **Sub** procedure. The **Return** statement causes the execution to resume at the statement immediately following the **GoSub** statement. The **Exit Sub** statement is used to prevent control from accidentally flowing into the subroutine.

```
Sub GosubDemo()
Dim Num
    ' Solicit a number from the user.
    Num = InputBox("Enter a positive number to be divided by 2.")
    ' Only use routine if user enters a positive number.
    If Num > 0 Then GoSub MyRoutine
    Debug.Print Num
    Exit Sub                            ' Use Exit to prevent an error.
MyRoutine:
    Num = Num/2                         ' Perform the division.
    Return                      ' Return control to statement.
End Sub                                 ' following the GoSub statement.
```

GoTo Statement

Description

Branches unconditionally to a specified line within a procedure.

Syntax

GoTo *line*

The required *line* argument can be any line label or line number.

Remarks

GoTo can branch only to lines within the procedure where it appears.

Note Too many **GoTo** statements can make code difficult to read and debug. Use structured control statements (**Do...Loop**, **For...Next**, **If...Then...Else**, **Select Case**) whenever possible.

See Also

Do...Loop statement, **For...Next** statement, **GoSub...Return** statement, **If...Then...Else** statement, **Select Case** statement.

Example

This example uses the **GoTo** statement to branch to line labels within a procedure.

```
Sub GotoStatementDemo()
Dim Number, MyString
   Number = 1                              ' Initialize variable.
   ' Evaluate Number and branch to appropriate label.
   If Number = 1 Then GoTo Line1 Else GoTo Line2

Line1:
   MyString = "Number equals 1"
   GoTo LastLine                           ' Go to LastLine.
Line2:
   ' The following statement never gets executed.
   MyString = "Number equals 2"
LastLine:
   Debug.Print MyString                    ' Print "Number equals 1" in
                                           ' Debug window.
End Sub
```

HelpContext Property

Applies To

Err object.

Description

Returns or sets a string expression containing the context ID for a topic in a Microsoft Windows Help file. Read/write.

Remarks

The **HelpContext** property is used to automatically display the Help topic specified in the **HelpFile** property. If both **HelpFile** and **HelpContext** are empty, the value of **Number** is checked. If **Number** corresponds to a Visual Basic run-time error value, then the Visual Basic Help context ID for the error is used. If the **Number** value doesn't correspond to a Visual Basic error, the contents screen for the Visual Basic Help file is displayed.

Note You should write routines in your application to handle typical errors. When programming with an object, you can use the object's Help file to improve the quality of your error handling, or to display a meaningful message to your user if the error isn't recoverable.

See Also

Description property, **Err** object, **HelpFile** property, **LastDLLError** property, **Number** property, **Source** property.

Example

This example uses the **HelpContext** property of the **Err** object to show the Visual Basic Help topic for the `Overflow` error.

```
Dim Msg
Err.Clear
On Error Resume Next
Err.Raise 6                           ' Generate "Overflow" error.
If Err.Number <> 0 Then
   Msg = "Press F1 or Help to see " & Err.HelpFile & " topic for" & _
      " the following HelpContext: " & Err.HelpContext
   MsgBox Msg, , "Error: " & Err.Description, Err.HelpFile, _
      Err.HelpContext
End If
```

HelpFile Property

Applies To

Err object.

Description

Returns or sets a string expression the fully qualified path to a Microsoft Windows Help file. Read/write.

Remarks

If a Help file is specified in **HelpFile**, it is automatically called when the user presses the **Help** button (or the F1 key) in the error message dialog box. If the **HelpContext** property contains a valid context ID for the specified file, that topic is automatically displayed. If no **HelpFile** is specified, the Visual Basic Help file is displayed.

Note You should write routines in your application to handle typical errors. When programming with an object, you can use the object's Help file to improve the quality of your error handling, or to display a meaningful message to your user if the error isn't recoverable.

See Also

Description property, **Err** object, **HelpContext** property, **LastDLLError** property, **Number** property, **Source** property.

Example

This example uses the **HelpFile** property of the **Err** object to start the Microsoft Windows Help system. By default, the **HelpFile** property contains the name of the Visual Basic Help file.

```
Dim Msg
Err.Clear
On Error Resume Next     ' Suppress errors for demonstration purposes.
Err.Raise 6              ' Generate "Overflow" error.
Msg = "Press F1 or Help to see " & Err.HelpFile & _
   " topic for this error"
MsgBox Msg, , "Error: " & Err.Description,Err.HelpFile, Err.HelpContext
```

Hex Function

Description

Returns a **String** representing the hexadecimal value of a number.

Syntax

Hex(*number*)

The required *number* argument is any valid numeric expression or string expression.

Remarks

If *number* is not already a whole number, it is rounded to the nearest whole number before being evaluated.

If *number* is	Hex returns
Null	Null
Empty	Zero (0)
Any other number	Up to eight hexadecimal characters

You can represent hexadecimal numbers directly by preceding numbers in the proper range with `&H`. For example, `&H10` represents decimal 16 in hexadecimal notation.

See Also

Oct function.

Example

This example uses the **Hex** function to return the hexadecimal value of a number.

```
Dim MyHex
MyHex = Hex(5)                                ' Returns 5.
MyHex = Hex(10)                               ' Returns A.
MyHex = Hex(459)                              ' Returns 1CB.
```

Hide Method

Applies To

UserForm object.

Description

Hides an object but doesn't unload it.

Syntax

object.**Hide**

The *object* placeholder represents an object expression that evaluates to an object in the Applies To list. If *object* is omitted, the **UserForm** with the focus is assumed to be *object*.

Remarks

When an object is hidden, it's removed from the screen and its **Visible** property is set to **False**. A hidden object's controls aren't accessible to the user, but they are available programmatically to the running application, to other processes that may be communicating with the application through dynamic data exchange (DDE) or Automation, and to **Timer** control events.

When a **UserForm** is hidden, the user can't interact with the application until all code in the event procedure that caused the **UserForm** to be hidden has finished executing.

If the **UserForm** isn't loaded when the **Hide** method is invoked, the **Hide** method loads the **UserForm** but doesn't display it.

See Also

Load statement, **Show** method, **Unload** statement.

Example

The following example assumes two **UserForms** in a program. In UserForm1's Initialize event, UserForm2 is loaded and shown. When the user clicks UserForm2, it is hidden and UserForm1 appears. When UserForm1 is clicked, UserForm2 is shown again.

```
' This is the Initialize event procedure for UserForm1.
Private Sub UserForm_Initialize()
   Load UserForm2
   UserForm2.Show
End Sub
' This is the Click event of UserForm2.
Private Sub UserForm_Click()
   UserForm2.Hide
End Sub

' This is the click event for UserForm1.
Private Sub UserForm_Click()
   UserForm2.Show
End Sub
```

Hour Function

Description

Returns a **Variant** (**Integer**) specifying a whole number between 0 and 23, inclusive, representing the hour of the day.

Syntax

Hour(*time***)**

The required *time* argument is any **Variant**, numeric expression, string expression, or any combination, that can represent a time. If *time* contains **Null**, **Null** is returned.

See Also

Day function, **Minute** function, **Now** function, **Second** function, **Time** function, **Time** statement.

Example

This example uses the **Hour** function to obtain the hour from a specified time. In the development environment, the time literal is displayed in short time format using the locale settings of your code.

```
Dim MyTime, MyHour
MyTime = #4:35:17 PM#                          ' Assign a time.
MyHour = Hour(MyTime)                          ' MyHour contains 16.
```

If...Then...Else Statement

Description

Conditionally executes a group of statements, depending on the value of an expression.

Syntax

If *condition* **Then** [*statements*] [**Else** *elsestatements*]

Or, you can use the block form syntax:

If *condition* **Then**
    [*statements*]
[**ElseIf** *condition-n* **Then**
    [*elseifstatements*] . . .
[**Else**
    [*elsestatements*]]
End If

The **If...Then...Else** statement syntax has these parts

Part	Description
condition	Required. One or more of the following two types of expressions: A numeric expression or string expression that evaluates to **True** or **False**. If *condition* is **Null**, *condition* is treated as **False**. An expression of the form **TypeOf** *objectname* **Is** *objecttype*. The *objectname* is any object reference and *objecttype* is any valid object type. The expression is **True** if *objectname* is of the object type specified by *objecttype*; otherwise it is **False**.
statements	Optional in block form; required in single-line form that has no **Else** clause. One or more statements separated by colons; executed if *condition* is **True**.
condition-n	Optional. Same as *condition*.
elseifstatements	Optional. One or more statements executed if associated *condition-n* is **True**.
elsestatements	Optional. One or more statements executed if no previous *condition* or *condition-n* expression is **True**.

Remarks

You can use the single-line form (first syntax) for short, simple tests. However, the block form (second syntax) provides more structure and flexibility than the single-line form and is usually easier to read, maintain, and debug.

Note With the single-line form, it is possible to have multiple statements executed as the result of an **If...Then** decision. All statements must be on the same line and separated by colons, as in the following statement:

```
If A > 10 Then A = A + 1 : B = B + A : C = C + B
```

A block form **If** statement must be the first statement on a line. The **Else**, **ElseIf**, and **End If** parts of the statement can have only a line number or line label preceding them. The block **If** must end with an **End If** statement.

To determine whether or not a statement is a block **If**, examine what follows the **Then** keyword. If anything other than a comment appears after **Then** on the same line, the statement is treated as a single-line **If** statement.

The **Else** and **ElseIf** clauses are both optional. You can have as many **ElseIf** clauses as you want in a block **If**, but none can appear after an **Else** clause. Block **If** statements can be nested; that is, contained within one another.

When executing a block **If** (second syntax), *condition* is tested. If *condition* is **True**, the statements following **Then** are executed. If *condition* is **False**, each **ElseIf** condition (if any) is evaluated in turn. When a **True** condition is found, the statements immediately following the associated **Then** are executed. If none of the **ElseIf** conditions are **True** (or if there are no **ElseIf** clauses), the statements following **Else** are executed. After executing the statements following **Then** or **Else**, execution continues with the statement following **End If**.

Tip **Select Case** may be more useful when evaluating a single expression that has several possible actions. However, the **TypeOf** *objectname* **Is** *objecttype* clause can't be used with the **Select Case** statement.

See Also

#If...Then...#Else directive, **Choose** function, **Select Case** statement, **Switch** function.

Example

This example shows both the block and single-line forms of the **If...Then...Else** statement. It also illustrates the use of **If TypeOf...Then...Else**.

```
Dim Number, Digits, MyString
Number = 53                          ' Initialize variable.
If Number < 10 Then
   Digits = 1
ElseIf Number < 100 Then
' Condition evaluates to True so the next statement is executed.
   Digits = 2
Else
   Digits = 3
End If

' Assign a value using the single-line form of syntax.
If Digits = 1 Then MyString = "One" Else MyString = "More than one"
```

Use **If TypeOf** construct to determine whether the Control passed into a procedure is a text box.

```
Sub ControlProcessor(MyControl As Control)
   If TypeOf MyControl Is CommandButton Then
      Debug.Print "You passed in a " & TypeName(MyControl)
   ElseIf TypeOf MyControl Is CheckBox Then
      Debug.Print "You passed in a " & TypeName(MyControl)
   ElseIf TypeOf MyControl Is TextBox Then
      Debug.Print "You passed in a " & TypeName(MyControl)
   End If
End Sub
```

Example (Microsoft Excel)

This example loops on cells A1:D10 on Sheet1. If one of the cells has a value less than 0.001, the code replaces the value with 0 (zero).

```
For Each c in Worksheets("Sheet1").Range("A1:D10")
   If c.Value < .001 Then
      c.Value = 0
   End If
Next c
```

This example loops on the range named "TestRange" and then displays the number of empty cells in the range.

```
numBlanks = 0
For Each c In Range("TestRange")
   If c.Value = "" Then
      numBlanks = numBlanks + 1
   End If
Next c
MsgBox "There are " & numBlanks & " empty cells in this range."
```

This example sets the standard font to Geneva (on the Macintosh) or Arial (in Windows).

```
If Application.OperatingSystem Like "*Macintosh*" Then
   Application.StandardFont = "Geneva"
Else
   Application.StandardFont = "Arial"
End If
```

IIf Function

Description

Returns one of two parts, depending on the evaluation of an expression.

Syntax

IIf(*expr*, *truepart*, *falsepart*)

The **IIf** function syntax has these named arguments

Part	Description
expr	Required. Expression you want to evaluate.
truepart	Required. Value or expression returned if ***expr*** is **True**.
falsepart	Required. Value or expression returned if ***expr*** is **False**.

Remarks

IIf always evaluates both ***truepart*** and ***falsepart***, even though it returns only one of them. Because of this, you should watch for undesirable side effects. For example, if evaluating ***falsepart*** results in a division by zero error, an error occurs even if ***expr*** is **True**.

See Also

Choose function, **If...Then...Else** statement, **Select Case** statement, **Switch** function.

Specifics (Microsoft Access)

You can also use the **IIf** function (immediate if) in a calculated control on a Microsoft Access form or report. You can use the **IIf** function to evaluate an expression and return either of two other values, depending on whether the expression evaluates to **True** (–1) or **False** (0). For example, you can use the **IIf** function to inspect a field on a form and determine whether its value is **Null**. If it is, you can force the function return an empty string. If the field has a value that is not **Null**, the function could return the field's contents.

The following example checks the ShipCountry field in an Orders table, and returns an empty string if it is **Null**.

```
=IIf(IsNull(Forms!Orders![ShipCountry]), "", Forms!Orders![ShipCountry])
```

In Visual Basic, the **IIf** function evaluates both *truepart* and *falsepart*, even though it returns only one of them. In a Microsoft Access form or report, however, the **IIf** function evaluates either *truepart* or *falsepart*, whichever is appropriate. Therefore, you need not be concerned about the undesirable side effects of evaluating both arguments if you use the **IIf** function in a calculated control, query expression, or macro.

Note The Microsoft Access **Nz** function converts **Null** values to zero, a zero-length string, or another value that you specify. If your expression handles **Null** values, you may be able use the **Nz** function as an alternative to the **IIf** function.

The **IIf** function is most useful within expressions that are in a form or report, rather than in Visual Basic code. In Visual Basic, the more full-featured **If...Then...Else** statement offers greater versatility.

Example

This example uses the **IIf** function to evaluate the `TestMe` parameter of the `CheckIt` procedure and returns the word "Large" if the amount is greater than 1000; otherwise, it returns the word "Small".

```
Function CheckIt (TestMe As Integer)
   CheckIt = IIf(TestMe > 1000, "Large", "Small")
End Function
```

Example (Microsoft Access)

This example uses the **IIf** function to evaluate an OrderAmount field and returns the word "Large" if the amount is greater than 1000; otherwise, it returns the word "Small". You can enter the following expression in the **ControlSource** property of a calculated control.

```
=IIf([OrderAmount] > 1000, "Large", "Small")
```

IMEStatus Function

Description

Returns an **Integer** specifying the current Input Method Editor (IME) mode of Microsoft Windows; available in Far East versions only.

Syntax

IMEStatus

Return Values

The return values for the Japanese locale are as follows

Constant	Value	Description
vbIMENoOP	0	No IME installed
vbIMEOn	1	IME on
vbIMEOff	2	IME off
vbIMEDisable	3	IME disabled
vbIMEHiragana	4	Hiragana double-byte characters (DBC)
vbIMEKatakanaDbl	5	Katakana DBC
vbIMEKatakanaSng	6	Katakana single-byte characters (SBC)
vbIMEAlphaDbl	7	Alphanumeric DBC
vbIMEAlphaSng	8	Alphanumeric SBC

The return values for the Chinese (traditional and simplified) locale are as follows

Constant	Value	Description
vbIMENoOP	0	No IME installed
vbIMEOn	1	IME on
vbIMEOff	2	IME off

For the Korean locale, the first five bits of the return are set as follows

Bit	Value	Description	Value	Description
0	0	No IME installed	1	IME installed
1	0	IME disabled	1	IME enabled
2	0	IME English mode	1	Hangeul mode
3	0	Banja mode (SB)	1	Junja mode (DB)
4	0	Normal mode	1	Hanja conversion mode

Imp Operator

Description

Used to perform a logical implication on two expressions.

Syntax

result = *expression1* **Imp** *expression2*

The **Imp** operator syntax has these parts

Part	Description
result	Required; any numeric variable.
expression1	Required; any expression.
expression2	Required; any expression.

Remarks

The following table illustrates how *result* is determined

If *expression1* is	And *expression2* is	The *result* is
True	**True**	**True**
True	**False**	**False**
True	**Null**	**Null**
False	**True**	**True**
False	**False**	**True**
False	**Null**	**True**
Null	**True**	**True**
Null	**False**	**Null**
Null	**Null**	**Null**

The **Imp** operator performs a bitwise comparison of identically positioned bits in two numeric expressions and sets the corresponding bit in *result* according to the following table

If bit in *expression1* is	And bit in *expression2* is	The *result* is
0	0	1
0	1	1
1	0	0
1	1	1

See Also

Operator precedence.

Example

This example uses the **Imp** Operator to perform logical implication on two expressions.

```
Dim A, B, C, D, MyCheck
A = 10: B = 8: C = 6: D = Null        ' Initialize variables.
MyCheck = A > B Imp B > C             ' Returns True.
MyCheck = A > B Imp C > B             ' Returns False.
MyCheck = B > A Imp C > B             ' Returns True.
MyCheck = B > A Imp C > D             ' Returns True.
MyCheck = C > D Imp B > A             ' Returns Null.
MyCheck = B Imp A                     ' Returns -1 (bitwise comparison).
```

Initialize Event

Applies To

UserForm object.

Description

Occurs after an object is loaded, but before it's shown.

Syntax

Private Sub *object*_**Initialize( )**

The *object* placeholder represents an object expression that evaluates to an object in the Applies To list.

Remarks

The Initialize event is typically used to prepare an application or **UserForm** for use. Variables are assigned initial values, and controls may be moved or resized to accommodate initialization data.

Example

The following example assumes two **UserForms** in a program. In UserForm1's Initialize event, UserForm2 is loaded and shown. When the user clicks UserForm2, it is hidden and UserForm1 appears. When UserForm1 is clicked, UserForm2 is shown again.

```
' This is the Initialize event procedure for UserForm1.
Private Sub UserForm_Initialize()
   Load UserForm2
   UserForm2.Show
End Sub
' This is the Click event of UserForm2.
Private Sub UserForm_Click()
   UserForm2.Hide
End Sub
```

```
' This is the click event for UserForm1.
Private Sub UserForm_Click()
   UserForm2.Show
End Sub
```

Input # Statement

Description

Reads data from an open sequential file and assigns the data to variables.

Syntax

Input #*filenumber, varlist*

The **Input #** statement syntax has these parts

Part	Description
filenumber	Required. Any valid file number.
varlist	Required. Comma-delimited list of variables that are assigned values read from the file—can't be an array or object variable. However, variables that describe an element of an array or user-defined type may be used.

Remarks

Data read with **Input #** is usually written to a file with **Write #**. Use this statement only with files opened in **Input** or **Binary** mode.

When read, standard string or numeric data is assigned to variables without modification. The following table illustrates how other input data is treated

Data	Value assigned to variable
Delimiting comma or blank line	**Empty**.
#NULL#	**Null**.
#TRUE# or #FALSE#	**True** or **False**.
#*yyyy-mm-dd hh:mm:ss*#	The date and/or time represented by the expression.
#ERROR *errornumber*#	*errornumber* (variable is a **Variant** tagged as an error).

Double quotation marks (" ") within input data are ignored.

Data items in a file must appear in the same order as the variables in *varlist* and match variables of the same data type. If a variable is numeric and the data is not numeric, a value of zero is assigned to the variable.

If you reach the end of the file while you are inputting a data item, the input is terminated and an error occurs.

Note To be able to correctly read data from a file into variables using **Input #**, use the **Write #** statement instead of the **Print #** statement to write the data to the files. Using **Write #** ensures each separate data field is properly delimited.

See Also

Input function, **Open** statement, **Print** # statement, **Write** # statement.

Example

This example uses the **Input #** statement to read data from a file into two variables. This example assumes that `TESTFILE` is a file with a few lines of data written to it using the **Write #** statement; that is, each line contains a string in quotations and a number separated by a comma, for example, ("Hello", 234).

```
Dim MyString, MyNumber
Open "TESTFILE" For Input As #1         ' Open file for input.
Do While Not EOF(1)                     ' Loop until end of file.
   Input #1, MyString, MyNumber         ' Read data into two variables.
   Debug.Print MyString, MyNumber       ' Print data to Debug window.
Loop
Close #1                                ' Close file.
```

Input Function

Description

Returns **String** containing characters from a file opened in **Input** or **Binary** mode.

Syntax

Input(*number***,** [#]*filenumber*)

The **Input** function syntax has these parts

Part	Description
number	Required. Any valid numeric expression specifying the number of characters to return.
filenumber	Required. Any valid file number.

Remarks

Data read with the **Input** function is usually written to a file with **Print #** or **Put**. Use this function only with files opened in **Input** or **Binary** mode.

Unlike the **Input #** statement, the **Input** function returns all of the characters it reads, including commas, carriage returns, linefeeds, quotation marks, and leading spaces.

With files opened for **Binary** access, an attempt to read through the file using the **Input** function until **EOF** returns **True** generates an error. Use the **LOF** and **Loc** functions instead of **EOF** when reading binary files with **Input**, or use **Get** when using the **EOF** function.

Note Use the **InputB** function for byte data contained within text files. With **InputB**, *number* specifies the number of bytes to return rather than the number of characters to return.

See Also

Input # statement.

Example

This example uses the **Input** function to read one character at a time from a file and print it to the **Debug** window. This example assumes that `TESTFILE` is a text file with a few lines of sample data.

```
Dim MyChar
Open "TESTFILE" For Input As #1                 ' Open file.
Do While Not EOF(1)                             ' Loop until end of file.
   MyChar = Input(1, #1)                        ' Get one character.
   Debug.Print MyChar                           ' Print to Debug window.
Loop
Close #1                                        ' Close file.
```

InputBox Function

Description

Displays a prompt in a dialog box, waits for the user to input text or click a button, and returns a **String** containing the contents of the text box.

Syntax

InputBox(*prompt*[, *title*] [, *default*] [, *xpos*] [, *ypos*] [, *helpfile*, *context*])

The **InputBox** function syntax has these named arguments

Part	Description
prompt	Required. String expression displayed as the message in the dialog box. The maximum length of ***prompt*** is approximately 1024 characters, depending on the width of the characters used. If ***prompt*** consists of more than one line, you can separate the lines using a carriage return character (**Chr**(13)), a linefeed character (**Chr**(10)), or carriage return–linefeed character combination (**Chr**(13) & **Chr**(10)) between each line.
title	Optional. String expression displayed in the title bar of the dialog box. If you omit ***title***, the application name is placed in the title bar.
default	Optional. String expression displayed in the text box as the default response if no other input is provided. If you omit ***default***, the text box is displayed empty.
xpos	Optional. Numeric expression that specifies, in twips, the horizontal distance of the left edge of the dialog box from the left edge of the screen. If ***xpos*** is omitted, the dialog box is horizontally centered.

(continued)

ypos	Optional. Numeric expression that specifies, in twips, the vertical distance of the upper edge of the dialog box from the top of the screen. If ***ypos*** is omitted, the dialog box is vertically positioned approximately one-third of the way down the screen.
helpfile	Optional. String expression that identifies the Help file to use to provide context-sensitive Help for the dialog box. If ***helpfile*** is provided, ***context*** must also be provided.
context	Optional. Numeric expression that is the Help context number assigned to the appropriate Help topic by the Help author. If ***context*** is provided, ***helpfile*** must also be provided.

Remarks

When both ***helpfile*** and ***context*** are provided, the user can press F1 to view the Help topic corresponding to the **context**. Some host applications, for example, Microsoft Excel, also automatically add a **Help** button to the dialog box. If the user clicks **OK** or presses ENTER, the **InputBox** function returns whatever is in the text box. If the user clicks **Cancel**, the function returns a zero-length string ("").

Note To specify more than the first named argument, you must use **InputBox** in an expression. To omit some positional arguments, you must include the corresponding comma delimiter.

See Also

MsgBox function.

Specifics (Microsoft Access)

You can't open a Help file from a dialog box created by the **InputBox** function in Microsoft Access. If you specify values for the *helpfile* and *context* arguments, they will be ignored, and no **Help** button appears on the input box. However, Microsoft Access won't generate an error.

Specifics (Microsoft Excel)

In Microsoft Excel, the ***prompt*** string cannot contain more than 256 characters.

Example

This example shows various ways to use the **InputBox** function to prompt the user to enter a value. If the x and y positions are omitted, the dialog box is automatically centered for the respective axes. The variable `MyValue` contains the value entered by the user if the user clicks **OK** or presses the ENTER key. If the user clicks **Cancel**, a zero-length string is returned.

```
Dim Message, Title, Default, MyValue
Message = "Enter a value between 1 and 3"    ' Set prompt.
Title = "InputBox Demo"                      ' Set title.
Default = "1"                                ' Set default.
' Display message, title, and default value.
MyValue = InputBox(Message, Title, Default)
```

```
' Use Helpfile and context. The Help button is added automatically.
MyValue = InputBox(Message, Title, , , , "DEMO.HLP", 10)

' Display dialog box at position 100, 100.
MyValue = InputBox(Message, Title, Default, 100, 100)
```

Example (Microsoft Access)

The following example uses the **InputBox** function to return the user's name. Note that you can't open a Help file from a dialog box created by the **InputBox** function in Microsoft Access.

```
Sub Greeting()
   Dim strInput As String, strMsg As String

   strMsg = "Enter your name."
   strInput = InputBox(Prompt:=strMsg, Title:="User Info", XPos:=2000, _
      YPos:=2000)
   MsgBox "Hello, " & strInput
End Sub
```

InStr Function

Description

Returns a **Variant** (**Long**) specifying the position of the first occurrence of one string within another.

Syntax

InStr([*start*,]*string1*, *string2*[, *compare*])

The **InStr** function syntax has these arguments

Part	Description
start	Optional. Numeric expression that sets the starting position for each search. If omitted, search begins at the first character position. If *start* contains **Null**, an error occurs. The *start* argument is required if *compare* is specified.
string1	Required. String expression being searched.
string2	Required. String expression sought.
compare	Optional. Specifies the type of string comparison. The *compare* argument can be omitted, or it can be 0, 1 or 2. Specify **0** (default) to perform a binary comparison. Specify **1** to perform a textual, noncase-sensitive comparison. For Microsoft Access only, specify **2** to perform a comparison based on information contained in your database. If *compare* is Null, an error occurs. If *compare* is omitted, the **Option Compare** setting determines the type of comparison.

Return Values

If	InStr returns
string1 is zero-length	0
string1 is **Null**	Null
string2 is zero-length	*start*
string2 is **Null**	Null
string2 is not found	0
string2 is found within *string1*	Position at which match is found
start > *string2*	0

Remarks

The **InStrB** function is used with byte data contained in a string. Instead of returning the character position of the first occurrence of one string within another, **InStrB** returns the byte position.

See Also

Option Compare statement, **StrComp** function.

Example

This example uses the **InStr** function to return the position of the first occurrence of one string within another.

```
Dim SearchString, SearchChar, MyPos
SearchString ="XXpXXpXXPXXP"                    ' String to search in.
SearchChar = "P"                                ' Search for "P".

' A textual comparison starting at position 4. Returns 6.
MyPos = Instr(4, SearchString, SearchChar, 1)

' A binary comparison starting at position 1. Returns 9.
MyPos = Instr(1, SearchString, SearchChar, 0)

' Comparison is binary by default (last argument is omitted).
MyPos = Instr(SearchString, SearchChar)         ' Returns 9.

MyPos = Instr(1, SearchString, "W")             ' Returns 0.
```

Int, Fix Functions

Description

Returns a value of the type passed to it containing the integer portion of a number.

Syntax

Int(*number*)
Fix(*number*)

The required *number* argument is a **Double** or any valid numeric expression. If *number* contains **Null**, **Null** is returned.

Remarks

Both **Int** and **Fix** remove the fractional part of *number* and return the resulting integer value.

The difference between **Int** and **Fix** is that if *number* is negative, **Int** returns the first negative integer less than or equal to *number,* whereas **Fix** returns the first negative integer greater than or equal to *number.* For example, **Int** converts –8.4 to –9, and **Fix** converts –8.4 to –8.

Fix(*number*) is equivalent to:

```
Sgn(number) * Int(Abs(number))
```

See Also

Integer data type.

Specifics (Microsoft Access)

If you use the **Fix** function to create a new field in a make-table query, the data type of the new field will be **dbDouble**. You can determine the data type using the DAO **Type** property.

Example

This example illustrates how the **Int** and **Fix** functions return integer portions of numbers. In the case of a negative number argument, the **Int** function returns the first negative integer less than or equal to the number; the **Fix** function returns the first negative integer greater than or equal to the number.

```
Dim MyNumber
MyNumber = Int(99.8)                        ' Returns 99.
MyNumber = Fix(99.2)                        ' Returns 99.

MyNumber = Int(-99.8)                       ' Returns -100.
MyNumber = Fix(-99.8)                       ' Returns -99.

MyNumber = Int(-99.2)                       ' Returns -100.
MyNumber = Fix(-99.2)                       ' Returns -99.
```

Integer Data Type

Description

Integer variables are stored as 16-bit (2-byte) numbers ranging in value from –32,768 to 32,767. The type-declaration character for **Integer** is the percent sign (%).

You can also use **Integer** variables to represent enumerated values. An enumerated value can contain a finite set of unique whole numbers, each of which has special meaning in the context in which it is used. Enumerated values provide a convenient way to select among a known number of choices, for example, black = 0, white = 1, and so on. It is good programming practice to define constants using the **Const** statement for each enumerated value.

See Also

Data type summary, **Def*type*** statements, **Long** data type, **Variant** data type.

IPmt Function

Description

Returns a **Double** specifying the interest payment for a given period of an annuity based on periodic, fixed payments and a fixed interest rate.

Syntax

IPmt(*rate*, *per*, *nper*, *pv*[, *fv*[, *type*]])

The **IPmt** function has these named arguments

Part	Description
rate	Required. **Double** specifying interest rate per period. For example, if you get a car loan at an annual percentage rate (APR) of 10 percent and make monthly payments, the rate per period is 0.1/12, or 0.0083.
per	Required. **Double** specifying payment period in the range 1 through ***nper***.
nper	Required. **Double** specifying total number of payment periods in the annuity. For example, if you make monthly payments on a four-year car loan, your loan has a total of 4 * 12 (or 48) payment periods.
pv	Required. **Double** specifying present value, or value today, of a series of future payments or receipts. For example, when you borrow money to buy a car, the loan amount is the present value to the lender of the monthly car payments you will make.
fv	Optional. **Variant** specifying future value or cash balance you want after you've made the final payment. For example, the future value of a loan is $0 because that's its value after the final payment. However, if you want to save $50,000 over 18 years for your child's education, then $50,000 is the future value. If omitted, 0 is assumed.
type	Optional. **Variant** specifying when payments are due. Use 0 if payments are due at the end of the payment period, or use 1 if payments are due at the beginning of the period. If omitted, 0 is assumed.

Remarks

An annuity is a series of fixed cash payments made over a period of time. An annuity can be a loan (such as a home mortgage) or an investment (such as a monthly savings plan).

The ***rate*** and ***nper*** arguments must be calculated using payment periods expressed in the same units. For example, if ***rate*** is calculated using months, ***nper*** must also be calculated using months.

For all arguments, cash paid out (such as deposits to savings) is represented by negative numbers; cash received (such as dividend checks) is represented by positive numbers.

See Also

DDB function, **IRR** function, **MIRR** function, **NPer** function, **NPV** function, **Pmt** function, **PPmt** function, **PV** function, **Rate** function, **SLN** function, **SYD** function.

Example

This example uses the **IPmt** function to calculate how much of a payment is interest when all the payments are of equal value. Given are the interest percentage rate per period (`APR / 12`), the payment period for which the interest portion is desired (`Period`), the total number of payments (`TotPmts`), the present value or principal of the loan (`PVal`), the future value of the loan (`FVal`), and a number that indicates whether the payment is due at the beginning or end of the payment period (`PayType`).

```
Dim FVal, Fmt, PVal, APR, TotPmts, PayType, Period, IntPmt, TotInt, Msg
Const ENDPERIOD = 0, BEGINPERIOD = 1          ' When payments are made.
FVal = 0                                       ' Usually 0 for a loan.
Fmt = "###,###,##0.00"                         ' Define money format.
PVal = InputBox("How much do you want to borrow?")
APR = InputBox("What is the annual percentage rate of your loan?")
If APR > 1 Then APR = APR / 100                ' Ensure proper form.
TotPmts = InputBox("How many monthly payments?")
PayType = MsgBox("Do you make payments at end of the month?", vbYesNo)
If PayType = vbNo Then PayType = BEGINPERIOD Else PayType = ENDPERIOD
For Period = 1 To TotPmts                      ' Total all interest.
   IntPmt = IPmt(APR / 12, Period, TotPmts, -PVal, FVal, PayType)
   TotInt = TotInt + IntPmt
Next Period
Msg = "You'll pay a total of " & Format(TotInt, Fmt)
Msg = Msg & " in interest for this loan."
MsgBox Msg                                     ' Display results.
```

IRR Function

Description

Returns a **Double** specifying the internal rate of return for a series of periodic cash flows (payments and receipts).

Syntax

IRR(*values*( )[, *guess*])

The **IRR** function has these named arguments

Part	Description
values( )	Required. Array of **Double** specifying cash flow values. The array must contain at least one negative value (a payment) and one positive value (a receipt).
guess	Optional. **Variant** specifying value you estimate will be returned by **IRR**. If omitted, *guess* is 0.1 (10 percent).

Remarks

The internal rate of return is the interest rate received for an investment consisting of payments and receipts that occur at regular intervals.

The **IRR** function uses the order of values within the array to interpret the order of payments and receipts. Be sure to enter your payment and receipt values in the correct sequence. The cash flow for each period doesn't have to be fixed, as it is for an annuity.

IRR is calculated by iteration. Starting with the value of ***guess***, **IRR** cycles through the calculation until the result is accurate to within 0.00001 percent. If **IRR** can't find a result after 20 tries, it fails.

See Also

DDB function, **FV** function, **IPmt** function, **MIRR** function, **NPer** function, **NPV** function, **Pmt** function, **PPmt** function, **PV** function, **Rate** function, **SLN** function, **SYD** function.

Example

In this example, the **IRR** function returns the internal rate of return for a series of 5 cash flows contained in the array `Values()`. The first array element is a negative cash flow representing business start-up costs. The remaining 4 cash flows represent positive cash flows for the subsequent 4 years. `Guess` is the estimated internal rate of return.

```
Dim Guess, Fmt, RetRate, Msg
Static Values(5) As Double            ' Set up array.
Guess = .1                            ' Guess starts at 10 percent.
Fmt = "#0.00"                         ' Define percentage format.
Values(0) = -70000                    ' Business start-up costs.
' Positive cash flows reflecting income for four successive years.
Values(1) = 22000 : Values(2) = 25000
Values(3) = 28000 : Values(4) = 31000
RetRate = IRR(Values(), Guess) * 100  ' Calculate internal rate.
Msg = "The internal rate of return for these five cash flows is "
Msg = Msg & Format(RetRate, Fmt) & " percent."
MsgBox Msg                            ' Display internal return rate.
```

Is Operator

Description

Used to compare two object reference variables.

Syntax

result = *object1* **Is** *object2*

The **Is** operator syntax has these parts

Part	Description
result	Required; any numeric variable.
object1	Required; any object name.
object2	Required; any object name.

Remarks

If *object1* and *object2* both refer to the same object, *result* is **True**; if they do not, *result* is **False**. Two variables can be made to refer to the same object in several ways.

In the following example, A has been set to refer to the same object as B:

```
Set A = B
```

The following example makes A and B refer to the same object as C:

```
Set A = C
Set B = C
```

See Also

Comparison operators, Operator precedence.

Example

This example uses the **Is** operator to compare two object references. The object variable names are generic and used for illustration purposes only.

```
Dim MyObject, YourObject, ThisObject, OtherObject, ThatObject, MyCheck
Set YourObject = MyObject               ' Assign object references.
Set ThisObject = MyObject
Set ThatObject = OtherObject
MyCheck = YourObject Is ThisObject      ' Returns True.
MyCheck = ThatObject Is ThisObject      ' Returns False.
' Assume MyObject <> OtherObject
MyCheck = MyObject Is ThatObject        ' Returns False.
```

Example (Microsoft Excel)

This example selects the intersection of two named ranges ("rg1" and "rg2") on Sheet1. If the ranges don't intersect, the example displays a message.

```
Worksheets("Sheet1").Activate
Set isect = Application.Intersect(Range("rg1"), Range("rg2"))
If isect Is Nothing Then
   MsgBox "Ranges do not intersect"
Else
   isect.Select
End If
```

This example finds the first occurrence of the word "Phoenix" in column B on Sheet1 and then displays the address of the cell that contains this word. If the word isn't found, the example displays a message.

```
Set foundCell = Worksheets("Sheet1").Columns("B").Find("Phoenix")
If foundCell Is Nothing Then
   MsgBox "The word was not found"
Else
   MsgBox "The word was found in cell " & foundCell.Address
End If
```

IsArray Function

Description

Returns a **Boolean** value indicating whether a variable is an array.

Syntax

IsArray(*varname***)**

The required *varname* argument is an identifier specifying a variable.

Remarks

IsArray returns **True** if the variable is an array; otherwise, it returns **False**. **IsArray** is especially useful with variants containing arrays.

See Also

Array function, **IsDate** function, **IsEmpty** function, **IsError** function, **IsMissing** function, **IsNull** function, **IsNumeric** function, **IsObject** function, **TypeName** function, **Variant** data type, **VarType** function.

Example

This example uses the **IsArray** function to check if a variable is an array.

```
Dim MyArray(1 To 5) As Integer, YourArray, MyCheck   ' Declare array variables.
YourArray = Array(1, 2, 3)                           ' Use Array function.
MyCheck = IsArray(MyArray)                           ' Returns True.
MyCheck = IsArray(YourArray)                         ' Returns True.
```

IsDate Function

Description

Returns a **Boolean** value indicating whether an expression can be converted to a date.

Syntax

IsDate(*expression***)**

The required *expression* argument is a **Variant** containing a date expression or string expression recognizable as a date or time.

Remarks

IsDate returns **True** if the expression is a date or can be converted to a valid date; otherwise, it returns **False**. In Microsoft Windows, the range of valid dates is January 1, 100 A.D. through December 31, 9999 A.D.; the ranges vary among operating systems.

See Also

Date data type, **IsArray** function, **IsEmpty** function, **IsError** function, **IsMissing** function, **IsNull** function, **IsNumeric** function, **IsObject** function, **TypeName** function, **Variant** data type, **VarType** function.

Example

This example uses the **IsDate** function to determine if an expression can be converted to a date.

```
Dim MyDate, YourDate, NoDate, MyCheck
MyDate = "February 12, 1969": YourDate = #2/12/69#: NoDate = "Hello"
MyCheck = IsDate(MyDate)                              ' Returns True.
MyCheck = IsDate(YourDate)                            ' Returns True.
MyCheck = IsDate(NoDate)                              ' Returns False.
```

Example (Microsoft Access)

The following example prompts the user for a string value, uses the **IsDate** function to determine whether the string can be converted to a date, and then displays an appropriate message.

```
Sub CheckDate()
   Dim strDate As String

   strDate = InputBox("Enter string to display as a date.")
   ' Test variable.
   If IsDate(strDate) Then
      ' If string is date, format and display in dialog.
      MsgBox "The date is: " & Format(DateValue(strDate), "Long Date")
   Else
      MsgBox "The value you entered is not a date."
   End If
End Sub
```

IsEmpty Function

Description

Returns a **Boolean** value indicating whether a variable has been initialized.

Syntax

IsEmpty(*expression*)

The required *expression* argument is a **Variant** containing a numeric or string expression. However, because **IsEmpty** is used to determine if individual variables are initialized, the *expression* argument is most often a single variable name.

Remarks

IsEmpty returns **True** if the variable is uninitialized, or is explicitly set to **Empty**; otherwise, it returns **False**. **False** is always returned if *expression* contains more than one variable. **IsEmpty** only returns meaningful information for variants.

See Also

IsArray function, **IsDate** function, **IsError** function, **IsMissing** function, **IsNull** function, **IsNumeric** function, **IsObject** function, **TypeName** function, **Variant** data type, **VarType** function.

Example

This example uses the **IsEmpty** function to determine whether a variable has been initialized.

```
Dim MyVar, MyCheck
MyCheck = IsEmpty(MyVar)                        ' Returns True.

MyVar = Null                                    ' Assign Null.
MyCheck = IsEmpty(MyVar)                        ' Returns False.

MyVar = Empty                                   ' Assign Empty.
MyCheck = IsEmpty(MyVar)                        ' Returns True.
```

Example (Microsoft Excel)

This example sorts the data in the first column on Sheet1 and then deletes any rows that contain duplicate data.

```
Worksheets("Sheet1").Range("A1").Sort _
   key1:=Worksheets("Sheet1").Range("A1")
Set currentCell = Worksheets("Sheet1").Range("A1")
Do While Not IsEmpty(currentCell)
   Set nextCell = currentCell.Offset(1, 0)
   If nextCell.Value = currentCell.Value Then
      currentCell.EntireRow.Delete
   End If
   Set currentCell = nextCell
Loop
```

IsError Function

Description

Returns a **Boolean** value indicating whether an expression is an error value.

Syntax

IsError(*expression***)**

The required *expression* argument must be a **Variant** of **VarType vbError**.

Remarks

Error values are created by converting real numbers to error values using the **CVErr** function. The **IsError** function is used to determine if a numeric expression represents an error. **IsError** returns **True** if the *expression* argument indicates an error; otherwise, it returns **False**. **IsError** only returns meaningful information for variants of **VarType vbError**.

See Also

CVErr function, **IsArray** function, **IsDate** function, **IsEmpty** function, **IsMissing** function, **IsNull** function, **IsNumeric** function, **IsObject** function, **TypeName** function, **Variant** data type, **VarType** function.

Example

This example uses the **IsError** function to check if a numeric expression is an error value. The **CVErr** function is used to return an **Error Variant** from a user-defined function. Assume `UserFunction` is a user-defined function procedure that returns an error value; for example, a return value assigned with the statement `UserFunction = CVErr(32767)`, where 32767 is a user-defined number.

```
Dim ReturnVal, MyCheck
ReturnVal = UserFunction()
MyCheck = IsError(ReturnVal)                    ' Returns True.
```

IsMissing Function

Description

Returns a **Boolean** value indicating whether an optional **Variant** argument has been passed to a procedure.

Syntax

IsMissing(*argname***)**

The required *argname* argument contains the name of an optional **Variant** procedure argument.

Remarks

Use the **IsMissing** function to detect whether or not optional **Variant** arguments have been provided in calling a procedure. **IsMissing** returns **True** if no value has been passed for the specified argument; otherwise, it returns **False**. If **IsMissing** returns **True** for an argument, use of the missing argument in other code may cause a user-defined error. If **IsMissing** is used on a **ParamArray** argument, it always returns **False**. To detect an empty **ParamArray**, test to see if the array's upper bound is less than its lower bound.

See Also

Function statement, **IsArray** function, **IsDate** function, **IsEmpty** function, **IsError** function, **IsNull** function, **IsNumeric** function, **IsObject** function, **Property Get** statement, **Property Let** statement, **Property Set** statement, **Sub** statement, **TypeName** function, **Variant** data type, **VarType** function.

Example

This example uses the **IsMissing** function to check if an optional argument has been passed to a user-defined procedure. Note that **Optional** arguments can now have default values and types other than **Variant**.

```
Dim ReturnValue
' The following statements call the user-defined function procedure.
ReturnValue = ReturnTwice()                       ' Returns Null.
ReturnValue = ReturnTwice(2)                      ' Returns 4.

' Function procedure definition.
Function ReturnTwice(Optional A)
   If IsMissing(A) Then
      ' If argument is missing, return a Null.
      ReturnTwice = Null
   Else
      ' If argument is present, return twice the value.
      ReturnTwice = A * 2
   End If
End Function
```

IsNull Function

Description

Returns a **Boolean** value that indicates whether an expression contains no valid data (**Null**).

Syntax

IsNull(*expression***)**

The required *expression* argument is a **Variant** containing a numeric expression or string expression.

Remarks

IsNull returns **True** if *expression* is **Null**; otherwise, **IsNull** returns **False**. If *expression* consists of more than one variable, **Null** in any constituent variable causes **True** to be returned for the entire expression.

The **Null** value indicates that the **Variant** contains no valid data. **Null** is not the same as **Empty**, which indicates that a variable has not yet been initialized. It is also not the same as a zero-length string (""), which is sometimes referred to as a null string.

Important Use the **IsNull** function to determine whether an expression contains a **Null** value. Expressions that you might expect to evaluate to **True** under some circumstances, such as `If Var = Null` and `If Var <> Null`, are always **False**. This is because any expression containing a **Null** is itself **Null** and, therefore, **False**.

See Also

IsArray function, **IsDate** function, **IsEmpty** function, **IsError** function, **IsMissing** function, **IsNumeric** function, **IsObject** function, **TypeName** function, **Variant** data type, **VarType** function.

Example

This example uses the **IsNull** function to determine if a variable contains a **Null**.

```
Dim MyVar, MyCheck
MyCheck = IsNull(MyVar)              ' Returns False.

MyVar = ""
MyCheck = IsNull(MyVar)              ' Returns False.

MyVar = Null
MyCheck = IsNull(MyVar)              ' Returns True.
```

Example (Microsoft Access)

The following example uses the **IsNull** function to determine whether the value of a control is **Null**. If it is, a message prompts the user to enter data. If the value is not **Null**, a message displays the value of the control.

```
Sub ControlValue(ctlText As Control)
   Dim strMsg As String

   ' Check that control is text box.
   If ctlText.ControlType = acTextBox Then
      ' If value of control is Null, prompt for data.
      If IsNull(ctlText.Value) Then
         strMsg = "No data in the field '" & ctlText.Name & "'." _
               & vbCrLf & "Please enter data for this field now."
            If MsgBox(strMsg, vbQuestion) = vbOK Then
               Exit Sub
            End If
      ' If value is not Null, display value.
      Else
         MsgBox (ctlText.Value)
      End If
   End If
End Sub
```

Example (Microsoft Excel)

This example creates a list of registered functions, placing each one in a separate row on Sheet1. Column A contains the full path and file name of the DLL or code resource, column B contains the function name, and column C contains the code for the argument data type.

```
theArray = Application.RegisteredFunctions
If IsNull(theArray) Then
   MsgBox "No registered functions"
Else
   For i = LBound(theArray) To UBound(theArray)
      For j = 1 To 3
         Worksheets("Sheet1").Cells(i, j).Formula = theArray(i, j)
      Next j
   Next i
End If
```

IsNumeric Function

Description

Returns a **Boolean** value indicating whether an expression can be evaluated as a number.

Syntax

IsNumeric(*expression*)

The required *expression* argument is a **Variant** containing a numeric expression or string expression.

Remarks

IsNumeric returns **True** if the entire *expression* is recognized as a number; otherwise, it returns **False**.

IsNumeric returns **False** if *expression* is a date expression.

See Also

IsArray function, **IsDate** function, **IsEmpty** function, **IsError** function, **IsMissing** function, **IsNull** function, **IsObject** function, **TypeName** function, **Variant** data type, **VarType** function.

Example

This example uses the **IsNumeric** function to determine if a variable can be evaluated as a number.

```
Dim MyVar, MyCheck
MyVar = "53"                                ' Assign value.
MyCheck = IsNumeric(MyVar)                  ' Returns True.

MyVar = "459.95"                            ' Assign value.
MyCheck = IsNumeric(MyVar)                  ' Returns True.

MyVar = "45 Help"                           ' Assign value.
MyCheck = IsNumeric(MyVar)                  ' Returns False.
```

IsObject Function

Description

Returns a **Boolean** value indicating whether an identifier represents an object variable.

Syntax

IsObject(*identifier***)**

The required *identifier* argument is a variable name.

Remarks

IsObject is useful only in determining whether a **Variant** is of **VarType vbObject**. This could occur if the **Variant** actually references (or once referenced) an object, or if it contains **Nothing**.

IsObject returns **True** if *identifier* is a variable declared with **Object** type or any valid class type, or if *identifier* is a **Variant** of **VarType vbObject**, or a user-defined object; otherwise, it returns **False**. **IsObject** returns **True** even if the variable has been set to **Nothing**.

Use error trapping to be sure that an object reference is valid. You can use the **IsNothing** function determine if an object reference has been set to **Nothing**.

See Also

IsArray function, **IsDate** function, **IsEmpty** function, **IsError** function, **IsMissing** function, **IsNull** function, **IsNumeric** function, **Object** data type, **Set** statement, **TypeName** function, **Variant** data type, **VarType** function.

Example

This example uses the **IsObject** function to determine if an identifier represents an object variable. `MyObject` and `YourObject` are object variables of the same type. They are generic names used for illustration purposes only.

```
Dim MyInt As Integer, YourObject, MyCheck    ' Declare variables.
Dim MyObject As Object
Set YourObject = MyObject                    ' Assign an object reference.
MyCheck = IsObject(YourObject)               ' Returns True.
MyCheck = IsObject(MyInt)                    ' Returns False.
```

Example (Microsoft Access)

The following example uses the **IsObject** function to check whether an argument passed to the function is an object.

```
Sub CheckObject(varAny As Variant)
   Dim varX as Variant

   If IsObject(varAny) Then
      Set varX = varAny
   Else
      varX = varAny
   End If
End Sub
```

Item Method

Applies To

Collection object.

Description

Returns a specific member of a **Collection** object either by position or by key.

Syntax

object.**Item(***index***)**

The **Item** method syntax has the following object qualifier and part

Part	Description
object	Required. An object expression that evaluates to an object in the Applies To list.
index	Required. An expression that specifies the position of a member of the collection. If a numeric expression, *index* must be a number from 1 to the value of the collection's **Count** property. If a string expression, *index* must correspond to the ***key*** argument specified when the member referred to was added to the collection.

Remarks

If the value provided as *index* doesn't match any existing member of the collection, an error occurs.

The **Item** method is the default method for a collection. Therefore, the following lines of code are equivalent:

```
Print MyCollection(1)
Print MyCollection.Item(1)
```

See Also

Add method, **Caption** property ("Extensibility Object Model Language Reference"), **Count** property ("Extensibility Object Model Language Reference"), **Name** property ("Extensibility Object Model Language Reference"), **Remove** method.

Example

This example uses the **Item** method to retrieve a reference to an object in a collection. Assuming `Birthdays` is a **Collection** object, the following code retrieves from the collection references to the objects representing Bill Smith's birthday and Adam Smith's birthday, using the keys "SmithBill" and "SmithAdam" as the *index* arguments. Note that the first call explicitly specifies the **Item** method, but the second does not. Both calls work because the **Item** method is the default for a **Collection** object. The references, assigned to `SmithBillBD` and `SmithAdamBD` using **Set**, can be used to access the properties and methods of the specified objects. To run this code, create the collection and populate it with at least the two referenced members.

```
Dim SmithBillBD As Object
Dim SmithAdamBD As Object
Dim Birthdays
Set SmithBillBD = Birthdays.Item("SmithBill")
Set SmithAdamBD = Birthdays("SmithAdam")
```

Example (Extensibility Object Model)

The following example contains two ways to display a specific member of the **CodePanes** collection, one using the **Item** method.

```
Application.VBE.CodePanes.Item(2).Show
Application.VBE.CodePanes(2).Show
```

Kill Statement

Description

Deletes files from a disk.

Syntax

Kill *pathname*

The required *pathname* argument is a string expression that specifies one or more file names to be deleted. The *pathname* may include the directory or folder, and the drive.

Remarks

Kill supports the use of multiple-character (*) and single-character (?) wildcards to specify multiple files.

An error occurs if you try to use **Kill** to delete an open file.

Note To delete directories, use the **RmDir** statement.

See Also

MacID function, **RmDir** statement.

Specifics (Macintosh)

In Microsoft Windows, **Kill** supports the use of multiple character (*) and single character (?) wildcards to specify multiple files. However, on the Macintosh, these characters are treated as valid file name characters and can't be used as wildcards to specify multiple files.

Since the Macintosh doesn't support the wildcards, use the file type to identify groups of files to delete. You can use the **MacID** function to specify file type instead of repeating the command with separate file names. For example, the following statement deletes all TEXT files in the current folder.

```
Kill MacID("TEXT")
```

If you use the **MacID** function with **Kill** in Microsoft Windows, an error occurs.

Example

This example uses the **Kill** statement to delete a file from a disk. Since the Macintosh doesn't support wildcards, you can use the **MacID** function to specify the file type instead of the file name.

```
' Assume TESTFILE is a file containing some data.
Kill "TestFile"' Delete file.

' In Microsoft Windows:
' Delete all *.TXT files in current directory.
Kill "*.TXT"

' On the Macintosh:
' Use the MacID function to delete all PICT files in current folder
Kill MacID("PICT")
```

LastDLLError Property

Applies To

Err object.

Description

Returns a system error code produced by a call to a dynamic-link library (DLL). Read-only.

Remarks

The **LastDLLError** property applies only to DLL calls made from Visual Basic code. When such a call is made, the called function usually returns a code indicating success or failure, and the **LastDLLError** property is filled. Check the documentation for the DLL's functions to determine the return values that indicate success or failure. Whenever the failure code is returned, the Visual Basic application should immediately check the **LastDLLError** property. No exception is raised when the **LastDLLError** property is set.

See Also

Declare statement, **Description** property, **Err** object, **HelpContext** property, **HelpContextID** property ("Extensibility Object Model Language Reference"), **HelpFile** property, **Number** property, **Source** property.

Example

When pasted into a **UserForm** module, the following code causes an attempt to call a DLL function. The call fails because the argument that is passed in (a null pointer) generates an error, and in any event, SQL can't be cancelled if it isn't running. The code following the call checks the return of the call, and then prints at the **LastDLLError** property of the **Err** object to reveal the error code.

```
Private Declare Function SQLCancel Lib "ODBC32.dll" _
   (ByVal hstmt As Long) As Integer

Private Sub UserForm_Click()
   Dim RetVal
   ' Call with invalid argument.
   RetVal = SQLCancel(myhandle&)
   ' Check for SQL error code.
   If RetVal = -2 Then
      ' Display the information code.
      MsgBox "Error code is :" & Err.LastDllError
   End If
End Sub
```

LBound Function

Description

Returns a **Long** containing the smallest available subscript for the indicated dimension of an array.

Syntax

LBound(*arrayname*[, *dimension*])

The **LBound** function syntax has these parts:

Part	Description
arrayname	Required. Name of the array variable; follows standard variable naming conventions.
dimension	Optional; **Variant** (**Long**). Whole number indicating which dimension's lower bound is returned. Use 1 for the first dimension, 2 for the second, and so on. If *dimension* is omitted, 1 is assumed.

Remarks

The **LBound** function is used with the **UBound** function to determine the size of an array. Use the **UBound** function to find the upper limit of an array dimension.

LBound returns the values in the following table for an array with the following dimensions:

```
Dim A(1 To 100, 0 To 3, -3 To 4)
```

Statement	Return Value
`LBound(A, 1)`	1
`LBound(A, 2)`	0
`LBound(A, 3)`	–3

The default lower bound for any dimension is either 0 or 1, depending on the setting of the **Option Base** statement. The base of an array created with the **Array** function is zero; it is unaffected by **Option Base**.

Arrays for which dimensions are set using the **To** clause in a **Dim**, **Private**, **Public**, **ReDim**, or **Static** statement can have any integer value as a lower bound.

See Also

Dim statement, **Option Base** statement, **Private** statement, **Public** statement, **ReDim** statement, **Static** statement, **UBound** function.

Example

This example uses the **LBound** function to determine the smallest available subscript for the indicated dimension of an array. Use the **Option Base** statement to override the default base array subscript value of 0.

```
Dim Lower
Dim MyArray(1 To 10, 5 To 15, 10 To 20)      ' Declare array variables.
Dim AnyArray(10)
Lower = Lbound(MyArray, 1)                    ' Returns 1.
Lower = Lbound(MyArray, 3)                    ' Returns 10.
Lower = Lbound(AnyArray)                      ' Returns 0 or 1, depending
                                              ' on setting of Option Base.
```

Example (Microsoft Excel)

This example writes the elements of the first custom list in column one on Sheet1.

```
listArray = Application.GetCustomListContents(1)
For i = LBound(listArray, 1) To UBound(listArray, 1)
   Worksheets("sheet1").Cells(i, 1).Value = listArray(i)
Next i
```

This example assumes that you used an external data source to create a PivotTable on Sheet1 in the active workbook. The example inserts the SQL connection string and query string into a new worksheet.

```
Set newSheet = ActiveWorkbook.Worksheets.Add
sdArray = Worksheets("Sheet1").UsedRange.PivotTable.SourceData
For i = LBound(sdArray) To UBound(sdArray)
   newSheet.Cells(i, 1) = sdArray(i)
Next i
```

LCase Function

Description

Returns a **String** that has been converted to lowercase.

Syntax

LCase(*string*)

The required *string* argument is any valid string expression. If *string* contains **Null**, Null is returned.

Remarks

Only uppercase letters are converted to lowercase; all lowercase letters and nonletter characters remain unchanged.

See Also

UCase function.

Example

This example uses the **LCase** function to return a lowercase version of a string.

```
Dim UpperCase, LowerCase
Uppercase = "Hello World 1234"      ' String to convert.
Lowercase = Lcase(UpperCase)        ' Returns "hello world 1234".
```

Left Function

Description

Returns a **Variant** (**String**) containing a specified number of characters from the left side of a string.

Syntax

Left(*string*, *length*)

The **Left** function syntax has these named arguments:

Part	Description
string	Required. String expression from which the leftmost characters are returned. If ***string*** contains **Null**, Null is returned.
length	Required; **Variant** (**Long**). Numeric expression indicating how many characters to return. If 0, a zero-length string ("") is returned. If greater than or equal to the number of characters in ***string***, the entire string is returned.

Remarks

To determine the number of characters in ***string***, use the **Len** function.

Note Use the **LeftB** function with byte data contained in a string. Instead of specifying the number of characters to return, ***length*** specifies the number of bytes.

See Also

Len function, **Mid** function, **Right** function.

Example

This example uses the **Left** function to return a specified number of characters from the left side of a string.

```
Dim AnyString, MyStr
AnyString = "Hello World"          ' Define string.
MyStr = Left(AnyString, 1)         ' Returns "H".
MyStr = Left(AnyString, 7)         ' Returns "Hello W".
MyStr = Left(AnyString, 20)        ' Returns "Hello World".
```

Len Function

Description

Returns a **Long** containing the number of characters in a string or the number of bytes required to store a variable.

Syntax

Len(*string* | *varname***)**

The **Len** function syntax has these parts:

Part	Description
string	Any valid string expression. If *string* contains **Null**, Null is returned.
Varname	Any valid variable name. If *varname* contains **Null**, **Null** is returned. If *varname* is a **Variant**, **Len** treats it the same as a **String** and always returns the number of characters it contains.

Remarks

One (and only one) of the two possible arguments must be specified. With user-defined types, **Len** returns the size as it will be written to the file.

Note Use the **LenB** function with byte data contained in a string. Instead of returning the number of characters in a string, **LenB** returns the number of bytes used to represent that string. With user-defined types, **LenB** returns the in-memory size, including any padding between elements.

Note **Len** may not be able to determine the actual number of storage bytes required when used with variable-length strings in user-defined data types.

See Also

Data type summary, **InStr** function.

Example

This example uses the **Len** function to return the number of characters in a string or the number of bytes required to store a variable. The **Type...End Type** block defining `CustomerRecord` must be preceded by the keyword **Private** if it appears in a class module. In a standard module, a **Type** statement can be **Public**.

```
Type CustomerRecord                      ' Define user-defined type.
   ID As Integer                         ' Place this definition in a
   Name As String * 10                   ' standard module.
   Address As String * 30
End Type

Dim Customer As CustomerRecord           ' Declare variables.
Dim MyInt As Integer, MyCur As Currency
Dim MyString, MyLen
MyString = "Hello World"                 ' Initialize variable.
MyLen = Len(MyInt)                       ' Returns 2.
MyLen = Len(Customer)                    ' Returns 42.
MyLen = Len(MyString)                    ' Returns 11.
MyLen = Len(MyCur)                       ' Returns 8.
```

Let Statement

Description

Assigns the value of an expression to a variable or property.

Syntax

[**Let**] *varname* = *expression*

The **Let** statement syntax has these parts:

Part	Description
Let	Optional. Explicit use of the **Let** keyword is a matter of style, but it is usually omitted.
varname	Required. Name of the variable or property; follows standard variable naming conventions.
expression	Required. Value assigned to the variable or property.

Remarks

A value expression can be assigned to a variable or property only if it is of a data type that is compatible with the variable. You can't assign string expressions to numeric variables, and you can't assign numeric expressions to string variables. If you do, an error occurs at compile time.

Variant variables can be assigned either string or numeric expressions. However, the reverse is not always true. Any **Variant** except a **Null** can be assigned to a string variable, but only a **Variant** whose value can be interpreted as a number can be assigned to a numeric variable. Use the **IsNumeric** function to determine if the **Variant** can be converted to a number.

Caution Assigning an expression of one numeric type to a variable of a different numeric type coerces the value of the expression into the numeric type of the resulting variable.

Let statements can be used to assign one record variable to another only when both variables are of the same user-defined type. Use the **LSet** statement to assign record variables of different user-defined types. Use the **Set** statement to assign object references to variables.

See Also

Const statement, Data type summary, **IsNumeric** function, **LSet** statement, **Set** statement, **Variant** data type.

Example

This example assigns the values of expressions to variables using both the explicit and implicit **Let** statement.

```
Dim MyStr, MyInt
' The following variable assignments use the Let statement.
Let MyStr = "Hello World"
Let MyInt = 5
```

The following are the same assignments without the **Let** statement.

```
Dim MyStr, MyInt
MyStr = "Hello World"
MyInt = 5
```

Like Operator

Description

Used to compare two strings.

Syntax

result = *string* **Like** *pattern*

The **Like** operator syntax has these parts:

Part	Description
result	Required; any numeric variable.
string	Required; any string expression.
pattern	Required; any string expression conforming to the pattern-matching conventions described in Remarks.

Remarks

If *string* matches *pattern*, *result* is **True**; if there is no match, *result* is **False**. If either *string* or *pattern* is **Null**, *result* is **Null**.

The behavior of the **Like** operator depends on the **Option Compare** statement. The default string-comparison method for each module is **Option Compare Binary**.

Option Compare Binary results in string comparisons based on a sort order derived from the internal binary representations of the characters. In Microsoft Windows, sort order is determined by the code page. In the following example, a typical binary sort order is shown:

A < B < E < Z < a < b < e < z < À < Ê < Ø < à < ê < ø

Option Compare Text results in string comparisons based on a case-insensitive, textual sort order determined by your system's locale. When you sort The same characters using **Option Compare Text**, the following text sort order is produced:

(A=a) < (À=à) < (B=b) < (E=e) < (Ê=ê) < (Z=z) < (Ø=ø)

Built-in pattern matching provides a versatile tool for string comparisons. The pattern-matching features allow you to use wildcard characters, character lists, or character ranges, in any combination, to match strings. The following table shows the characters allowed in *pattern* and what they match:

Characters in *pattern*	Matches in *string*
?	Any single character.
*	Zero or more characters.
#	Any single digit (0–9).
[*charlist*]	Any single character in *charlist*.
[**!***charlist*]	Any single character not in *charlist*.

A group of one or more characters (*charlist*) enclosed in brackets (**[ ]**) can be used to match any single character in *string* and can include almost any character code, including digits.

Note To match the special characters left bracket (**[**), question mark (**?**), number sign (**#**), and asterisk (*****), enclose them in brackets. The right bracket (**]**) can't be used within a group to match itself, but it can be used outside a group as an individual character.

By using a hyphen (**-**) to separate the upper and lower bounds of the range, *charlist* can specify a range of characters. For example, `[A-Z]` results in a match if the corresponding character position in *string* contains any uppercase letters in the range A–Z. Multiple ranges are included within the brackets without delimiters.

The meaning of a specified range depends on the character ordering valid at run time (as determined by **Option Compare** and the locale setting of the system the code is running on). Using the **Option Compare Binary** example, the range `[A-E]` matches A, B and E. With **Option Compare Text**, `[A-E]` matches A, a, À, à, B, b, E, e. The range does not match Ê or ê because accented characters fall after unaccented characters in the sort order.

Other important rules for pattern matching include the following:

- An exclamation point (**!**) at the beginning of *charlist* means that a match is made if any character except the characters in *charlist* is found in *string*. When used outside brackets, the exclamation point matches itself.
- A hyphen (**-**) can appear either at the beginning (after an exclamation point if one is used) or at the end of *charlist* to match itself. In any other location, the hyphen is used to identify a range of characters.
- When a range of characters is specified, they must appear in ascending sort order (from lowest to highest). `[A-Z]` is a valid pattern, but `[Z-A]` is not.
- The character sequence `[]` is considered a zero-length string ("").

In some languages, there are special characters in the alphabet that represent two separate characters. For example, several languages use the character "æ" to represent the characters "a" and "e" when they appear together. The **Like** operator recognizes that the single special character and the two individual characters are equivalent.

When a language that uses a special character is specified in the system locale settings, an occurrence of the single special character in either *pattern* or *string* matches the equivalent 2-character sequence in the other string. Similarly, a single special character in *pattern* enclosed in brackets (by itself, in a list, or in a range) matches the equivalent 2-character sequence in *string*.

See Also

Comparison operators, **InStr** function, Operator precedence, **Option Compare** statement, **StrComp** function.

Specifics (Macintosh)

On the Macintosh, sort order is determined by the character set.

Specifics (Microsoft Access)

In Microsoft Access, you can use the **Like** operator in a query expression or in a calculated control on a form or report.

You can use the **Like** operator to specify inexact criteria in the query design grid. For example, if you type **Like "C*"** in the **Criteria** row of the query design grid, the query returns all field values beginning with the letter C.

In a parameter query, you can use the **Like** operator to prompt the user for a pattern to search for. For example, suppose you have an Employees table that includes a LastName field. In the Query window, create a new query by adding the Employees table and dragging the LastName field to the grid. Enter the following expression in the **Criteria** cell:

```
Like [Enter first few letters of name:]&"*"
```

When the query is run, a dialog box prompts the user with "Enter first few letters of name:". If the user types **Sm** in the dialog box, the query looks for the pattern Sm*—that is, all names beginning with the letters Sm.

You can use the **Like** operator in an expression as a setting for the **ValidationRule** property. For example, you can restrict data entered in a text box control to an inexact specification. In the **ValidationRule** property of the text box, enter the following expression:

```
Like "P[A-F]###"
```

Data entered in this text box must now begin with the letter P, followed by any letter between A and F and three digits.

Example

This example uses the **Like** operator to compare a string to a pattern.

```
Dim MyCheck
MyCheck = "aBBBa" Like "a*a"                    ' Returns True.
MyCheck = "F" Like "[A-Z]"                      ' Returns True.
MyCheck = "F" Like "[!A-Z]"                     ' Returns False.
MyCheck = "a2a" Like "a#a"                      ' Returns True.
MyCheck = "aM5b" Like "a[L-P]#[!c-e]"           ' Returns True.
MyCheck = "BAT123khg" Like "B?T*"               ' Returns True.
MyCheck = "CAT123khg" Like "B?T*"               ' Returns False.
```

Example (Microsoft Excel)

This example deletes every defined name that contains "temp". The Option Compare Text statement must be included at the top of any module that contains this example.

```
For Each nm In ActiveWorkbook.Names
   If nm.Name Like "*temp*" Then
      nm.Delete
   End If
Next nm
```

This example adds an arrowhead to every shape on Sheet1 that has the word "Line" in its name.

```
For Each d In Worksheets("Sheet1").DrawingObjects
   If d.Name Like "*Line*" Then
      d.ArrowHeadLength = xlLong
      d.ArrowHeadStyle = xlOpen
      d.ArrowHeadWidth = xlNarrow
   End If
Next
```

Line Input # Statement

Description

Reads a single line from an open sequential file and assigns it to a **String** variable.

Syntax

Line Input #*filenumber*, *varname*

The **Line Input #** statement syntax has these parts:

Part	Description
filenumber	Required. Any valid file number.
varname	Required. Valid **Variant** or **String** variable name.

Remarks

Data read with **Line Input #** is usually written from a file with **Print #**.

The **Line Input #** statement reads from a file one character at a time until it encounters a carriage return (**Chr**(13)) or carriage return–linefeed (**Chr**(13) + **Chr**(10)) sequence. Carriage return–linefeed sequences are skipped rather than appended to the character string.

See Also

Chr function, **Input #** statement.

Example

This example uses the **Line Input #** statement to read a line from a sequential file and assign it to a variable. This example assumes that `TESTFILE` is a text file with a few lines of sample data.

```
Dim TextLine
Open "TESTFILE" For Input As #1          ' Open file.
Do While Not EOF(1)                      ' Loop until end of file.
   Line Input #1, TextLine               ' Read line into variable.
   Debug.Print TextLine                  ' Print to Debug window.
Loop
Close #1                                 ' Close file.
```

Load Statement

Description

Loads an object but doesn't show it.

Syntax

Load *object*

The *object* placeholder represents an object expression that evaluates to an object in the Applies To list.

Remarks

When an object is loaded, it is placed in memory, but isn't visible. Use the **Show** method to make the object visible. Until an object is visible, a user can't interact with it. The object can be manipulated programatically in its Initialize event procedure.

See Also

Activate, Deactivate events, **Hide** method, **StartUpPosition** property, **Unload** statement.

Example

In the following example, UserForm2 is loaded during UserForm1's Initialize event. Subsequent clicking on UserForm2 reveals UserForm1.

```
' This is the Initialize event procedure for UserForm1.
Private Sub UserForm_Initialize()
   Load UserForm2
   UserForm2.Show
End Sub
' This is the Click event of UserForm2.
Private Sub UserForm_Click()
   UserForm2.Hide
End Sub

' This is the click event for UserForm1.
Private Sub UserForm_Click()
   UserForm2.Show
End Sub
```

Loc Function

Description

Returns a **Long** specifying the current read/write position within an open file.

Syntax

Loc(*filenumber*)

The required *filenumber* argument is any valid **Integer** file number.

Remarks

The following describes the return value for each file access mode:

Mode	Return value
Random	Number of the last record read from or written to the file.
Sequential	Current byte position in the file divided by 128. However, information returned by **Loc** for sequential files is neither used nor required.
Binary	Position of the last byte read or written.

See Also

EOF function, **LOF** function, **Seek** function, **Seek** statement.

Example

This example uses the **Loc** function to return the current read/write position within an open file. This example assumes that `TESTFILE` is a text file with a few lines of sample data.

```
Dim MyLocation, MyLine
Open "TESTFILE" For Binary As #1        ' Open file just created.
Do While MyLocation < LOF(1)            ' Loop until end of file.
   MyLine = MyLine & Input(1, #1)       ' Read character into variable.
   MyLocation = Loc(1)                  ' Get current position within file.
' Print to Debug window.
   Debug.Print MyLine; Tab; MyLocation
Loop
Close #1                                ' Close file.
```

Lock, Unlock Statements

Description

Controls access by other processes to all or part of a file opened using the **Open** statement.

Syntax

Lock [#]*filenumber*[, *recordrange*]

. . .

Unlock [#]*filenumber*[, *recordrange*]

The **Lock** and **Unlock** statement syntax has these parts:

Part	Description
filenumber	Required. Any valid file number.
recordrange	Optional. The range of records to lock or unlock.

Settings

The *recordrange* argument settings are:

recnumber | [*start*] **To** *end*

Setting	Description
recnumber	Record number (**Random** mode files) or byte number (**Binary** mode files) at which locking or unlocking begins.
start	Number of the first record or byte to lock or unlock.
end	Number of the last record or byte to lock or unlock.

Remarks

The **Lock** and **Unlock** statements are used in environments where several processes might need access to the same file.

Lock and **Unlock** statements are always used in pairs. The arguments to **Lock** and **Unlock** must match exactly.

The first record or byte in a file is at position 1, the second record or byte is at position 2, and so on. If you specify just one record, then only that record is locked or unlocked. If you specify a range of records and omit a starting record (*start*), all records from the first record to the end of the range (*end*) are locked or unlocked. Using **Lock** without *recnumber* locks the entire file; using **Unlock** without *recnumber* unlocks the entire file.

If the file has been opened for sequential input or output, **Lock** and **Unlock** affect the entire file, regardless of the range specified by *start* and *end*.

Caution Be sure to remove all locks with an **Unlock** statement before closing a file or quitting your program. Failure to remove locks produces unpredictable results.

See Also

Open statement.

Example

This example illustrates the use of the **Lock** and **Unlock** statements. While a record is being modified, access by other processes to the record is denied. This example assumes that `TESTFILE` is a file containing five records of the user-defined type `Record`.

```
Type Record                                     ' Define user-defined type.
   ID As Integer
   Name As String * 20
End Type
```

```
Dim MyRecord As Record, RecordNumber          ' Declare variables.
' Open sample file for random access.
Open "TESTFILE" For Random Shared As #1 Len = Len(MyRecord)
RecordNumber = 4                              ' Define record number.
Lock #1, RecordNumber                         ' Lock record.
Get #1, RecordNumber, MyRecord                ' Read record.
MyRecord.ID = 234                             ' Modify record.
MyRecord.Name = "John Smith"
Put #1, RecordNumber, MyRecord                ' Write modified record.
Unlock #1, RecordNumber                       ' Unlock current record.
Close #1                                      ' Close file.
```

LOF Function

Description

Returns a **Long** representing the size, in bytes, of a file opened using the **Open** statement.

Syntax

LOF(*filenumber*)

The required *filenumber* argument is an **Integer** containing a valid file number.

Note Use the **FileLen** function to obtain the length of a file that is not open.

See Also

EOF function, **FileLen** function, **Loc** function, **Open** statement.

Example

This example uses the **LOF** function to determine the size of an open file. This example assumes that `TESTFILE` is a text file containing sample data.

```
Dim FileLength
Open "TESTFILE" For Input As #1               ' Open file.
FileLength = LOF(1)                           ' Get length of file.
Close #1                                      ' Close file.
```

Log Function

Description

Returns a **Double** specifying the natural logarithm of a number.

Syntax

Log(*number*)

The required *number* argument is a **Double** or any valid numeric expression greater than zero.

Remarks

The natural logarithm is the logarithm to the base *e*. The constant *e* is approximately 2.718282.

You can calculate base-*n* logarithms for any number *x* by dividing the natural logarithm of *x* by the natural logarithm of *n* as follows:

Log*n(x)* = **Log**(*x*) / **Log**(*n*)

The following example illustrates a custom **Function** that calculates base-10 logarithms:

```
Static Function Log10(X)
   Log10 = Log(X) / Log(10#)
End Function
```

See Also

Exp function.

Example

This example uses the **Log** function to return the natural logarithm of a number.

```
Dim MyAngle, MyLog
' Define angle in radians.
MyAngle = 1.3
' Calculate inverse hyperbolic sine.
MyLog = Log(MyAngle + Sqr(MyAngle * MyAngle + 1))
```

Long Data Type

Description

Long (**Long Integer**) variables are stored as signed 32-bit (4-byte) numbers ranging in value from –2,147,483,648 to 2,147,483,647. The type-declaration character for **Long** is the ampersand (**&**).

See Also

Data Type Summary, **Def***type* statements, **Integer** data type.

LSet Statement

Description

Left aligns a string within a string variable, or copies a variable of one user-defined type to another variable of a different user-defined type.

Syntax

LSet *stringvar* = *string*
LSet *varname1* = *varname2*

The **LSet** statement syntax has these parts:

Part	Description
stringvar	Required. Name of string variable.
string	Required. String expression to be left-aligned within *stringvar*.
varname1	Required. Variable name of the user-defined type being copied to.
varname2	Required. Variable name of the user-defined type being copied from.

Remarks

LSet replaces any leftover characters in *stringvar* with spaces.

If *string* is longer than *stringvar*, **LSet** places only the leftmost characters, up to the length of the *stringvar*, in *stringvar*.

Warning Using **LSet** to copy a variable of one user-defined type into a variable of a different user-defined type is not recommended. Copying data of one data type into space reserved for a different data type can cause unpredictable results.

When you copy a variable from one user-defined type to another, the binary data from one variable is copied into the memory space of the other, without regard for the data types specified for the elements.

See Also

Data type summary, **RSet** statement.

Example

This example uses the **LSet** statement to left align a string within a string variable. Although **LSet** can also be used to copy a variable of one user-defined type to another variable of a different, but compatible, user-defined type, this practice is not recommended. Due to the varying implementations of data structures among platforms, such a use of **LSet** can't be guaranteed to be portable.

```
Dim MyString
MyString = "0123456789"                 ' Initialize string.
Lset MyString = "<-Left"                ' MyString contains "<-Left    ".
```

LTrim, RTrim, and Trim Functions

Description

Returns a **Variant** (**String**) containing a copy of a specified string without leading spaces (**LTrim**), trailing spaces (**RTrim**), or both leading and trailing spaces (**Trim**).

Syntax

LTrim(*string*)
RTrim(*string*)
Trim(*string*)

The required *string* argument is any valid string expression. If *string* contains **Null**, **Null** is returned.

See Also

Left function, **Right** function.

Example

This example uses the **LTrim** function to strip leading spaces and the **RTrim** function to strip trailing spaces from a string variable. It uses the **Trim** function to strip both types of spaces.

```
Dim MyString, TrimString
MyString = "  <-Trim->  "              ' Initialize string.
TrimString = LTrim(MyString)           ' TrimString = "<-Trim->  ".
TrimString = RTrim(MyString)           ' TrimString = "  <-Trim->".
TrimString = LTrim(RTrim(MyString))    ' TrimString = "<-Trim->".
' Using the Trim function alone achieves the same result.
TrimString = Trim(MyString)            ' TrimString = "<-Trim->".
```

MacID Function

Description

Used on the Macintosh to convert a 4-character constant to a value that may be used by **Dir**, **Kill**, **Shell**, and **AppActivate**.

Syntax

MacID(constant)

The required *constant* argument consists of 4 characters used to specify a resource type, file type, application signature, or Apple Event, for example, TEXT, OBIN, MSWD (Microsoft Word), XCEL (Microsoft Excel), and so on.

Remarks

MacID is used with **Dir** and **Kill** to specify a Macintosh file type. Since the Macintosh does not support * and **?** as wildcards, you can use a four-character constant instead to identify groups of files. For example, the following statement returns TEXT type files from the current folder:

```
Dir("SomePath", MacID("TEXT"))
```

MacID is used with **Shell** and **AppActivate** to specify an application using the application's unique signature.

See Also

AppActivate statement, **Dir** function, **Kill** statement.

Example

This example shows various uses of the **MacID** function. The **MacID** function is not available in Microsoft Windows.

```
Dim filename, ReturnValue
' Return the first text file in folder HD:MY FOLDER.
FileName = Dir("HD:MY FOLDER:", MacId("TEXT"))

' Deletes all "TEXT" files in the current folder.
Kill MacId("TEXT")

' Run Microsoft Excel.
ReturnValue = Shell(MacId("XCEL"))

' Activate Microsoft Word.
AppActivate MacId("MSWD")
```

MacScript Function

Description

Executes an AppleScript script and returns a value returned by the script, if any.

Syntax

MacScript *script*

The *script* argument is a **String** expression. The **String** expression either can be a series of AppleScript commands or can specify the name of an AppleScript script or a script file.

Remarks

Multiline scripts can be created by embedding carriage-return characters (**Chr**(13)).

See Also

Chr Function.

Example

This example uses the **MacScript** function to open the **Choose File** dialog box (the Macintosh standard-file dialog). The full path of the file chosen by the user is returned. If appropriate, the path specification is preceded by the type of the file.

```
ThePath$ = Macscript("ChooseFile")
```

Mid Function

Description

Returns a **Variant** (**String**) containing a specified number of characters from a string.

Syntax

Mid(*string*, *start*[, *length*])

The **Mid** function syntax has these named arguments:

Part	Description
string	Required. String expression from which characters are returned. If ***string*** contains **Null**, **Null** is returned.
start	Required; **Long**. Character position in ***string*** at which the part to be taken begins. If ***start*** is greater than the number of characters in ***string***, **Mid** returns a zero-length string (" ").
length	Optional; **Variant** (**Long**). Number of characters to return. If omitted or if there are fewer than ***length*** characters in the text (including the character at ***start***), all characters from the ***start*** position to the end of the string are returned.

Remarks

To determine the number of characters in ***string***, use the **Len** function.

Note Use the **MidB** function with byte data contained in a string. Instead of specifying the number of characters, the arguments specify numbers of bytes.

See Also

Left function, **Len** function, **LTrim**, **RTrim**, and **Trim** functions, **Mid** statement, **Right** function.

Example

This example uses the **Mid** function to return a specified number of characters from a string.

```
Dim MyString, FirstWord, LastWord, MidWords
MyString = "Mid Function Demo"              ' Create text string.
FirstWord = Mid(MyString, 1, 3)             ' Returns "Mid".
LastWord = Mid(MyString, 14, 4)             ' Returns "Demo".
MidWords = Mid(MyString, 5)                 ' Returns "Function Demo".
```

Mid Statement

Description

Replaces a specified number of characters in a **Variant** (**String**) variable with characters from another string.

Syntax

Mid(*stringvar*, *start*[, *length*]) = *string*

The **Mid** statement syntax has these parts:

Part	Description
stringvar	Required. Name of string variable to modify.
start	Required; **Variant** (**Long**). Character position in *stringvar* where the replacement of text begins.
length	Optional; **Variant** (**Long**). Number of characters to replace. If omitted, all of *string* is used.
string	Required. String expression that replaces part of *stringvar*.

Remarks

The number of characters replaced is always less than or equal to the number of characters in *stringvar*.

Note Use the **MidB** statement with byte data contained in a string. In the **MidB** statement, *start* specifies the byte position within *stringvar* where replacement begins and *length* specifies the numbers of bytes to replace.

See Also

Mid function.

Example

This example uses the **Mid** statement to replace a specified number of characters in a string variable with characters from another string.

```
Dim MyString
MyString = "The dog jumps"                ' Initialize string.
Mid(MyString, 5, 3) = "fox"               ' MyString = "The fox jumps".
Mid(MyString, 5) = "cow"                  ' MyString = "The cow jumps".
Mid(MyString, 5) = "cow jumped over"      ' MyString = "The cow jumpe".
Mid(MyString, 5, 3) = "duck"              ' MyString = "The duc jumpe".
```

Minute Function

Description

Returns a **Variant** (**Integer**) specifying a whole number between 0 and 59, inclusive, representing the minute of the hour.

Syntax

Minute(*time***)**

The required *time* argument is any **Variant**, numeric expression, string expression, or any combination, that can represent a time. If *time* contains **Null**, **Null** is returned.

See Also

Day function, **Hour** function, **Now** function, **Second** function, **Time** function, **Time** statement.

Example

This example uses the **Minute** function to obtain the minute of the hour from a specified time. In the development environment, the time literal is displayed in short time format using the locale settings of your code.

```
Dim MyTime, MyMinute
MyTime = #4:35:17 PM#                    ' Assign a time.
MyMinute = Minute(MyTime)                ' MyMinute contains 35.
```

MIRR Function

Description

Returns a **Double** specifying the modified internal rate of return for a series of periodic cash flows (payments and receipts).

Syntax

MIRR(*values***( ),***finance_rate***,** ***reinvest_rate***)**

The **MIRR** function has these named arguments:

Part	Description
values( )	Required. Array of **Double** specifying cash flow values. The array must contain at least one negative value (a payment) and one positive value (a receipt).
finance_rate	Required. **Double** specifying interest rate paid as the cost of financing.
reinvest_rate	Required. **Double** specifying interest rate received on gains from cash reinvestment.

Remarks

The modified internal rate of return is the internal rate of return when payments and receipts are financed at different rates. The **MIRR** function takes into account both the cost of the investment (***finance_rate***) and the interest rate received on reinvestment of cash (***reinvest_rate***).

The ***finance_rate*** and ***reinvest_rate*** arguments are percentages expressed as decimal values. For example, 12 percent is expressed as 0.12.

The **MIRR** function uses the order of values within the array to interpret the order of payments and receipts. Be sure to enter your payment and receipt values in the correct sequence.

See Also

DDB function, **FV** function, **IPmt** function, **IRR** function, **NPer** function, **NPV** function, **Pmt** function, **PPmt** function, **PV** function, **Rate** function, **SLN** function, **SYD** function.

Example

This example uses the **MIRR** function to return the modified internal rate of return for a series of cash flows contained in the array `Values()`. `LoanAPR` represents the financing interest, and `InvAPR` represents the interest rate received on reinvestment.

```
Dim LoanAPR, InvAPR, Fmt, RetRate, Msg
Static Values(5) As Double                     ' Set up array.
LoanAPR = .1                                   ' Loan rate.
InvAPR = .12                                   ' Reinvestment rate.
Fmt = "#0.00"                                  ' Define money format.
Values(0) = -70000                             ' Business start-up costs.
' Positive cash flows reflecting income for four successive years.
Values(1) = 22000 : Values(2) = 25000
Values(3) = 28000 : Values(4) = 31000
RetRate = MIRR(Values(), LoanAPR, InvAPR)      ' Calculate internal rate.
Msg = "The modified internal rate of return for these five cash flows is"
Msg = Msg & Format(Abs(RetRate) * 100, Fmt) & "%."
MsgBox Msg                                     ' Display internal return
                                               ' rate.
```

MkDir Statement

Description

Creates a new directory or folder.

Syntax

MkDir *path*

The required *path* argument is a string expression that identifies the directory or folder to be created. The *path* may include the drive. If no drive is specified, **MkDir** creates the new directory or folder on the current drive.

See Also

ChDir statement, **CurDir** function, **RmDir** statement.

Example

This example uses the **MkDir** statement to create a directory or folder. If the drive is not specified, the new directory or folder is created on the current drive.

```
MkDir "MYDIR"                    ' Make new directory or folder.
```

Mod Operator

Description

Used to divide two numbers and return only the remainder.

Syntax

result = *number1* **Mod** *number2*

The **Mod** operator syntax has these parts:

Part	Description
result	Required; any numeric variable.
number1	Required; any numeric expression.
number2	Required; any numeric expression.

Remarks

The modulus, or remainder, operator divides *number1* by *number2* (rounding floating-point numbers to integers) and returns only the remainder as *result*. For example, in the following expression, A (*result*) equals 5.

```
A = 19 Mod 6.7
```

Usually, the data type of *result* is a **Byte**, **Byte** variant, **Integer**, **Integer** variant, **Long**, or **Variant** containing a **Long**, regardless of whether or not *result* is a whole number. Any fractional portion is truncated. However, if any expression is **Null**, *result* is **Null**. Any expression that is **Empty** is treated as 0.

See Also

Operator precedence.

Example

This example uses the **Mod** operator to divide two numbers and return only the remainder. If either number is a floating-point number, it is first rounded to an integer.

```
Dim MyResult
MyResult = 10 Mod 5                        ' Returns 0.
MyResult = 10 Mod 3                        ' Returns 1.
MyResult = 12 Mod 4.3                      ' Returns 0.
MyResult = 12.6 Mod 5                      ' Returns 3.
```

Example (Microsoft Excel)

This example sets the column width of every other column on Sheet1 to 4 points.

```
For Each col In Worksheets("Sheet1").Columns
   If col.Column Mod 2 = 0 Then
      col.ColumnWidth = 4
   End If
Next col
```

This example sets the row height of every other row on Sheet1 to 4 points.

```
For Each rw In Worksheets("Sheet1").Rows
   If rw.Row Mod 2 = 0 Then
      rw.RowHeight = 4
   End If
Next rw
```

This example selects every other item in list box one on Sheet1.

```
Dim items() As Boolean
Set lbox = Worksheets("Sheet1").ListBoxes(1)
ReDim items(1 To lbox.ListCount)
For i = 1 To lbox.ListCount
   If i Mod 2 = 1 Then
      items(i) = True
   Else
      items(i) = False
   End If
Next
lbox.MultiSelect = xlExtended
lbox.Selected = items
```

Month Function

Description

Returns a **Variant** (**Integer**) specifying a whole number between 1 and 12, inclusive, representing the month of the year.

Syntax

Month(*date***)**

The required *date* argument is any **Variant**, numeric expression, string expression, or any combination, that can represent a date. If *date* contains **Null**, **Null** is returned.

See Also

Date function, **Date** statement, **Day** function, **Now** function, **Weekday** function, **Year** function.

Example

This example uses the **Month** function to obtain the month from a specified date. In the development environment, the date literal is displayed in short date format using the locale settings of your code.

```
Dim MyDate, MyMonth
MyDate = #February 12, 1969#                ' Assign a date.
MyMonth = Month(MyDate)                     ' MyMonth contains 2.
```

Example (Microsoft Access)

See the **DateSerial** function example (Microsoft Access).

MsgBox Function

Description

Displays a message in a dialog box, waits for the user to click a button, and returns an **Integer** indicating which button the user clicked.

Syntax

MsgBox(*prompt*[, *buttons*] [, *title*] [,, *helpfile*, *context*])

The **MsgBox** function syntax has these named arguments:

Part	Description
prompt	Required. String expression displayed as the message in the dialog box. The maximum length of ***prompt*** is approximately 1024 characters, depending on the width of the characters used. If ***prompt*** consists of more than one line, you can separate the lines using a carriage return character (**Chr**(13)), a linefeed character (**Chr**(10)), or carriage return–linefeed character combination (**Chr**(13) & **Chr**(10)) between each line.
buttons	Optional. Numeric expression that is the sum of values specifying the number and type of buttons to display, the icon style to use, the identity of the default button, and the modality of the message box. If omitted, the default value for ***buttons*** is 0.
title	Optional. String expression displayed in the title bar of the dialog box. If you omit ***title***, the application name is placed in the title bar.
helpfile	Optional. String expression that identifies the Help file to use to provide context-sensitive Help for the dialog box. If ***helpfile*** is provided, ***context*** must also be provided.
context	Optional. Numeric expression that is the Help context number assigned to the appropriate Help topic by the Help author. If ***context*** is provided, ***helpfile*** must also be provided.

Settings

The ***buttons*** argument settings are:

Constant	Value	Description
vbOKOnly	0	Display **OK** button only.
vbOKCancel	1	Display **OK** and **Cancel** buttons.
vbAbortRetryIgnore	2	Display **Abort**, **Retry**, and **Ignore** buttons.
vbYesNoCancel	3	Display **Yes**, **No**, and **Cancel** buttons.
vbYesNo	4	Display **Yes** and **No** buttons.
vbRetryCancel	5	Display **Retry** and **Cancel** buttons.
vbCritical	16	Display **Critical Message** icon.
vbQuestion	32	Display **Warning Query** icon.
vbExclamation	48	Display **Warning Message** icon.
vbInformation	64	Display **Information Message** icon.
vbDefaultButton1	0	First button is default.
vbDefaultButton2	256	Second button is default.
vbDefaultButton3	512	Third button is default.
vbDefaultButton4	768	Fourth button is default.
vbApplicationModal	0	Application modal; the user must respond to the message box before continuing work in the current application.
vbSystemModal	4096	System modal; all applications are suspended until the user responds to the message box.

The first group of values (0 – 5) describes the number and type of buttons displayed in the dialog box; the second group (16, 32, 48, 64) describes the icon style; the third group (0, 256, 512) determines which button is the default; and the fourth group (0, 4096) determines the modality of the message box. When adding numbers to create a final value for the ***buttons*** argument, use only one number from each group.

Note These constants are specified by Visual Basic for Applications. As a result, the names can be used anywhere in your code in place of the actual values.

Return Values

Constant	Value	Description
vbOK	1	**OK**
vbCancel	2	**Cancel**
vbAbort	3	**Abort**
vbRetry	4	**Retry**
vbIgnore	5	**Ignore**
vbYes	6	**Yes**
vbNo	7	**No**

Remarks

When both ***helpfile*** and ***context*** are provided, the user can press F1 to view the Help topic corresponding to the **context**. Some host applications, for example, Microsoft Excel, also automatically add a **Help** button to the dialog box.

If the dialog box displays a **Cancel** button, pressing the ESC key has the same effect as clicking **Cancel**. If the dialog box contains a **Help** button, context-sensitive Help is provided for the dialog box. However, no value is returned until one of the other buttons is clicked.

Note To specify more than the first named argument, you must use **MsgBox** in an expression. To omit some positional arguments, you must include the corresponding comma delimiter.

See Also

InputBox function, **MsgBox** action.

Specifics (Microsoft Access)

You can use the **MsgBox** function in Microsoft Access to create a formatted error message similar to built-in error messages displayed by Microsoft Access. This function permits you to supply a string in three sections for the *prompt* argument. You separate the sections with the at sign (@).

The following example displays a formatted dialog box with a sectioned string. The first section of text in the string is displayed as a bold heading. The second section is displayed as plain text beneath that heading. The third section is displayed as plain text beneath the heading "Solution," which the function provides for you.

```
MsgBox "Wrong button!@This button doesn't work.@Try another.", _
    vbOKOnly + vbExclamation
```

Note To display a message box without an icon in Microsoft Access, simply omit any constant that would denote an icon, or supply a value of zero for the *buttons* argument, as in the following example.

```
MsgBox "No icons included.", 0
```

Specifics (Microsoft Excel)

In Microsoft Excel, the ***prompt*** string cannot contain more than 256 characters.

Example

This example uses the **MsgBox** function to display a critical-error message in a dialog box with Yes and No buttons. The No button is specified as the default response. The value returned by the **MsgBox** function depends on the button chosen by the user. This example assumes that `DEMO.HLP` is a Help file that contains a topic with a Help context number equal to `1000`.

```
Dim Msg, Style, Title, Help, Ctxt, Response, MyString
Msg = "Do you want to continue ?"                      ' Define message.
Style = vbYesNo + vbCritical + vbDefaultButton2        ' Define buttons.
Title = "MsgBox Demonstration"                         ' Define title.
Help = "DEMO.HLP"                                      ' Define Help file.
Ctxt = 1000                                            ' Define topic
                                                       ' context.
                                                       ' Display message.
Response = MsgBox(Msg, Style, Title, Help, Ctxt)
If Response = vbYes Then                               ' User chose Yes.
   MyString = "Yes"                                    ' Perform some action.
Else                                                   ' User chose No.
   MyString = "No"                                     ' Perform some action.
End If
```

Example (Microsoft Access)

The following example uses the **MsgBox** function to create a formatted error message in Microsoft Access. Note the use of the at sign (@) to denote the different sections of the string.

```
Sub CustomMessage()
   Dim strMsg As String, strInput As String

   ' Initialize string.
   strMsg = "Number outside range.@You entered a number that is " _
      & "less than 1 or greater than 10.@Press OK to enter " _
      & "the number again."
   ' Prompt user for input.
   strInput = InputBox("Enter a number between 1 and 10.")
   ' Determine if user chose "Cancel".
   If strInput <> "" Then
      ' Test value of user input.
      Do While strInput < 0 Or strInput > 10
         If MsgBox(strMsg, vbOKCancel, "Error!") = vbOK Then
            strInput = InputBox("Enter a number between 1 and 10.")
         Else
            Exit Sub
         End If
      Loop
      ' Display user's correct input.
      MsgBox "You entered the number " & strInput & "."
   Else
      Exit Sub
   End If
End Sub
```

Name Statement

Description

Renames a disk file, directory, or folder.

Syntax

Name *oldpathname* **As** *newpathname*

The **Name** statement syntax has these parts:

Part	Description
oldpathname	Required. String expression that specifies the existing file name and location—may include directory or folder, and drive.
newpathname	Required. String expression that specifies the new file name and location—may include directory or folder, and drive. The file name specified by *newpathname* can't already exist.

Remarks

Both *newpathname* and *oldpathname* must be on the same drive. If the path in *newpathname* exists and is different from the path in *oldpathname*, the **Name** statement moves the file to the new directory or folder and renames the file, if necessary. If *newpathname* and *oldpathname* have different paths and the same file name, **Name** moves the file to the new location and leaves the file name unchanged. Using **Name**, you can move a file from one directory or folder to another, but you can't move a directory or folder.

Using **Name** on an open file produces an error. You must close an open file before renaming it. **Name** arguments cannot include multiple-character (*) and single-character (?) wildcards.

See Also

Kill statement.

Example

This example uses the **Name** statement to rename a file. For purposes of this example, assume that the directories or folders that are specified already exist.

```
Dim OldName, NewName
OldName = "OLDFILE": NewName = "NEWFILE"      ' Define filenames.
Name OldName As NewName                       ' Rename file.

' In Microsoft Windows:
OldName = "C:\MYDIR\OLDFILE": NewName = "C:\YOURDIR\NEWFILE"
Name OldName As NewName                       ' Move and rename file.

' On the Macintosh:
OldName = "HD:MY FOLDER:OLDFILE": NewName = "HD:YOUR FOLDER:NEWFILE"
Name OldName As NewName                       ' Move and rename file.
```

Not Operator

Description

Used to perform logical negation on an expression.

Syntax

result = **Not** *expression*

The **Not** operator syntax has these parts:

Part	Description
result	Required; any numeric variable.
expression	Required; any expression.

Remarks

The following table illustrates how *result* is determined:

If *expression* is	Then *result* is
True	**False**
False	**True**
Null	**Null**

In addition, the **Not** operator inverts the bit values of any variable and sets the corresponding bit in *result* according to the following table:

If bit in *expression* is	Then bit in *result* is
0	1
1	0

See Also

Operator precedence.

Example

This example uses the **Not** operator to perform logical negation on an expression.

```
Dim A, B, C, D, MyCheck
A = 10: B = 8: C = 6: D = Null       ' Initialize variables.
MyCheck = Not(A > B)                 ' Returns False.
MyCheck = Not(B > A)                 ' Returns True.
MyCheck = Not(C > D)                 ' Returns Null.
MyCheck = Not A                      ' Returns -11 (bitwise comparison).
```

Now Function

Description

Returns a **Variant** (**Date**) specifying the current date and time according your computer's system date and time.

Syntax

Now

See Also

Date function, **Date** statement, **Day** function, **Hour** function, **Minute** function, **Month** function, **Second** function, **Time** function, **Time** statement, **Weekday** function, **Year** function.

Example

This example uses the **Now** function to return the current system date and time.

```
Dim Today
Today = Now                     ' Assign current system date and time.
```

Example (Microsoft Access)

You can use the **Now** function in a calculated control to return the current system date and time. For example, you can create a text box and set its **ControlSource** property to the following expression.

```
=Now()
```

NPer Function

Description

Returns a **Double** specifying the number of periods for an annuity based on periodic, fixed payments and a fixed interest rate.

Syntax

NPer(*rate*, *pmt*, *pv*[, *fv*[, *type*]])

The **NPer** function has these named arguments:

Part	Description
rate	Required. **Double** specifying interest rate per period. For example, if you get a car loan at an annual percentage rate (APR) of 10 percent and make monthly payments, the rate per period is 0.1/12, or 0.0083.
pmt	Required. **Double** specifying payment to be made each period. Payments usually contain principal and interest that doesn't change over the life of the annuity.

(continued)

pv Required. **Double** specifying present value, or value today, of a series of future payments or receipts. For example, when you borrow money to buy a car, the loan amount is the present value to the lender of the monthly car payments you will make.

fv Optional. **Variant** specifying future value or cash balance you want after you've made the final payment. For example, the future value of a loan is $0 because that's its value after the final payment. However, if you want to save $50,000 over 18 years for your child's education, then $50,000 is the future value. If omitted, 0 is assumed.

type Optional. **Variant** specifying when payments are due. Use 0 if payments are due at the end of the payment period, or use 1 if payments are due at the beginning of the period. If omitted, 0 is assumed.

Remarks

An annuity is a series of fixed cash payments made over a period of time. An annuity can be a loan (such as a home mortgage) or an investment (such as a monthly savings plan).

For all arguments, cash paid out (such as deposits to savings) is represented by negative numbers; cash received (such as dividend checks) is represented by positive numbers.

See Also

DDB function, **FV** function, **IPmt** function, **IRR** function, **MIRR** function, **NPV** function, **Pmt** function, **PPmt** function, **PV** function, **Rate** function, **SLN** function, **SYD** function.

Example

This example uses the **NPer** function to return the number of periods during which payments must be made to pay off a loan whose value is contained in `PVal`. Also provided are the interest percentage rate per period (`APR / 12`), the payment (`Payment`), the future value of the loan (`FVal`), and a number that indicates whether the payment is due at the beginning or end of the payment period (`PayType`).

```
Dim FVal, PVal, APR, Payment, PayType, TotPmts
Const ENDPERIOD = 0, BEGINPERIOD = 1        ' When payments are made.
FVal = 0                                    ' Usually 0 for a loan.
PVal = InputBox("How much do you want to borrow?")
APR = InputBox("What is the annual percentage rate of your loan?")
If APR > 1 Then APR = APR / 100             ' Ensure proper form.
Payment = InputBox("How much do you want to pay each month?")
PayType = MsgBox("Do you make payments at the end of month?", vbYesNo)
If PayType = vbNo Then PayType = BEGINPERIOD Else PayType = ENDPERIOD
TotPmts = NPer(APR / 12, -Payment, PVal, FVal, PayType)
If Int(TotPmts) <> TotPmts Then TotPmts = Int(TotPmts) + 1
MsgBox "It will take you " & TotPmts & " months to pay off your loan."
```

NPV Function

Description

Returns a **Double** specifying the net present value of an investment based on a series of periodic cash flows (payments and receipts) and a discount rate.

Syntax

NPV(*rate*, *values*( ))

The **NPV** function has these named arguments:

Part	Description
rate	Required. **Double** specifying discount rate over the length of the period, expressed as a decimal.
values( )	Required. Array of **Double** specifying cash flow values. The array must contain at least one negative value (a payment) and one positive value (a receipt).

Remarks

The net present value of an investment is the current value of a future series of payments and receipts.

The **NPV** function uses the order of values within the array to interpret the order of payments and receipts. Be sure to enter your payment and receipt values in the correct sequence.

The **NPV** investment begins one period before the date of the first cash flow value and ends with the last cash flow value in the array.

The net present value calculation is based on future cash flows. If your first cash flow occurs at the beginning of the first period, the first value must be added to the value returned by **NPV** and must not be included in the cash flow values of ***values***( ).

The **NPV** function is similar to the **PV** function (present value) except that the **PV** function allows cash flows to begin either at the end or the beginning of a period. Unlike the variable **NPV** cash flow values, **PV** cash flows must be fixed throughout the investment.

See Also

DDB function, **FV** function, **IPmt** function, **IRR** function, **MIRR** function, **NPer** function, **Pmt** function, **PPmt** function, **PV** function, **Rate** function, **SLN** function, **SYD** function.

Example

This example uses the **NPV** function to return the net present value for a series of cash flows contained in the array `Values()`. `RetRate` represents the fixed internal rate of return.

```
Dim Fmt, Guess, RetRate, NetPVal, Msg
Static Values(5) As Double                    ' Set up array.
Fmt = "###,##0.00"                            ' Define money format.
Guess = .1                                    ' Guess starts at 10 percent.
RetRate = .0625                               ' Set fixed internal rate.
Values(0) = -70000                            ' Business start-up costs.
' Positive cash flows reflecting income for four successive years.
Values(1) = 22000 : Values(2) = 25000
Values(3) = 28000 : Values(4) = 31000
NetPVal = NPV(RetRate, Values())              ' Calculate net present value.
Msg = "The net present value of these cash flows is "
Msg = Msg & Format(NetPVal, Fmt) & "."
MsgBox Msg                                    ' Display net present value.
```

Number Property

Applies To

Err object.

Description

Returns or sets a numeric value specifying an error. **Number** is the **Err** object's default property. Read/write.

Remarks

When returning a user-defined error from an object, set **Err.Number** by adding the number you selected as an error code to the **vbObjectError** constant. For example, you use the following code to return the number 1051 as an error code:

```
Err.Raise Number := vbObjectError + 1051, Source:= "SomeClass"
```

See Also

Description property, **Err** object, **HelpContext** property, **HelpContextID** property ("Extensibility Object Model Language Reference"), **HelpFile** property, **LastDLLError** property, **Source** property.

Example

The first example illustrates a typical use of the **Number** property in an error-handling routine. The second example examines the **Number** property of the **Err** object to determine whether an error returned by an Automation object was defined by the object, or whether it was mapped to an error defined by Visual Basic. Note that the constant **vbObjectError** is a very large negative number that an object adds to its own error code to indicate that the error is defined by the server. Therefore, subtracting it from **Err.Number** strips it out of the result. If the error is object-defined, the base number is left in `MyError`, which is displayed in a message box along with the original source of the error. If **Err.Number** represents a Visual Basic error, then the Visual Basic error number is displayed in the message box.

```
' Typical use of Number property.
Sub test()
   On Error GoTo out

   Dim x, y
   x = 1 / y                           ' Create division by zero error.
   Exit Sub
   out:
   MsgBox Err.Number
   MsgBox Err.Description
   ' Check for division by zero error.
   If Err.Number = 11 Then
      y = y + 1
   End If
   Resume
End Sub

' Using Number property with an error from an
' Automation object.
Dim MyError, Msg
' First, strip off the constant added by the object to indicate one
' of its own errors.
MyError = Err.Number - vbObjectError
' If you subtract the vbObjectError constant, and the number is still
' in the range 0-65,535, it is an object-defined error code.
If MyError > 0 And MyError < 65535 Then
   Msg = "The object you accessed assigned this number to the error: " _
      & MyError & ". The originator of the error was: " _
      & Err.Source & ". Press F1 to see originator's Help topic."
' Otherwise it is a Visual Basic error number.
Else
   Msg = "This error (# " & Err.Number & ") is a Visual Basic error" & _
      " number. Press Help button or F1 for the Visual Basic Help" _
      & " topic for this error."
End If
   MsgBox Msg, , "Object Error", Err.HelpFile, Err.HelpContext
```

Object Data Type

Description

Object variables are stored as 32-bit (4-byte) addresses that refer to objects. Using the **Set** statement, a variable declared as an **Object** can have any object reference assigned to it.

Note Although a variable declared with **Object** type is flexible enough to contain a reference to any object, binding to the object referenced by that variable is always late (run-time binding). To force early binding (compile-time binding), assign the object reference to a variable declared with a specific class name.

See Also

Data type summary, **Def***type* statements, **IsObject** function, **Variant** data type.

Oct Function

Description

Returns a **Variant** (**String**) representing the octal value of a number.

Syntax

Oct(*number*)

The required *number* argument is any valid numeric expression or string expression.

Remarks

If *number* is not already a whole number, it is rounded to the nearest whole number before being evaluated.

If *number* is	Oct returns
Null	**Null**
Empty	Zero (0)
Any other number	Up to 11 octal characters

You can represent octal numbers directly by preceding numbers in the proper range with `&O`. For example, `&O10` is the octal notation for decimal 8.

See Also

Hex function.

Example

This example uses the **Oct** function to return the octal value of a number.

```
Dim MyOct
MyOct = Oct(4)                              ' Returns 4.
MyOct = Oct(8)                              ' Returns 10.
MyOct = Oct(459)                            ' Returns 713.
```

On Error Statement

Description

Enables an error-handling routine and specifies the location of the routine within a procedure; can also be used to disable an error-handling routine.

Syntax

On Error GoTo *line*
On Error Resume Next
On Error GoTo 0

The **On Error** statement syntax can have any of the following forms:

Statement	Description
On Error GoTo *line*	Enables the error-handling routine that starts at *line* specified in the required *line* argument. The *line* argument is any line label or line number. If a run-time error occurs, control branches to *line*, making the error handler active. The specified *line* must be in the same procedure as the **On Error** statement; otherwise, a compile-time error occurs.
On Error Resume Next	Specifies that when a run-time error occurs, control goes to the statement immediately following the statement where the error occurred where execution continues. Use this form rather than **On Error GoTo** when accessing objects.
On Error GoTo 0	Disables any enabled error handler in the current procedure.

Remarks

If you don't use an **On Error** statement, any run-time error that occurs is fatal; that is, an error message is displayed and execution stops.

An "enabled" error handler is one that is turned on by an **On Error** statement; an "active" error handler is an enabled handler that is in the process of handling an error. If an error occurs while an error handler is active (between the occurrence of the error and a **Resume**, **Exit Sub**, **Exit Function**, or **Exit Property** statement), the current procedure's error handler can't handle the error. Control returns to the calling procedure. If the calling procedure has an enabled error handler, it is activated to handle the error. If the calling procedure's error handler is also active, control passes back through previous calling procedures until an enabled, but inactive, error handler is found. If no inactive, enabled error handler is found, the error is fatal at the point at which it actually occurred. Each time the error handler passes control back to a calling procedure, that procedure becomes the current procedure. Once an error is handled by an error handler in any procedure, execution resumes in the current procedure at the point designated by the **Resume** statement.

Note An error-handling routine is not a **Sub** procedure or **Function** procedure. It is a section of code marked by a line label or line number.

Error-handling routines rely on the value in the **Number** property of the **Err** object to determine the cause of the error. The error-handling routine should test or save relevant property values in the **Err** object before any other error can occur or before a procedure that might cause an error is called. The property values in the **Err** object reflect only the most recent error. The error message associated with **Err.Number** is contained in **Err.Description**.

On Error Resume Next causes execution to continue with the statement immediately following the statement that caused the run-time error, or with the statement immediately following the most recent call out of the procedure containing the **On Error Resume Next** statement. This statement allows execution to continue despite a run-time error. You can place the error-handling routine where the error would occur, rather than transferring control to another location within the procedure. An **On Error Resume Next** statement becomes inactive when another procedure is called, so you should execute an **On Error Resume Next** statement in each called routine if you want inline error handling within that routine.

Note The **On Error Resume Next** construct may be preferable to **On Error GoTo** when handling errors generated during access to other objects. Checking **Err** after each interaction with an object removes ambiguity about which object was accessed by the code. You can be sure which object placed the error code in **Err.Number**, as well as which object originally generated the error (the object specified in **Err.Source**).

On Error GoTo 0 disables error handling in the current procedure. It doesn't specify line 0 as the start of the error-handling code, even if the procedure contains a line numbered 0. Without an **On Error GoTo 0** statement, an error handler is automatically disabled when a procedure is exited.

To prevent error-handling code from running when no error has occurred, place an **Exit Sub**, **Exit Function**, or **Exit Property** statement immediately before the error-handling routine, as in the following fragment:

```
Sub InitializeMatrix(Var1, Var2, Var3, Var4)
   On Error GoTo ErrorHandler
   . . .
   Exit Sub
ErrorHandler:
   . . .
   Resume Next
End Sub
```

Here, the error-handling code follows the **Exit Sub** statement and precedes the **End Sub** statement to separate it from the procedure flow. Error-handling code can be placed anywhere in a procedure.

Untrapped errors in objects are returned to the controlling application when the object is running as an executable file. Within the development environment, untrapped errors are only returned to the controlling application if the proper options are set. See your host application's documentation for a description of which options should be set during debugging, how to set them, and whether the host can create classes.

If you create an object that accesses other objects, you should try to handle errors passed back from them unhandled. If you cannot handle such errors, map the error code in **Err.Number** to one of your own errors, and then pass them back to the caller of your object. You should specify your error by adding your error code to the **vbObjectError** constant. For example, if your error code is 1052, assign it as follows:

```
Err.Number = vbObjectError + 1052
```

Note System errors during calls to dynamic-link libraries (DLL) do not raise exceptions and cannot be trapped with Visual Basic error trapping. When calling DLL functions, you should check each return value for success or failure (according to the API specifications), and in the event of a failure, check the value in the **Err** object's **LastDLLError** property.

See Also

End statement, **Err** object, **Exit** statement, **LastDLLError** property, **Resume** statement.

Example

This example first uses the **On Error GoTo** statement to specify the location of an error-handling routine within a procedure. In the example, an attempt to delete an open file generates error number 55. The error is handled in the error-handling routine, and control is then returned to the statement that caused the error. The **On Error GoTo 0** statement turns off error trapping. Then the **On Error Resume Next** statement is used to defer error trapping so that the context for the error generated by the next statement can be known for certain. Note that **Err.Clear** is used to clear the **Err** object's properties after the error is handled.

```
Sub OnErrorStatementDemo()
   On Error GoTo ErrorHandler                ' Enable error-handling routine.
   Open "TESTFILE" For Output As #1          ' Open file for output.
   Kill "TESTFILE"                           ' Attempt to delete open
                                             ' file.
   On Error Goto 0                           ' Turn off error trapping.
   On Error Resume Next                      ' Defer error trapping.
   ObjectRef = GetObject("MyWord.Basic")     ' Try to start nonexistent
                                             ' object, then test for
'Check for likely Automation errors.
   If Err.Number = 440 Or Err.Number = 432 Then
      ' Tell user what happened. Then clear the Err object.
      Msg = "There was an error attempting to open the Automation object!"
      MsgBox Msg, , "Deferred Error Test"
      Err.Clear                              ' Clear Err object fields
   End If
Exit Sub                                     ' Exit to avoid handler.
ErrorHandler:                                ' Error-handling routine.
   Select Case Err.Number                    ' Evaluate error number.
      Case 55                                ' "File already open" error.
         Close #1                            ' Close open file.
      Case Else
         ' Handle other situations here...
   End Select
   Resume                                    ' Resume execution at same line
                                             ' that caused the error.
End Sub
```

On...GoSub, On...GoTo Statements

Description

Branch to one of several specified lines, depending on the value of an expression.

Syntax

On *expression* **GoSub** *destinationlist*
On *expression* **GoTo** *destinationlist*

The **On...GoSub** and **On...GoTo** statement syntax has these parts:

Part	Description
expression	Required. Any numeric expression that evaluates to a whole number between 0 and 255, inclusive. If *expression* is any number other than a whole number, it is rounded before it is evaluated.
destinationlist	Required. List of line numbers or line labels separated by commas.

Remarks

The value of *expression* determines which line is branched to in *destinationlist*. If the value of *expression* is less than 1 or greater than the number of items in the list, one of the following results occurs:

If *expression* is	Then
Equal to 0	Control drops to the statement following **On...GoSub** or **On...GoTo**.
Greater than number of items in list	Control drops to the statement following **On...GoSub** or **On...GoTo**.
Negative	An error occurs.
Greater than 255	An error occurs.

You can mix line numbers and line labels in the same list. You can use as many line labels and line numbers as you like with **On...GoSub** and **On...GoTo**. However, if you use more labels or numbers than fit on a single line, you must use the line-continuation character to continue the logical line onto the next physical line.

Tip **Select Case** provides a more structured and flexible way to perform multiple branching.

See Also

GoSub...Return statement, **GoTo** statement, **Select Case** statement.

Example

This example uses the **On...GoSub** and **On...GoTo** statements to branch to subroutines and line labels, respectively.

```
Sub OnGosubGotoDemo()
Dim Number, MyString
   Number = 2                        ' Initialize variable.
   ' Branch to Sub2.
   On Number GoSub Sub1, Sub2        ' Execution resumes here after
                                     ' On...GoSub.
   On Number GoTo Line1, Line2       ' Branch to Line2.
   ' Execution does not resume here after On...GoTo.
   Exit Sub
```

```
Sub1:
   MyString = "In Sub1" : Return
Sub2:
   MyString = "In Sub2" : Return
Line1:
   MyString = "In Line1"
Line2:
   MyString = "In Line2"
End Sub
```

Open Statement

Description

Enables input/output (I/O) to a file.

Syntax

Open *pathname* **For** *mode* [**Access** *access*] [*lock*] **As** [**#**]*filenumber* [**Len**=*reclength*]

The **Open** statement syntax has these parts:

Part	Description
pathname	Required. String expression that specifies a file name—may include directory or folder, and drive.
mode	Required. Keyword specifying the file mode: **Append**, **Binary**, **Input**, **Output**, or **Random**. If unspecified, the file is opened for **Random** access.
access	Optional. Keyword specifying the operations permitted on the open file: **Read**, **Write**, or **Read Write**.
lock	Optional. Keyword specifying the operations permitted on the open file by other processes: **Shared**, **Lock Read**, **Lock Write**, and **Lock Read Write**.
filenumber	Required. A valid file number in the range 1 to 511, inclusive. Use the **FreeFile** function to obtain the next available file number.
reclength	Optional. Number less than or equal to 32,767 (bytes). For files opened for random access, this value is the record length. For sequential files, this value is the number of characters buffered.

Remarks

You must open a file before any I/O operation can be performed on it. **Open** allocates a buffer for I/O to the file and determines the mode of access to use with the buffer.

If the file specified by *pathname* doesn't exist, it is created when a file is opened for **Append**, **Binary**, **Output**, or **Random** modes.

If the file is already opened by another process and the specified type of access is not allowed, the **Open** operation fails and an error occurs.

The **Len** clause is ignored if *mode* is **Binary**.

Important In **Binary**, **Input**, and **Random** modes, you can open a file using a different file number without first closing the file. In **Append** and **Output** modes, you must close a file before opening it with a different file number.

See Also

Close statement, **FreeFile** function.

Example

This example illustrates various uses of the **Open** statement to enable input and output to a file.

The following code opens the file TESTFILE in sequential-input mode.

```
Open "TESTFILE" For Input As #1
' Close before reopening in another mode.
Close #1
```

This example opens the file in Binary mode for writing operations only.

```
Open "TESTFILE" For Binary Access Write As #1
' Close before reopening in another mode.
Close #1
```

The following example opens the file in Random mode. The file contains records of the user-defined type Record.

```
Type Record                             ' Define user-defined type.
   ID As Integer
   Name As String * 20
End Type

Dim MyRecord As Record                  ' Declare variable.
Open "TESTFILE" For Random As #1 Len = Len(MyRecord)
' Close before reopening in another mode.
Close #1
```

This code example opens the file for sequential output; any process can read or write to file.

```
Open "TESTFILE" For Output Shared As #1
' Close before reopening in another mode.
Close #1
```

This code example opens the file in Binary mode for reading; other processes can't read file.

```
Open "TESTFILE" For Binary Access Read Lock Read As #1
```

Operator Precedence

Description

When several operations occur in an expression, each part is evaluated and resolved in a predetermined order called operator precedence.

When expressions contain operators from more than one category, arithmetic operators are evaluated first, comparison operators are evaluated next, and logical operators are evaluated last. Comparison operators all have equal precedence; that is, they are evaluated in the left-to-right order in which they appear. Arithmetic and logical operators are evaluated in the following order of precedence:

Arithmetic	Comparison	Logical
Exponentiation (^)	Equality (=)	**Not**
Negation (–)	Inequality (<>)	**And**
Multiplication and division (*, /)	Less than (<)	**Or**
Integer division (\)	Greater than (>)	**Xor**
Modulus arithmetic (**Mod**)	Less than or equal to (<=)	**Eqv**
Addition and subtraction (+, –)	Greater than or equal to (>=)	**Imp**
String concatenation (**&**)	**Like**	
	Is	

When multiplication and division occur together in an expression, each operation is evaluated as it occurs from left to right. When addition and subtraction occur together in an expression, each operation is evaluated in order of appearance from left to right. Parentheses can be used to override the order of precedence and force some parts of an expression to be evaluated before others. Operations within parentheses are always performed before those outside. Within parentheses, however, operator precedence is maintained.

The string concatenation operator (**&**) is not an arithmetic operator, but in precedence, it does follow all arithmetic operators and precede all comparison operators.

The **Like** operator is equal in precedence to all comparison operators, but is actually a pattern-matching operator.

The **Is** operator is an object reference comparison operator. It does not compare objects or their values; it checks only to determine if two object references refer to the same object.

See Also

Is operator, **Like** operator.

Option Base Statement

Description

Used at module level to declare the default lower bound for array subscripts.

Syntax

Option Base {**0** | **1**}

Remarks

Because the default base is **0**, the **Option Base** statement is never required. If used, the statement must appear in a module before any procedures. **Option Base** can appear only once in a module and must precede array declarations that include dimensions.

Note The **To** clause in the **Dim**, **Private**, **Public**, **ReDim**, and **Static** statements provides a more flexible way to control the range of an array's subscripts. However, if you don't explicitly set the lower bound with a **To** clause, you can use **Option Base** to change the default lower bound to 1. The base of an array created with the **Array** function or the **ParamArray** keyword is zero; **Option Base** does not affect **Array** or **ParamArray**.

The **Option Base** statement only affects the lower bound of arrays in the module where the statement is located.

See Also

Dim statement, **LBound** function, **Option Compare** statement, **Option Explicit** statement, **Option Private** statement, **Private** statement, **Public** statement, **ReDim** statement, **Static** statement.

Example

This example uses the **Option Base** statement to override the default base array subscript value of 0. The **LBound** function returns the smallest available subscript for the indicated dimension of an array. The **Option Base** statement is used at the module level only.

```
Option base 1                       ' Set default array subscripts to 1.

Dim Lower
Dim MyArray(20), TwoDArray(3, 4)    ' Declare array variables.
Dim ZeroArray(0 To 5)               ' Override default base subscript.
' Use LBound function to test lower bounds of arrays.
Lower = LBound(MyArray)             ' Returns 1.
Lower = LBound(TwoDArray, 2)        ' Returns 1.
Lower = LBound(ZeroArray)           ' Returns 0.
```

Option Compare Statement

Description

Used at module level to declare the default comparison method to use when string data is compared.

Syntax

Option Compare {**Binary** | **Text** | **Database**}

Remarks

If used, the **Option Compare** statement must appear in a module before any procedures.

The **Option Compare** statement specifies the string comparison method (**Binary**, **Text**, or **Database**) for a module. If a module doesn't include an **Option Compare** statement, the default text comparison method is **Binary**.

Option Compare Binary results in string comparisons based on a sort order derived from the internal binary representations of the characters. In Microsoft Windows, sort order is determined by the code page. A typical binary sort order is shown in the following example:

```
A < B < E < Z < a < b < e < z < À < Ê < Ø < à < ê < ø
```

Option Compare Text results in string comparisons based on a case-insensitive text sort order determined by your system's locale. When the same characters are sorted using **Option Compare Text**, the following text sort order is produced:

```
(A=a) < ( À=à) < (B=b) < (E=e) < (Ê=ê) < (Z=z) < (Ø=ø)
```

Option Compare Database can only be used within Microsoft Access. This results in string comparisons based on the sort order determined by the locale ID of the database where the string comparisons occur.

See Also

Comparison operators, **InStr** function, **Option Base** statement, **Option Explicit** statement, **Option Private** statement, **StrComp** function.

Specifics (Macintosh)

On the Macintosh, sort order is determined by the character set.

Specifics (Microsoft Access)

In Microsoft Access, all modules by default contain the **Option Compare Database** statement in the Declarations section. This statement sets the string comparison method for the module to the one specified for the entire database.

You can change the string comparison method for all new databases by clicking **Options** on the **Tools** menu and changing the value in the **New Database Sort Order** box on the **General** tab of the **Options** dialog box. By default this value is set to General, which specifies a case-insensitive sort order based on the English alphabet.

Changing the **New Database Sort Order** option doesn't affect the string comparison method for the current database. It only affects databases that are created after the option has been set.

To specify a string comparison method for an individual module that is different from the one specified for the database, change **Option Compare Database** to **Option Compare Binary** or **Option Compare Text**. The **Option Compare Binary** statement compares strings by evaluating the ASCII values corresponding to the characters they contain, so the statement is case-sensitive. **Option Compare Text** is case-insensitive.

Note If you are using the **Bookmark** property of a **Recordset** object, you must include an **Option Compare Binary** statement in the Declarations section of the module. The setting and return value for the **Bookmark** property is a **Variant** array of **Byte** data. If you use a case-insensitive string comparison method, the **Bookmark** property may point you to the wrong record.

Example

This example uses the **Option Compare** statement to set the default string comparison method. The **Option Compare** statement is used at the module level only.

```
' Set the string comparison method to Binary.
Option compare Binary                ' That is, "AAA" is less than "aaa"
' Set the string comparison method to Text.
Option compare Text                  ' That is, "AAA" is equal to "aaa".
```

Option Explicit Statement

Description

Used at module level to force explicit declaration of all variables in that module.

Syntax

Option Explicit

Remarks

If used, the **Option Explicit** statement must appear in a module before any procedures.

When **Option Explicit** appears in a module, you must explicitly declare all variables using the **Dim**, **Private**, **Public**, **ReDim**, or **Static** statements. If you attempt to use an undeclared variable name, an error occurs at compile time.

If you don't use the **Option Explicit** statement, all undeclared variables are of **Variant** type unless the default type is otherwise specified with a **Def*type*** statement.

Note Use **Option Explicit** to avoid incorrectly typing the name of an existing variable or to avoid confusion in code where the scope of the variable is not clear.

See Also

Const statement, **Def*type*** statements, **Dim** statement, **Function** statement, **Option Base** statement, **Option Compare** statement, **Option Private** statement, **Private** statement, **Public** statement, **ReDim** statement, **Static** statement, **Sub** statement.

Specifics (Microsoft Access)

In Microsoft Access, you can ensure that all new modules will automatically include the **Option Explicit** statement. Click **Options** on the **Tool** menu, click the **Module** tab, and select the **Require Variable Declaration** option.

Once you select this option, it will automatically be set for all other databases which you create or open with Microsoft Access.

Note When you select this option, only new modules will have the **Option Explicit** setting. You must enter the **Option Explicit** statement into the Declarations section of any existing modules. Or, when the module is open, click **Options** on the **Tools** menu, click the **Module** tab, and select the **Require Variable Declaration** option.

Example

This example uses the **Option Explicit** statement to force you to explicitly declare all variables. Attempting to use an undeclared variable causes an error at compile time. The **Option Explicit** statement is used at the module level only.

```
Option explicit             ' Force explicit variable declaration.
Dim MyVar                ' Declare variable.
MyInt = 10                  ' Undeclared variable generates error.
MyVar = 10                  ' Declared variable does not generate error.
```

Option Private Statement

Description

When used in host applications that allow references across multiple projects, **Option Private Module** prevents a module's contents from being referenced outside its project. In host applications that don't permit such references, for example, standalone versions of Visual Basic, **Option Private** has no effect.

Syntax

Option Private Module

Remarks

If used, the **Option Private** statement must appear at module level, before any procedures.

When a module contains **Option Private Module**, the public parts, for example, variables, objects, and user-defined types declared at module level, are still available within the project containing the module, but they are not available to other applications or projects.

Note **Option Private** is only useful for host applications that support simultaneous loading of multiple projects and permit references between the loaded projects. For example, Microsoft Excel permits loading of multiple projects and **Option Private Module** can be used to restrict cross-project visibility. Although Visual Basic permits loading of multiple projects, references between projects are never permitted in Visual Basic.

See Also

Option Base statement, **Option Compare** statement, **Option Explicit** statement, **Private** statement, **Public** statement.

Specifics (Microsoft Access)

When you include the **Option Private** statement in a standard module in Microsoft Access, any public variables or procedures in the module are still available to all other procedures in the current database. However, they are not available to procedures in other databases.

Since class modules are private by default, including the **Option Private** statement in a class module generates an error.

Example

This example demonstrates the **Option Private** statement, which is used at the module level to indicate that the entire module is private. With **Option Private Module**, module-level symbols not declared **Private** are still available to other modules in the project, but not to other projects or applications.

```
Option private Module                   ' Indicate that module is private.
```

Or Operator

Description

Used to perform a logical disjunction on two expressions.

Syntax

result = *expression1* **Or** *expression2*

The **Or** operator syntax has these parts:

Part	Description
result	Required; any numeric variable.
expression1	Required; any expression.
expression2	Required; any expression.

Remarks

If either or both expressions evaluate to **True**, *result* is **True**. The following table illustrates how *result* is determined:

If *expression1* is	And *expression2* is	Then *result* is
True	**True**	**True**
True	**False**	**True**
True	**Null**	**True**
False	**True**	**True**
False	**False**	**False**

(continued)

False	**Null**	**Null**
Null	**True**	**True**
Null	**False**	**Null**
Null	**Null**	**Null**

The **Or** operator also performs a bitwise comparison of identically positioned bits in two numeric expressions and sets the corresponding bit in *result* according to the following table:

If bit in *expression1* is	And bit in *expression2* is	Then *result* is
0	0	0
0	1	1
1	0	1
1	1	1

See Also

Operator precedence.

Example

This example uses the **Or** operator to perform logical disjunction on two expressions.

```
Dim A, B, C, D, MyCheck
A = 10: B = 8: C = 6: D = Null         ' Initialize variables.
MyCheck = A > B Or B > C               ' Returns True.
MyCheck = B > A Or B > C               ' Returns True.
MyCheck = A > B Or B > D               ' Returns True.
MyCheck = B > D Or B > A               ' Returns Null.
MyCheck = A Or B                       ' Returns 10 (bitwise comparison).
```

Partition Function

Description

Returns a **Variant** (**String**) indicating where a number occurs within a calculated series of ranges.

Syntax

Partition(*number*, *start*, *stop*, *interval*)

The **Partition** function syntax has these named arguments.

Part	Description
number	Required. Whole number that you want to evaluate against the ranges.
start	Required. Whole number that is the start of the overall range of numbers. The number can't be less than 0.
stop	Required. Whole number that is the end of the overall range of numbers. The number can't be equal to or less than ***start***.
interval	Required. Whole number that is the interval spanned by each range in the series from ***start*** to ***stop***. The number can't be less than 1.

Remarks

The **Partition** function identifies the particular range in which ***number*** falls and returns a **Variant** (**String**) describing that range. The **Partition** function is most useful in queries. You can create a select query that shows how many orders fall within various ranges, for example, order values from 1 to 1000, 1001 to 2000, and so on.

The following table shows how the ranges are determined using three sets of ***start***, ***stop***, and ***interval*** parts. The First Range and Last Range columns show what **Partition** returns. The ranges are represented by *lowervalue*:*uppervalue*, where the low end (*lowervalue*) of the range is separated from the high end (*uppervalue*) of the range with a colon (**:**).

start	*stop*	*interval*	Before First	First Range	Last Range	After Last
0	99	5	" :-1"	" 0: 4"	" 95: 99"	" 100: "
20	199	10	" : 19"	" 20: 29"	" 190: 199"	" 200: "
100	1010	20	" : 99"	" 100: 119"	" 1000: 1010"	" 1011: "

In the table shown above, the third line shows the result when ***start*** and ***stop*** define a set of numbers that can't be evenly divided by ***interval***. The last range extends to ***stop*** (11 numbers) even though ***interval*** is 20.

If necessary, **Partition** returns a range with enough leading spaces so that there are the same number of characters to the left and right of the colon as there are characters in ***stop***, plus one. This ensures that if you use **Partition** with other numbers, the resulting text will be handled properly during any subsequent sort operation.

If ***interval*** is 1, the range is ***number:number***, regardless of the ***start*** and ***stop*** arguments. For example, if ***interval*** is 1, ***number*** is 100 and ***stop*** is 1000, **Partition** returns " 100: 100".

If any of the parts is **Null**, **Partition** returns a **Null**.

Example

This example assumes you have an Orders table that contains a Freight field. It creates a select procedure that counts the number of orders for which freight cost falls into each of several ranges. The **Partition** function is used first to establish these ranges, then the SQL Count function counts the number of orders in each range. In this example, the arguments to the **Partition** function are *start* = 0, *stop* = 500, *interval* = 50. The first range would therefore be 0:49, and so on up to 500.

```
SELECT DISTINCTROW Partition([freight],0, 500, 50) AS Range,
Count(Orders.Freight) AS Count
FROM Orders
GROUP BY Partition([freight],0,500,50);
```

Example (Microsoft Access)

You can use the **Partition** function in the query design grid as well as in the SQL view of the Query window. In the query design grid, you can use the **Partition** function in a calculated field or to specify criteria for a select query.

The following example shows how you can use the **Partition** function to create a calculated field that lists how many records fall into each specified range. Suppose you have an Orders table that contains a Freight field. In the Query window, create a new Totals query by adding the Orders table and clicking on the **Totals** button in the **Query** command bar. Drag the Freight field to the first **Field** cell on the query design grid, and set the value of the **Total** cell to Count. In another field cell, enter the following expression.

```
Range: Partition([Freight], 0, 1000, 50)
<BREAK>
```

Set the **Total** cell below this field to Group By, and run the query. The **Partition** function returns eleven ranges (0:99, 100:199, 200:299, and so on). The query shows the number of orders with freight charges falling into each range.

The next example shows how you can use the **Partition** function in the SQL view of the Query window. It creates a crosstab query that evaluates a Freight field in an Orders table. It calculates the number of orders for each customer for which freight cost falls within one of several ranges. The ranges are defined by the arguments to the **Partition** function: *start* = 0, *stop* = 1000, *interval* = 50.

Enter the following expression in SQL view. When you run this query, each range will appear as a column heading.

```
TRANSFORM Count(Orders.[OrderID]) AS [CountOfOrderID]
SELECT Orders.[CustomerID]
FROM Orders
GROUP BY Orders.[CustomerID]
PIVOT Partition(Int([Freight]), 0, 1000, 50);
```

Pmt Function

Description

Returns a **Double** specifying the payment for an annuity based on periodic, fixed payments and a fixed interest rate.

Syntax

Pmt(*rate*, *nper*, *pv*[, *fv*[, *type*]])

The **Pmt** function has these named arguments.

Part	Description
rate	Required. **Double** specifying interest rate per period. For example, if you get a car loan at an annual percentage rate (APR) of 10 percent and make monthly payments, the rate per period is 0.1/12, or 0.0083.
nper	Required. **Integer** specifying total number of payment periods in the annuity. For example, if you make monthly payments on a four-year car loan, your loan has a total of 4 * 12 (or 48) payment periods.
pv	Required. **Double** specifying present value (or lump sum) that a series of payments to be paid in the future is worth now. For example, when you borrow money to buy a car, the loan amount is the present value to the lender of the monthly car payments you will make.
fv	Optional. **Variant** specifying future value or cash balance you want after you've made the final payment. For example, the future value of a loan is $0 because that's its value after the final payment. However, if you want to save $50,000 over 18 years for your child's education, then $50,000 is the future value. If omitted, 0 is assumed.
type	Optional. **Variant** specifying when payments are due. Use 0 if payments are due at the end of the payment period, or use 1 if payments are due at the beginning of the period. If omitted, 0 is assumed.

Remarks

An annuity is a series of fixed cash payments made over a period of time. An annuity can be a loan (such as a home mortgage) or an investment (such as a monthly savings plan).

The ***rate*** and ***nper*** arguments must be calculated using payment periods expressed in the same units. For example, if ***rate*** is calculated using months, ***nper*** must also be calculated using months.

For all arguments, cash paid out (such as deposits to savings) is represented by negative numbers; cash received (such as dividend checks) is represented by positive numbers.

See Also

DDB function, **FV** function, **IPmt** function, **IRR** function, **MIRR** function, **NPer** function, **NPV** function, **PPmt** function, **PV** function, **Rate** function, **SLN** function, **SYD** function.

Example

This example uses the **Pmt** function to return the monthly payment for a loan over a fixed period. Given are the interest percentage rate per period (`APR / 12`), the total number of payments (`TotPmts`), the present value or principal of the loan (`PVal`), the future value of the loan (`FVal`), and a number that indicates whether the payment is due at the beginning or end of the payment period (`PayType`).

```
Dim Fmt, FVal, PVal, APR, TotPmts, PayType, Payment
Const ENDPERIOD = 0, BEGINPERIOD = 1          ' When payments are made.
Fmt = "###,###,##0.00"                        ' Define money format.
FVal = 0                                      ' Usually 0 for a loan.
PVal = InputBox("How much do you want to borrow?")
APR = InputBox("What is the annual percentage rate of your loan?")
If APR > 1 Then APR = APR / 100               ' Ensure proper form.
TotPmts = InputBox("How many monthly payments will you make?")
PayType = MsgBox("Do you make payments at the end of month?", vbYesNo)
If PayType = vbNo Then PayType = BEGINPERIOD Else PayType = ENDPERIOD
Payment = Pmt(APR / 12, TotPmts, -PVal, FVal, PayType)
MsgBox "Your payment will be " & Format(Payment, Fmt) & " per month."
```

PPmt Function

Description

Returns a **Double** specifying the principal payment for a given period of an annuity based on periodic, fixed payments and a fixed interest rate.

Syntax

PPmt(*rate*, *per*, *nper*, *pv*[, *fv*[, *type*]])

The **PPmt** function has these named arguments.

Part	Description
rate	Required. **Double** specifying interest rate per period. For example, if you get a car loan at an annual percentage rate (APR) of 10 percent and make monthly payments, the rate per period is 0.1/12, or 0.0083.
per	Required. **Integer** specifying payment period in the range 1 through ***nper***.
nper	Required. **Integer** specifying total number of payment periods in the annuity. For example, if you make monthly payments on a four-year car loan, your loan has a total of 4 * 12 (or 48) payment periods.
pv	Required. **Double** specifying present value, or value today, of a series of future payments or receipts. For example, when you borrow money to buy a car, the loan amount is the present value to the lender of the monthly car payments you will make.

(continued)

Part	Description
fv	Optional. **Variant** specifying future value or cash balance you want after you've made the final payment. For example, the future value of a loan is $0 because that's its value after the final payment. However, if you want to save $50,000 over 18 years for your child's education, then $50,000 is the future value. If omitted, 0 is assumed.
type	Optional. **Variant** specifying when payments are due. Use 0 if payments are due at the end of the payment period, or use 1 if payments are due at the beginning of the period. If omitted, 0 is assumed.

Remarks

An annuity is a series of fixed cash payments made over a period of time. An annuity can be a loan (such as a home mortgage) or an investment (such as a monthly savings plan).

The ***rate*** and ***nper*** arguments must be calculated using payment periods expressed in the same units. For example, if ***rate*** is calculated using months, ***nper*** must also be calculated using months.

For all arguments, cash paid out (such as deposits to savings) is represented by negative numbers; cash received (such as dividend checks) is represented by positive numbers.

See Also

DDB function, **FV** function, **IPmt** function, **IRR** function, **MIRR** function, **NPer** function, **NPV** function, **Pmt** function, **PV** function, **Rate** function, **SLN** function, **SYD** function.

Example

This example uses the **PPmt** function to calculate how much of a payment for a specific period is principal when all the payments are of equal value. Given are the interest percentage rate per period (`APR / 12`), the payment period for which the principal portion is desired (`Period`), the total number of payments (`TotPmts`), the present value or principal of the loan (`PVal`), the future value of the loan (`FVal`), and a number that indicates whether the payment is due at the beginning or end of the payment period (`PayType`).

```
Dim NL, TB, Fmt, FVal, PVal, APR, TotPmts, PayType, Payment, Msg, _
   MakeChart, Period, P, I
Const ENDPERIOD = 0, BEGINPERIOD = 1         ' When payments are made.
NL = Chr(13) & Chr(10)                       ' Define newline.
TB = Chr(9)                                  ' Define tab.
Fmt = "###,###,##0.00"                       ' Define money format.
FVal = 0                                     ' Usually 0 for a loan.
PVal = InputBox("How much do you want to borrow?")
APR = InputBox("What is the annual percentage rate of your loan?")
If APR > 1 Then APR = APR / 100              ' Ensure proper form.
TotPmts = InputBox("How many monthly payments do you have to make?")
PayType = MsgBox("Do you make payments at the end of month?", vbYesNo)
```

```
If PayType = vbNo Then PayType = BEGINPERIOD Else PayType = ENDPERIOD
Payment = Abs(-Pmt(APR / 12, TotPmts, PVal, FVal, PayType))
Msg = "Your monthly payment is " & Format(Payment, Fmt) & ". "
Msg = Msg & "Would you like a breakdown of your principal and "
Msg = Msg & "interest per period?"
MakeChart = MsgBox(Msg, vbYesNo)          ' See if chart is desired.
If MakeChart <> vbNo Then
   If TotPmts > 12 Then MsgBox "Only first year will be shown."
   Msg = "Month  Payment  Principal  Interest" & NL
   For Period = 1 To TotPmts
      If Period > 12 Then Exit For        ' Show only first 12.
      P = PPmt(APR / 12, Period, TotPmts, -PVal, FVal, PayType)
      P = (Int((P + .005) * 100) / 100)     ' Round principal.
      I = Payment - P
      I = (Int((I + .005) * 100) / 100)     ' Round interest.
      Msg = Msg & Period & TB & Format(Payment, Fmt)
      Msg = Msg & TB & Format(P, Fmt) & TB & Format(I, Fmt) & NL
   Next Period
   MsgBox Msg                             ' Display amortization table.
End If
```

Print # Statement

Description

Writes display-formatted data to a sequential file.

Syntax

Print #*filenumber***,** [*outputlist*]

The **Print #** statement syntax has these parts.

Part	Description
filenumber	Required. Any valid file number.
outputlist	Optional. Expression or list of expressions to print.

Settings

The *outputlist* argument settings are

[{**Spc(***n***)** | **Tab**[**(***n***)**]}] [*expression*] [*charpos*]

Setting	Description
Spc(*n***)**	Used to insert space characters in the output, where *n* is the number of space characters to insert.
Tab(*n***)**	Used to position the insertion point to an absolute column number, where *n* is the column number. Use **Tab** with no argument to position the insertion point at the beginning of the next print zone.

(continued)

Setting	Description
expression	Numeric expressions or string expressions to print.
charpos	Specifies the insertion point for the next character. Use a semicolon to position the insertion point immediately after the last character displayed. Use **Tab**(*n*) to position the insertion point to an absolute column number. Use **Tab** with no argument to position the insertion point at the beginning of the next print zone. If *charpos* is omitted, the next character is printed on the next line.

Remarks

Data written with **Print #** is usually read from a file with **Line Input #** or **Input**.

If you omit *outputlist* and include only a list separator after *filenumber*, a blank line is printed to the file. Multiple expressions can be separated with either a space or a semicolon. A space has the same effect as a semicolon.

For **Boolean** data, either `True` or `False` is printed. The **True** and **False** keywords are not translated, regardless of the locale.

Date data is written to the file using the standard short date format recognized by your system. When either the date or the time component is missing or zero, only the part provided gets written to the file.

Nothing is written to the file if *outputlist* data is **Empty**. However, if *outputlist* data is **Null**, **Null** is written to the file.

For **Error** data, the output appears as `Error errorcode`. The **Error** keyword is not translated regardless of the locale.

All data written to the file using **Print #** is internationally aware; that is, the data is properly formatted using the appropriate decimal separator.

Because **Print #** writes an image of the data to the file, you must delimit the data so it prints correctly. If you use **Tab** with no arguments to move the print position to the next print zone, **Print #** also writes the spaces between print fields to the file.

Note If, at some future time, you want to read the data from a file using the **Input #** statement, use the **Write #** statement instead of the **Print #** statement to write the data to the file. Using **Write #** ensures the integrity of each separate data field by properly delimiting it, so it can be read back in using **Input #**. Using **Write #** also ensures it can be correctly read in any locale.

See Also

Open statement, **Print** method, **Spc** function, **Tab** function, **Write #** statement.

Example

This example uses the **Print #** statement to write data to a file.

```
Open "TESTFILE" For Output As #1                ' Open file for output.
Print #1, "This is a test"                      ' Print text to file.
Print #1,                                       ' Print blank line to file.
Print #1, "Zone 1"; Tab ; "Zone 2"              ' Print in two print zones.
Print #1, "Hello" ; " " ; "World"               ' Separate strings with space.
Print #1, Spc(5) ; "5 leading spaces "          ' Print five leading spaces.
Print #1, Tab(10) ; "Hello"                     ' Print word at column 10.

' Assign Boolean, Date, Null and Error values.
Dim MyBool, MyDate, MyNull, MyError
MyBool = False : MyDate = #February 12, 1969# : MyNull = Null
MyError = CVErr(32767)
' True, False, Null, and Error are translated using locale settings of
' your system. Date literals are written using standard short date
' format.
Print #1, MyBool ; " is a Boolean value"
Print #1, MyDate ; " is a date"
Print #1, MyNull ; " is a null value"
Print #1, MyError ; " is an error value"
Close #1                                        ' Close file.
```

Print Method

Applies To

Debug object.

Description

Prints text in the **Immediate** pane of the **Debug** window.

Syntax

object.**Print** [*outputlist*]

The **Print** method syntax has the following object qualifier and part.

Part	Description
object	Optional. An object expression that evaluates to an object in the Applies To list.
outputlist	Optional. Expression or list of expressions to print. If omitted, a blank line is printed.

The *outputlist* argument has the following syntax and parts.

{**Spc**(*n*) | **Tab**(*n*)} *expression charpos*

Part	Description
Spc(*n*)	Optional. Used to insert space characters in the output, where *n* is the number of space characters to insert.
Tab(*n*)	Optional. Used to position the insertion point at an absolute column number where *n* is the column number. Use **Tab** with no argument to position the insertion point at the beginning of the next print zone.
expression	Optional. Numeric expression or string expression to print.
charpos	Optional. Specifies the insertion point for the next character. Use a semicolon (;) to position the insertion point immediately following the last character displayed. Use **Tab**(*n*) to position the insertion point at an absolute column number. Use **Tab** with no argument to position the insertion point at the beginning of the next print zone. If *charpos* is omitted, the next character is printed on the next line.

Remarks

Multiple expressions can be separated with either a space or a semicolon.

All data printed to the **Immediate** window is properly formatted using the decimal separator for the locale settings specified for your system. The keywords are output in the appropriate language for the host application.

For **Boolean** data, either `True` or `False` is printed. The **True** and **False** keywords are translated according to the locale setting for the host application.

Date data is written using the standard short date format recognized by your system. When either the date or the time component is missing or zero, only the data provided is written.

Nothing is written if *outputlist* data is **Empty**. However, if *outputlist* data is **Null**, `Null` is output. The **Null** keyword is appropriately translated when it is output.

For error data, the output is written as `Error errorcode`. The **Error** keyword is appropriately translated when it is output.

The *object* is required if the method is used outside a module having a default display space. For example an error occurs if the method is called in a standard module without specifying an *object*, but if called in a form module, *outputlist* is displayed on the form.

Note Because the **Print** method typically prints with proportionally-spaced characters, there is no correlation between the number of characters printed and the number of fixed-width columns those characters occupy. For example, a wide letter, such as a "W", occupies more than one fixed-width column, and a narrow letter, such as an "i", occupies less. To allow for cases where wider than average characters are used, your tabular columns must be positioned far enough apart. Alternatively, you can print using a fixed-pitch font (such as Courier) to ensure that each character uses only one column.

See Also

Print # statement, **Spc** function, **Tab** function.

Specifics (Microsoft Access)

The Visual Basic **Print** method applies only to the **Debug** object in Microsoft Access, never to a **Form** object. The **Debug** object is required when you use the **Print** method in Microsoft Access.

Don't confuse the Visual Basic **Print** method with the Microsoft Access **Print** method, which applies only to a **Report** object.

Example

Using the **Print** method, this example displays the value of the variable `MyVar` in the **Immediate** pane of the **Debug** window. Note that the **Print** method only applies to objects that can display text.

```
Dim MyVar
MyVar = "Come see me in the Immediate pane."
Debug.Print MyVar
```

PrintForm Method

Applies To

UserForm object.

Description

Sends a bit-by-bit image of a **UserForm** object to the printer.

Syntax

object.**PrintForm**

The *object* placeholder represents an object expression that evaluates to an object in the Applies To list. If *object* is omitted, the **UserForm** with the focus is assumed to be *object*.

Remarks

PrintForm prints all visible objects and bitmaps of the **UserForm** object. **PrintForm** also prints graphics added to a **UserForm** object.

The printer used by **PrintForm** is determined by the operating system's **Control Panel** settings.

Example

In the following example, the client area of the form is printed when the user clicks the form.

```
' This is the click event for UserForm1
Private Sub UserForm_Click()
   UserForm1.PrintForm
End Sub
```

Private Statement

Description

Used at module level to declare private variables and allocate storage space.

Syntax

Private [**WithEvents**] *varname*[([*subscripts*])] [**As** [**New**] *type*] [,[**WithEvents**]
➥ *varname*[([*subscripts*])] [**As** [**New**] *type*]] **. . .**

The **Private** statement syntax has these parts.

Part	Description
WithEvents	Optional. Keyword that specifies that *varname* is an object variable used to respond to events triggered by an ActiveX object. Valid only in class modules. You can declare as many individual variables as you like using **WithEvents**, but you can't create arrays with **WithEvents**. You can't use **New** with **WithEvents**.
varname	Required. Name of the variable; follows standard variable naming conventions.
subscripts	Optional. Dimensions of an array variable; up to 60 multiple dimensions may be declared. The *subscripts* argument uses the following syntax: [*lower* **To**] *upper* [,[*lower* **To**] *upper*] **. . .** When not explicitly stated in *lower*, the lower bound of an array is controlled by the **Option Base** statement. The lower bound is zero if no **Option Base** statement is present.
New	Optional. Keyword that enables implicit creation of an object. If you use **New** when declaring the object variable, a new instance of the object is created on first reference to it, so you don't have to use the **Set** statement to assign the object reference. The **New** keyword can't be used to declare variables of any intrinsic data type, can't be used to declare instances of dependent objects, and can't be used with **WithEvents**.
type	Optional. Data type of the variable; may be **Byte**, **Boolean**, **Integer**, **Long**, **Currency**, **Single**, **Double**, **Decimal** (not currently supported), **Date**, **String** (for variable-length strings), **String** * *length* (for fixed-length strings), **Object**, **Variant**, a user-defined type, or an object type. Use a separate **As** *type* clause for each variable being defined.

Remarks

Private variables are available only to the module in which they are declared.

Use the **Private** statement to declare the data type of a variable. For example, the following statement declares a variable as an **Integer**:

```
Private NumberOfEmployees As Integer
```

You can also use a **Private** statement to declare the object type of a variable. The following statement declares a variable for a new instance of a worksheet.

```
Private X As New Worksheet
```

If the **New** keyword is not used when declaring an object variable, the variable that refers to the object must be assigned an existing object using the **Set** statement before it can be used. Until it is assigned an object, the declared object variable has the special value **Nothing**, which indicates that it doesn't refer to any particular instance of an object.

If you don't specify a data type or object type, and there is no **Def***type* statement in the module, the variable is **Variant** by default.

You can also use the **Private** statement with empty parentheses to declare a dynamic array. After declaring a dynamic array, use the **ReDim** statement within a procedure to define the number of dimensions and elements in the array. If you try to redeclare a dimension for an array variable whose size was explicitly specified in a **Private**, **Public**, or **Dim** statement, an error occurs.

When variables are initialized, a numeric variable is initialized to 0, a variable-length string is initialized to a zero-length string (" "), and a fixed-length string is filled with zeros. **Variant** variables are initialized to **Empty**. Each element of a user-defined type variable is initialized as if it were a separate variable.

Note When you use the **Private** statement in a procedure, you generally put the **Private** statement at the beginning of the procedure.

See Also

Array function, **Const** statement, **Dim** statement, **Function** statement, **Option Base** statement, **Option Private** statement, **Property Get** statement, **Property Let** statement, **Property Set** statement, **Public** statement, **ReDim** statement, **Set** statement, **Static** statement, **Sub** statement, **Type** statement.

Example

This example shows the **Private** statement being used at the module level to declare variables as private; that is, they are available only to the module in which they are declared.

```
Private Number As Integer                   ' Private Integer variable.
Private NameArray(1 To 5) As String         ' Private array variable.
' Multiple declarations, two Variants and one Integer, all Private.
Private MyVar, YourVar, ThisVar As Integer
```

Property Get Statement

Description

Declares the name, arguments, and code that form the body of a **Property** procedure, which gets the value of a property.

Syntax

[**Public** | **Private**] [**Static**] **Property Get** *name* [(*arglist*)] [**As** *type*]
↳ [*statements*]
↳ [*name* = *expression*]
↳ [**Exit Property**]
↳ [*statements*]
↳ [*name* = *expression*]
End Property

The **Property Get** statement syntax has these parts.

Part	Description
Public	Optional. Indicates that the **Property Get** procedure is accessible to all other procedures in all modules. If used in a module that contains an **Option Private** statement, the procedure is not available outside the project.
Private	Optional. Indicates that the **Property Get** procedure is accessible only to other procedures in the module where it is declared.
Static	Optional. Indicates that the **Property Get** procedure's local variables are preserved between calls. The **Static** attribute doesn't affect variables that are declared outside the **Property Get** procedure, even if they are used in the procedure.
name	Required. Name of the **Property Get** procedure; follows standard variable naming conventions, except that the name can be the same as a **Property Let** or **Property Set** procedure in the same module.
arglist	Optional. List of variables representing arguments that are passed to the **Property Get** procedure when it is called. Multiple arguments are separated by commas. The name and data type of each argument in a **Property Get** procedure must be the same as the corresponding argument in a **Property Let** procedure (if one exists).
type	Optional. Data type of the value returned by the **Property Get** procedure; may be **Byte**, **Boolean**, **Integer**, **Long**, **Currency**, **Single**, **Double**, **Decimal** (not currently supported), **Date**, **String** (except fixed length), **Object**, **Variant**, or user-defined type. Arrays of any type can't be returned, but a **Variant** containing an array can. The return *type* of a **Property Get** procedure must be the same data type as the last (or sometimes the only) argument in a corresponding **Property Let** procedure (if one exists) that defines the value assigned to the property on the right side of an expression.

(continued)

statements	Optional. Any group of statements to be executed within the body of the **Property Get** procedure.
expression	Optional. Value of the property returned by the procedure defined by the **Property Get** statement.

The *arglist* argument has the following syntax and parts.

[**Optional**] [**ByVal** | **ByRef**] *varname*[( )] [**As** *type*] [= *defaultvalue*]

Part	Description
Optional	Optional. Indicates that an argument is not required. If used, all subsequent arguments in *arglist* must also be optional and declared using the **Optional** keyword.
ByVal	Optional. Indicates that the argument is passed by value.
ByRef	Optional. Indicates that the argument is passed by reference. **ByRef** is the default in Visual Basic.
ParamArray	Optional. Used only as the last argument in *arglist* to indicate that the final argument is an **Optional** array of **Variant** elements. The **ParamArray** keyword allows you to provide an arbitrary number of arguments. It may not be used with **ByVal**, **ByRef**, or **Optional**.
varname	Required. Name of the variable representing the argument; follows standard variable naming conventions.
type	Optional. Data type of the argument passed to the procedure; may be **Byte**, **Boolean**, **Integer**, **Long**, **Currency**, **Single**, **Double**, **Decimal** (not currently supported), **Date**, **String** (variable length only), **Object**, **Variant**. If the parameter is not **Optional**, a user-defined type or an object type may also be specified.
defaultvalue	Optional. Any constant or constant expression. Valid for **Optional** parameters only. If the type is an **Object**, an explicit default value can only be **Nothing**.

Remarks

If not explicitly specified using either **Public** or **Private**, **Property** procedures are public by default. If **Static** is not used, the value of local variables is not preserved between calls.

All executable code must be in procedures. You can't define a **Property Get** procedure inside another **Property**, **Sub**, or **Function** procedure.

The **Exit Property** statement causes an immediate exit from a **Property Get** procedure. Program execution continues with the statement following the statement that called the **Property Get** procedure. Any number of **Exit Property** statements can appear anywhere in a **Property Get** procedure.

Like a **Sub** and **Property Let** procedure, a **Property Get** procedure is a separate procedure that can take arguments, perform a series of statements, and change the values of its arguments. However, unlike a **Sub** or **Property Let** procedure, you can use a **Property Get** procedure on the right side of an expression in the same way you use a **Function** or a property name when you want to return the value of a property.

See Also

Function statement, **Property Let** statement, **Property Set** statement, **Sub** statement.

Specifics (Microsoft Access)

You can use the **Property Get** statement to define a property procedure that returns the value of a property. You will probably want to use the **Property Get** and **Property Let** statements together to create a property in a class module. For example, you could define a **Property Let** procedure in a class module to set a new property, and a **Property Get** procedure to return the value of that setting. When you create a new instance of this class, the property procedures behave like custom properties for the new object.

Property procedures in a class module are public by default, and will be available to procedures in other modules in the current database, unless you preface them with the **Private** keyword.

Example

This example uses the **Property Get** statement to define a property procedure that gets the value of a property. The property identifies the current color of a pen in a drawing package as a string.

```
Dim CurrentColor As Integer
Const BLACK = 0, RED = 1, GREEN = 2, BLUE = 3

' Returns the current color of the pen as a string.
Property Get PenColor() As String
   Select Case CurrentColor
      Case RED
         PenColor = "Red"
      Case GREEN
         PenColor = "Green"
      Case BLUE
         PenColor = "Blue"
   End Select
End Property

' The following code gets the color of the pen
' calling the Property get procedure.
ColorName = PenColor
```

Property Let Statement

Description

Declares the name, arguments, and code that form the body of a **Property Let** procedure, which assigns a value to a property.

Syntax

[Public | Private] [Static] Property Let *name* **(**[*arglist*,] *value*)
↪ [*statements*]
↪ [**Exit Property**]
↪ [*statements*]
End Property

The **Property Let** statement syntax has these parts.

Part	Description
Public	Optional. Indicates that the **Property Let** procedure is accessible to all other procedures in all modules. If used in a module that contains an **Option Private** statement, the procedure is not available outside the project.
Private	Optional. Indicates that the **Property Let** procedure is accessible only to other procedures in the module where it is declared.
Static	Optional. Indicates that the **Property Let** procedure's local variables are preserved between calls. The **Static** attribute doesn't affect variables that are declared outside the **Property Let** procedure, even if they are used in the procedure.
name	Required. Name of the **Property Let** procedure; follows standard variable naming conventions, except that the name can be the same as a **Property Get** or **Property Set** procedure in the same module.
arglist	Required. List of variables representing arguments that are passed to the **Property Let** procedure when it is called. Multiple arguments are separated by commas. The name and data type of each argument in a **Property Let** procedure must be the same as the corresponding argument in a **Property Get** procedure.
value	Required. Variable to contain the value to be assigned to the property. When the procedure is called, this argument appears on the right side of the calling expression. The data type of *value* must be the same as the return type of the corresponding **Property Get** procedure.
statements	Optional. Any group of statements to be executed within the **Property Let** procedure.

The *arglist* argument has the following syntax and parts.

[**Optional**] [**ByVal** | **ByRef**] [**ParamArray**] *varname*[( )] [**As** *type*] [= *defaultvalue*]

Part	Description
Optional	Optional. Indicates that an argument is not required. If used, all subsequent arguments in *arglist* must also be optional and declared using the **Optional** keyword. Note that it is not possible for the right side of a **Property Let** expression to be **Optional**.
ByVal	Optional. Indicates that the argument is passed by value.
ByRef	Optional. Indicates that the argument is passed by reference. **ByRef** is the default in Visual Basic.
ParamArray	Optional. Used only as the last argument in *arglist* to indicate that the final argument is an **Optional** array of **Variant** elements. The **ParamArray** keyword allows you to provide an arbitrary number of arguments. It may not be used with **ByVal**, **ByRef**, or **Optional**.
varname	Required. Name of the variable representing the argument; follows standard variable naming conventions.
type	Optional. Data type of the argument passed to the procedure; may be **Byte**, **Boolean**, **Integer**, **Long**, **Currency**, **Single**, **Double**, **Decimal** (not currently supported), **Date**, **String** (variable length only), **Object**, **Variant**. If the parameter is not **Optional**, a user-defined type, or an object type may also be specified.
defaultvalue	Optional. Any constant or constant expression. Valid for **Optional** parameters only. If the type is an **Object**, an explicit default value can only be **Nothing**.

Note Every **Property Let** statement must define at least one argument for the procedure it defines. That argument (or the last argument if there is more than one) contains the actual value to be assigned to the property when the procedure defined by the **Property Let** statement is invoked. That argument is referred to as *value* in the preceding syntax.

Remarks

If not explicitly specified using either **Public** or **Private**, **Property** procedures are public by default. If **Static** is not used, the value of local variables is not preserved between calls.

All executable code must be in procedures. You can't define a **Property Let** procedure inside another **Property**, **Sub**, or **Function** procedure.

The **Exit Property** statement causes an immediate exit from a **Property Let** procedure. Program execution continues with the statement following the statement that called the **Property Let** procedure. Any number of **Exit Property** statements can appear anywhere in a **Property Let** procedure.

Like a **Function** and **Property Get** procedure, a **Property Let** procedure is a separate procedure that can take arguments, perform a series of statements, and change the value of its arguments. However, unlike a **Function** and **Property Get** procedure, both of which return a value, you can only use a **Property Let** procedure on the left side of a property assignment expression or **Let** statement.

See Also

Function statement, **Let** statement, **Property Get** statement, **Property Set** statement, **Sub** statement.

Specifics (Microsoft Access)

You can use the **Property Let** statement to define a property procedure that assigns the value of a property. You will probably want to use the **Property Let** and **Property Get** statements together to create a property in a class module. For example, you could define a **Property Let** procedure in a class module to set a new property, and a **Property Get** procedure to return the value of that setting. When you create a new instance of this class, the property procedures behave like custom properties for the new object.

Property procedures in a class module are public by default, and will be available to procedures in other modules in the current database, unless you preface them with the **Private** keyword.

Example

This example uses the **Property Let** statement to define a procedure that assigns a value to a property. The property identifies the pen color for a drawing package.

```
Dim CurrentColor As Integer
Const BLACK = 0, RED = 1, GREEN = 2, BLUE = 3

' Set the pen color property for a Drawing package.
' The module-level variable CurrentColor is set to
' a numeric value that identifies the color used for drawing.
Property Let PenColor(ColorName As String)
   Select Case ColorName                        ' Check color name string.
      Case "Red"
         CurrentColor = RED                     ' Assign value for Red.
      Case "Green"
         CurrentColor = GREEN                   ' Assign value for Green.
      Case "Blue"
         CurrentColor = BLUE                    ' Assign value for Blue.
      Case Else
         CurrentColor = BLACK                   ' Assign default value.
   End Select
End Property

' The following code sets the PenColor property for a drawing package
' by calling the Property let procedure.
PenColor = "Red"
```

Property Set Statement

Description

Declares the name, arguments, and code that form the body of a **Property** procedure, which sets a reference to an object.

Syntax

[Public | Private] [Static] Property Set *name* ([*arglist*,] *reference*)
→ [*statements*]
→ **[Exit Property]**
→ [*statements*]
End Property

The **Property Set** statement syntax has these parts.

Part	Description
Optional	Optional. Indicates that the argument may or may not be supplied by the caller.
Public	Optional. Indicates that the **Property Set** procedure is accessible to all other procedures in all modules. If used in a module that contains an **Option Private** statement, the procedure is not available outside the project.
Private	Optional. Indicates that the **Property Set** procedure is accessible only to other procedures in the module where it is declared.
Static	Optional. Indicates that the **Property Set** procedure's local variables are preserved between calls. The **Static** attribute doesn't affect variables that are declared outside the **Property Set** procedure, even if they are used in the procedure.
name	Required. Name of the **Property Set** procedure; follows standard variable naming conventions, except that the name can be the same as a **Property Get** or **Property Let** procedure in the same module.
arglist	Required. List of variables representing arguments that are passed to the **Property Set** procedure when it is called. Multiple arguments are separated by commas.
reference	Required. Variable containing the object reference used on the right side of the object reference assignment.
statements	Optional. Any group of statements to be executed within the body of the **Property** procedure.

The *arglist* argument has the following syntax and parts.

[Optional] [ByVal | ByRef] [ParamArray] *varname*[( )] **[As** *type*] [= *defaultvalue*]

Part	Description
Optional	Optional. Indicates that an argument is not required. If used, all subsequent arguments in *arglist* must also be optional and declared using the **Optional** keyword. Note that it is not possible for the right side of a **Property Set** expression to be **Optional**.
ByVal	Optional. Indicates that the argument is passed by value.
ByRef	Optional. Indicates that the argument is passed by reference. **ByRef** is the default in Visual Basic.
ParamArray	Optional. Used only as the last argument in *arglist* to indicate that the final argument is an **Optional** array of **Variant** elements. The **ParamArray** keyword allows you to provide an arbitrary number of arguments. It may not be used with **ByVal**, **ByRef**, or **Optional**.
varname	Required. Name of the variable representing the argument; follows standard variable naming conventions.
type	Optional. Data type of the argument passed to the procedure; may be **Byte**, **Boolean**, **Integer**, **Long**, **Currency**, **Single**, **Double**, **Decimal** (not currently supported), **Date**, **String** (variable length only), **Object**, **Variant**. If the parameter is not **Optional**, a user-defined type, or an object type may also be specified.
defaultvalue	Optional. Any constant or constant expression. Valid for **Optional** parameters only. If the type is an **Object**, an explicit default value can only be **Nothing**.

Note Every **Property Set** statement must define at least one argument for the procedure it defines. That argument (or the last argument if there is more than one) contains the actual object reference for the property when the procedure defined by the **Property Set** statement is invoked. It is referred to as *reference* in the preceding syntax. It can't be **Optional**.

Remarks

If not explicitly specified using either **Public** or **Private**, **Property** procedures are public by default. If **Static** is not used, the value of local variables is not preserved between calls.

All executable code must be in procedures. You can't define a **Property Set** procedure inside another **Property**, **Sub**, or **Function** procedure.

The **Exit Property** statement causes an immediate exit from a **Property Set** procedure. Program execution continues with the statement following the statement that called the **Property Set** procedure. Any number of **Exit Property** statements can appear anywhere in a **Property Set** procedure.

Like a **Function** and **Property Get** procedure, a **Property Set** procedure is a separate procedure that can take arguments, perform a series of statements, and change the value of its arguments. However, unlike a **Function** and **Property Get** procedure, both of which return a value, you can only use a **Property Set** procedure on the left side of an object reference assignment (**Set** statement).

See Also

Function statement, **Property Get** statement, **Property Let** statement, **Set** statement, **Sub** statement.

Example

This example uses the **Property Set** statement to define a property procedure that sets a reference to an object.

```
' The Pen property may be set to different Pen implementations.
Property Set Pen(P As Object)
   Set CurrentPen = P                        ' Assign Pen to object.
End Property
```

Public Statement

Description

Used at module level to declare public variables and allocate storage space.

Syntax

Public [**WithEvents**] *varname*[([*subscripts*])] [**As** [**New**] *type*] [,[**WithEvents**] ➥ *varname*[([*subscripts*])] [**As** [**New**] *type*]] **. . .**

The **Public** statement syntax has these parts

Part	Description
WithEvents	Optional. Keyword specifying that *varname* is an object variable used to respond to events triggered by an ActiveX object. Valid only in class modules. You can declare as many individual variables as you like using **WithEvents**, but you can't create arrays with **WithEvents**. You can't use **New** with **WithEvents**.
varname	Required. Name of the variable; follows standard variable naming conventions.
subscripts	Optional. Dimensions of an array variable; up to 60 multiple dimensions may be declared. The *subscripts* argument uses the following syntax: [*lower* **To**] *upper* [,[*lower* **To**] *upper*] **. . .** When not explicitly stated in *lower*, the lower bound of an array is controlled by the **Option Base** statement. The lower bound is zero if no **Option Base** statement is present.

(continued)

New	Optional. Keyword that enables implicit creation of an object. If you use **New** when declaring the object variable, a new instance of the object is created on first reference to it, so you don't have to use the **Set** statement to assign the object reference. The **New** keyword can't be used to declare variables of any intrinsic data type, can't be used to declare instances of dependent objects, and can't be used with **WithEvents**.
type	Optional. Data type of the variable; may be **Byte**, **Boolean**, **Integer**, **Long**, **Currency**, **Single**, **Double**, **Decimal** (not currently supported), **Date**, **String**, (for variable-length strings), **String** * *length* (for fixed-length strings), **Object**, **Variant**, a user-defined type, or an object type. Use a separate **As** *type* clause for each variable being defined.

Remarks

Variables declared using the **Public** statement are available to all procedures in all modules in all applications unless **Option Private Module** is in effect; in which case, the variables are public only within the project in which they reside.

Caution The **Public** statement can't be used in a class module to declare a fixed-length string variable.

Use the **Public** statement to declare the data type of a variable. For example, the following statement declares a variable as an **Integer**:

```
Public NumberOfEmployees As Integer
```

Also use a **Public** statement to declare the object type of a variable. The following statement declares a variable for a new instance of a worksheet.

```
Public X As New Worksheet
```

If the **New** keyword is not used when declaring an object variable, the variable that refers to the object must be assigned an existing object using the **Set** statement before it can be used. Until it is assigned an object, the declared object variable has the special value **Nothing**, which indicates that it doesn't refer to any particular instance of an object.

You can also use the **Public** statement with empty parentheses to declare a dynamic array. After declaring a dynamic array, use the **ReDim** statement within a procedure to define the number of dimensions and elements in the array. If you try to redeclare a dimension for an array variable whose size was explicitly specified in a **Private**, **Public**, or **Dim** statement, an error occurs.

If you don't specify a data type or object type and there is no **Def***type* statement in the module, the variable is **Variant** by default.

When variables are initialized, a numeric variable is initialized to 0, a variable-length string is initialized to a zero-length string (" "), and a fixed-length string is filled with zeros. **Variant** variables are initialized to **Empty**. Each element of a user-defined type variable is initialized as if it were a separate variable.

See Also

Array function, **Const** statement, **Dim** statement, **Option Base** statement, **Option Private** statement, **Private** statement, **Property Get** statement, **Property Let** statement, **Property Set** statement, **ReDim** statement, **Set** statement, **Static** statement, **Type** statement.

Specifics (Microsoft Access)

By default, module-level variables are private to that module. You must explicitly declare a public variable with the **Public** statement.

Module-level variables declared in standard modules with the **Public** statement are available to all other procedures in all modules in the current database and in referencing Microsoft Access databases. However, they are not available to any applications other than Microsoft Access.

If a public variable is declared in a module that contains the **Option Private** statement or in a class module, the variable is available to all procedures in the current database, but not to procedures in other databases.

Note The **Public** statement can't be used in a class module to declare a constant, a fixed-length string, or an array. In addition, if you include a **Declare** statement in a class module, you must precede it with the **Private** keyword. For more information about the **Declare** statement, see Declare Statement.

Example

This example uses the **Public** statement at the module level (General section) of a standard module to explicitly declare variables as public; that is, they are available to all procedures in all modules in all applications unless **Option Private Module** is in effect.

```
Public Number As Integer                    ' Public Integer variable.
Public NameArray(1 To 5) As String          ' Public array variable.
' Multiple declarations, two Variants and one Integer, all Public.
Public MyVar, YourVar, ThisVar As Integer
```

Put Statement

Description

Writes data from a variable to a disk file.

Syntax

Put [#]*filenumber*, [*recnumber*], *varname*

The **Put** statement syntax has these parts

Part	Description
filenumber	Required. Any valid file number.
recnumber	Optional. **Variant** (**Long**). Record number (**Random** mode files) or byte number (**Binary** mode files) at which writing begins.
varname	Required. Name of variable containing data to be written to disk.

Remarks

Data written with **Put** is usually read from a file with **Get**.

The first record or byte in a file is at position 1, the second record or byte is at position 2, and so on. If you omit *recnumber*, the next record or byte after the last **Get** or **Put** statement or pointed to by the last **Seek** function is written. You must include delimiting commas, for example:

```
Put #4,,FileBuffer
```

For files opened in **Random** mode, the following rules apply:

- If the length of the data being written is less than the length specified in the **Len** clause of the **Open** statement, **Put** writes subsequent records on record-length boundaries. The space between the end of one record and the beginning of the next record is padded with the existing contents of the file buffer. Because the amount of padding data can't be determined with any certainty, it is generally a good idea to have the record length match the length of the data being written. If the length of the data being written is greater than the length specified in the **Len** clause of the **Open** statement, an error occurs.
- If the variable being written is a variable-length string, **Put** writes a 2-byte descriptor containing the string length and then the variable. The record length specified by the **Len** clause in the **Open** statement must be at least 2 bytes greater than the actual length of the string.

- If the variable being written is a **Variant** of a numeric type, **Put** writes 2 bytes identifying the **VarType** of the **Variant** and then writes the variable. For example, when writing a **Variant** of **VarType** 3, **Put** writes 6 bytes: 2 bytes identifying the **Variant** as **VarType** 3 (**Long**) and 4 bytes containing the **Long** data. The record length specified by the **Len** clause in the **Open** statement must be at least 2 bytes greater than the actual number of bytes required to store the variable.

  Note You can use the **Put** statement to write a **Variant** array to disk, but you can't use **Put** to write a scalar **Variant** containing an array to disk. You also can't use **Put** to write objects to disk.

- If the variable being written is a **Variant** of **VarType** 8 (**String**), **Put** writes 2 bytes identifying the **VarType**, 2 bytes indicating the length of the string, and then writes the string data. The record length specified by the **Len** clause in the **Open** statement must be at least 4 bytes greater than the actual length of the string.
- If the variable being written is a dynamic array, **Put** writes a descriptor whose length equals 2 plus 8 times the number of dimensions, that is, 2 + 8 * *NumberOfDimensions*. The record length specified by the **Len** clause in the **Open** statement must be greater than or equal to the sum of all the bytes required to write the array data and the array descriptor. For example, the following array declaration requires 118 bytes when the array is written to disk.

  ```
  Dim MyArray(1 To 5,1 To 10) As Integer
  ```

- The 118 bytes are distributed as follows: 18 bytes for the descriptor (2 + 8 * 2), and 100 bytes for the data (5 * 10 * 2).
- If the variable being written is a fixed-size array, **Put** writes only the data. No descriptor is written to disk.
- If the variable being written is any other type of variable (not a variable-length string or a **Variant**), **Put** writes only the variable data. The record length specified by the **Len** clause in the **Open** statement must be greater than or equal to the length of the data being written.
- **Put** writes elements of user-defined types as if each were written individually, except there is no padding between elements. On disk, a dynamic array in a user-defined type written with **Put** is prefixed by a descriptor whose length equals 2 plus 8 times the number of dimensions, that is, 2 + 8 * *NumberOfDimensions*. The record length specified by the **Len** clause in the **Open** statement must be greater than or equal to the sum of all the bytes required to write the individual elements, including any arrays and their descriptors.

For files opened in **Binary** mode, all of the **Random** rules apply, except:

- The **Len** clause in the **Open** statement has no effect. **Put** writes all variables to disk contiguously; that is, with no padding between records.
- For any array other than an array in a user-defined type, **Put** writes only the data. No descriptor is written.

- **Put** writes variable-length strings that are not elements of user-defined types without the 2-byte length descriptor. The number of bytes written equals the number of characters in the string. For example, the following statements write 10 bytes to file number 1:

```
VarString$ = String$(10," ")
Put #1,,VarString$
```

See Also

Get statement, **Open** statement, **Seek** function, **Type** statement, **VarType** function.

Example

This example uses the **Put** statement to write data to a file. Five records of the user-defined type `Record` are written to the file.

```
Type Record                                   ' Define user-defined type.
   ID As Integer
   Name As String * 20
End Type

Dim MyRecord As Record, RecordNumber          ' Declare variables.
' Open file for random access.
Open "TESTFILE" For Random As #1 Len = Len(MyRecord)
For RecordNumber = 1 To 5                     ' Loop 5 times.
   MyRecord.ID = RecordNumber                 ' Define ID.
   MyRecord.Name = "My Name" & RecordNumber   ' Create a string.
   Put #1, RecordNumber, MyRecord             ' Write record to file.
Next RecordNumber
Close #1                                      ' Close file.
```

PV Function

Description

Returns a **Double** specifying the present value of an annuity based on periodic, fixed payments to be paid in the future and a fixed interest rate.

Syntax

PV(*rate*, *nper*, *pmt*[, *fv*[, *type*]])

The **PV** function has these named arguments

Part	Description
rate	Required. **Double** specifying interest rate per period. For example, if you get a car loan at an annual percentage rate (APR) of 10 percent and make monthly payments, the rate per period is 0.1/12, or 0.0083.
nper	Required. **Integer** specifying total number of payment periods in the annuity. For example, if you make monthly payments on a four-year car loan, your loan has a total of 4 * 12 (or 48) payment periods.
pmt	Required. **Double** specifying payment to be made each period. Payments usually contain principal and interest that doesn't change over the life of the annuity.

(continued)

Part	Description
fv	Optional. **Variant** specifying future value or cash balance you want after you've made the final payment. For example, the future value of a loan is $0 because that's its value after the final payment. However, if you want to save $50,000 over 18 years for your child's education, then $50,000 is the future value. If omitted, 0 is assumed.
type	Optional. **Variant** specifying when payments are due. Use 0 if payments are due at the end of the payment period, or use 1 if payments are due at the beginning of the period. If omitted, 0 is assumed.

Remarks

An annuity is a series of fixed cash payments made over a period of time. An annuity can be a loan (such as a home mortgage) or an investment (such as a monthly savings plan).

The ***rate*** and ***nper*** arguments must be calculated using payment periods expressed in the same units. For example, if ***rate*** is calculated using months, ***nper*** must also be calculated using months.

For all arguments, cash paid out (such as deposits to savings) is represented by negative numbers; cash received (such as dividend checks) is represented by positive numbers.

See Also

DDB function, **FV** function, **IPmt** function, **IRR** function, **MIRR** function, **NPer** function, **NPV** function, **Pmt** function, **PPmt** function, **Rate** function, **SLN** function, **SYD** function.

Example

In this example, the **PV** function returns the present value of an $1,000,000 annuity that will provide $50,000 a year for the next 20 years. Provided are the expected annual percentage rate (`APR`), the total number of payments (`TotPmts`), the amount of each payment (`YrIncome`), the total future value of the investment (`FVal`), and a number that indicates whether each payment is made at the beginning or end of the payment period (`PayType`). Note that `YrIncome` is a negative number because it represents cash paid out from the annuity each year.

```
Dim Fmt, APR, TotPmts, YrIncome, FVal, PayType, PVal
Const ENDPERIOD = 0, BEGINPERIOD = 1          ' When payments are made.
Fmt = "###,##0.00"                            ' Define money format.
APR = .0825                                   ' Annual percentage rate.
TotPmts = 20                                  ' Total number of payments.
YrIncome = 50000                              ' Yearly income.
FVal = 1000000                                ' Future value.
PayType = BEGINPERIOD                         ' Payment at beginning of month.
PVal = PV(APR, TotPmts, -YrIncome, FVal, PayType)
MsgBox "The present value is " & Format(PVal, Fmt) & "."
```

QBColor Function

Description

Returns a **Long** representing the RGB color code corresponding to the specified color number.

Syntax

QBColor(*color***)**

The required *color* argument is a whole number in the range 0–15.

Settings

The *color* argument has these settings

Number	Color	Number	Color
0	Black	8	Gray
1	Blue	9	Light Blue
2	Green	10	Light Green
3	Cyan	11	Light Cyan
4	Red	12	Light Red
5	Magenta	13	Light Magenta
6	Yellow	14	Light Yellow
7	White	15	Bright White

Remarks

The *color* argument represents color values used by earlier versions of Basic (such as Microsoft Visual Basic for MS-DOS and the Basic Compiler). Starting with the least-significant byte, the returned value specifies the red, green, and blue values used to set the appropriate color in the RGB system used by Visual Basic for Applications.

See Also

RGB function.

Example

This example uses the **QBColor** function to change the **BackColor** property of the form passed in as `MyForm` to the color indicated by `ColorCode`. **QBColor** accepts integer values between 0 and 15.

```
Sub ChangeBackColor (ColorCode As Integer, MyForm As Form)
   MyForm.BackColor = QBColor(ColorCode)
End Sub
```

QueryClose Event

Applies To

UserForm object.

Description

Occurs before a **UserForm** closes.

Syntax

Private Sub UserForm_QueryClose(*cancel* **As Integer,** *closemode* **As Integer)**

The QueryClose event syntax has these parts

Part	Description
cancel	An integer. Setting this argument to any value other than 0 stops the QueryClose event in all loaded user forms and prevents the **UserForm** and application from closing.
closemode	A value or constant indicating the cause of the QueryClose event.

Return Values

The *closemode* argument returns the following values

Constant	Value	Description
vbFormControlMenu	0	The user has chosen the **Close** command from the **Control** menu on the **UserForm**.
vbFormCode	1	The **Unload** statement is invoked from code.
vbAppWindows	2	The current Windows operating environment session is ending.
vbAppTaskManager	3	The Windows **Task Manager** is closing the application.

These constants are listed in the Visual Basic for Applications object library in the **Object Browser**. Note that **vbFormMDIForm** is also specified in the **Object Browser**, but is not yet supported.

Remarks

This event is typically used to make sure there are no unfinished tasks in the user forms included in an application before that application closes. For example, if a user hasn't saved new data in any **UserForm**, the application can prompt the user to save the data.

When an application closes, you can use the QueryClose event procedure to set the **Cancel** property to **True**, stopping the closing process.

Example

The following code forces the user to click the **UserForm**'s client area to close it. If the user tries to use the **Close** box in the title bar, the Cancel parameter is set to a nonzero value, preventing termination. However, if the user has clicked the client area, `CloseMode` has the value 1 and the Unload Me is completed.

```
Private Sub UserForm_Activate()
   UserForm1.Caption = "You must Click me to kill me!"
End Sub

Private Sub UserForm_Click()
   Unload Me
End Sub

Private Sub UserForm_QueryClose(Cancel As Integer, CloseMode As Integer)
' Prevent user from closing with the Close box in the title bar.
   If CloseMode <> 1 Then Cancel = 1
   UserForm1.Caption = "The Close box won't work! Click me!"
End Sub
```

Raise Method

Applies To

Err object.

Description

Generates a run-time error.

Syntax

object.**Raise** ***number*, *source*, *description*, *helpfile*, *helpcontext***

The **Raise** method has the following object qualifier and named arguments

Argument	Description
object	Required. Always the **Err** object.
number	Required. **Long** integer that identifies the nature of the error. Visual Basic errors (both Visual Basic-defined and user-defined errors) are in the range 0–65535. When setting the **Number** property to your own error code in a class module, you add your error code number to the **vbObjectError** constant. For example, to generate the error number 1050, assign **vbObjectError** + 1050 to the **Number** property.
source	Optional. String expression naming the object or application that generated the error. When setting this property for an object, use the form *project.class*. If *source* is not specified, the programmatic ID of the current Visual Basic project is used.

(continued)

Argument	Description
description	Optional. String expression describing the error. If unspecified, the value in **Number** is examined. If it can be mapped to a Visual Basic run-time error code, the string that would be returned by the **Error** function is used as **Description**. If there is no Visual Basic error corresponding to **Number**, the "Application-defined or object-defined error" message is used.
helpfile	Optional. The fully qualified path to the Microsoft Windows Help file in which help on this error can be found. If unspecified, Visual Basic uses the fully qualified drive, path, and file name of the Visual Basic Help file.
helpcontext	Optional. The context ID identifying a topic within ***helpfile*** that provides help for the error. If omitted, the Visual Basic Help file context ID for the error corresponding to the **Number** property is used, if it exists.

Remarks

All of the arguments are optional except ***number***. If you use **Raise** without specifying some arguments, and the property settings of the **Err** object contain values that have not been cleared, those values serve as the values for your error.

Raise is used for generating run-time errors and can be used instead of the **Error** statement. **Raise** is useful for generating errors when writing class modules, because the **Err** object gives richer information than is possible if you generate errors with the **Error** statement. For example, with the **Raise** method, the source that generated the error can be specified in the **Source** property, online Help for the error can be referenced, and so on.

See Also

Clear method, **Description** property, **Err** object, **Error** statement, **HelpContext** property, **HelpContextID** property ("Extensibility Object Model Language Reference"), **HelpFile** property, **LastDLLError** property, **Number** property, **Source** property.

Specifics (Microsoft Access)

The **Raise** method raises a specified Visual Basic error. The properties of the **Err** object are set as though the error had actually occurred in running code. However, this works only for Visual Basic errors, not for Microsoft Access errors or Microsoft Jet database engine errors.

If you use the **Raise** method with an error number reserved by Microsoft Access or by the Microsoft Jet database engine, the value of the **Err** object's **Description** property is "Application-defined or object-defined error." To determine the descriptive string for a Microsoft Access or Jet database engine error that hasn't actually occurred in running code, use the **AccessError** method.

The **AccessError** method takes a **Long** value that represents an error number and returns the descriptive string associated with the error.

Example

This example uses the **Err** object's **Raise** method to generate an error within an Automation object written in Visual Basic. It has the programmatic ID `MyProj.MyObject`.

```
Const MyContextID = 1010407          ' Define a constant for contextID.
Function TestName(CurrentName, NewName)
   If Instr(NewName, "bob") Then     ' Test the validity of NewName.
      ' Raise the exception.
      Err.Raise vbObjectError + 27, "MyProj.MyObject", _
         "No ""bob"" allowed in your name", "c:\MyProj\MyHelp.Hlp", _
         MyContextID
   End If
End Function
```

Randomize Statement

Description

Initializes the random-number generator.

Syntax

Randomize [*number*]

The optional *number* argument is a **Variant** or any valid numeric expression.

Remarks

Randomize uses *number* to initialize the **Rnd** function's random-number generator, giving it a new seed value. If you omit *number,* the value returned by the system timer is used as the new seed value.

If **Randomize** is not used, the **Rnd** function (with no arguments) uses the same number as a seed the first time it is called, and thereafter uses the last generated number as a seed value.

Note To repeat sequences of random numbers, call **Rnd** with a negative argument immediately before using **Randomize** with a numeric argument. Using **Randomize** with the same value for *number* does not repeat the previous sequence.

See Also

Rnd function, **Timer** function.

Example

This example uses the **Randomize** statement to initialize the random-number generator. Because the number argument has been omitted, **Randomize** uses the return value from the **Timer** function as the new seed value.

```
Dim MyValue
Randomize                          ' Initialize random-number generator.

MyValue = Int((6 * Rnd) + 1)       ' Generate random value between 1 and 6.
```

Rate Function

Description

Returns a **Double** specifying the interest rate per period for an annuity.

Syntax

Rate(*nper*, *pmt*, *pv*[, *fv*[, *type*[, *guess*]]])

The **Rate** function has these named arguments

Part	Description
nper	Required. **Double** specifying total number of payment periods in the annuity. For example, if you make monthly payments on a four-year car loan, your loan has a total of 4 * 12 (or 48) payment periods.
pmt	Required. **Double** specifying payment to be made each period. Payments usually contain principal and interest that doesn't change over the life of the annuity.
pv	Required. **Double** specifying present value, or value today, of a series of future payments or receipts. For example, when you borrow money to buy a car, the loan amount is the present value to the lender of the monthly car payments you will make.
fv	Optional. **Variant** specifying future value or cash balance you want after you make the final payment. For example, the future value of a loan is $0 because that's its value after the final payment. However, if you want to save $50,000 over 18 years for your child's education, then $50,000 is the future value. If omitted, 0 is assumed.
type	Optional. **Variant** specifying a number indicating when payments are due. Use 0 if payments are due at the end of the payment period, or use 1 if payments are due at the beginning of the period. If omitted, 0 is assumed.
guess	Optional. **Variant** specifying value you estimate will be returned by **Rate**. If omitted, ***guess*** is 0.1 (10 percent).

Remarks

An annuity is a series of fixed cash payments made over a period of time. An annuity can be a loan (such as a home mortgage) or an investment (such as a monthly savings plan).

For all arguments, cash paid out (such as deposits to savings) is represented by negative numbers; cash received (such as dividend checks) is represented by positive numbers.

Rate is calculated by iteration. Starting with the value of ***guess***, **Rate** cycles through the calculation until the result is accurate to within 0.00001 percent. If **Rate** can't find a result after 20 tries, it fails. If your guess is 10 percent and **Rate** fails, try a different value for ***guess***.

See Also

DDB function, **FV** function, **IPmt** function, **IRR** function, **MIRR** function, **NPer** function, **NPV** function, **Pmt** function, **PPmt** function, **PV** function, **SLN** function, **SYD** function.

Example

This example uses the **Rate** function to calculate the interest rate of a loan given the total number of payments (`TotPmts`), the amount of the loan payment (`Payment`), the present value or principal of the loan (`PVal`), the future value of the loan (`FVal`), a number that indicates whether the payment is due at the beginning or end of the payment period (`PayType`), and an approximation of the expected interest rate (`Guess`).

```
Dim Fmt, FVal, Guess, PVal, Payment, TotPmts, PayType, APR
Const ENDPERIOD = 0, BEGINPERIOD = 1         ' When payments are made.
Fmt = "##0.00"                               ' Define percentage format.
FVal = 0                                     ' Usually 0 for a loan.
Guess = .1                                   ' Guess of 10 percent.
PVal = InputBox("How much did you borrow?")
Payment = InputBox("What's your monthly payment?")
TotPmts = InputBox("How many monthly payments do you have to make?")
PayType = MsgBox("Do you make payments at the end of the month?", _
   vbYesNo)
If PayType = vbNo Then PayType = BEGINPERIOD Else PayType = ENDPERIOD
APR = (Rate(TotPmts, -Payment, PVal, FVal, PayType, Guess) * 12) * 100
MsgBox "Your interest rate is " & Format(CInt(APR), Fmt) & " percent."
```

ReDim Statement

Description

Used at procedure level to reallocate storage space for dynamic array variables.

Syntax

ReDim [Preserve] *varname*(*subscripts*) [**As** *type*] [, *varname*(*subscripts*) [**As** *type*]] . . .

The **ReDim** statement syntax has these parts

Part	Description
Preserve	Optional. Keyword used to preserve the data in an existing array when you change the size of the last dimension.
varname	Required. Name of the variable; follows standard variable naming conventions.

(continued)

Part	Description
subscripts	Required. Dimensions of an array variable; up to 60 multiple dimensions may be declared. The *subscripts* argument uses the following syntax: [*lower* **To**] *upper* [,[*lower* **To**] *upper*] **. . .** When not explicitly stated in *lower*, the lower bound of an array is controlled by the **Option Base** statement. The lower bound is zero if no **Option Base** statement is present.
type	Optional. Data type of the variable; may be **Byte**, **Boolean**, **Integer**, **Long**, **Currency**, **Single**, **Double**, **Decimal** (not currently supported), **Date**, **String** (for variable-length strings), **String** * *length* (for fixed-length strings), **Object**, **Variant**, a user-defined type, or an object type. Use a separate **As** *type* clause for each variable being defined. For a **Variant** containing an array, *type* describes the type of each element of the array, but doesn't change the **Variant** to some other type.

Remarks

The **ReDim** statement is used to size or resize a dynamic array that has already been formally declared using a **Private**, **Public**, or **Dim** statement with empty parentheses (without dimension subscripts).

You can use the **ReDim** statement repeatedly to change the number of elements and dimensions in an array. However, you can't declare an array of one data type and later use **ReDim** to change the array to another data type, unless the array is contained in a **Variant**. If the array is contained in a **Variant**, the type of the elements can be changed using an **As** *type* clause, unless you're using the **Preserve** keyword, in which case, no changes of data type are permitted.

If you use the **Preserve** keyword, you can resize only the last array dimension and you can't change the number of dimensions at all. For example, if your array has only one dimension, you can resize that dimension because it is the last and only dimension. However, if your array has two or more dimensions, you can change the size of only the last dimension and still preserve the contents of the array. The following example shows how you can increase the size of the last dimension of a dynamic array without erasing any existing data contained in the array.

```
ReDim X(10, 10, 10)
. . .
ReDim Preserve X(10, 10, 15)
```

Similarly, when you use **Preserve**, you can change the size of the array only by changing the upper bound; changing the lower bound causes an error.

Caution If you make an array smaller than it was, data in the eliminated elements will be lost. If you pass an array to a procedure by reference, you can't redimension the array within the procedure.

When variables are initialized, a numeric variable is initialized to 0, a variable-length string is initialized to a zero-length string (" "), and a fixed-length string is filled with zeros. **Variant** variables are initialized to **Empty**. Each element of a user-defined type variable is initialized as if it were a separate variable. A variable that refers to an object must be assigned an existing object using the **Set** statement before it can be used. Until it is assigned an object, the declared object variable has the special value **Nothing**, which indicates that it doesn't refer to any particular instance of an object.

Caution The **ReDim** statement acts as a declarative statement if the variable it declares doesn't exist at module level or procedure level. If another variable with the same name is created later, even in a wider scope, **ReDim** will refer to the later variable and won't necessarily cause a compilation error, even if **Option Explicit** is in effect. To avoid such conflicts, **ReDim** should not be used as a declarative statement, but simply for redimensioning arrays.

Note To resize an array contained in a **Variant**, you must explicitly declare the **Variant** variable before attempting to resize its array.

See Also

Array function, **Dim** statement, **Option Base** statement, **Private** statement, **Public** statement, **Set** statement, **Static** statement.

Example

This example uses the **ReDim** statement to allocate and reallocate storage space for dynamic-array variables. It assumes the **Option Base** is 1.

```
Dim MyArray() As Integer                    ' Declare dynamic array.
Redim MyArray(5)                            ' Allocate 5 elements.
For I = 1 To 5                              ' Loop 5 times.
   MyArray(I) = I                           ' Initialize array.
Next I
```

The next statement resizes the array and erases the elements.

```
Redim MyArray(10)                           ' Resize to 10 elements.
For I = 1 To 10                             ' Loop 10 times.
   MyArray(I) = I                           ' Initialize array.
Next I
```

The following statement resizes the array but does not erase elements.

```
Redim Preserve MyArray(15)                  ' Resize to 15 elements.
```

Rem Statement

Description

Used to include explanatory remarks in a program.

Syntax

Rem *comment*

You can also use the following syntax:

' *comment*

The optional *comment* argument is the text of any comment you want to include. A space is required between the **Rem** keyword and *comment*.

Remarks

If you use line numbers or line labels, you can branch from a **GoTo** or **GoSub** statement to a line containing a **Rem** statement. Execution continues with the first executable statement following the **Rem** statement. If the **Rem** keyword follows other statements on a line, it must be separated from the statements by a colon (**:**).

You can use a apostrophe (**'**) instead of the **Rem** keyword. When you use a apostrophe, the colon is not required after other statements.

Example

This example illustrates the various forms of the **Rem** statement, which is used to include explanatory remarks in a program.

```
Rem This is the first form of the syntax.
```

The following shows the second form of the syntax.

```
Dim MyStr1, MyStr2
MyStr1 = "Hello": Rem Comment after a statement separated by a colon.
MyStr2 = "Goodbye"      ' This is also a comment; no colon is needed.
```

Remove Method

Applies To

Collection object.

Description

Removes a member from a **Collection** object.

Syntax

object.**Remove** *index*

The **Remove** method syntax has the following object qualifier and part

Part	Description
object	Required. An object expression that evaluates to an object in the Applies To list.
index	Required. An expression that specifies the position of a member of the collection. If a numeric expression, *index* must be a number from 1 to the value of the collection's **Count** property. If a string expression, *index* must correspond to the ***key*** argument specified when the member referred to was added to the collection.

Remarks

If the value provided as *index* doesn't match an existing member of the collection, an error occurs.

See Also

Add method, **Add** method ("Extensibility Object Model Language Reference"), **Item** method, **Item** method ("Extensibility Object Model Language Reference"), ItemAdded event ("Extensibility Object Model Language Reference"), ItemRemoved event ("Extensibility Object Model Language Reference").

Example

This example illustrates the use of the **Remove** method to remove objects from a **Collection** object, `MyClasses`. This code removes the object whose index is 1 on each iteration of the loop.

```
Dim Num, MyClasses
For Num = 1 To MyClasses.Count
   MyClasses.Remove 1                ' Remove the first object each time
                                     ' through the loop until there are
                                     ' no objects left in the collection.
Next Num
```

Example (Extensibility Object Model)

The example verifies that a particular member of the **VBComponents** collection is a module, and then it uses the **Remove** method to remove the module.

```
Debug.Print Application.VBE.ActiveVBProject.VBComponents(4).Name
Application.VBE.ActiveVBProject.VBComponents.Remove _
   Application.VBE.ActiveVBProject.VBComponents(4)
```

Reset Statement

Description

Closes all disk files opened using the **Open** statement.

Syntax

Reset

Remarks

The **Reset** statement closes all active files opened by the **Open** statement and writes the contents of all file buffers to disk.

See Also

Close statement, **End** statement, **Open** statement.

Example

This example uses the **Reset** statement to close all open files and write the contents of all file buffers to disk. Note the use of the **Variant** variable `FileNumber` as both a string and a number.

```
Dim FileNumber
For FileNumber = 1 To 5               ' Loop 5 times.
   ' Open file for output. FileNumber is concatenated into the string
   ' TEST for the filename, but is a number following a #.
   Open "TEST" & FileNumber For Output As #FileNumber
   Write #FileNumber, "Hello World"   ' Write data to file.
Next FileNumber
Reset                                 ' Close files and write contents
                                      ' to disk.
```

Resize Event

Applies To

UserForm object.

Description

Occurs when a user form is resized.

Syntax

Private Sub UserForm_Resize( )

Remarks

Use a Resize event procedure to move or resize controls when the parent **UserForm** is resized. You can also use this event procedure to recalculate variables or properties.

Example

The following example uses the Activate and Click events to illustrate triggering of the **UserForm**'s Resize event. As the user clicks the client area of the form, it grows or shrinks and the new height is specified in the title bar. Note that the **Tag** property is used to store the **UserForm**'s initial height.

```
' Activate event for UserForm1
Private Sub UserForm_Activate()
   UserForm1.Caption = "Click me to make me taller!"
   Tag = Height                               ' Save the initial height.
End Sub
```

```
' Click event for UserForm1
Private Sub UserForm_Click()
   Dim NewHeight As Single
   NewHeight = Height
   ' If the form is small, make it tall.
   If NewHeight = Val(Tag) Then
      Height = Val(Tag) * 2
   Else
   ' If the form is tall, make it small.
      Height = Val(Tag)
   End If
End Sub

' Resize event for UserForm1
Private Sub UserForm_Resize()
   UserForm1.Caption = "New Height: " & Height & "  " _
      & "Click to resize me!"
End Sub
```

Resume Statement

Description

Resumes execution after an error-handling routine is finished.

Syntax

Resume [0]
Resume Next
Resume *line*

The **Resume** statement syntax can have any of the following forms

Statement	Description
Resume	If the error occurred in the same procedure as the error handler, execution resumes with the statement that caused the error. If the error occurred in a called procedure, execution resumes at the statement that last called out of the procedure containing the error-handling routine.
Resume Next	If the error occurred in the same procedure as the error handler, execution resumes with the statement immediately following the statement that caused the error. If the error occurred in a called procedure, execution resumes with the statement immediately following the statement that last called out of the procedure containing the error-handling routine (or **On Error Resume Next** statement).
Resume *line*	Execution resumes at *line* specified in the required *line* argument. The *line* argument is a line label or line number and must be in the same procedure as the error handler.

Remarks

If you use a **Resume** statement anywhere except in an error-handling routine, an error occurs.

See Also

End statement, **Err** object, **Exit** statement, **On Error** statement.

Example

This example uses the **Resume** statement to end error handling in a procedure, and then resume execution with the statement that caused the error. Error number 55 is generated to illustrate using the **Resume** statement.

```
Sub ResumeStatementDemo()
   On Error GoTo ErrorHandler          ' Enable error-handling routine.
   Open "TESTFILE" For Output As #1    ' Open file for output.
   Kill "TESTFILE"                     ' Attempt to delete open file.
   Exit Sub                            ' Exit Sub to avoid error handler.
ErrorHandler:                          ' Error-handling routine.
   Select Case Err.Number              ' Evaluate error number.
      Case 55                          ' "File already open" error.
         Close #1                      ' Close open file.
      Case Else
         ' Handle other situations here....
   End Select
   Resume                              ' Resume execution at same line
                                       ' that caused the error.
End Sub
```

RGB Function

Description

Returns a **Long** whole number representing an RGB color value.

Syntax

RGB(*red*, *green*, *blue*)

The **RGB** function syntax has these named arguments.

Part	Description
red	Required; **Variant** (**Integer**). Number in the range 0–255, inclusive, that represents the red component of the color.
green	Required; **Variant** (**Integer**). Number in the range 0–255, inclusive, that represents the green component of the color.
blue	Required; **Variant** (**Integer**). Number in the range 0–255, inclusive, that represents the blue component of the color.

Remarks

Application methods and properties that accept a color specification expect that specification to be a number representing an RGB color value. An RGB color value specifies the relative intensity of red, green, and blue to cause a specific color to be displayed.

The value for any argument to **RGB** that exceeds 255 is assumed to be 255.

The following table lists some standard colors and the red, green, and blue values they include

Color	Red value	Green value	Blue value
Black	0	0	0
Blue	0	0	255
Green	0	255	0
Cyan	0	255	255
Red	255	0	0
Magenta	255	0	255
Yellow	255	255	0
White	255	255	255

See Also

QBColor function.

Specifics (Macintosh)

The RGB color values returned by this function are incompatible with those used by the Macintosh operating system. They may be used within the context of Microsoft applications for the Macintosh, but should not be used when communicating color changes directly to the Macintosh operating system.

Example

This example shows how the **RGB** function is used to return a whole number representing an **RGB** color value. It is used for those application methods and properties that accept a color specification. The object `MyObject` and its property are used for illustration purposes only. If `MyObject` does not exist, or if it does not have a Color property, an error occurs.

```
Dim RED, I, RGBValue, MyObject
Red = RGB(255, 0, 0)                    ' Return the value for Red.
I = 75                                  ' Initialize offset.
RGBValue = RGB(I, 64 + I, 128 + I)      ' Same as RGB(75, 139, 203).
MyObject.Color = RGB(255, 0, 0)         ' Set the Color property of
                                        ' MyObject to Red.
```

Example (Microsoft Excel)

This example sets the gridline color in the active window in Book1.xls to red.

```
Workbooks("BOOK1.XLS").Worksheets("Sheet1").Activate
ActiveWindow.GridlineColor = RGB(255,0,0)
```

This example sets the color of the tick labels on the value axis in Chart1 to green.

```
Charts("Chart1").Axes(xlValue).TickLabels.Font.Color = RGB(0, 255, 0)
```

This example sets the marker background and foreground colors for the second point in series one in Chart1 to green and red, respectively.

```
With Charts("Chart1").SeriesCollection(1).Points(2)
    .MarkerBackgroundColor = RGB(0,255,0)      ' Green.
    .MarkerForegroundColor = RGB(255,0,0)      ' Red.
End With
```

This example sets the interior pattern color for rectangle one on Sheet1 to red.

```
With Worksheets("Sheet1").Rectangles(1).Interior
    .Pattern = xlGrid
    .PatternColor = RGB(255,0,0)
End With
```

Right Function

Description

Returns a **Variant** (**String**) containing a specified number of characters from the right side of a string.

Syntax

Right(*string*, *length*)

The **Right** function syntax has these named arguments.

Part	Description
string	Required. String expression from which the rightmost characters are returned. If ***string*** contains **Null**, **Null** is returned.
length	Required; **Variant** (**Long**). Numeric expression indicating how many characters to return. If 0, a zero-length string ("") is returned. If greater than or equal to the number of characters in ***string***, the entire string is returned.

Remarks

To determine the number of characters in ***string***, use the **Len** function.

Note Use the **RightB** function with byte data contained in a string. Instead of specifying the number of characters to return, ***length*** specifies the number of bytes.

See Also

Left function, **Len** function, **Mid** function.

Example

This example uses the **Right** function to return a specified number of characters from the right side of a string.

```
Dim AnyString, MyStr
AnyString = "Hello World"                        ' Define string.
MyStr = Right(AnyString, 1)                      ' Returns "d".
MyStr = Right(AnyString, 6)                      ' Returns " World".
MyStr = Right(AnyString, 20)                     ' Returns "Hello World".
```

RmDir Statement

Description

Removes an existing directory or folder.

Syntax

RmDir *path*

The required *path* argument is a string expression that identifies the directory or folder to be removed. The *path* may include the drive. If no drive is specified, **RmDir** removes the directory or folder on the current drive.

Remarks

An error occurs if you try to use **RmDir** on a directory or folder containing files. Use the **Kill** statement to delete all files before attempting to remove a directory or folder.

See Also

ChDir statement, **CurDir** function, **Kill** statement, **MkDir** statement.

Example

This example uses the **RmDir** statement to remove an existing directory or folder.

```
' Assume that MYDIR is an empty directory or folder.
RmDir "MYDIR"                                    ' Remove MYDIR.
```

Rnd Function

Description

Returns a **Single** containing a random number.

Syntax

Rnd[(*number*)]

The optional *number* argument is a **Single** or any valid numeric expression.

Return Values

If *number* is	Rnd generates
Less than zero	The same number every time, using *number* as the seed.
Greater than zero	The next random number in the sequence.
Equal to zero	The most recently generated number.
Not supplied	The next random number in the sequence.

Remarks

The **Rnd** function returns a value less than 1 but greater than or equal to zero.

The value of *number* determines how **Rnd** generates a random number:

For any given initial seed, the same number sequence is generated because each successive call to the **Rnd** function uses the previous number as a seed for the next number in the sequence.

Before calling **Rnd**, use the **Randomize** statement without an argument to initialize the random-number generator with a seed based on the system timer.

To produce random integers in a given range, use this formula:

```
Int((upperbound - lowerbound + 1) * Rnd + lowerbound)
```

Here, *upperbound* is the highest number in the range, and *lowerbound* is the lowest number in the range.

Note To repeat sequences of random numbers, call **Rnd** with a negative argument immediately before using **Randomize** with a numeric argument. Using **Randomize** with the same value for *number* does not repeat the previous sequence.

See Also

Randomize statement, **Timer** function.

Example

This example uses the **Rnd** function to generate a random integer value from 1 to 6.

```
Dim MyValue
MyValue = Int((6 * Rnd) + 1)    ' Generate random value between 1 and 6.
```

RSet Statement

Description

Right aligns a string within a string variable.

Syntax

RSet *stringvar* = *string*

The **RSet** statement syntax has these parts.

Part	Description
stringvar	Required. Name of string variable.
string	Required. String expression to be right-aligned within *stringvar*.

Remarks

If *stringvar* is longer than *string*, **RSet** replaces any leftover characters in *stringvar* with spaces, back to its beginning.

Note **RSet** can't be used with user-defined types.

See Also

Data type summary, **LSet** statement.

Example

This example uses the **RSet** statement to right align a string within a string variable.

```
Dim MyString
MyString = "0123456789"              ' Initialize string.
Rset MyString = "Right->"            ' MyString contains "   Right->".
```

RTrim Function

See LTrim, RTrim, and Trim Functions.

SaveSetting Statement

Description

Saves or creates an application entry in the Windows registry.

Syntax

SaveSetting ***appname*****,** ***section*****,** ***key*****,** ***setting***

The **SaveSetting** statement syntax has these named arguments.

Part	Description
appname	Required. String expression containing the name of the application or project to which the setting applies.
section	Required. String expression containing the name of the section where the key setting is being saved.
key	Required. String expression containing the name of the key setting being saved.
setting	Required. Expression containing the value that ***key*** is being set to.

Remarks

An error occurs if the key setting can't be saved for any reason.

See Also

DeleteSetting statement, **GetAllSettings** function, **GetSetting** function.

Example

The following example first uses the **SaveSetting** statement to make entries in the Windows registry (or .ini file on 16-bit Windows platforms) for the `MyApp` application, and then uses the **DeleteSetting** statement to remove them.

```
' Place some settings in the registry.
SaveSetting appname := "MyApp", section := "Startup", _
   key := "Top", setting := 75
SaveSetting "MyApp","Startup", "Left", 50
' Remove section and all its settings from registry.
DeleteSetting "MyApp", "Startup"
```

Second Function

Description

Returns a **Variant** (**Integer**) specifying a whole number between 0 and 59, inclusive, representing the second of the minute.

Syntax

Second(*time***)**

The required *time* argument is any **Variant**, numeric expression, string expression, or any combination, that can represent a time. If *time* contains **Null**, **Null** is returned.

See Also

Day function, **Hour** function, **Minute** function, **Now** function, **Time** function, **Time** statement.

Example

This example uses the **Second** function to obtain the second of the minute from a specified time. In the development environment, the time literal is displayed in short time format using the locale settings of your code.

```
Dim MyTime, MySecond
MyTime = #4:35:17 PM#                       ' Assign a time.
MySecond = Second(MyTime)                   ' MySecond contains 17.
```

Seek Function

Description

Returns a **Long** specifying the current read/write position within a file opened using the **Open** statement.

Syntax

Seek(*filenumber***)**

The required *filenumber* argument is an **Integer** containing a valid file number.

Remarks

Seek returns a value between 1 and 2,147,483,647 (equivalent to 2^31–1), inclusive.

The following describes the return values for each file access mode.

Mode	Return Value
Random	Number of the next record read or written.
Binary, **Output**, **Append**, **Input**	Byte position at which the next operation takes place. The first byte in a file is at position 1, the second byte is at position 2, and so on.

See Also

Get statement, **Loc** function, **Open** statement, **Put** statement, **Seek** statement.

Example

This example uses the **Seek** function to return the current file position. The example assumes `TESTFILE` is a file containing records of the user-defined type `Record`.

```
Type Record                             ' Define user-defined type.
   ID As Integer
   Name As String * 20
End Type
```

For files opened in Random mode, **Seek** returns number of next record.

```
Dim MyRecord As Record                  ' Declare variable.
Open "TESTFILE" For Random As #1 Len = Len(MyRecord)
Do While Not EOF(1)                     ' Loop until end of file.
   Get #1, , MyRecord                   ' Read next record.
   Debug.Print Seek(1)                  ' Print record number to Debug
                                        ' window.
Loop
Close #1                                ' Close file.
```

For files opened in modes other than Random mode, **Seek** returns the byte position at which the next operation takes place. Assume `TESTFILE` is a file containing a few lines of text.

```
Dim MyChar
Open "TESTFILE" For Input As #1         ' Open file for reading.
Do While Not EOF(1)                     ' Loop until end of file.
   MyChar = Input(1, #1)                ' Read next character of data.
   Debug.Print Seek(1)                  ' Print byte position to Debug
                                        ' window.
Loop
Close #1                                ' Close file.
```

Seek Statement

Description

Sets the position for the next read/write operation within a file opened using the **Open** statement.

Syntax

Seek [#]*filenumber*, *position*

The **Seek** statement syntax has these parts:

Part	Description
filenumber	Required. Any valid file number.
position	Required. Number in the range 1–2,147,483,647, inclusive, that indicates where the next read/write operation should occur.

Remarks

Record numbers specified in **Get** and **Put** statements override file positioning performed by **Seek**.

Performing a file-write operation after a **Seek** operation beyond the end of a file extends the file. If you attempt a **Seek** operation to a negative or zero position, an error occurs.

See Also

Get statement, **Loc** function, **Open** statement, **Put** statement, **Seek** function.

Example

This example uses the **Seek** statement to set the position for the next read or write within a file. This example assumes `TESTFILE` is a file containing records of the user-defined type `Record`.

```
Type Record                                   ' Define user-defined type.
   ID As Integer
   Name As String * 20
End Type
```

For files opened in Random mode, **Seek** sets the next record.

```
Dim MyRecord As Record, MaxSize, RecordNumber        ' Declare variables.
' Open file in random-file mode.
Open "TESTFILE" For Random As #1 Len = Len(MyRecord)
MaxSize = LOF(1) \ Len(MyRecord)              ' Get number of records in file.
' The loop reads all records starting from the last.
For RecordNumber = MaxSize To 1 Step - 1
   Seek #1, RecordNumber                      ' Set position.
   Get #1, , MyRecord                         ' Read record.
Next RecordNumber
Close #1                                      ' Close file.
```

For files opened in modes other than Random mode, **Seek** sets the byte position at which the next operation takes place. Assume `TESTFILE` is a file containing a few lines of text.

```
Dim MaxSize, NextChar, MyChar
Open "TESTFILE" For Input As #1               ' Open file for input.
MaxSize = LOF(1)                              ' Get size of file in bytes.
' The loop reads all characters starting from the last.
For NextChar = MaxSize To 1 Step -1
   Seek #1, NextChar                          ' Set position.
   MyChar = Input(1, #1)                      ' Read character.
Next NextChar
Close #1                                      ' Close file.
```

Select Case Statement

Description

Executes one of several groups of statements, depending on the value of an expression.

Syntax

Select Case *testexpression*
  [**Case** *expressionlist-n*
    [*statements-n*]] . . .
  [**Case Else**
    [*elsestatements*]]
End Select

The **Select Case** statement syntax has these parts:

Part	Description
testexpression	Required. Any numeric expression or string expression.
expressionlist-n	Required if a **Case** appears. Delimited list of one or more of the following forms: *expression*, *expression* **To** *expression*, **Is** *comparisonoperator expression*. The **To** keyword specifies a range of values. If you use the **To** keyword, the smaller value must appear before **To**. Use the **Is** keyword with comparison operators (except **Is** and **Like**) to specify a range of values. If not supplied, the **Is** keyword is automatically inserted.
statements-n	Optional. One or more statements executed if *testexpression* matches any part of *expressionlist-n*.
elsestatements	Optional. One or more statements executed if *testexpression* doesn't match any of the **Case** clause.

Remarks

If *testexpression* matches any **Case** *expressionlist* expression, the *statements* following that **Case** clause are executed up to the next **Case** clause, or, for the last clause, up to **End Select**. Control then passes to the statement following **End Select**. If *testexpression* matches an *expressionlist* expression in more than one **Case** clause, only the statements following the first match are executed.

The **Case Else** clause is used to indicate the *elsestatements* to be executed if no match is found between the *testexpression* and an *expressionlist* in any of the other **Case** selections. Although not required, it is a good idea to have a **Case Else** statement in your **Select Case** block to handle unforeseen *testexpression* values. If no **Case** *expressionlist* matches *testexpression* and there is no **Case Else** statement, execution continues at the statement following **End Select**.

You can use multiple expressions or ranges in each **Case** clause. For example, the following line is valid:

```
Case 1 To 4, 7 To 9, 11, 13, Is > MaxNumber
```

Note The **Is** comparison operator is not the same as the **Is** keyword used in the **Select Case** statement.

You also can specify ranges and multiple expressions for character strings. In the following example, **Case** matches strings that are exactly equal to `everything`, strings that fall between `nuts` and `soup` in alphabetic order, and the current value of `TestItem`:

```
Case "everything", "nuts" To "soup", TestItem
```

Select Case statements can be nested. Each nested **Select Case** statement must have a matching **End Select** statement.

See Also

Choose function, **End** statement, **If...Then...Else** statement, **On...GoSub**, **On...GoTo** statements.

Example

This example uses the **Select Case** statement to evaluate the value of a variable. The second **Case** clause contains the value of the variable being evaluated, and therefore only the statement associated with it is executed.

```
Dim Number
Number = 8                                    ' Initialize variable.
Select Case Number                            ' Evaluate Number.
Case 1 To 5                                   ' Number between 1 and 5.
   Debug.Print "Between 1 and 5"
' The following is the only Case clause that evaluates to True.
Case 6, 7, 8                                  ' Number between 6 and 8.
   Debug.Print "Between 6 and 8"
Case Is > 8 And Number < 11                   ' Number is 9 or 10.
Debug.Print "Greater than 8"
Case Else                                     ' Other values.
   Debug.Print "Not between 1 and 10"
End Select
```

Example (Microsoft Excel)

This example displays the name of the mail system installed on the computer.

```
Select Case Application.MailSystem
   Case Is = xlMAPI
      MsgBox "Mail system is Microsoft Mail"
   Case Is = xlPowerTalk
      MsgBox "Mail system is PowerTalk"
   Case Is = xlNoMailSystem
      MsgBox "No mail system installed"
End Select
```

This example displays a message box that indicates the location of the active cell in the PivotTable.

```
Worksheets("Sheet1").Activate
Select Case ActiveCell.LocationInTable
Case Is = xlRowHeader
   MsgBox "Active cell is part of a row header"
Case Is = xlColumnHeader
   MsgBox "Active cell is part of a column header"
Case Is = xlPageHeader
   MsgBox "Active cell is part of a page header"
Case Is = xlDataHeader
   MsgBox "Active cell is part of a data header"
Case Is = xlRowItem
   MsgBox "Active cell is part of a row item"
Case Is = xlColumnItem
   MsgBox "Active cell is part of a column item"
Case Is = xlPageItem
   MsgBox "Active cell is part of a page item"
Case Is = xlDataItem
   MsgBox "Active cell is part of a data item"
Case Is = xlTableBody
   MsgBox "Active cell is part of the table body"
End Select
```

This example displays a message if the active cell on Sheet1 contains a cell error value. You can use this example as a framework for a cell-error-value error handler.

```
Worksheets("Sheet1").Activate
If IsError(ActiveCell.Value) Then
   errval = ActiveCell.Value
   Select Case errval
      Case CVErr(xlErrDiv0)
         MsgBox "#DIV/0! error"
      Case CVErr(xlErrNA)
         MsgBox "#N/A error"
      Case CVErr(xlErrName)
         MsgBox "#NAME? error"
      Case CVErr(xlErrNull)
         MsgBox "#NULL! error"
      Case CVErr(xlErrNum)
         MsgBox "#NUM! error"
      Case CVErr(xlErrRef)
         MsgBox "#REF! error"
      Case CVErr(xlErrValue)
         MsgBox "#VALUE! error"
      Case Else
         MsgBox "This should never happen!!"
   End Select
End If
```

SendKeys Statement

Description

Sends one or more keystrokes to the active window as if typed at the keyboard.

Syntax

SendKeys ***string***[, ***wait***]

The **SendKeys** statement syntax has these named arguments:

Part	Description
string	Required. String expression specifying the keystrokes to send.
wait	Optional. **Boolean** value specifying the wait mode. If **False** (default), control is returned to the procedure immediately after the keys are sent. If **True**, keystrokes must be processed before control is returned to the procedure.

Remarks

Each key is represented by one or more characters. To specify a single keyboard character, use the character itself. For example, to represent the letter A, use `"A"` for ***string***. To represent more than one character, append each additional character to the one preceding it. To represent the letters A, B, and C, use `"ABC"` for ***string***.

The plus sign (+), caret (^), percent sign (%), tilde (~), and parentheses ( ) have special meanings to **SendKeys**. To specify one of these characters, enclose it within braces ({}). For example, to specify the plus sign, use `{+}`. Brackets ([ ]) have no special meaning to **SendKeys**, but you must enclose them in braces. In other applications, brackets do have a special meaning that may be significant when dynamic data exchange (DDE) occurs. To specify brace characters, use `{{}` and `{}}`.

To specify characters that aren't displayed when you press a key, such as ENTER or TAB, and keys that represent actions rather than characters, use the codes shown below:

Key	Code
BACKSPACE	`{BACKSPACE}`, `{BS}`, or `{BKSP}`
BREAK	`{BREAK}`
CAPS LOCK	`{CAPSLOCK}`
DEL or DELETE	`{DELETE}` or `{DEL}`
DOWN ARROW	`{DOWN}`
END	`{END}`
ENTER	`{ENTER}` or ~
ESC	`{ESC}`
HELP	`{HELP}`
HOME	`{HOME}`

(continued)

INS or INSERT	`{INSERT}` or `{INS}`
LEFT ARROW	`{LEFT}`
NUM LOCK	`{NUMLOCK}`
PAGE DOWN	`{PGDN}`
PAGE UP	`{PGUP}`
PRINT SCREEN	`{PRTSC}`
RIGHT ARROW	`{RIGHT}`
SCROLL LOCK	`{SCROLLLOCK}`
TAB	`{TAB}`
UP ARROW	`{UP}`
F1	`{F1}`
F2	`{F2}`
F3	`{F3}`
F4	`{F4}`
F5	`{F5}`
F6	`{F6}`
F7	`{F7}`
F8	`{F8}`
F9	`{F9}`
F10	`{F10}`
F11	`{F11}`
F12	`{F12}`
F13	`{F13}`
F14	`{F14}`
F15	`{F15}`
F16	`{F16}`

To specify keys combined with any combination of the SHIFT, CTRL, and ALT keys, precede the key code with one or more of the following codes:

Key	Code
SHIFT	`+`
CTRL	`^`
ALT	`%`

To specify that any combination of SHIFT, CTRL, and ALT should be held down while several other keys are pressed, enclose the code for those keys in parentheses. For example, to specify to hold down SHIFT while E and C are pressed, use "`+(EC)`". To specify to hold down SHIFT while E is pressed, followed by C without SHIFT, use "`+EC`".

To specify repeating keys, use the form `{key number}`. You must put a space between `key` and `number`. For example, `{LEFT 42}` means press the LEFT ARROW key 42 times; `{h 10}` means press H 10 times.

Note You can't use **SendKeys** to send keystrokes to an application that is not designed to run in Microsoft Windows. **SendKeys** also can't send the PRINT SCREEN key `{PRTSC}` to any application.

See Also

AppActivate statement, **DoEvents** function.

Example

This example uses the **Shell** function to run the Calculator application included with Microsoft Windows. It uses the **SendKeys** statement to send keystrokes to add some numbers, and then quit the Calculator. The **SendKeys** statement is not available on the Macintosh. (To see the example, paste it into a procedure, then run the procedure. Because **AppActivate** changes the focus to the Calculator application, you can't single step through the code.)

```
Dim ReturnValue, I
ReturnValue = Shell("CALC.EXE", 1)    ' Run Calculator.
AppActivate ReturnValue               ' Activate the Calculator.
For I = 1 To 100                      ' Set up counting loop.
   SendKeys I & "{+}", True           ' Send keystrokes to Calculator
Next I                                ' to add each value of I.
SendKeys "=", True                    ' Get grand total.
SendKeys "%{F4}", True                ' Send ALT+F4 to close Calculator.
```

Set Statement

Description

Assigns an object reference to a variable or property.

Syntax

Set *objectvar* = {[**New**] *objectexpression* | **Nothing**}

The **Set** statement syntax has these parts:

Part	Description
objectvar	Required. Name of the variable or property; follows standard variable naming conventions.
New	Optional. **New** is usually used during declaration to enable implicit object creation. When **New** is used with **Set**, it creates a new instance of the class. If *objectvar* contained a reference to an object, that reference is released when the new one is assigned. The **New** keyword can't be used to create new instances of any intrinsic data type and can't be used to create dependent objects.

(continued)

objectexpression	Required. Expression consisting of the name of an object, another declared variable of the same object type, or a function or method that returns an object of the same object type.
Nothing	Optional. Discontinues association of *objectvar* with any specific object. Assigning **Nothing** to *objectvar* releases all the system and memory resources associated with the previously referenced object when no other variable refers to it.

Remarks

To be valid, *objectvar* must be an object type consistent with the object being assigned to it.

The **Dim**, **Private**, **Public**, **ReDim**, and **Static** statements only declare a variable that refers to an object. No actual object is referred to until you use the **Set** statement to assign a specific object.

The following example illustrates how **Dim** is used to declare an array with the type `Form1`. No instance of `Form1` actually exists. **Set** then assigns references to new instances of `Form1` to the `myChildForms` variable. Such code might be used to create child forms in an MDI application.

```
Dim myChildForms(1 to 4) As Form1
Set myChildForms(1) = New Form1
Set myChildForms(2) = New Form1
Set myChildForms(3) = New Form1
Set myChildForms(4) = New Form1
```

Generally, when you use **Set** to assign an object reference to a variable, no copy of the object is created for that variable. Instead, a reference to the object is created. More than one object variable can refer to the same object. Because such variables are references to the object rather than copies of the object, any change in the object is reflected in all variables that refer to it. However, when you use the **New** keyword in the **Set** statement, you are actually creating an instance of the object.

See Also

Dim statement, **Let** statement, **Private** statement, **Public** statement, **ReDim** statement, **Static** statement.

Example

This example uses the **Set** statement to assign object references to variables. `YourObject` is assumed to be a valid object with a **Text** property.

```
Dim YourObject, MyObject, MyStr
Set MyObject = YourObject                   ' Assign object reference.
' MyObject and YourObject refer to the same object.
YourObject.Text = "Hello World"             ' Initialize property.
MyStr = MyObject.Text                       ' Returns "Hello World".

' Discontinue association. MyObject no longer refers to YourObject.
Set MyObject = Nothing                      ' Release the object.
```

Example (Microsoft Excel)

This example adds a new worksheet to the active workbook and then sets the name of the worksheet.

```
Set newSheet = Worksheets.Add
newSheet.Name = "1995 Budget"
```

This example creates a new worksheet and then inserts into it a list of all the names in the active workbook, including their formulas in A1-style notation in the language of the user.

```
Set newSheet = ActiveWorkbook.Worksheets.Add
i = 1
For Each nm In ActiveWorkbook.Names
   newSheet.Cells(i, 1).Value = nm.NameLocal
   newSheet.Cells(i, 2).Value = "'" & nm.RefersToLocal
   i = i + 1
Next
```

SetAttr Statement

Description

Sets attribute information for a file.

Syntax

SetAttr ***pathname*****,** ***attributes***

The **SetAttr** statement syntax has these named arguments:

Part	Description
pathname	Required. String expression that specifies a file name—may include directory or folder, and drive.
attributes	Required. Constant or numeric expression, whose sum specifies file attributes.

Settings

The ***attributes*** argument settings are:

Constant	Value	Description
vbNormal	0	Normal (default).
vbReadOnly	1	Read-only.
vbHidden	2	Hidden.
vbSystem	4	System file.
vbArchive	32	File has changed since last backup.

Note These constants are specified by Visual Basic for Applications. The names can be used anywhere in your code in place of the actual values.

Remarks

A run-time error occurs if you try to set the attributes of an open file.

See Also

FileAttr function, **GetAttr** function.

Specifics (Macintosh)

The following constants aren't available on the Macintosh:

Constant	Value	Description
vbSystem	4	System file.
vbArchive	32	File has changed since last backup.

The following constant is available only on the Macintosh.

Constant	Value	Description
vbAlias	64	Specified file name is an alias.

Example

This example uses the **SetAttr** statement to set attributes for a file.

```
SetAttr "TESTFILE", vbHidden                ' Set hidden attribute.
SetAttr "TESTFILE", vbHidden + vbReadOnly   ' Set hidden and read-only
                                            ' attributes.
```

Sgn Function

Description

Returns a **Variant** (**Integer**) indicating the sign of a number.

Syntax

Sgn(*number***)**

The required *number* argument can be any valid numeric expression.

Return Values

If *number* is	Sgn returns
Greater than zero	1
Equal to zero	0
Less than zero	–1

Remarks

The sign of the *number* argument determines the return value of the **Sgn** function.

See Also

Abs function.

Example

This example uses the **Sgn** function to determine the sign of a number.

```
Dim MyVar1, MyVar2, MyVar3, MySign
MyVar1 = 12: MyVar2 = -2.4: MyVar3 = 0
MySign = Sgn(MyVar1)                              ' Returns 1.
MySign = Sgn(MyVar2)                              ' Returns -1.
MySign = Sgn(MyVar3)                              ' Returns 0.
```

Shell Function

Description

Runs an executable program and returns a **Variant** (**Double**) representing the program's task ID if successful, otherwise it returns zero.

Syntax

Shell(*pathname*[,*windowstyle*])

The **Shell** function syntax has these named arguments:

Part	Description
pathname	Required; **Variant** (**String**). Name of the program to execute and any required arguments or command-line switches; may include directory or folder and drive.
windowstyle	Optional. **Variant** (**Integer**) corresponding to the style of the window in which the program is to be run. If ***windowstyle*** is omitted, the program is started minimized with focus.

The ***windowstyle*** named argument has these values:

Constant	Value	Description
vbHide	0	Window is hidden and focus is passed to the hidden window.
vbNormalFocus	1	Window has focus and is restored to its original size and position.
vbMinimizedFocus	2	Window is displayed as an icon with focus.
vbMaximizedFocus	3	Window is maximized with focus.
vbNormalNoFocus	4	Window is restored to its most recent size and position. The currently active window remains active.
vbMinimizedNoFocus	6	Window is displayed as an icon. The currently active window remains active.

Remarks

If the **Shell** function successfully executes the named file, it returns the task ID of the started program. The task ID is a unique number that identifies the running program. If the **Shell** function can't start the named program, an error occurs. If you use the **MacID** function with **Shell** in Microsoft Windows, an error occurs.

Note The **Shell** function runs other programs asynchronously. This means that a program started with **Shell** might not finish executing before the statements following the **Shell** function are executed.

See Also

AppActivate statement, **MacID** function.

Specifics (Macintosh)

The **Shell** function syntax has these named arguments:

Part	Description
pathname	On the Macintosh, you can use the **MacID** function to specify an application's signature instead of its name. The following example uses the signature for Microsoft Word: `Shell MacID("MSWD")`
windowstyle	On the Macintosh (System 7.0 or later), ***windowstyle*** only determines whether or not the application gets the focus when it is run.

The **vbHide** constant is not applicable on Apple Macintosh platforms.

Example

This example uses the **Shell** function to run an application specified by the user. On the Macintosh, using the **MacID** function ensures that the application can be launched even if the file name of the application has been changed. The **Shell** function is not available on Macintosh versions earlier than System 7.0.

```
' In Microsoft Windows:
' Specifying 1 as the second argument opens the application in
' normal size and gives it the focus.
Dim RetVal
RetVal = Shell("C:\WINDOWS\CALC.EXE", 1)      ' Run Calculator.

' On the Macintosh:
' Both statements launch Microsoft Excel.
RetVal = Shell("Microsoft Excel")              ' Specify filename.
RetVal = Shell(MacID("XCEL"))                  ' Specify signature.
```

Show Method

Applies To

CodePane object, **UserForm** object.

Description

Displays a **UserForm** object.

Syntax

[*object*.]**Show**

The optional *object* is an object expression that evaluates to an object in the Applies To list. If *object* is omitted, the **UserForm** associated with the active **UserForm** module is assumed to be *object.*

Remarks

If the specified object isn't loaded when the **Show** method is invoked, Visual Basic automatically loads it.

A **UserForm** is always modal; therefore, the user must respond before using any other part of the application. No subsequent code is executed until the **UserForm** is hidden or unloaded.

Although other forms in the application are disabled when a **UserForm** is displayed, other applications are not.

See Also

Hide method, **Load** statement, **Unload** statement.

Example

The following example assumes two **UserForms** in a program. In UserForm1's Initialize event, UserForm2 is loaded and shown. When the user clicks UserForm2, it is hidden and UserForm1 appears. When UserForm1 is clicked, UserForm2 is shown again.

```
' This is the Initialize event procedure for UserForm1.
Private Sub UserForm_Initialize()
   Load UserForm2
   UserForm2.Show
End Sub
' This is the Click event for UserForm2.
Private Sub UserForm_Click()
   UserForm2.Hide
End Sub

' This is the click event for UserForm1.
Private Sub UserForm_Click()
   UserForm2.Show
End Sub
```

Example (Extensibility Object Model)

The following example uses the **Show** method to move the specified code pane to the foreground.

```
Application.VBE.CodePanes(2).Show
```

Sin Function

Description

Returns a **Double** specifying the sine of an angle.

Syntax

Sin(*number*)

The required *number* argument is a **Double** or any valid numeric expression that expresses an angle in radians.

Remarks

The **Sin** function takes an angle and returns the ratio of two sides of a right triangle. The ratio is the length of the side opposite the angle divided by the length of the hypotenuse.

The result lies in the range –1 to 1.

To convert degrees to radians, multiply degrees by pi/180. To convert radians to degrees, multiply radians by 180/pi.

See Also

Atn function, **Cos** function, **Tan** function.

Example

This example uses the **Sin** function to return the sine of an angle.

```
Dim MyAngle, MyCosecant
MyAngle = 1.3                                ' Define angle in radians.
MyCosecant = 1 / Sin(MyAngle)                ' Calculate cosecant.
```

Single Data Type

Description

Single (single-precision floating-point) variables are stored as IEEE 32-bit (4-byte) floating-point numbers, ranging in value from –3.402823E38 to –1.401298E–45 for negative values and from 1.401298E–45 to 3.402823E38 for positive values. The type-declaration character for **Single** is the exclamation point (**!**).

See Also

Data type summary, **Def***type* statements, **Double** data type, **Variant** data type.

SLN Function

Description

Returns a **Double** specifying the straight-line depreciation of an asset for a single period.

Syntax

SLN(*cost, salvage, life*)

The **SLN** function has these named arguments:

Part	Description
cost	Required. **Double** specifying initial cost of the asset.
salvage	Required. **Double** specifying value of the asset at the end of its useful life.
life	Required. **Double** specifying length of the useful life of the asset.

Remarks

The depreciation period must be expressed in the same unit as the ***life*** argument. All arguments must be positive numbers.

See Also

DDB function, **FV** function, **IPmt** function, **IRR** function, **MIRR** function, **NPer** function, **NPV** function, **Pmt** function, **PPmt** function, **PV** function, **Rate** function, **SYD** function.

Example

This example uses the **SLN** function to return the straight-line depreciation of an asset for a single period given the asset's initial cost (`InitCost`), the salvage value at the end of the asset's useful life (`SalvageVal`), and the total life of the asset in years (`LifeTime`).

```
Dim Fmt, InitCost, SalvageVal, MonthLife, LifeTime, PDepr
Const YEARMONTHS = 12                   ' Number of months in a year.
Fmt = "###,##0.00"                      ' Define money format.
InitCost = InputBox("What's the initial cost of the asset?")
SalvageVal = InputBox("What's the asset's value at the end of its " _
   & "useful life?")
MonthLife = InputBox("What's the asset's useful life in months?")
Do While MonthLife < YEARMONTHS         ' Ensure period is >= 1 year.
   MsgBox "Asset life must be a year or more."
   MonthLife = InputBox("What's the asset's useful life in months?")
Loop
LifeTime = MonthLife / YEARMONTHS       ' Convert months to years.
If LifeTime <> Int(MonthLife / YEARMONTHS) Then
   LifeTime = Int(LifeTime + 1)         ' Round up to nearest year.
End If
PDepr = SLN(InitCost, SalvageVal, LifeTime)
MsgBox "The depreciation is " & Format(PDepr, Fmt) & " per year."
```

Source Property

Applies To

Err object.

Description

Returns or sets a string expression specifying the name of the object or application that originally generated the error. Read/write.

Remarks

The **Source** property specifies a string expression representing the object that generated the error; the expression is usually the object's class name or programmatic ID. Use **Source** to provide information when your code is unable to handle an error generated in an accessed object. For example, if you access Microsoft Excel and it generates a `Division by zero` error, Microsoft Excel sets **Err.Number** to its error code for that error and sets **Source** to Excel.Application.

When generating an error from code, **Source** is your application's programmatic ID. For class modules, **Source** should contain a name having the form *project.class*. When an unexpected error occurs in your code, the **Source** property is automatically filled in. For errors in a standard module, **Source** contains the project name. For errors in a class module, **Source** contains a name with the *project.class* form.

See Also

Description property, **Err** object, **GetObject** function, **HelpContext** property, **HelpContextID** property ("Extensibility Object Model Language Reference"), **HelpFile** property, **LastDLLError** property, **Number** property, **On Error** statement.

Example

This example assigns the Programmatic ID of an Automation object created in Visual Basic to the variable `MyObjectID`, and then assigns that to the **Source** property of the **Err** object when it generates an error with the **Raise** method. When handling errors, you should not use the **Source** property (or any **Err** properties other than **Number**) programatically. The only valid use of properties other than **Number** is for displaying rich information to an end user in cases where you can't handle an error. The example assumes that `App` and `MyClass` are valid references.

```
Dim MyClass, MyObjectID, MyHelpFile, MyHelpContext
' An object of type MyClass generates an error and fills all Err object
' properties, including Source, which receives MyObjectID, which is a
' combination of the Title property of the App object and the Name
' property of the MyClass object.
MyObjectID = App.Title & "." & MyClass.Name
Err.Raise Number := vbObjectError + 894, Source := MyObjectID, _
   Description := "Was not able to complete your task", _
   HelpFile := MyHelpFile, HelpContext := MyHelpContext
```

Space Function

Description

Returns a **Variant** (**String**) consisting of the specified number of spaces.

Syntax

Space(*number*)

The required *number* argument is the number of spaces you want in the string.

Remarks

The **Space** function is useful for formatting output and clearing data in fixed-length strings.

See Also

Spc function, **String** function.

Example

This example uses the **Space** function to return a string consisting of a specified number of spaces.

```
Dim MyString
' Returns a string with 10 spaces.
MyString = Space(10)

' Insert 10 spaces between two strings.
MyString = "Hello" & Space(10) & "World"
```

Spc Function

Description

Used with the **Print #** statement or the **Print** method to position output.

Syntax

Spc(*n*)

The required *n* argument is the number of spaces to insert before displaying or printing the next expression in a list.

Remarks

If *n* is less than the output line width, the next print position immediately follows the number of spaces printed. If *n* is greater than the output line width, **Spc** calculates the next print position using the formula:

currentprintposition + (*n* **Mod** *width*)

For example, if the current print position is 24, the output line width is 80, and you specify **Spc**(90), the next print will start at position 34 (current print position + the remainder of 90/80). If the difference between the current print position and the output line width is less than *n* (or *n* **Mod** *width*), the **Spc** function skips to the beginning of the next line and generates spaces equal to *n* – (*width* – *currentprintposition*).

Note Make sure your tabular columns are wide enough to accommodate wide letters.

When you use the **Print** method with a proportionally spaced font, the width of space characters printed using the **Spc** function is always an average of the width of all characters in the point size for the chosen font. However, there is no correlation between the number of characters printed and the number of fixed-width columns those characters occupy. For example, the uppercase letter W occupies more than one fixed-width column and the lowercase letter i occupies less than one fixed-width column.

See Also

Mod operator, **Print** # statement, **Print** method, **Space** function, **Tab** function, **Width** # statement.

Example

This example uses the **Spc** function to position output in a file and in the **Debug** window.

```
' The Spc function can be used with the Print # statement.
Open "TESTFILE" For Output As #1              ' Open file for output.
Print #1, "10 spaces between here"; Spc(10); "and here."
Close #1                                      ' Close file.
```

The following statement causes the text to be printed in the **Debug** window (using the **Print** method), preceded by 30 spaces.

```
Debug.Print Spc(30); "Thirty spaces later..."
```

Sqr Function

Description

Returns a **Double** specifying the square root of a number.

Syntax

Sqr(*number*)

The required *number* argument is a **Double** or any valid numeric expression greater than or equal to zero.

Example

This example uses the **Sqr** function to calculate the square root of a number.

```
Dim MySqr
MySqr = Sqr(4)                              ' Returns 2.
MySqr = Sqr(23)                             ' Returns 4.79583152331272.
MySqr = Sqr(0)                              ' Returns 0.
MySqr = Sqr(-4)                             ' Generates a run-time error.
```

StartUpPosition Property

Applies To

UserForm object.

Description

Returns or sets a value specifying the position of a **UserForm** when it first appears.

You can use one of four settings for **StartUpPosition**:

Setting	Value	Description
Manual	0	No initial setting specified.
CenterOwner	1	Center on the item to which the **UserForm** belongs.
CenterScreen	2	Center on the whole screen.
Windows Default	3	Position in upper-left corner of screen.

Remarks

You can set the **StartUpPosition** property programmatically or from the **Properties** window.

See Also

Load statement.

Example

The following example uses the **Load** statement and the **Show** method in UserForm1's Click event to load UserForm2 with the **StartUpPosition** property set to 3 (the Windows default position). The **Show** method then makes UserForm2 visible.

```
Private Sub UserForm_Click()
    Load UserForm2
    UserForm2.StartUpPosition = 3
    UserForm2.Show
End Sub
```

Static Statement

Description

Used at procedure level to declare variables and allocate storage space. Variables declared with the **Static** statement retain their values as long as the code is running.

Syntax

Static *varname*[([*subscripts*])] [**As** [**New**] *type*] [**,** *varname*[([*subscripts*])]
↳ [**As** [**New**] *type*]] **. . .**

The **Static** statement syntax has these parts:

Part	Description
varname	Required. Name of the variable; follows standard variable naming conventions.
subscripts	Optional. Dimensions of an array variable; up to 60 multiple dimensions may be declared. The *subscripts* argument uses the following syntax: [*lower* **To**] *upper* [,[*lower* **To**] *upper*] **. . .** When not explicitly stated in *lower*, the lower bound of an array is controlled by the **Option Base** statement. The lower bound is zero if no **Option Base** statement is present.
New	Optional. Keyword that enables implicit creation of an object. If you use **New** when declaring the object variable, a new instance of the object is created on first reference to it, so you don't have to use the **Set** statement to assign the object reference. The **New** keyword can't be used to declare variables of any intrinsic data type and can't be used to declare instances of dependent objects.
type	Optional. Data type of the variable; may be **Byte**, **Boolean**, **Integer**, **Long**, **Currency**, **Single**, **Double**, **Decimal** (not currently supported), **Date**, **String**, (for variable-length strings), **String** * *length* (for fixed-length strings), **Object**, **Variant**, a user-defined type, or an object type. Use a separate **As** *type* clause for each variable being defined.

Remarks

Once module code is running, variables declared with the **Static** statement retain their value until the module is reset or restarted. Use the **Static** statement in nonstatic procedures to explicitly declare variables that are visible only within the procedure, but whose lifetime is the same as the module in which the procedure is defined.

Use a **Static** statement within a procedure to declare the data type of a variable that retains its value between procedure calls. For example, the following statement declares a fixed-size array of integers:

```
Static EmployeeNumber(200) As Integer
```

The following statement declares a variable for a new instance of a worksheet:

```
Static X As New Worksheet
```

If the **New** keyword is not used when declaring an object variable, the variable that refers to the object must be assigned an existing object using the **Set** statement before it can be used. Until it is assigned an object, the declared object variable has the special value **Nothing**, which indicates that it doesn't refer to any particular instance of an object. When you use the **New** keyword in the declaration, an instance of the object is created on the first reference to the object.

If you don't specify a data type or object type, and there is no **Def***type* statement in the module, the variable is **Variant** by default.

Note The **Static** statement and the **Static** keyword are similar, but used for different effects. If you declare a procedure using the **Static** keyword (as in `Static Sub CountSales ()`), the storage space for all local variables within the procedure is allocated once, and the value of the variables is preserved for the entire time the program is running. For nonstatic procedures, storage space for variables is allocated each time the procedure is called and released when the procedure is exited. The **Static** statement is used to declare specific variables within nonstatic procedures to preserve their value for as long as the program is running.

When variables are initialized, a numeric variable is initialized to 0, a variable-length string is initialized to a zero-length string (" "), and a fixed-length string is filled with zeros. **Variant** variables are initialized to **Empty**. Each element of a user-defined type variable is initialized as if it were a separate variable.

Note When you use **Static** statements within a procedure, put them at the beginning of the procedure with other declarative statements such as **Dim**.

See Also

Array function, **Dim** statement, **Function** statement, **Option Base** statement, **Private** statement, **Public** statement, **ReDim** statement, **Sub** statement.

Example

This example uses the **Static** statement to retain the value of a variable for as long as module code is running.

```
' Function definition.
Function KeepTotal(Number)
   ' Only the variable Accumulate preserves its value between calls.
   Static Accumulate
   Accumulate = Accumulate + Number
   KeepTotal = Accumulate
End Function

' Static function definition.
Static Function MyFunction(Arg1, Arg2, Arg3)
   ' All local variables preserve value between function calls.
   Accumulate = Arg1 + Arg2 + Arg3
   Half = Accumulate / 2
   MyFunction = Half
End Function
```

Example (Microsoft Excel)

This example uses the worksheet function **Pmt** to calculate a home mortgage loan payment. Note that this example uses the **InputBox** method instead of the **InputBox** function so that the method can perform type checking. The **Static** statements cause Visual Basic to retain the values of the three variables; these are displayed as default values the next time you run the example.

```
Static loanAmt
Static loanInt
Static loanTerm
loanAmt = Application.InputBox _
   (Prompt:="Loan amount (100,000 for example)", _
   Default:=loanAmt, Type:=1)
loanInt = Application.InputBox _
   (Prompt:="Annual interest rate (8.75 for example)", _
   Default:=loanInt, Type:=1)
loanTerm = Application.InputBox _
   (Prompt:="Term in years (30 for example)", _
   Default:=loanTerm, Type:=1)
payment = Application.Pmt(loanInt / 1200, loanTerm * 12, loanAmt)
MsgBox "Monthly payment is " & Format(payment, "Currency")
```

Stop Statement

Description

Suspends execution.

Syntax

Stop

Remarks

You can place **Stop** statements anywhere in procedures to suspend execution. Using the **Stop** statement is similar to setting a breakpoint in the code.

The **Stop** statement suspends execution, but unlike **End**, it doesn't close any files or clear variables, unless it is in a compiled executable (.exe) file.

See Also

End statement.

Example

This example uses the **Stop** statement to suspend execution for each iteration through the **For...Next** loop.

```
Dim I
For I = 1 To 10                        ' Start For...Next loop.
   Debug.Print I                       ' Print I to Debug window.
   Stop                                ' Stop during each iteration.
Next I
```

Str Function

Description

Returns a **Variant** (**String**) representation of a number.

Syntax

Str(*number*)

The required *number* argument is a **Long** containing any valid numeric expression.

Remarks

When numbers are converted to strings, a leading space is always reserved for the sign of *number*. If *number* is positive, the returned string contains a leading space and the plus sign is implied.

Use the **Format** function to convert numeric values you want formatted as dates, times, or currency or in other user-defined formats. Unlike **Str**, the **Format** function doesn't include a leading space for the sign of *number*.

Note The **Str** function recognizes only the period (**.**) as a valid decimal separator. When different decimal separators may be used (for example, in international applications), use **CStr** to convert a number to a string.

See Also

Format function, **Val** function.

Example

This example uses the **Str** function to return a string representation of a number. When a number is converted to a string, a leading space is always reserved for its sign.

```
Dim MyString
MyString = Str(459)                          ' Returns " 459".
MyString = Str(-459.65)                      ' Returns "-459.65".
MyString = Str(459.001)                      ' Returns " 459.001".
```

StrComp Function

Description

Returns a **Variant** (**Integer**) indicating the result of a string comparison.

Syntax

StrComp(***string1***, ***string2***[, ***compare***])

The **StrComp** function syntax has these named arguments:

Part	Description
string1	Required. Any valid string expression.
string2	Required. Any valid string expression.
compare	Optional. Specifies the type of string comparison. The ***compare*** argument can be omitted, or it can be 0, 1 or 2. Specify **0** (default) to perform a binary comparison. Specify **1** to perform a textual comparison. For Microsoft Access only, specify **2** to perform a comparison based on information contained in your database. If ***compare*** is **Null**, an error occurs. If ***compare*** is omitted, the **Option Compare** setting determines the type of comparison.

Return Values

The **StrComp** function has the following return values:

If	StrComp returns
string1 is less than ***string2***	–1
string1 is equal to ***string2***	0
string1 is greater than ***string2***	1
string1 or ***string2*** is **Null**	**Null**

See Also

InStr function, **Option Compare** statement.

Example

This example uses the **StrComp** function to return the results of a string comparison. If the third argument is 1, a textual comparison is performed; if the third argument is 0 or omitted, a binary comparison is performed.

```
Dim MyStr1, MyStr2, MyComp
MyStr1 = "ABCD": MyStr2 = "abcd"                ' Define variables.
MyComp = StrComp(MyStr1, MyStr2, 1)             ' Returns 0.
MyComp = StrComp(MyStr1, MyStr2, 0)             ' Returns -1.
MyComp = StrComp(MyStr2, MyStr1)                ' Returns 1.
```

StrConv Function

Description

Returns a **Variant** (**String**) converted as specified.

Syntax

StrConv(***string***, ***conversion***)

The **StrConv** function syntax has these named arguments:

Part	Description
string	Required. String expression to be converted.
conversion	Required; **Integer**. The sum of values specifying the type of conversion to perform.

Settings

The ***conversion*** argument settings are:

Constant	Value	Description
vbUpperCase	1	Converts the string to uppercase characters.
vbLowerCase	2	Converts the string to lowercase characters.
vbProperCase	3	Converts the first letter of every word in string to uppercase.
vbWide*	4*	Converts narrow (single-byte) characters in string to wide (double-byte) characters.
vbNarrow*	8*	Converts wide (double-byte) characters in string to narrow (single-byte) characters.
vbKatakana**	16**	Converts Hiragana characters in string to Katakana characters.
vbHiragana**	32**	Converts Katakana characters in string to Hiragana characters.
vbUnicode	64	Converts the string to Unicode using the default code page of the system.
vbFromUnicode	128	Converts the string from Unicode to the default code page of the system.

* Applies to Far East locales.

** Applies to Japan only.

Note These constants are specified by Visual Basic for Applications. As a result, they may be used anywhere in your code in place of the actual values. Most can be combined, for example, **vbUpperCase + vbWide**, except when they are mutually exclusive, for example, **vbUnicode + vbFromUnicode**. The constants **vbWide**, **vbNarrow**, **vbKatakana**, and **vbHiragana** cause run-time errors when used in locales where they do not apply.

The following are valid word separators for proper casing: **Null** (**Chr$**(0)), horizontal tab (**Chr$**(9)), linefeed (**Chr$**(10)), vertical tab (**Chr$**(11)), form feed (**Chr$**(12)), carriage return (**Chr$**(13)), space (SBCS) (**Chr$**(32)). The actual value for a space varies by country for DBCS.

See Also

Chr function, **String** data type.

String Data Type

Description

There are two kinds of strings: variable-length and fixed-length strings.

- A variable-length string can contain up to approximately 2 billion (2^31) characters.
- A fixed-length string can contain 1 to approximately 64K (2^16) characters.

Note A **Public** fixed-length string can't be used in a class module.

The codes for **String** characters range from 0–255. The first 128 characters (0–127) of the character set correspond to the letters and symbols on a standard U.S. keyboard. These first 128 characters are the same as those defined by the ASCII character set. The second 128 characters (128–255) represent special characters, such as letters in international alphabets, accents, currency symbols, and fractions. The type-declaration character for **String** is the dollar sign (**$**).

See Also

Data type summary, **Def***type* statements, **String** function, **Variant** data type.

String Function

Description

Returns a **Variant** (**String**) containing a repeating character string of the length specified.

Syntax

String(*number*, *character*)

The **String** function syntax has these named arguments:

Part	Description
number	Required; **Long**. Length of the returned string. If ***number*** contains **Null**, **Null** is returned.
character	Required; **Variant**. Character code specifying the character or string expression whose first character is used to build the return string. If ***character*** contains **Null**, **Null** is returned.

Remarks

If you specify a number for ***character*** greater than 255, **String** converts the number to a valid character code using the formula:

character **Mod** 256

See Also

Mod operator, **Space** function, **String** data type.

Example

This example uses the **String** function to return repeating character strings of the length specified.

```
Dim MyString
MyString = String(5, "*")                  ' Returns "*****".
MyString = String(5, 42)                   ' Returns "*****".
MyString = String(10, "ABC")               ' Returns "AAAAAAAAAA".
```

Sub Statement

Description

Declares the name, arguments, and code that form the body of a **Sub** procedure.

Syntax

[**Private** | **Public**] [**Static**] **Sub** *name* [(*arglist*)]
↳ [*statements*]
↳ [**Exit Sub**]
↳ [*statements*]
End Sub

The **Sub** statement syntax has these parts:

Part	Description
Public	Optional. Indicates that the **Sub** procedure is accessible to all other procedures in all modules. If used in a module that contains an **Option Private** statement, the procedure is not available outside the project.
Private	Optional. Indicates that the **Sub** procedure is accessible only to other procedures in the module where it is declared.
Static	Optional. Indicates that the **Sub** procedure's local variables are preserved between calls. The **Static** attribute doesn't affect variables that are declared outside the **Sub**, even if they are used in the procedure.
name	Required. Name of the **Sub**; follows standard variable naming conventions.
arglist	Optional. List of variables representing arguments that are passed to the **Sub** procedure when it is called. Multiple variables are separated by commas.
statements	Optional. Any group of statements to be executed within the **Sub** procedure.

The *arglist* argument has the following syntax and parts:

[**Optional**] [**ByVal** | **ByRef**] [**ParamArray**] *varname*[( )] [**As** *type*] [= *defaultvalue*]

Part	Description
Optional	Optional. Keyword indicating that an argument is not required. If used, all subsequent arguments in *arglist* must also be optional and declared using the **Optional** keyword. **Optional** can't be used for any argument if **ParamArray** is used.
ByVal	Optional. Indicates that the argument is passed by value.
ByRef	Optional. Indicates that the argument is passed by reference. **ByRef** is the default in Visual Basic.
ParamArray	Optional. Used only as the last argument in *arglist* to indicate that the final argument is an **Optional** array of **Variant** elements. The **ParamArray** keyword allows you to provide an arbitrary number of arguments. **ParamArray** can't be used with **ByVal**, **ByRef**, or **Optional**.
varname	Required. Name of the variable representing the argument; follows standard variable naming conventions.
type	Optional. Data type of the argument passed to the procedure; may be **Byte**, **Boolean**, **Integer**, **Long**, **Currency**, **Single**, **Double**, **Decimal** (not currently supported), **Date**, **String** (variable-length only), **Object**, **Variant**. If the parameter is not **Optional**, a user-defined type, or an object type may also be specified.
defaultvalue	Optional. Any constant or constant expression. Valid for **Optional** parameters only. If the type is an **Object**, an explicit default value can only be **Nothing**.

Remarks

If not explicitly specified using either **Public** or **Private**, **Sub** procedures are public by default. If **Static** is not used, the value of local variables is not preserved between calls.

Caution **Sub** procedures can be recursive; that is, they can call themselves to perform a given task. However, recursion can lead to stack overflow. The **Static** keyword usually is not used with recursive **Sub** procedures.

All executable code must be in procedures. You can't define a **Sub** procedure inside another **Sub**, **Function**, or **Property** procedure.

The **Exit Sub** keywords cause an immediate exit from a **Sub** procedure. Program execution continues with the statement following the statement that called the **Sub** procedure. Any number of **Exit Sub** statements can appear anywhere in a **Sub** procedure.

Like a **Function** procedure, a **Sub** procedure is a separate procedure that can take arguments, perform a series of statements, and change the value of its arguments. However, unlike a **Function** procedure, which returns a value, a **Sub** procedure can't be used in an expression.

You call a **Sub** procedure using the procedure name followed by the argument list. See the **Call** statement for specific information on how to call **Sub** procedures.

Variables used in **Sub** procedures fall into two categories: those that are explicitly declared within the procedure and those that are not. Variables that are explicitly declared in a procedure (using **Dim** or the equivalent) are always local to the procedure. Variables that are used but not explicitly declared in a procedure are also local unless they are explicitly declared at some higher level outside the procedure.

Caution A procedure can use a variable that is not explicitly declared in the procedure, but a naming conflict can occur if anything you defined at the module level has the same name. If your procedure refers to an undeclared variable that has the same name as another procedure, constant or variable, it is assumed that your procedure is referring to that module-level name. To avoid this kind of conflict, explicitly declare variables. You can use an **Option Explicit** statement to force explicit declaration of variables.

Note You can't use **GoSub**, **GoTo**, or **Return** to enter or exit a **Sub** procedure.

See Also

Call statement, **Dim** statement, **Function** statement, **Option Explicit** statement, **Property Get** statement, **Property Let** statement, **Property Set** statement.

Specifics (Microsoft Access)

In Microsoft Access, a public **Sub** procedure in a standard module is available to all other procedures in the current database and in referencing Microsoft Access databases. However, it is not available to any other applications.

If you declare a **Sub** procedure as private in any module, that procedure is available only to other procedures within the same module.

If a **Sub** procedure is declared as public within a private module, such as a class module, then the procedure is available to all other procedures in that database, but is not available to other Microsoft Access databases.

When you create an event procedure for a form or report, Microsoft Access automatically inserts a code stub for a **Sub** procedure and precedes it with the **Private** keyword. For example, create a command button on a new form, set its **OnClick** property to [Event Procedure], and click the **Build** button to view the form's module. Microsoft Access inserts the following code for you in the module.

```
Private Sub Command0_Click

End Sub
```

You can then enter the code that you want to execute when that button's Click event occurs.

Example

This example uses the **Sub** statement to define the name, arguments, and code that form the body of a **Sub** procedure.

```
' Sub procedure definition.
' Sub procedure with two arguments.
Sub SubComputeArea(Length, TheWidth)
   Dim Area As Double                            ' Declare local variable.
   If Length = 0 Or TheWidth = 0 Then
   ' If either argument = 0.
      Exit Sub                                   ' Exit Sub immediately.
   End If
   Area = Length * TheWidth                      ' Calculate area of rectangle.
   Debug.Print Area                              ' Print Area to Debug window.
End Sub
```

Switch Function

Description

Evaluates a list of expressions and returns a **Variant** value or an expression associated with the first expression in the list that is **True**.

Syntax

Switch(*expr-1***,** *value-1*[**,** *expr-2***,** *value-2* **...** [**,** *expr-n***,** *value-n*]]**)**

The **Switch** function syntax has these parts:

Part	Description
expr	Required. **Variant** expression you want to evaluate.
value	Required. Value or expression to be returned if the corresponding expression is **True**.

Remarks

The **Switch** function argument list consists of pairs of expressions and values. The expressions are evaluated from left to right, and the value associated with the first expression to evaluate to **True** is returned. If the parts aren't properly paired, a run-time error occurs. For example, if *expr-1* is **True**, **Switch** returns *value-1*. If *expr-1* is **False**, but *expr-2* is **True**, **Switch** returns *value-2*, and so on.

Switch returns a **Null** value if:

- None of the expressions is **True**.
- The first **True** expression has a corresponding value that is **Null**.

Switch evaluates all of the expressions, even though it returns only one of them. For this reason, you should watch for undesirable side effects. For example, if the evaluation of any expression results in a division by zero error, an error occurs.

See Also

Choose function, **IIf** function, **Select Case** statement.

Specifics (Microsoft Access)

You can also use the **Switch** function in a calculated control on a Microsoft Access form or report. For example, you can use the **Switch** function to set the value of a control based on the value of another field. Set the **ControlSource** property of the control to an expression containing the **Switch** function.

In the following example, the **Switch** function returns a string that is the name of a shipper based on the value of the Freight field. If the value of the Freight field is less than $25, the **Switch** function returns “Speedy”; if it is greater than or equal to $25 but less than or equal to $50, the **Switch** function returns “United”; if it is greater than $50, the **Switch** function returns “Federal”.

```
=Switch([Freight] < 25, "Speedy", ([Freight] >= 25 and [Freight] <= 50), _
   "United", [Freight] > 50, "Federal")
```

Note In Visual Basic code, you may want to use the more full-featured **Select Case** statement to return a value from a set of several choices.

Example

This example uses the **Switch** function to return the name of a language that matches the name of a city.

```
Function MatchUp (CityName As String)
   Matchup = Switch(CityName = "London", "English", CityName _
      = "Rome", "Italian", CityName = "Paris", "French")
End Function
```

Example (Microsoft Access)

The following example uses the **Switch** function to determine the appropriate language for a specified city based on the values of the ShipCountry and ShipCity fields in an Orders table. You can enter the following expression in a calculated control on a form or report. The expression is shown on multiple lines for clarity; you can also enter it on a single line.

```
=Switch([ShipCity] = "Madrid", "Spanish", _
   [ShipCity] = "Berlin", "German", _
   [ShipCity] = "Torino", "Italian", _
   [ShipCountry] = "France", "French", _
   True, "English")
```

If the city is Madrid, the **Switch** function returns “Spanish”; if it is Berlin, it returns “German”; and so on. If the city is not one of those listed, but the country is France, it returns “French”. If the city in question is not in the list, the **Switch** function returns “English”.

SYD Function

Description

Returns a **Double** specifying the sum-of-years' digits depreciation of an asset for a specified period.

Syntax

SYD(*cost*, *salvage*, *life*, *period*)

The **SYD** function has these named arguments:

Part	Description
cost	Required. **Double** specifying initial cost of the asset.
salvage	Required. **Double** specifying value of the asset at the end of its useful life.
life	Required. **Double** specifying length of the useful life of the asset.
period	Required. **Double** specifying period for which asset depreciation is calculated.

Remarks

The ***life*** and ***period*** arguments must be expressed in the same units. For example, if ***life*** is given in months, ***period*** must also be given in months. All arguments must be positive numbers.

See Also

DDB function, **FV** function, **IPmt** function, **IRR** function, **MIRR** function, **NPer** function, **NPV** function, **Pmt** function, **PPmt** function, **PV** function, **Rate** function, **SLN** function.

Example

This example uses the **SYD** function to return the depreciation of an asset for a specified period given the asset's initial cost (`InitCost`), the salvage value at the end of the asset's useful life (`SalvageVal`), and the total life of the asset in years (`LifeTime`). The period in years for which the depreciation is calculated is `PDepr`.

```
Dim Fmt, InitCost, SalvageVal, MonthLife, LifeTime, DepYear, PDepr
Const YEARMONTHS = 12                   ' Number of months in a year.
Fmt = "###,##0.00"                      ' Define money format.
InitCost = InputBox("What's the initial cost of the asset?")
SalvageVal = InputBox("What's the asset's value at the end of its life?")
MonthLife = InputBox("What's the asset's useful life in months?")
Do While MonthLife < YEARMONTHS          ' Ensure period is >= 1 year.
   MsgBox "Asset life must be a year or more."
   MonthLife = InputBox("What's the asset's useful life in months?")
Loop
LifeTime = MonthLife / YEARMONTHS       ' Convert months to years.
If LifeTime <> Int(MonthLife / YEARMONTHS) Then
   LifeTime = Int(LifeTime + 1)         ' Round up to nearest year.
End If
```

```
DepYear = CInt(InputBox("For which year do you want depreciation?"))
Do While DepYear < 1 Or DepYear > LifeTime
   MsgBox "You must enter at least 1 but not more than " & LifeTime
   DepYear = CInt(InputBox("For what year do you want depreciation?"))
Loop
PDepr = SYD(InitCost, SalvageVal, LifeTime, DepYear)
MsgBox "The depreciation for year " & DepYear & " is " _
   & Format(PDepr, Fmt) & "."
```

Tab Function

Description

Used with the **Print #** statement or the **Print** method to position output.

Syntax

Tab[(*n*)]

The optional *n* argument is the column number moved to before displaying or printing the next expression in a list. If omitted, **Tab** moves the insertion point to the beginning of the next print zone. This allows **Tab** to be used instead of a comma in locales where the comma is used as a decimal separator.

Remarks

If the current print position on the current line is greater than *n*, **Tab** skips to the *n*th column on the next output line. If *n* is less than 1, **Tab** moves the print position to column 1. If *n* is greater than the output line width, **Tab** calculates the next print position using the formula:

n **Mod** *width*

For example, if *width* is 80 and you specify **Tab**(90), the next print will start at column 10 (the remainder of 90/80). If *n* is less than the current print position, printing begins on the next line at the calculated print position. If the calculated print position is greater than the current print position, printing begins at the calculated print position on the same line.

The leftmost print position on an output line is always 1. When you use the **Print #** statement to print to files, the rightmost print position is the current width of the output file, which you can set using the **Width #** statement.

Note Make sure your tabular columns are wide enough to accommodate wide letters.

When you use the **Tab** function with the **Print** method, the print surface is divided into uniform, fixed-width columns. The width of each column is an average of the width of all characters in the point size for the chosen font. However, there is no correlation between the number of characters printed and the number of fixed-width columns those characters occupy. For example, the uppercase letter W occupies more than one fixed-width column and the lowercase letter i occupies less than one fixed-width column.

See Also

Mod operator, **Print** # statement, **Print** method, **Space** function, **Spc** function, **Width** # statement.

Example

This example uses the **Tab** function to position output in a file and in the **Debug** window.

```
' The Tab function can be used with the Print # statement.
Open "TESTFILE" For Output As #1            ' Open file for output.
' The second word prints at column 20.
Print #1, "Hello"; Tab(20); "World."
' If the argument is omitted, cursor is moved to the next print zone.
Print #1, "Hello"; Tab; "World"
Close #1                                    ' Close file.
```

The **Tab** function can also be used with the **Print** method. The following statement prints text starting at column 10.

```
Debug.Print Tab(10); "10 columns from start."
```

Tan Function

Description

Returns a **Double** specifying the tangent of an angle.

Syntax

Tan(*number***)**

The required *number* argument is a **Double** or any valid numeric expression that expresses an angle in radians.

Remarks

Tan takes an angle and returns the ratio of two sides of a right triangle. The ratio is the length of the side opposite the angle divided by the length of the side adjacent to the angle.

To convert degrees to radians, multiply degrees by pi/180. To convert radians to degrees, multiply radians by 180/pi.

See Also

Atn function, **Cos** function, **Sin** function.

Example

This example uses the **Tan** function to return the tangent of an angle.

```
Dim MyAngle, MyCotangent
MyAngle = 1.3                               ' Define angle in radians.
MyCotangent = 1 / Tan(MyAngle)              ' Calculate cotangent.
```

Terminate Event

Applies To

UserForm object.

Description

Occurs when all references to an instance of an object are removed from memory by setting all variables that refer to the object to **Nothing** or when the last reference to the object goes out of scope.

Syntax

Private Sub *object*_**Terminate( )**

The *object* placeholder represents an object expression that evaluates to an object in the Applies To list.

Remarks

The Terminate event occurs after the object is unloaded. The Terminate event isn't triggered if the instances of the **UserForm** or class are removed from memory because the application terminated abnormally. For example, if your application invokes the **End** statement before removing all existing instances of the class or **UserForm** from memory, the Terminate event isn't triggered for that class or **UserForm**.

Example

The following event procedures cause a **UserForm** to beep for a few seconds after the user clicks the client area to dismiss the form.

```
Private Sub UserForm_Activate()
   UserForm1.Caption = "Click me to kill me!"
End Sub

Private Sub UserForm_Click()
   Unload Me
End Sub

Private Sub UserForm_Terminate()
   Dim Count As Integer
   For Count = 1 To 100
      Beep
   Next
End Sub
```

Time Function

Description

Returns a **Variant** (**Date**) indicating the current system time.

Syntax

Time

Remarks

To set the system time, use the **Time** statement.

See Also

Date function, **Date** statement, **Time** statement, **Timer** function.

Specifics (Microsoft Access)

You can insert the current time on a form or report by clicking **Date And Time** on the **Insert** menu. This command creates a text box on a form or report and sets the **ControlSource** property of the text box to an expression containing the **Time** function. This expression will vary according to the format you have chosen to display the time. This command is available only in form Design view and report Design view.

You can also use the **Time** function in a query expression or in a macro. However, you must include the parentheses after the function when you use it anywhere other than in a Visual Basic module, as in the expression `Time()`.

Example

This example uses the **Time** function to return the current system time.

```
Dim MyTime
MyTime = Time                         ' Return current system time.
```

Example (Microsoft Access)

You can use the **Time** function in a calculated control to return the current system time. For example, you can create a text box and set its **ControlSource** property to the following expression.

```
=Time()
```

Time Statement

Description

Sets the system time.

Syntax

Time = *time*

The required *time* argument is any numeric expression, string expression, or any combination, that can represent a time.

Remarks

If *time* is a string, **Time** attempts to convert it to a time using the time separators you specified for your system. If it can't be converted to a valid time, an error occurs.

See Also

Date function, **Date** statement, **Time** function.

Example

This example uses the **Time** statement to set the computer system time to a user-defined time.

```
Dim MyTime
MyTime = #4:35:17 PM#                   ' Assign a time.
Time = MyTime                           ' Set system time to MyTime.
```

Timer Function

Description

Returns a **Single** representing the number of seconds elapsed since midnight.

Syntax

Timer

See Also

Randomize statement, **Time** function.

Example

This example uses the **Timer** function to pause the application. The example also uses **DoEvents** to yield to other processes during the pause.

```
Dim PauseTime, Start, Finish, TotalTime
If (MsgBox("Press Yes to pause for 5 seconds", 4)) = vbYes Then
   PauseTime = 5                           ' Set duration.
   Start = Timer                           ' Set start time.
   Do While Timer < Start + PauseTime
      DoEvents                             ' Yield to other processes.
   Loop
   Finish = Timer                          ' Set end time.
   TotalTime = Finish - Start              ' Calculate total time.
   MsgBox "Paused for " & TotalTime & " seconds"
Else
   End
End If
```

Example (Microsoft Access)

You can use the **Timer** function to time operations and events in your Microsoft Access application by placing the **Timer** function immediately before and after the operation in your code that you wish to time. The following example uses the name of a query as its argument, then calculates how long it takes the query to run.

```
Sub QueryTimer (strQueryName As String)
   Dim sngStart As Single, sngEnd As Single
   Dim sngElapsed As Single

   sngStart = Timer                                ' Get start time.
```

```
    DoCmd.OpenQuery strQueryName, acNormal            ' Run query.
    sngEnd = Timer                                    ' Get end time.
    sngElapsed = Format(sngEnd - sngStart, "Fixed")   ' Elapsed time.
    MsgBox ("The query " & strQueryName & " took " & sngElapsed _
        & " seconds to run.")
End Sub
```

TimeSerial Function

Description

Returns a **Variant** (**Date**) containing the time for a specific hour, minute, and second.

Syntax

TimeSerial(*hour, minute, second*)

The **TimeSerial** function syntax has these named arguments:

Part	Description
hour	Required; **Variant** (**Integer**). Number between 0 (12:00 A.M.) and 23 (11:00 P.M.), inclusive, or a numeric expression.
minute	Required; **Variant** (**Integer**). Any numeric expression.
second	Required; **Variant** (**Integer**). Any numeric expression.

Remarks

To specify a time, such as 11:59:59, the range of numbers for each **TimeSerial** argument should be in the normal range for the unit; that is, 0–23 for hours and 0–59 for minutes and seconds. However, you can also specify relative times for each argument using any numeric expression that represents some number of hours, minutes, or seconds before or after a certain time. The following example uses expressions instead of absolute time numbers. The **TimeSerial** function returns a time for 15 minutes before (`-15`) six hours before noon (`12 - 6`), or 5:45:00 A.M.

```
TimeSerial(12 - 6, -15, 0)
```

When any argument exceeds the normal range for that argument, it increments to the next larger unit as appropriate. For example, if you specify 75 minutes, it is evaluated as one hour and 15 minutes. If any single argument is outside the range –32,768 to 32,767, an error occurs. If the time specified by the three arguments causes the date to fall outside the acceptable range of dates, an error occurs.

See Also

DateSerial function, **DateValue** function, **Hour** function, **Minute** function, **Now** function, **Second** function, **TimeValue** function.

Example

This example uses the **TimeSerial** function to return a time for the specified hour, minute, and second.

```
Dim MyTime
MyTime = TimeSerial(16, 35, 17)      ' MyTime contains serial
                                     ' representation of 4:35:17 PM.
```

TimeValue Function

Description

Returns a **Variant** (**Date**) containing the time.

Syntax

TimeValue(*time***)**

The required *time* argument is normally a string expression representing a time from 0:00:00 (12:00:00 A.M.) to 23:59:59 (11:59:59 P.M.), inclusive. However, *time* can also be any expression that represents a time in that range. If *time* contains **Null**, **Null** is returned.

Remarks

You can enter valid times using a 12-hour or 24-hour clock. For example, `"2:24PM"` and `"14:24"` are both valid *time* arguments.

If the *time* argument contains date information, **TimeValue** doesn't return it. However, if *time* includes invalid date information, an error occurs.

See Also

DateSerial function, **DateValue** function, **Hour** function, **Minute** function, **Now** function, **Second** function, **TimeSerial** function.

Example

This example uses the **TimeValue** function to convert a string to a time. You can also use date literals to directly assign a time to a **Variant** or **Date** variable, for example, MyTime = #4:35:17 PM#.

```
Dim MyTime
MyTime = TimeValue("4:35:17 PM")                 ' Return a time.
```

Trim Function

See LTrim, RTrim, and Trim Functions.

Type Conversion Functions

Description

Each function coerces an expression to a specific data type.

Syntax

CBool(*expression*)
CByte(*expression*)
CCur(*expression*)
CDate(*expression*)
CDbl(*expression*)
CDec(*expression*)
CInt(*expression*)
CLng(*expression*)
CSng(*expression*)
CVar(*expression*)
CStr(*expression*)

The required *expression* argument is any string expression or numeric expression.

Return Types

The function name determines the return type as shown in the following:

Function	Return type	Range for *expression* argument
CBool	**Boolean**	Any valid string or numeric expression.
CByte	**Byte**	0 to 255.
CCur	**Currency**	–922,337,203,685,477.5808 to 922,337,203,685,477.5807.
CDate	**Date**	Any valid date expression.
CDbl	**Double**	–1.79769313486232E308 to –4.94065645841247E–324 for negative values; 4.94065645841247E–324 to 1.79769313486232E308 for positive values.
CDec	**Decimal**	+/-79,228,162,514,264,337,593,543,950,335 for zero-scaled numbers, that is, numbers with no decimal places. For numbers with 28 decimal places, the range is +/-7.9228162514264337593543950335. The smallest possible non-zero number is 0.0000000000000000000000000001.

(continued)

Function	Return type	Range for *expression* argument
CInt	**Integer**	–32,768 to 32,767; fractions are rounded.
CLng	**Long**	–2,147,483,648 to 2,147,483,647; fractions are rounded.
CSng	**Single**	–3.402823E38 to –1.401298E–45 for negative values; 1.401298E–45 to 3.402823E38 for positive values.
CVar	**Variant**	Same range as **Double** for numerics. Same range as **String** for non-numerics.
CStr	**String**	Returns for CStr depend on the *expression* argument.

Remarks

If the *expression* passed to the function is outside the range of the data type being converted to, an error occurs.

In general, you can document your code using the data-type conversion functions to show that the result of some operation should be expressed as a particular data type rather than the default data type. For example, use **CCur** to force currency arithmetic in cases where single-precision, double-precision, or integer arithmetic normally would occur.

You should use the data-type conversion functions instead of **Val** to provide internationally aware conversions from one data type to another. For example, when you use **CCur**, different decimal separators, different thousand separators, and various currency options are properly recognized depending on the locale setting of your computer.

When the fractional part is exactly 0.5, **CInt** and **CLng** always round it to the nearest even number. For example, 0.5 rounds to 0, and 1.5 rounds to 2. **CInt** and **CLng** differ from the **Fix** and **Int** functions, which truncate, rather than round, the fractional part of a number. Also, **Fix** and **Int** always return a value of the same type as is passed in.

Use the **IsDate** function to determine if *date* can be converted to a date or time. **CDate** recognizes date literals and time literals as well as some numbers that fall within the range of acceptable dates. When converting a number to a date, the whole number portion is converted to a date. Any fractional part of the number is converted to a time of day, starting at midnight.

CDate recognizes date formats according to the locale setting of your system. The correct order of day, month, and year may not be determined if it is provided in a format other than one of the recognized date settings. In addition, a long date format is not recognized if it also contains the day-of-the-week string.

A **CVDate** function is also provided for compatibility with previous versions of Visual Basic. The syntax of the **CVDate** function is identical to the **CDate** function, however, **CVDate** returns a **Variant** whose subtype is **Date** instead of an actual **Date** type. Since there is now an intrinsic **Date** type, there is no further need for **CVDate**. The same effect can be achieved by converting an expression to a **Date**, and then assigning it to a **Variant**. This technique is consistent with the conversion of all other intrinsic types to their equivalent **Variant** subtypes.

Note The **CDec** function does not return a discrete data type; instead, it always returns a **Variant** whose value has been converted to a **Decimal** subtype.

Example

This example uses the **CBool** function to convert an expression to a **Boolean**. If the expression evaluates to a nonzero value, **CBool** returns **True**; otherwise, it returns **False**.

```
Dim A, B, Check
A = 5: B = 5                            ' Initialize variables.
Check = CBool(A = B)                    ' Check contains True.

A = 0                                   ' Define variable.
Check = CBool(A)                        ' Check contains False.
```

Example

This example uses the **CByte** function to convert an expression to a **Byte**.

```
Dim MyDouble, MyByte
MyDouble = 125.5678                     ' MyDouble is a Double.
MyByte = CByte(MyDouble)                ' MyByte contains 126.
```

Example

This example uses the **CCur** function to convert an expression to a **Currency**.

```
Dim MyDouble, MyCurr
MyDouble = 543.214588                   ' MyDouble is a Double.
MyCurr = CCur(MyDouble * 2)             ' Convert result of MyDouble * 2
                                        ' (1086.429176) to a
                                        ' Currency (1086.4292).
```

Example

This example uses the **CDate** function to convert a string to a **Date**. In general, hard-coding dates and times as strings (as shown in this example) is not recommended. Use date literals and time literals, such as #2/12/1969# and #4:45:23 PM#, instead.

```
Dim MyDate, MyShortDate, MyTime, MyShortTime
MyDate = "February 12, 1969"            ' Define date.
MyShortDate = CDate(MyDate)             ' Convert to Date data type.

MyTime = "4:35:47 PM"                   ' Define time.
MyShortTime = CDate(MyTime)             ' Convert to Date data type.
```

Example

This example uses the **CDbl** function to convert an expression to a **Double**.

```
Dim MyCurr, MyDouble
MyCurr = CCur(234.456784)                    ' MyCurr is a Currency.
MyDouble = CDbl(MyCurr * 8.2 * 0.01)         ' Convert result to a Double.
```

Example

This example uses the **CInt** function to convert a value to an **Integer**.

```
Dim MyDouble, MyInt
MyDouble = 2345.5678                         ' MyDouble is a Double.
MyInt = CInt(MyDouble)                       ' MyInt contains 2346.
```

Example

This example uses the **CLng** function to convert a value to a **Long**.

```
Dim MyVal1, MyVal2, MyLong1, MyLong2
MyVal1 = 25427.45: MyVal2 = 25427.55        ' MyVal1, MyVal2 are Doubles.
MyLong1 = CLng(MyVal1)                       ' MyLong1 contains 25427.
MyLong2 = CLng(MyVal2)                       ' MyLong2 contains 25428.
```

Example

This example uses the **CSng** function to convert a value to a **Single**.

```
Dim MyDouble1, MyDouble2, MySingle1, MySingle2
' MyDouble1, MyDouble2 are Doubles.
MyDouble1 = 75.3421115: MyDouble2 = 75.3421555
MySingle1 = CSng(MyDouble1)                  ' MySingle1 contains 75.34211.
MySingle2 = CSng(MyDouble2)                  ' MySingle2 contains 75.34216.
```

Example

This example uses the **CStr** function to convert a numeric value to a **String**.

```
Dim MyDouble, MyString
MyDouble = 437.324                           ' MyDouble is a Double.
MyString = CStr(MyDouble)                    ' MyString contains "437.324".
```

Example

This example uses the **CVar** function to convert an expression to a **Variant**.

```
Dim MyInt, MyVar
MyInt = 4534                                 ' MyInt is an Integer.
MyVar = CVar(MyInt & "000")                  ' MyVar contains the string
                                             ' 4534000.
```

Type Statement

Description

Used at module level to define a user-defined data type containing one or more elements.

Syntax

[Private | Public] Type *varname*
↳ *elementname* [([*subscripts*])] **As** *type*
↳ [*elementname* [([*subscripts*])] **As** *type*]
↳ . . .
End Type

The **Type** statement syntax has these parts:

Part	Description
Public	Optional. Used to declare user-defined types that are available to all procedures in all modules in all projects.
Private	Optional. Used to declare user-defined types that are available only within the module where the declaration is made.
varname	Required. Name of the user-defined type; follows standard variable naming conventions.
elementname	Required. Name of an element of the user-defined type. Element names also follow standard variable naming conventions, except that keywords can be used.
subscripts	Optional. Dimensions of an array element. Use only parentheses when declaring an array whose size can change. The *subscripts* argument uses the following syntax: [*lower* **To**] *upper* [,[*lower* **To**] *upper*] . . . When not explicitly stated in *lower*, the lower bound of an array is controlled by the **Option Base** statement. The lower bound is zero if no **Option Base** statement is present.
type	Required. Data type of the element; may be **Byte**, **Boolean**, **Integer**, **Long**, **Currency**, **Single**, **Double**, **Decimal** (not currently supported), **Date**, **String**(for variable-length strings), **String** * *length* (for fixed-length strings), **Object**, **Variant**, another user-defined type, or an object type.

Remarks

The **Type** statement can be used only at module level. Once you have declared a user-defined type using the **Type** statement, you can declare a variable of that type anywhere within the scope of the declaration. Use **Dim**, **Private**, **Public**, **ReDim**, or **Static** to declare a variable of a user-defined type.

In standard modules, user-defined types are public by default. This visibility can be changed using the **Private** keyword. In class modules, however, user-defined types can only be private and the visibility can't be changed using the **Public** keyword.

Line numbers and line labels aren't allowed in **Type...End Type** blocks.

User-defined types are often used with data records, which frequently consist of a number of related elements of different data types.

The following example shows the use of fixed-size arrays in a user-defined type:

```
Type StateData
   CityCode (1 To 100) As Integer     ' Declare a static array.
   County As String * 30
End Type

Dim Washington(1 To 100) As StateData
```

In the preceding example, `StateData` includes the `CityCode` static array, and the record `Washington` has the same structure as `StateData`.

When you declare a fixed-size array within a user-defined type, its dimensions must be declared with numeric literals or constants rather than variables.

The setting of the **Option Base** statement determines the lower bound for arrays within user-defined types.

See Also

Data type summary, **Dim** statement, **Option Base** statement, **Private** statement, **Public** statement, **ReDim** statement, **Static** statement.

Specifics (Microsoft Access)

In Microsoft Access, user-defined types are public by default. You cannot define a public user-defined type within a class module. To declare a user-defined type within a class module, precede the **Type** statement with the **Private** keyword. If you fail to include the **Private** keyword, Microsoft Access generates a compile-time error.

Example

This example uses the **Type** statement to define a user-defined data type. The **Type** statement is used at the module level only. If it appears in a class module, a **Type** statement must be preceded by the keyword **Private**.

```
Type EmployeeRecord                     ' Create user-defined type.
   ID As Integer                        ' Define elements of data type.
   Name As String * 20
   Address As String * 30
   Phone As Long
   HireDate As Date
End Type
Sub CreateRecord()
   Dim MyRecord As EmployeeRecord       ' Declare variable.

   ' Assignment to EmployeeRecord variable must occur in a procedure.
   MyRecord.ID = 12003                  ' Assign a value to an element.
End Sub
```

TypeName Function

Description

Returns a **String** that provides information about a variable.

Syntax

TypeName(*varname*)

The required *varname* argument is a **Variant** containing any variable except a variable of a user-defined type.

Remarks

The string returned by **TypeName** can be any one of the following:

String returned	Variable
object type	An object whose type is *objecttype*
Byte	Byte value
Integer	Integer
Long	Long integer
Single	Single-precision floating-point number
Double	Double-precision floating-point number
Currency	Currency value
Decimal	Decimal value
Date	Date value
String	String
Boolean	Boolean value
Error	An error value
Empty	Uninitialized
Null	No valid data
Object	An object
Unknown	An object whose type is unknown
Nothing	Object variable that doesn't refer to an object

If *varname* is an array, the returned string can be any one of the possible returned strings (or **Variant**) with empty parentheses appended. For example, if *varname* is an array of integers, **TypeName** returns "`Integer()`".

See Also

Data type summary, **IsArray** function, **IsDate** function, **IsEmpty** function, **IsError** function, **IsMissing** function, **IsNull** function, **IsNumeric** function, **IsObject** function, **Variant** data type, **VarType** function.

Example

This example uses the **TypeName** function to return information about a variable.

```
' Declare variables.
Dim NullVar, MyType, StrVar As String, IntVar As Integer, CurVar As Currency
Dim ArrayVar (1 To 5) As Integer
NullVar = Null                              ' Assign Null value.
MyType = TypeName(StrVar)                   ' Returns "String".
MyType = TypeName(IntVar)                   ' Returns "Integer".
MyType = TypeName(CurVar)                   ' Returns "Currency".
MyType = TypeName(NullVar)                  ' Returns "Null".
MyType = TypeName(ArrayVar)                 ' Returns "Integer()".
```

Example (Microsoft Access)

The following example creates several object variables and passes them to the **TypeName** function.

```
Sub ObjectTypes()
   Dim dbs As Database, tdf As TableDef
   Dim fld As Field

   ' Get current database.
   Set dbs = CurrentDb
   ' Return TableDef object pointing to Orders table.
   Set tdf = dbs.TableDefs("Orders")
   ' Return Field object pointing to OrderDate field.
   Set fld = tdf.Fields("OrderDate")
   ' Print value returned by TypeName for each object.
   Debug.Print TypeName(dbs)
   Debug.Print TypeName(tdf)
   Debug.Print TypeName(fld)
End Sub
```

Example (Microsoft Excel)

This example displays the Visual Basic object type of the selection. You can run this example with cells selected, with a single oval selected, or with several different graphic objects selected.

```
Worksheets("Sheet1").Activate
MsgBox "The selection object type is " & TypeName(Selection)
```

UBound Function

Description

Returns a **Long** containing the largest available subscript for the indicated dimension of an array.

Syntax

UBound(*arrayname*[, *dimension*])

The **UBound** function syntax has these parts:

Part	Description
arrayname	Required, Name of the array variable; follows standard variable naming conventions.
dimension	Optional; **Variant** (**Long**). Whole number indicating which dimension's upper bound is returned. Use 1 for the first dimension, 2 for the second, and so on. If *dimension* is omitted, 1 is assumed.

Remarks

The **UBound** function is used with the **LBound** function to determine the size of an array. Use the **LBound** function to find the lower limit of an array dimension.

UBound returns the following values for an array with these dimensions:

```
Dim A(1 To 100, 0 To 3, -3 To 4)
```

Statement	Return Value
`UBound(A, 1)`	100
`UBound(A, 2)`	3
`UBound(A, 3)`	4

See Also

Dim statement, **LBound** function, **Option Base** statement, **Public** statement, **ReDim** statement.

Example

This example uses the **UBound** function to determine the largest available subscript for the indicated dimension of an array.

```
Dim Upper
Dim MyArray(1 To 10, 5 To 15, 10 To 20)      ' Declare array variables.
Dim AnyArray(10)
Upper = UBound(MyArray, 1)                   ' Returns 10.
Upper = UBound(MyArray, 3)                   ' Returns 20.
Upper = UBound(AnyArray)                     ' Returns 10.
```

Example (Microsoft Excel)

This example writes the elements of the first custom list in column one on Sheet1.

```
listArray = Application.GetCustomListContents(1)
For i = LBound(listArray, 1) To UBound(listArray, 1)
   Worksheets("sheet1").Cells(i, 1).Value = listArray(i)
Next i
```

This example assumes that you used an external data source to create a PivotTable on Sheet1. The example inserts the SQL connection string and query string into a new worksheet.

```
Set newSheet = ActiveWorkbook.Worksheets.Add
sdArray = Worksheets("Sheet1").UsedRange.PivotTable.SourceData
For i = LBound(sdArray) To UBound(sdArray)
   newSheet.Cells(i, 1) = sdArray(i)
Next i
```

UCase Function

Description

Returns a **Variant** (**String**) containing the specified string, converted to uppercase.

Syntax

UCase(*string***)**

The required *string* argument is any valid string expression. If *string* contains **Null**, **Null** is returned.

Remarks

Only lowercase letters are converted to uppercase; all uppercase letters and nonletter characters remain unchanged.

See Also

LCase function.

Example

This example uses the **UCase** function to return an uppercase version of a string.

```
Dim LowerCase, UpperCase
LowerCase = "Hello World 1234"       ' String to convert.
UpperCase = UCase(LowerCase)         ' Returns "HELLO WORLD 1234".
```

Unload Statement

Description

Removes an object from memory.

Syntax

Unload *object*

The required *object* placeholder represents an object expression that evaluates to an object in the Applies To list.

Remarks

When an object is unloaded, it's removed from memory and all memory associated with the object is reclaimed. Until it is placed in memory again using the **Load** statement, a user can't interact with an object, and the object can't be manipulated programmatically.

See Also

Activate, Deactivate events, **Hide** method, **Load** statement.

Example

The following example assumes two **UserForms** in a program. In UserForm1's Initialize event, UserForm2 is loaded and shown. When the user clicks UserForm2, it is unloaded and UserForm1 appears. When UserForm1 is clicked, it is unloaded in turn.

```
' This is the Initialize event procedure for UserForm1.
Private Sub UserForm_Initialize()
   Load UserForm2
   UserForm2.Show
End Sub
' This is the Click event for UserForm2.
Private Sub UserForm_Click()
   Unload UserForm2
End Sub

' This is the click event for UserForm1.
Private Sub UserForm_Click()
   Unload UserForm1
End Sub
```

Unlock Statement

See Lock, Unlock Statements.

User-Defined Data Type

Description

Any data type you define using the **Type** statement. User-defined data types can contain one or more elements of a data type, an array, or a previously defined user-defined type. For example:

```
Type MyType
   MyName As String          ' String variable stores a name.
   MyBirthDate As Date       ' Date variable stores a birthdate.
   MySex As Integer          ' Integer variable stores sex (0 for
End Type                     ' female, 1 for male).
```

See Also

Data type summary, **Type** statement.

UserForm Object, UserForms Collection

Description

A **UserForm** object is a window or dialog box that makes up part of an application's user interface.

The **UserForms** collection is a collection whose elements represent each loaded **UserForm** in an application. The **UserForms** collection has a **Count** property, an **Item** property, and an **Add** method. **Count** specifies the number of elements in the collection; **Item** (the default member) specifies a specific collection member; and **Add** places a new **UserForm** element in the collection.

Syntax

UserForm
UserForms[.Item](*index*)

The placeholder *index* represents an integer with a range from 0 to **UserForms.Count –** 1. **Item** is the default member of the **UserForms** collection and need not be specified.

Remarks

You can use the **UserForms** collection to iterate through all loaded user forms in an application. It identifies an intrinsic global variable named **UserForms**. You can pass **UserForms(***index***)** to a function whose argument is specified as a **UserForm** class.

User forms have properties that determine appearance such as position, size, and color; and aspects of their behavior.

User forms can also respond to events initiated by a user or triggered by the system. For example, you can write code in the **Initialize** event procedure of the **UserForm** to initialize module-level variables before the **UserForm** is displayed.

In addition to properties and events, you can use methods to manipulate user forms using code. For example, you can use the **Move** method to change the location and size of a **UserForm**.

When designing user forms, set the **BorderStyle** property to define borders, and set the **Caption** property to put text in the title bar. In code, you can use the **Hide** and **Show** methods to make a **UserForm** invisible or visible at run time.

UserForm is an **Object** data type. You can declare variables as type **UserForm** before setting them to an instance of a type of **UserForm** declared at design time. Similarly, you can pass an argument to a procedure as type **UserForm**. You can create multiple instances of user forms in code by using the **New** keyword in **Dim**, **Set**, and **Static** statements.

You can access the collection of controls on a **UserForm** using the **Controls** collection. For example, to hide all the controls on a **UserForm**, use code similar to the following:

```
For Each Control in UserForm1.Controls
   Control.Visible = False
Next Control
```

Note You can't use the **UserForm** object and **UserForms** collection in Microsoft Access, even though it's part of the Visual Basic for Applications type library. The properties, methods, and events listed below for this object are part of the Forms type library.

Properties

ActiveControl property, **BackColor** property, **BorderColor** property, **BorderStyle** property, **CanPaste** property, **CanRedo** property, **CanUndo** property, **Caption** property, **Cycle** property, **DrawBuffer** property, **Enabled** property, **Font** object, **ForeColor** property, **Height**, **Width** properties, **HelpContextID** property, **InsideHeight**, **InsideWidth** properties, **KeepScrollBarsVisible** property, **Left**, **Top** properties, **MouseIcon** property, **MousePointer** property, **Name** property, **Picture** property, **PictureAlignment** property, **PictureSizeMode** property, **PictureTiling** property, **ScrollBars** property, **ScrollHeight**, **ScrollWidth** properties, **ScrollLeft**, **ScrollTop** properties, **SpecialEffect** property, **StartUpPosition** property, **Tag** property, **VerticalScrollbarSide** property, **Visible** property, **WhatsThisButton** property, **WhatsThisHelp** property, **Zoom** property.

Methods

Copy method, **Cut** method, **Hide** method, **Move** method, **Paste** method, **PrintForm** method, **RedoAction** method, **Repaint** method, **Scroll** method, **SetDefaultTabOrder** method, **Show** method, **UndoAction** method, **WhatsThisMode** method.

Events

Activate, Deactivate events, AddControl event, BeforeDragOver event, BeforeDropOrPaste event, Click event, DblClick event, Error event, KeyDown, KeyUp events, KeyPress event, Layout event, MouseDown, MouseUp events, MouseMove event, RemoveControl event, Scroll event, Terminate Event, Zoom event.

See Also

Unload statement.

Val Function

Description

Returns the numbers contained in a string as a numeric value of appropriate type.

Syntax

Val(*string*)

The required *string* argument is any valid string expression.

Remarks

The **Val** function stops reading the string at the first character it can't recognize as part of a number. Symbols and characters that are often considered parts of numeric values, such as dollar signs and commas, are not recognized. However, the function recognizes the radix prefixes &O (for octal) and &H (for hexadecimal). Blanks, tabs, and linefeed characters are stripped from the argument.

The following returns the value 1615198:

```
Val("    1615 198th Street N.E.")
```

In the code below, **Val** returns the decimal value -1 for the hexadecimal value shown:

```
Val("&HFFFF")
```

Note The **Val** function recognizes only the period (.) as a valid decimal separator. When different decimal separators can be used, for example, in international applications, use **CDbl** instead to convert a string to a number.

See Also

Str function.

Example

This example uses the **Val** function to return the numbers contained in a string.

```
Dim MyValue
MyValue = Val("2457")                                   ' Returns 2457.
MyValue = Val(" 2 45 7")                                ' Returns 2457.
MyValue = Val("24 and 57")                              ' Returns 24.
```

Variant Data Type

Description

The **Variant** data type is the data type for all variables that are not explicitly declared as some other type (using statements such as **Dim**, **Private**, **Public**, or **Static**). The **Variant** data type has no type-declaration character.

A **Variant** is a special data type that can contain any kind of data except fixed-length **String** data and user-defined types. A **Variant** can also contain the special values **Empty**, **Error**, **Nothing**, and **Null**. You can determine how the data in a **Variant** is treated using the **VarType** function or **TypeName** function.

Numeric data can be any integer or real number value ranging from -1.797693134862315E308 to -4.94066E-324 for negative values and from 4.94066E-324 to 1.797693134862315E308 for positive values. Generally, numeric **Variant** data is maintained in its original data type within the **Variant**. For example, if you assign an **Integer** to a **Variant**, subsequent operations treat the **Variant** as an **Integer**. However, if an arithmetic operation is performed on a **Variant** containing a **Byte**, an **Integer**, a **Long**, or a **Single**, and the result exceeds the normal range for the original data type, the result is promoted within the **Variant** to the next larger data type. A **Byte** is promoted to an **Integer**, an **Integer** is promoted to a **Long**, and a **Long** and a **Single** are promoted to a **Double**. An error occurs when **Variant** variables containing **Currency**, **Decimal**, and **Double** values exceed their respective ranges.

You can use the **Variant** data type in place of any data type to work with data in a more flexible way. If the contents of a **Variant** variable are digits, they may be either the string representation of the digits or their actual value, depending on the context. For example:

```
Dim MyVar As Variant
MyVar = 98052
```

In the preceding example, `MyVar` contains a numeric representation—the actual value `98052`. Arithmetic operators work as expected on **Variant** variables that contain numeric values or string data that can be interpreted as numbers. If you use the **+** operator to add `MyVar` to another **Variant** containing a number or to a variable of a numeric type, the result is an arithmetic sum.

The value **Empty** denotes a **Variant** variable that hasn't been initialized (assigned an initial value). A **Variant** containing **Empty** is 0 if it is used in a numeric context and a zero-length string (" ") if it is used in a string context.

Don't confuse **Empty** with **Null**. **Null** indicates that the **Variant** variable intentionally contains no valid data.

In a **Variant**, **Error** is a special value used to indicate that an error condition has occurred in a procedure. However, unlike for other kinds of errors, normal application-level error handling does not occur. This allows you, or the application itself, to take some alternative action based on the error value. **Error** values are created by converting real numbers to error values using the **CVErr** function.

See Also

CVErr function, Data type summary, **Def*type*** statements, **Dim** statement, **Private** statement, **Public** statement, **Static** statement, **TypeName** function.

VarType Function

Description

Returns an **Integer** indicating the subtype of a variable.

Syntax

VarType(*varname***)**

The required *varname* argument is a **Variant** containing any variable except a variable of a user-defined type.

Return Values

Constant	Value	Description
vbEmpty	0	**Empty** (uninitialized)
vbNull	1	**Null** (no valid data)
vbInteger	2	Integer
vbLong	3	Long integer
vbSingle	4	Single-precision floating-point number
vbDouble	5	Double-precision floating-point number
vbCurrency	6	Currency value
vbDate	7	Date value
vbString	8	String
vbObject	9	Object
vbError	10	Error value
vbBoolean	11	Boolean value
vbVariant	12	**Variant** (used only with arrays of variants)
vbDataObject	13	A data access object
vbDecimal	14	Decimal value
vbByte	17	Byte value
vbArray	8192	Array

Note These constants are specified by Visual Basic for Applications. The names can be used anywhere in your code in place of the actual values.

Remarks

The **VarType** function never returns the value for **vbArray** by itself. It is always added to some other value to indicate an array of a particular type. The constant **vbVariant** is only returned in conjunction with **vbArray** to indicate that the argument to the **VarType** function is an array of type **Variant**. For example, the value returned for an array of integers is calculated as **vbInteger** + **vbArray**, or 8194. If an object has a default property, **VarType** (*object*) returns the type of the object's default property.

See Also

Data type summary, **IsArray** function, **IsDate** function, **IsEmpty** function, **IsError** function, **IsMissing** function, **IsNull** function, **IsNumeric** function, **IsObject** function, **TypeName** function, **Variant** data type.

Example

This example uses the **VarType** function to determine the subtype of a variable.

```
Dim IntVar, StrVar, DateVar, MyCheck
' Initialize variables.
IntVar = 459: StrVar = "Hello World": DateVar = #2/12/69#
MyCheck = VarType(IntVar)                          ' Returns 2.
MyCheck = VarType(DateVar)                         ' Returns 7.
MyCheck = VarType(StrVar)                          ' Returns 8.
```

Weekday Function

Description

Returns a **Variant** (**Integer**) containing a whole number representing the day of the week.

Syntax

Weekday(*date***, [***firstdayofweek***])**

The **Weekday** function syntax has these named arguments:

Part	Description
date	Required. **Variant**, numeric expression, string expression, or any combination, that can represent a date. If ***date*** contains **Null**, **Null** is returned.
firstdayofweek	Optional. A constant that specifies the first day of the week. If not specified, **vbSunday** is assumed.

Settings

The ***firstdayofweek*** argument has these settings:

Constant	Value	Description
vbUseSystem	0	Use the NLS API setting.
vbSunday	1	Sunday (default).
vbMonday	2	Monday.
vbTuesday	3	Tuesday.
vbWednesday	4	Wednesday.
vbThursday	5	Thursday.
vbFriday	6	Friday.
vbSaturday	7	Saturday.

Return Values

The **Weekday** function can return any of these values:

Constant	Value	Description
vbSunday	1	Sunday.
vbMonday	2	Monday.
vbTuesday	3	Tuesday.
vbWednesday	4	Wednesday.
vbThursday	5	Thursday.
vbFriday	6	Friday.
vbSaturday	7	Saturday.

See Also

Date function, **Date** statement, **Day** function, **Month** function, **Now** function, **Year** function.

Example

This example uses the **Weekday** function to obtain the day of the week from a specified date.

```
Dim MyDate, MyWeekDay
MyDate = #February 12, 1969#            ' Assign a date.
MyWeekDay = Weekday(MyDate)             ' MyWeekDay contains 4 because
                                        ' MyDate represents a Wednesday.
```

WhatsThisButton Property

Applies To

UserForm object.

Description

Returns a **Boolean** value that determines whether the **What's This** button appears on the title bar of a **UserForm** object. Read-only at run time.

Remarks

The settings for the **WhatsThisButton** property are:

Setting	Description
True	Turns on display of the **What's This Help** button.
False	(Default) Turns off display of the **What's This Help** button.

Remarks

The **WhatsThisHelp** property must be **True** for the **WhatsThisButton** property to be **True**.

See Also

WhatsThisHelp property, **WhatsThisMode** method.

WhatsThisHelp Property

Applies To

UserForm object.

Description

Returns a **Boolean** value that determines whether context-sensitive Help uses the pop-up window provided by Windows 95 Help or the main Help window. Read-only at run time.

Remarks

The settings for the **WhatsThisHelp** property are:

Setting	Description
True	The application uses one of the What's This access techniques to start Windows Help and load a topic identified by the **WhatsThisHelpID** property.
False	(Default) The application uses the F1 key to start Windows Help and load the topic identified by the **HelpContextID** property.

Remarks

There are two access techniques for providing What's This Help in an application. The **WhatsThisHelp** property must be set to **True** for any of these techniques to work.

- Providing a **What's This** button on the title bar of the **UserForm** using the **WhatsThisButton** property. The mouse pointer changes to the What's This state (arrow with question mark). The topic displayed is identified by the **WhatsThisHelpID** property of the control clicked by the user.
- Invoking the **WhatsThisMode** method of a **UserForm**. This produces the same behavior as clicking the **What's This** button without using a button. For example, you can invoke this method from a command on a menu in the menu bar of the application.

See Also

WhatsThisButton property, **WhatsThisMode** method.

WhatsThisMode Method

Applies To

UserForm object.

Description

Causes the mouse pointer to change to the **What's This** pointer and prepares the application to display Help on a selected object.

Syntax

object.**WhatsThisMode**

The *object* placeholder represents an object expression that evaluates to an object in the Applies To list. If *object* is omitted, the **UserForm** with the focus is assumed to be *object*.

Remarks

Executing the **WhatsThisMode** method places the application in the same state as clicking the **What's This** button on the title bar. The mouse pointer changes to the **What's This** pointer. When the user clicks an object, the **WhatsThisHelpID** property of the clicked object is used to invoke the context-sensitive Help.

See Also

WhatsThisButton property, **WhatsThisHelp** property.

Example

The following example changes the mouse pointer to the **What's This** (question mark) pointer when the user clicks the **UserForm**. If neither the **WhatsThisHelp** or the **WhatsThisButton** property is set to **True** in the **Properties** window, the following invocation has no effect.

```
Private Sub UserForm_Click()
    ' Turn mouse pointer to What's This question mark.
    WhatsThisMode
End Sub
```

While...Wend Statement

Description

Executes a series of statements as long as a given condition is **True**.

Syntax

While *condition*
  [*statements*]
Wend

The **While...Wend** statement syntax has these parts:

Part	Description
condition	Required. Numeric expression or string expression that evaluates to **True** or **False**. If *condition* is **Null**, *condition* is treated as **False**.
statements	Optional. One or more statements executed while condition is **True**.

Remarks

If *condition* is **True**, all *statements* are executed until the **Wend** statement is encountered. Control then returns to the **While** statement and *condition* is again checked. If *condition* is still **True**, the process is repeated. If it is not **True**, execution resumes with the statement following the **Wend** statement.

While...Wend loops can be nested to any level. Each **Wend** matches the most recent **While**.

Tip The **Do...Loop** statement provides a more structured and flexible way to perform looping.

See Also

Do...Loop statement, **With** statement.

Example

This example uses the **While...Wend** statement to increment a counter variable. The statements in the loop are executed as long as the condition evaluates to **True**.

```
Dim Counter
Counter = 0                             ' Initialize variable.
While Counter < 20                      ' Test value of Counter.
   Counter = Counter + 1                ' Increment Counter.
Wend                                    ' End While loop when Counter > 19.
Debug.Print Counter                     ' Prints 20 in Debug window.
```

Width # Statement

Description

Assigns an output line width to a file opened using the **Open** statement.

Syntax

Width #*filenumber***,** *width*

The **Width #** statement syntax has these parts:

Part	Description
filenumber	Required. Any valid file number.
width	Required. Numeric expression in the range 0–255, inclusive, that indicates how many characters appear on a line before a new line is started. If *width* equals 0, there is no limit to the length of a line. The default value for *width* is 0.

See Also

Open statement, **Print #** statement.

Example

This example uses the **Width #** statement to set the output line width for a file.

```
Dim I
Open "TESTFILE" For Output As #1          ' Open file for output.
Width #1, 5                               ' Set output line width to 5.
For I = 0 To 9                            ' Loop 10 times.
   Print #1, Chr(48 + I);                 ' Prints five characters per line.
Next I
Close #1                                  ' Close file.
```

With Statement

Description

Executes a series of statements on a single object or a user-defined type.

Syntax

With *object*
  [*statements*]
End With

The **With** statement syntax has these parts:

Part	Description
object	Required. Name of an object or a user-defined type.
statements	Optional. One or more statements to be executed on *object*.

Remarks

The **With** statement allows you to perform a series of statements on a specified object without requalifying the name of the object. For example, to change a number of different properties on a single object, place the property assignment statements within the **With** control structure, referring to the object once instead of referring to it with each property assignment. The following example illustrates use of the **With** statement to assign values to several properties of the same object.

```
With MyLabel
   .Height = 2000
   .Width = 2000
   .Caption = "This is MyLabel"
End With
```

Note Once a **With** block is entered, *object* can't be changed. As a result, you can't use a single **With** statement to affect a number of different objects.

You can nest **With** statements by placing one **With** block within another. However, because members of outer **With** blocks are masked within the inner **With** blocks, you must provide a fully qualified object reference in an inner **With** block to any member of an object in an outer **With** block.

Important Do not jump into or out of **With** blocks. If statements in a **With** block are executed, but either the **With** or **End With** statement is not executed, you may get errors or unpredictable behavior.

See Also

Do...Loop statement.

Example

This example uses the **With** statement to execute a series of statements on a single object. The object `MyObject` and its properties are generic names used for illustration purposes only.

```
With MyObject
   .Height = 100               ' Same as MyObject.Height = 100.
   .Caption = "Hello World"    ' Same as MyObject.Caption = "Hello World".
   With .Font
      .Color = Red             ' Same as MyObject.Font.Color = Red.
      .Bold = True             ' Same as MyObject.Font.Bold = True.
   End With
End With
```

Example (Microsoft Excel)

This example creates a formatted multiplication table in cells A1:K11 on Sheet1.

```
Set dataTableRange = Worksheets("Sheet1").Range("A1:K11")
Set rowInputCell = Worksheets("Sheet1").Range("A12")
Set columnInputCell = Worksheets("Sheet1").Range("A13")

Worksheets("Sheet1").Range("A1").Formula = "=A12*A13"
For i = 2 To 11
   Worksheets("Sheet1").Cells(i, 1) = i - 1
   Worksheets("Sheet1").Cells(1, i) = i - 1
Next i
dataTableRange.Table rowInputCell, columnInputCell
With Worksheets("Sheet1").Range("A1").CurrentRegion
   .Rows(1).Font.Bold = True
   .Columns(1).Font.Bold = True
   .Columns.AutoFit
End With
```

Write # Statement

Description

Writes data to a sequential file.

Syntax

Write **#***filenumber***,** [*outputlist*]

The **Write #** statement syntax has these parts:

Part	Description
filenumber	Required. Any valid file number.
outputlist	Optional. One or more comma-delimited numeric expressions or string expressions to write to a file.

Remarks

Data written with **Write #** is usually read from a file with **Input #**.

If you omit *outputlist* and include a comma after *filenumber*, a blank line is printed to the file. Multiple expressions can be separated with a space, a semicolon, or a comma. A space has the same effect as a semicolon.

When **Write #** is used to write data to a file, several universal assumptions are followed so the data can always be read and correctly interpreted using **Input #**, regardless of locale:

- Numeric data is always written using the period as the decimal separator.
- For **Boolean** data, either `#TRUE#` or `#FALSE#` is printed. The **True** and **False** keywords are not translated, regardless of locale.
- **Date** data is written to the file using the universal date format. When either the date or the time component is missing or zero, only the part provided gets written to the file.
- Nothing is written to the file if *outputlist* data is **Empty**. However, for **Null** data, `#NULL#` is written.
- If *outputlist* data is **Null** data, `#NULL#` is written to the file.
- For **Error** data, the output appears as `#ERROR errorcode#`. The **Error** keyword is not translated, regardless of locale.

Unlike the **Print #** statement, the **Write #** statement inserts commas between items and quotation marks around strings as they are written to the file. You don't have to put explicit delimiters in the list. **Write #** inserts a newline character, that is, a carriage return–linefeed (**Chr**(13) + **Chr**(10)), after it has written the final character in *outputlist* to the file.

See Also

Input # statement, **Open** statement, **Print #** statement.

Example

This example uses the **Write #** statement to write raw data to a sequential file.

```
Open "TESTFILE" For Output As #1      ' Open file for output.
Write #1, "Hello World", 234         ' Write comma-delimited data.
Write #1,                       ' Write blank line.

Dim MyBool, MyDate, MyNull, MyError
' Assign Boolean, Date, Null, and Error values.
MyBool = False : MyDate = #February 12, 1969# : MyNull = Null
MyError = CVErr(32767)
' Boolean data is written as #TRUE# or #FALSE#. Date literals are
' written in universal date format, for example, #1994-07-13#
' represents July 13, 1994. Null data is written as #NULL#.
' Error data is written as #ERROR errorcode#.
Write #1, MyBool ; " is a Boolean value"
Write #1, MyDate ; " is a date"
Write #1, MyNull ; " is a null value"
Write #1, MyError ; " is an error value"
Close #1                             ' Close file.
```

Xor Operator

Description

Used to perform a logical exclusion on two expressions.

Syntax

[*result* =] *expression1* **Xor** *expression2*

The **Xor** operator syntax has these parts:

Part	Description
result	Optional; any numeric variable.
expression1	Required; any expression.
expression2	Required; any expression.

Remarks

If one, and only one, of the expressions evaluates to **True**, *result* is **True**. However, if either expression is **Null**, *result* is also **Null**. When neither expression is **Null**, *result* is determined according to the following table:

If *expression1* is	And *expression2* is	Then *result* is
True	**True**	**False**
True	**False**	**True**
False	**True**	**True**
False	**False**	**False**

The **Xor** operator performs as both a logical and bitwise operator. A bit-wise comparison of two expressions using exclusive-or logic to form the result, as shown in the following table:

If bit in *expression1* is	And bit in *expression2* is	Then *result* is
0	0	0
0	1	1
1	0	1
1	1	0

See Also

Operator precedence.

Example

This example uses the **Xor** operator to perform logical exclusion on two expressions.

```
Dim A, B, C, D, MyCheck
A = 10: B = 8: C = 6: D = Null       ' Initialize variables.
MyCheck = A > B Xor B > C            ' Returns False.
MyCheck = B > A Xor B > C            ' Returns True.
MyCheck = B > A Xor C > B            ' Returns False.
MyCheck = B > D Xor A > B            ' Returns Null.
MyCheck = A Xor B                    ' Returns 2 (bitwise comparison).
```

Year Function

Description

Returns a **Variant** (**Integer**) containing a whole number representing the year.

Syntax

Year(*date***)**

The required *date* argument is any **Variant**, numeric expression, string expression, or any combination, that can represent a date. If *date* contains **Null**, **Null** is returned.

See Also

Date function, **Date** statement, **Day** function, **Month** function, **Now** function, **Weekday** function.

Example

This example uses the **Year** function to obtain the year from a specified date. In the development environment, the date literal is displayed in short date format using the locale settings of your code.

```
Dim MyDate, MyYear
MyDate = #February 12, 1969#          ' Assign a date.
MyYear = Year(MyDate)                 ' MyYear contains 1969.
```

Example (Microsoft Access)

See the **DateSerial** function example (Microsoft Access).

Microsoft Office Language Reference

Microsoft Office Assistant

Default location: \Program Files\Microsoft Office\Office

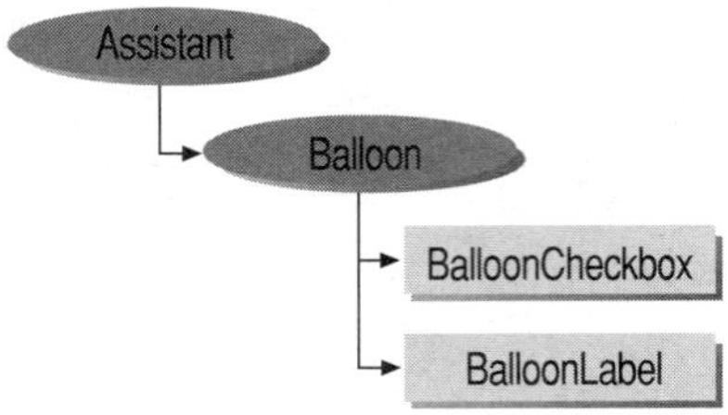

Source (Type Library)

The Microsoft Office Assistant object model is provided by MSO97.DLL, which is included when you install Microsoft Office 97.

Microsoft Office Command Bars

Default location: \Program Files\Microsoft Office\Office

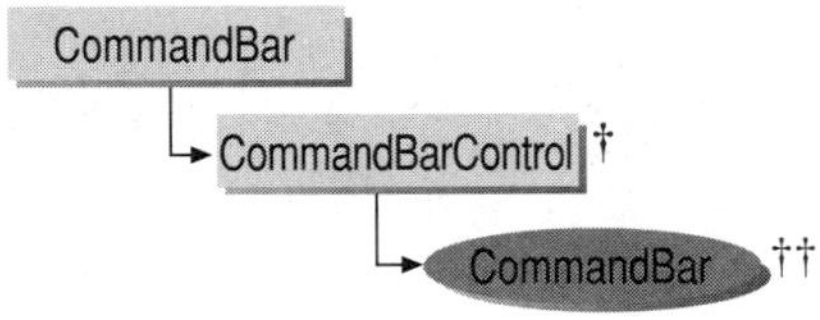

Source (Type Library)

The Microsoft Office 97 CommandBars object model is provided by MSO97.DLL, which is included when you install Microsoft Office 97.

Notes

Items marked by a single (†) indicate the CommandBarControl class has three derived classes which are used to represent a certain subset of control types. The derived classes are CommandBarButton, CommandBarComboBox, and CommandBarPopup. Given a base CommandBarControl object you can determine if it is really one of the derived object types by using the Visual Basic TypeName() function. The derived classes add several properties and methods which only apply to certain control types.

Items marked by a double (††) contain objects that only appear in the CommandBarControlPopup derived class.

Microsoft Office FileSearch

Default location: \Program Files\Microsoft Office\Office

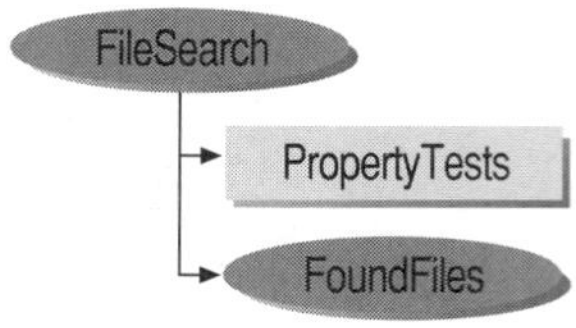

Source (Type Library)

The Microsoft Office 97 FileSearch object model is provided by MSO97.DLL, which is included when you install Microsoft Office 97.

ActionControl Property

Applies To

CommandBars collection object.

Description

Returns the **CommandBarControl** object whose **OnAction** property is set to the running procedure. If the running procedure was not initiated by a command bar control, this property returns **Nothing**. Read-only.

Example

This example disables the command bar control that initiated the running procedure while a series of statements runs, and then enables the control.

```
Set theCtrl = CommandBars.ActionControl
theCtrl.Enabled = False
   'insert OnAction process here
theCtrl.Enabled = True
```

ActivateWizard Method

Applies To

Assistant object.

Description

Resumes or suspends an Office Assistant wizard session.

Note This method is used as part of the process begun with the **StartWizard** method.

Syntax

expression.**ActivateWizard(*WizardID, Act, Animation*)**

expression Required. An expression that returns an **Assistant** object.

WizardID Required **Long**. A number that uniquely identifies the Office Assistant wizard session, as returned by the **StartWizard** method.

Act Required **Variant**. Specifies the way the Office Assistant wizard session changes. Can be one of the following constants: **msoWizardActTypes**: **msoWizardActActive**, **msoWizardActInactive**, **msoWizardActResume**, or **msoWizardActSuspend**.

Animation Optional **Variant**. The type of animation that the Office Assistant performs when it resumes or suspends the wizard session.

See Also

EndWizard method, **StartWizard** method.

Example

This example suspends the Office Assistant wizard session begun with the **StartWizard** method. The variable `helpForWiz` was set to the return value of the **StartWizard** method.

```
Assistant.ActivateWizard WizardID:=helpForWiz, _
   Act:=msoWizardActSuspend, Animation:=msoAnimationGoodbye
```

ActiveMenuBar Property

Applies To

CommandBars collection object.

Description

Returns a **CommandBar** object that represents the active menu bar in the container application. Read-only.

See Also

Add method (**CommandBars** collection).

Example

This example adds a temporary pop-up control named "Custom" to the end of the active menu bar, and then it adds a button control named "Import" to the command bar displayed by the control.

```
Set myMenuBar = CommandBars.ActiveMenuBar
Set newMenu = myMenuBar.Controls.Add(Type:=msoControlPopup, _
   Temporary:=True)
newMenu.Caption = "Custom"
Set ctrl1 = newMenu.CommandBar.Controls _
   .Add(Type:=msoControlButton, Id:=1)
With ctrl1
   .Caption = "Import"
   .TooltipText = "Import"
   .Style = msoButtonCaption
End With
```

Add Method (CommandBarControls Collection)

Applies To

CommandBarControls collection object.

Description

Creates a new command bar control and adds it to the collection of controls on the specified command bar. Returns a **CommandBarButton**, **CommandBarComboBox**, or **CommandBarPopup** object.

Syntax

expression.**Add**(***Type, Id, Parameter, Before, Temporary***)

expression Required. An expression that returns a **CommandBarControls** object.

Type Optional **Variant**. The type of control to be added to the specified command bar. Can be one of the following **MsoControlType** constants: **msoControlButton**, **msoControlEdit**, **msoControlDropdown**, **msoControlComboBox**, or **msoControlPopup**.

Id Optional **Variant**. An integer that specifies a built-in control. If the value of this argument is 1, or if this argument is omitted, a blank custom control of the specified type will be added to the command bar.

Parameter Optional **Variant**. For built-in controls, this argument is used by the container application to run the command. For custom controls, you can use this argument to send information to Visual Basic procedures, or you can use it to store information about the control (similar to a second **Tag** property value).

Before Optional **Variant**. A number that indicates the position of the new control on the command bar. The new control will be inserted before the control at this position. If this argument is omitted, the control is added at the end of the specified command bar.

Temporary Optional **Variant**. **True** to make the new control temporary. Temporary controls are automatically deleted when the container application is closed. The default value is **False**.

See Also

CustomizationContext property.

Specifics (Microsoft Access)

You can set the ***Id*** argument of this method to an **Integer** value that corresponds to a built-in command button or menu item. This will cause the new control to have the appearance and functionality of the existing command button or menu item.

However, if you set the ***Id*** argument to the **Integer** value of a Microsoft Office command button or menu item that has been modified by Microsoft Access (for example, Microsoft Access uses a different label, different shortcut text, or uses text instead of an icon), you won't see the Microsoft Access modifications to the command button or menu item. If you want to make sure a control you're adding to a command bar looks and functions exactly like the Microsoft Access version of the control, use the **Copy** method to copy the control to the command bar.

Example

This example adds a button control with a charting face to the command bar named "Custom," and then it assigns the control the procedure named "Analyze."

```
Set custBar = CommandBars("Custom")
custBar.Visible = True
Set graphBtn = custBar.Controls.Add(Type:=msoControlButton)
graphBtn.FaceId = 17
graphBtn.OnAction = "Analyze"
```

Add Method (CommandBars Collection)

Applies To

CommandBars collection object.

Description

Creates a new command bar and adds it to the collection of command bars. Returns a **CommandBar** object.

Syntax

expression.**Add**(***Name, Position, MenuBar, Temporary***)

expression Required. An expression that returns a **CommandBars** object.

Name Optional **Variant**. The name of the new command bar. If this argument is omitted, Word assigns a default name to the command bar (such as "Custom 1").

Position Optional **Variant**. The position of the new command bar. Can be one of the following **MsoBarPosition** constants.

Constant	Description
msoBarLeft, **msoBarTop**, **msoBarRight**, **msoBarBottom**	Indicate the left, top, right, and bottom coordinates of the new command bar
msoBarFloating	Indicates that the new command bar won't be docked
msoBarPopup	Indicates that the new command bar will be a shortcut menu
msoBarMenuBar	Indicates that the new command bar will replace the system menu bar on the Macintosh

MenuBar Optional **Variant**. **True** to replace the active menu bar with the new command bar. The default value is **False**.

Temporary Optional **Variant**. **True** to make the new command bar temporary. Temporary command bars are deleted when the container application is closed. The default value is **False**.

See Also

CommandBars collection object, **CustomizationContext** property.

Example

This example adds a top-level command bar named "Custom" that won't be saved when the session ends. The example also adds a built-in spelling-checker button to the command bar.

```
Set mybar = CommandBars _
    .Add(Name:="Custom", Position:=msoBarTop, Temporary:=True)
With mybar
    .Controls.Add Type:=msoControlButton, Id:=2
    .Visible = True
End With
```

Add Method (DocumentProperties Collection)

Applies To

DocumentProperties collection object.

Description

Creates a new custom document property. You can use this method only with the collection of custom document properties.

Syntax

expression.**Add**(***Name, LinkToContent, Type, Value, LinkSource***)

expression Required. The custom **DocumentProperties** object.

Name Required **String**. The name of the property.

LinkToContent Required **Boolean**. Specifies whether the property is linked to the contents of the container document. If this argument is **True**, the ***LinkSource*** argument is required; if it's **False**, the value argument is required.

Type Required **Long**. The data type of the property. Can be one of the following **MsoDocProperties** constants: **msoPropertyTypeBoolean**, **msoPropertyTypeDate**, **msoPropertyTypeFloat**, **msoPropertyTypeNumber**, or **msoPropertyTypeString**.

Value Optional **Variant**. The value of the property if it's not linked to the contents of the container document. The value is converted to match the data type specified by the type argument, if possible; otherwise, an error occurs. If ***LinkToContent*** is **True**, the ***Value*** argument is ignored and the new document property has a default value until linked property values are updated by the container application (usually when the document is saved).

LinkSource Optional **Boolean**. Ignored if ***LinkToContent*** is **False**. The source of the linked property. The container application determines what types of source linking you can use.

See Also

DocumentProperties collection object.

Example

This example adds a new custom document property and names it "Complete." You must pass the custom **DocumentProperties** collection to the procedure.

```
Sub AddCustomProperty(dp As DocumentProperties)
    dp.Add name:="Complete", linkToContent:=False, _
    type:=msoPropertyTypeBoolean, value:=False
End Sub
```

Add Method (PropertyTests Collection)

Applies To

PropertyTests collection object.

Description

Adds a **PropertyTest** object to the **PropertyTests** collection.

Syntax

expression.**Add**(***Name, Condition, Value, SecondValue, Connector***)

expression An expression that returns a **PropertyTests** object.

Name Required **String**. The name of the property criterion. The name corresponds to a value in the **Property** box in the **Advanced Find** dialog box.

Condition Required **Variant**. The condition of the search criteria. Can be one of the following **MsoCondition** constants:

msoConditionAnyNumberBetween	**msoConditionAnytime**
msoConditionAnytimeBetween	**msoConditionAtLeast**
msoConditionAtMost	**msoConditionBeginsWith**
msoConditionDoesNotEqual	**msoConditionEndsWith**
msoConditionEquals	**msoConditionFileTypeAllFiles**
msoConditionFileTypeBinders	**msoConditionFileTypeDatabases**

(continued)

msoConditionFileTypeExcelWorkbooks
msoConditionFileTypeOfficeFiles
msoConditionFileTypePowerPointPresentations
msoConditionFileTypeTemplates
msoConditionFileTypeWordDocuments
msoConditionIncludesNearEachOther
msoConditionIncludesPhrase
msoConditionInTheLast
msoConditionInTheNext
msoConditionIsExactly
msoConditionIsNo
msoConditionIsNot
msoConditionIsYes
msoConditionLastMonth
msoConditionLastWeek
msoConditionLessThan
msoConditionMoreThan
msoConditionNextMonth
msoConditionNextWeek
msoConditionOn
msoConditionOnorAfter
msoConditionOnorBefore
msoConditionThisMonth
msoConditionThisWeek
msoConditionToday
msoConditionTomorrow
msoConditionYesterday

Value Optional **Variant**. The value of the search criterion to test for.

SecondValue Optional **Variant**. An upper value for the search range. You can use this argument only if ***Condition*** is **msoConditionAnyTimeBetween** or **msoConditionAnyNumberBetween**.

Connector Optional **Variant**. Specifies the way two search criteria are combined. Can be either of the following **MsoConnector** constants: **msoConnectorAnd** or **msoConnectorOr**.

Example

This example adds two property tests to the search criteria. The first test is that the found files must be Word documents, and the second test is that the found files must have been modified between January 1, 1996 and June 30, 1996.

```
Set fs = Application.FileSearch
fs.NewSearch
With fs.PropertyTests
    .Add Name:="Files of Type", Condition:= _
        msoConditionFileTypeWordDocuments, Connector:=msoConnectorOr
    .Add Name:="Last Modified", Condition:= _
        msoConditionAnytimeBetween, Value:="1/1/96", SecondValue:= _
            "6/30/96", Connector:=msoConnectorAnd
End With
```

AddItem Method

Applies To

CommandBarComboBox object.

Description

Adds a list item to the specified command bar combo box control. The combo box control must be a custom control and it must be either a drop-down list box or a combo box.

Note This method will fail if it's applied to a combo box control that's either an edit box or a built-in combo box control.

Syntax

expression.**AddItem**(***Text, Index***)

expression Required. An expression that returns a **CommandBarComboBox** object.

Text Required **String**. The item to be added to the specified control.

Index Optional **Variant**. The position of the specified item in the list of items. If this argument is omitted, the item is added at the end of the list.

See Also

Add method (**CommandBarControls** collection), **Clear** method, **CommandBarComboBox** object, **Visible** property.

Example

This example adds a combo box control to the command bar named "Custom," and then it adds two items to the list. The example also sets the number of line items, the width of the combo box, and an empty default for the combo box.

```
Set myBar = CommandBars("Custom")
Set myControl = myBar.Controls.Add(Type:=msoControlComboBox, Id:=1)
With myControl
    .AddItem "First Item", 1
    .AddItem "Second Item", 2
    .DropDownLines = 3
    .DropDownWidth = 75
    .ListHeaderCount = 0
End With
```

Animation Property

Applies To

Assistant object, **Balloon** object.

Description

Returns or sets the animation action for the Office Assistant. When this property is applied to the **Assistant** object, the Assistant is animated immediately (if the Assistant is visible). When this property is applied to the **Balloon** object, the Assistant is animated only while the balloon is displayed. Read/write **Long**.

Can be one of the following **MsoAnimationType** constants:

msoAnimationAppear	**msoAnimationBeginSpeaking**
msoAnimationCharacterSuccessMajor	**msoAnimationCheckingSomething**
msoAnimationDisappear	**msoAnimationEmptyTrash**
msoAnimationGestureDown	**msoAnimationGestureLeft**
msoAnimationGestureRight	**msoAnimationGestureUp**
msoAnimationGetArtsy	**msoAnimationGetAttentionMajor**
msoAnimationGetAttentionMinor	**msoAnimationGetTechy**
msoAnimationGetWizardy	**msoAnimationGoodbye**
msoAnimationGreeting	**msoAnimationIdle**
msoAnimationListensToComputer	**msoAnimationLookDown**
msoAnimationLookDownLeft	**msoAnimationLookDownRight**
msoAnimationLookLeft	**msoAnimationLookRight**
msoAnimationLookUp	**msoAnimationLookUpLeft**
msoAnimationLookUpRight	**msoAnimationPrinting**
msoAnimationSaving	**msoAnimationSearching**
msoAnimationSendingMail	**msoAnimationThinking**
msoAnimationWorkingAtSomething	**msoAnimationWritingNotingSomething**

Remarks

Clippit is the default Assistant, and **msoAnimationIdle** is the default animation type for the Assistant.

Depending on the selected Assistant, setting the **Animation** property may or may not result in any obvious animation. However, all **MsoAnimationType** constants are valid for all Assistants.

The following **MsoAnimationType** constants represent animations that repeat the specified action until the Assistant is dismissed, or until the **Animation** property is reset with another animation.

msoAnimationCheckingSomething	**msoAnimationGetArtsy**
msoAnimationGetTechy	**msoAnimationSaving**
msoAnimationSearching	**msoAnimationThinking**
msoAnimationWorkingAtSomething	**msoAnimationWritingNotingSomething**

See Also

Assistant object, **FileName** property, **Visible** property.

Example

This example displays the Office Assistant in a specific location, and it sets several options before making the Assistant visible.

```
With Assistant
   .Reduced = True
   .Move xLeft:= 400, yTop:= 300
   .MoveWhenInTheWay = True
   .TipOfDay = True
   .Visible = True
   .Animation = msoAnimationGreeting
End With
```

Application Property

Applies To

Assistant object, **Balloon** object, **BalloonCheckbox** object, **BalloonCheckboxes** collection object, **BalloonLabel** object, **BalloonLabels** collection object, **CommandBar** object, **CommandBarButton** object, **CommandBarComboBox** object, **CommandBarControl** object, **CommandBarControls** collection object, **CommandBarPopup** object, **CommandBars** collection object, **DocumentProperties** collection object, **DocumentProperty** object, **FileSearch** object, **FoundFiles** object, **PropertyTest** object, **PropertyTests** collection object.

Description

Returns an **Application** object that represents the container application for the specified object (you can use this property with an Automation object to return that object's container application). Read-only.

Example

This example returns the application in which the command bar named "Documents" was created.

```
Set Appobj = CommandBars("Document").Application
```

Assistant Object

Description

Represents the Microsoft Office Assistant.

Using the Assistant Object

Use the **Assistant** property to return the **Assistant** object. There's no collection for the **Assistant** object; only one **Assistant** object can be active at a time. Use the **Visible** property to display the Assistant.

Remarks

The default Assistant is Clippit. To select a different Assistant programatically, use the **FileName** property.

The following example displays a previously selected Assistant and animates it with the associated sound. If your computer doesn't have a sound card installed, this example won't generate an error, but the sound won't be heard.

```
With Assistant
    .Visible = True
    .Sounds = True
    .Animation = msoAnimationBeginSpeaking
End With
```

Properties

Animation property, **Application** property, **AssistWithAlerts** property, **AssistWithHelp** property, **AssistWithWizards** property, **BalloonError** property, **Creator** property, **FeatureTips** property, **FileName** property, **GuessHelp** property, **HighPriorityTips** property, **Item** property (**Assistant**, **BalloonLabel**, and **BalloonCheckbox** objects), **KeyboardShortcutTips** property, **Left** property, **MouseTips** property, **MoveWhenInTheWay** property, **Name** property, **NewBalloon** property, **Parent** property, **Reduced** property, **SearchWhenProgramming** property, **Sounds** property, **TipOfDay** property, **Top** property, **Visible** property.

Methods

ActivateWizard method, **EndWizard** method, **Help** method, **Move** method, **ResetTips** method, **StartWizard** method.

Example (Microsoft Access)

The following function creates a custom balloon for the Office Assistant and determines how the user responded to the balloon:

```
Function AssistantBalloon(Optional varCheck As Variant, _
      Optional varLabel As Variant)
   Dim bch As BalloonCheckbox
   Dim intI As Integer
   Dim intReturn As Integer
   Dim strCheck(5) As String
   Dim strList As String

   ' Create new balloon.
   Set bal = Assistant.NewBalloon
   ' Specify balloon type.
   bal.BalloonType = msoBalloonTypeButtons
   ' Specify that balloon is modal.
   bal.Mode = msoModeModal

   ' Make Assistant visible.
   If Assistant.Visible = False Then Assistant.Visible = True
   ' Check if first argument has been passed.
   If Not IsMissing(varCheck) Then
      ' If too large, set to maximum number of check boxes (5).
      If varCheck > 6 Then
         varCheck = 5
      End If
      ' Set text property to alphabet character.
      For intI = 1 To varCheck
         bal.Checkboxes(intI).Text = Chr(64 + intI)
      Next intI
   End If

   If Not IsMissing(varLabel) Then
      ' If too large, set to maximum number of labels (5).
      If varLabel > 6 Then
         varLabel = 5
      End If
      For intI = 1 To varLabel
         ' Set text property to alphabet character.
         bal.Labels(intI).Text = Chr(64 + intI)
      Next intI
   End If
   ' Store return value.
   intReturn = bal.Show

   intI = 0
   ' Determine which check boxes were checked, if any.
```

```
    For Each bch In bal.Checkboxes
        If bch.Checked = True Then
            strCheck(intI) = bch.Text
            strList = strList & "'" & strCheck(intI) & "'" & Chr(32)
        End If
        intI = intI + 1
    Next
    If Len(strList) <> 0 Then
        MsgBox "You selected checkboxes " & strList & "."
    End If
    ' Determine which label was selected, if any.
    If intReturn > 0 Then
        MsgBox "You selected label " & bal.Labels(intReturn).Text & "."
    End If
End Function
```

You could call this function from the Debug window as follows:

```
? AssistantBalloon(4, 5)
```

AssistWithAlerts Property

Applies To

Assistant object.

Description

True if application alerts are delivered by the Office Assistant balloon whenever the Office Assistant is visible. Read/write **Boolean**.

Remarks

The **AssistWithAlerts** property corresponds to the **Display alerts** option under **Assistant capabilities** on the **Options** tab in the **Office Assistant** dialog box.

If this property is **False**, the application displays alerts in dialog boxes without the Office Assistant.

Example

This example sets the Office Assistant to be displayed whenever an application alert is generated.

```
With Assistant
    .AssistWithHelp = True
    .AssistWithAlerts = True
    .Animation = msoAnimationGreeting
    .Visible = True
End With
```

AssistWithHelp Property

Applies To

Assistant object.

Description

True if the Office Assistant appears whenever the user presses the F1 key to display Help. Read/write **Boolean**.

Remarks

The **AssistWithHelp** property corresponds to the **Respond to F1 key** option under **Assistant capabilities** on the **Options** tab in the **Office Assistant** dialog box.

If this property is set to **False**, the **Help Topics** dialog box appears instead of the Office Assistant.

Example

This example displays the Office Assistant whenever the user presses the F1 key to display Help.

```
With Assistant
    .AssistWithHelp = True
    .AssistWithAlerts = True
    .Animation = msoAnimationGreeting
    .Visible = True
End With
```

AssistWithWizards Property

Applies To

Assistant object.

Description

True if the Office Assistant provides Help information about wizards. Read/write **Boolean**.

Remarks

The **AssistWithWizards** property corresponds to the **Help with wizards** option under **Assistant capabilities** on the **Options** tab in the **Office Assistant** dialog box.

Example

This example sets the Office Assistant to provide Help information about wizards.

```
Assistant.AssistWithWizards = True
```

Author Property

Applies To

FileFind object.

Description

Macintosh only. Returns or sets a string (up to 80 characters long) that represents the author listed in the properties of the document to be searched for. Read/write **String**.

See Also

DateCreatedFrom property, **DateCreatedTo** property, **DateSavedFrom** property, **DateSavedTo** property.

Balloon Object

Description

Represents the balloon in which the Office Assistant displays headings and text information. A balloon can contain controls such as check boxes and labels.

Using the Balloon Object

Use the **NewBalloon** property to return a **Balloon** object. There's no collection for the **Balloon** object; only one balloon can be visible at a time. However, it's possible to define several balloons and call any one of them when needed. For more information, see "Defining and Reusing Balloons" later in this topic.

Use the **Show** method to make the specified balloon visible. Use the **Callback** property to run procedures based on selections from modeless balloons (balloons that remain visible while a user works in the application). Use the **Close** method to close modeless balloons.

The following example creates a balloon that contains tips for saving entered data.

```
With Assistant.NewBalloon
    .BalloonType = msoBalloonTypeBullets
    .Icon = msoIconTip
    .Button = msoButtonSetOkCancel
    .Heading = "Tips for Saving Information."
    .Labels(1).Text = "Save your work often."
    .Labels(2).Text = "Install a surge protector."
    .Labels(3).Text = "Exit your application properly."
    .Show
End With
```

Defining and Reusing Balloons

You can reuse balloons by assigning them to object variables and calling them when needed throughout your procedure. This example defines `balloon1`, `balloon2`, and `balloon3` as separate balloons, and it displays the balloons at various points in the procedure.

```
Set balloon1 = Assistant.NewBalloon
balloon1.Heading = "First balloon"
Set balloon2 = Assistant.NewBalloon
balloon2.Heading = "Second balloon"
Set balloon3 = Assistant.NewBalloon
balloon3.Heading = "Third balloon"
balloon1.Show
balloon3.Show
balloon2.Show
```

You can also combine balloon object variables in an array and index into the array.

Properties

Animation property, **Application** property, **BalloonType** property, **Button** property, **Callback** property, **Checkboxes** property, **Creator** property, **Heading** property, **Icon** property, **Labels** property, **Mode** property, **Name** property, **Parent** property, **Private** property, **Text** property.

Methods

Close method, **SetAvoidRectangle** method, **Show** method.

Example (Microsoft Access)

See the **Assistant** object example (Microsoft Access).

BalloonCheckbox Object

Description

Represents a check box in the Office Assistant balloon. The **BalloonCheckbox** object is a member of the **BalloonCheckboxes** collection.

Using the BalloonCheckbox Object

Use **Checkboxes**(*index*), where *index* is a number from 1 through 5, to return a single **BalloonCheckbox** object. There can be up to five check boxes in one balloon; each check box appears when a value is assigned to its **Text** property.

The following example creates a balloon with a heading, text, and three region choices. When the user selects a check box and then clicks **OK**, the appropriate procedure is run.

```
With Assistant.NewBalloon
   .Heading = "Regional Sales Data"
   .Text = "Select your region"
   For i = 1 To 3
      .CheckBoxes(i).Text = "Region " & i
   Next
   .Button = msoButtonSetOkCancel
   .Show
   Select Case True
      Case .CheckBoxes(1).Checked
         runregion1
      Case .CheckBoxes(2).Checked
         runregion2
      Case .CheckBoxes(3).Checked
         runregion3
   End Select
End With
```

Remarks

Balloon check boxes display the user's choices until the user dismisses the balloon. Balloon labels record the user's choice as soon as the user clicks the button beside the label.

Properties

Application property, **Checked** property, **Creator** property, **Item** property (**Assistant**, **BalloonLabel**, and **BalloonCheckbox** objects), **Name** property, **Parent** property, **Text** property.

Example (Microsoft Access)

See the **Assistant** object example (Microsoft Access).

BalloonCheckboxes Collection Object

Description

A collection of **BalloonCheckbox** objects that represent all the check boxes in the Office Assistant balloon.

Using the BalloonCheckboxes Collection

Use the **Checkboxes** property to return the **BalloonCheckboxes** collection.

Use **Checkboxes**(*index*), where *index* is a number from 1 through 5, to return a single **BalloonCheckbox** object. There can be up to five check boxes in one balloon; each check box appears when a value is assigned to its **Text** property.

The following example writes the checkbox text of all visible checkboxes, in an existing balloon, to the debug window.

```
For Each box In .CheckBoxes
   If box.Text <> "" Then
      Debug.Print box.Text
   End If
Next
```

You cannot add check boxes to or remove check boxes from the **BalloonCheckboxes** collection.

Remarks

Balloon check boxes display the user's choices until he or she dismisses the balloon. Balloon labels record the user's choice as soon as he or she clicks the button beside the label.

Properties

Application property, **Count** property, **Creator** property, **Item** property (**BalloonCheckboxes** collection), **Name** property, **Parent** property.

Example (Microsoft Access)

See the **Assistant** object example (Microsoft Access).

BalloonError Property

Applies To

Assistant object.

Description

Returns a value that indicates the last recorded balloon error. Read-only **String**.

Can be one of the following **MsoBalloonErrorType** constants.

Constant	Description
msoBalloonErrorBadPictureRef	The balloon contains a bitmap that couldn't be displayed because the file doesn't exist or because the bitmap isn't a valid .BMP or .WMF file (or PICT file on the Macintosh).
msoBalloonErrorBadReference	The balloon contains an unrecognized or unsupported reference.
msoBalloonErrorButtonlessModal	The balloon you attempted to display is modal, but it contains no buttons. The balloon won't be shown because it cannot be dismissed.

(continued)

msoBalloonErrorButtonModeless	The balloon you attempted to display is modeless, contains no buttons, and has no procedure assigned to the **Callback** property. The balloon won't be shown because a procedure is required to evaluate the button clicked in the balloon.
msoBalloonErrorNone	The property succeeded in displaying the balloon; no error was encountered.
msoBalloonErrorBadCharacter	The balloon contains an ASCII control character other than CR or LF and greater than 32.
msoBalloonErrorOutOfMemory	The balloon won't appear because there is insufficient memory.
msoBalloonErrorTooBig	The balloon is too big to appear on the screen.
msoBalloonErrorOther	The balloon won't appear because some other error occurred, such as another modal balloon is already active.

See Also

Balloon object, **BalloonType** property, **Show** method.

Example

This example creates a balloon that generates an error. The error is caused because the balloon is created without a way to dismiss it: the button type was set to **msoButtonSetNone** and the default balloon mode is **msoModeModal**, resulting in a buttonless balloon. Note that there's no way to dismiss a buttonless modal balloon.

```
With Application.Assistant
With .NewBalloon
   .Heading = "This will never show."
   .Text = "Imagine a balloon here."
   .Button = msoButtonSetNone
   .Show
End With
.Visible = True
If .BalloonError = msoBalloonErrorButtonlessModal Then
   MsgBox "You need a button to dismiss the balloon."
End If
End With
```

BalloonLabel Object

Description

Represents a label in the Office Assistant balloon. The **BalloonLabel** object is a member of the **BalloonLabels** collection.

Using the BalloonLabel Object

Use **Labels**(*index*), where *index* is a number from 1 through 5, to return a **BalloonLabel** object. There can be up to five labels on one balloon; each label appears when a value is assigned to its **Text** property.

The following example creates a balloon that asks the user to click the label corresponding to his or her age.

```
With Assistant.NewBalloon
    .Heading = "Check Your Age Group."
    .Labels(1).Text = "Under 30."
    .Labels(2).Text = "Over 30."
    .Labels(3).Text = "None of your business."
    .Text = "Which of the following " _
        & .Labels.Count & " choices apply to you?"
    .Show
End With
```

Remarks

Balloon check boxes display the user's choices until he or she dismisses the balloon. Balloon labels record the user's choice as soon as he or she clicks the button beside the label.

Properties

Application property, **Creator** property, **Item** property (**Assistant**, **BalloonLabel**, and **BalloonCheckbox** objects), **Name** property, **Parent** property, **Text** property.

Example (Microsoft Access)

See the **Assistant** object example (Microsoft Access).

BalloonLabels Collection Object

Description

A collection of **BalloonLabel** objects that represent all the labels in the Office Assistant balloon.

Using the BalloonLabels Collection

Use the **Labels** property to return the **BalloonLabels** collection.

Use **Labels**(*index*), where *index* is a number from 1 through 5, to return a **BalloonLabel** object. There can be up to five labels in one balloon; each label appears when a value is assigned to its **Text** property.

The following example creates a balloon containing three choices. The variable x is set to the return value of the **Show** method, which will be 1, 2, or 3, corresponding to the label the user clicks. The example displays the value of the variable x, but you can pass the value to another procedure, or you can use the value in a **Select Case** statement.

```
Set b = Assistant.NewBalloon
With b
   .Heading = "This is my heading"
   .Text = "Select one of these things:"
   .Labels(1).Text = "Choice One"
   .Labels(2).Text = "Choice Two"
   .Labels(3).Text = "Choice Three"
    x = .Show
End With
MsgBox x
```

Remarks

Balloon check boxes display the user's choices until the user dismisses the balloon. Balloon labels record the user's choice as soon as the user clicks the button beside the label.

Properties

Application property, **Count** property, **Creator** property, **Item** property (**BalloonLabels** collection), **Name** property, **Parent** property.

Example (Microsoft Access)

See the **Assistant** object example (Microsoft Access).

BalloonType Property

Applies To

Balloon object.

Description

Returns or sets the type of balloon the Office Assistant uses. Can be one of the following **MsoBalloonType** constants: **msoBalloonTypeButtons**, **msoBalloonTypeBullets**, or **msoBalloonTypeNumbers**. When you create a new balloon with the **NewBalloon** method, this property is initially set to **msoBalloonTypeButtons**. Read/write **Long**.

See Also

Balloon object, **BalloonError** property.

Example

This example creates an instruction balloon that explains how to select a printer. The balloon is modeless, so the user can follow the instructions in the balloon and keep the balloon visible as he or she works.

```
Set bln = Assistant.NewBalloon
With bln
   .Heading = "Instructions for Choosing a Printer."
   .Text = "Click OK when you've chosen a printer."
   .Labels(1).Text = "From the File menu, choose Print."
   .Labels(2).Text = "Click Setup."
   .Labels(3).Text = "Select the name of the printer."
   .BalloonType = msoBalloonTypeNumbers
   .Mode = msoModeModeless
   .Callback = "ProcessPrinter"
   .Button = msoButtonSetOK
   .Show
End With
```

Example (Microsoft Access)

The following function creates a custom balloon for the Office Assistant and determines how the user responded to the balloon:

```
Function AssistantBalloon(Optional varCheck As Variant, Optional _
   varLabel As Variant)
   Dim bch As BalloonCheckbox
   Dim intI As Integer
   Dim intReturn As Integer
   Dim strCheck(5) As String
   Dim strList As String

   ' Create new balloon.
   Set bal = Assistant.NewBalloon
   ' Specify balloon type.
   bal.BalloonType = msoBalloonTypeButtons
   ' Specify that balloon is modal.
   bal.Mode = msoModeModal

   ' Make Assistant visible.
   If Assistant.Visible = False Then Assistant.Visible = True
   ' Check if first argument has been passed.
   If Not IsMissing(varCheck) Then
      ' If too large, set to maximum number of check boxes (5).
      If varCheck > 6 Then
         varCheck = 5
      End If
      ' Set text property to alphabet character.
      For intI = 1 To varCheck
         bal.Checkboxes(intI).Text = Chr(64 + intI)
      Next intI
   End If
```

```
    If Not IsMissing(varLabel) Then
        ' If too large, set to maximum number of labels (5).
        If varLabel > 6 Then
            varLabel = 5
        End If
        For intI = 1 To varLabel
            ' Set text property to alphabet character.
            bal.Labels(intI).Text = Chr(64 + intI)
        Next intI
    End If
    ' Store return value.
    intReturn = bal.Show

    intI = 0
    ' Determine which check boxes were checked, if any.
    For Each bch In bal.Checkboxes
        If bch.Checked = True Then
            strCheck(intI) = bch.Text
            strList = strList & "'" & strCheck(intI) & "'" & Chr(32)
        End If
        intI = intI + 1
    Next
    If Len(strList) <> 0 Then
        MsgBox "You selected checkboxes " & strList & "."
    End If
    ' Determine which label was selected, if any.
    If intReturn > 0 Then
        MsgBox "You selected label " & bal.Labels(intReturn).Text & "."
    End If
End Function
```

You could call this function from the Debug window as follows:

```
? AssistantBalloon(4, 5)
```

BeginGroup Property

Applies To

CommandBarButton object, **CommandBarComboBox** object, **CommandBarControl** object, **CommandBarPopup** object.

Description

True if the specified command bar control is at the beginning of a group of controls on the command bar. Read/write **Boolean**.

Specifics (Microsoft Access)

In Microsoft Access 97, you can use the *Toolbar* **Control Properties** dialog box for command bar controls to determine whether or not a control on a command bar is at the beginning of a group of controls. A separator bar is displayed before the control on the command bar. Display the **Customize** dialog box by pointing to **Toolbars** on the **View** menu and clicking **Customize**. For menu bar and toolbar controls, display the menu bar or toolbar, and then right-click the control whose **BeginGroup** property you want to set. For shortcut menu controls, select the **Shortcut Menus** check box on the **Toolbars** tab of the **Customize** dialog box, then find the shortcut menu control you want on the menu bar that's displayed and right-click the control. Click the **Properties** command. Select or clear the **Begin A Group** check box.

The separator bar that appears at the beginning of a group of controls isn't a control itself, and doesn't affect item counts or indexes in the **CommandBarControls** collection.

Example

This example sets the last control on the active menu bar to be at the beginning of its own group.

```
Set myMenuBar = CommandBars.ActiveMenuBar
Set lastMenu = myMenuBar.Controls(myMenuBar.Controls.Count)
lastMenu.BeginGroup = True
```

BuiltIn Property

Applies To

CommandBar object, **CommandBarButton** object, **CommandBarComboBox** object, **CommandBarControl** object, **CommandBarPopup** object.

Description

True if the specified command bar or command bar control is a built-in command bar or control of the container application. **False** if it's a custom command bar or control, or if it's a built-in control who's **OnAction** property has been set. Read-only **Boolean**.

See Also

CommandBar object, **CommandBarControl** object, **FaceId** property, **PasteFace** method.

Example

This example deletes all custom command bars that aren't visible.

```
foundFlag = False
deletedBars = 0
For Each bar In CommandBars
   If (bar.BuiltIn = False) And (bar.Visible = False) Then
      bar.Delete
      foundFlag = True
      deletedBars = deletedBars + 1
   End If
Next
If Not foundFlag Then
   MsgBox "No command bars have been deleted."
Else
   MsgBox deletedBars & " custom command bar(s) deleted."
End If
```

BuiltInFace Property

Applies To

CommandBarButton object.

Description

True if the face of the specified command bar button control is its built-in face. This property can only be set to **True**, which will reset the face to the built-in one. Read/write **Boolean**.

See Also

CommandBarControl object, **FaceId** property, **PasteFace** method.

Example

This example determines whether the face of the first control on the command bar named "Custom" is its built-in button face. If it is, the example copies the button face to the Clipboard.

```
Set myControl = CommandBars("My Custom Bar").Controls(1)
With myControl
   If .BuiltInFace = True Then .CopyFace
End With
```

Button Property

Applies To

Balloon object.

Description

Returns or sets the type of button displayed at the bottom of the Office Assistant balloon. When you create a new balloon with the **NewBalloon** method, this property is initially set to **msoButtonSetOK**. Read/write **Long**.

Can be one of the following **MsoButtonSetType** constants:

msoButtonSetAbortRetryIgnore
msoButtonSetBackClose
msoButtonSetBackNextClose
msoButtonSetBackNextSnooze
msoButtonSetCancel
msoButtonSetNextClose
msoButtonSetNone
msoButtonSetOK
msoButtonSetOkCancel
msoButtonSetRetryCancel
msoButtonSetSearchClose
msoButtonSetTipsOptionsClose
msoButtonSetYesAllNoCancel
msoButtonSetYesNo
msoButtonSetYesNoCancel

See Also

BuiltIn property, **BuiltInFace** property, **FaceId** property, **PasteFace** method, **Show** method.

Example

This example creates a balloon with a heading, text, and three region choices, and then displays it.

```
With Assistant.NewBalloon
    .Heading = "Regional Sales Data"
    .Text = "Select a region"
    For i = 1 To 3
        .CheckBoxes(i).Text = "Region " & i
    Next
    .Button = msoButtonSetOkCancel
    .Show
End With
```

Callback Property

Applies To

Balloon object.

Description

Sets the name of the procedure to be run whenever a modeless balloon is displayed. Read/write **String**.

Note If you specify a macro that exists behind an Excel worksheet, you must include the worksheet in the reference, as in "`Sheet1.myCallback`" instead of "`myCallback`".

See Also

Balloon object, **BalloonCheckbox** object, **BalloonLabel** object, **Checked** property, **Show** method.

Specifics (Microsoft Access)

You set the **Callback** property when you're working with a modeless balloon. A modeless balloon is one that allows the user to switch back to the application in which they're working without first closing the balloon. A modeless balloon may be useful if you're creating help that the user will want to leave open while performing several steps in the application. To make a balloon modeless, set the **Mode** property of the **Balloon** object to **msoModeModeless**.

The **Callback** property specifies a function or a macro to run when the user clicks a button on a balloon. If you write a function to be called by the **Callback** property, you can use that function to determine which button was clicked.

You set the **Callback** property to the name of a function or macro. For example, the following line of code sets the **Callback** property:

```
Assistant.NewBalloon.Callback = "EvaluateCheckboxes"
```

Note that you must set the **Callback** property to the name of a **Function** procedure; you can't set it to the name of a **Sub** procedure. The **Function** procedure must be public.

Example

This example displays a balloon that contains a selection of three printers. After the user clicks the **OK** button on the balloon, the `ProcessPrinter` procedure is run and the balloon is closed.

```
Sub shar()
Set bln = Assistant.NewBalloon
With bln
   .Heading = "Select a Printer."
   .Text = "Click OK when you've selected a printer."
   .Labels(1).Text = "Network Printer"
   .Labels(2).Text = "Local Printer"
   .Labels(3).Text = "Local Color Printer"
   .BalloonType = msoBalloonTypeButtons
   .Mode = msoModeModeless
   .Callback = "ProcessPrinter"
   .Button = msoButtonSetOK
   .Show
End With
End Sub
```

(Every procedure specified in the **Callback** property is passed three arguments: the balloon that activated the procedure, the return value of the button the user pressed, and an integer that uniquely identifies the balloon that called the procedure.)

```
Sub ProcessPrinter(bln As Balloon, ibtn As Long, Priv As Long)
   Assistant.Animation = msoAnimationPrinting
   Select Case ibtn
   Case 1
      ' Insert printer-specific code
      bln.Close
   Case 2
      ' Insert printer-specific code
      bln.Close
   Case 3
      ' Insert printer-specific code
      bln.Close
   End Select
   End Sub
```

Caption Property

Applies To

CommandBarButton object, **CommandBarComboBox** object, **CommandBarControl** object, **CommandBarPopup** object.

Description

Returns or sets the caption text for the specified command bar control. Read/write **String**.

Note The caption for a control is also displayed as its default ScreenTip.

See Also

Add method (**CommandBarControls** collection), **CommandBarControl** object, **DescriptionText** property, **Enabled** property, **TooltipText** property.

Specifics (Microsoft Access)

In Microsoft Access 97, you can use the *Toolbar* **Control Properties** dialog box for command bar controls to set the caption for a control on a command bar. Display the **Customize** dialog box by pointing to **Toolbars** on the **View** menu and clicking **Customize**. For menu bar and toolbar controls, display the menu bar or toolbar, and then right-click the control whose **Caption** property you want to set. For shortcut menu controls, select the **Shortcut Menus** check box on the **Toolbars** tab of the **Customize** dialog box, then find the shortcut menu control you want on the menu bar that's displayed and right-click the control. Click the **Properties** command. Enter the caption you want in the **Caption** box.

When you display a control's **Caption** property setting in the *Toolbar* **Control Properties** dialog box or in Visual Basic, the ampersand (&) for the accelerator key is displayed (for example, &Paste). When you reference the control in Visual Basic, you can choose to include the ampersand (or not). For example, the following references are identical:

```
CommandBars("Menu Bar").Controls("Tools")
```

```
CommandBars("Menu Bar").Controls("&Tools")
```

When setting the **Caption** property, you must include the ampersand if you want the control to have an accelerator key.

Example

This example adds a command bar control with a spelling checker button face to a custom command bar, and then it sets the caption to "Spelling checker."

```
Set myBar = CommandBars.Add(Name:="Custom", _
    Position:=msoBarTop, Temporary:=True)
myBar.Visible = True
Set myControl = myBar.Controls.Add(Type:=msoControlButton, Id:=2)
```

```
With myControl
    .DescriptionText = "Starts the spelling checker"
    .Caption = "Spelling checker"
End With
```

Checkboxes Property

Applies To

Balloon object.

Description

Returns the **BalloonCheckboxes** collection that represents all the check boxes contained in the specified balloon. Read-only.

See Also

Balloon object, **Checked** property.

Example

This example creates a balloon with a heading, text, and three region choices. When the user selects a check box and then clicks **OK** in the balloon, the appropriate procedure is run.

```
With Assistant.NewBalloon
    .Heading = "Regional Sales Data"
    .Text = "Select your region"
    For i = 1 To 3
        .CheckBoxes(i).Text = "Region " & i
    Next
    .Button = msoButtonSetOkCancel
    .Show
Select Case True
    Case .CheckBoxes(1).Checked
        runregion1
    Case .CheckBoxes(2).Checked
        runregion2
    Case .CheckBoxes(3).Checked
        runregion3
End Select
End With
```

Example (Microsoft Access)

The following function creates a custom balloon for the Office Assistant and determines how the user responded to the balloon:

```
Function AssistantBalloon(Optional varCheck As Variant, _
    Optional varLabel As Variant)
    Dim bch As BalloonCheckbox
    Dim intI As Integer
    Dim intReturn As Integer
    Dim strCheck(5) As String
    Dim strList As String
```

```
    ' Create new balloon.
    Set bal = Assistant.NewBalloon
    ' Specify balloon type.
    bal.BalloonType = msoBalloonTypeButtons
    ' Specify that balloon is modal.
    bal.Mode = msoModeModal

    ' Make Assistant visible.
    If Assistant.Visible = False Then Assistant.Visible = True
    ' Check if first argument has been passed.
    If Not IsMissing(varCheck) Then
       ' If too large, set to maximum number of check boxes (5).
       If varCheck > 6 Then
          varCheck = 5
       End If
       ' Set text property to alphabet character.
       For intI = 1 To varCheck
          bal.Checkboxes(intI).Text = Chr(64 + intI)
       Next intI
    End If

    If Not IsMissing(varLabel) Then
       ' If too large, set to maximum number of labels (5).
       If varLabel > 6 Then
          varLabel = 5
       End If
       For intI = 1 To varLabel
          ' Set text property to alphabet character.
          bal.Labels(intI).Text = Chr(64 + intI)
       Next intI
    End If
    ' Store return value.
    intReturn = bal.Show

    intI = 0
    ' Determine which check boxes were checked, if any.
    For Each bch In bal.Checkboxes
       If bch.Checked = True Then
          strCheck(intI) = bch.Text
          strList = strList & "'" & strCheck(intI) & "'" & Chr(32)
       End If
       intI = intI + 1
    Next
    If Len(strList) <> 0 Then
       MsgBox "You selected checkboxes " & strList & "."
    End If
    ' Determine which label was selected, if any.
    If intReturn > 0 Then
       MsgBox "You selected label " & bal.Labels(intReturn).Text & "."
    End If
End Function
```

You could call this function from the Debug window as follows:

```
? AssistantBalloon(4, 5)
```

Checked Property

Applies To

BalloonCheckbox object.

Description

True if the specified check box in the Office Assistant balloon is selected. Read/write **Boolean**.

See Also

Balloon object, **BalloonCheckboxes** collection object.

Example

This example creates a balloon with a heading, text, and three region choices. When the user selects a check box and then clicks **OK** in the balloon, the appropriate procedure is run.

```
With Assistant.NewBalloon
   .Heading = "Regional Sales Data"
   .Text = "Select your region"
   For i = 1 To 3
      .CheckBoxes(i).Text = "Region " & i
   Next
   .Button = msoButtonSetOkCancel
   .Show
Select Case True
   Case .CheckBoxes(1).Checked
      runregion1
   Case .CheckBoxes(2).Checked
      runregion2
   Case .CheckBoxes(3).Checked
      runregion3
End Select
End With
```

Example (Microsoft Access)

The following function creates a custom balloon for the Office Assistant and determines how the user responded to the balloon:

```
Function AssistantBalloon(Optional varCheck As Variant, Optional _
   varLabel As Variant)
   Dim bch As BalloonCheckbox
   Dim intI As Integer
   Dim intReturn As Integer
   Dim strCheck(5) As String
   Dim strList As String
```

```
    ' Create new balloon.
    Set bal = Assistant.NewBalloon
    ' Specify balloon type.
    bal.BalloonType = msoBalloonTypeButtons
    ' Specify that balloon is modal.
    bal.Mode = msoModeModal

    ' Make Assistant visible.
    If Assistant.Visible = False Then Assistant.Visible = True
    ' Check if first argument has been passed.
    If Not IsMissing(varCheck) Then
        ' If too large, set to maximum number of check boxes (5).
        If varCheck > 6 Then
            varCheck = 5
        End If
        ' Set text property to alphabet character.
        For intI = 1 To varCheck
            bal.Checkboxes(intI).Text = Chr(64 + intI)
        Next intI
    End If

    If Not IsMissing(varLabel) Then
        ' If too large, set to maximum number of labels (5).
        If varLabel > 6 Then
            varLabel = 5
        End If
        For intI = 1 To varLabel
            ' Set text property to alphabet character.
            bal.Labels(intI).Text = Chr(64 + intI)
        Next intI
    End If
    ' Store return value.
    intReturn = bal.Show

    intI = 0
    ' Determine which check boxes were checked, if any.
    For Each bch In bal.Checkboxes
        If bch.Checked = True Then
            strCheck(intI) = bch.Text
            strList = strList & "'" & strCheck(intI) & "'" & Chr(32)
        End If
        intI = intI + 1
    Next
    If Len(strList) <> 0 Then
        MsgBox "You selected checkboxes " & strList & "."
    End If
    ' Determine which label was selected, if any.
    If intReturn > 0 Then
        MsgBox "You selected label " & bal.Labels(intReturn).Text & "."
    End If
End Function
```

You could call this function from the Debug window as follows:

```
? AssistantBalloon(4, 5)
```

Clear Method

Applies To

CommandBarComboBox object.

Description

Removes all list items from the specified command bar combo box control (drop-down list box or combo box) and clears the text box (edit box or combo box).

Note This method will fail if it's applied to a built-in command bar control.

Syntax

expression.**Clear**

expression Required. An expression that returns a **CommandBarComboBox** object.

See Also

Add method (**CommandBarControls** collection), **AddItem** method, **CommandBarComboBox** object, **Enabled** property.

Example

This example checks the number of items in the combo box control named "Names" on the command bar named "Custom." If there are more than three items in the list, the example clears the list, adds a new first item to the list, and displays this new item as the default for the combo box control.

```
Set myBar = CommandBars("Custom Bar")
Set myControl = myBar.Controls("Names")
With myControl
    If .ListCount > 3 Then
        .Clear
        .AddItem Text:="Bendel", Index:=1
        .ListIndex = 1
    End If
End With
```

Close Method

Applies To

Balloon object.

Description

Closes the active modeless balloon.

Syntax

expression.**Close**

expression Required. An expression that returns a **Balloon** object.

Example

This example displays a balloon that contains instructions for selecting a printer. After the user clicks the OK button on the balloon, the `ProcessPrinter` procedure is run and the balloon is closed.

```
Sub shar()
Set bln = Assistant.NewBalloon
With bln
    .Heading = "Instructions for Choosing a Printer."
    .Text = "Click OK when you've chosen a printer."
    .Labels(1).Text = "Choose File, Print."
    .Labels(2).Text = "Click Setup."
    .Labels(3).Text = "Select the name of the printer."
    .BalloonType = msoBalloonTypeNumbers
    .Mode = msoModeModeless
    .Callback = "ProcessPrinter"
    .Button = msoButtonSetOK
    .Show
End With
End Sub

Sub ProcessPrinter(bln As Balloon, ibtn As Long, _
    iPriv As Long)
    Assistant.Animation = msoAnimationSearching
    'Insert printer-specific code
    bln.Close
End Sub
```

CommandBar Object

Description

Represents a command bar in the container application. The **CommandBar** object is a member of the **CommandBars** collection.

Using the CommandBar Object

Use **CommandBars**(*index*), where *index* is the name or index number of a command bar, to return a single **CommandBar** object. The following example steps through the collection of command bars to find the command bar named “Forms.” If it finds this command bar, the example makes it visible and protects its docking state. In this example, the variable `cb` represents a **CommandBar** object.

```
foundFlag = False
For Each cb In CommandBars
   If cb.Name = "Forms" Then
      cb.Protection = msoBarNoChangeDock
      cb.Visible = True
      foundFlag = True
   End If
Next cb
If Not foundFlag Then
   MsgBox "The collection does not contain a Forms command bar."
End If
```

You can use a name or index number to specify a menu bar or toolbar in the list of available menu bars and toolbars in the container application. However, you must use a name to specify a menu, shortcut menu, or submenu (all of which are represented by **CommandBar** objects). This example adds a new menu item to the bottom of the **Tools** menu. When clicked, the new menu item runs the procedure named "qtrReport."

```
Set newItem = CommandBars("Tools").Controls.Add(Type:=msoControlButton)
With newItem
   .BeginGroup = True
   .Caption = "Make Report"
   .FaceID = 0
   .OnAction = "qtrReport"
End With
```

If two or more custom menus or submenus have the same name, **CommandBars**(*index*) returns the first one. To ensure that you return the correct menu or submenu, locate the pop-up control that displays that menu. Then apply the **CommandBar** property to the pop-up control to return the command bar that represents that menu.

Assuming that the third control on the toolbar named "Custom Tools" is a pop-up control, this example adds the **Save** command to the bottom of that menu.

```
Set viewMenu = CommandBars("Custom Tools").Controls(3).CommandBar
viewMenu.Controls.Add ID:=3          'ID of Save command is 3
```

Properties

Application property, **BuiltIn** property, **Context** property, **Controls** property, **Creator** property, **Enabled** property, **Height** property, **Index** property, **Left** property, **Name** property, **NameLocal** property, **Parent** property, **Position** property, **Protection** property, **RowIndex** property, **Top** property, **Type** property, **Visible** property, **Width** property.

Methods

Delete method, **FindControl** method, **Reset** method, **ShowPopup** method.

CommandBar Property

Applies To

CommandBarPopup object.

Description

Returns a **CommandBar** object that represents the menu displayed by the specified pop-up control. Read-only.

Example

This example sets `thirdLevel` to the fourth control on the command bar named "Drawing."

```
Set thirdLevel = CommandBars("Drawing") _
   .Controls(1).CommandBar.Controls(4)
```

CommandBarButton Object

Description

Represents a button control on a command bar.

Using the CommandBarButton Object

Use **Controls**(*index*), where *index* is the index number of the control, to return a **CommandBarButton** object. (The **Type** property of the control must be **msoControlButton**.)

Assuming that the second control on the command bar named "Custom" is a button, the following example changes the style of that button.

```
Set c = CommandBars("Custom").Controls(2)
With c
If .Type = msoControlButton Then
   If .Style = msoButtonIcon Then
      .Style = msoButtonIconAndCaption
   Else
      .Style = msoButtonIcon
   End If
End If
End With
```

You can also use the **FindControl** method to return a **CommandBarButton** object.

Properties

Application property, **BeginGroup** property, **BuiltIn** property, **BuiltInFace** property, **Caption** property, **Creator** property, **DescriptionText** property, **Enabled** property,

FaceId property, **Height** property, **HelpContextId** property, **HelpFile** property, **Id** property, **Index** property, **Left** property, **OLEUsage** property, **OnAction** property, **Parameter** property, **Parent** property, **Priority** property, **ShortcutText** property, **State** property, **Style** property, **Tag** property, **TooltipText** property, **Top** property, **Type** property, **Visible** property, **Width** property.

Methods

Copy method, **CopyFace** method, **Delete** method, **Execute** method (**CommandBar** controls), **Move** method, **PasteFace** method, **Reset** method, **SetFocus** method.

CommandBarComboBox Object

Description

Represents a combo box control on a command bar.

Using the CommandBarComboBox Object

Use **Controls**(*index*), where *index* is the index number of the control, to return a **CommandBarComboBox** object. (The **Type** property of the control must be **msoControlEdit**, **msoControlDropdown**, **msoControlComboBox**, **msoControlButtonDropdown**, **msoControlSplitDropdown**, **msoControlOCXDropdown**, **msoControlGraphicCombo**, or **msoControlGraphicDropdown**.)

The following example adds two items to the second control on the command bar named "Custom," and then it adjusts the size of the control.

```
Set combo = CommandBars("Custom").Controls(2)
With combo
   .AddItem "First Item", 1
   .AddItem "Second Item", 2
   .DropDownLines = 3
   .DropDownWidth = 75
   .ListIndex = 0
End With
```

You can also use the **FindControl** method to return a **CommandBarComboBox** object. The following example searches all command bars for a visible **CommandBarComboBox** object whose tag is "sheet assignments."

```
Set myControl = CommandBars.FindControl _
   (Type:=msoControlComboBox, Tag:="sheet assignments", Visible:=True)
```

Properties

Application property, **BeginGroup** property, **BuiltIn** property, **Caption** property, **Creator** property, **DescriptionText** property, **DropDownLines** property, **DropDownWidth** property, **Enabled** property, **Height** property, **HelpContextId** property, **HelpFile** property, **Id** property, **Index** property, **Left** property, **List** property, **ListCount** property, **ListHeaderCount** property, **ListIndex** property, **OLEUsage** property, **OnAction** property, **Parameter** property, **Parent** property, **Priority**

property, **Style** property, **Tag** property, **Text** property, **TooltipText** property, **Top** property, **Type** property, **Visible** property, **Width** property.

Methods

AddItem method, **Clear** method, **Copy** method, **Delete** method, **Execute** method (Command Bar controls), **Move** method, **RemoveItem** method, **Reset** method, **SetFocus** method.

See Also

Add method (**CommandBarControls** collection), **AddItem** method.

CommandBarControl Object

Description

Represents a command bar control. The **CommandBarControl** object is a member of the **CommandBarControls** collection. The properties and methods of the **CommandBarControl** object are all shared by the **CommandBarButton**, **CommandBarComboBox**, and **CommandBarPopup** objects.

Note When writing Visual Basic code to work with custom command bar controls, you use the **CommandBarButton**, **CommandBarComboBox**, and **CommandBarPopup** objects. When writing code to work with built-in controls in the container application that cannot be represented by one of those three objects, you use the **CommandBarControl** object.

Using the CommandBarControl Object

Use **Controls**(*index*), where *index* is the index number of a control, to return a **CommandBarControl** object. (The **Type** property of the control must be **msoControlLabel**, **msoControlExpandingGrid**, **msoControlSplitExpandingGrid**, **msoControlGrid**, or **msoControlGauge**.)

Note Variables declared as **CommandBarControl** can be assigned **CommandBarButton**, **CommandBarComboBox**, and **CommandBarPopup** values.

You can also use the **FindControl** method to return a **CommandBarControl** object. The following example searches for a control of type **msoControlGauge**; if it finds one, it displays the index number of the control and the name of the command bar that contains it. In this example, the variable `lbl` represents a **CommandBarControl** object.

```
Set lbl = CommandBars.FindControl(Type:= msoControlGauge)
If lbl Is Nothing Then
   MsgBox "A control of type msoControlGauge was not found."
Else
   MsgBox "Control " & lbl.Index & " on command bar " _
      & lbl.Parent.Name & " is type msoControlGauge"
End If
```

Properties

Application property, **BeginGroup** property, **BuiltIn** property, **Caption** property, **Creator** property, **DescriptionText** property, **Enabled** property, **Height** property, **HelpContextId** property, **HelpFile** property, **Id** property, **Index** property, **Left** property, **OLEUsage** property, **OnAction** property, **Parameter** property, **Parent** property, **Priority** property, **Tag** property, **TooltipText** property, **Top** property, **Type** property, **Visible** property, **Width** property.

Methods

Copy method, **Delete** method, **Execute** method (Command Bar controls), **Move** method, **Reset** method, **SetFocus** method.

CommandBarControls Collection Object

Description

A collection of **CommandBarControl** objects that represent the command bar controls on a command bar.

Using the CommandBarControls Collection

Use the **Controls** property to return the **CommandBarControls** collection. The following example changes the caption of every control on the toolbar named "Standard" to the current value of the **Id** property for that control.

```
For Each ctl In CommandBars("Standard").Controls
   ctl.Caption = CStr(ctl.Id)
Next ctl
```

Use the **Add** method to add a new command bar control to the **CommandBarControls** collection. This example adds a new, blank button to the command bar named "Custom."

```
Set myBlankBtn = CommandBars("Custom").Controls.Add
```

Use **Controls**(*index*), where *index* is the caption or index number of a control, to return a **CommandBarControl**, **CommandBarButton**, **CommandBarComboBox**, or **CommandBarPopup** object. The following example copies the first control from the command bar named "Standard" to the command bar named "Custom."

```
Set myCustomBar = CommandBars("Custom")
Set myControl = CommandBars("Standard").Controls(1)
myControl.Copy Bar:=myCustomBar, Before:=1
```

Properties

Application property, **Count** property, **Creator** property, **Item** property (**CommandBars** and **CommandBarControls** collections), **Parent** property.

Methods

Add method (**CommandBarControls** collection).

Specifics (Microsoft Access)

Although most Access collections are zero-based, all command bar collections are 1-based. Note, however, that you can use the **For Each...Next** syntax to iterate through the objects in a collection without having to worry about specific index numbers.

CommandBarPopup Object

Description

Represents a pop-up control on a command bar.

Using the CommandBarPopup Object

Use **Controls**(*index*), where *index* is the number of the control, to return a **CommandBarPopup** object. (The **Type** property of the control must be **msoControlPopup**, **msoControlGraphicPopup**, **msoControlButtonPopup**, **msoControlSplitButtonPopup**, or **msoControlSplitButtonMRUPopup**.)

You can also use the **FindControl** method to return a **CommandBarPopup** object. The following example searches all command bars for a **CommandBarPopup** object whose tag is "Graphics."

```
Set myControl = Application.CommandBars.FindControl _
    (Type:=msoControlPopup, Tag:="Graphics")
```

Remarks

Every pop-up control contains a **CommandBar** object. To return the command bar from a pop-up control, apply the **CommandBar** property to the **CommandBarPopup** object.

Properties

Application property, **BeginGroup** property, **BuiltIn** property, **Caption** property, **CommandBar** property, **Controls** property, **Creator** property, **DescriptionText** property, **Enabled** property, **Height** property, **HelpContextId** property, **HelpFile** property, **Id** property, **Index** property, **Left** property, **OLEMenuGroup** property, **OLEUsage** property, **OnAction** property, **Parameter** property, **Parent** property, **Priority** property, **Tag** property, **TooltipText** property, **Top** property, **Type** property, **Visible** property, **Width** property.

Methods

Copy method, **Delete** method, **Execute** method (Command Bar controls), **Move** method, **Reset** method, **SetFocus** method.

CommandBars Collection Object

Description

A collection of **CommandBar** objects that represent the command bars in the container application.

Using the CommandBars Collection

Use the **CommandBars** property to return the **CommandBars** collection. The following example displays in the **Immediate** window both the name and local name of each menu bar and toolbar, and it displays a value that indicates whether the menu bar or toolbar is visible.

```
For Each cbar in CommandBars
   Debug.Print cbar.Name, cbar.NameLocal, cbar.Visible
Next
```

Use the **Add** method to add a new command bar to the collection. The following example creates a custom toolbar named "Custom1" and displays it as a floating toolbar.

```
Set cbar1 = CommandBars.Add(Name:="Custom1", Position:=msoBarFloating)
cbar1.Visible = True
```

Use **CommandBars(***index***)**, where *index* is the name or index number of a command bar, to return a single **CommandBar** object. The following example docks the toolbar named "Custom1" at the bottom of the application window.

```
CommandBars("Custom1").Position = msoBarBottom
```

Note You can use the name or index number to specify a menu bar or toolbar in the list of available menu bars and toolbars in the container application. However, you must use the name to specify a menu, shortcut menu, or submenu (all of which are represented by **CommandBar** objects).

If two or more custom menus or submenus have the same name, **CommandBars(***index***)** returns the first one. To ensure that you return the correct menu or submenu, locate the pop-up control that displays that menu. Then apply the **CommandBar** property to the pop-up control to return the command bar that represents that menu.

Properties

ActionControl property, **ActiveMenuBar** property, **Application** property, **Count** property, **Creator** property, **DisplayKeysInTooltips** property, **DisplayTooltips** property, **Item** property (**CommandBars** and **CommandBarControls** collections), **LargeButtons** property, **MenuAnimationStyle** property, **Parent** property.

Methods

Add method (**CommandBars** collection), **FindControl** method, **ReleaseFocus** method.

Specifics (Microsoft Access)

Although most Access collections are zero-based, all command bar collections are 1-based. Note, however, that you can use the **For Each...Next** syntax to iterate through the objects in a collection without having to worry about specific index numbers.

Condition Property

Applies To

PropertyTest object.

Description

Returns the condition of the specified search criteria. Read-only **Variant**.

Can be one of the following **MsoCondition** constants:

msoConditionAnyNumberBetween
msoConditionAnytime
msoConditionAnytimeBetween
msoConditionAtLeast
msoConditionAtMost
msoConditionBeginsWith
msoConditionDoesNotEqual
msoConditionEndsWith
msoConditionEquals
msoConditionFileTypeAllFiles
msoConditionFileTypeBinders
msoConditionFileTypeDatabases
msoConditionFileTypeExcelWorkbooks
msoConditionFileTypeOfficeFiles
msoConditionFileTypePowerPointPresentations
msoConditionFileTypeTemplates
msoConditionFileTypeWordDocuments
msoConditionIncludesNearEachOther
msoConditionIncludesPhrase
msoConditionInTheLast
msoConditionInTheNext
msoConditionIsExactly
msoConditionIsNo
msoConditionIsNot
msoConditionIsYes
msoConditionLastMonth
msoConditionLastWeek
msoConditionLessThan
msoConditionMoreThan
msoConditionNextMonth
msoConditionNextWeek
msoConditionOn
msoConditionOnorAfter
msoConditionOnorBefore
msoConditionThisMonth
msoConditionThisWeek
msoConditionToday
msoConditionTomorrow
msoConditionYesterday

See Also

NewSearch method.

Example

This example returns the connection value for search criteria for the first property test.

```
With Application.FileSearch.PropertyTests(1)
   MsgBox "The condition you've set is: " & .Condition
End With
```

Connector Property

Applies To

PropertyTest object.

Description

Returns the connector between two similar property test values. Can be either of the following **MsoConnector** constants: **msoConnectorAnd** or **msoConnectorOr**. The default value is **msoConnectorAnd**. Read-only **Variant**.

Remarks

A connector specifies whether two similar search criteria will be combined to form one property test (as with **msoConnectorAnd**), or treated independently (as with **msoConnectorOr**).

See Also

SecondValue property, **Value** property.

Example

This example displays a message that describes how the search criteria will be evaluated in a file search.

```
With Application.FileSearch.PropertyTests(1)
If .Connector = msoConnectorAnd Then
   MsgBox "All search criteria will be combined."
Else
   MsgBox "Criteria will be treated independently"
End If
End With
```

Context Property

Applies To

CommandBar object.

Description

Returns or sets a string that determines where the specified command bar will be saved. The string is defined and interpreted by the application. Read/write **String**.

Remarks

You can set the **Context** property only for custom command bars. This property will fail if the application doesn't recognize the context string, or if the application doesn't support changing context strings programmatically.

Controls Property

Applies To

CommandBar object, **CommandBarPopup** object.

Description

Returns a **CommandBarControls** object that represents all the controls on the specified command bar or popup control. Read-only.

Example

This example adds a combo box control to the command bar named "Custom" and adds two items to the combo box list. The example also sets the number of line items, the width of the combo box, and an empty default for the combo box.

```
Set myControl = CommandBars("Custom").Controls _
   .Add(Type:=msoControlComboBox, Before:=1)
With myControl
   .AddItem Text:="First Item", Index:=1
   .AddItem Text:="Second Item", Index:=2
   .DropDownLines = 3
   .DropDownWidth = 75
   .ListHeaderCount = 0
End With
```

Copy Method

Applies To

CommandBarButton object, **CommandBarComboBox** object, **CommandBarControl** object, **CommandBarPopup** object.

Description

Copies the specified command bar control to an existing command bar.

Syntax

expression.**Copy**(***Bar, Before***)

expression Required. An expression that returns a **CommandBarControl**, **CommandBarButton**, **CommandBarPopup**, or **CommandBarComboBox** object.

Bar Optional **Variant**. A **CommandBar** object that represents the destination command bar. If this argument is omitted, the control is copied to the same command bar (the command bar it's already on).

Before Optional **Variant**. A number that indicates the position for the new control on the specified command bar. The new control will be inserted before the control at this position. If this argument is omitted, the control is copied to the end of the command bar.

Example

This example copies the first control from the command bar named "Standard" to the command bar named "Custom" and positions it as the first control there too. The example assigns a new parameter to the control and sets the focus to the new button.

```
Set myCustomBar = CommandBars("Custom")
Set myControl = CommandBars("Standard").Controls(1)
With myControl
    .Copy Bar:=myCustomBar, Before:=1
    .Parameter = "2"
    .SetFocus
End With
```

CopyFace Method

Applies To

CommandBarButton object.

Description

Copies the face of the specified command bar button control to the Clipboard.

Syntax

expression.**CopyFace**

expression Required. An expression that returns a **CommandBarButton** object.

Remarks

Use the **PasteFace** method to paste the contents of the Clipboard onto a button face.

See Also

BuiltInFace property, **FaceId** property, **PasteFace** method.

Example

This example finds the built-in **Open** button and copies its button face to the Clipboard.

```
Set myControl = CommandBars.FindControl(Type:=msoControlButton, Id:=23)
myControl.CopyFace
```

Count Property

Applies To

BalloonCheckboxes collection object, **BalloonLabels** collection object, **CommandBarControls** collection object, **CommandBars** collection object, **DocumentProperties** collection object, **FoundFiles** object, **PropertyTests** collection object.

Description

Returns the number of items in the specified collection. Read-only **Long**.

Remarks

For the **CommandBars** collection, the count includes only menu bars, toolbars, and shortcut menus. Menus and submenus aren't included.

Example

This example uses the **Count** property to display the number of command bars in the collection.

```
MsgBox "There are " & CommandBars.Count & " bars in your collection."
```

This example uses the **Count** property to display the number of check boxes in the Office Assistant balloon.

```
With Assistant.NewBalloon
    .CheckBoxes(1).Text = "First Choice"
    .CheckBoxes(2).Text = "Second Choice"
    .Text = "You have the following " _
       & .CheckBoxes.Count & " choices."
    .Show
End With
```

This example uses the **Count** property to display the number of labels in the Office Assistant balloon.

```
With Assistant.NewBalloon
    .Heading = "Check Your Age Group."
    .Labels(1).Text = "20 to 29."
    .Labels(2).Text = "30 to 39."
    .Labels(3).Text = "40 or over"
    .Text = "Which of the following " _
       & .Labels.Count & " choices apply to you?"
    .Show
End With
```

This example displays the number of document properties in the **DocumentProperties** collection that was passed to the procedure.

```
Sub CountDocumentProperties(dp As DocumentProperties)
   MsgBox "There are " & dp.Count & " properties in the collection."
End Sub
```

Creator Property

Applies To

Assistant object, **Balloon** object, **BalloonCheckbox** object, **BalloonCheckboxes** collection object, **BalloonLabel** object, **BalloonLabels** collection object, **CommandBar** object, **CommandBarButton** object, **CommandBarComboBox** object, **CommandBarControl** object, **CommandBarControls** collection object, **CommandBarPopup** object, **CommandBars** collection object, **DocumentProperties** collection object, **DocumentProperty** object, **FileSearch** object, **FoundFiles** object, **PropertyTest** object, **PropertyTests** collection object.

Description

Returns the four-character code for the application in which the specified object was created. Macintosh only. Read-only **Long**.

DateCreatedFrom Property

Applies To

FileFind object.

Description

Macintosh only. Returns or sets the date on which the file to be searched for was created; this will be the lower limit for the file search. Read/write **Variant**.

Remarks

You can use the **DateCreatedTo** property to set an upper limit for the file search, or you can omit it to conduct an open-ended search.

See Also

DateCreatedTo property, **DateSavedFrom** property, **DateSavedTo** property.

DateCreatedTo Property

Applies To

FileFind object.

Description

Macintosh only. Returns or sets the date on which the file to be searched for was created; this will be the upper limit for the file search. Read/write **Variant**.

See Also

DateCreatedFrom property, **DateSavedFrom** property, **DateSavedTo** property.

DateSavedFrom Property

Applies To

FileFind object.

Description

Macintosh only. Returns or sets the date on which the file to be searched for was last saved; this will be the lower limit for the file search. Read/write **Variant**.

Remarks

You can use the **DateSavedTo** property to set an upper limit for the file search, or you can omit it to conduct an open-ended search.

See Also

DateCreatedFrom property, **DateCreatedTo** property, **DateSavedTo** property.

DateSavedTo Property

Applies To

FileFind object.

Description

Macintosh only. Returns or sets the date on which the file to be searched for was last saved; this will be the upper limit for the file search. Read/write **Variant**.

See Also

DateCreatedFrom property, **DateCreatedTo** property, **DateSavedFrom** property.

Delete Method

Applies To

CommandBar object, **CommandBarButton** object, **CommandBarComboBox** object, **CommandBarControl** object, **CommandBarPopup** object, **DocumentProperty** object, **FileFind** object.

Description

Deletes the specified object from the collection it's contained in.

Syntax 1

expression.**Delete**

Syntax 2

expression.**Delete(*Temporary*)**

Syntax 3

expression.**Delete(*BstrQueryName*)**

expression Required. An expression that returns a **CommandBar** or **DocumentProperty** object (Syntax 1), a **CommandBarControl** object (Syntax 2), or a **FileFind** object (Syntax 3).

Temporary Optional **Variant**. **True** to delete the control for the current session. The application will display the control again in the next session.

BstrQueryName Required **String**. A string containing up to 31 characters that indicates the name of the saved search criterion to be deleted.

Remarks

You cannot delete a built-in document property.

Example

This example deletes all custom command bars that aren't visible.

```
foundFlag = False
delBars = 0
For Each bar In CommandBars
   If (bar.BuiltIn = False) And (bar.Visible = False) Then
      bar.Delete
      foundFlag = True
      delBars = delBars + 1
   End If
Next
If Not foundFlag Then
   MsgBox "No command bars have been deleted."
Else
   MsgBox delBars & " custom bar(s) deleted."
End If
```

This example deletes a custom document property. You must pass a **DocumentProperty** object to the procedure.

```
Sub DeleteCustomDocumentProperty(dp As DocumentProperty)
   dp.Delete
End Sub
```

DescriptionText Property

Applies To

CommandBarButton object, **CommandBarComboBox** object, **CommandBarControl** object, **CommandBarPopup** object.

Description

Returns or sets the description for the specified command bar control. The description is displayed in the status bar of the container application when the user positions the pointer over a command bar control. Read/write **String**.

Remarks

Not all applications display a status bar. This property is also used for Balloon Help on the Macintosh.

See Also

Caption property, **DisplayKeysInTooltips** property, **DisplayTooltips** property.

Example

This example adds a command bar control with a spelling checker button face to a custom command bar. The example also sets the text "Starts the spelling checker" to appear in the status bar whenever the user positions the pointer over the button.

```
Set myBar = CommandBars.Add("Custom", msoBarTop, , True)
myBar.Visible = True
Set myControl = myBar.Controls.Add(Type:=msoControlButton, Id:=2)
With myControl
    .DescriptionText = "Starts the spelling checker"
    .Caption = "Spelling checker"
End With
```

DisplayKeysInTooltips Property

Applies To

CommandBars collection object.

Description

True if shortcut keys are displayed in the ToolTips for each command bar control . Read/write **Boolean**.

Remarks

To display shortcut keys in ToolTips, you must also set the **DisplayTooltips** property to **True**.

See Also

Caption property, **DescriptionText** property, **DisplayTooltips** property.

Example

This example sets the options for all command bars in Microsoft Office.

```
With CommandBars
    .LargeButtons = True
    .DisplayTooltips = True
    .DisplayKeysInTooltips = True
    .MenuAnimationStyle = msoMenuAnimationUnfold
End With
```

DisplayTooltips Property

Applies To

CommandBars collection object.

Description

True if ScreenTips are displayed whenever the user positions the pointer over command bar controls. Read/write **Boolean**.

Remarks

Setting the **DisplayTooltips** property in a container application immediately affects all the command bars in that application, in any other Office 97 application running at that time, and in any Office 97 application opened after that time, until the property is set again.

See Also

Caption property, **DescriptionText** property, **DisplayKeysInTooltips** property.

Example

This example displays large controls and ScreenTips on all command bars if the menu bar named "Custom Menu Bar" is the active menu bar.

```
Set allBars = CommandBars
If allBars.ActiveMenuBar.Name = "Custom Menu Bar" Then
   allBars.LargeButtons = True
   allBars.DisplayTooltips = True
End If
```

DocumentProperties Collection Object

Description

A collection of **DocumentProperty** objects. Each **DocumentProperty** object represents a built-in or custom property of a container document.

Using the DocumentProperties Collection

Use the **BuiltinDocumentProperties** property to return a **DocumentProperties** collection that contains all the built-in properties of a container document. Use the **CustomDocumentProperties** property to return a **DocumentProperties** collection that contains all the custom properties of the document.

Use the **Add** method to create a new custom property and add it to the **DocumentProperties** collection. You cannot use the **Add** method to create a built-in document property.

Use **BuiltinDocumentProperties(***index***)**, where *index* is the index number of the built-in document property, to return a single **DocumentProperty** object that represents a specific built-in document property. Use

CustomDocumentProperties(*index*), where *index* is the number of the custom document property, to return a **DocumentProperty** object that represents a specific custom document property.

Properties

Application property, **Count** property, **Creator** property, **Item** property (**DocumentProperties** collection), **Parent** property.

Methods

Add method (**DocumentProperties** collection).

Specifics (Microsoft Excel)

Each workbook has a collection of built-in document properties and a collection of custom document properties. Each collection is represented by a **DocumentProperties** object, and each collection contains individual **DocumentProperty** objects.

Use the **BuiltinDocumentProperties** property to return the collection of built-in document properties, and use the **CustomDocumentProperties** property to return the collection of custom document properties.

The following example displays the names of the built-in document properties as a list on worksheet one.

```
rw = 1
Worksheets(1).Activate
For Each p In ActiveWorkbook.BuiltinDocumentProperties
   Cells(rw, 1).Value = p.Name
   rw = rw + 1
Next
```

DocumentProperty Object

Description

Represents a custom or built-in document property of a container document. The **DocumentProperty** object is a member of the **DocumentProperties** collection.

Using the DocumentProperty Object

Use **BuiltinDocumentProperties**(*index*), where *index* is the name or index number of the built-in document property, to return a single **DocumentProperty** object that represents a specific built-in document property. Use **CustomDocumentProperties**(*index*), where *index* is the name or index number of the custom document property, to return a **DocumentProperty** object that represents a specific custom document property.

The names of all the available built-in document properties are shown in the following list:

Title	Subject
Author	Keywords
Comments	Template
Last Author	Revision Number
Application Name	Last Print Date
Creation Date	Last Save Time
Total Editing Time	Number of Pages
Number of Words	Number of Characters
Security	Category
Format	Manager
Company	Number of Bytes
Number of Lines	Number of Paragraphs
Number of Slides	Number of Notes
Number of Hidden Slides	Number of Multimedia Clips

Container applications don't necessarily define a value for every built-in document property. If a given application doesn't define a value for one of the built-in document properties, returning the **Value** property for that document property causes an error.

Properties

Application property, **Creator** property, **LinkSource** property, **LinkToContent** property, **Name** property, **Parent** property, **Type** property, **Value** property.

Methods

Delete method.

Specifics (Microsoft Excel)

Each workbook has a collection of built-in document properties and a collection of custom document properties. Each collection is represented by a **DocumentProperties** object, and each collection contains individual **DocumentProperty** objects.

Use the **BuiltinDocumentProperties** property to return the collection of built-in document properties, and use the **CustomDocumentProperties** property to return the collection of custom document properties. Use the **Item** property to return a single member of the collection.

The following example sets the value of the built-in document property named "Title."

```
ActiveWorkbook.BuiltinDocumentProperties.Item("Title") _
    .Value = "Year-End Sales Results"
```

DropDownLines Property

Applies To

CommandBarComboBox object.

Description

Returns or sets the number of lines in the specified command bar combo box control. The combo box control must be a custom control and it must be either a drop-down list box or a combo box. Read/write **Long**.

Note If this property is set for a combo box control that's either an edit box or a built-in combo box control, an error occurs.

Remarks

If this property is set to 0 (zero), the number of lines in the control will be based on the number of items in the list.

See Also

Add method (**CommandBarControls** Collection), **AddItem** method, **Clear** method, **DropDownWidth** property.

Example

This example adds a combo box control to the command bar named "Custom" and then adds two items to the combo box list. The example also sets the number of line items, the width of the combo box, and an empty default for the combo box.

```
Set myBar = CommandBars("Custom")
Set myControl = myBar.Controls.Add(Type:=msoControlComboBox, Id:=1)
With myControl
    .AddItem Text:="First Item", Index:=1
    .AddItem "Second Item", 2
    .DropDownLines = 3
    .DropDownWidth = 75
    .ListHeaderCount = 0
End With
```

DropDownWidth Property

Applies To

CommandBarComboBox object.

Description

Returns or sets the width (in pixels) of the list for the specified command bar combo box control. Read/write **Long**.

Note If this property is set for a built-in combo box control, an error occurs.

Remarks

If this property is set to -1, the width of the list is based on the length of the longest item in the combo box list. If this property is set to 0, the width of the list is based on the width of the control.

See Also

Add method (**CommandBarControls** collection), **AddItem** method, **Clear** method, **DropDownLines** property.

Example

This example adds a combo box control to the command bar named "Custom" and then adds two items to the combo box list. The example also sets the number of line items, the width of the combo box, and an empty default for the combo box.

```
Set myBar = CommandBars("Custom")
Set myControl = myBar.Controls.Add(Type:=msoControlComboBox, Id:=1)
With myControl
    .AddItem "First Item", 1
    .AddItem "Second Item", 2
    .DropDownLines = 3
    .DropDownWidth = 75
    .ListHeaderCount = 0
End With
```

Enabled Property

Applies To

CommandBar object, **CommandBarButton** object, **CommandBarComboBox** object, **CommandBarControl** object, **CommandBarPopup** object.

Description

True if the specified command bar or command bar control is enabled. Read/write **Boolean**.

Remarks

For command bars, setting this property to **True** causes the name of the command bar to appear in the list of available command bars.

For built-in controls, if you set the **Enabled** property to **True** the application determines its state but setting it to **False** will force it to be disabled.

Specifics (Microsoft Access)

You can use this property to disable (dimmed) or enable a menu item or command button. This property applies to menu names, submenu names, and items on submenus. The **Enabled** property replaces the functionality supplied by the SetMenuItem action and **SetMenuItem** method in Microsoft Access 95.

You can disable a menu item that Microsoft Access would normally enable, but you can't enable a menu item that Microsoft Access would normally disable.

Example

This example adjusts the command bars according to the user level specified by `user`. If `user` is "Level 1," the command bar named "VB Custom Bar" is displayed. If `user` is any other value, the built-in command bar "Visual Basic" is reset to its default state and the command bar named "VB Custom Bar" is disabled.

```
Set myBar = CommandBars("VB Custom Bar")
If user = "Level 1" Then
   myBar.Visible = True
Else
   CommandBars("Visual Basic").Reset
   myBar.Enabled = False
End If
```

This example adds two command bar buttons to the command bar represented by the variable `myBar`. The first control is disabled and will appear grey. The second control is enabled by default.

```
With myBar
   .Controls.Add Type:=msoControlButton, Id:=3
   .Controls(1).Enabled = False
   .Controls.Add Type:=msoControlButton, Id:=3
End With
myBar.Visible = True
```

EndWizard Method

Applies To

Assistant object.

Description

Closes the Office Assistant window and releases the variable that uniquely identifies the wizard session.

Note You use this method to complete the process begun with the **StartWizard** method.

Syntax

expression.**EndWizard(*WizardID, varfSuccess, Animation*)**

expression Required. An expression that returns an **Assistant** object.

WizardID Required **Long**. A number that uniquely identifies the Office Assistant wizard session, as returned by the **StartWizard** method.

varfSuccess Required **Boolean**. When the method returns, this argument is **True** if the user completes the wizard successfully.

Animation Optional **Variant**. The type of animation that the Office Assistant performs when the wizard session ends.

See Also

ActivateWizard method, **Assistant** object, **StartWizard** method.

Example

This example closes the Office Assistant for a wizard session that was completed successfully by the user. The variable `helpForWiz` was assigned the return value of the **StartWizard** method.

```
Assistant.EndWizard WizardId:=helpForWiz, _
    varfSuccess:=True, Animation:=msoAnimationGoodbye
```

Execute Method (Command Bar Controls)

Applies To

CommandBarButton object, **CommandBarComboBox** object, **CommandBarControl** object, **CommandBarPopup** object.

Description

Runs the macro or built-in command assigned to the specified command bar control. For custom controls, use the **OnAction** property to specify the macro to run.

Syntax

expression.**Execute**

expression Required. An expression that returns a **CommandBarControl**, **CommandBarButton**, **CommandBarPopup**, or **CommandBarComboBox** object.

Example

This example checks the value of the combo box control on the custom command bar named "My Command Bar." If the value is "First," the example runs the macro specified by the **OnAction** property of the command bar control.

```
Set mycontrol = CommandBars("My Custom Bar").Controls(1)
With mycontrol
    If .List(.ListIndex) = "First" Then
        mycontrol.Execute
    End If
End With
```

Execute Method (FileSearch and FileFind Objects)

Applies To

FileFind object, **FileSearch** object.

Description

FileSearch object: Begins the search for the specified files.

FileFind object: Begins the search for the specified files and updates the **FindFileResults** collection. Macintosh only.

Syntax 1

expression.**Execute(*SortBy, SortOrder, AlwaysAccurate*)**

Syntax 2

expression.**Execute**

expression Required. An expression that returns a **FileSearch** object (Syntax 1) or a **FileFind** object (Syntax 2).

SortBy Optional **Variant**. The method used to sort the returned files. Can be one of the following **MsoSortBy** constants: **msoSortbyFileName**, **msoSortbyFileType**, **msoSortbyLastModified**, or **msoSortbySize**.

SortOrder Optional **Variant**. The order in which the returned files are to be sorted. Can be either of the following **MsoSortOrder** constants: **msoSortOrderAscending** or **msoSortOrderDescending**.

AlwaysAccurate Optional **Boolean**. **True** to have the file search include files that have been added, modified, or deleted since the file index was last updated. The default value is **True**.

Example

This example searches for all files that begin with "cmd" in the My Documents folder and displays the location and name of each file that's found. The example sorts the list of returned files in ascending alphabetic order, by file name.

```
Set fs = Application.FileSearch
With fs
   .LookIn = "C:\My Documents"
   .FileName = "cmd*"
   If .Execute(SortBy:=msoSortbyFileName, _
         SortOrder:=msoSortOrderAscending) > 0 Then
      MsgBox "There were " & .FoundFiles.Count & _
         " file(s) found."
      For i = 1 To .FoundFiles.Count
         MsgBox .FoundFiles(i)
      Next i
   Else
      MsgBox "There were no files found."
   End If
End With
```

FaceId Property

Applies To

CommandBarButton object.

Description

Returns or sets the ID number for the button face that's currently assigned to the specified command bar button control. Read/write **Long**.

Remarks

The **FaceId** property dictates the look, but not the function, of a command bar button. The **Id** property of the **CommandBarControl** object determines the function of the button.

The value of the **FaceId** property for a command bar button with a custom face is 0 (zero).

See Also

BuiltInFace property, **CopyFace** method, **PasteFace** method.

Example

This example adds a command bar button to a custom command bar. Clicking this button is equivalent to clicking the **Open** command on the **File** menu because the ID number is 23, yet the button has the same button face as the built-in **Charting** button. When you click this button, the **Open** dialog box is displayed.

```
Set newBar = CommandBars.Add(Name:="Custom2", _
    Position:=msoBarTop, Temporary:=True)
newBar.Visible = True
Set con = newBar.Controls.Add(Type:=msoControlButton, Id:=23)
con.FaceId = 17
```

FeatureTips Property

Applies To

Assistant object.

Description

True if the Office Assistant provides information about using application features more effectively. Read/write **Boolean**.

Remarks

The **FeatureTips** property corresponds to the **Using features more effectively** check box on the **Options** tab in the **Assistant** dialog box.

Specifics (Microsoft Access)

This property isn't available in Microsoft Access.

Example

This example sets the Office Assistant to provide information about using application features more effectively.

```
Assistant.FeatureTips = True
```

FileFind Object

Description

Represents the functionality of the **File Find** dialog box.

Using the FileFind Object

Use the **FileFind** property to return the **FileFind** object.

FileFindResults Object

Description

Represents the list of files returned from a file search.

Using the FileFindResults Object

Use the **Results** property to return the **FileFindResults** object.

Use **FileFindResults**(*item*), where *item* is the index number, to return the path and file name of a found file.

Use the **Execute** method to begin the file search and update the list.

Use the **View** property to display the list of found files in a dialog box.

FileName Property

Applies To

Assistant object, **FileSearch** object.

Description

Assistant object: Returns or sets the name of the file for the active Office Assistant. Read/write **String**.

FileSearch object: Returns or sets the name of the file to look for during a file search. The name of the file may include the * (asterisk) or ? (question mark) wildcards. Use the question mark wildcard to match any single character. For example, type **gr?y** to match both “gray” and “grey.” Use the asterisk wildcard to match any number of characters. For example, type ***.txt** to find all files that have the .TXT extension. Read/write **String**.

Remarks

In Windows, the file name extension for Assistant files is .act, and the files are installed in the \Program Files\Microsoft Office\Office\Actors folder in Windows 95, in the \Windows\MsApps\Actors folder in Windows NT, and in the Microsoft:Assistants folder on the Macintosh.

The following file names correspond to the Assistants in Office 97.

Character	File name
Office Logo	Logo.act
PowerPup	Powerpup.act
The Genius	Genius.act
Hoverbot	Hoverbot.act
Scribble	Scribble.act
The Dot	Dot.act
Clippit	Clippit.act
Mother Nature	MNature.act
Will	Will.act

See Also

Animation property.

Example

This example uses the **FileName** property to customize balloon text for specific Office Assistants. The variable `btext` can be used for the value of the **Text** property in a Print Wizard balloon.

```
Select Case Assistant.FileName
Case "will.act"
   btext = "To Print, or Not to Print. That is the question."
Case "genius.act"
   btext = "The sum of the checkboxes equals the document to print."
Case Else
   btext = "Choose the document you want to print."
End Select
```

This example searches for all files located in the My Documents folder that begin with "cmd." The example displays the name and location of each found file.

```
Set fs = Application.FileSearch
With fs
   .LookIn = "C:\My Documents"
   .FileName = "cmd*"
   If .Execute > 0 Then
      MsgBox "There were " & .FoundFiles.Count & _
         " file(s) found."
      For i = 1 To .FoundFiles.Count
         MsgBox .FoundFiles(i)
      Next i
   Else
      MsgBox "There were no files found."
   End If
End With
```

FileSearch Object

Description

Represents the functionality of the **Open** dialog box (**File** menu).

Using the FileSearch Object

Use the **FileSearch** property to return the **FileSearch** object. The following example searches for the specified files and displays both the number of files found and the title of each found file.

```
With Application.FileSearch
    If .Execute() > 0 Then
        MsgBox "There were " & .FoundFiles.Count & _
            " file(s) found."
        For i = 1 To .FoundFiles.Count
            MsgBox .FoundFiles(i)
        Next i
    Else
        MsgBox "There were no files found."
    End If
End With
```

Use the **NewSearch** method to reset the search criteria to the default settings. All property values are retained after each search is run, and by using the **NewSearch** method you can selectively set properties for the next file search without manually resetting previous property values. The following example resets the search criteria to the default settings before beginning a new search.

```
With Application.FileSearch
    .NewSearch
    .LookIn = "C:\My Documents"
    .SearchSubFolders = True
    .FileName = "Run"
    .MatchTextExactly = True
    .FileType = msoFileTypeAllFiles
End With
```

Properties

Application property, **Creator** property, **FileName** property, **FileType** property, **FoundFiles** property, **LastModified** property, **LookIn** property, **MatchAllWordForms** property, **MatchTextExactly** property, **PropertyTests** property, **SearchSubFolders** property, **TextOrProperty** property.

Methods

Execute method (**FileSearch** and **FileFind** objects), **NewSearch** method.

FileType Property

Applies To

FileFind object, **FileSearch** object.

Description

FileSearch object: Returns or sets the type of file to be searched for during a file search. Can be one of the following **MsoFileType** constants: **msoFileTypeAllFiles**, **msoFileTypeBinders**, **msoFileTypeDatabases**, **msoFileTypeExcelWorkbooks**, **msoFileTypeOfficeFiles**, **msoFileTypePowerPointPresentations**, **msoFileTypeTemplates**, or **msoFileTypeWordDocuments**. The default value is **msoFileTypeOfficeFiles**. Read/write **Variant**.

FileFind object: Returns or sets the type of file to be searched for. Can be set to a number returned by the **MacID** function. Macintosh only. Read/write **Long**.

Remarks

Use the arguments listed in the following table with the **MacID** function to return the appropriate Macintosh file type.

File type	Argument
Word document	MSWD
Microsoft Excel workbook	XCEL
PowerPoint presentation	PPT3 (for use with all versions of PowerPoint)
Text file	TTXT

See Also

Execute method, **NewSearch** method.

Example

This example searches for all Binder files located in the My Documents folder. The example displays the name and location of each found file in a message dialog.

```
Set fs = Application.FileSearch
With fs
    .LookIn = "C:\My Documents"
    .FileType = msoFileTypeBinders
    If .Execute > 0 Then
        MsgBox "There were " & .FoundFiles.Count & _
            " Binder file(s) found."
        For i = 1 To .FoundFiles.Count
            MsgBox .FoundFiles(i)
        Next i
    Else
        MsgBox "There were no Binder files found."
    End If
End With
```

FindControl Method

Applies To

CommandBar object, **CommandBars** collection object.

Description

Returns a **CommandBarControl** object that fits the specified criteria.

Syntax

expression.**FindControl(*Type, Id, Tag, Visible, Recursive*)**

expression Required. An expression that returns a **CommandBars** object.

Type Optional **Variant**. The type of control to be searched for. Can be one of the following **MsoControlType** constants:

msoControlButton	**msoControlButtonDropdown**
msoControlButtonPopup	**msoControlComboBox**
msoControlCustom	**msoControlDropdown**
msoControlEdit	**msoControlExpandingGrid**
msoControlGauge	**msoControlGenericDropdown**
msoControlGraphicCombo	**msoControlGraphicDropdown**
msoControlGraphicPopup	**msoControlGrid**
msoControlLabel	**msoControlOCXDropDown**
msoControlPopup	**msoControlSplitButtonMRUPopup**
msoControlSplitButtonPopup	**msoControlSplitDropdown**
msoControlSplitExpandingGrid	

Id Optional **Variant**. The identifier of the control to be searched for.

Tag Optional **Variant**. The tag value of the control to be searched for.

Visible Optional **Variant**. **True** to include only visible command bar controls in the search. The default value is **False**.

Recursive Optional **Boolean**. **True** to include the command bar and all of its popup sub-toolbars in the search. The default value is **False**.

Remarks

If the **CommandBars** collection contains two or more controls that fit the search criteria, **FindControl** returns the first control that's found. If no control that fits the criteria is found, **FindControl** returns **Nothing**. None of the arguments for the **FindControl** method have a default value.

Example

This example adds the **Save** button to the **Help** menu on the menu bar. Using the **FindControl** method ensures that the **Help** menu will be found even if the user has customized the menu bar.

```
Set helpMenu = CommandBars.FindControl _
   (Type:=msoControlPopup, Id:=helpId)
Set helpMenuDrop = helpMenu.Control.CommandBar
helpMenuDrop.Controls.Add Type:=msoControlButton, Id:=saveId
```

FoundFiles Object

Description

Represents the list of files returned from a file search.

Using the FoundFiles Object

Use the **FoundFiles** property to return the **FoundFiles** object. This example steps through the list of found files and displays the path and file name of each found file.

```
With Application.FileSearch
   For i = 1 To .FoundFiles.Count
      MsgBox .FoundFiles(i)
   Next I
End With
```

Use **FoundFiles**(*index*), where *index* is the index number, to return the path and file name of a found file. The following example steps through the collection of found files and displays the path and file name of each one.

```
With Application.FileSearch
For i = 1 To .FoundFiles.Count
   MsgBox .FoundFiles(i)
Next I
End With
```

Use the **Execute** method to begin the file search and update the **FoundFiles** object. The following example searches the My Documents folder for all files whose names begin with "Cmd" and displays the name and location of each file that's found. The example also sorts the returned files in ascending alphabetic order by file name.

```
Set fs = Application.FileSearch
With fs
   .LookIn = "C:\My Documents"
   .FileName = "cmd*"
   If .Execute(SortBy:=msoSortbyFileName, _
      SortOrder:=msoSortOrderAscending) > 0 Then
      MsgBox "There were " & .FoundFiles.Count & _
         " file(s) found."
      For i = 1 To .FoundFiles.Count
         MsgBox .FoundFiles(i)
      Next i
   Else
      MsgBox "There were no files found."
   End If
End With
```

FoundFiles Property

Applies To

FileSearch object.

Description

Returns a **FoundFiles** object that contains the names of all files found in a search operation. Read-only.

Example

This example steps through the list of found files and displays the path for each file.

```
With Application.FileSearch
For i = 1 To .FoundFiles.Count
   MsgBox .FoundFiles(i)
Next I
End With
```

GuessHelp Property

Applies To

Assistant object.

Description

True if the Office Assistant displays a list of relevant Help topics based on the context immediately before the user clicks the Assistant window or presses F1. Read/write **Boolean**.

Remarks

The **GuessHelp** property corresponds to the **Guess help topics** option under **Assistant capabilities** on the **Options** tab in the **Office Assistant** dialog box.

Example

This example sets the Office Assistant to guess at Help topics.

```
Assistant.GuessHelp = True
```

Heading Property

Applies To

Balloon object.

Description

Returns or sets the heading that appears in the Office Assistant balloon. Read/write **String**.

Remarks

You can specify a graphic to display by using the following syntax: {*type location sizing_factor*}, where *type* is bmp (bitmap), wmf (Windows metafile), or pict (Macintosh PICT file); *location* is the resource id or the path and file name; and *sizing_factor* specifies the width of the wmf or pict (omitted for bmp).

See Also

Show method, **Text** property.

Example

This example creates a balloon with a heading, text, and three region choices, and then displays it.

```
With Assistant.NewBalloon
    .Button = msoButtonSetOkCancel
    .Heading = "Regional Sales Data"
    .Text = "Select a region"
    For i = 1 To 3
        .CheckBoxes(i).Text = "Region " & i
    Next
    .Show
End With
```

Height Property

Applies To

CommandBar object, **CommandBarButton** object, **CommandBarComboBox** object, **CommandBarControl** object, **CommandBarPopup** object.

Description

Returns or sets the height of the specified command bar or command bar control, in pixels. Read/write **Long**.

Remarks

Setting the **Height** property will cause an error if the command bar isn't in a resizable state (that is, if it's docked or protected from resizing).

See Also

Controls property.

Example

This example adds a custom control before the second control on the command bar named "Custom." The example sets the height of the control to half the height of the command bar and sets its width to 50 pixels.

```
Set myBar = cmdbar.CommandBars("Custom")
barHeight = myBar.Height
Set myControl = myBar.Controls _
    .Add(Type:=msoControlComboBox, Before:=2, Temporary:=True)
With myControl
    .Height = barHeight / 2
    .Width = 50
End With
myBar.Visible = True
```

Help Method

Applies To

Assistant object.

Description

Displays the Office Assistant and the built-in Assistant balloon.

Syntax

expression.**Help**

expression Required. An expression that returns an **Assistant** object.

See Also

HelpContextId property, **HelpFile** property.

Example

This example displays the built-in Assistant balloon when the user selects the "I need more information" checkbox.

```
Set b = Assistant.NewBalloon
With b
   .Heading = "User Information"
   .Text = "Select your skill level"
   .CheckBoxes(1).Text = "Beginner."
   .CheckBoxes(2).Text = "Advanced."
   .CheckBoxes(3).Text = "I need more information."
   .Show
End With
If b.CheckBoxes(3).Checked = True Then
   Assistant.Help
End If
```

HelpContextId Property

Applies To

CommandBarButton object, **CommandBarComboBox** object, **CommandBarControl** object, **CommandBarPopup** object.

Description

Returns or sets the Help context ID number for the Help topic attached to the command bar control. Read/write **Long**.

Remarks

To use this property, you must also set the **HelpFile** property.

See Also

Help method, **HelpFile** property.

Specifics (Microsoft Access)

In Microsoft Access 97, you can use the *Toolbar* **Control Properties** dialog box for command bar controls to set the **HelpContextId** property for a control on a command bar. Display the **Customize** dialog box by pointing to **Toolbars** on the **View** menu and clicking **Customize**. For menu bar and toolbar controls, display the menu bar or toolbar, and then right-click the control whose **HelpContextId** property you want to set. For shortcut menu controls, select the **Shortcut Menus** check box on the **Toolbars** tab of the **Customize** dialog box, then find the shortcut menu control you want on the menu bar that's displayed and right-click the control. Click the **Properties** command. Enter the context ID number of the Help topic you want in the **Help ContextID** box.

Example

This example adds a custom report manager button to the **File** menu and specifies a Help topic to be displayed as that button's context-sensitive Help.

```
Set fileMenu = CommandBars _
   .FindControl(Type:=msoControlPopup, Id:=fileID)
Set fileMenuDropdown = fileMenu.CommandBar
Set newButton = fileMenuDropdown.Controls _
   .Add(Type:=msoControlButton, Before:=3)
With newButton
   .Caption = "Open Report"
   .DescriptionText = "Opens a quarterly report form"
   .OnAction = "ReportManager"
   .HelpFile = "C:\corphelp\custom.hlp"
   .HelpContextID = 47
End With
```

HelpFile Property

Applies To

CommandBarButton object, **CommandBarComboBox** object, **CommandBarControl** object, **CommandBarPopup** object.

Description

Returns or sets the Help file name for the Help topic attached to the command bar control. Read/write **String**.

Remarks

To use this property, you must also set the **HelpContextID** property.

See Also

Help method, **HelpContextId** property.

Specifics (Microsoft Access)

In Microsoft Access 97, you can use the *Toolbar* **Control Properties** dialog box for command bar controls to set the **HelpFile** property for a control on a command bar. Display the **Customize** dialog box by pointing to **Toolbars** on the **View** menu and clicking **Customize**. For menu bar and toolbar controls, display the menu bar or toolbar, and then right-click the control whose **HelpFile** property you want to set. For shortcut menu controls, select the **Shortcut Menus** check box on the **Toolbars** tab of the **Customize** dialog box, then find the shortcut menu control you want on the menu bar that's displayed and right-click the control. Click the **Properties** command. Enter the name of the Help file you want in the **Help File** box.

Example

This example adds a custom report manager button to the **File** menu and specifies a Help topic to be displayed as that button's context-sensitive Help.

```
Set fileMenu = CommandBars _
    .FindControl(Type:=msoControlPopup, Id:=fileId)
Set fileMenuDropdown = fileMenu.CommandBar
Set newbutton = fileMenuDropdown.Controls _
    .Add(Type:=msoControlButton, Id:=customId, Before:=3)
With newButton
    .Caption = "Open Report"
    .DescriptionText = "Opens a quarterly report form"
    .OnAction = "ReportManager"
    .HelpFile = "C:\corphelp\custom.hlp"
    .HelpContextID = 47
End With
```

HighPriorityTips Property

Applies To

Assistant object.

Description

True if the Office Assistant displays high-priority tips. Read/write **Boolean**.

Remarks

The **HighPriorityTips** property corresponds to the **Only show high priority tips** option under **Other tip options** on the **Options** tab in the **Office Assistant** dialog box.

Specifics (Microsoft Access)

This property isn't available in Microsoft Access.

Example

This example sets the Office Assistant to display high-priority tips.

```
Assistant.HighPriorityTips = True
```

Icon Property

Applies To

Balloon object.

Description

Returns or sets the type of icon that appears in the upper-left portion of the Office Assistant balloon. Can be one of the following **MsoIconType** constants: **msoIconAlert**, **msoIconNone**, or **msoIconTip**. Read/write **String**.

Example

This example creates a balloon with an alert icon that instructs the user to select a printer.

```
With Assistant.NewBalloon
    .Heading = "Select A Printer"
    .Text = "You must select a printer before printing."
    .Icon = msoIconAlert
    .CheckBoxes(1).Text = "Local printer"
    .CheckBoxes(2).Text = "Network printer"
    .Show
End With
```

Id Property

Applies To

CommandBarButton object, **CommandBarComboBox** object, **CommandBarControl** object, **CommandBarPopup** object.

Description

Returns the ID for the specified built-in command bar control. Read-only **Long**.

Remarks

A control's ID determines the built-in action for that control. The value of the **Id** property for all custom controls is 1.

See Also

FindControl method.

Specifics (Microsoft Access)

The **Id** property can only be set when you create a new control. Set the ***Id*** argument of the **Add** method of the **CommandBarControls** collection to an **Integer** value that corresponds to a built-in command button or menu item, or to one of the equivalent intrinsic constants used with the **RunCommand** method in Microsoft Access. For a custom control, set the ***Id*** argument to 1 or leave it blank.

You can use the **Id** property to determine the **Integer** value corresponding to a built-in control. For example, to determine the **Integer** value corresponding to the **Paste** command on the **Edit** menu of the main menu bar, use the following reference:

```
CommandBars("Menu Bar").Controls("Edit").Controls("Paste").Id
```

Example

This example changes the button face of the first control on the command bar named "Custom2" if the button's ID value is less than 25.

```
Set ctrl = CommandBars("Custom2").Controls(1)
With ctrl
   If .Id < 25 Then
      .FaceId = 17
      .Tag = "Changed control"
   End If
End With
```

The following example changes the caption of every control on the toolbar named "Standard" to the current value of the **Id** property for that control.

```
For Each ctl In CommandBars("Standard").Controls
   ctl.Caption = CStr(ctl.Id)
Next ctl
```

Index Property

Applies To

CommandBar object, **CommandBarButton** object, **CommandBarComboBox** object, **CommandBarControl** object, **CommandBarPopup** object.

Description

Returns the index number of the specified object in the collection. Read-only **Long**.

Remarks

The position of the first command bar control is 1. Separators are not counted in the **CommandBarControls** collection.

Example

This example searches the command bar named "Custom2" for a control with an ID value of 23. If such a control is found and the index number of the found control is greater than 5, the control will be positioned as the first control on the command bar.

```
Set myBar = CommandBars("Custom2")
Set ctrl1 = myBar.FindControl(Id:=23)
If ctrl1.Index > 5 Then
   ctrl1.Move before:=1
End If
```

Item Property (Assistant, BalloonLabel, and BalloonCheckbox Objects)

Applies To

Assistant object, **BalloonCheckbox** object, **BalloonLabel** object.

Description

Returns the text associated with the specified object. Read-only **String**.

Syntax

expression.**Item**

expression Required. An expression that returns an **Assistant**, **BalloonCheckbox**, or **BalloonLabel** object.

Item Property (BalloonCheckboxes Collection)

Applies To

BalloonCheckboxes collection object.

Description

Returns a **BalloonCheckbox** object from a **BalloonCheckboxes** collection. Read-only.

Syntax

expression.**Item(*iCbx*)**

expression An expression that returns a **BalloonCheckboxes** object.

iCbx Required **Long**. The index number of the check box to be returned.

Item Property (BalloonLabels Collection)

Applies To

BalloonLabels collection object.

Description

Returns a **BalloonLabel** object from a **BalloonLabels** collection. Read-only.

Syntax

expression.**Item(*iLbl*)**

expression   An expression that returns a **BalloonLabels** object.

iLbl   Required **Long**. The index number of the label to be returned.

Item Property (CommandBars and CommandBarControls Collections)

Applies To

CommandBarControls collection object, **CommandBars** collection object.

Description

Returns a **CommandBar** object from a **CommandBars** collection, or returns a **CommandBarControl** object from a **CommandBarControls** collection. Read-only.

Syntax

expression.**Item(*Index*)**

expression   Required. An expression that returns a **CommandBars** or **CommandBarControls** object.

Index   Required **Variant**. The name or index number of the object to be returned. Note that you can only use index numbers to return **PropertyTest** objects from the **PropertyTests** collection.

Item Property (DocumentProperties Collection)

Applies To

DocumentProperties collection object.

Description

Returns an **DocumentProperty** object from a **DocumentProperties** collection. Read-only.

Syntax

expression.**Item(*Index*)**

expression   Required. An expression that returns a **DocumentProperties** object.

Index   Required **Variant**. The name or index number of the document property to be returned.

Item Property (FoundFiles and FileFindResults Objects)

Applies To

FoundFiles object.

Description

Returns a file name from the list of file names represented by the **FoundFiles** or **FileFindResults** object. Read-only **String**.

Syntax

expression.**Item(*Index*)**

expression Required. An expression that returns a **FoundFiles** or **FileFindResults** object (**FileFindResults** is Macintosh only).

Index Required **Variant**. The index number of the file name to be returned.

Item Property (PropertyTests Collection)

Applies To

PropertyTests collection object.

Description

Returns an **PropertyTest** object from a **PropertyTests** collection. Read-only.

Syntax

expression.**Item(*Index*)**

expression Required. An expression that returns a **PropertyTests** object.

Index Required **Variant**. The index number of the property test to be returned.

KeyboardShortcutTips Property

Applies To

Assistant object.

Description

True if the Office Assistant provides Help information about keyboard shortcuts. Read/write **Boolean**.

Remarks

The **KeyboardShortcutTips** property corresponds to the **Keyboard shortcuts** option under **Show tips about** on the **Options** tab in the **Office Assistant** dialog box.

Specifics (Microsoft Access)

This property isn't available in Microsoft Access.

Example

This example sets the Office Assistant to provide Help information about keyboard shortcuts.

```
Assistant.KeyboardShortcutTips = True
```

Keywords Property

Applies To

FileFind object.

Description

Macintosh only. Returns or sets a string (up to 80 characters long) that represents keywords listed in the properties of the document to be searched for. Read/write **String**.

See Also

Execute method.

<break>

Labels Property

Applies To

Balloon object.

Description

Returns a **BalloonLabels** collection that represents the button labels, number labels, and bullet labels contained in the specified Office Assistant balloon. Read-only.

Example

This example creates a balloon containing three choices. The variable x is set to the return value of the **Show** method, which will be 1, 2 or 3, corresponding to the label the user clicks. In the example, a simple message box displays the value of the variable x, but you can pass the value to another procedure, or you can use the value in a **Select Case** statement.

```
Set b = Assistant.NewBalloon
With b
   .Heading = "This is my heading"
   .Text = "Select one of these things:"
   .Labels(1).Text = "Choice One"
   .Labels(2).Text = "Choice Two"
   .Labels(3).Text = "Choice Three"
   x = .Show
End With
MsgBox x
```

Example (Microsoft Access)

The following function creates a custom balloon for the Office Assistant and determines how the user responded to the balloon:

```
Function AssistantBalloon(Optional varCheck As Variant, Optional _
   varLabel As Variant)
   Dim bch As BalloonCheckbox
   Dim intI As Integer
   Dim intReturn As Integer
   Dim strCheck(5) As String
   Dim strList As String

   ' Create new balloon.
   Set bal = Assistant.NewBalloon
   ' Specify balloon type.
   bal.BalloonType = msoBalloonTypeButtons
   ' Specify that balloon is modal.
   bal.Mode = msoModeModal

   ' Make Assistant visible.
   If Assistant.Visible = False Then Assistant.Visible = True
   ' Check if first argument has been passed.
   If Not IsMissing(varCheck) Then
      ' If too large, set to maximum number of check boxes (5).
      If varCheck > 6 Then
         varCheck = 5
      End If
      ' Set text property to alphabet character.
      For intI = 1 To varCheck
         bal.Checkboxes(intI).Text = Chr(64 + intI)
      Next intI
   End If
```

```
If Not IsMissing(varLabel) Then
      ' If too large, set to maximum number of labels (5).
      If varLabel > 6 Then
         varLabel = 5
      End If
      For intI = 1 To varLabel
         ' Set text property to alphabet character.
         bal.Labels(intI).Text = Chr(64 + intI)
      Next intI
   End If
   ' Store return value.
   intReturn = bal.Show

   intI = 0
   ' Determine which check boxes were checked, if any.
   For Each bch In bal.Checkboxes
      If bch.Checked = True Then
         strCheck(intI) = bch.Text
         strList = strList & "'" & strCheck(intI) & "'" & Chr(32)
      End If
      intI = intI + 1
   Next
   If Len(strList) <> 0 Then
      MsgBox "You selected checkboxes " & strList & "."
   End If
   ' Determine which label was selected, if any.
   If intReturn > 0 Then
      MsgBox "You selected label " & bal.Labels(intReturn).Text & "."
   End If
End Function
```

You could call this function from the Debug window as follows:

```
? AssistantBalloon(4, 5)
```

LargeButtons Property

Applies To

CommandBars collection object.

Description

True if large toolbar buttons are displayed. Read/write **Boolean**.

Example

This example displays large toolbar buttons and ScreenTips on all command bars if the main menu bar that's active is named "Custom."

```
Set allBars = CommandBars
If allBars.ActiveMenuBar.Name = "Custom" Then
   allBars.LargeButtons = True
   allBars.ShowToolTips = True
End If
```

LastModified Property

Applies To

FileSearch object.

Description

Returns or sets a constant that represents the amount of time since the specified file was last modified and saved. Can be one of the following **MsoLastModified** constants: **msoLastModifiedAnyTime**, **msoLastModifiedLastMonth**, **msoLastModifiedLastWeek**, **msoLastModifiedThisMonth**, **msoLastModifiedThisWeek**, **msoLastModifiedToday**, or **msoLastModifiedYesterday**. The default value is **msoLastModifiedAnyTime**. Read/write **Variant**.

See Also

NewSearch method.

Example

This example sets options for a file search. The files that this search will return have been previously modified and are located in the C:\My Documents folder or in a subfolder of that folder.

```
Set fs = Application.FileSearch
With fs
    .LookIn = "C:\My Documents"
    .SearchSubFolders = True
    .LastModified = msoLastModifiedYesterday
End With
```

Left Property

Applies To

Assistant object, **CommandBar** object, **CommandBarButton** object, **CommandBarComboBox** object, **CommandBarControl** object, **CommandBarPopup** object.

Description

CommandBar or **CommandBarControl** object: Returns or sets the distance (in pixels) from the left edge of the specified command bar or command bar control to the left edge of the screen. Returns the distance from the left side of the docking area. Read/write **Long** for **CommandBar**, read-only **Long** for **CommandBarControl**.

Assistant object: Sets or returns the horizontal position of the Office Assistant window (in points), relative to the screen. Read/write **Long**.

See Also

Top property.

Example

This example adjusts the position of the custom command bar named "Custom" by moving it to the left 110 pixels more than the default. The example also makes this command bar the first one to be docked by changing the row index number to 1.

```
Set myBar = CommandBars("Custom")
With myBar
   .RowIndex = 1
   .Left = 140
End With
```

This example displays the Office Assistant and moves it to the specified position.

```
With Assistant
   .Visible = True
   .Left = 300
   .Top = 300
End With
```

LinkSource Property

Applies To

DocumentProperty object.

Description

Returns or sets the source of the specified linked custom document property. Read/write **String**.

Remarks

This property applies only to custom document properties; you cannot use it with built-in document properties.

The source of the specified link is defined by the container application.

Setting the **LinkSource** property sets the **LinkToContent** property to **True**.

See Also

LinkToContent property.

Example

This example displays the linked status of a custom document property. For the example to work, dp must be a valid **DocumentProperty** object.

```
Sub DisplayLinkStatus(dp As DocumentProperty)
   Dim stat As String, tf As String
   If dp.LinkToContent Then
      tf = ""
   Else
      tf = "not "
   End If
   stat = "This property is " & tf & "linked"
   If dp.LinkToContent Then
      stat = stat + Chr(13) & "The link source is " & dp.LinkSource
   End If
   MsgBox stat
End Sub
```

LinkToContent Property

Applies To

DocumentProperty object.

Description

True if the value of the specified custom document property is linked to the content of the container document. **False** if the value is static. Read/write **Boolean**.

Remarks

This property applies only to custom document properties. For built-in document properties, this property is always **False**.

Use the **LinkSource** property to set the source for the specified linked property. Setting the **LinkSource** property sets the **LinkToContent** property to **True**.

See Also

LinkSource property.

Example

This example displays the linked status of the custom document property. For the example to work, dp must be a valid **DocumentProperty** object.

```
Sub DisplayLinkStatus(dp As DocumentProperty)
   Dim stat As String, tf As String
   If dp.LinkToContent Then
      tf = ""
   Else
      tf = "not "
   End If
   stat = "This property is " & tf & "linked"
```

```
If dp.LinkToContent Then
        stat = stat + Chr(13) & "The link source is " & dp.LinkSource
    End If
    MsgBox stat
End Sub
```

List Property

Applies To

CommandBarComboBox object.

Description

Returns or sets the value of a list item in the command bar combo box control. Read/write **String**.

Note This property is read-only for built-in combo box controls.

Syntax

expression.**List(*Index*)**

expression Required. An expression that returns a **CommandBarComboBox** object.

Index Required **Long**. The list item to be set.

See Also

Execute method, **ListBy** property, **ListCount** property, **ListHeaderCount** property, **ListIndex** property.

Example

This example checks the value of the fourth list item in the combo box control named "Vegetables" on the command bar named "Custom." If the value is "Tomato," the code specified by the **OnAction** property of the command bar control is run.

```
Set myBar = CommandBars("Custom")
Set myControl = myBar.Controls("Vegetables")
If myControl.List(4) = "Tomatoes" Then myControl.Execute
```

ListBy Property

Applies To

FileFind object.

Description

Macintosh only. Returns or sets the way the found files are displayed in the results dialog box. Can be either of the following **MsoFileFindListBy** constants: **msoFileFindListByName** (which lists found files by their system file name) or **msoFileFindListByTitle** (which lists found files by their title property). Read/write.

See Also

Execute method, **List** property, **ListCount** property, **ListHeaderCount** property, **ListIndex** property.

ListCount Property

Applies To

CommandBarComboBox object.

Description

Returns the number of list items in the specified command bar combo box control. Read-only **Long**.

See Also

Execute method, **List** property, **ListBy** property, **ListHeaderCount** property, **ListIndex** property.

Example

This example checks the number of items in the combo box control on the command bar named "Custom." If there are more than three items in the list, the list is cleared and a new first item is added and displayed as the default for the combo box control.

```
Set myBar = CommandBars("Custom")
Set myControl = myBar.Controls(2)
With myControl
   If .ListCount > 3 Then
   .Clear
   .AddItem Text:="Floyd", Index:=1
   .ListIndex = 1
   End If
End With
```

ListHeaderCount Property

Applies To

CommandBarComboBox object.

Description

Returns or sets the number of list items in the command bar combo box control that appear above the separator line. Read/write **Long**.

Note This property is read-only for built-in combo box controls.

Remarks

A **ListHeaderCount** property value of –1 indicates that there's no separator line in the combo box control.

See Also

Execute method, **List** property, **ListBy** property, **ListCount** property, **ListIndex** property.

Example

The following example adds a combo box control to the command bar named "Custom," and then it adds two items to the combo box list. The example also sets the number of line items, the width of the combo box, and an empty default for the combo box.

```
Set myBar = CommandBars("Custom")
Set myControl = myBar.Controls.Add(Type:=msoControlComboBox)
With myControl
   .AddItem Text:="First Item", Index:=1
   .AddItem Text:="Second Item", Index:=2
   .DropDownLines = 3
   .DropDownWidth = 75
   .ListHeaderCount = 1
End With
```

ListIndex Property

Applies To

CommandBarComboBox object.

Description

Returns or sets the index number of the selected item in the list portion of the command bar combo box control. If nothing is selected in the list, this property returns zero. Read/write **Long**.

Note This property fails when applied to controls other than list controls.

Remarks

Setting the **ListIndex** property causes the specified control to select the given item and execute the appropriate action in the application.

See Also

Execute method, **List** property, **ListBy** property, **ListCount** property, **ListHeaderCount** property.

Example

This example runs an existing procedure, based on the selection in the combo box. The text in the combo box can be anything, because the example uses either the **ListIndex** property or the index number of the text entry to determine which procedure to run.

```
With myControl
   Select Case .ListIndex
      Case 1
         chartcourse
      Case 2
         displaygraph
      Case Else
         MsgBox "invalid choice"
   End Select
End With
```

Load Method

Applies To

FileFind object.

Description

Macintosh only. Loads the specified file search query into memory.

Syntax

expression.**Load**(*bstrQueryName*)

expression   Required. An expression that returns a **FileFind** object.

bstrQueryName   Required **String**. A string containing 31 characters or fewer that indicates the name of the saved search criteria to be loaded.

Remarks

Use the **Execute** method to run a loaded query.

LookIn Property

Applies To

FileSearch object.

Description

Returns or sets the folder to be searched during the specified file search. Read/write **String**.

Example

This example searches the My Documents folders for all files whose names begin with "Cmd" and displays the name and location of each file that's found.

```
Set fs = Application.FileSearch
With fs
   .LookIn = "C:\My Documents"
   .FileName = "cmd.*"
   If .Execute > 0 Then
      MsgBox "There were " & .FoundFiles.Count & _
            " file(s) found."
         For i = 1 To .FoundFiles.Count
            MsgBox .FoundFiles(i)
      Next i
   Else
         MsgBox "There were no files found."
   End If
End With
```

MatchAllWordForms Property

Applies To

FileSearch object.

Description

True if the specified file search will be expanded to include all forms of the specified word in the body of the file, or in the file's properties. Read/write **Boolean**.

Remarks

This property is available only if the file Mswds_en.lex has been installed and registered. Note that this file isn't installed as part of a Typical setup.

See Also

MatchCase property, **MatchTextExactly** property, **NewSearch** method.

Example

This example returns all files that contain the word "run," "running," "runs," or "ran" in the body of the file, or in the file properties. The **TextOrProperty** property sets the word to be matched, and limits the search to either the body of the file or the file properties.

```
With Application.FileSearch
   .NewSearch
   .LookIn = "C:\My Documents"
   .SearchSubFolders = True
   .TextOrProperty = "run"
   .MatchAllWordForms = True
   .FileType = msoFileTypeAllFiles
End With
```

MatchCase Property

Applies To

FileFind object.

Description

Macintosh only. **True** if the file search will be case sensitive. Read/write **Boolean**.

See Also

MatchAllWordForms property, **MatchTextExactly** property, **NewSearch** method.

MatchTextExactly Property

Applies To

FileSearch object.

Description

True if the specified file search will find only files whose body text or file properties contain the exact word or phrase that you've specified. Read/write **Boolean**.

See Also

MatchAllWordForms property, **MatchCase** property, **NewSearch** method.

Example

This example searches the C:\My Documents folder and returns all files that contain the word "Run" either in their body text or in their file properties.

```
With Application.FileSearch
    .NewSearch
    .LookIn = "C:\My Documents"
    .TextOrProperty = "Run"
    .MatchTextExactly = True
    .FileType = msoFileTypeAllFiles
End With
```

MenuAnimationStyle Property

Applies To

CommandBars collection object.

Description

Returns or sets the way the specified command bar is animated. Can be one of the following **MsoMenuAnimation** types: **msoMenuAnimationNone**, **msoMenuAnimationRandom**, **msoMenuAnimationUnfold**, or **msoMenuAnimationSlide**. Read/write.

Example

This example sets the options for all command bars in Microsoft Office.

```
With CommandBars
    .LargeButtons = True
    .DisplayTooltips = True
    .DisplayKeysInTooltips = True
    .MenuAnimationStyle = msoMenuAnimationUnfold
End With
```

Mode Property

Applies To

Balloon object.

Description

Returns or sets the type of balloon displayed. Can be one of the following **MsoModeType** constants: **msoModeAutoDown**, **msoModeModal**, or **msoModeModeless**. When you create a new balloon with the **NewBalloon** method, this property is initially set to **msoModeModal**. Read/write **Long**.

Remarks

If the **Mode** property for a balloon is set to **msoModeModeless**, the user can work in the application while the balloon is visible. If the property is set to **msoModeModal**, the user must dismiss the balloon before he or she can return to working in the application. If the property is set to **msoModeAutoDown**, the balloon is instantly dismissed when the user clicks anywhere on the screen.

If the **Mode** property for a balloon is set to **msoModeModeless**, a value for the **Callback** property is required. The **Close** method can only be used if the property is set to **msoModeModeless**.

See Also

Balloon object, **BalloonError** property.

Example

This example creates a balloon with an alert icon that instructs the user to select a printer. Because the balloon is modeless, the user has access to printer commands while the balloon is visible.

```
With Assistant.NewBalloon
    .Heading = "Select A Printer"
    .Text = "You must select a printer before printing."
    .Icon = msoIconAlert
    .CheckBoxes(1).Text = "Local printer"
    .CheckBoxes(2).Text = "Network printer"
    .Mode = msoModeModeless
    .Callback = "ProcessPrinter"
    .Show
End With
```

MouseTips Property

Applies To

Assistant object.

Description

True if the Office Assistant provides suggestions for using the mouse more effectively. Read/write. **Boolean**.

Remarks

The **MouseTips** property corresponds to the **Using the mouse more effectively** option under **Show tips about** on the **Options** tab in the **Office Assistant** dialog box.

Specifics (Microsoft Access)

This property isn't available in Microsoft Access.

Example

This example sets the Office Assistant to provide suggestions for using the mouse more effectively.

```
Assistant.MouseTips = True
```

Move Method

Applies To

Assistant object, **CommandBarButton** object, **CommandBarComboBox** object, **CommandBarControl** object, **CommandBarPopup** object.

Description

CommandBarControl object: Moves the specified command bar control to an existing command bar.

Assistant object: Moves the Office Assistant to the specified location.

Syntax 1

expression.**Move**(***Bar, Before***)

Syntax 2

expression.**Move**(***xLeft, yTop***)

expression Syntax 1: Required. An expression that returns a **CommandBarControl**, **CommandBarButton**, **CommandBarPopup**, or **CommandBarComboBox** object.

Syntax 2: Required. An expression that returns an **Assistant** object.

Bar Optional **Variant**. A **CommandBar** object that represents the destination command bar for the control. If this argument is omitted, the control is moved to the end of the same command bar (the command bar that the control currently resides on).

Before Optional **Variant**. A number that indicates the position for the control. The control is inserted before the control currently occupying this position. If this argument is omitted, the control is inserted on the same command bar.

xLeft Required **Integer**. The left position of the Office Assistant window, in points.

yTop Required **Integer**. The top position of the Office Assistant window, in points.

Example

This example moves the first combo box control from the custom command bar named "Custom" to the position before the seventh control on that command bar. The example sets the tag to "Selection box" and assigns the control a low priority so that it will likely be dropped from the command bar if all the controls don't fit in one row.

```
Set allcontrols = CommandBars("Custom").Controls
For Each ctrl In allControls
   If ctrl.Type = msoControlComboBox Then
      With ctrl
         .Move Before:=7
         .Tag = "Selection box"
      .Priority = 5
      End With
      Exit For
   End If
Next
```

This example displays the Office Assistant in the specified location and sets several options before making it visible.

```
With Assistant
   .Reduced = True
   .Move xLeft:= 400, yTop:= 300
   .MoveWhenInTheWay = True
   .TipOfDay = True
   .Visible = True
   .Animation = msoAnimationGreeting
End With
```

MoveWhenInTheWay Property

Applies To

Assistant object.

Description

True if the Office Assistant window automatically moves when it's in the way of the user's work area. For example, the Assistant will move if it's in the way of dragging or dropping or in the way of keystroke entries. Read/write **Boolean**.

Remarks

The **MoveWhenInTheWay** property corresponds to the **Move when in the way** option under **Assistant capabilities** on the **Options** tab in the **Office Assistant** dialog box.

Example

This example displays the Office Assistant in a specific location, and it sets several options before making the Assistant visible.

```
With Assistant
    .Reduced = True
    .Left = 400
    .MoveWhenInTheWay = True
    .TipOfDay = True
    .Visible = True
    .Animation = msoAnimGreeting
End With
```

Name Property

Applies To

Assistant object, **Balloon** object, **BalloonCheckbox** object, **BalloonCheckboxes** collection object, **BalloonLabel** object, **BalloonLabels** collection object, **CommandBar** object, **DocumentProperty** object, **FileFind** object, **PropertyTest** object.

Description

Returns or sets the name of the specified object. Read/write **String** for the **CommandBar** object, read-only **String** for all other objects.

Remarks

The local name of a built-in command bar is displayed in the title bar (when the command bar isn't docked) and in the list of available command bars—wherever that list is displayed in the container application.

For a built-in command bar, the **Name** property returns the command bar's U.S. English name. Use the **NameLocal** property to return the localized name.

If you change the value of the **LocalName** property for a custom command bar, the value of **Name** changes as well, and vice versa.

See Also

NameLocal property.

Specifics (Microsoft Access)

In Microsoft Access 97, you can use the **Toolbar Properties** dialog box to change the name of a custom menu bar, toolbar, or shortcut menu. Point to **Toolbars** on the **View** menu and click **Customize**, then click the **Properties** button in the **Customize** dialog box. Select the custom menu bar, toolbar, or shortcut menu you want in the **Selected Toolbar** box, and then enter the new name in the **Toolbar Name** box. You can't change the name of a built-in menu bar, toolbar, or shortcut menu.

Example

This example searches the collection of command bars for the command bar named "Custom." If this command bar is found, the example makes it visible.

```
foundFlag = False
For Each bar In CommandBars
   If bar.Name = "Custom" Then
      foundFlag = True
      bar.Visible = True
   End If
Next
If Not foundFlag Then
   MsgBox "'Custom' bar isn't in collection."
Else
   MsgBox "'Custom' bar is now visible."
End If
```

This example displays the name, type, and value of a document property. You must pass a valid **DocumentProperty** object to the procedure.

```
Sub DisplayPropertyInfo(dp As DocumentProperty)
   MsgBox "value = " & dp.Value & Chr(13) & _
      "type = " & dp.Type & Chr(13) & "name = " & dp.Name
End Sub
```

NameLocal Property

Applies To

CommandBar object.

Description

Returns the name of a built-in command bar as it's displayed in the language version of the container application, or returns or sets the name of a custom command bar. Read/write **String**.

Note If you attempt to set this property for a built-in command bar, an error occurs.

Remarks

The local name of a built-in command bar is displayed in the title bar (when the command bar isn't docked) and in the list of available command bars, wherever that list is displayed in the container application.

If you change the value of the **LocalName** property for a custom command bar, the value of **Name** changes as well, and vice versa.

See Also

Name property.

Example

This example displays the name and localized name of the first command bar in the container application.

```
With CommandBars(1)
   MsgBox "The name of the command bar is " & .Name
   MsgBox "The localized name of the command bar is " & .NameLocal
End With
```

NewBalloon Property

Applies To

Assistant object.

Description

Creates a new Office Assistant balloon. Returns a **Balloon** object.

See Also

Assistant object, **Balloon** object, **BalloonError** property, **Show** method.

Example

This example creates a balloon with a heading, text, and three region choices, and then displays it.

```
With Assistant.NewBalloon
    .Button = msoButtonSetOK
    .Heading = "Regional Sales Data"
    .Text = "Select a region"
    For i = 1 To 3
        .CheckBoxes(i).Text = "Region " & i
    Next
    .Show
End With
```

Example (Microsoft Access)

The following function creates a custom balloon for the Office Assistant and determines how the user responded to the balloon:

```
Function AssistantBalloon(Optional varCheck As Variant, Optional _
   rLabel As Variant)
   Dim bch As BalloonCheckbox
   Dim intI As Integer
   Dim intReturn As Integer
   Dim strCheck(5) As String
   Dim strList As String

   ' Create new balloon.
   Set bal = Assistant.NewBalloon
   ' Specify balloon type.
   bal.BalloonType = msoBalloonTypeButtons
   ' Specify that balloon is modal.
   bal.Mode = msoModeModal

   ' Make Assistant visible.
   If Assistant.Visible = False Then Assistant.Visible = True
   ' Check if first argument has been passed.
   If Not IsMissing(varCheck) Then
      ' If too large, set to maximum number of check boxes (5).
      If varCheck > 6 Then
         varCheck = 5
      End If
      ' Set text property to alphabet character.
      For intI = 1 To varCheck
         bal.Checkboxes(intI).Text = Chr(64 + intI)
      Next intI
   End If

   If Not IsMissing(varLabel) Then
      ' If too large, set to maximum number of labels (5).
      If varLabel > 6 Then
         varLabel = 5
      End If
      For intI = 1 To varLabel
         ' Set text property to alphabet character.
         bal.Labels(intI).Text = Chr(64 + intI)
      Next intI
   End If
   ' Store return value.
   intReturn = bal.Show

   intI = 0
   ' Determine which check boxes were checked, if any.
```

```
For Each bch In bal.Checkboxes
      If bch.Checked = True Then
         strCheck(intI) = bch.Text
         strList = strList & "'" & strCheck(intI) & "'" & Chr(32)
      End If
      intI = intI + 1
   Next
   If Len(strList) <> 0 Then
      MsgBox "You selected checkboxes " & strList & "."
   End If
   ' Determine which label was selected, if any.
   If intReturn > 0 Then
      MsgBox "You selected label " & bal.Labels(intReturn).Text & "."
   End If
End Function
```

You could call this function from the Debug window as follows:

```
? AssistantBalloon(4, 5)
```

NewSearch Method

Applies To

FileSearch object.

Description

Resets all the search criteria settings to their default settings.

Syntax

expression.**NewSearch**

expression   Required. An expression that returns a **FileSearch** object.

Remarks

Search criteria settings are retained throughout an application session. Use this method every time you change search criteria. This method will not reset the value of the **LookIn** property.

See Also

FileSearch object.

Example

This example uses the **NewSearch** method to reset the default search criteria before beginning a new search.

```
With Application.FileSearch
   .NewSearch
   .LookIn = "C:\My Documents"
   .SearchSubFolders = True
   .FileName = "run"
   .MatchAllWordForms = True
   .FileType = msoFileTypeAllFiles
```

```
    If .Execute() > 0 Then
        MsgBox "There were " & .FoundFiles.Count & " file(s) found."
        For i = 1 To .FoundFiles.Count
            MsgBox .FoundFiles(i)
        Next i
    Else
        MsgBox "There were no files found."
    End If
End With
```

OLEMenuGroup Property

Applies To

CommandBarPopup object.

Description

Returns or sets the menu group that the specified command bar pop-up control belongs to when the menu groups of the OLE server are merged with the menu groups of an OLE client (that is, when an object of the container application type is embedded in another application). Can be one of the following **MsoOLEMenuGroup** constants: **msoOleMenuGroupNone**, **msoOleMenuGroupFile**, **msoOleMenuGroupEdit**, **msoOleMenuGroupContainer**, **msoOleMenuGroupObject**, **msoOleMenuGroupWindow**, or **msoOleMenuGroupHelp**. Read/write **Long**.

Note This property is read-only for built-in controls.

Remarks

This property is intended to allow add-in applications to specify how their command bar controls will be represented in the Office application. If either the container or the server does not implement command bars, normal OLE menu merging will occur: the menu bar will be merged, as well as all the toolbars from the server, and none of the toolbars from the container. This property is relevant only for pop-up controls on the menu bar because menus are merged on the basis of their menu group category.

If both of the merging applications implement command bars, command bar controls are merged according to the **OLEUsage** property.

Example

This example checks the **OLEMenuGroup** property of a new custom popup control on the active menu bar, and sets it to **msoOLEMenuGroupNone**.

```
Set myControl = ActiveMenuBar.Controls _
    .Add(Type:=msoControlPopup,Temporary:=False)
myControl.OLEMenuGroup = msoOLEMenuGroupNone
```

OLEUsage Property

Applies To

CommandBarButton object, **CommandBarComboBox** object, **CommandBarControl** object, **CommandBarPopup** object.

Description

Returns or sets the OLE client and OLE server roles in which a command bar control will be used when two Microsoft Office applications are merged. Can be one of the following **MsoControlOLEUsage** constants: **msoControlOLEUsageNeither**, **msoControlOLEUsageServer**, **msoControlOLEUsageClient**, or **msoControlOLEUsageBoth**. Read/write **Long**.

Remarks

This property is intended to allow you to specify how individual add-in applications' command bar controls will be represented in one Office application when it is merged with another Office application. If both the client and server implement command bars, the command bar controls are embedded in the client control by control. Custom controls marked as client-only (or neither client nor server) are dropped from the server, and controls marked as server-only (or neither server nor client) are dropped from the client. The remaining controls are merged.

If one of the merging applications isn't an Office application, normal OLE menu merging is used, which is controlled by the **OLEMenuGroup** property.

Example

This example adds a new button to the command bar named `Tools`, and sets its **OLEUsage** property.

```
Set myControl = CommandBars("Tools").Controls _
    .Add(Type:=msoControlButton,Temporary:=True)
myControl.OLEUsage = msoControlOLEUsageNeither
```

OnAction Property

Applies To

CommandBarButton object, **CommandBarComboBox** object, **CommandBarControl** object, **CommandBarPopup** object.

Description

Returns or sets the name of the Visual Basic macro that will be run when the user clicks or changes the value of a command bar control. Read/write **String**.

Note The container application determines whether the value is a valid macro name.

Specifics (Microsoft Access)

In Microsoft Access 97, you can use the *Toolbar* **Control Properties** dialog box for command bar controls to set the **OnAction** property for a control on a command bar. Display the **Customize** dialog box by pointing to **Toolbars** on the **View** menu and clicking **Customize**. For menu bar and toolbar controls, display the menu bar or toolbar, and then right-click the control whose **OnAction** property you want to set. For shortcut menu controls, select the **Shortcut Menus** check box on the **Toolbars** tab of the **Customize** dialog box, then find the shortcut menu control you want on the menu bar that's displayed and right-click the control. Click the **Properties** command. Enter the macro or function you want to run in the **On Action** box.

You can use the **OnAction** property only to run a macro or a function. To run a macro, select it from the drop-down list in the **On Action** box, or enter its name in the box. To run a function, enter its name in the form *=functionname*( ) in the box.

You can also set the **OnAction** property to an expression. The expression can contain a built-in or user-defined function or combination of functions. When Microsoft Access evaluates an expression, it performs all of the operations in the expression. For example, the following is an expression that runs the user-defined function "CustomControlFunction":

```
=CustomControlFunction()
```

In Visual Basic, the **OnAction** property takes a string, so to set it to an expression, you must pass it a string that contains the expression. In passing the string, be careful to enclose strings within the string in quotation marks ("). (Note that in the **On Action** box in the *Toolbar* **Control Properties** dialog box, an enclosed string in the expression should only have one set of quotation marks around it.) Also, make sure you include the equal sign (=) to specify that the string contains an expression. If your function takes no arguments, remember to include parentheses [( )] within the string. You can set the **OnAction** property to the previous expression with the following string:

```
"=CustomControlFunction()"
```

Note that you must set the **OnAction** property to the name of a **Function** procedure; you can't set it to the name of a **Sub** procedure.

For custom command bar controls, you must set this property in order for the control to perform any action. If you set this property for a built-in control, the **OnAction** property setting overrides the normal actions that the control performs; that is, you can force a built-in control to perform different actions from its default actions. The control becomes in effect a custom control.

Example

This example adds a command bar control to the command bar named "Custom" and sets the macro named "MySub" to run whenever the button is clicked.

```
Set myBar = .CommandBars("Custom")
Set myControl = myBar.Controls.Add(Type:=msocontrolButton)
With myControl
    .FaceId = 2
    .OnAction = "MySub"
End With
myBar.Visible = True
```

Options Property

Applies To

FileFind object.

Description

Macintosh only. Returns or sets the way the most recent group of found files are displayed in relation to the list of previous results. Can be one of the following **MsoFileFindOptions** constants: **msoFileFindOptionsNew**, **msoFileFindOptionsAdd**, or **msoFileFindOptionsWithin**. Read/write **Variant**.

Parameter Property

Applies To

CommandBarButton object, **CommandBarComboBox** object, **CommandBarControl** object, **CommandBarPopup** object.

Description

Returns or sets a string that an application can use to execute a command associated with a command bar control. Read/write **String**.

Remarks

If the specified parameter is set for a built-in control, the application can modify its default behavior if it's able to parse and use the new value. If the parameter is set for custom controls, it can be used to send information to Visual Basic procedures, or it can be used to hold information about the control (similar to a second **Tag** property value).

Specifics (Microsoft Access)

In Microsoft Access 97, you can use the *Toolbar* **Control Properties** sheet for command bar controls to set the **Parameter** property for a control on a command bar. Display the **Customize** dialog box by pointing to **Toolbars** on the **View** menu and clicking **Customize**. For menu bar and toolbar controls, display the menu bar or toolbar, and then right-click the control whose **Parameter** property you want to set. For shortcut menu controls, select the **Shortcut Menus** check box on the **Toolbars** tab of the **Customize** dialog box, then find the shortcut menu control you want on the menu bar that's displayed and right-click the control. Click the **Properties** command. Enter the parameter information you want in the **Parameter** box.

Example

This example copies the fourth control from the custom command bar named "Custom" and pastes it onto the same command bar as the new first control. The example assigns a new parameter and sets the focus to the new button.

```
Set myControl = CommandBars("Custom").Controls(4)
With myControl
    .Copy , 1
    .Parameter = "2"
    .SetFocus
End With
```

Parent Property

Applies To

Assistant object, **Balloon** object, **BalloonCheckbox** object, **BalloonCheckboxes** collection object, **BalloonLabel** object, **BalloonLabels** collection object, **CommandBar** object, **CommandBarButton** object, **CommandBarComboBox** object, **CommandBarControl** object, **CommandBarControls** collection object, **CommandBarPopup** object, **CommandBars** collection object, **DocumentProperties** collection object, **DocumentProperty** object.

Description

Returns the parent object for the specified object. Read-only.

Example

This example displays the name of the parent object for a document property. You must pass a valid **DocumentProperty** object to the procedure.

```
Sub DisplayParent(dp as DocumentProperty)
    MsgBox dp.Parent.Name
End Sub
```

PasteFace Method

Applies To

CommandBarButton object.

Description

Pastes the contents of the Clipboard onto the specified command bar button control.

Syntax

expression.**PasteFace**

expression Required. An expression that returns a **CommandBarButton** object.

See Also

BuiltInFace property, **CopyFace** method, **FaceId** property, **Id** property.

Example

This example finds the built-in **FileOpen** button and pastes a custom face onto it from the Clipboard, where the user had previously altered it. This example will fail if a custom face doesn't already exist in the Clipboard; use the **CopyFace** method to copy a specified button face to the Clipboard.

```
Set myControl = CommandBars.FindControl(Type:=msoControlButton, Id:=23)
myControl.PasteFace
```

PatternMatch Property

Applies To

FileFind object.

Description

True if the search for files that match the **Text** property string is expanded to include the wildcard characters * (asterisk) and ? (question mark). Macintosh only. Read/write **Boolean**.

Remarks

Use the question mark wildcard character to match any single character. For example, type **gr?y** to return all files that contain at least one instance of either "gray" or "grey."

Use the asterisk wildcard character to match any number of characters. For example, type **San*** to return all files that contain at least one word that begins with "San."

Position Property

Applies To

CommandBar object.

Description

Returns or sets the position of the specified command bar. Can be one of the following **MsoBarPosition** constants: **msoBarLeft**, **msoBarTop**, **msoBarRight**, **msoBarBottom**, **msoBarFloating**, **msoBarPopup**, or **msoBarMenu**. Read/write **Long**.

Specifics (Microsoft Access)

You can't set the **Position** property to the intrinsic constant **msoBarPopup**. To create a shortcut menu, use the ***Position*** argument of the **Add** method of the **CommandBars** collection.

The **msoBarMenuBar** constant is used only with the Macintosh.

Example

This example steps through the collection of command bars, docking the custom command bars at the bottom of the application window and docking the built-in command bars at the top of the window.

```
For Each bar In CommandBars
   If bar.Visible = True Then
      If bar.BuiltIn Then
         bar.Position = msoBarTop
      Else
         bar.Position = msoBarBottom
      End If
   End If
Next
```

Priority Property

Applies To

CommandBarButton object, **CommandBarComboBox** object, **CommandBarControl** object, **CommandBarPopup** object.

Description

Returns or sets the priority of the specified command bar control. A control's priority determines whether it can be dropped from a docked command bar if the command bar controls don't fit in a single row. Read/write **Long**.

Remarks

A priority of 1 means the control cannot be dropped. Controls with the highest priority numbers are dropped first.

A priority of 0 indicates an "automatic" value, which will choose an effective priority based on the control type. A priority of 1 means that the control will never be dropped. The other valid priorities are from 2 through 7, and these controls will be dropped in order of their values (starting with the highest values).

Example

This example moves the first combo box control from the custom command bar named "Custom" to the position before the seventh control on the command bar, sets the tag to "selection box," and then assigns the control a high priority so that it will likely be dropped from the command bar if the controls don't all fit in one row.

```
Set allcontrols = CommandBars("Custom").Controls
For Each ctrl In allControls
   If ctrl.Type = msoControlComboBox Then
      With ctrl
         .Move Before:=7
         .Tag = "Selection box"
         .Priority = 5
      End With
   Exit For
End If
Next
```

Private Property

Applies To

Balloon object.

Description

Returns or sets an integer that uniquely identifies the Office Assistant balloon that initiates the callback procedure. Read/write **Long**.

Remarks

It may be helpful to use this property if you use the same callback procedure for a variety of circumstances.

Example

This example identifies the Office Assistant balloon by setting the **Private** property to 129. The callback procedure, `myCallback`, is used in a variety of circumstances, and the integer 129 will be used to identify this circumstance.

```
With myBalloon
   .Heading = "Select a region"
   .Private = 129
   .Callback = "myCallback"
   .Show
End With
```

PropertyTest Object

Description

Represents a single file search criterion. Search criteria are listed in the **Advanced Find** dialog box (**File** menu, **Open** command, **Advanced Find** button). The **PropertyTest** object is a member of the **PropertyTests** collection.

Using the PropertyTest Object

Use **PropertyTests**(*index*), where *index* is the index number, to return a single **PropertyTest** object. The following example displays all the search criteria for the first property test in the **PropertyTests** collection.

```
With Application.FileSearch.PropertyTests(1)
myString = "This is the search criteria: " _
   & " The name is: " & .Name & ". The condition is: " _
   & .Condition
If .Value <> "" Then
   myString = myString & ". The value is: " & .Value
   If .SecondValue <> "" Then
      myString = myString & ". The second value is: " _
         & .SecondValue & ", and the connector is " _
         & .Connector
   End If
End If
MsgBox myString
End With
```

Properties

Application property, **Condition** property, **Connector** property, **Creator** property, **Name** property, **SecondValue** property, **Value** property.

PropertyTests Collection Object

Description

A collection of **PropertyTest** objects that represent all the search criteria of a file search. Search criteria are listed in the **Advanced Find** dialog box (**File** menu, **Open** command, **Advanced Find** button).

Using the PropertyTests Collection

Use the **PropertyTests** property to return the **PropertyTests** collection. The following example displays the number of advanced-find search criteria that will be used for one file search.

```
FileSearch.PropertyTests.Count
```

Use the **Add** method to add a new **PropertyTest** object to the **PropertyTests** collection. The following example adds two property tests to the search criteria. The first criterion specifies that the found files must be Word documents, and the second one specifies that the found files must have been modified between January 1, 1996 and June 30, 1996.

```
Set fs = Application.FileSearch
fs.NewSearch
With fs.PropertyTests
   .Add Name:="Files of Type", _
      Condition:=msoConditionFileTypeWordDocuments, _
      Connector:=msoConnectorOr
   .Add Name:="Last Modified", _
      Condition:=msoConditionAnytimeBetween, _
      Value:="1/1/96", SecondValue:="6/30/96", _
      Connector:=msoConnectorAnd
End With
```

Use **PropertyTests**(*index*), where *index* is the index number, to return a single **PropertyTest** object. The following example displays all the search criteria for the first property test in the **PropertyTests** collection.

```
With Application.FileSearch.PropertyTests(1)
myString = "This is the search criteria: " _
   & " The name is: " & .Name & ". The condition is: " _
   & .Condition
If .Value <> "" Then
   myString = myString & ". The value is: " & .Value
   If .SecondValue <> "" Then
      myString = myString _
         & ". The second value is: " _
         & .SecondValue & ", and the connector is" _
         & .Connector
   End If
End If
MsgBox myString
End With
```

Methods

Add method (**PropertyTests** collection), **Remove** method.

PropertyTests Property

Applies To

FileSearch object.

Description

Returns a **PropertyTests** collection that represents all the search criteria for a file search. Read-only.

See Also

NewSearch method.

Example

This example displays all the search criteria for the first property test in the collection.

```
With Application.FileSearch.PropertyTests(1)
myString = "This is the search criteria: " _
   & " The name is: " & .Name & ". The condition is: " _
   & .Condition
If .Value <> "" Then
   myString = myString & ". The value is: " & .Value
   If .SecondValue <> "" Then
      myString = myString _
         & ". The second value is: " _
         & .SecondValue & ", and the connector is" _
         & .Connector
   End If
End If
MsgBox myString
End With
```

Protection Property

Applies To

CommandBar object.

Description

Returns or sets the way the specified command bar is protected from user customization. Can be one of or a sum of the following **MsoBarProtection** constants: **msoBarNoProtection**, **msoBarNoCustomize**, **msoBarNoResize**, **msoBarNoMove**, **msoBarNoChangeVisible**, **msoBarNoChangeDock**, **msoBarNoVerticalDock**, or **msoBarNoHorizontalDock**. Read/write **Long**.

Specifics (Microsoft Access)

In Microsoft Access 97, you can use the **Toolbar Properties** sheet to set the various options of the **Protection** property that prevent or allow user customization of a menu bar, toolbar, or custom shortcut menu. Point to **Toolbars** on the **View** menu and click **Customize**, then click the **Properties** button in the **Customize** dialog box. Select the menu bar, toolbar, or custom shortcut menu you want in the **Selected Toolbar** box, and then use the **Docking** combo box and the **Allow Customizing**, **Allow Resizing**, **Allow Moving**, and **Allow Showing/Hiding** check boxes to set the protection you want. For custom shortcut menus, the only option that's available is **Allow Customizing**.

Example

This example steps through the collection of command bars to find the command bar named "Forms." If this command bar is found, the example makes it visible and protects its docking state.

```
foundFlag = False
For i = 1 To .CommandBars.Count
   If .CommandBars(i).Name = "Forms" Then
      .CommandBars(i).Protection = msoBarNoChangeDock
      .CommandBars(i).Visible = True
      foundFlag = True
   End If
Next
If Not foundFlag Then
   MsgBox "'Forms' command bar is not in the collection."
End If
```

Reduced Property

Applies To

Assistant object.

Description

True if the Office Assistant window appears in its smaller size. Read/write **Boolean**.

Example

This example displays the Office Assistant in a specific location, and it sets several options before making the Assistant visible.

```
With Assistant
   .Reduced = True
   .Left = 400
   .MoveWhenInTheWay = True
   .TipOfDay = True
   .Visible = True
   .Animation = msoAnimationGreeting
End With
```

ReleaseFocus Method

Applies To

CommandBars collection object.

Description

Releases the user interface focus from all command bars.

Syntax

expression.**ReleaseFocus**

expression Required. An expression that returns a **CommandBars** object.

See Also

SetFocus method.

Example

This example releases the user interface focus from all command bars.

```
CommandBars.ReleaseFocus
```

Remove Method

Applies To

PropertyTests collection object.

Description

Removes a **PropertyTest** object from the **PropertyTests** collection.

Syntax

expression.**Remove(*Index*)**

expression Required. An expression that returns a **PropertyTests** object.

Index Required **Long**. The index number of the property test to remove.

Example

This example removes the first search criterion from the collection.

```
Application.FileSearch.PropertyTests.Remove(1)
```

RemoveItem Method

Applies To

CommandBarComboBox object.

Description

Removes a list item from the specified command bar combo box control.

Note The property fails when applied to controls other than list controls.

Syntax

expression.**RemoveItem(*Index*)**

expression Required. An expression that returns a **CommandBarComboBox** object.

Index Required **Long**. The item to be removed from the list.

Example

The following example determines whether there are more than three items in the combo box control named "Combo1" on the custom command bar named "Custom." If there are more than three items, the example removes the second item, alters the style to not show the combo box label, and sets a new value. It also sets the **Tag** property of the parent object (the **CommandBarControl** object) to show that the list has changed.

```
Set myBar = CommandBars("Custom")
Set myControl = myBar.Controls("Combo1")
With myControl
   If .ListCount > 3 Then
      .RemoveItem 2
      .Style = msoComboNormal
      .Text = "New Default"
      Set ctrl = .Parent
      ctrl.Tag = "Contents Changed"
   End If
End With
```

Reset Method

Applies To

CommandBar object, **CommandBarButton** object, **CommandBarComboBox** object, **CommandBarControl** object, **CommandBarPopup** object.

Description

Resets the specified built-in command bar to its default configuration of controls, or resets the specified built-in command bar control to its default function and face.

Syntax

expression.**Reset**

expression Required. An expression that returns a **CommandBar**, **CommandBarControl**, **CommandBarButton**, **CommandBarPopup**, or **CommandBarComboBox** object.

Remarks

Resetting a built-in control restores the actions originally intended for the control and resets each of the control's properties back to its original state. Resetting a built-in command bar removes custom controls and restores built-in controls.

See Also

ResetTips method.

Specifics (Microsoft Access)

In Microsoft Access 97, you can use the **Toolbar Properties** sheet to reset a built-in menu bar or toolbar. Point to **Toolbars** on the **View** menu and click **Customize**, then click the **Properties** button in the **Customize** dialog box. Select the built-in menu bar or toolbar you want in the **Selected Toolbar** box, and then click the **Restore Defaults** button. You can't reset a custom menu bar or toolbar, or a specific shortcut menu.

The **Reset** button in the **Customize** dialog box resets the selected built-in menu bar or toolbar, or all built-in shortcut menus if you select **Shortcut Menus** in the **Customize** dialog box. The **Reset** command on the shortcut menu that's displayed when you right-click a particular built-in control on a menu bar or toolbar while the **Customize** dialog box is open resets that control to its original state. The **Reset** button and **Reset** command are equivalent to the **Reset** method.

The **Restore Defaults** button not only resets the menu bar or toolbar controls' image, text, and the commands they run, but also restores all of the original settings for the menu bar or toolbar, including its original position and visibility.

Example

This example uses the value of `user` to adjust the command bars according to the user level. If `user` is "Level 1," the command bar named "Custom" is displayed. If `user` is any other value, the built-in Visual Basic command bar is reset to its default state and the command bar named "Custom" is disabled.

```
Set myBar = CommandBars("Custom")
If user = "Level 1" Then
   myBar.Visible = True
Else
   .CommandBars("Visual Basic").Reset
   myBar.Enabled = False
End If
```

ResetTips Method

Applies To

Assistant object.

Description

Resets the application tips that will appear in the Office Assistant balloon.

Syntax

expression.**ResetTips**

expression   Required. An expression that returns an **Assistant** object.

Remarks

The **ResetTips** method corresponds to the **Reset my tips** button on the **Options** tab in the **Office Assistant** dialog box.

See Also

Reset method.

Example

This example resets the application tips before making the Office Assistant visible. A confirmation balloon will appear, telling the user that his or her application tips have been reset.

```
With Application.Assistant
    .Visible = True
    .Animation = msoAnimationGreeting
    .ResetTips
End With
```

Results Property

Applies To

FileFind object.

Description

Macintosh only. Returns the **FileFindResults** object. Read-only.

RowIndex Property

Applies To

CommandBar object.

Description

Returns or sets the docking order of the specified command bar in relation to other command bars in the same docking area. Can be an integer greater than zero, or either of the following **MsoBarRow** constants: **msoBarRowFirst** or **msoBarRowLast**. Read/write **Long**.

Remarks

Command bars with lower numbers are docked first. Several command bars can share the same row index. If two or more command bars share the same row index, the command bar most recently assigned will be displayed first in its group.

Example

This example adjusts the position of the command bar named "Custom" by moving it to the left 110 pixels more than the default, and it makes this command bar the first to be docked by changing its row index to 1.

```
Set myBar = CommandBars("Custom")
With myBar
    .RowIndex = 1
    .Left = 140
End With
```

Save Method

Applies To

FileFind object.

Description

Macintosh only. Saves the specified file search criteria.

Syntax

expression.**Save(*bstrQueryName*)**

expression Required. An expression that returns a **FileFind** object.

bstrQueryName Required **String**. A string (up to 31 characters long) that indicates the name of the search criteria to be saved.

SavedBy Property

Applies To

FileFind object.

Description

Macintosh only. Returns or sets a string (up to 80 characters long) that represents the name of the user who last saved the file to be searched for. Read/write **String**.

SearchPath Property

Applies To

FileFind object.

Description

Macintosh only. Returns or sets the folder to be searched during the specified file search. Read/write **String**.

Remarks

The search path can be up to 255 characters long.

SearchSubFolders Property

Applies To

FileSearch object.

Description

True if the specified search includes all the subfolders in the folder specified by the **LookIn** property. Read/write **Boolean**.

Example

This example searches the My Documents folder and all of its subfolders for all files whose names begin with "Cmd." The example also displays the name and location of each file that's found.

```
Set fs = Application.FileSearch
With fs
    .LookIn = "C:\My Documents"
    .SearchSubFolders = True
    .FileName = "cmd*"
    If .Execute() > 0 Then
        MsgBox "There were " & .FoundFiles.Count & " file(s) found."
        For i = 1 To .FoundFiles.Count
            MsgBox .FoundFiles(i)
        Next i
    Else
        MsgBox "There were no files found."
    End If
End With
```

SearchWhenProgramming Property

Applies To

Assistant object.

Description

True if the Office Assistant displays application help as well as programming help while the user is working in Visual Basic. Read/write **Boolean**.

Remarks

The **SearchWhenProgramming** property corresponds to the **Search for both product and programming help when programming** option under **Assistant capabilities** on the **Options** tab in the **Office Assistant** dialog box.

Example

This example enables you to search both application and programming help while you're working in Visual Basic.

```
Assistant.SearchWhenProgramming = True
```

SecondValue Property

Applies To

PropertyTest object.

Description

Returns an optional second value property test (as in a range) for the specified file search. Read-only **Variant**.

Remarks

This property is intended to be used to specify a range, and it can only be used with the **MsoCondition** constants **msoConditionAnyTimeBetween** or **msoConditionAnyNumberBetween**.

See Also

Value property.

Example

This example displays the second value of the search criteria (if it exists) in a dialog box. If the second value doesn't exist, the example displays another message.

```
With Application.FileSearch.PropertyTests(1)
If .SecondValue = "" Then
   MsgBox "You haven't specified a second value."
Else
   MsgBox "The second value you've set is: " & .SecondValue
End If
End With
```

SelectedFile Property

Applies To

FileFind object.

Description

Macintosh only. Returns or sets a number that represents the file highlighted in the **Find File** dialog box. Read/write **Integer**.

Remarks

Use the **Show** method to display the **Find File** dialog box.

SetAvoidRectangle Method

Applies To

Balloon object.

Description

Prevents the Office Assistant balloon from being displayed in a specified area of the screen.

Syntax

expression.**SetAvoidRectangle(*Left, Top, Right, Bottom*)**

expression Required. An expression that returns an **Assistant** object.

Left*, *Top*, *Right*, *Bottom Required **Long**. The coordinates (in points and relative to the screen) of the area of the screen that the Office Assistant balloon will be excluded from when it's displayed.

Remarks

This property is intended to prevent the Office Assistant balloon from overlapping with custom dialog boxes and wizards.

See Also

ActivateWizard method, **EndWizard** method, **StartWizard** method.

Example

This example prevents the Office Assistant balloon represented by the variable `myBalloon` from being displayed in the region of the screen denoted by the specified coordinates (measured in pixels).

```
With myBalloon
    .SetAvoidRectangle 300, 250, 700, 500
    .Show
End With
```

SetFocus Method

Applies To

CommandBarButton object, **CommandBarComboBox** object, **CommandBarControl** object, **CommandBarPopup** object.

Description

Moves the keyboard focus to the specified command bar control so that it can receive keyboard input. The kind of keyboard input you can direct to the control depends on what type of control it is.

Note If the control is disabled or isn't visible from the current state, this method will fail.

Syntax

expression.**SetFocus**

expression Required. An expression that returns a **CommandBarControl**, **CommandBarButton**, **CommandBarPopup**, or **CommandBarComboBox** object.

Example

This example copies the fourth control from the My Custom Bar custom command bar and pastes it onto the same command bar as the first control. The example also assigns a new parameter to the control and sets the focus to the new button.

```
Set mycontrol = CommandBars("My Custom Bar").Controls(4)
With mycontrol
    .Copy Before:=1
    .Parameter = "2"
    .SetFocus
End With
```

ShortcutText Property

Applies To

CommandBarButton object.

Description

Returns or sets the shortcut key text displayed next to the specified button control when that button appears on a menu, submenu, or shortcut menu. Read/write **String**.

Remarks

You can set this property only for command bar buttons that have an attached **OnAction** macro.

Specifics (Microsoft Access)

In Microsoft Access 97, you can use the *Toolbar* **Control Properties** dialog box for command bar controls to set the shortcut text that's displayed to the right of a built-in button control on a menu, submenu, or shortcut menu. Display the **Customize** dialog box by pointing to **Toolbars** on the **View** menu and clicking **Customize**. For menu bar and toolbar controls, display the menu bar or toolbar, and then right-click the button control whose **ShortcutText** property you want to set. For shortcut menu controls, select the **Shortcut Menus** check box on the **Toolbars** tab of the **Customize** dialog box, then find the shortcut menu control you want on the menu bar that's displayed and right-click the control. Click the **Properties** command. Enter the shortcut text you want in the **Shortcut Text** box. You can set this property for any built-in button control in Microsoft Access, but not for custom button controls.

Setting this property in Microsoft Access just causes the shortcut text to be displayed next to the control. If you change or add shortcut text for a built-in control, typing this shortcut key or key combination doesn't run the command associated with this control. To run this command, you must assign the shortcut key or key combination in an AutoKeys macro. In the AutoKeys macro, assign the key or key combination to a macro that uses the RunCommand action to run the command.

For custom commands, you can't display the shortcut text next to the control, but you can use the AutoKeys macro to assign a shortcut key or key combination that will run the same set of actions as the macro or function that's the setting of the control's

OnAction property. Assign the key or key combination to the desired set of macro actions, or use the RunMacro or RunCode action to run the macro or function you want this key or key combination to carry out.

Example

This example places a charting button on the command bar named "Custom" and assigns an **OnAction** macro to the button, along with a shortcut key and a caption.

```
Set myControl = CommandBars("Custom").Controls _
    .Add(Type:=msoControlButton, Id:= 17)
With myControl
    .OnAction = "MySub"
    .Caption = "Graph Results"
    .Control.ShortcutText = "CTRL+SHIFT+M"
End With
```

Show Method

Applies To

Balloon object, **FileFind** object.

Description

Balloon object: Displays the specified balloon object. Returns an **msoBalloonType** constant that indicates which balloon the user clicks.

FileFind object: Displays the **Find File** dialog and the current search criteria. Macintosh only.

Syntax

expression.**Show**

expression Required. An expression that returns a **Balloon** object or a **FileFind** object.

Remarks

For the **Balloon** object, you can use the return value of the **Show** method to display a user's button selection. The **Show** method returns one of the following **MsoBalloonType** constants:

msoBalloonButtonAbort	**msoBalloonButtonBack**
msoBalloonButtonCancel	**msoBalloonButtonClose**
msoBalloonButtonIgnore	**msoBalloonButtonNext**
msoBalloonButtonNo	**msoBalloonButtonNull**
msoBalloonButtonOK	**msoBalloonButtonOptions**
msoBalloonButtonRetry	**msoBalloonButtonSearch**
msoBalloonButtonSnooze	**msoBalloonButtonTips**
msoBalloonButtonYes	**msoBalloonButtonYesToAll**

See Also

Balloon object, **BalloonCheckboxes** collection object, **NewBalloon** property.

Example

This example creates a balloon containing three choices. The variable x is set to the return value of the **Show** method, which will be 1, 2 or 3, corresponding to the label the user clicks. In the example, a simple message box displays the value of the variable x, but you can pass the value to another procedure, or you can use the value in a **Select Case** statement.

```
Set b = Assistant.NewBalloon
With b
   .Heading = "This is my heading"
   .Text = "Select one of these things:"
   .Labels(1).Text = "Choice One"
   .Labels(2).Text = "Choice Two"
   .Labels(3).Text = "Choice Three"
   x = .Show
End With
MsgBox x
```

ShowPopup Method

Applies To

CommandBar object.

Description

Displays the specified command bar as a shortcut menu at the specified coordinates or at the current pointer coordinates.

Note If the **Position** property of the command bar is not set to **msoBarPopup**, this method fails.

Syntax

expression.**ShowPopup(***x*, *y***)**

expression Required. An expression that returns a **CommandBar** object.

x Optional **Variant**. The x-coordinate for the location of the shortcut menu. If this argument is omitted, the current x-coordinate of the pointer is used.

y Optional **Variant**. The y-coordinate for the location of the shortcut menu. If this argument is omitted, the current y-coordinate of the pointer is used.

Example

This example creates a shortcut menu containing two controls. The **ShowPopup** method is used to make the shortcut menu visible.

```
Set myBar = CommandBars _
    .Add(Name:="Custom1", Position:=msoBarPopup, Temporary:=False)
With myBar
    .Controls.Add Type:=msoControlButton, Id:=3
    .Controls.Add Type:=msoControlComboBox
End With
myBar.ShowPopup
```

SortBy Property

Applies To

FileFind object.

Description

Macintosh only. Returns or sets the method used to sort the files returned from the specified file search. Can be one of the following **MsoFileFindSortBy** constants: **msoFileFindSortByAuthor**, **msoFileFindSortByDateCreated**, **msoFileFindSortByDateSaved**, **msoFileFindSortByFileName**, **msoFileFindSortByLastSavedBy**, **msoFileFindSortBySize**, or **msoFileFindSortByTitle**. Read/write.

Sounds Property

Applies To

Assistant object.

Description

True if the Office Assistant produces the sounds that correspond to animations. Read/write **Boolean**.

Remarks

If a sound card is not installed, this property has no effect.

Example

This example displays the Office Assistant, animates it, and generates sound.

```
With Assistant
    .Visible = True
    .Sounds = True
    .Animation = msoAnimationBeginSpeaking
End With
```

StartWizard Method

Applies To

Assistant object.

Description

Starts the Office Assistant as part of a process to provide additional explanation for existing custom wizard panels. Returns a number that uniquely identifies the Office Assistant wizard session.

Syntax

expression.**StartWizard(*On, Callback, PrivateX, Animation, CustomTeaser, Top,*
↪ ***Left, Bottom, Right*)**

expression Required. An expression that returns an **Assistant** object.

On Required **Boolean**. The wizard's local state. When the method returns, this argument is **True** if the user requests help for the wizard from the standard balloon that asks the user whether he or she wants help.

Callback Required **String**. The name of the callback procedure to be run.

PrivateX Required **Long**. The unique identifier of the Office Assistant balloon panel that initiates the callback procedure.

Animation Optional **Variant**. The type of animation that the Office Assistant performs when it appears. The default value is **msoAnimationGetWizardy**.

CustomTeaser Optional **Variant**. **True** to have the standard balloon that asks the user whether he or she wants help be replaced with a custom balloon.

Top*, *Left*, *Bottom*, *Right Optional **Variant**. The position of the corners (in points and relative to the screen) of the custom wizard panel that the Office Assistant will avoid when the user starts it or switches to it.

Remarks

It isn't necessary to use the **Visible** property to display the Office Assistant if you use the **StartWizard** method.

See Also

ActivateWizard method, **Assistant** object, **EndWizard** method.

Example

This example starts the Office Assistant as part of a process to provide additional explanation for existing custom wizards. If the user clicks the selection in the balloon that requests additional help, the callback procedure will be run. The variable `helpForWiz` is set to the return value of the **StartWizard** method.

```
helpForWiz = Assistant.StartWizard(on:=True, _
   PrivateX:=23, Callback:="myCallback", _
   Animation:=msoAnimationGetAttentionMajor, _
   CustomTeaser:=False, Top:=100, Left:=200, _
   Bottom:=50, Right:=200)
```

State Property

Applies To

CommandBarButton object.

Description

Returns or sets the appearance of the specified command bar button control. Can be one of the following **MsoButtonState** constants: **msoButtonUp**, **msoButtonDown**, or **msoButtonMixed**. Read/write **Long**.

Specifics (Microsoft Access)

You can use the **State** property to place or remove a check beside a menu item or command button. This property replaces the functionality supplied by the SetMenuItem action and **SetMenuItem** method in Microsoft Access 95.

Example

This example determines whether the first control on the command bar named "Custom" has a built-in button face. If it does, the example copies the button face to the Clipboard so that it can be customized with an application such as Microsoft Paint. The example then sets the button state to **msoButtonUp**.

```
Set myControl = CommandBars("Custom").Controls(1)
With myControl
   If .BuiltInFace = True Then
      .CopyFace
   End If
   .State = msoButtonUp
End With
```

Style Property

Applies To

CommandBarButton object, **CommandBarComboBox** object.

Description

CommandBarButton object: Returns or sets the way the specified command bar button control is displayed. Can be one of the following **MsoButtonStyle** constants: **msoButtonAutomatic**, **msoButtonIcon**, **msoButtonCaption**, or **msoButtonIconandCaption**. Read/write **Long**.

CommandBarComboBox object: Returns or sets the way the specified command bar combo box control is displayed. Can be either of the following **MsoComboStyle** constants: **msoComboLabel** or **msoComboNormal**. Read/write **Long**.

Specifics (Microsoft Access)

In Microsoft Access 97, you can use the *Toolbar* **Control Properties** dialog box for command bar controls to set the display style for a button control on a command bar. Display the **Customize** dialog box by pointing to **Toolbars** on the **View** menu and clicking **Customize**. For menu bar and toolbar controls, display the menu bar or toolbar, and then right-click the control whose **Style** property you want to set. For shortcut menu controls, select the **Shortcut Menus** check box on the **Toolbars** tab of the **Customize** dialog box, then find the shortcut menu control you want on the menu bar that's displayed and right-click the control. Click the **Properties** command. Select the style you want in the **Style** box.

The settings in the **Style** box correspond to the intrinsic constants used as the setting of the **Style** property in the following way.

Style box setting	Style property constant
Default Style	**msoButtonAutomatic**
Text Only (Always)	**msoButtonCaption**
Text Only (in Menus)	**msoButtonIcon**
Image and Text	**msoButtonIconAndCaption**
No Label	**msoComboNormal**
Show Label	**msoComboLabel**

Example

This example creates a shortcut menu containing a button control and a combo box control and sets the style of each.

```
Set myBar = CommandBars _
   .Add(Name:="Custom1", Position:=msoBarPopup, Temporary:=False)
With myBar
   .Controls.Add Type:=msoControlButton, Id:=3
   .Controls(1).Style = msoButtonCaption
   .Controls.Add Type:=msoControlComboBox
   With .Controls(2)
      .Style = msoComboLabel
      .AddItem "vanilla"
      .AddItem "chocolate"
      .AddItem "cookie dough"
   End With
End With
myBar.ShowPopup
```

SubDir Property

Applies To

FileFind object.

Description

Macintosh only. **True** if the specified file search includes all subfolders in the folder specified by the **SearchPath** property. Read/write **Boolean**.

Subject Property

Applies To

FileFind object.

Description

Macintosh only. Returns or sets a string (up to 80 characters long) that represents the subject listed in the properties of the file to be searched for. Read/write **String**.

Tag Property

Applies To

CommandBarButton object, **CommandBarComboBox** object, **CommandBarControl** object, **CommandBarPopup** object.

Description

Returns or sets information about the command bar control, such as data that can be used as an argument in procedures, or information that identifies the control. Read/write **String**.

See Also

FindControl method.

Specifics (Microsoft Access)

In Microsoft Access 97, you can use the *Toolbar* **Control Properties** dialog box for command bar controls to set the **Tag** property for a control on a command bar. Display the **Customize** dialog box by pointing to **Toolbars** on the **View** menu and clicking **Customize**. For menu bar and toolbar controls, display the menu bar or toolbar, and then right-click the control whose **Tag** property you want to set. For shortcut menu controls, select the **Shortcut Menus** check box on the **Toolbars** tab of the **Customize** dialog box, then find the shortcut menu control you want on the menu bar that's displayed and right-click the control. Click the **Properties** command. Enter the information you want in the **Tag** box.

Example

This example moves the first combo box control from the custom command bar named "My Custom Bar" to the position before the seventh control on the command bar, sets the tag to "selection box," and assigns the control a high priority so that it will likely be dropped from the command bar if the controls don't all fit in one row.

```
Set allControls = CommandBars("My Custom Bar").Controls
For Each ctrl In allControls
   If ctrl.Type = msoControlComboBox Then
      With ctrl
         .Move Before:=7
         .Tag = "Selection box"
         .Priority = 5
      End With
      Exit For
   End If
Next
```

Text Property

Applies To

Balloon object, **BalloonCheckbox** object, **BalloonLabel** object, **CommandBarComboBox** object, **FileFind** object.

Description

CommandBarComboBox object: Returns or sets the text in the display or edit portion of the command bar combo box control. Read/write **String**.

BalloonLabel or **BalloonCheckbox** object: Returns or sets the text displayed next to the specified check box or label in the Office Assistant balloon. Read/write **String**.

Balloon object: Returns or sets the text displayed after the heading but before the labels or check boxes in the Office Assistant balloon. Read/write **String**.

FileFind object: Returns or sets the string to look for, up to 80 characters, in a the body of a document during a file search. Macintosh only. Read/write **String**.

Remarks

For the **Balloon**, **BalloonLabel**, and **BalloonCheckbox** objects, you can specify a graphic to display by using the following syntax: {*type location sizing_factor*}, where *type* is bmp (bitmap), wmf (Windows metafile), or pict (Macintosh PICT file); *location* is the resource id or the path and file name; and *sizing_factor* specifies the width of the wmf or pict (omitted for bmp).

See Also

Heading property, **Show** method.

Example

This example checks the number of items in the combo box control on the command bar named "Custom." If there are more than three items in the list, the example clears the list and adds a new first item to it. The new default item for this control is "Floyd."

```
Set myBar = CommandBars("Custom")
Set myControl = myBar.Controls(2)
With myControl
   If .ListCount > 3 Then
      .Clear
      .AddItem "Floyd", 1
      .Text = "Floyd"
   End If
End With
```

This example creates a new Office Assistant balloon with a heading, text, and three region choices. The example uses the **Text** property to provide a label for each check box.

```
With Assistant.NewBalloon
   .Heading = "Regional Sales Data"
   .Text = "Select a region"
   For i = 1 To 3
      .CheckBoxes(i).Text = "Region " & i
   Next
   .Show
End With
```

This example creates a new Office Assistant balloon with a heading, text, and three region choices. The example uses the **Text** property to provide balloon-related instructions to the user.

```
With Assistant.NewBalloon
   .Heading = "Regional Sales Data"
   .Text = "Select a region"
   For i = 1 To 3
      .CheckBoxes(i).Text = "Region " & i
   Next
   .Show
End With
```

TextOrProperty Property

Applies To

FileSearch object.

Description

Returns or sets the word or phrase to be searched for, in either the body of a file or the file's properties, during the specified file search. The word or phrase can include the * (asterisk) or ? (question mark) wildcard character. Read/write **String**.

Remarks

Use the question mark wildcard character to match any single character. For example, type **gr?y** to find all files that contain at least one instance of either "gray" or "grey."

Use the asterisk wildcard character to match any number of characters. For example, type **San*** to return all files that contain at least one word that begins with t "San."

See Also

NewSearch method.

Example

This example searches the C:\My Documents folder and all of its subfolders and returns all files whose body text or file properties contain any words that begin with "San." The **TextOrProperty** property sets the word to be searched for and limits the search to either the body of the file or the file properties.

```
With Application.FileSearch
    .NewSearch
    .LookIn = "C:\My Documents"
    .SearchSubFolders = True
    .TextOrProperty = "San*"
    .FileType = msoFileTypeAllFiles
End With
```

TipOfDay Property

Applies To

Assistant object.

Description

True if the Office Assistant displays a special tip each time the Office application is opened. Read/write **Boolean**.

Remarks

The **TipOfDay** property corresponds to the **Show the Tip of the Day at startup** option under **Other tip options** on the **Options** tab in the **Office Assistant** dialog box.

Example

This example displays the Office Assistant in a specific location, and it sets several options before making the Assistant visible.

```
With Assistant
    .Reduced = True
    .Left = 400
    .MoveWhenInTheWay = True
    .TipOfDay = True
    .Visible = True
    .Animation = msoAnimGreeting
End With
```

Title Property

Applies To

FileFind object.

Description

Macintosh only. Returns or sets a string (up to 80 characters long) that represents the document title in the properties of the file to be searched for. Read/write **String**.

See Also

Execute method.

TooltipText Property

Applies To

CommandBarButton object, **CommandBarComboBox** object, **CommandBarControl** object, **CommandBarPopup** object.

Description

Returns or sets the text displayed in the specified command bar control's ScreenTip. Read/write **String**.

Remarks

By default, the value of the **Caption** property is used as the ScreenTip.

See Also

Caption property, **DescriptionText** property.

Specifics (Microsoft Access)

In Microsoft Access 97, you can use the *Toolbar* **Control Properties** dialog box for command bar controls to set the ToolTip (ScreenTip) for a control on a command bar. Display the **Customize** dialog box by pointing to **Toolbars** on the **View** menu and clicking **Customize**. For menu bar and toolbar controls, display the menu bar or toolbar, and then right-click the control whose **TooltipText** property you want to set. For shortcut menu controls, select the **Shortcut Menus** check box on the **Toolbars** tab of the **Customize** dialog box, then find the shortcut menu control you want on the menu bar that's displayed and right-click the control. Click the **Properties** command. Enter the text you want in the **ToolTip** box.

Example

This example sets the last control on the active menu bar to begin its own group, and then adds a ScreenTip to it.

```
Set myMenuBar = CommandBars.ActiveMenuBar
Set lastCtrl = myMenuBar.Controls(myMenuBar.Controls.Count)
lastCtrl.BeginGroup = True
lastCtrl.TooltipText = "Click for help on UI feature"
End With
```

Top Property

Applies To

Assistant object, **CommandBar** object, **CommandBarButton** object, **CommandBarComboBox** object, **CommandBarControl** object, **CommandBarPopup** object.

Description

CommandBar or **CommandBarControl** object: Returns or sets the distance (in pixels) from the top edge of the specified command bar or command bar control to the top edge of the screen. For docked command bars, this property returns or sets the distance from the command bar to the top of the docking area. Read/write **Long** for **CommandBar**, read-only **Long** for **CommandBarControl**.

Assistant object: Sets or returns the vertical position of the Office Assistant window (in points), relative to the screen. Read/write **Integer**.

See Also

Left property.

Example

This example positions the upper-left corner of the floating command bar named "Custom" 140 pixels from the left edge of the screen and 100 pixels from the top of the screen.

```
Set myBar = CommandBars("Custom")
myBar.Position = msoBarFloating
With myBar
    .Left = 140
    .Top = 100
End With
```

This example moves the Office Assistant to the specified coordinate.

```
Assistant.Top = 500
```

Type Property

Applies To

CommandBar object, **CommandBarButton** object, **CommandBarComboBox** object, **CommandBarControl** object, **CommandBarPopup** object, **DocumentProperty** object.

Description

DocumentProperty object: Returns or sets the document property type. Can be one of the following **MsoDocProperties** constants: **msoPropertyTypeBoolean**, **msoPropertyTypeDate**, **msoPropertyTypeFloat**, **msoPropertyTypeNumber**, or **msoPropertyTypeString**. Read-only for built-in document properties; read/write for custom document properties.

CommandBar object: Returns the type of command bar. Can be one of the following **MsoBarType** constants: **msoBarTypeNormal**, **msoBarTypeMenuBar**, or **msoBarTypePopup**. Read-only **Long**.

CommandBarControl object: Returns the type of command bar control. Read-only **Long**.

Can be one of the following **MsoControlType** constants.

<table>
<tr><th>Constant</th><th>Control type</th></tr>
<tr><td>msoControlButton</td><td></td></tr>
<tr><td>msoControlButtonDropdown</td><td>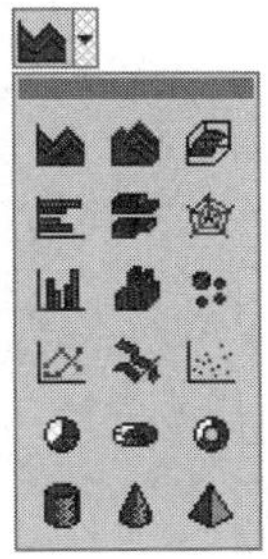</td></tr>
<tr><td>msoControlButtonPopup</td><td>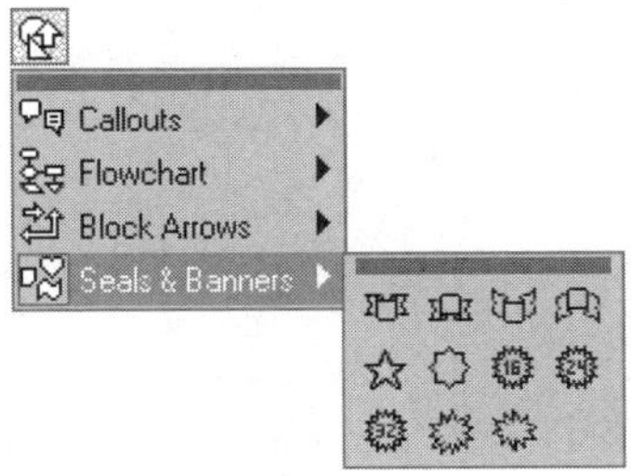
</td></tr>
<tr><td>msoControlComboBox</td><td>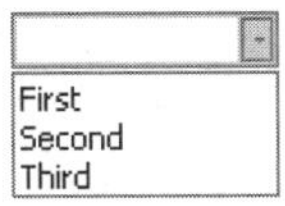
</td></tr>
<tr><td>msoControlCustom</td><td>Reserved for future use.</td></tr>
<tr><td>MsoControlDropdown</td><td>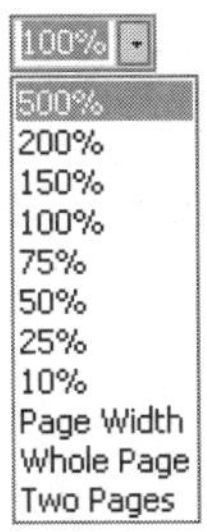
</td></tr>
<tr><td>msoControlEdit</td><td>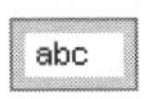
</td></tr>
</table>

(continued)

Constant	Control type
msoControlExpandingGrid	
msoControlGauge	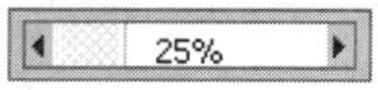
msoControlGenericDropdown	Reserved for future use.
msoControlGraphicCombo	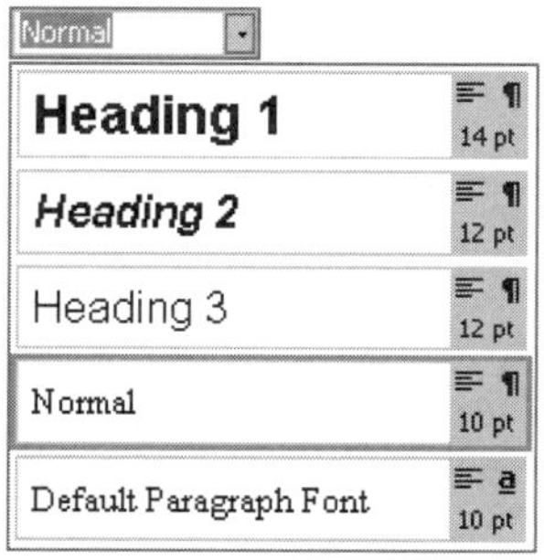
msoControlGraphicDropdown	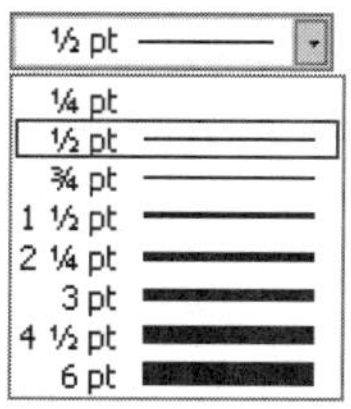
msoControlGraphicPopup	Reserved for future use.
msoControlGrid	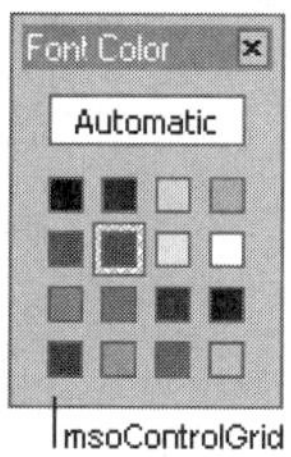
msoControlLabel	Reserved for future use.

(continued)

Constant	Control type
msoControlOCXDropDown	
msoControlPopup	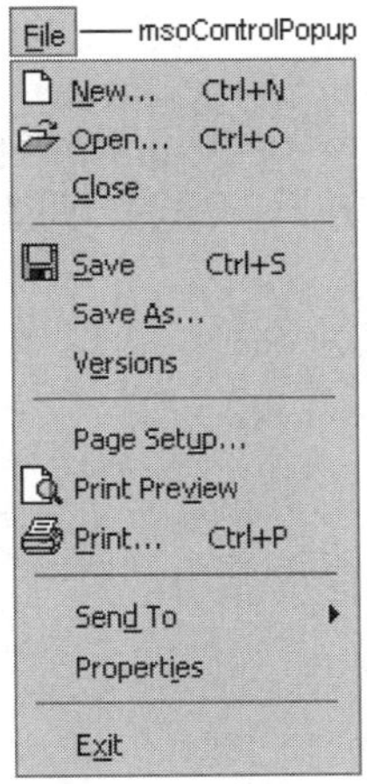
msoControlSplitButtonMRUPopup	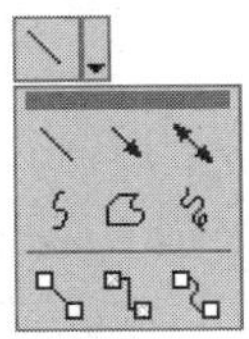
msoControlSplitButtonPopup	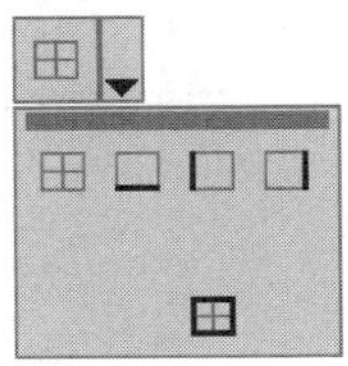
msoControlSplitDropdown	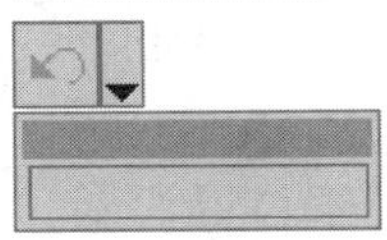
msoControlSplitExpandingGrid	Reserved for future use.

Specifics (Microsoft Access)

In Microsoft Access 97, you can use the **Toolbar Properties** dialog box to change the type of a custom menu bar, toolbar, or shortcut menu. Point to **Toolbars** on the **View** menu and click **Customize**, then click the **Properties** button in the **Customize** dialog box. Select the custom menu bar, toolbar, or shortcut menu you want in the **Selected Toolbar** box, and then select the new type for the menu bar, toolbar, or shortcut menu in the **Type** box. You can't change the type of a built-in menu bar, toolbar, or shortcut menu.

If you set the type of a command bar to "Popup", the command bar disappears from the **Toolbars** list in the **Customize** dialog box, and moves to the menu bar that's displayed when you select the **Shortcut Menus** box in the **Toolbars** list (this menu bar displays all the shortcut menus in Microsoft Access).

Example

This example finds the first control with the tag value "Change this bar." If the control with that tag value is a command bar button, the example adds a new combo box control to the end of the command bar and changes the tag value of the found button to "Changed."

```
Set ctrl = CommandBars _
   .FindControl(Tag:="Change this bar")
If ctrl Is Nothing Then Goto notFound
If ctrl.Type = msoControlButton Then
   Set br = ctrl.Parent
   br.Controls.Add(Type:=msoControlComboBox)
   ctrl.Tag = "Changed"
End If
```

This example displays the name, type, and value of a document property. You must pass a valid **DocumentProperty** object to the procedure.

```
Sub DisplayPropertyInfo(dp As DocumentProperty)
   MsgBox "value = " & dp.Value & Chr(13) & _
      "type = " & dp.Type & Chr(13) & _
      "name = " & dp.Name
End Sub
```

Value Property

Applies To

DocumentProperty object, **PropertyTest** object.

Description

DocumentProperty object: Returns or sets the value of the specified document property. Read/write **Variant**.

PropertyTest object: Returns the value of a property test for a file search. Read-only **Variant**.

Remarks

If the container application doesn't define a value for one of the built-in document properties, reading the **Value** property for that document property causes an error.

Example

This example displays the name, type, and value of a document property. For the example to work, dp must be a valid **DocumentProperty** object.

```
Sub DisplayPropertyInfo(dp As DocumentProperty)
   MsgBox "value = " & dp.Value & Chr(13) & _
      "type = " & dp.Type & Chr(13) & _
      "name = " & dp.Name
End Sub
```

This example displays the value of the search criteria (if it exists) in a dialog box. If the second value doesn't exist, the example displays another message.

```
With Application.FileSearch.PropertyTests(1)
If .Value = "" Then
   MsgBox "You haven't specified a value."
Else
   MsgBox "The value you've set is: " & .Value
End If
End With
```

View Property

Applies To

FileFind object.

Description

Macintosh only. Returns or sets the style used to display information about the found files in the dialog box. Can be one of the following **MsoFileFindView** constants: **msoFileFindViewFileInfo**, **msoFileFindViewPreview**, or **msoFileFindViewSummary**. Read-only **Variant**.

Visible Property

Applies To

Assistant object, **CommandBar** object, **CommandBarButton** object, **CommandBarComboBox** object, **CommandBarControl** object, **CommandBarPopup** object.

Description

CommandBar and **CommandBarControl** object: **True** if the specified command bar or command bar control is visible. Read/write **Boolean**.

Assistant object: **True** if the Office Assistant is visible. Read/write **Boolean**.

Remarks

The **Visible** property for newly created custom command bars is **False** by default.

The **Enabled** property for a command bar must be set to **True** before the visible property is set to **True**.

See Also

Add Method (**CommandBarControls** collection), **Add** Method (**CommandBars** collection).

Example

This example steps through the collection of command bars to find the Forms command bar. If the Forms command bar is found, the example makes it visible and protects its docking state.

```
foundFlag = False
For Each cmdbar In CommandBars
   If cmdbar.Name = "Forms" Then
      cmdbar.Protection = msoBarNoChangeDock
      cmdbar.Visible = True
      foundFlag = True
   End If
Next
If Not foundFlag Then
   MsgBox "'Forms'command bar is not in the collection."
End If
```

This example makes the Office Assistant visible and sets its animation.

```
With Application.Assistant
   .Visible = True
   .Sounds = True
   .Animation = msoAnimationBeginSpeaking
End With
```

Width Property

Applies To

CommandBar object, **CommandBarButton** object, **CommandBarComboBox** object, **CommandBarControl** object, **CommandBarPopup** object.

Description

Returns or sets the width (in pixels) of the specified command bar or command bar control. Read/write **Long**.

See Also

Height property.

Example

This example adds a custom control before the second control on the command bar named "Custom." The example sets the height of the custom control to half the height of the command bar and sets its width to 50 pixels.

```
Set myBar = cmdbar.CommandBars("Custom")
barheight = myBar.Height
Set myControl = myBar.Controls _
   .Add(Type:=msoControlComboBox, Id:=4, Before:=2, Temporary:=True)
With myControl
   .Height = barheight / 2
   .Width = 50
End With
myBar.Visible = True
```

Microsoft Forms Language Reference

Microsoft Forms

Default location: \Windows\System32

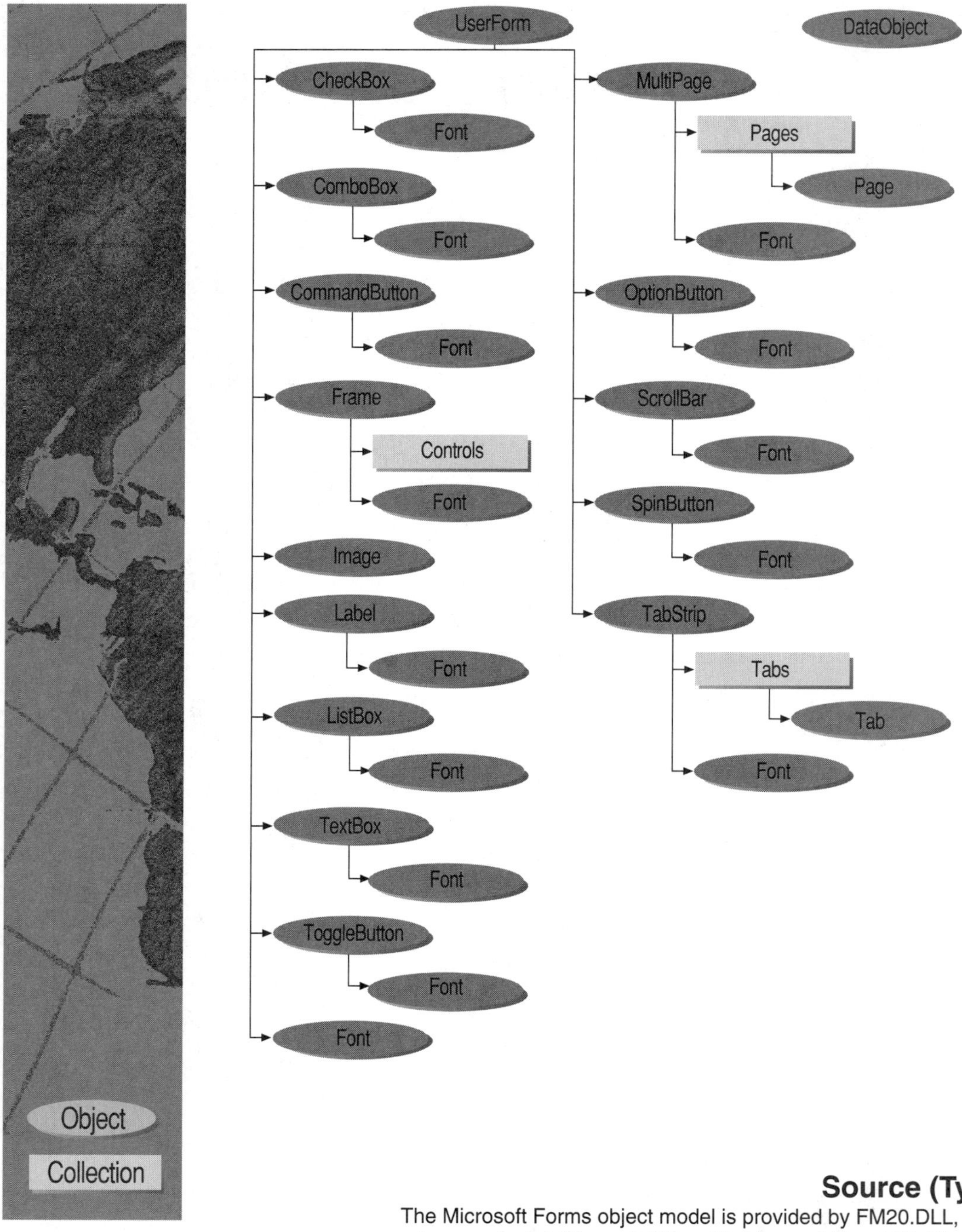

Source (Type Library)

The Microsoft Forms object model is provided by FM20.DLL, which is included when you install Microsoft Office 97, Microsoft Excel 97, Microsoft Outlook 97, Microsoft PowerPoint 97, or Microsoft Word 97.

Accelerator Property

Applies To

CheckBox control, **CommandButton** control, **Label** control, **OptionButton** control, **Page** object, **Tab** object, **ToggleButton** control.

Description

Sets or retrieves the accelerator key for a control.

Syntax

object.**Accelerator** [= *String*]

The **Accelerator** property syntax has these parts:

Part	Description
object	Required. A valid object.
String	Optional. The character to use as the accelerator key.

Remarks

To designate an accelerator key, enter a single character for the **Accelerator** property. You can set **Accelerator** in the control's property sheet or in code. If the value of this property contains more than one character, the first character in the string becomes the value of **Accelerator**.

When an accelerator key is used, there is no visual feedback (other than focus) to indicate that the control initiated the Click event. For example, if the accelerator key applies to a **CommandButton**, the user will not see the button pressed in the interface. The button receives the focus, however, when the user presses the accelerator key.

If the accelerator applies to a **Label**, the control following the **Label** in the tab order, rather than the **Label** itself, receives the focus.

Example

This example changes the **Accelerator** and **Caption** properties of a **CommandButton** each time the user clicks the button by using the mouse or the accelerator key. The Click event contains the code to change the **Accelerator** and **Caption** properties.

To try this example, paste the code into the Declarations section of a form containing a **CommandButton** named CommandButton1.

```
Private Sub UserForm_Initialize()
   CommandButton1.Accelerator= "C"          'Set accelerator key to ALT + C
End Sub

Private Sub CommandButton1_Click ()
   If CommandButton1.Caption = "OK" Then      'Check caption, then change it.
      CommandButton1.Caption = "Clicked"
      CommandButton1.Accelerator  = "C"       'Set accelerator key to ALT + C
   Else
      CommandButton1.Caption = "OK"
      CommandButton1.Accelerator  = "O"       'Set accelerator key to ALT + O
   End If
End Sub
```

ActiveControl Property

Applies To

Frame control, **Page** object, **UserForm** object.

Description

Identifies and allows manipulation of the control that has the focus.

Syntax

object.**ActiveControl**

The **ActiveControl** property syntax has these parts:

Part	Description
object	Required. A valid object.

Remarks

The **ActiveControl** property is read-only and is set when you select a control in the interface. You can use **ActiveControl** as a substitute for the control name when setting properties or calling methods.

Example

The following example uses the **ActiveControl** property in a subroutine that tracks the controls a user visits. The Enter event for each control calls the TraceFocus subroutine to identify the control that has the focus.

To use this example, copy this sample code to the Declarations portion of a form. Make sure that the form contains the following controls:

- A **ScrollBar** named ScrollBar1.
- A **ListBox** named ListBox1.

- Two **OptionButton** controls named OptionButton1 and OptionButton2.
- A **Frame** named Frame1.

```
Dim MyControl As Control

Private Sub TraceFocus()
   ListBox1.AddItem ActiveControl.Name
   ListBox1.List(ListBox1.ListCount - 1, 1) = ActiveControl.TabIndex
End Sub

Private Sub UserForm_Initialize()
   ListBox1.ColumnCount = 2
   ListBox1.AddItem "Controls Visited"
   ListBox1.List(0, 1) = "Control Index"
End Sub

Private Sub Frame1_Enter()
   TraceFocus
End Sub

Private Sub ListBox1_Enter()
   TraceFocus
End Sub

Private Sub OptionButton1_Enter()
   TraceFocus
End Sub

Private Sub OptionButton2_Enter()
   TraceFocus
End Sub

Private Sub ScrollBar1_Enter()
   TraceFocus
End Sub
```

Add Method

Applies To

Controls collection, **Pages** collection, **Tabs** collection.

Description

Adds or inserts a **Tab** or **Page** in a **TabStrip** or **MultiPage**, or adds a control by its programmatic identifier (*ProgID*) to a page or form.

Syntax

For MultiPage, TabStrip

Set *Object* = *object*.**Add(** [*Name* [, *Caption* [, *index*]]])

For other controls

Set *Control* = *object*.**Add**(*ProgID* [, *Name* [, *Visible*]])

The **Add** method syntax has these parts:

Part	Description
object	Required. A valid object name.
Name	Optional. Specifies the name of the object being added. If a name is not specified, the system generates a default name based on the rules of the application where the form is used.
Caption	Optional. Specifies the caption to appear on a tab or a control. If a caption is not specified, the system generates a default caption based on the rules of the application where the form is used.
index	Optional. Identifies the position of a page or tab within a **Pages** or **Tabs** collection. If an index is not specified, the system appends the page or tab to the end of the **Pages** or **Tabs** collection and assigns the appropriate index value.
ProgID	Required. Programmatic identifier. A text string with no spaces that identifies an object class. The standard syntax for a *ProgID* is <Vendor>.<Component>.<Version>. A *ProgID* is mapped to a class identifier (CLSID).
Visible	Optional. **True** if the object is visible (default). **False** if the object is hidden.

Settings

ProgID values for individual controls are:

CheckBox	Forms.CheckBox.1
ComboBox	Forms.ComboBox.1
CommandButton	Forms.CommandButton.1
Frame	Forms.Frame.1
Image	Forms.Image.1
Label	Forms.Label.1
ListBox	Forms.ListBox.1
MultiPage	Forms.MultiPage.1
OptionButton	Forms.OptionButton.1
ScrollBar	Forms.ScrollBar.1
SpinButton	Forms.SpinButton.1
TabStrip	Forms.TabStrip.1
TextBox	Forms.TextBox.1
ToggleButton	Forms.ToggleButton.1

Remarks

For a **MultiPage** control, the **Add** method returns a **Page** object. For a **TabStrip**, it returns a **Tab** object. The index value for the first **Page** or **Tab** of a collection is 0, the value for the second **Page** or **Tab** is 1, and so on.

For the **Controls** collection of an object, the **Add** method returns a control corresponding to the specified *ProgID*. The AddControl event occurs after the control is added.

The following syntax will return the **Text** property of a control added at design time:

```
userform1.thebox.text
```

If you add a control at run time, you must use the exclamation syntax to reference properties of that control. For example, to return the **Text** property of a control added at run time, use the following syntax:

```
userform1!thebox.text
```

Note You can change a control's **Name** property at run time only if you added that control at run time with the **Add** method.

See Also

AddControl event, **Clear** method, **Page** object, **Remove** method, **Tab** object.

Example

The following example uses the **Add** method to add a control to a form at run time and uses the AddControl event as confirmation that the control was added.

To use this example, copy this sample code to the Declarations portion of a form. Make sure that the form contains:

- A **CommandButton** named CommandButton1.
- A **Label** named Label1.

```
Dim Mycmd As Control
Private Sub CommandButton1_Click()

   Set Mycmd = Controls.Add("Forms.CommandButton.1") ', CommandButton2, Visible)
   Mycmd.Left = 18
   Mycmd.Top = 150
   Mycmd.Width = 175
   Mycmd.Height = 20
   Mycmd.Caption = "This is fun." & Mycmd.Name

End Sub

Private Sub UserForm_AddControl(ByVal Control As MSForms.Control)
   Label1.Caption = "Control was Added."
End Sub
```

Example

The following example uses the **Add**, **Clear**, and **Remove** methods to add and remove a control to a **Page** of a **MultiPage** at run time.

To use this example, copy this sample code to the Declarations portion of a form. Make sure that the form contains:

- A **MultiPage** named MultiPage1.
- Three **CommandButton** controls named CommandButton1 through CommandButton3.

```
Dim MyTextBox As Control

Private Sub CommandButton1_Click()
Set MyTextBox = MultiPage1.Pages(0).Controls.Add("Forms.TextBox.1", _
   "MyTextBox", Visible)
End Sub

Private Sub CommandButton2_Click()
   MultiPage1.Pages(0).Controls.Clear
End Sub

Private Sub CommandButton3_Click()
   If MultiPage1.Pages(0).Controls.Count > 0  Then
      MultiPage1.Pages(0).Controls.Remove "MyTextBox"
   End If
End Sub

Private Sub UserForm_Initialize()
   CommandButton1.Caption = "Add control"
   CommandButton2.Caption = "Clear controls"
   CommandButton3.Caption = "Remove control"
End Sub
```

Example

See the **Cut** method example.

AddControl Event

Applies To

Frame control, **MultiPage** control, **UserForm** object.

Description

Occurs when a control is inserted onto a form, a **Frame**, or a **Page** of a **MultiPage**.

Syntax

For Frame

Private Sub *object*_**AddControl( )**

For MultiPage

Private Sub *object*_**AddControl(** *index* **As Long**, *ctrl* **As Control)**

The **AddControl** event syntax has these parts:

Part	Description
object	Required. A valid object.
index	Required. The index of the **Page** that will contain the new control.
ctrl	Required. The control to be added.

Remarks

The AddControl event occurs when a control is added at run time. This event is not initiated when you add a control at design time, nor is it initiated when a form is initially loaded and displayed at run time.

The default action of this event is to add a control to the specified form, **Frame**, or **MultiPage**.

The **Add** method initiates the AddControl event.

See Also

Add method.

Example

See the **Add** method example.

AddItem Method

Applies To

ComboBox control, **ListBox** control.

Description

For a single-column list box or combo box, adds an item to the list. For a multicolumn list box or combo box, adds a row to the list.

Syntax

Variant = *object*.**AddItem(** [*item* [, *varIndex*]])

The **AddItem** method syntax has these parts:

Part	Description
object	Required. A valid object.
Item	Optional. Specifies the item or row to add. The number of the first item or row is 0; the number of the second item or row is 1, and so on.
varIndex	Optional. Integer specifying the position within the object where the new item or row is placed.

Remarks

If you supply a valid value for *varIndex*, the **AddItem** method places the item or row at that position within the list. If you omit *varIndex*, the method adds the item or row at the end of the list.

The value of *varIndex* must not be greater than the value of the **ListCount** property.

For a multicolumn **ListBox** or **ComboBox**, **AddItem** inserts an entire row, that is, it inserts an item for each column of the control. To assign values to an item beyond the first column, use the **List** or **Column** property and specify the row and column of the item.

If the control is bound to data, the **AddItem** method fails.

Note You can add more than one row at a time to a **ComboBox** or **ListBox** by using **List**.

See Also

Column property, **List** property, **ListCount** property.

Example

The following example adds and deletes the contents of a **ListBox** using the **AddItem**, **RemoveItem**, and **SetFocus** methods, and the **ListIndex** and **ListCount** properties.

To use this example, copy this sample code to the Declarations portion of a form. Make sure that the form contains:

- A **ListBox** named ListBox1.
- Two **CommandButton** controls named CommandButton1 and CommandButton2.

```
Dim EntryCount As Single
Private Sub CommandButton1_Click()
   EntryCount = EntryCount + 1
   ListBox1.AddItem (EntryCount & " - Selection")
End Sub

Private Sub CommandButton2_Click()
   ListBox1.SetFocus

   'Ensure ListBox contains list items.
   If ListBox1.ListCount >= 1 Then
      'If no selection, choose last list item.
      If ListBox1.ListIndex = -1 Then
         ListBox1.ListIndex = ListBox1.ListCount - 1
      End If
      ListBox1.RemoveItem (ListBox1.ListIndex)
   End If
End Sub
```

```
Private Sub UserForm_Initialize()
    EntryCount = 0
    CommandButton1.Caption = "Add Item"
    CommandButton2.Caption = "Remove Item"
End Sub
```

AfterUpdate Event

Applies To

CheckBox control, **ComboBox** control, **ListBox** control, **OptionButton** control, **ScrollBar** control, **SpinButton** control, **TextBox** control, **ToggleButton** control.

Description

Occurs after data in a control is changed through the user interface.

Syntax

Private Sub *object*_**AfterUpdate( )**

The **AfterUpdate** event syntax has these parts:

Part	Description
object	Required. A valid object.

Remarks

The AfterUpdate event occurs regardless of whether the control is bound (that is, when the **RowSource** property specifies a data source for the control). This event cannot be canceled. If you want to cancel the update (to restore the previous value of the control), use the BeforeUpdate event and set the *Cancel* argument to **True**.

The AfterUpdate event occurs after the BeforeUpdate event and before the Exit event for the current control and before the Enter event for the next control in the tab order.

See Also

BeforeUpdate event, **BoundValue** property, Change event, **RowSource** property.

Alignment Property

Applies To

CheckBox control, **OptionButton** control, **ToggleButton** control.

Description

Specifies the position of a control relative to its caption.

Syntax

object.**Alignment** [= *fmAlignment*]

The **Alignment** property syntax has these parts:

Part	Description
object	Required. A valid object.
fmAlignment	Optional. Caption position.

Settings

The settings for *fmAlignment* are:

Constant	Value	Description
fmAlignmentLeft	0	Places the caption to the left of the control.
fmAlignmentRight	1	Places the caption to the right of the control (default).

Remarks

The caption text for a control is left-aligned.

Note Although the **Alignment** property exists on the **ToggleButton**, the property is disabled. You cannot set or return a value for this property on the **ToggleButton**.

Example

The following example demonstrates the **Alignment** property used with several **OptionButton** controls. In this example, the user can change the alignment by clicking a **ToggleButton**.

To use this example, copy this sample code to the Declarations portion of a form. Make sure that the form contains the following controls:

- Two **OptionButton** controls named OptionButton1 and OptionButton2.
- A **ToggleButton** named ToggleButton1.

```
Private Sub UserForm_Initialize()
   OptionButton1.Alignment = fmAlignmentLeft
   OptionButton2.Alignment = fmAlignmentLeft

   OptionButton1.Caption = "Alignment with AutoSize"
   OptionButton2.Caption = "Choice 2"
   OptionButton1.AutoSize = True
   OptionButton2.AutoSize = True

   ToggleButton1.Caption = "Left Align"
   ToggleButton1.WordWrap = True
   ToggleButton1.Value = True
End Sub
```

```
Private Sub ToggleButton1_Click()
   If ToggleButton1.Value = True Then
      ToggleButton1.Caption = "Left Align"
      OptionButton1.Alignment = fmAlignmentLeft
      OptionButton2.Alignment = fmAlignmentLeft
   Else
      ToggleButton1.Caption = "Right Align"
      OptionButton1.Alignment = fmAlignmentRight
      OptionButton2.Alignment = fmAlignmentRight
   End If
End Sub
```

AutoSize Property

Applies To

CheckBox control, **ComboBox** control, **CommandButton** control, **Image** control, **Label** control, **OptionButton** control, **TextBox** control, **ToggleButton** control.

Description

Specifies whether an object automatically resizes to display its entire contents.

Syntax

object.**AutoSize** [= *Boolean*]

The **AutoSize** property syntax has these parts:

Part	Description
object	Required. A valid object.
Boolean	Optional. Whether the control is resized.

Settings

The settings for *Boolean* are:

Value	Description
True	Automatically resizes the control to display its entire contents.
False	Keeps the size of the control constant. Contents are clipped when they exceed the area of the control (default).

Remarks

For controls with captions, the **AutoSize** property specifies whether the control automatically adjusts to display the entire caption.

For controls without captions, this property specifies whether the control automatically adjusts to display the information stored in the control. In a **ComboBox**, for example, setting **AutoSize** to **True** automatically sets the width of the display area to match the length of the current text.

For a single-line text box, setting **AutoSize** to **True** automatically sets the width of the display area to the length of the text in the text box.

For a multiline text box that contains no text, setting **AutoSize** to **True** automatically displays the text as a column. The width of the text column is set to accommodate the widest letter of that font size. The height of the text column is set to display the entire text of the **TextBox**.

For a multiline text box that contains text, setting **AutoSize** to **True** automatically enlarges the **TextBox** vertically to display the entire text. The width of the **TextBox** does not change.

Note If you manually change the size of a control while **AutoSize** is **True**, the manual change overrides the size previously set by **AutoSize**.

See Also

Caption property, **MultiLine** property, **WordWrap** property.

Example

The following example demonstrates the effects of the **AutoSize** property with a single-line **TextBox** and a multiline **TextBox**. The user can enter text into either **TextBox** and turn **AutoSize** on or off independently of the contents of the **TextBox**. This code sample also uses the **Text** property.

To use this example, copy this sample code to the Declarations portion of a form. Make sure that the form contains:

- Two **TextBox** controls named TextBox1 and TextBox2.
- A **ToggleButton** named ToggleButton1.

```
Private Sub UserForm_Initialize()
   TextBox1.Text = "Single-line TextBox. Type your text here."

   TextBox2.MultiLine = True
   TextBox2.Text = "Multi-line TextBox. Type your text here. " _
       & "Use CTRL+ENTER to start a new line."

   ToggleButton1.Value = True
   ToggleButton1.Caption = "AutoSize On"
   TextBox1.AutoSize = True
   TextBox2.AutoSize = True
End Sub

Private Sub ToggleButton1_Click()
   If ToggleButton1.Value = True Then
      ToggleButton1.Caption = "AutoSize On"
      TextBox1.AutoSize = True
      TextBox2.AutoSize = True
   Else
      ToggleButton1.Caption = "AutoSize Off"
      TextBox1.AutoSize = False
      TextBox2.AutoSize = False
   End If
End Sub
```

AutoTab Property

Applies To

ComboBox control, **TextBox** control.

Description

Specifies whether an automatic tab occurs when a user enters the maximum allowable number of characters into a **TextBox** or the text box portion of a **ComboBox**.

Syntax

object.**AutoTab** [= *Boolean*]

The **AutoTab** property syntax has these parts:

Part	Description
object	Required. A valid object.
Boolean	Optional. Specifies whether an automatic tab occurs.

Settings

The settings for *Boolean* are:

Value	Description
True	Tab occurs.
False	Tab does not occur (default).

Remarks

The **MaxLength** property specifies the maximum number of characters allowed in a **TextBox** or the text box portion of a **ComboBox**.

You can specify the **AutoTab** property for a **TextBox** or **ComboBox** on a form for which you usually enter a set number of characters. Once a user enters the maximum number of characters, the focus automatically moves to the next control in the tab order. For example, if a **TextBox** displays inventory stock numbers that are always five characters long, you can use **MaxLength** to specify the maximum number of characters to enter into the **TextBox** and **AutoTab** to automatically tab to the next control after the user enters five characters.

Support for **AutoTab** varies from one application to another. Not all containers support this property.

See Also

MaxLength property.

AutoWordSelect Property

Applies To

ComboBox control, **TextBox** control.

Description

Specifies whether a word or a character is the basic unit used to extend a selection.

Syntax

object.**AutoWordSelect** [= *Boolean*]

The **AutoWordSelect** property syntax has these parts:

Part	Description
object	Required. A valid object.
Boolean	Optional. Specifies the basic unit used to extend a selection.

Settings

The settings for *Boolean* are:

Value	Description
True	Uses a word as the basic unit (default).
False	Uses a character as the basic unit.

Remarks

The **AutoWordSelect** property specifies how the selection extends or contracts in the edit region of a **TextBox** or **ComboBox**.

If the user places the insertion point in the middle of a word and then extends the selection while **AutoWordSelect** is **True**, the selection includes the entire word.

BackColor Property

Applies To

CheckBox control, **ComboBox** control, **CommandButton** control, **Frame** control, **Image** control, **Label** control, **ListBox** control, **MultiPage** control, **OptionButton** control, **ScrollBar** control, **SpinButton** control, **TabStrip** control, **TextBox** control, **ToggleButton** control, **UserForm** object.

Description

Specifies the background color of the object.

Syntax

object.**BackColor** [= *Long*]

The **BackColor** property syntax has these parts:

Part	Description
object	Required. A valid object.
Long	Optional. A value or constant that determines the background color of an object.

Settings

You can use any integer that represents a valid color. You can also specify a color by using the RGB function with red, green, and blue color components. The value of each color component is an integer that ranges from zero to 255. For example, you can specify teal blue as the integer value 4966415 or as red, green, and blue color components 15, 200, 75.

Remarks

You can only see the background color of an object if the **BackStyle** property is set to **fmBackStyleOpaque**.

See Also

BackStyle property, **ForeColor** property.

Example

The following example demonstrates the **BorderStyle** and **SpecialEffect** properties, showing each border available through these properties. The example also demonstrates how to control color settings by using the **BackColor**, **BackStyle**, **BorderColor**, and **ForeColor** properties.

To use this example, copy this sample code to the Declarations portion of a form. Make sure that the form contains:

- Six **TextBox** controls named TextBox1 through TextBox6.
- Two **ToggleButton** controls named ToggleButton1 and ToggleButton2.

```
Private Sub UserForm_Initialize()
'Initialize each TextBox with a border style or special effect,
'and foreground and background colors.

'TextBox1 initially uses a borderstyle.
TextBox1.Text = "BorderStyle-Single"
TextBox1.BorderStyle = fmBorderStyleSingle
TextBox1.BorderColor = RGB(255, 128, 128)   'Color - Salmon
TextBox1.ForeColor = RGB(255, 255, 0)       'Color - Yellow
TextBox1.BackColor = RGB(0, 128, 64)        'Color - Green #2

'TextBoxes 2 through 6 initially use special effects.
TextBox2.Text = "Flat"
TextBox2.SpecialEffect = fmSpecialEffectFlat
TextBox2.ForeColor = RGB(64, 0, 0)          'Color - Brown
TextBox2.BackColor = RGB(0, 0, 255)         'Color - Blue
```

```
'Ensure the background style for TextBox2 is initially opaque.
TextBox2.BackStyle = fmBackStyleOpaque

TextBox3.Text = "Etched"
TextBox3.SpecialEffect = fmSpecialEffectEtched
TextBox3.ForeColor = RGB(128, 0, 255)       'Color - Purple
TextBox3.BackColor = RGB(0, 255, 255)       'Color - Cyan

'Define BorderColor for later use (when borderstyle=fmBorderStyleSingle).
TextBox3.BorderColor = RGB(0, 0, 0)         'Color - Black

TextBox4.Text = "Bump"
TextBox4.SpecialEffect = fmSpecialEffectBump
TextBox4.ForeColor = RGB(255, 0, 255)       'Color - Magenta
TextBox4.BackColor = RGB(0, 0, 100)         'Color - Navy blue

TextBox5.Text = "Raised"
TextBox5.SpecialEffect = fmSpecialEffectRaised
TextBox5.ForeColor = RGB(255, 0, 0)         'Color - Red
TextBox5.BackColor = RGB(128, 128, 128)     'Color - Gray

TextBox6.Text = "Sunken"
TextBox6.SpecialEffect = fmSpecialEffectSunken
TextBox6.ForeColor = RGB(0, 64, 0)          'Color - Olive
TextBox6.BackColor = RGB(0, 255, 0)         'Color - Green #1

ToggleButton1.Caption = "Swap styles"
ToggleButton2.Caption = "Transparent/Opaque background"
End Sub

Private Sub ToggleButton1_Click()

'Swap borders between TextBox1 and TextBox3.
If ToggleButton1.Value = True Then
   'Change TextBox1 from BorderStyle to Etched.
   TextBox1.Text = "Etched"
   TextBox1.SpecialEffect = fmSpecialEffectEtched

   'Change TextBox3 from Etched to BorderStyle.
   TextBox3.Text = "BorderStyle-Single"
   TextBox3.BorderStyle = fmBorderStyleSingle
Else
   'Change TextBox1 back to BorderStyle.
   TextBox1.Text = "BorderStyle-Single"
   TextBox1.BorderStyle = fmBorderStyleSingle

   'Change TextBox3 back to Etched.
   TextBox3.Text = "Etched"
   TextBox3.SpecialEffect = fmSpecialEffectEtched
End If
End Sub

Private Sub ToggleButton2_Click()
```

```
'Set background to Opaque or Transparent.
If ToggleButton2.Value = True Then
   'Change TextBox2 to a transparent background.
   TextBox2.BackStyle = fmBackStyleTransparent
Else
   'Change TextBox2 back to opaque background.
   TextBox2.BackStyle = fmBackStyleOpaque
End If

End Sub
```

BackStyle Property

Applies To

CheckBox control, **ComboBox** control, **CommandButton** control, **Image** control, **Label** control, **OptionButton** control, **TextBox** control, **ToggleButton** control.

Description

Returns or sets the background style for an object.

Syntax

object.**BackStyle** [= *fmBackStyle*]

The **BackStyle** property syntax has these parts:

Part	Description
object	Required. A valid object.
fmBackStyle	Optional. Specifies the control background.

Settings

The settings for *fmBackStyle* are:

Constant	Value	Description
fmBackStyleTransparent	0	The background is transparent.
fmBackStyleOpaque	1	The background is opaque (default).

Remarks

The **BackStyle** property determines whether a control is transparent. If **BackStyle** is **fmBackStyleOpaque**, the control is not transparent and you cannot see anything behind the control on a form. If **BackStyle** is **fmBackStyleTransparent**, you can see through the control and look at anything on the form located behind the control.

Note **BackStyle** does not affect the transparency of bitmaps. You must use a picture editor such as Paintbrush to make a bitmap transparent. Not all controls support transparent bitmaps.

See Also

BackColor property.

Example

See the **BackColor** property example.

BeforeDragOver Event

Applies To

CheckBox control, **ComboBox** control, **CommandButton** control, **Frame** control, **Image** control, **Label** control, **ListBox** control, **MultiPage** control, **OptionButton** control, **ScrollBar** control, **SpinButton** control, **TabStrip** control, **TextBox** control, **ToggleButton** control, **UserForm** object.

Description

Occurs when a drag-and-drop operation is in progress.

Syntax

For Frame

Private Sub *object*_**BeforeDragOver(ByVal** *Cancel* **As MSForms.ReturnBoolean,**
↪ *ctrl* **As Control, ByVal** *Data* **As DataObject, ByVal** *X* **As Single, ByVal** *Y* **As**
↪ **Single, ByVal** *DragState* **As fmDragState, ByVal** *Effect* **As**
↪ **MSForms.ReturnEffect, ByVal** *Shift* **As fmShiftState)**

For MultiPage

Private Sub *object*_**BeforeDragOver(** *index* **As Long, ByVal** *Cancel* **As**
↪ **MSForms.ReturnBoolean,** *ctrl* **As Control, ByVal** *Data* **As DataObject,**
↪ **ByVal** *X* **As Single, ByVal** *Y* **As Single, ByVal** *DragState* **As fmDragState,**
↪ **ByVal** *Effect* **As MSForms.ReturnEffect, ByVal** *Shift* **As fmShiftState)**

For TabStrip

Private Sub *object*_**BeforeDragOver(** *index* **As Long, ByVal** *Cancel* **As**
↪ **MSForms.ReturnBoolean, ByVal** *Data* **As DataObject, ByVal** *X* **As Single,**
↪ **ByVal** *Y* **As Single, ByVal** *DragState* **As fmDragState, ByVal** *Effect* **As**
↪ **MSForms.ReturnEffect, ByVal** *Shift* **As fmShiftState)**

For other controls

Private Sub *object*_**BeforeDragOver(ByVal** *Cancel* **As MSForms.ReturnBoolean,**
↪ **ByVal** *Data* **As DataObject, ByVal** *X* **As Single, ByVal** *Y* **As Single, ByVal**
↪ *DragState* **As fmDragState, ByVal** *Effect* **As MSForms.ReturnEffect, ByVal**
↪ *Shift* **As fmShiftState)**

The **BeforeDragOver** event syntax has these parts:

Part	Description
object	Required. A valid object name.
index	Required. The index of the **Page** in a **MultiPage** that the drag-and-drop operation will affect.
Cancel	Required. Event status. **False** indicates that the control should handle the event (default). **True** indicates the application handles the event.
ctrl	Required. The control being dragged over.
Data	Required. Data that is dragged in a drag-and-drop operation. The data is packaged in a **DataObject**.
X, Y	Required. The horizontal and vertical coordinates of the control's position. Both coordinates are measured in points. *X* is measured from the left edge of the control; *Y* is measured from the top of the control..
DragState	Required. Transition state of the data being dragged.
Effect	Required. Operations supported by the drop source.
Shift	Required. Specifies the state of SHIFT, CTRL, and ALT.

Settings

The settings for *DragState* are:

Constant	Value	Description
fmDragStateEnter	0	Mouse pointer is within range of a target.
fmDragStateLeave	1	Mouse pointer is outside the range of a target.
fmDragStateOver	2	Mouse pointer is at a new position, but remains within range of the same target.

The settings for *Effect* are:

Constant	Value	Description
fmDropEffectNone	0	Does not copy or move the drop source to the drop target.
fmDropEffectCopy	1	Copies the drop source to the drop target.
fmDropEffectMove	2	Moves the drop source to the drop target.
fmDropEffectCopyOrMove	3	Copies or moves the drop source to the drop target.

The settings for *Shift* are:

Constant	Value	Description
fmShiftMask	1	SHIFT was pressed.
fmCtrlMask	2	CTRL was pressed.
fmAltMask	4	ALT was pressed.

Remarks

Use this event to monitor the mouse pointer as it enters, leaves, or rests directly over a valid target. When a drag-and-drop operation is in progress, the system initiates this event when the user moves the mouse, or presses or releases the mouse buttons. The mouse pointer position determines the target object that receives this event. You can determine the state of the mouse pointer by examining the *DragState* argument.

When a control handles this event, you can use the *Effect* argument to identify the drag-and-drop action to perform. When *Effect* is set to **fmDropEffectCopyOrMove**, the drop source supports a copy (**fmDropEffectCopy**), move (**fmDropEffectMove**), or cancel (**fmDropEffectNone**) operation.

When *Effect* is set to **fmDropEffectCopy**, the drop source supports a copy or a cancel (**fmDropEffectNone**) operation.

When *Effect* is set to **fmDropEffectMove**, the drop source supports a move or a cancel (**fmDropEffectNone**) operation.

When *Effect* is set to **fmDropEffectNone**. the drop source supports a cancel operation.

Most controls do not support drag-and-drop while *Cancel* is **False**, which is the default setting. This means the control rejects attempts to drag or drop anything on the control, and the control does not initiate the BeforeDropOrPaste event. The **TextBox** and **ComboBox** controls are exceptions to this; these controls support drag-and-drop operations even when *Cancel* is **False**.

See Also

BeforeDropOrPaste event, **DataObject** object.

BeforeDropOrPaste Event

Applies To

CheckBox control, **ComboBox** control, **CommandButton** control, **Frame** control, **Image** control, **Label** control, **ListBox** control, **MultiPage** control, **OptionButton** control, **TabStrip** control, **TextBox** control, **ToggleButton** control, **UserForm** object.

Description

Occurs when the user is about to drop or paste data onto an object.

Syntax

For Frame

Private Sub *object*_**BeforeDropOrPaste(ByVal** *Cancel* **As**
➥ **MSForms.ReturnBoolean**, *ctrl* **As Control**, **ByVal** *Action* **As fmAction**,
➥ **ByVal** *Data* **As DataObject**, **ByVal** *X* **As Single**, **ByVal** *Y* **As Single**, **ByVal** *Effect* **As**
➥ **MSForms.ReturnEffect**, **ByVal** *Shift* **As fmShiftState)**

For MultiPage

Private Sub *object*_**BeforeDropOrPaste(** *index* **As Long**, **ByVal** *Cancel* **As**
➥ **MSForms.ReturnBoolean**, *ctrl* **As Control**, **ByVal** *Action* **As fmAction**, **ByVal**
➥ *Data* **As DataObject**, **ByVal** *X* **As Single**, **ByVal** *Y* **As Single**, **ByVal** *Effect* **As**
➥ **MSForms.ReturnEffect**, **ByVal** *Shift* **As fmShiftState)**

For TabStrip

Private Sub *object*_**BeforeDropOrPaste(** *index* **As Long**, **ByVal** *Cancel* **As**
➥ **MSForms.ReturnBoolean**, **ByVal** *Action* **As fmAction**, **ByVal** *Data* **As DataObject**,
➥ **ByVal** *X* **As Single**, **ByVal** *Y* **As Single**, **ByVal** *Effect* **As MSForms.ReturnEffect**,
➥ **ByVal** *Shift* **As fmShiftState)**

For other controls

Private Sub *object*_**BeforeDropOrPaste(** **ByVal** *Cancel* **As MSForms.ReturnBoolean**,
➥ **ByVal** *Action* **As fmAction**, **ByVal** *Data* **As DataObject**, **ByVal** *X* **As Single**, **ByVal**
➥ *Y* **As Single**, **ByVal** *Effect* **As MSForms.ReturnEffect**, **ByVal** *Shift* **As fmShiftState)**

The **BeforeDropOrPaste** event syntax has these parts:

Part	Description
object	Required. A valid object name.
index	Required. The index of the **Page** in a **MultiPage** that the drop or paste operation will affect.
Cancel	Required. Event status. **False** indicates that the control should handle the event (default). **True** indicates the application handles the event.
ctrl	Required. The target control.
Action	Required. Indicates the result, based on the current keyboard settings, of the pending drag-and-drop operation.
Data	Required. Data that is dragged in a drag-and-drop operation. The data is packaged in a **DataObject**.
X, Y	Required. The horizontal and vertical position of the mouse pointer when the drop occurs. Both coordinates are measured in points. *X* is measured from the left edge of the control; *Y* is measured from the top of the control..
Effect	Required. Effect of the drag-and-drop operation on the target control.
Shift	Required. Specifies the state of SHIFT, CTRL, and ALT.

Settings

The settings for *Action* are:

Constant	Value	Description
fmActionPaste	2	Pastes the selected object into the drop target.
fmActionDragDrop	3	Indicates the user has dragged the object from its source to the drop target and dropped it on the drop target.

The settings for *Effect* are:

Constant	Value	Description
fmDropEffectNone	0	Does not copy or move the drop source to the drop target.
fmDropEffectCopy	1	Copies the drop source to the drop target.
fmDropEffectMove	2	Moves the drop source to the drop target.
fmDropEffectCopyOrMove	3	Copies or moves the drop source to the drop target.

The settings for *Shift* are:

Constant	Value	Description
fmShiftMask	1	SHIFT was pressed.
fmCtrlMask	2	CTRL was pressed.
fmAltMask	4	ALT was pressed.

Remarks

For a **MultiPage** or **TabStrip**, Visual Basic for Applications initiates this event when it transfers a data object to the control.

For other controls, the system initiates this event immediately prior to the drop or paste operation.

When a control handles this event, you can update the *Action* argument to identify the drag-and-drop action to perform. When *Effect* is set to **fmDropEffectCopyOrMove**, you can assign *Action* to **fmDropEffectNone**, **fmDropEffectCopy**, or **fmDropEffectMove**. When *Effect* is set to **fmDropEffectCopy** or **fmDropEffectMove**, you can reassign *Action* to **fmDropEffectNone**. You cannot reassign *Action* when *Effect* is set to **fmDropEffectNone**.

See Also

BeforeDragOver event, **DataObject** object.

BeforeUpdate Event

Applies To

CheckBox control, **ComboBox** control, **ListBox** control, **OptionButton** control, **ScrollBar** control, **SpinButton** control, **TextBox** control, **ToggleButton** control.

Description

Occurs before data in a control is changed.

Syntax

Private Sub *object*_**BeforeUpdate(ByVal** *Cancel* **As MSForms.ReturnBoolean)**

The **BeforeUpdate** event syntax has these parts:

Part	Description
object	Required. A valid object.
Cancel	Required. Event status. **False** indicates that the control should handle the event (default). **True** cancels the update and indicates the application should handle the event.

Remarks

The BeforeUpdate event occurs regardless of whether the control is bound (that is, when the **RowSource** property specifies a data source for the control). This event occurs before the AfterUpdate and Exit events for the control (and before the Enter event for the next control that receives focus).

If you set the *Cancel* argument to **True**, the focus remains on the control and neither the AfterUpdate event nor the Exit event occurs.

See Also

AfterUpdate event, **BoundValue** property, Change event, **RowSource** property, **UndoAction** method.

Bold, Italic, Size, StrikeThrough, Underline, Weight Properties

Applies To

Font object.

Description

Specifies the visual attributes of text on a displayed or printed form.

Syntax

object.**Bold** [= *Boolean*]
object.**Italic** [= *Boolean*]
object.**Size** [= *Currency*]
object.**StrikeThrough** [= *Boolean*]
object.**Underline** [= *Boolean*]
object.**Weight** [= *Integer*]

The **Bold**, **Italic**, **Size**, **StrikeThrough**, **Underline**, and **Weight** property syntaxes have these parts:

Part	Description
object	Required. A valid object name.
Boolean	Optional. Specifies the font style.
Currency	Optional. A number indicating the font size.
Integer	Optional. Specifies the font style.

The settings for *Boolean* are:

Value	Description
True	The text has the specified attribute (that is bold, italic, size, strikethrough or underline marks, or weight).
False	The text does not have the specified attribute (default).

The **Weight** property accepts values from 0 to 1000. A value of zero allows the system to pick the most appropriate weight. A value from 1 to 1000 indicates a specific weight, where 1 represents the lightest type and 1000 represents the darkest type.

Remarks

These properties define the visual characteristics of text. The **Bold** property determines whether text is normal or bold. The **Italic** property determines whether text is normal or italic. The **Size** property determines the height, in points, of displayed text. The **Underline** property determines whether text is underlined. The **StrikeThrough** property determines whether the text appears with strikethrough marks. The **Weight** property determines the darkness of the type.

The font's appearance on screen and in print may differ, depending on your computer and printer. If you select a font that your system can't display with the specified attribute or that isn't installed, Windows substitutes a similar font. The substitute font will be as similar as possible to the font originally requested.

Changing the value of **Bold** also changes the value of **Weight**. Setting **Bold** to **True** sets **Weight** to 700; setting **Bold** to **False** sets **Weight** to 400. Conversely, setting **Weight** to anything over 550 sets **Bold** to **True**; setting **Weight** to 550 or less sets **Bold** to **False**.

The default point size is determined by the operating system.

See Also

Name property.

Example

The following example demonstrates a **Font** object and the **Bold**, **Italic**, **Size**, **StrikeThrough**, **Underline**, and **Weight** properties related to fonts. You can manipulate font properties of an object directly or by using an alias, as this example also shows.

To use this example, copy this sample code to the Declarations portion of a form. Make sure that the form contains:

- A **Label** named Label1.
- Four **ToggleButton** controls named ToggleButton1 through ToggleButton4.
- A second **Label** and a **TextBox** named Label2 and TextBox1.

```
Dim MyFont As StdFont

Private Sub ToggleButton1_Click()
   If ToggleButton1.Value = True Then
      MyFont.Bold = True              'Using MyFont alias to control font
      ToggleButton1.Caption = "Bold On"
      MyFont.Size = 22                'Increase the font size.
   Else
      MyFont.Bold = False
      ToggleButton1.Caption = "Bold Off"
      MyFont.Size = 8                 'Return font size to initial size.
   End If

   TextBox1.Text = Str(MyFont.Weight)  'Bold and Weight are related.
End Sub

Private Sub ToggleButton2_Click()
   If ToggleButton2.Value = True Then
      Label1.Font.Italic = True              'Using Label1.Font directly
      ToggleButton2.Caption = "Italic On"
   Else
      Label1.Font.Italic = False
      ToggleButton2.Caption = "Italic Off"
   End If
End Sub

Private Sub ToggleButton3_Click()
   If ToggleButton3.Value = True Then
      Label1.Font.Strikethrough = True   'Using Label1.Font directly
      ToggleButton3.Caption = "StrikeThrough On"
   Else
      Label1.Font.Strikethrough = False
      ToggleButton3.Caption = "StrikeThrough Off"
   End If
End Sub

Private Sub ToggleButton4_Click()
   If ToggleButton4.Value = True Then
      MyFont.Underline = True   'Using MyFont alias for Label1.Font
      ToggleButton4.Caption = "Underline On"
   Else
      Label1.Font.Underline = False
      ToggleButton4.Caption = "Underline Off"
   End If
End Sub
```

```
Private Sub UserForm_Initialize()
   Set MyFont = Label1.Font

   ToggleButton1.Value = True
   ToggleButton1.Caption = "Bold On"

   Label1.AutoSize = True     'Set size of Label1
   Label1.AutoSize = False

   ToggleButton2.Value = False
   ToggleButton2.Caption = "Italic Off"

   ToggleButton3.Value = False
   ToggleButton3.Caption = "StrikeThrough Off"

   ToggleButton4.Value = False
   ToggleButton4.Caption = "Underline Off"

   Label2.Caption = "Font Weight"
   TextBox1.Text = Str(Label1.Font.Weight)
   TextBox1.Enabled = False

End Sub
```

BorderColor Property

Applies To

ComboBox control, **Frame** control, **Image** control, **Label** control, **ListBox** control, **TextBox** control, **UserForm** object.

Description

Specifies the color of an object's border.

Syntax

object.**BorderColor** [= *Long*]

The **BorderColor** property syntax has these parts:

Part	Description
object	Required. A valid object.
Long	Optional. A value or constant that determines the border color of an object.

Settings

You can use any integer that represents a valid color. You can also specify a color by using the RGB function with red, green, and blue color components. The value of each color component is an integer that ranges from zero to 255. For example, you can specify teal blue as the integer value 4966415 or as RGB color component values 15, 200, 75.

Remarks

To use the **BorderColor** property, the **BorderStyle** property must be set to a value other than **fmBorderStyleNone**.

BorderStyle uses **BorderColor** to define the border colors. The **SpecialEffect** property uses system colors exclusively to define its border colors. For Windows operating systems, system color settings are part of the **Control Panel** and are found in the **Appearance** tab of the **Display** folder. In Windows NT 3.51, system color settings are stored in the **Color** folder of the **Control Panel**.

See Also

BorderStyle property.

Example

See the **BackColor** property example.

BorderStyle Property

Applies To

ComboBox control, **Frame** control, **Image** control, **Label** control, **ListBox** control, **TextBox** control, **UserForm** object.

Description

Specifies the type of border used by a control or a form.

Syntax

object.**BorderStyle** [= *fmBorderStyle*]

The **BorderStyle** property syntax has these parts:

Part	Description
object	Required. A valid object.
fmBorderStyle	Optional. Specifies the border style.

Settings

The settings for *fmBorderStyle* are:

Constant	Value	Description
fmBorderStyleNone	0	The control has no visible border line.
fmBorderStyleSingle	1	The control has a single-line border (default).

The default value for a **ComboBox**, **Frame**, **Label**, **ListBox** or **TextBox** is 0 (*None*). The default value for an **Image** is 1 (*Single*).

Remarks

For a **Frame**, the **BorderStyle** property is ignored if the **SpecialEffect** property is *None*.

You can use either **BorderStyle** or **SpecialEffect** to specify the border for a control, but not both. If you specify a nonzero value for one of these properties, the system sets the value of the other property to zero. For example, if you set **BorderStyle** to **fmBorderStyleSingle**, the system sets **SpecialEffect** to zero (*Flat*). If you specify a nonzero value for **SpecialEffect**, the system sets **BorderStyle** to zero.

BorderStyle uses **BorderColor** to define the colors of its borders.

See Also

BorderColor property, **SpecialEffect** property.

Example

See the **BackColor** property example.

BoundColumn Property

Applies To

ComboBox control, **ListBox** control.

Description

Identifies the source of data in a multicolumn **ComboBox** or **ListBox**.

Syntax

object.**BoundColumn** [= *Variant*]

The **BoundColumn** property syntax has these parts:

Part	Description
object	Required. A valid object.
Variant	Optional. Indicates how the **BoundColumn** value is selected.

Settings

The settings for *Variant* are:

Value	Description
0	Assigns the value of the **ListIndex** property to the control.
1 or greater	Assigns the value from the specified column to the control. Columns are numbered from 1 when using this property (default).

Remarks

When the user chooses a row in a multicolumn **ListBox** or **ComboBox**, the **BoundColumn** property identifies which item from that row to store as the value of the control. For example, if each row contains 8 items and **BoundColumn** is 3, the system stores the information in the third column of the currently-selected row as the value of the object.

You can display one set of data to users but store different, associated values for the object by using the **BoundColumn** and the **TextColumn** properties. **TextColumn** identifies the column of data displayed in a **ComboBox** or **ListBox**; **BoundColumn** identifies the column of associated data values stored for the control. For example, you could set up a multicolumn **ListBox** that contains the names of holidays in one column and dates for the holidays in a second column. To present the holiday names to users, specify the first column as the **TextColumn**. To store the dates of the holidays, specify the second column as the **BoundColumn**.

If the control is bound to a data source, the value in the column specified by **BoundColumn** is stored in the data source named in the **ControlSource** property.

The **ListIndex** value retrieves the number of the selected row. For example, if you want to know the row of the selected item, set **BoundColumn** to 0 to assign the number of the selected row as the value of the control. Be sure to retrieve a current value, rather than relying on a previously saved value, if you are referencing a list whose contents might change.

The **Column**, **List**, and **ListIndex** properties all use zero-based numbering. That is, the value of the first item (column or row) is zero; the value of the second item is one, and so on. This means that if **BoundColumn** is set to 3, you could access the value stored in that column using the expression Column(2).

See Also

ControlSource property, **ListIndex** property, **TextColumn** property, **Value** property.

Example

The following example demonstrates how the **BoundColumn** property influences the value of a **ListBox**. The user can choose to set the value of the **ListBox** to the index value of the specified row, or to a specified column of data in the **ListBox**.

To use this example, copy this sample code to the Declarations portion of a form. Make sure that the form contains:

- A **ListBox** named ListBox1.
- A **Label** named Label1.

- Three **OptionButton** controls named OptionButton1, OptionButton2, and OptionButton3.

```
Private Sub UserForm_Initialize()
   ListBox1.ColumnCount = 2

   ListBox1.AddItem "Item 1, Column 1"
   ListBox1.List(0, 1) = "Item 1, Column 2"
   ListBox1.AddItem "Item 2, Column 1"
   ListBox1.List(1, 1) = "Item 2, Column 2"

   ListBox1.Value = "Item 1, Column 1"

   OptionButton1.Caption = "List Index"
   OptionButton2.Caption = "Column 1"
   OptionButton3.Caption = "Column 2"
   OptionButton2.Value = True
End Sub

Private Sub OptionButton1_Click()
   ListBox1.BoundColumn = 0
   Label1.Caption = ListBox1.Value
End Sub

Private Sub OptionButton2_Click()
   ListBox1.BoundColumn = 1
   Label1.Caption = ListBox1.Value
End Sub

Private Sub OptionButton3_Click()
   ListBox1.BoundColumn = 2
   Label1.Caption = ListBox1.Value
End Sub

Private Sub ListBox1_Click()
   Label1.Caption = ListBox1.Value
End Sub
```

BoundValue Property

Applies To

CheckBox control, **ComboBox** control, **CommandButton** control, **ListBox** control, **MultiPage** control, **OptionButton** control, **ScrollBar** control, **SpinButton** control, **TabStrip** control, **TextBox** control, **ToggleButton** control.

Description

Contains the value of a control when that control receives the focus.

Syntax

object.**BoundValue** [= *Variant*]

The **BoundValue** property syntax has these parts:

Part	Description
object	Required. A valid object.
Variant	Optional. The current state or content of the control.

Settings

Control	Description
CheckBox	An integer value indicating whether the item is selected: Null Indicates the item is in a null state, neither selected nor cleared. –1 True. Indicates the item is selected. 0 False. Indicates the item is cleared.
OptionButton	Same as **CheckBox**.
ToggleButton	Same as **CheckBox**.
ScrollBar	An integer between the values specified for the **Max** and **Min** properties.
SpinButton	Same as **ScrollBar**.
ComboBox, ListBox	The value in the **BoundColumn** of the currently selected rows.
CommandButton	Always **False**.
MultiPage	An integer indicating the currently active page. Zero (0) indicates the first page. The maximum value is one less than the number of pages.
TextBox	The text in the edit region.

Remarks

BoundValue applies to the control that has the focus.

The contents of the **BoundValue** and **Value** properties are identical most of the time. When the user edits a control so that its value changes, the contents of **BoundValue** and **Value** are different until the change is final.

Several things occur when the user changes the value of a control. For example, if a user changes the text in a **TextBox**, the following things occur:

1. The Change event is initiated. At this time the **Value** property contains the new text and **BoundValue** contains the previous text.

2. The BeforeUpdate event is initiated.
3. The AfterUpdate event is initiated. The values for **BoundValue** and **Value** are once again identical, containing the new text.

BoundValue cannot be used with a multi-select list box.

See Also

AfterUpdate event, BeforeUpdate event, Change event, **Value** property.

Cancel Property

Applies To

CommandButton control.

Description

Returns or sets a value indicating whether a command button is the Cancel button on a form.

Syntax

object.**Cancel** [= *Boolean*]

The **Cancel** property syntax has these parts:

Part	Description
object	Required. A valid object.
Boolean	Optional. Whether the object is the Cancel button.

Settings

The settings for *Boolean* are:

Value	Description
True	The **CommandButton** is the Cancel button.
False	The **CommandButton** is not the Cancel button (default).

Remarks

A **CommandButton** or an object that acts like a command button can be designated as the default command button. For OLE container controls, the **Cancel** property is provided only for those objects that specifically behave as command buttons.

Only one **CommandButton** on a form can be the Cancel button. Setting **Cancel** to **True** for one command button automatically sets it to **False** for all other objects on the form. When a **CommandButton**'s **Cancel** property is set to **True** and the form is the active form, the user can choose the command button by clicking it, pressing ESC, or pressing ENTER when the button has the focus.

A typical use of **Cancel** is to give the user the option of canceling uncommitted changes and returning the form to its previous state.

You should consider making the Cancel button the default button for forms that support operations that can't be undone (such as delete). To do this, set both **Cancel** and the **Default** property to **True**.

See Also

Default property.

CanPaste Property

Applies To

ComboBox control, **Frame** control, **Page** object, **TextBox** control, **UserForm** object.

Description

Specifies whether the Clipboard contains data that the object supports.

Syntax

object.**CanPaste**

The **CanPaste** property syntax has these parts:

Part	Description
object	Required. A valid object.

Return Values

The **CanPaste** property return values are:

Value	Description
True	The object underneath the mouse pointer can receive information pasted from the Clipboard (default).
False	The object underneath the mouse pointer cannot receive information pasted from the Clipboard.

Remarks

CanPaste is read-only.

If the Clipboard data is in a format that the current target object does not support, the **CanPaste** property is **False**. For example, if you try to paste a bitmap into an object that only supports text, **CanPaste** will be **False**.

See Also

Paste method.

Example

The following example uses the **CanPaste** property and the **Paste** method to paste a **ComboBox** from the Clipboard to a **Page** of a **MultiPage**. This sample also uses the **SetFocus** and **Copy** methods to copy a control from the form to the Clipboard.

The user clicks CommandButton1 to copy the **ComboBox** to the Clipboard. The user double-clicks (using the DblClick event) CommandButton1 to paste the **ComboBox** to the **MultiPage**.

To use this example, copy this sample code to the Declarations portion of a form. Make sure that the form contains:

- A **TextBox** named TextBox1.
- A **ComboBox** named ComboBox1.
- A **MultiPage** named MultiPage1.
- A **CommandButton** named CommandButton1.

Note This example also includes a subroutine to illustrate pasting text into a control.

```
Private Sub UserForm_Initialize()
   ComboBox1.AddItem "It's a beautiful day!"

   CommandButton1.Caption = "Copy ComboBox to Clipboard"
   CommandButton1.AutoSize = True
End Sub

Private Sub MultiPage1_DblClick(ByVal Index As Long, ByVal Cancel _
        As MSForms.ReturnBoolean)
   If MultiPage1.Pages(MultiPage1.Value).CanPaste = True Then
      MultiPage1.Pages(MultiPage1.Value).Paste
   Else
      TextBox1.Text = "Can't Paste"
   End If
End Sub

Private Sub CommandButton1_Click()
      UserForm1.ComboBox1.SetFocus
      UserForm1.Copy
End Sub

'Code for pasting text into a control
'Private Sub ComboBox1_DblClick(ByVal Cancel As MSForms.ReturnBoolean)
'   If ComboBox1.CanPaste = True Then
'        ComboBox1.Paste
'    Else
'        TextBox1.Text = "Can't Paste"
'    End If
'End Sub
```

CanRedo Property

Applies To

Frame control, **Page** object, **UserForm** object.

Description

Indicates whether the most recent Undo can be reversed.

Syntax

object.**CanRedo**

The **CanRedo** property syntax has these parts:

Part	Description
object	Required. A valid object.

Return Values

The **CanRedo** property return values are:

Value	Description
True	The most recent Undo can be reversed.
False	The most recent Undo is irreversible.

Remarks

CanRedo is read-only.

To Redo an action means to reverse an Undo; it does not necessarily mean to repeat the last user action.

The following user actions illustrate using Undo and Redo:

1. Change the setting of an option button.
2. Enter text into a text box.
3. Click Undo. The text disappears from the text box.
4. Click Undo. The option button reverts to its previous setting.
5. Click Redo. The value of the option button changes.
6. Click Redo. The text reappears in the text box.

See Also

CanUndo property, **RedoAction** method, **UndoAction** method.

Example

The following example demonstrates how to undo or redo text editing within a text box or within the text area of a **ComboBox**. This sample checks whether an undo or redo operation can occur and then performs the appropriate action. The sample uses the **CanUndo** and **CanRedo** properties, and the **UndoAction** and **RedoAction** methods.

To use this example, copy this sample code to the Declarations portion of a form. Make sure that the form contains:

- A **TextBox** named TextBox1.
- A **ComboBox** named ComboBox1.
- Two **CommandButton** controls named CommandButton1 and CommandButton2.

```
Private Sub CommandButton1_Click()
   If UserForm1.CanUndo = True Then
      UserForm1.UndoAction
      MsgBox "Undid IT"
   Else
      MsgBox "No undo performed."
   End If
End Sub

Private Sub CommandButton2_Click()
   If UserForm1.CanRedo = True Then
      UserForm1.RedoAction
      MsgBox "Redid IT"
   Else
      MsgBox "No redo performed."
   End If
End Sub

Private Sub UserForm_Initialize()
   TextBox1.Text = "Type your text here."

   ComboBox1.ColumnCount = 3
   ComboBox1.AddItem "Choice 1, column 1"
   ComboBox1.List(0, 1) = "Choice 1, column 2"
   ComboBox1.List(0, 2) = "Choice 1, column 3"

   CommandButton1.Caption = "Undo"
   CommandButton2.Caption = "Redo"
End Sub
```

CanUndo Property

Applies To

Frame control, **Page** object, **UserForm** object.

Description

Indicates whether the last user action can be undone.

Syntax

object.**CanUndo**

The **CanUndo** property syntax has these parts:

Part	Description
object	Required. A valid object.

Return Values

The **CanUndo** property return values are:

Value	Description
True	The most recent user action can be undone.
False	The most recent user action cannot be undone.

Remarks

CanUndo is read-only.

Many user actions can be undone with the **Undo** command. The **CanUndo** property indicates whether the most recent action can be undone.

See Also

CanRedo property, **RedoAction** method, **UndoAction** method.

Example

See the **CanRedo** property example.

Caption Property

Applies To

CheckBox control, **CommandButton** control, **Frame** control, **Label** control, **OptionButton** control, **Page** object, **Tab** object, **ToggleButton** control, **UserForm** object.

Description

Descriptive text that appears on an object to identify or describe it.

Syntax

object.**Caption** [= *String*]

The **Caption** property syntax has these parts:

Part	Description
object	Required. A valid object.
String	Optional. A string expression that evaluates to the text displayed as the caption.

Settings

The default setting for a control is a unique name based on the type of control. For example, CommandButton1 is the default caption for the first command button in a form.

Remarks

The text identifies or describes the object with which it is associated. For buttons and labels, the **Caption** property specifies the text that appears in the control. For **Page** and **Tab** objects, it specifies the text that appears on the tab.

If a control's caption is too long, the caption is truncated. If a form's caption is too long for the title bar, the title is displayed with an ellipsis.

The **ForeColor** property of the control determines the color of the text in the caption.

Tip If a control has both the **Caption** and **AutoSize** properties, setting **AutoSize** to **True** automatically adjusts the size of the control to frame the entire caption.

See Also

AutoSize property, **BorderStyle** property, **ForeColor** property.

Example

See the **Accelerator** property example.

Change Event

Applies To

CheckBox control, **ComboBox** control, **ListBox** control, **MultiPage** control, **OptionButton** control, **ScrollBar** control, **SpinButton** control, **TabStrip** control, **TextBox** control, **ToggleButton** control.

Description

Occurs when the **Value** property changes.

Syntax

Private Sub *object*_**Change( )**

The **Change** event syntax has these parts:

Part	Description
object	Required. A valid object.

Settings

The Change event occurs when the setting of the **Value** property changes, regardless of whether the change results from execution of code or a user action in the interface.

Here are some examples of actions that change the **Value** property:

- Clicking a **CheckBox**, **OptionButton**, or **ToggleButton**.
- Entering or selecting a new text value for a **ComboBox**, **ListBox**, or **TextBox**.
- Selecting a different tab on a **TabStrip**.
- Moving the scroll box in a **ScrollBar**.
- Clicking the up arrow or down arrow on a **SpinButton**.
- Selecting a different page on a **MultiPage**.

Remarks

The Change event procedure can synchronize or coordinate data displayed among controls. For example, you can use the Change event procedure of a **ScrollBar** to update the contents of a **TextBox** that displays the value of the **ScrollBar**. Or you can use a Change event procedure to display data and formulas in a work area and results in another area.

Note In some cases, the Click event may also occur when the **Value** property changes. However, using the Change event is the preferred technique for detecting a new value for a property.

See Also

AfterUpdate event, BeforeUpdate event, **BoundValue** property, Click event, **UndoAction** method, **Value** property.

Example

See the **MatchFound** property example.

CheckBox Control

Description

Displays the selection state of an item.

Remarks

Use a **CheckBox** to give the user a choice between two values such as *Yes/No*, *True/False*, or *On/Off*. When the user selects a **CheckBox**, it displays a special mark (such as an X) and its current setting is *Yes*, *True*, or *On*; if the user does not select the **CheckBox**, it is empty and its setting is *No*, *False*, or *Off*. Depending on the value of the **TripleState** property, a **CheckBox** can also have a null value.

If a **CheckBox** is bound to a data source, changing the setting changes the value of that source. A disabled **CheckBox** shows the current value, but is dimmed and does not allow changes to the value from the user interface.

You can also use check boxes inside a group box to select one or more of a group of related items. For example, you can create an order form that contains a list of available items, with a **CheckBox** preceding each item. The user can select a particular item or items by checking the corresponding **CheckBox**.

The default property of a **CheckBox** is the **Value** property.

The default event of a **CheckBox** is the Click event.

Note The **ListBox** also lets you put a check mark by selected options. Depending on your application, you can use the **ListBox** instead of using a group of **CheckBox** controls.

Properties

Accelerator property, **Alignment** property, **AutoSize** property, **BackColor** property, **BackStyle** property, **BoundValue** property, **Caption** property, **ControlSource** property, **ControlTipText** property, **Enabled** property, **Font** object, **ForeColor** property, **Height**, **Width** properties, **HelpContextID** property, **LayoutEffect** property, **Left**, **Top** properties, **Locked** property, **MouseIcon** property, **MousePointer** property, **Name** property, **Object** property, **OldHeight**, **OldWidth** properties, **OldLeft**, **OldTop** properties, **Parent** property, **Picture** property, **PicturePosition** property, **SpecialEffect** property, **TabIndex** property, **TabStop** property, **Tag** property, **TripleState** property, **Value** property, **Visible** property, **WordWrap** property.

Methods

Move method, **SetFocus** method, **ZOrder** method.

Events

AfterUpdate event, BeforeDragOver event, BeforeDropOrPaste event, BeforeUpdate event, Change event, Click event, DblClick event, Enter, Exit events, Error event, KeyDown, KeyUp events, KeyPress event, MouseDown, MouseUp events, MouseMove event.

See Also

ListBox control.

Example

See the **Enabled** property example.

Example

See the **MatchFound** property example.

Clear Method

Applies To

ComboBox control, **Controls** collection, **DataObject** object, **ListBox** control, **Pages** collection, **Tabs** collection.

Description

Removes all objects from an object or collection.

Syntax

object.**Clear**

The **Clear** method syntax has these parts:

Part	Description
object	Required. A valid object.

Remarks

For a **MultiPage** or **TabStrip**, the **Clear** method deletes individual pages or tabs.

For a **ListBox** or **ComboBox**, **Clear** removes all entries in the list.

For a **Controls** collection, **Clear** deletes controls that were created at run time with the **Add** method. Using **Clear** on controls created at design time causes an error.

If the control is bound to data, the **Clear** method fails.

See Also

Add method, **Remove** method.

Example

See the **Add** method example.

Click Event

Applies To

CheckBox control, **ComboBox** control, **CommandButton** control, **Frame** control, **Image** control, **Label** control, **ListBox** control, **MultiPage** control, **OptionButton** control, **TabStrip** control, **ToggleButton** control, **UserForm** object.

Description

Occurs in one of two cases:

- The user clicks a control with the mouse.

- The user definitively selects a value for a control with more than one possible value.

Syntax

For MultiPage, TabStrip

Private Sub *object*_**Click(** *index* **As Long)**

For all other controls

Private Sub *object*_**Click( )**

The Click event syntax has these parts:

Part	Description
object	Required. A valid object.
index	Required. The index of the page or tab in a **MultiPage** or **TabStrip** associated with this event.

Remarks

Of the two cases where the Click event occurs, the first case applies to the **CommandButton**, **Frame**, **Image**, **Label**, **ScrollBar**, and **SpinButton**. The second case applies to the **CheckBox**, **ComboBox**, **ListBox**, **MultiPage**, **TabStrip**, and **ToggleButton**. It also applies to an **OptionButton** when the value changes to **True**.

The following are examples of actions that initiate the Click event:

- Clicking a blank area of a form or a disabled control (other than a list box) on the form.
- Clicking a **CommandButton**. If the command button doesn't already have the focus, the Enter event occurs before the Click event.
- Pressing the SPACEBAR when a **CommandButton** has the focus.
- Clicking a control with the left mouse button (left-clicking).
- Pressing ENTER on a form that has a command button whose **Default** property is set to **True**, as long as no other command button has the focus.
- Pressing ESC on a form that has a command button whose **Cancel** property is set to **True**, as long as no other command button has the focus.
- Pressing a control's accelerator key.

When the Click event results from clicking a control, the sequence of events leading to the Click event is:

1. MouseDown
2. MouseUp
3. Click

For some controls, the Click event occurs when the **Value** property changes. However, using the Change event is the preferred technique for detecting a new value for a property. The following are examples of actions that initiate the Click event due to assigning a new value to a control:

- Clicking a different page or tab in a **MultiPage** or **TabStrip**. The **Value** property for these controls reflects the current **Page** or **Tab**. Clicking the current page or tab does not change the control's value and does not initiate the Click event.
- Clicking a **CheckBox** or **ToggleButton**, pressing the SPACEBAR when one of these controls has the focus, pressing the accelerator key for one of these controls, or changing the value of the control in code.
- Changing the value of an **OptionButton** to **True**. Setting one **OptionButton** in a group to **True** sets all other buttons in the group to **False**, but the Click event occurs only for the button whose value changes to **True**.
- Selecting a value for a **ComboBox** or **ListBox** so that it unquestionably matches an item in the control's drop-down list. For example, if a list is not sorted, the first match for characters typed in the edit region may not be the only match in the list, so choosing such a value does not initiate the Click event. In a sorted list, you can use entry-matching to ensure that a selected value is a unique match for text the user types.

The Click event is not initiated when **Value** is set to **Null**.

Note Left-clicking changes the value of a control, thus it initiates the Click event. Right-clicking does not change the value of the control, so it does not initiate the Click event.

See Also

Cancel property, Change event, DblClick event, **Default** property, **Enabled** property, MouseDown, MouseUp events, **Value** property.

Example

See the **Accelerator** property example.

ClientHeight, ClientLeft, ClientTop, ClientWidth Properties

Applies To

TabStrip control.

Description

Define the dimensions and location of the display area of a **TabStrip**.

Syntax

object.**ClientHeight** [=*Single*]
object.**ClientLeft** [=*Single*]
object.**ClientTop** [=*Single*]
object.**ClientWidth** [=*Single*]

The **ClientHeight**, **ClientLeft**, **ClientTop**, and **ClientWidth** property syntaxes have these parts:

Part	Description
object	Required. A valid object.
Single	Optional. For **ClientHeight** and **ClientWidth**, specifies the height or width, in points, of the display area. For **ClientLeft** and **ClientTop**, specifies the distance, in points, from the top or left edge of the **TabStrip**'s container.

Remarks

At run time, **ClientLeft**, **ClientTop**, **ClientHeight**, and **ClientWidth** automatically store the coordinates and dimensions of the **TabStrip**'s internal area, which is shared by objects in the **TabStrip**.

Example

The following example sets the dimensions of an **Image** to the size of a **TabStrip**'s client area when the user clicks a **CommandButton**. This code sample uses the following properties: **Height**, **Left**, **Top**, **Width**, **ClientHeight**, **ClientLeft**, **ClientTop**, and **ClientWidth**.

To use this example, copy this sample code to the Declarations portion of a form. Make sure that the form contains:

- A **CommandButton** named CommandButton1.
- A **TabStrip** named TabStrip1.
- An **Image** named Image1.

```
Private Sub UserForm_Initialize()
   CommandButton1.Caption = "Size Image to Tab Area"
   CommandButton1.WordWrap = True
   CommandButton1.AutoSize = True
End Sub

Private Sub CommandButton1_Click()
   Image1.ZOrder (fmFront)             'Place Image in front of TabStrip

   'ClientLeft and ClientTop are measured from the edge of the TabStrip,
   'not from the edges of the form containing the TabStrip.
   Image1.Left = TabStrip1.Left + TabStrip1.ClientLeft
   Image1.Top = TabStrip1.Top + TabStrip1.ClientTop
   Image1.Width = TabStrip1.ClientWidth
   Image1.Height = TabStrip1.ClientHeight

End Sub
```

Column Property

Applies To

ComboBox control, **ListBox** control.

Description

Specifies one or more items in a **ListBox** or **ComboBox**.

Syntax

object.**Column(** *column, row* **)** [= *Variant*]

The **Column** property syntax has these parts:

Part	Description
object	Required. A valid object.
column	Optional. An integer with a range from 0 to one less than the total number of columns.
row	Optional. An integer with a range from 0 to one less than the total number of rows.
Variant	Optional. Specifies a single value, a column of values, or a two-dimensional array to load into a **ListBox** or **ComboBox**.

Settings

If you specify both the column and row values, **Column** reads or writes a specific item.

If you specify only the column value, the **Column** property reads or writes the specified column in the current row of the object. For example, MyListBox.Column (3) reads or writes the third column in MyListBox.

Column returns a *Variant* from the cursor. When a built-in cursor provides the value for *Variant* (such as when using the **AddItem** method), the value is a string. When an external cursor provides the value for *Variant*, formatting associated with the data is not included in the *Variant*.

Remarks

You can use **Column** to assign the contents of a combo box or list box to another control, such as a text box. For example, you can set the **ControlSource** property of a text box to the value in the second column of a list box.

If the user makes no selection when you refer to a column in a combo box or list box, the **Column** setting is **Null**. You can check for this condition by using the **IsNull** function.

You can also use **Column** to copy an entire two-dimensional array of values to a control. This syntax lets you quickly load a list of choices rather than individually loading each element of the list using **AddItem**.

Note When copying data from a two-dimensional array, **Column** transposes the contents of the array in the control so that the contents of ListBox1.Column(*X*, *Y*) is the same as MyArray(*Y*, *X*). You can also use **List** to copy an array without transposing it.

See Also

AddItem method, **List** property.

Example

The following example loads a two-dimensional array with data and, in turn, loads two **ListBox** controls using the **Column** and **List** properties. Note that the **Column** property transposes the array elements during loading.

To use this example, copy this sample code to the Declarations portion of a form. Make sure that the form contains two **ListBox** controls named ListBox1 and ListBox2.

```
Dim MyArray(6,3)

Private Sub UserForm_Initialize()
   Dim i As Single

   ListBox1.ColumnCount = 3     'The 1st list box contains 3 data columns
   ListBox2.ColumnCount = 6     'The 2nd list box contains 6 data columns

   'Load integer values into first column of MyArray
   For i = 0 To 5
      MyArray(i, 0) = i
   Next i

   'Load columns 2 and 3 of MyArray
   MyArray(0, 1) = "Zero"
   MyArray(1, 1) = "One"
   MyArray(2, 1) = "Two"
   MyArray(3, 1) = "Three"
   MyArray(4, 1) = "Four"
   MyArray(5, 1) = "Five"

   MyArray(0, 2) = "Zero"
   MyArray(1, 2) = "Un ou Une"
   MyArray(2, 2) = "Deux"
   MyArray(3, 2) = "Trois"
   MyArray(4, 2) = "Quatre"
   MyArray(5, 2) = "Cinq"

   'Load data into ListBox1 and ListBox2
   ListBox1.List() = MyArray
   ListBox2.Column() = MyArray

End Sub
```

ColumnCount Property

Applies To

ComboBox control, **ListBox** control.

Description

Specifies the number of columns to display in a list box or combo box.

Syntax

object.**ColumnCount** [= *Long*]

The **ColumnCount** property syntax has these parts:

Part	Description
object	Required. A valid object.
Long	Optional. Specifies the number of columns to display.

Remarks

If you set the **ColumnCount** property for a list box to 3 on an employee form, one column can list last names, another can list first names, and the third can list employee ID numbers.

Setting **ColumnCount** to 0 displays zero columns, and setting it to -1 displays all the available columns. For an unbound data source, there is a 10-column limit (0 to 9).

You can use the **ColumnWidths** property to set the width of the columns displayed in the control.

See Also

Column property, **ColumnHeads** property, **ColumnWidths** property.

Example

See the **Column** property example.

Example

See the **ColumnWidths** property example.

ColumnHeads Property

Applies To

ComboBox control, **ListBox** control.

Description

Displays a single row of column headings for list boxes, combo boxes, and objects that accept column headings.

Syntax

object.**ColumnHeads** [= *Boolean*]

The **ColumnHeads** property syntax has these parts:

Part	Description
object	Required. A valid object.
Boolean	Optional. Specifies whether the column headings are displayed.

Settings

The settings for *Boolean* are:

Value	Description
True	Display column headings.
False	Do not display column headings (default).

Headings in combo boxes appear only when the list drops down.

Remarks

When the system uses the first row of data items as column headings, they can't be selected.

See Also

ColumnCount property, **ColumnWidths** property, **ControlSource** property.

ColumnWidths Property

Applies To

ComboBox control, **ListBox** control.

Description

Specifies the width of each column in a multicolumn combo box or list box.

Syntax

object.**ColumnWidths** [= *String*]

The **ColumnWidths** property syntax has these parts:

Part	Description
object	Required. A valid object.
String	Optional. Sets the column width in points. A setting of –1 or blank results in a calculated width. A width of 0 hides a column. To specify a different unit of measurement, include the unit of measure. A value greater than 0 explicitly specifies the width of the column.

Settings

To separate column entries, use semicolons (;) as list separators. Or use the list separator specified in the Regional Settings section of the Windows Control Panel.

Any or all of the **ColumnWidths** property settings can be blank. You create a blank setting by typing a list separator without a preceding value.

If you specify a –1 in the property page, the displayed value in the property page is a blank.

To calculate column widths when **ColumnWidths** is blank or –1, the width of the control is divided equally among all columns of the list. If the sum of the specified column widths exceeds the width of the control, the list is left-aligned within the control and one or more of the rightmost columns are not displayed. Users can scroll the list using the horizontal scroll bar to display the rightmost columns.

The minimum calculated column width is 72 points (1 inch). To produce columns narrower than this, you must specify the width explicitly.

Unless specified otherwise, column widths are measured in points. To specify another unit of measure, include the units as part of the values. The following examples specify column widths in several units of measure and describe how the various settings would fit in a three-column list box that is 4 inches wide.

Setting	Effect
90;72;90	The first column is 90 points (1.25 inch); the second column is 72 points (1 inch); the third column is 90 points.
6 cm;0;6 cm	The first column is 6 centimeters; the second column is hidden; the third column is 6 centimeters. Because only part of the third column is visible, a horizontal scroll bar appears.
1.5 in;0;2.5 in	The first column is 1.5 inches, the second column is hidden, and the third column is 2.5 inches.
2 in;;2 in	The first column is 2 inches, the second column is 1 inch (default), and the third column is 2 inches. Because only half of the third column is visible, a horizontal scroll bar appears.
(Blank)	All three columns are the same width (1.33 inches).

Remarks

In a combo box, the system displays the column designated by the **TextColumn** property in the text box portion of the control.

See Also

ColumnCount property, **ColumnHeads** property, **TextColumn** property.

Example

The following example uses the **ColumnWidths** property to change the column widths of a multicolumn **ListBox**. The example uses three **TextBox** controls to specify the individual column widths and uses the Exit event to specify the units of measure of each **TextBox**.

To use this example, copy this sample code to the Declarations portion of a form. Make sure that the form contains:

- A **ListBox** named ListBox1.
- Three **TextBox** controls named TextBox1 through TextBox3.
- A **CommandButton** named CommandButton1.

Try entering the value 0 to hide a column.

```
Dim MyArray(2, 3) As String

Private Sub CommandButton1_Click()
   'ColumnWidths requires a value for each column separated by semicolons
   ListBox1.ColumnWidths = TextBox1.Text & ";" & TextBox2.Text & ";" _
      & TextBox3.Text
End Sub

Private Sub TextBox1_Exit(ByVal Cancel as MSForms.ReturnBoolean)
   'ColumnWidths accepts points (no units), inches or centimeters;
   'make inches the default
   If Not (InStr(TextBox1.Text, "in") > 0 Or InStr(TextBox1.Text, "cm") _
         > 0) Then
      TextBox1.Text = TextBox1.Text & " in"
   End If
End Sub

Private Sub TextBox2_Exit(ByVal Cancel as MSForms.ReturnBoolean)
   'ColumnWidths accepts points (no units), inches or centimeters; make
   'inches the default
   If Not (InStr(TextBox2.Text, "in") > 0 Or InStr(TextBox2.Text, "cm") _
          > 0) Then
      TextBox2.Text = TextBox2.Text & " in"
   End If
End Sub

Private Sub TextBox3_Exit(ByVal Cancel as MSForms.ReturnBoolean)
   'ColumnWidths accepts points (no units), inches or centimeters; make
   'inches the default
   If Not (InStr(TextBox3.Text, "in") > 0 Or InStr(TextBox3.Text, "cm") _
         > 0) Then
      TextBox3.Text = TextBox3.Text & " in"
   End If
End Sub

Private Sub UserForm_Initialize()
Dim i, j, Rows As Single

ListBox1.ColumnCount = 3
Rows = 2
```

```
For j = 0 To ListBox1.ColumnCount - 1
   For i = 0 To Rows - 1
      MyArray(i, j) = "Row " & i & ", Column " & j
   Next i
Next j

ListBox1.List() = MyArray          'Load MyArray into ListBox1

TextBox1.Text = "1 in"             '1-inch columns initially
TextBox2.Text = "1 in"
TextBox3.Text = "1 in"

End Sub
```

ComboBox Control

Description

Combines the features of a **ListBox** and a **TextBox**. The user can enter a new value, as with a **TextBox**, or the user can select an existing value as with a **ListBox**.

Remarks

If a **ComboBox** is bound to a data source, then the **ComboBox** inserts the value the user enters or selects into that data source. If a multicolumn combo box is bound, then the **BoundColumn** property determines which value is stored in the bound data source.

The list in a **ComboBox** consists of rows of data. Each row can have one or more columns, which can appear with or without headings. Some applications do not support column headings, others provide only limited support.

The default property of a **ComboBox** is the **Value** property.

The default event of a **ComboBox** is the Change event.

Note If you want more than a single line of the list to appear at all times, you might want to use a **ListBox** instead of a **ComboBox**. If you want to use a **ComboBox** and limit values to those in the list, you can set the **Style** property of the **ComboBox** so the control looks like a drop-down list box.

Properties

AutoSize property, **AutoTab** property, **AutoWordSelect** property, **BackColor** property, **BackStyle** property, **BorderColor** property, **BorderStyle** property, **BoundColumn** property, **BoundValue** property, **CanPaste** property, **Column** property, **ColumnCount** property, **ColumnHeads** property, **ColumnWidths** property, **ControlSource** property, **ControlTipText** property, **CurTargetX** property, **CurX** property, **DragBehavior** property, **DropButtonStyle** property, **Enabled** property, **EnterFieldBehavior** property, **Font** object, **ForeColor** property, **Height**, **Width** properties, **HelpContextID** property, **HideSelection** property, **IMEMode** property,

LayoutEffect property, **Left**, **Top** properties, **LineCount** property, **List** property, **ListCount** property, **ListIndex** property, **ListRows** property, **ListStyle** property, **ListWidth** property, **Locked** property, **MatchEntry** property, **MatchFound** property, **MatchRequired** property, **MaxLength** property, **MouseIcon** property, **MousePointer** property, **Name** property, **Object** property, **OldHeight**, **OldWidth** properties, **OldLeft**, **OldTop** properties, **Parent** property, **RowSource** property, **SelectionMargin** property, **SelLength** property, **SelStart** property, **SelText** property, **ShowDropButtonWhen** property, **SpecialEffect** property, **Style** property, **TabIndex** property, **TabStop** property, **Tag** property, **Text** property, **TextAlign** property, **TextColumn** property, **TextLength** property, **TopIndex** property, **Value** property, **Visible** property.

Methods

AddItem method, **Clear** method, **Copy** method, **Cut** method, **DropDown** method, **Move** method, **Paste** method, **RemoveItem** method, **SetFocus** method, **ZOrder** method.

Events

AfterUpdate event, BeforeDragOver event, BeforeDropOrPaste event, BeforeUpdate event, Change event, Click event, DblClick event, DropButtonClick event, Enter, Exit events, Error event, KeyDown, KeyUp events, KeyPress event, MouseDown, MouseUp events, MouseMove event.

See Also

ListBox control, **TextBox** control.

Example

The following example uses a **ComboBox** to show the picture placement options for a control. Each time the user clicks a list choice, the picture and caption are updated on the **CommandButton**. This code sample also uses the **AddItem** method to populate the **ComboBox** choices.

To use this example, copy this sample code to the Declarations portion of a form. Make sure that the form contains:

- A **Label** named Label1.
- A **CommandButton** named CommandButton1.
- A **ComboBox** named ComboBox1.

```
Private Sub UserForm_Initialize()
   Label1.Left = 18
   Label1.Top = 12
   Label1.Height = 12
   Label1.Width = 190
   Label1.Caption = "Select picture placement relative to the caption."

   'Add list entries to combo box. The value of each entry matches the
   'corresponding ListIndex value in the combo box.
```

```
ComboBox1.AddItem "Left Top"          'ListIndex = 0
   ComboBox1.AddItem "Left Center"     'ListIndex = 1
   ComboBox1.AddItem "Left Bottom"     'ListIndex = 2
   ComboBox1.AddItem "Right Top"       'ListIndex = 3
   ComboBox1.AddItem "Right Center"    'ListIndex = 4
   ComboBox1.AddItem "Right Bottom"    'ListIndex = 5

   ComboBox1.AddItem "Above Left"      'ListIndex = 6
   ComboBox1.AddItem "Above Center"    'ListIndex = 7
   ComboBox1.AddItem "Above Right"     'ListIndex = 8
   ComboBox1.AddItem "Below Left"      'ListIndex = 9
   ComboBox1.AddItem "Below Center"    'ListIndex = 10
   ComboBox1.AddItem "Below Right"     'ListIndex = 11

   ComboBox1.AddItem "Centered"        'ListIndex = 12

   ComboBox1.Style = fmStyleDropDownList   'Use drop-down list

   ComboBox1.BoundColumn = 0    'Combo box values are ListIndex values
   ComboBox1.ListIndex = 0             'Set combo box to first entry


   ComboBox1.Left = 18
   ComboBox1.Top = 36
   ComboBox1.Width = 90
   ComboBox1.ListWidth = 90

   'Initialize CommandButton1
   CommandButton1.Left = 230
   CommandButton1.Top = 36
   CommandButton1.Height = 120
   CommandButton1.Width = 120

   'Note: Be sure to refer to a bitmap file that is present on your
   'Note: system, and to include the path in the filename.
   CommandButton1.Picture = LoadPicture("c:\windows\argyle.bmp")
   CommandButton1.PicturePosition = ComboBox1.Value
End Sub

Private Sub ComboBox1_Click()
   Select Case ComboBox1.Value
   Case 0  'Left Top
      CommandButton1.Caption = "Left Top"
      CommandButton1.PicturePosition = fmPicturePositionLeftTop

   Case 1  'Left Center
      CommandButton1.Caption = "Left Center"
      CommandButton1.PicturePosition = fmPicturePositionLeftCenter

   Case 2  'Left Bottom
      CommandButton1.Caption = "Left Bottom"
      CommandButton1.PicturePosition = fmPicturePositionLeftBottom
```

```
        Case 3  'Right Top
            CommandButton1.Caption = "Right Top"
            CommandButton1.PicturePosition = fmPicturePositionRightTop

        Case 4  'Right Center
            CommandButton1.Caption = "Right Center"
            CommandButton1.PicturePosition = fmPicturePositionRightCenter

        Case 5  'Right Bottom
            CommandButton1.Caption = "Right Bottom"
            CommandButton1.PicturePosition = fmPicturePositionRightBottom

        Case 6  'Above Left
            CommandButton1.Caption = "Above Left"
            CommandButton1.PicturePosition = fmPicturePositionAboveLeft

        Case 7  'Above Center
            CommandButton1.Caption = "Above Center"
            CommandButton1.PicturePosition = fmPicturePositionAboveCenter

        Case 8  'Above Right
            CommandButton1.Caption = "Above Right"
            CommandButton1.PicturePosition = fmPicturePositionAboveRight

        Case 9  'Below Left
            CommandButton1.Caption = "Below Left"
            CommandButton1.PicturePosition = fmPicturePositionBelowLeft

        Case 10 'Below Center
            CommandButton1.Caption = "Below Center"
            CommandButton1.PicturePosition = fmPicturePositionBelowCenter

        Case 11 'Below Right
            CommandButton1.Caption = "Below Right"
            CommandButton1.PicturePosition = fmPicturePositionBelowRight

        Case 12 'Centered
            CommandButton1.Caption = "Centered"
            CommandButton1.PicturePosition = fmPicturePositionCenter

        End Select

    End Sub
```

CommandButton Control

Description

Starts, ends, or interrupts an action or series of actions.

Remarks

The macro or event procedure assigned to the **CommandButton**'s Click event determines what the **CommandButton** does. For example, you can create a **CommandButton** that opens another form. You can also display text, a picture, or both on a **CommandButton**.

The default property of a **CommandButton** is the **Value** property.

The default event for a **CommandButton** is the Click event.

Properties

Accelerator property, **AutoSize** property, **BackColor** property, **BackStyle** property, **BoundValue** property, **Cancel** property, **Caption** property, **ControlTipText** property, **Default** property, **Enabled** property, **Font** object, **ForeColor** property, **Height**, **Width** properties, **HelpContextID** property, **LayoutEffect** property, **Left**, **Top** properties, **Locked** property, **MouseIcon** property, **MousePointer** property, **Name** property, **Object** property, **OldHeight**, **OldWidth** properties, **OldLeft**, **OldTop** properties, **Parent** property, **Picture** property, **PicturePosition** property, **TabIndex** property, **TabStop** property, **Tag** property, **TakeFocusOnClick** property, **Value** property, **Visible** property, **WordWrap** property.

Methods

Move method, **SetFocus** method, **ZOrder** method.

Events

BeforeDragOver event, BeforeDropOrPaste event, Click event, DblClick event, Enter, Exit events, Error event, KeyDown, KeyUp events, KeyPress event, MouseDown, MouseUp events, MouseMove event.

Example

See the **Accelerator** property example.

Example

See the **ControlTipText** property example.

Controls Collection

Applies To

Frame control, **MultiPage** control, **Page** object.

Description

Includes all the controls contained in an object.

Remarks

Each control in the **Controls** collection of an object has a unique index whose value can be either an integer or a string. The index value for the first control in a collection is 0; the value for the second control is 1, and so on. This value indicates the order in which controls were added to the collection.

If the index is a string, it represents the name of the control. The **Name** property of a control also specifies a control's name.

You can use the **Controls** collection to enumerate or count individual controls, and to set their properties. For example, you can enumerate the **Controls** collection of a particular form and set the **Height** property of each control to a specified value.

Note The **For Each...Next** statement is useful for enumerating a collection.

Properties

Count property.

Methods

Add method, **Clear** method, **Item** method, **Move** method, **Remove** method.

See Also

Name property.

Example

The following example accesses individual controls from the **Controls** collection using a **For Each...Next** loop. When the user presses CommandButton1, the other controls are placed in a column along the left edge of the form using the **Move** method.

To use this example, copy this sample code to the Declarations portion of a form. Make sure that the form contains a **CommandButton** named CommandButton1 and several other controls.

```
Dim CtrlHeight As Single
Dim CtrlTop As Single
Dim CtrlGap As Single

Private Sub CommandButton1_Click()
   Dim MyControl As Control
   CtrlTop = 5
```

```
    For Each MyControl In Controls
        If MyControl.Name = "CommandButton1" Then
            'Don't move or resize this control.
        Else
            'Move method using named arguments
        MyControl.Move Top:=CtrlTop, Height:=CtrlHeight, Left:=5

        'Move method using unnamed arguments (left, top, width, height)
        'MyControl.Move 5, CtrlTop, ,CtrlHeight

            'Calculate top coordinate for next control
            CtrlTop = CtrlTop + CtrlHeight + CtrlGap
        End If
    Next

End Sub

Private Sub UserForm_Initialize()
    CtrlHeight = 20
    CtrlGap = 5

    CommandButton1.Caption = "Click to move controls"
    CommandButton1.AutoSize = True
    CommandButton1.Left = 120
    CommandButton1.Top = CtrlTop
End Sub
```

Example

See the **Move** method example.

ControlSource Property

Applies To

CheckBox control, **ComboBox** control, **ListBox** control, **OptionButton** control, **ScrollBar** control, **SpinButton** control, **TextBox** control, **ToggleButton** control.

Description

Identifies the data location used to set or store the **Value** property of a control.

Syntax

object.**ControlSource** [= *String*]

The **ControlSource** property syntax has these parts:

Part	Description
object	Required. A valid object.
String	Optional. Specifies the worksheet cell linked to the **Value** property of a control.

Remarks

The **ControlSource** property identifies a cell or field; it does not contain the data stored in the cell or field. If you change the **Value** of the control, the change is automatically reflected in the linked cell or field. Similarly, if you change the value of the linked cell or field, the change is automatically reflected in the **Value** of the control.

You cannot specify another control for the **ControlSource**. Doing so causes an error.

The default value for **ControlSource** is an empty string. If **ControlSource** contains a value other than an empty string, it identifies a linked cell or field. The contents of that cell or field are automatically copied to the **Value** property when the control is loaded.

Note If the **Value** property is **Null**, no value appears in the location identified by **ControlSource**.

See Also

ColumnHeads property, **Value** property.

Example

The following example uses a range of worksheet cells in a **ListBox** and, when the user selects a row from the list, displays the row index in another worksheet cell. This code sample uses the **RowSource**, **BoundColumn**, and **ControlSource** properties.

To use this example, copy this sample code to the Declarations portion of a form. Make sure that the form contains a **ListBox** named ListBox1. In the worksheet, enter data in cells A1:E4. You also need to make sure cell A6 contains no data.

```
Private Sub UserForm_Initialize()

ListBox1.ColumnCount = 5
ListBox1.RowSource = "a1:e4"

ListBox1.ControlSource = "a6"
ListBox1.BoundColumn = 0          'Place the ListIndex into cell a6
End Sub
```

ControlTipText Property

Applies To

CheckBox control, **ComboBox** control, **CommandButton** control, **Image** control, **Label** control, **ListBox** control, **MultiPage** control, **OptionButton** control, **Page** object, **ScrollBar** control, **SpinButton** control, **Tab** object, **TabStrip** control, **TextBox** control, **ToggleButton** control.

Description

Specifies text that appears when the user briefly holds the mouse pointer over a control without clicking.

Syntax

object.**ControlTipText** [= *String*]

The **ControlTipText** property syntax has these parts:

Part	Description
object	Required. A valid object.
String	Optional. The text that appears when the user holds the mouse pointer over a control.

Remarks

The **ControlTipText** property lets you give users tips about a control in a running form. The property can be set during design time but only appears by the control during run time.

The default value of **ControlTipText** is an empty string. When the value of **ControlTipText** is set to an empty string, no tip is available for that control.

Example

The following example defines the **ControlTipText** property for three **CommandButton** controls and two **Page** objects in a **MultiPage**.

To use this example, copy this sample code to the Declarations portion of a form. Make sure that the form contains:

- A **MultiPage** named MultiPage1.
- Three **CommandButton** controls named CommandButton1 through CommandButton3.

Note For an individual **Page** of a **MultiPage**, **ControlTipText** becomes enabled when the **MultiPage** or a control on the current page of the **MultiPage** has the focus.

```
Private Sub UserForm_Initialize()
   MultiPage1.Page1.ControlTipText = "Here in page 1"
   MultiPage1.Page2.ControlTipText = "Now in page 2"

   CommandButton1.ControlTipText = "And now here's"
   CommandButton2.ControlTipText = "a tip from"
   CommandButton3.ControlTipText = "your controls!"
End Sub
```

Copy Method

Applies To

ComboBox control, **Frame** control, **Page** object, **TextBox** control, **UserForm** object.

Description

Copies the contents of an object to the Clipboard.

Syntax

object.**Copy**

The **Copy** method syntax has these parts:

Part	Description
object	Required. A valid object.

Remarks

The original content remains on the object.

The actual content that is copied depends on the object. For example, on a **Page**, the **Copy** method copies the currently selected control or controls. On a **TextBox** or **ComboBox**, it copies the currently selected text.

Using **Copy** for a form, **Frame**, or **Page** copies the currently-active control.

See Also

Cut method, **Paste** method.

Example

See the **CanPaste** property example.

Count Property

Applies To

Controls collection, **Pages** collection, **Tabs** collection.

Description

Returns the number of objects in a collection.

Syntax

object.**Count**

The **Count** property syntax has these parts:

Part	Description
object	Required. A valid object.

Remarks

The **Count** property is read-only.

Note that the index value for the first page or tab of a collection is zero, the value for the second page or tab is one, and so on. For example, if a **MultiPage** contains two pages, the indexes of the pages are 0 and 1, and the value of **Count** is 2.

Example

The following example displays the **Count** property of the **Controls** collection for the form, and the **Count** property identifying the number of pages and tabs of each **MultiPage** and **TabStrip**.

To use this example, copy this sample code to the Declarations portion of a form. The form can contain any number of controls, with the following restrictions:

- Names of **MultiPage** controls must start with "MultiPage".
- Names of **TabStrip** controls must start with "TabStrip".

Note You can add pages to a **MultiPage** or add tabs to a **TabStrip**. Double-click on the control, then right-click in the tab area of the control and choose **New Page** from the shortcut menu.

```
Private Sub UserForm_Initialize()
    Dim MyControl As Control

    MsgBox "UserForm1.Controls.Count = " & Controls.Count

    For Each MyControl In Controls
        If (MyControl.Name Like "MultiPage*") Then
            MsgBox MyControl.Name & ".Pages.Count = " & MyControl.Pages.Count
        ElseIf (MyControl.Name Like "TabStrip*") Then
            MsgBox MyControl.Name & ".Tabs.Count = " & MyControl.Tabs.Count
        End If
    Next

End Sub
```

CurLine Property

Applies To

TextBox control.

Description

Specifies the current line of a control.

Syntax

object.**CurLine** [= *Long*]

The **CurLine** property syntax has these parts:

Part	Description
object	Required. A valid object.
Long	Optional. Specifies the current line of a control.

Remarks

The current line of a control is the line that contains the insertion point. The number of the first line is zero.

The **CurLine** property is valid when the control has the focus.

Example

The following example tracks the **CurLine**, **CurTargetX**, and **CurX** property settings in a multiline **TextBox**. These settings change in the KeyUp event as the user types into the **Text** property, moves the insertion point, and extends the selection using the keyboard.

To use this example, follow these steps:

1. Copy this sample code to the Declarations portion of a form.
2. Add one large **TextBox** named TextBox1 to the form.
3. Add three **TextBox** controls named TextBox2, TextBox3, and TextBox4 in a column.

```
Private Sub TextBox1_KeyUp(ByVal KeyCode As MSForms.ReturnInteger, _
      ByVal Shift As Integer)
   TextBox2.Text = TextBox1.CurLine
   TextBox3.Text = TextBox1.CurX
   TextBox4.Text = TextBox1.CurTargetX
End Sub

Private Sub UserForm_Initialize()
   TextBox1.MultiLine = True

   TextBox1.Text = "Type your text here. User CTRL + ENTER to start a new line."
End Sub
```

CurTargetX Property

Applies To

ComboBox control, **TextBox** control.

Description

Retrieves the preferred horizontal position of the insertion point in a multiline **TextBox** or **ComboBox**.

Syntax

object.**CurTargetX**

The **CurTargetX** property syntax has these parts:

Part	Description
object	Required. A valid object.

Return Values

The **CurTargetX** property retrieves the preferred position, measured in himetric units. A himetric is 0.0001 meter.

Remarks

The target position is relative to the left edge of the control. If the length of a line is less than the value of the **CurTargetX** property, you can place the insertion point at the end of the line. The value of **CurTargetX** changes when the user sets the insertion point or when the **CurX** property is set. **CurTargetX** is read-only.

The return value is valid when the object has focus.

You can use **CurTargetX** and **CurX** to move the insertion point as the user scrolls through the contents of a multiline **TextBox** or **ComboBox**. When the user moves the insertion point to another line of text by scrolling the content of the object, **CurTargetX** specifies the preferred position for the insertion point. **CurX** is set to this value if the line of text is longer than the value of **CurTargetX**. Otherwise, **CurX** is set to the end of the line of text.

See Also

CurX property.

Example

See the **CurLine** property example.

CurX Property

Applies To

ComboBox control, **TextBox** control.

Description

Specifies the current horizontal position of the insertion point in a multiline **TextBox** or **ComboBox**.

Syntax

object.**CurX** [= *Long*]

The **CurX** property syntax has these parts:

Part	Description
object	Required. A valid object.
Long	Optional. Indicates the current position, measured in himetrics. A himetric is 0.0001 meter.

Remarks

The **CurX** property applies to a multiline **TextBox** or **ComboBox**. The return value is valid when the object has the focus.

You can use **CurTargetX** and **CurX** to position the insertion point as the user scrolls through the contents of a multiline **TextBox** or **ComboBox**. When the user moves the insertion point to another line of text by scrolling the content of the object, **CurTargetX** specifies the preferred position for the insertion point. **CurX** is set to this value if the line of text is longer than the value of **CurTargetX**. Otherwise, **CurX** is set to the end of the line of text.

See Also

CurTargetX property.

Example

See the **CurLine** property example.

Cut Method

Applies To

ComboBox control, **Frame** control, **Page** object, **TextBox** control, **UserForm** object.

Description

Removes selected information from an object and transfers it to the Clipboard.

Syntax

object.**Cut**

The **Cut** method syntax has these parts:

Part	Description
object	Required. A valid object.

Remarks

For a **ComboBox** or **TextBox**, the **Cut** method removes currently selected text in the control to the Clipboard. This method does not require that the control have the focus.

On a **Page**, **Frame**, or form, **Cut** removes currently selected controls to the Clipboard. This method only removes controls created at run time.

See Also

Copy method, **Paste** method.

Example

The following example uses the **Add**, **Cut**, and **Paste** methods to cut and paste a control from a **Page** of a **MultiPage**. The control involved in the cut and paste operations is dynamically added to the form.

This example assumes the user will add, then cut, then paste the new control.

To use this example, copy this sample code to the Declarations portion of a form. Make sure that the form contains:

- Three **CommandButton** controls named CommandButton1 through CommandButton3.
- A **MultiPage** named MultiPage1.

```
Dim MyTextBox As Control

Private Sub CommandButton1_Click()
   Set MyTextBox = MultiPage1.Pages(MultiPage1.Value).Controls.Add( _
      "Forms.TextBox.1", "MyTextBox", Visible)
   CommandButton2.Enabled = True
   CommandButton1.Enabled = False
End Sub
Private Sub CommandButton2_Click()
   MultiPage1.Pages(MultiPage1.Value).Controls.Cut
   CommandButton3.Enabled = True
   CommandButton2.Enabled = False
End Sub
Private Sub CommandButton3_Click()
   Dim MyPage As Object
   Set MyPage = MultiPage1.Pages.Item(MultiPage1.Value)

   MyPage.Paste
   CommandButton3.Enabled = False
End Sub
Private Sub UserForm_Initialize()
   CommandButton1.Caption = "Add"
   CommandButton2.Caption = "Cut"
   CommandButton3.Caption = "Paste"

   CommandButton1.Enabled = True
   CommandButton2.Enabled = False
   CommandButton3.Enabled = False
End Sub
```

Example

The following example uses the **Cut** and **Paste** methods to cut text from one **TextBox** and paste it into another **TextBox**.

To use this example, copy this sample code to the Declarations portion of a form. Make sure that the form contains:

- Two **TextBox** controls named TextBox1 and TextBox2.
- A **CommandButton** named CommandButton1.

```
Private Sub UserForm_Initialize()
   TextBox1.Text = "From TextBox1!"
   TextBox2.Text = "Hello "

   CommandButton1.Caption = "Cut and Paste"
   CommandButton1.AutoSize = True
End Sub

Private Sub CommandButton1_Click()
   TextBox2.SelStart = 0
   TextBox2.SelLength = TextBox2.TextLength
   TextBox2.Cut

   TextBox1.SetFocus
   TextBox1.SelStart = 0

   TextBox1.Paste
   TextBox2.SelStart = 0
End Sub
```

Cycle Property

Applies To

Frame control, **Page** object, **UserForm** object.

Description

Specifies the action to take when the user leaves the last control on a **Frame** or **Page**.

Syntax

object.**Cycle** [= *fmCycle*]

The **Cycle** property syntax has these parts:

Part	Description
object	Required. A valid object.
fmCycle	Optional. Specifies whether cycling includes controls nested in a **Frame** or **MultiPage**.

Settings

The settings for *fmCycle* are:

Constant	Value	Description
fmCycleAllForms	0	Cycles through the controls on the form and the controls of the **Frame** and **MultiPage** controls that are currently displayed on the form.
fmCycleCurrentForm	2	Cycles through the controls on the form, **Frame**, or **MultiPage**. The focus stays within the form, **Frame**, or **MultiPage** until the focus is explicitly set to a control outside the form, **Frame**, or **MultiPage**.

If you specify a non-integer value for **Cycle**, the value is rounded up to the nearest integer.

Remarks

The tab order identifies the order in which controls receive the focus as the user tabs through a form or subform. The **Cycle** property determines the action to take when a user tabs from the last control in the tab order.

The **fmCycleAllForms** setting transfers the focus to the first control of the next **Frame** or **MultiPage** on the form when the user tabs from the last control in the tab order.

The **fmCycleCurrentForm** setting transfers the focus to the first control of the same form, **Frame**, or **MultiPage** when the user tabs from the last control in the tab order.

Example

The following example defines the **Cycle** property for a **Frame** and two **Page** objects in a **MultiPage**.

To use this example, copy this sample code to the Declarations portion of a form. Make sure that the form contains:

- A **Frame** named Frame1.
- A **MultiPage** named MultiPage1 that contains two objects named Page1 and Page2.
- Two **CommandButton** controls named CommandButton1 and CommandButton2.

In the form, the **Frame**, and each **Page** of the **MultiPage**, place a couple of controls, so you can see how **Cycle** affects the tab order of the **Frame** and **MultiPage**.

The user should tab through the controls to observe how **Cycle** affects the tab order. Pressing CommandButton1 extends the tab order to include controls in the **Frame** and **Page** objects. Pressing CommandButton2 restricts the tab order.

```
Private Sub RestrictCycles()
'Limit tab order for the Frame and Page objects
   Frame1.Cycle = fmCycleCurrentForm
   MultiPage1.Page1.Cycle = fmCycleCurrentForm
   MultiPage1.Page2.Cycle = fmCycleCurrentForm
End Sub
```

```
Private Sub UserForm_Initialize()
   RestrictCycles
End Sub

Private Sub CommandButton1_Click()
'Extend tab order subforms (the Frame and Page objects)
   Frame1.Cycle = fmCycleAllForms
   MultiPage1.Page1.Cycle = fmCycleAllForms
   MultiPage1.Page2.Cycle = fmCycleAllForms
End Sub

Private Sub CommandButton2_Click()
   RestrictCycles
End Sub
```

DataObject Object

Description

A holding area for formatted text data used in transfer operations. Also holds a list of formats corresponding to the pieces of text stored in the **DataObject**.

Remarks

A **DataObject** can contain one piece of text for the Clipboard text format, and one piece of text for each additional text format, such as custom and user-defined formats.

A **DataObject** is distinct from the Clipboard. A **DataObject** supports commands that involve the Clipboard and drag-and-drop actions for text. When you start an operation involving the Clipboard (such as **GetText**) or a drag-and-drop operation, the data involved in that operation is moved to a **DataObject**.

The **DataObject** works like the Clipboard. If you copy a text string to a **DataObject**, the **DataObject** stores the text string. If you copy a second string of the same format to the **DataObject**, the **DataObject** discards the first text string and stores a copy of the second string. It stores one piece of text of a specified format and keeps the text from the most recent operation.

Methods

Clear method, **GetFormat** method, **GetFromClipboard** method, **GetText** method, **PutInClipboard** method, **SetText** method, **StartDrag** method.

See Also

BeforeDragOver event, **BeforeDropOrPaste** event.

Example

The following example demonstrates a drag-and-drop operation from one **ListBox** to another using a **DataObject** to contain the dragged text. This code sample uses the **SetText** and **StartDrag** methods in the **MouseMove** event to implement the drag-and-drop operation.

To use this example, copy this sample code to the Declarations portion of a form. Make sure that the form contains two **ListBox** controls named ListBox1 and ListBox2. You also need to add choices to the second **ListBox**.

```
Private Sub ListBox2_BeforeDragOver(ByVal Cancel As MSForms.ReturnBoolean, _
      ByVal Data As MSForms.DataObject, ByVal X As Single, ByVal Y As _
      Single, ByVal DragState As Long, ByVal Effect As MSForms.ReturnEffect, _
      ByVal Shift As Integer)
   Cancel = True
   Effect = 1
End Sub

Private Sub ListBox2_BeforeDropOrPaste(ByVal Cancel As MSForms.ReturnBoolean, _
      ByVal Action As Long, ByVal Data As MSForms.DataObject, ByVal X As  _
      Single, ByVal Y As Single, ByVal Effect As MSForms.ReturnEffect, ByVal  _
      Shift As Integer)
   Cancel = True
   Effect = 1
   ListBox2.AddItem Data.GetText
End Sub

Private Sub ListBox1_MouseMove(ByVal Button As Integer, ByVal Shift _
      As Integer, ByVal X As Single, ByVal Y As Single)
   Dim MyDataObject As DataObject
   If Button = 1 Then
      Set MyDataObject = New DataObject
      Dim Effect As Integer
      MyDataObject.SetText ListBox1.Value
      Effect = MyDataObject.StartDrag
   End If
End Sub

Private Sub UserForm_Initialize()
   For i = 1 To 10
      ListBox1.AddItem "Choice " & (ListBox1.ListCount + 1)
   Next i
End Sub
```

DblClick Event

Applies To

CheckBox control, **ComboBox** control, **CommandButton** control, **Frame** control, **Image** control, **Label** control, **ListBox** control, **MultiPage** control, **OptionButton** control, **TabStrip** control, **TextBox** control, **ToggleButton** control, **UserForm** object.

Description

Occurs when the user points to an object and then clicks a mouse button twice.

Syntax

For MultiPage, TabStrip

Private Sub *object*_**DblClick(** *index* **As Long, ByVal** *Cancel* **As MSForms.ReturnBoolean)**

For other controls

Private Sub *object*_**DblClick(ByVal** *Cancel* **As MSForms.ReturnBoolean)**

The DblClick event syntax has these parts:

Part	Description
object	Required. A valid object.
index	Required. The position of a **Page** or **Tab** object within a **Pages** or **Tabs** collection.
Cancel	Required. Event status. **False** indicates that the control should handle the event (default). **True** indicates the application handles the event.

Remarks

For this event to occur, the two clicks must occur within the time span specified by the system's double-click speed setting.

For controls that support Click, the following sequence of events leads to the DblClick event:

1. MouseDown
2. MouseUp
3. Click
4. DblClick

If a control, such as **TextBox**, does not support Click, Click is omitted from the order of events leading to the DblClick event.

If the return value of *Cancel* is **True** when the user clicks twice, the control ignores the second click. This is useful if the second click reverses the effect of the first, such as double-clicking a toggle button. The *Cancel* argument allows your form to ignore the second click, so that either clicking or double-clicking the button has the same effect.

See Also

Click event, MouseDown, MouseUp events.

Example

See the **CanPaste** property example.

Default Property

Applies To

CommandButton control.

Description

Designates the default command button on a form.

Syntax

object.**Default** [= *Boolean*]

The **Default** property syntax has these parts:

Part	Description
object	Required. A valid object.
Boolean	Optional. Whether the command button is the default.

Settings

The settings for *Boolean* are:

Value	Description
True	The **CommandButton** is the default button.
False	The **CommandButton** is not the default button (default).

Remarks

A **CommandButton** or an object that acts like a command button can be designated as the default command button. Only one object on a form can be the default command button. Setting the **Default** property to **True** for one object automatically sets it to **False** for all other objects on the form.

To choose the default command button on an active form, the user can click the button, or press ENTER when no other **CommandButton** has the focus. Pressing ENTER when no other **CommandButton** has the focus also initiates the KeyUp event for the default command button.

Default is provided for OLE container controls that specifically act like **CommandButton** controls.

Tip You should consider making the Cancel button the default button for forms that support operations that can't be undone (such as delete). To do this, set both **Default** and the **Cancel** property to **True**.

See Also

Cancel property.

Delay Property

Applies To

ScrollBar control, **SpinButton** control.

Description

Specifies the delay for the SpinUp, SpinDown, and Change events on a **SpinButton** or **ScrollBar**.

Syntax

object.**Delay** [= *Long*]

The **Delay** property syntax has these parts:

Part	Description
object	Required. A valid object.
Long	Optional. The delay, in milliseconds, between events.

Remarks

The **Delay** property affects the amount of time between consecutive SpinUp, SpinDown, and Change events generated when the user clicks and holds down a button on a **SpinButton** or **ScrollBar**. The first event occurs immediately. The delay to the second occurrence of the event is five times the value of the specified **Delay**. This initial lag makes it easy to generate a single event rather than a stream of events.

After the initial lag, the interval between events is the value specified for **Delay**.

The default value of **Delay** is 50 milliseconds. This means the object initiates the first event after 250 milliseconds (5 times the specified value) and initiates each subsequent event after 50 milliseconds.

See Also

Change event, SpinDown, SpinUp events.

Example

The following example demonstrates the time interval between successive Change, SpinUp, and SpinDown events that occur when a user holds down the mouse button to change the value of a **SpinButton** or **ScrollBar**.

In this example, the user chooses a delay setting, then clicks and holds down either side of a **SpinButton**. The SpinUp and SpinDown events are recorded in a **ListBox** as they are initiated.

To use this example, copy this sample code to the Declarations portion of a form. Make sure that the form contains:

- A **SpinButton** named SpinButton1.

- Two **OptionButton** controls named OptionButton1 and OptionButton2.
- A **ListBox** named ListBox1.

```
Dim EventCount As Long

Private Sub ResetControl()
   ListBox1.Clear
   EventCount = 0
   SpinButton1.Value = 5000
End Sub

Private Sub UserForm_Initialize()
   SpinButton1.Min = 0
   SpinButton1.Max = 10000
   ResetControl

   SpinButton1.Delay = 50
   OptionButton1.Caption = "50 millisecond delay"
   OptionButton2.Caption = "250 millisecond delay"

   OptionButton1.Value = True
End Sub

Private Sub OptionButton1_Click()
   SpinButton1.Delay = 50
   ResetControl
End Sub

Private Sub OptionButton2_Click()
   SpinButton1.Delay = 250
   ResetControl
End Sub

Private Sub SpinButton1_SpinDown()
   EventCount = EventCount + 1
   ListBox1.AddItem EventCount
End Sub

Private Sub SpinButton1_SpinUp()
   EventCount = EventCount + 1
   ListBox1.AddItem EventCount
End Sub
```

DragBehavior Property

Applies To

ComboBox control, **TextBox** control.

Description

Specifies whether the system enables the drag-and-drop feature for a **TextBox** or **ComboBox**.

Syntax

object
DragBehavior [= *fmDragBehavior*]

The **DragBehavior** property syntax has these parts:

Part	Description
object	Required. A valid object.
fmDragBehavior	Optional. Specifies whether the drag-and-drop feature is enabled.

Settings

The settings for *fmDragBehavior* are:

Constant	Value	Description
fmDragBehaviorDisabled	0	Does not allow a drag-and-drop action (default).
fmDragBehaviorEnabled	1	Allows a drag-and-drop action.

Remarks

If the **DragBehavior** property is enabled, dragging in a text box or combo box starts a drag-and-drop operation on the selected text. If **DragBehavior** is disabled, dragging in a text box or combo box selects text.

The drop-down portion of a **ComboBox** does not support drag-and-drop processes, nor does it support selection of list items within the text.

DragBehavior has no effect on a **ComboBox** whose **Style** property is set to **fmStyleDropDownList**.

Note You can combine the effects of the **EnterFieldBehavior** property and **DragBehavior** to create a large number of text box styles.

See Also

EnterFieldBehavior property, **Style** property.

Example

The following example uses the **DragBehavior** and **EnterFieldBehavior** properties to demonstrate the different effects that you can provide when entering a control and when dragging information from one control to another.

The sample uses two **TextBox** controls. You can set **DragBehavior** and **EnterFieldBehavior** for each control and see the effects of dragging from one control to another.

To use this example, copy this sample code to the Declarations portion of a form. Make sure that the form contains:

- A **TextBox** named TextBox1.
- Two **ToggleButton** controls named ToggleButton1 and ToggleButton2. These controls are associated with TextBox1.
- A **TextBox** named TextBox2.
- Two **ToggleButton** controls named ToggleButton3 and ToggleButton4. These controls are associated with TextBox2.

```
Private Sub UserForm_Initialize()
   TextBox1.Text = "Once upon a time in a land ...,"
   ToggleButton1.Value = True
   ToggleButton1.Caption = "Drag Enabled"
   ToggleButton1.WordWrap = True
   TextBox1.DragBehavior = fmDragBehaviorEnabled

   ToggleButton2.Value = True
   ToggleButton2.Caption = "Recall Selection"
   ToggleButton2.WordWrap = True
   TextBox1.EnterFieldBehavior = fmEnterFieldBehaviorRecallSelection

   TextBox2.Text = "XXX, YYYY"
   ToggleButton3.Value = False
   ToggleButton3.Caption = "Drag Disabled"
   ToggleButton3.WordWrap = True
   TextBox2.DragBehavior = fmDragBehaviorDisabled

   ToggleButton4.Value = False
   ToggleButton4.Caption = "Select All"
   ToggleButton4.WordWrap = True
   TextBox2.EnterFieldBehavior = fmEnterFieldBehaviorSelectAll
End Sub

Private Sub ToggleButton1_Click()
   If ToggleButton1.Value = True Then
      ToggleButton1.Caption = "Drag Enabled"
      TextBox1.DragBehavior = fmDragBehaviorEnabled
   Else
      ToggleButton1.Caption = "Drag Disabled"
      TextBox1.DragBehavior = fmDragBehaviorDisabled
   End If
End Sub
```

```
Private Sub ToggleButton2_Click()
    If ToggleButton2.Value = True Then
        ToggleButton2.Caption = "Recall Selection"
        TextBox1.EnterFieldBehavior = fmEnterFieldBehaviorRecallSelection
    Else
        ToggleButton2.Caption = "Select All"
        TextBox1.EnterFieldBehavior = fmEnterFieldBehaviorSelectAll
    End If
End Sub

Private Sub ToggleButton3_Click()
    If ToggleButton3.Value = True Then
        ToggleButton3.Caption = "Drag Enabled"
        TextBox2.DragBehavior = fmDragBehaviorEnabled
    Else
        ToggleButton3.Caption = "Drag Disabled"
        TextBox2.DragBehavior = fmDragBehaviorDisabled
    End If
End Sub

Private Sub ToggleButton4_Click()
    If ToggleButton4.Value = True Then
        ToggleButton4.Caption = "Recall Selection"
        TextBox2.EnterFieldBehavior = fmEnterFieldBehaviorRecallSelection
    Else
        ToggleButton4.Caption = "Select All"
        TextBox2.EnterFieldBehavior = fmEnterFieldBehaviorSelectAll
    End If
End Sub
```

DrawBuffer Property

Applies To

Frame control, **UserForm** object.

Description

Specifies the number of pixels set aside for off-screen memory in rendering a frame.

Syntax

object
DrawBuffer [= *value*]

Part	Description
object	Required. A valid object name.
value	An integer from 16,000 through 1,048,576 equal to the maximum number of pixels the object can render off-screen.

Remarks

The **DrawBuffer** property specifies the maximum number of pixels that can be drawn at one time as the display repaints. The actual memory used by the object depends upon the screen resolution of the display. If you set a large value for **DrawBuffer**, performance will be slower. A large buffer only helps when several large images overlap.

Use the **Properties** window to specify the value of **DrawBuffer**.

See Also

Repaint method.

DropButtonClick Event

Applies To

ComboBox control, **TextBox** control.

Description

Occurs whenever the drop-down list appears or disappears.

Syntax

Private Sub *object*_**DropButtonClick( )**

The DropButtonClick event syntax has these parts:

Part	Description
object	Required. A valid object.

Remarks

You can initiate the DropButtonClick event through code or by taking certain actions in the user interface.

In code, calling the **DropDown** method initiates the DropButtonClick event.

In the user interface, any of the following actions initiates the event:

- Clicking the drop-down button on the control.
- Pressing F4.

Any of the above actions, in code or in the interface, cause the drop-down box to appear on the control. The system initiates the DropButtonClick event when the drop-down box goes away.

See Also

DropButtonStyle property, **DropDown** method, **ShowDropButtonWhen** property.

DropButtonStyle Property

Applies To

ComboBox control, **TextBox** control.

Description

Specifies the symbol displayed on the drop button in a **ComboBox**.

Syntax

object.**DropButtonStyle** [= *fmDropButtonStyle*]

The **DropButtonStyle** property syntax has these parts:

Part	Description
object	Required. A valid object.
fmDropButtonStyle	Optional. The appearance of the drop button.

Settings

The settings for *fmDropButtonStyle* are:

Constant	Value	Description
fmDropButtonStylePlain	0	Displays a plain button, with no symbol.
fmDropButtonStyleArrow	1	Displays a down arrow (default).
fmDropButtonStyleEllipsis	2	Displays an ellipsis (...).
fmDropButtonStyleReduce	3	Displays a horizontal line like an underscore character.

Remarks

The recommended setting for showing items in a list is **fmDropButtonStyleArrow**. If you want to use the drop button in another way, such as to display a dialog box, specify **fmDropButtonStyleEllipsis**, **fmDropButtonStylePlain**, or **fmDropButtonStyleReduce** and trap the DropButtonClick event.

See Also

DropButtonClick event, **DropDown** method, **ShowDropButtonWhen** property.

Example

The following example demonstrates the different symbols that you can specify for a drop-down arrow in a **ComboBox** or **TextBox**. In this example, the user chooses a drop-down arrow style from a **ComboBox**. This example also uses the **Locked** property. To use this example, copy this sample code to the Declarations portion of a form. Make sure that the form contains:

- A **ComboBox** named ComboBox1.
- A **Label** named Label1.

- A **TextBox** named TextBox1 placed beneath Label1.

```
Private Sub ComboBox1_Click()
   ComboBox1.DropButtonStyle = ComboBox1.Value
   TextBox1.DropButtonStyle = ComboBox1.Value
End Sub

Private Sub UserForm_Initialize()
   ComboBox1.ColumnCount = 2
   ComboBox1.BoundColumn = 2
   ComboBox1.TextColumn = 1

   ComboBox1.AddItem "Blank Button"
   ComboBox1.List(0, 1) = 0
   ComboBox1.AddItem "Down Arrow"
   ComboBox1.List(1, 1) = 1
   ComboBox1.AddItem "Ellipsis"
   ComboBox1.List(2, 1) = 2
   ComboBox1.AddItem "Underscore"
   ComboBox1.List(3, 1) = 3

   ComboBox1.Value = 0

   TextBox1.Text = "TextBox1"
   TextBox1.ShowDropButtonWhen = fmShowDropButtonWhenAlways
   TextBox1.Locked = True

   Label1.Caption = "TheDropButton also applies to a TextBox."
   Label1.AutoSize = True
   Label1.WordWrap = False
End Sub
```

DropDown Method

Applies To

ComboBox control.

Description

Displays the list portion of a **ComboBox**.

Syntax

object.**DropDown**

The **DropDown** method syntax has these parts:

Part	Description
object	Required. A valid object.

Remarks

Use the **DropDown** method to open the list in a combo box.

See Also

DropButtonClick event, **DropButtonStyle** property, **ShowDropButtonWhen** property.

Example

The following example uses the **DropDown** method to display the list in a **ComboBox**. The user can display the list of a **ComboBox** by clicking the **CommandButton**.

To use this example, copy this sample code to the Declarations portion of a form. Make sure that the form contains:

- A **ComboBox** named ComboBox1.
- A **CommandButton** named CommandButton1.

```
Private Sub CommandButton1_Click()
   ComboBox1.DropDown
End Sub

Private Sub UserForm_Initialize()
   ComboBox1.AddItem "Turkey"
   ComboBox1.AddItem "Chicken"
   ComboBox1.AddItem "Duck"
   ComboBox1.AddItem "Goose"
   ComboBox1.AddItem "Grouse"
End Sub
```

Enabled Property

Applies To

CheckBox control, **ComboBox** control, **CommandButton** control, **Frame** control, **Image** control, **Label** control, **ListBox** control, **MultiPage** control, **OptionButton** control, **Page** object, **ScrollBar** control, **SpinButton** control, **Tab** object, **TabStrip** control, **TextBox** control, **ToggleButton** control, **UserForm** object.

Description

Specifies whether a control can receive the focus and respond to user-generated events.

Syntax

object.**Enabled** [= *Boolean*]

The **Enabled** property syntax has these parts:

Part	Description
object	Required. A valid object.
Boolean	Optional. Whether the object can respond to user-generated events.

Settings

The settings for *Boolean* are:

Value	Description
True	The control can receive the focus and respond to user-generated events, and is accessible through code (default).
False	The user cannot interact with the control by using the mouse, keystrokes, accelerators, or hot keys. The control is generally still accessible through code.

Remarks

Use the **Enabled** property to enable and disable controls. A disabled control appears dimmed, while an enabled control does not. Also, if a control displays a bitmap, the bitmap is dimmed whenever the control is dimmed. If **Enabled** is **False** for an **Image**, the control does not initiate events but does not appear dimmed.

The **Enabled** and **Locked** properties work together to achieve the following effects:

- If **Enabled** and **Locked** are both **True**, the control can receive focus and appears normally (not dimmed) in the form. The user can copy, but not edit, data in the control.
- If **Enabled** is **True** and **Locked** is **False**, the control can receive focus and appears normally in the form. The user can copy and edit data in the control.
- If **Enabled** is **False** and **Locked** is **True**, the control cannot receive focus and is dimmed in the form. The user can neither copy nor edit data in the control.
- If **Enabled** and **Locked** are both **False**, the control cannot receive focus and is dimmed in the form. The user can neither copy nor edit data in the control.

You can combine the settings of the **Enabled** and the **TabStop** properties to prevent the user from selecting a command button with TAB, while still allowing the user to click the button. Setting **TabStop** to **False** means that the command button won't appear in the tab order. However, if **Enabled** is **True**, then the user can still click the command button, as long as **TakeFocusOnClick** is set to **True**.

When the user tabs into an enabled **MultiPage** or **TabStrip**, the first page or tab in the control receives the focus. If the first page or tab of a **MultiPage** or **TabStrip** is disabled, the first enabled page or tab of that control receives the focus. If all pages or tabs of a **MultiPage** or **TabStrip** are disabled, the control is disabled and cannot receive the focus.

If a **Frame** is disabled, all controls it contains are disabled.

Clicking a disabled **ListBox** does not initiate the Click event.

See Also

Click event, **Locked** property, **TabStop** property, **TakeFocusOnClick** property.

Example

The following example demonstrates the **Enabled** and **Locked** properties and how they complement each other. This example exposes each property independently with a **CheckBox**, so you observe the settings individually and combined. This example also includes a second **TextBox** so you can copy and paste information between the **TextBox** controls and verify the activities supported by the settings of these properties.

Note You can copy the selection to the Clipboard using CTRL+C and paste using CTRL+V.

To use this example, copy this sample code to the Declarations portion of a form. Make sure that the form contains:

- A **TextBox** named TextBox1.
- Two **CheckBox** controls named CheckBox1 and CheckBox2.
- A second **TextBox** named TextBox2.

```
Private Sub CheckBox1_Change()
   TextBox2.Text = "TextBox2"
   TextBox1.Enabled = CheckBox1.Value
End Sub

Private Sub CheckBox2_Change()
   TextBox2.Text = "TextBox2"
   TextBox1.Locked = CheckBox2.Value
End Sub

Private Sub UserForm_Initialize()
   TextBox1.Text = "TextBox1"
   TextBox1.Enabled = True
   TextBox1.Locked = False

   CheckBox1.Caption = "Enabled"
   CheckBox1.Value = True

   CheckBox2.Caption = "Locked"
   CheckBox2.Value = False

   TextBox2.Text = "TextBox2"
End Sub
```

Enter, Exit Events

Applies To

CheckBox control, **ComboBox** control, **CommandButton** control, **Frame** control, **ListBox** control, **MultiPage** control, **OptionButton** control, **ScrollBar** control, **SpinButton** control, **TabStrip** control, **TextBox** control, **ToggleButton** control.

Description

Enter occurs before a control actually receives the focus from a control on the same form. Exit occurs immediately before a control loses the focus to another control on the same form.

Syntax

Private Sub *object*_**Enter( )**
Private Sub *object*_**Exit(ByVal** *Cancel* **As MSForms.ReturnBoolean)**

The Enter and Exit event syntaxes have these parts:

Part	Description
object	Required. A valid object name.
Cancel	Required. Event status. **False** indicates that the control should handle the event (default). **True** indicates the application handles the event and the focus should remain at the current control.

Remarks

The Enter and Exit events are similar to the GotFocus and LostFocus events in Visual Basic. Unlike GotFocus and LostFocus, the Enter and Exit events don't occur when a form receives or loses the focus.

For example, suppose you select the check box that initiates the Enter event. If you then select another control in the same form, the Exit event is initiated for the check box (because focus is moving to a different object in the same form) and then the Enter event occurs for the second control on the form.

Because the Enter event occurs before the focus moves to a particular control, you can use an Enter event procedure to display instructions; for example, you could use a macro or event procedure to display a small form or message box identifying the type of data the control typically contains.

Note To prevent the control from losing focus, assign **True** to the *Cancel* argument of the Exit event.

See Also

SetFocus method.

Example

See the **ActiveControl** property example.

Example

See the **ColumnWidths** property example.

EnterFieldBehavior Property

Applies To

ComboBox control, **TextBox** control.

Description

Specifies the selection behavior when entering a **TextBox** or **ComboBox**.

Syntax

object.**EnterFieldBehavior** [= *fmEnterFieldBehavior*]

The **EnterFieldBehavior** property syntax has these parts:

Part	Description
object	Required. A valid object.
fmEnterFieldBehavior	Optional. The desired selection behavior.

Settings

The settings for *fmEnterFieldBehavior* are:

Constant	Value	Description
fmEnterFieldBehaviorSelectAll	0	Selects the entire contents of the edit region when entering the control (default).
fmEnterFieldBehaviorRecallSelection	1	Leaves the selection unchanged. Visually, this uses the selection that was in effect the last time the control was active.

Remarks

The **EnterFieldBehavior** property controls the way text is selected when the user tabs to the control, not when the control receives focus as a result of the **SetFocus** method. Following **SetFocus**, the contents of the control are not selected and the insertion point appears after the last character in the control's edit region.

See Also

DragBehavior property, **HideSelection** property, **SetFocus** method.

Example

See the **DragBehavior** property example.

EnterKeyBehavior Property

Applies To

TextBox control.

Description

Defines the effect of pressing ENTER in a **TextBox**.

Syntax

object.**EnterKeyBehavior** [= *Boolean*]

The **EnterKeyBehavior** property syntax has these parts:

Part	Description
object	Required. A valid object.
Boolean	Optional. Specifies the effect of pressing ENTER.

Settings

The settings for *Boolean* are:

Value	Description
True	Pressing ENTER creates a new line.
False	Pressing ENTER moves the focus to the next object in the tab order (default).

Remarks

The **EnterKeyBehavior** and **MultiLine** properties are closely related. The values described above only apply if **MultiLine** is **True**. If **MultiLine** is **False**, pressing ENTER always moves the focus to the next control in the tab order regardless of the value of **EnterKeyBehavior**.

The effect of pressing CTRL+ENTER also depends on the value of **MultiLine**. If **MultiLine** is **True**, pressing CTRL+ENTER creates a new line regardless of the value of **EnterKeyBehavior**. If **MultiLine** is **False**, pressing CTRL+ENTER has no effect.

See Also

MultiLine property.

Example

The following example uses the **EnterKeyBehavior** property to control the effect of ENTER in a **TextBox**. In this example, the user can specify either a single-line or multiline **TextBox**.

To use this example, copy this sample code to the Declarations portion of a form. Make sure that the form contains:

- A **TextBox** named TextBox1.
- Two **ToggleButton** controls named ToggleButton1 and ToggleButton2.

```
Private Sub UserForm_Initialize()
   TextBox1.EnterKeyBehavior = True
   ToggleButton1.Caption = "EnterKeyBehavior is True"
   ToggleButton1.Width = 70
   ToggleButton1.Value = True

   TextBox1.MultiLine = True
   ToggleButton2.Caption = "MultiLine is True"
   ToggleButton2.Width = 70
   ToggleButton2.Value = True

   TextBox1.Height = 100
   TextBox1.WordWrap = True
   TextBox1.Text = "Type your text here. If EnterKeyBehavior is True,"& _
        " press ENTER to start a new line. Otherwise, press SHIFT+ENTER."
End Sub

Private Sub ToggleButton1_Click()
   If ToggleButton1.Value = True Then
      TextBox1.EnterKeyBehavior = True
      ToggleButton1.Caption = "EnterKeyBehavior is True"
   Else
      TextBox1.EnterKeyBehavior = False
      ToggleButton1.Caption = "EnterKeyBehavior is False"
   End If
End Sub

Private Sub ToggleButton2_Click()
   If ToggleButton2.Value = True Then
      TextBox1.MultiLine = True
      ToggleButton2.Caption = "MultiLine TextBox"
   Else
      TextBox1.MultiLine = False
      ToggleButton2.Caption = "Single-line TextBox"
   End If
End Sub
```

Error Event

Applies To

CheckBox control, **ComboBox** control, **CommandButton** control, **Frame** control, **Image** control, **Label** control, **ListBox** control, **MultiPage** control, **OptionButton** control, **ScrollBar** control, **SpinButton** control, **TabStrip** control, **TextBox** control, **ToggleButton** control, **UserForm** object.

Description

Occurs when a control detects an error and cannot return the error information to a calling program.

Syntax

For MultiPage

Private Sub *object*_**Error(** *index* **As Long**, **ByVal** *Number* **As Integer**, **ByVal**
➥ *Description* **As MSForms.ReturnString**, **ByVal** *SCode* **As SCode**, **ByVal**
➥ *Source* **As String**, **ByVal** *HelpFile* **As String**, **ByVal** *HelpContext* **As Long**,
➥ **ByVal** *CancelDisplay* **As MSForms.ReturnBoolean)**

For other controls

Private Sub *object*_**Error(** **ByVal** *Number* **As Integer**, **ByVal** *Description* **As**
➥ **MSForms.ReturnString**, **ByVal** *SCode* **As SCode**, **ByVal** *Source* **As String**,
➥ **ByVal** *HelpFile* **As String**, **ByVal** *HelpContext* **As Long**, **ByVal** *CancelDisplay*
➥ **As MSForms.ReturnBoolean)**

The Error event syntax has these parts:

Part	Description
object	Required. A valid object name.
index	Required. The index of the page in a **MultiPage** associated with this event.
Number	Required. Specifies a unique value that the control uses to identify the error.
Description	Required. A textual description of the error.
SCode	Required. Specifies the OLE status code for the error. The low-order 16 bits specify a value that is identical to the *Number* argument.
Source	Required. The string that identifies the control that initiated the event.
HelpFile	Required. Specifies a fully qualified path name for the Help file that describes the error.
HelpContext	Required. Specifies the context ID of the Help file topic that contains a description of the error.
CancelDisplay	Required. Specifies whether to display the error string in a message box.

Remarks

The code written for the Error event determines how the control responds to the error condition.

The ability to handle error conditions varies from one application to another. The Error event is initiated when an error occurs that the application is not equipped to handle.

Exit Event

See Enter, Exit Events.

Font Object

Applies To

CheckBox control, **ComboBox** control, **CommandButton** control, **Frame** control, **Label** control, **ListBox** control, **MultiPage** control, **OptionButton** control, **TabStrip** control, **TextBox** control, **ToggleButton** control.

Description

Defines the characteristics of the text used by a control or form.

Remarks

Each control or form has its own **Font** object to let you set its text characteristics independently of the characteristics defined for other controls and forms. Use font properties to specify the font name, to set bold or underlined text, or to adjust the size of the text.

Note The font properties of your form or container determine the default font attributes of controls you put on the form.

The default property for the **Font** object is the **Name** property. If the **Name** property contains a null string, the **Font** object uses the default system font.

Properties

Bold, **Italic**, **Size**, **StrikeThrough**, **Underline**, **Weight** properties, **Name** property.

Example

The following example demonstrates a **Font** object and the **Bold**, **Italic**, **Size**, **StrikeThrough**, **Underline**, and **Weight** properties related to fonts. You can manipulate font properties of an object directly or by using an alias, as this example also shows.

To use this example, copy this sample code to the Declarations portion of a form. Make sure that the form contains:

- A **Label** named Label1.
- Four **ToggleButton** controls named ToggleButton1 through ToggleButton4.
- A second **Label** and a **TextBox** named Label2 and TextBox1.

```
Dim MyFont As StdFont

Private Sub ToggleButton1_Click()
   If ToggleButton1.Value = True Then
      MyFont.Bold = True              'Using MyFont alias to control font
      ToggleButton1.Caption = "Bold On"
      MyFont.Size = 22                'Increase the font size
   Else
      MyFont.Bold = False
      ToggleButton1.Caption = "Bold Off"
      MyFont.Size = 8                 'Return font size to initial size
   End If

   TextBox1.Text = Str(MyFont.Weight)  'Bold and Weight are related
End Sub

Private Sub ToggleButton2_Click()
   If ToggleButton2.Value = True Then
      Label1.Font.Italic = True              'Using Label1.Font directly
      ToggleButton2.Caption = "Italic On"
   Else
      Label1.Font.Italic = False
      ToggleButton2.Caption = "Italic Off"
   End If
End Sub

Private Sub ToggleButton3_Click()
   If ToggleButton3.Value = True Then
      Label1.Font.Strikethrough = True       'Using Label1.Font directly
      ToggleButton3.Caption = "StrikeThrough On"
   Else
      Label1.Font.Strikethrough = False
      ToggleButton3.Caption = "StrikeThrough Off"
   End If
End Sub

Private Sub ToggleButton4_Click()
   If ToggleButton4.Value = True Then
      MyFont.Underline = True      'Using MyFont alias for Label1.Font
      ToggleButton4.Caption = "Underline On"
   Else
      Label1.Font.Underline = False
      ToggleButton4.Caption = "Underline Off"
   End If
End Sub
```

```
Private Sub UserForm_Initialize()
   Set MyFont = Label1.Font

   ToggleButton1.Value = True
   ToggleButton1.Caption = "Bold On"

   Label1.AutoSize = True     'Set size of Label1
   Label1.AutoSize = False

   ToggleButton2.Value = False
   ToggleButton2.Caption = "Italic Off"

   ToggleButton3.Value = False
   ToggleButton3.Caption = "StrikeThrough Off"

   ToggleButton4.Value = False
   ToggleButton4.Caption = "Underline Off"

   Label2.Caption = "Font Weight"
   TextBox1.Text = Str(Label1.Font.Weight)
   TextBox1.Enabled = False

End Sub
```

ForeColor Property

Applies To

CheckBox control, **ComboBox** control, **CommandButton** control, **Frame** control, **Label** control, **ListBox** control, **MultiPage** control, **OptionButton** control, **ScrollBar** control, **SpinButton** control, **TabStrip** control, **TextBox** control, **ToggleButton** control, **UserForm** object.

Description

Specifies the foreground color of an object.

Syntax

object.**ForeColor** [= *Long*]

The **ForeColor** property syntax has these parts:

Part	Description
object	Required. A valid object.
Long	Optional. A value or constant that determines the foreground color of an object.

Settings

You can use any integer that represents a valid color. You can also specify a color by using the RGB function with red, green, and blue color components. The value of each color component is an integer that ranges from zero to 255. For example, you can specify teal blue as the integer value 4966415 or as red, green, and blue color components 15, 200, 75.

Remarks

Use the **ForeColor** property for controls on forms to make them easy to read or to convey a special meaning. For example, if a text box reports the number of units in stock, you can change the color of the text when the value falls below the reorder level.

For a **ScrollBar** or **SpinButton**, **ForeColor** sets the color of the arrows. For a **Frame**, **ForeColor** changes the color of the caption. For a **Font** object, **ForeColor** determines the color of the text.

See Also

BackColor property.

Example

The following example demonstrates the **BorderStyle** and **SpecialEffect** properties, showing each border available through these properties. The example also demonstrates how to control color settings by using the **BackColor**, **BackStyle**, **BorderColor**, and **ForeColor** properties.

To use this example, copy this sample code to the Declarations portion of a form. Make sure that the form contains:

- Six **TextBox** controls named TextBox1 through TextBox6.
- Two **ToggleButton** controls named ToggleButton1 and ToggleButton2.

```
Private Sub UserForm_Initialize()
'Initialize each TextBox with a border style or special effect,
'and foreground and background colors

'TextBox1 initially uses a borderstyle
TextBox1.Text = "BorderStyle-Single"
TextBox1.BorderStyle = fmBorderStyleSingle
TextBox1.BorderColor = RGB(255, 128, 128)   'Color - Salmon
TextBox1.ForeColor = RGB(255, 255, 0)       'Color - Yellow
TextBox1.BackColor = RGB(0, 128, 64)        'Color - Green #2

'TextBoxes 2 through 6 initially use special effects
TextBox2.Text = "Flat"
TextBox2.SpecialEffect = fmSpecialEffectFlat
TextBox2.ForeColor = RGB(64, 0, 0)          'Color - Brown
TextBox2.BackColor = RGB(0, 0, 255)         'Color - Blue

'Ensure the background style for TextBox2 is initially opaque.
TextBox2.BackStyle = fmBackStyleOpaque
```

```
TextBox3.Text = "Etched"
TextBox3.SpecialEffect = fmSpecialEffectEtched
TextBox3.ForeColor = RGB(128, 0, 255)       'Color - Purple
TextBox3.BackColor = RGB(0, 255, 255)       'Color - Cyan

'Define BorderColor for later use (when borderstyle=fmBorderStyleSingle)
TextBox3.BorderColor = RGB(0, 0, 0)         'Color - Black

TextBox4.Text = "Bump"
TextBox4.SpecialEffect = fmSpecialEffectBump
TextBox4.ForeColor = RGB(255, 0, 255)       'Color - Magenta
TextBox4.BackColor = RGB(0, 0, 100)         'Color - Navy blue

TextBox5.Text = "Raised"
TextBox5.SpecialEffect = fmSpecialEffectRaised
TextBox5.ForeColor = RGB(255, 0, 0)         'Color - Red
TextBox5.BackColor = RGB(128, 128, 128)     'Color - Gray

TextBox6.Text = "Sunken"
TextBox6.SpecialEffect = fmSpecialEffectSunken
TextBox6.ForeColor = RGB(0, 64, 0)          'Color - Olive
TextBox6.BackColor = RGB(0, 255, 0)         'Color - Green #1

ToggleButton1.Caption = "Swap styles"
ToggleButton2.Caption = "Transparent/Opaque background"
End Sub

Private Sub ToggleButton1_Click()

'Swap borders between TextBox1 and TextBox3
If ToggleButton1.Value = True Then
   'Change TextBox1 from BorderStyle to Etched
   TextBox1.Text = "Etched"
   TextBox1.SpecialEffect = fmSpecialEffectEtched

   'Change TextBox3 from Etched to BorderStyle
   TextBox3.Text = "BorderStyle-Single"
   TextBox3.BorderStyle = fmBorderStyleSingle
Else
   'Change TextBox1 back to BorderStyle
   TextBox1.Text = "BorderStyle-Single"
   TextBox1.BorderStyle = fmBorderStyleSingle

   'Change TextBox3 back to Etched
   TextBox3.Text = "Etched"
   TextBox3.SpecialEffect = fmSpecialEffectEtched
End If
End Sub

Private Sub ToggleButton2_Click()

'Set background to Opaque or Transparent
```

```
If ToggleButton2.Value = True Then
   'Change TextBox2 to a transparent background
   TextBox2.BackStyle = fmBackStyleTransparent
Else
   'Change TextBox2 back to opaque background
   TextBox2.BackStyle = fmBackStyleOpaque
End If

End Sub
```

Frame Control

Description

Creates a functional and visual control group.

Remarks

All option buttons in a **Frame** are mutually exclusive, so you can use the **Frame** to create an option group. You can also use a **Frame** to group controls with closely related contents. For example, in an application that processes customer orders, you might use a **Frame** to group the name, address, and account number of customers.

You can also use a **Frame** to create a group of toggle buttons, but the toggle buttons are not mutually exclusive.

The default event for a **Frame** is the Click event.

Properties

ActiveControl property, **BackColor** property, **BorderColor** property, **BorderStyle** property, **CanPaste** property, **CanRedo** property, **CanUndo** property, **Caption** property, **ControlTipText** property, **Cycle** property, **DrawBuffer** property, **Enabled** property, **Font** object, **ForeColor** property, **Height**, **Width** properties, **HelpContextID** property, **InsideHeight**, **InsideWidth** properties, **KeepScrollBarsVisible** property, **LayoutEffect** property, **Left**, **Top** properties, **MouseIcon** property, **MousePointer** property, **Name** property, **Object** property, OldHeight, **OldWidth** properties, **OldLeft**, **OldTop** properties, **Parent** property, **Picture** property, **PictureAlignment** property, **PictureSizeMode** property, **PictureTiling** property, **ScrollBars** property, **ScrollHeight**, **ScrollWidth** properties, **ScrollLeft**, **ScrollTop** properties, **SpecialEffect** property, **TabIndex** property, **TabStop** property, **Tag** property, **VerticalScrollbarSide** property, **Visible** property, **Zoom** property.

Methods

Copy method, **Cut** method, **Move** method, **Paste** method, **RedoAction** method, **Repaint** method, **Scroll** method, **SetDefaultTabOrder** method, **SetFocus** method, **UndoAction** method, **ZOrder** method.

Events

AddControl event, BeforeDragOver event, BeforeDropOrPaste event, Click event, DblClick event, Enter, Exit events, Error event, KeyDown, KeyUp events, KeyPress event, Layout event, MouseDown, MouseUp events, MouseMove event, RemoveControl event, Scroll event, Zoom event.

See Also

Controls collection, **GroupName** property.

Example

The following example uses the **Zoom** property to shrink or enlarge the information displayed on a form, **Page**, or **Frame**. This example includes a **Frame**, a **TextBox** in the **Frame**, and a **ScrollBar**. The magnification level of the **Frame** changes through **Zoom**. The user can set **Zoom** by using the **ScrollBar**. The **TextBox** is present to demonstrate the effects of zooming.

This example also uses the **Max** and **Min** properties to identify the range of acceptable values for the **ScrollBar**.

To use this example, copy this sample code to the Declarations portion of a form. Make sure that the form contains:

- A **Label** named Label1.
- A **ScrollBar** named ScrollBar1.
- A second **Label** named Label2.
- A **Frame** named Frame1.
- A **TextBox** named TextBox1 that is located inside Frame1.

```
Private Sub UserForm_Initialize()
   ScrollBar1.Max = 400
   ScrollBar1.Min = 10
   ScrollBar1.Value = 100

   Label1.Caption = "10  -----Percent of Original Size---- 400"
   Label2.Caption = ScrollBar1.Value

   Frame1.TextBox1.Text = "Enter your text here."
   Frame1.TextBox1.MultiLine = True
   Frame1.TextBox1.WordWrap = True

   Frame1.Zoom = ScrollBar1.Value
End Sub

Private Sub ScrollBar1_Change()
   Frame1.Zoom = ScrollBar1.Value
   Label2.Caption = ScrollBar1.Value
End Sub
```

GetFormat Method

Applies To

DataObject object.

Description

Returns an integer value indicating whether a specific format is on the **DataObject**.

Syntax

Boolean = *object*.**GetFormat(***format***)**

The **GetFormat** method syntax has these parts:

Part	Description
object	Required. A valid object.
format	Required. An integer or string specifying a specific format that might exist in the **DataObject**. If the specified format exists in the **DataObject**, **GetFormat** returns **True**.

Settings

The settings for *format* are:

Value	Description
1	Text format.
A string or any integer other than 1	A user-defined **DataObject** format passed to the **DataObject** from **SetText**.

Remarks

The **GetFormat** method searches for a format in the current list of formats on the **DataObject**. If the format is on the **DataObject**, **GetFormat** returns **True**; if not, **GetFormat** returns **False**.

The **DataObject** currently supports only text formats.

See Also

GetFromClipboard method, **GetText** method, **SetText** method.

Example

The following example uses the **GetFormat**, **GetText**, and **SetText** methods to transfer text between a **DataObject** and the Clipboard.

The user types text into a **TextBox** and then can transfer it to a **DataObject** in a standard text format by clicking CommandButton1. Clicking CommandButton2 retrieves the text from the **DataObject**. Clicking CommandButton3 copies text from TextBox1 to the **DataObject** in a custom format. Clicking CommandButton4 retrieves the text from the **DataObject** in a custom format.

To use this example, copy this sample code to the Declarations portion of a form. Make sure that the form contains:

- A **TextBox** named TextBox1.
- Four **CommandButton** controls named CommandButton1 through CommandButton4.
- A **Label** named Label1.

```
Dim MyDataObject As DataObject

Private Sub CommandButton1_Click()
'Put standard format on Clipboard
   If TextBox1.TextLength > 0 Then
      Set MyDataObject = New DataObject
      MyDataObject.SetText TextBox1.Text
      Label1.Caption = "Put on D.O."
      CommandButton2.Enabled = True
      CommandButton4.Enabled = False
   End If
End Sub

Private Sub CommandButton2_Click()
'Get standard format from Clipboard
   If MyDataObject.GetFormat(1) = True Then
      Label1.Caption = "Std format - " & MyDataObject.GetText(1)
   End If
End Sub

Private Sub CommandButton3_Click()
'Put custom format on Clipboard
   If TextBox1.TextLength > 0 Then
      Set MyDataObject = New DataObject
      MyDataObject.SetText TextBox1.Text, 233
      Label1.Caption = "Custom on D.O."
      CommandButton4.Enabled = True
      CommandButton2.Enabled = False
   End If
End Sub

Private Sub CommandButton4_Click()
'Get custom format from Clipboard
   If MyDataObject.GetFormat(233) = True Then
      Label1.Caption = "Cust format - " & MyDataObject.GetText(233)
End If
End Sub

Private Sub UserForm_Initialize()
   CommandButton2.Enabled = False
   CommandButton4.Enabled = False
End Sub
```

GetFromClipboard Method

Applies To

DataObject object.

Description

Copies data from the Clipboard to a **DataObject**.

Syntax

String = *object*.**GetFromClipboard( )**

The **GetFromClipboard** method syntax has these parts:

Part	Description
object	Required. A valid object name.

Remarks

The **DataObject** can contain multiple data items, but each item must be in a different format. For example, the **DataObject** might include one text item and one item in a custom format; but cannot include two text items.

See Also

GetText method, **PutInClipboard** method.

Example

The following example demonstrates data movement from a **TextBox** to the Clipboard, from the Clipboard to a **DataObject**, and from a **DataObject** into another **TextBox**. The **GetFromClipboard** method transfers the data from the Clipboard to a **DataObject**. The **Copy** and **GetText** methods are also used.

To use this example, copy this sample code to the Declarations portion of a form. Make sure that the form contains:

- Two **TextBox** controls named TextBox1 and TextBox2.
- A **CommandButton** named CommandButton1.

```
Dim MyData as DataObject

Private Sub CommandButton1_Click()
    'Need to select text before copying it to Clipboard
    TextBox1.SelStart = 0
    TextBox1.SelLength = TextBox1.TextLength
    TextBox1.Copy

    MyData.GetFromClipboard
    TextBox2.Text = MyData.GetText(1)
End Sub
```

```
Private Sub UserForm_Initialize()
   Set MyData = New DataObject
   TextBox1.Text = "Move this data to the Clipboard, to a DataObject," _
      & " then to TextBox2!"
End Sub
```

GetText Method

Applies To

DataObject object.

Description

Retrieves a text string from the **DataObject** using the specified format.

Syntax

String = *object*.**GetText(** [*format*])

The **GetText** method syntax has these parts:

Part	Description
object	Required. A valid object name.
format	Optional. A string or integer specifying the format of the data to retrieve from the **DataObject**.

Settings

The settings for *format* are:

Value	Description
1	Text format.
A string or any integer other than 1	A user-defined **DataObject** format passed to the **DataObject** from **SetText**.

Remarks

The **DataObject** supports multiple formats, but only supports one data item of each format. For example, the **DataObject** might include one text item and one item in a custom format; but cannot include two text items.

If no format is specified, the **GetText** method requests information in the Text format from the **DataObject**.

See Also

GetFormat method, **GetFromClipboard** method, **PutInClipboard** method, **SetText** method.

Example

See the **GetFormat** method example.

GroupName Property

Applies To

OptionButton control.

Description

Creates a group of mutually exclusive **OptionButton** controls.

Syntax

object.**GroupName** [= *String*]

The **GroupName** property syntax has these parts:

Part	Description
object	Required. A valid **OptionButton**.
String	Optional. The name of the group that includes the **OptionButton**. Use the same setting for all buttons in the group. The default setting is an empty string.

Remarks

To create a group of mutually exclusive **OptionButton** controls, you can put the buttons in a **Frame** on your form, or you can use the **GroupName** property. **GroupName** is more efficient for the following reasons:

- You do not have to include a **Frame** for each group. By not using a **Frame**, you reduce the number of controls on the form, and in turn, improve performance and reduce the size of the form.
- You have more design flexibility. If you use a **Frame** to create the group, all the buttons must be inside the **Frame**. If you want more than one group, you must have one **Frame** for each group. However, if you use **GroupName** to create the group, the group can include option buttons anywhere on the form. If you want more than one group, specify a unique name for each group; you can still place the individual controls anywhere on the form.
- You can create buttons with transparent backgrounds, which can improve the visual appearance of your form. The **Frame** is not a transparent control.

Regardless of which method you use to create the group of buttons, clicking one button in a group sets all other buttons in the same group to **False**. All option buttons with the same **GroupName** within a single container are mutually exclusive. You can use the same group name in two containers, but doing so creates two groups (one in each container) rather than one group that includes both containers.

For example, assume your form includes some option buttons and a **MultiPage** that also includes option buttons. The option buttons on the **MultiPage** are one group and the buttons on the form are another group. The two groups do not affect each other. Changing the setting of a button on the **MultiPage** does not affect the buttons on the form.

See Also

Frame control.

Example

The following example uses the **GroupName** property to create two groups of **OptionButton** controls on the same form.

To use this example, copy this sample code to the Declarations portion of a form. Make sure that the form contains five **OptionButton** controls named OptionButton1 through OptionButton5.

```
Private Sub UserForm_Initialize()
   OptionButton1.GroupName = "Widgets"
   OptionButton2.GroupName = "Widgets"
   OptionButton4.GroupName = "Widgets"

   OptionButton3.GroupName = "Gadgets-Group2"
   OptionButton5.GroupName = "Gadgets-Group2"
End Sub
```

Height, Width Properties

Applies To

CheckBox control, **ComboBox** control, **CommandButton** control, **Image** control, **Label** control, **ListBox** control, **MultiPage** control, **OptionButton** control, **ScrollBar** control, **SpinButton** control, **TabStrip** control, **TextBox** control, **ToggleButton** control, **UserForm** object.

Description

The height or width, in points, of an object.

Syntax

object.**Height** [= *Single*]
object.**Width** [= *Single*]

The **Height** and **Width** property syntaxes have these parts:

Part	Description
object	Required. A valid object.
Single	Optional. A numeric expression specifying the dimensions of an object.

Remarks

The **Height** and **Width** properties are automatically updated when you move or size a control. If you change the size of a control, the **Height** or **Width** property stores the new height or width and the **OldHeight** or **OldWidth** property stores the previous height or width. If you specify a setting for the **Left** or **Top** property that is less than zero, that value will be used to calculate the height or width of the control, but a portion of the control will not be visible on the form.

If you move a control from one part of a form to another, the setting of **Height** or **Width** only changes if you size the control as you move it. The settings of the control's **Left** and **Top** properties will change to reflect the control's new position relative to the edges of the form that contains it.

The value assigned to **Height** or **Width** must be greater than or equal to zero. For most systems, the recommended range of values is from 0 to +32,767. Higher values may also work depending on your system configuration.

See Also

InsideHeight, **InsideWidth** properties, **Left**, **Top** properties.

Example

The following example sets the dimensions of an **Image** to the size of a **TabStrip**'s client area when the user clicks a **CommandButton**. This code sample uses the following properties: **Height**, **Left**, **Top**, **Width**, **ClientHeight**, **ClientLeft**, **ClientTop**, and **ClientWidth**.

To use this example, copy this sample code to the Declarations portion of a form. Make sure that the form contains:

- A **CommandButton** named CommandButton1.
- A **TabStrip** named TabStrip1.
- An **Image** named Image1.

```
Private Sub UserForm_Initialize()
   CommandButton1.Caption = "Size Image to Tab Area"
   CommandButton1.WordWrap = True
   CommandButton1.AutoSize = True
End Sub

Private Sub CommandButton1_Click()
   Image1.ZOrder (fmFront)             'Place Image in front of TabStrip

   'ClientLeft and ClientTop are measured from the edge of the TabStrip,
   'not from the edges of the form containing the TabStrip.
   Image1.Left = TabStrip1.Left + TabStrip1.ClientLeft
   Image1.Top = TabStrip1.Top + TabStrip1.ClientTop
   Image1.Width = TabStrip1.ClientWidth
   Image1.Height = TabStrip1.ClientHeight

End Sub
```

HelpContextID Property

Applies To

CheckBox control, **ComboBox** control, **CommandButton** control, **ListBox** control, **MultiPage** control, **OptionButton** control, **Page** object, **ScrollBar** control, **SpinButton** control, **TabStrip** control, **TextBox** control, **ToggleButton** control, **UserForm** object.

Description

Associates a specific topic in a custom Microsoft Windows Help file with a specific control.

Syntax

object.**HelpContextID** [= *Long*]

The **HelpContextID** property syntax has these parts:

Part	Description
object	Required. A valid object.
Long	Optional. A positive integer specifies the context ID of a topic in the Help file associated with the object. Zero indicates no Help topic is associated with the object (default). Must be a valid context ID in the specified Help file.

Remarks

The topic identified by the **HelpContextID** property is available to users when a form is running. To display the topic, the user must either select the control or set focus to the control, and then press F1.

The **HelpContextID** property refers to a topic in a custom Help file you have created to describe your form or application. In Visual Basic, the custom Help file is a property of the project.

HideSelection Property

Applies To

ComboBox control, **TextBox** control.

Description

Specifies whether selected text remains highlighted when a control does not have the focus.

Syntax

object.**HideSelection** [= *Boolean*]

The **HideSelection** property syntax has these parts:

Part	Description
object	Required. A valid object.
Boolean	Optional. Whether the selected text remains highlighted even when the control does not have the focus.

Settings

The settings for *Boolean* are:

Value	Description
True	Selected text is not highlighted unless the control has the focus (default).
False	Selected text always appears highlighted.

Remarks

You can use the **HideSelection** property to maintain highlighted text when another form or a dialog box receives the focus, such as in a spell-checking procedure.

See Also

EnterFieldBehavior property.

Example

The following example demonstrates the **HideSelection** property in the context of either a single form or more than one form. The user can select text in a **TextBox** and TAB to other controls on a form, as well as transfer the focus to a second form. This code sample also uses the **SetFocus** method, and the **EnterFieldBehavior**, **MultiLine**, and **Value** properties.

To use this example, follow these steps:

1. Copy this sample code (except for the last event subroutine) to the Declarations portion of a form.
2. Add a large **TextBox** named TextBox1, a **ToggleButton** named ToggleButton1, and a **CommandButton** named CommandButton1.
3. Insert a second form into this project named UserForm2.
4. Paste the last event subroutine of this listing into the Declarations section of UserForm2.
5. In this form, add a **CommandButton** named CommandButton1.
6. Run UserForm1.

```
' ***** Code for UserForm1 *****

Private Sub CommandButton1_Click()
    TextBox1.SetFocus
    UserForm2.Show                              'Bring up the second form.
End Sub
```

```
Private Sub ToggleButton1_Click()
   If ToggleButton1.Value = True Then
      TextBox1.HideSelection = False
      ToggleButton1.Caption = "Selection Visible"
   Else
      TextBox1.HideSelection = True
      ToggleButton1.Caption = "Selection Hidden"
   End If
End Sub

Private Sub UserForm_Initialize()
   TextBox1.MultiLine = True
   TextBox1.EnterFieldBehavior = fmEnterFieldBehaviorRecallSelection

'Fill the TextBox
   TextBox1.Text = "SelText indicates the starting point of selected " _
      & "text, or the insertion point if no text is selected." _
      & Chr$(10) & Chr$(13) & "The SelStart property is always valid, " _
      & "even when the control does not have focus. Setting SelStart " _
      & "to a value less than zero creates an error. " _
      & Chr$(10) & Chr$(13) & "Changing the value of SelStart cancels " _
      & "any existing selection in the control, places an insertion " _
      & "point in the text, and sets the SelLength property to zero."

   TextBox1.HideSelection = True
   ToggleButton1.Caption = "Selection Hidden"
   ToggleButton1.Value = False

End Sub

' ***** Code for UserForm2 *****

Private Sub CommandButton1_Click()
   UserForm2.Hide
End Sub
```

Image Control

Description

Displays a picture on a form.

Remarks

The **Image** lets you display a picture as part of the data in a form. For example, you might use an **Image** to display employee photographs in a personnel form.

The **Image** lets you crop, size, or zoom a picture, but does not allow you to edit the contents of the picture. For example, you cannot use the **Image** to change the colors in the picture, to make the picture transparent, or to refine the image of the picture. You must use image editing software for these purposes.

The **Image** supports the following file formats:

- *.bmp
- *.cur
- *.gif
- *.ico
- *.jpg
- *.wmf

Note You can also display a picture on a **Label**. However, a **Label** does not let you crop, size, or zoom the picture.

The default event for the **Image** is the Click event.

Properties

AutoSize property, **BackColor** property, **BackStyle** property, **BorderColor** property, **BorderStyle** property, **ControlTipText** property, **Enabled** property, **Height**, **Width** properties, **LayoutEffect** property, **Left**, **Top** properties, **MouseIcon** property, **MousePointer** property, **Name** property, **Object** property, **OldHeight**, **OldWidth** properties, **OldLeft**, **OldTop** properties, **Parent** property, **Picture** property, **PictureAlignment** property, **PictureSizeMode** property, **PictureTiling** property, **SpecialEffect** property, **Tag** property, **Visible** property.

Methods

Move method, **ZOrder** method.

Events

BeforeDragOver event, BeforeDropOrPaste event, Click event, DblClick event, Error event, MouseDown, MouseUp events, MouseMove event.

See Also

Label control.

Example

The following example sets the dimensions of an **Image** to the size of a **TabStrip**'s client area when the user clicks a **CommandButton**. This code sample uses the following properties: **Height**, **Left**, **Top**, **Width**, **ClientHeight**, **ClientLeft**, **ClientTop**, and **ClientWidth**.

To use this example, copy this sample code to the Declarations portion of a form. Make sure that the form contains:

- A **CommandButton** named CommandButton1.
- A **TabStrip** named TabStrip1.
- An **Image** named Image1.

```
Private Sub UserForm_Initialize()
   CommandButton1.Caption = "Size Image to Tab Area"
   CommandButton1.WordWrap = True
   CommandButton1.AutoSize = True
End Sub

Private Sub CommandButton1_Click()
   Image1.ZOrder (fmFront)             'Place Image in front of TabStrip

   'ClientLeft and ClientTop are measured from the edge of the TabStrip,
   'not from the edges of the form containing the TabStrip.
   Image1.Left = TabStrip1.Left + TabStrip1.ClientLeft
   Image1.Top = TabStrip1.Top + TabStrip1.ClientTop
   Image1.Width = TabStrip1.ClientWidth
   Image1.Height = TabStrip1.ClientHeight

End Sub
```

IMEMode Property

Applies To

ComboBox control, **ListBox** control, **TextBox** control.

Description

Specifies the default run time mode of the Input Method Editor (IME) for a control. This property applies only to applications written for the Far East and is ignored in other applications.

Syntax

object.**IMEMode** [= *fmIMEMode*]

The **IMEMode** property syntax has these parts:

Part	Description
object	Required. A valid object.
fmIMEMode	Optional. The mode of the Input Method Editor (IME).

Settings

The settings for *fmIMEMode* are:

Constant	Value	Description
fmIMEModeNoControl	0	Does not control IME (default).
fmIMEModeOn	1	IME on.
fmIMEModeOff	2	IME off. English mode.
fmIMEModeDisable	3	IME off. User can't turn on IME by keyboard.
fmIMEModeHiragana	4	IME on with Full-width Hiragana mode.
fmIMEModeKatakana	5	IME on with Full-width Katakana mode.
fmIMEModeKatakanaHalf	6	IME on with Half-width Katakana mode.
fmIMEModeAlphaFull	7	IME on with Full-width Alphanumeric mode.
fmIMEModeAlpha	8	IME on with Half-width Alphanumeric mode.
fmIMEModeHangulFull	9	IME on with Full-width Hangul mode.
fmIMEModeHangul	10	IME on with Half-width Hangul mode.

The **fmIMEModeNoControl** setting indicates that the mode of the IME does not change when the control receives focus at run time. For any other value, the mode of the IME is set to the value specified by the **IMEMode** property when the control receives focus at run time.

Remarks

There are two ways to set the mode of the IME. One is through the toolbar of the IME. The other is with the **IMEMode** property of a control, which sets or returns the current mode of the IME. This property allows dynamic control of the IME through code.

The following example explains how **IMEMode** interacts with the toolbar of the IME. Assume that you have designed a form with TextBox1 and CheckBox1. You have set TextBox1.IMEMode to 0, and you have set CheckBox1.IMEMode to 1. While in design mode you have used the IME toolbar to put the IME in mode 2.

When you run the form, the IME begins in mode 2. If you click TextBox1, the IME mode does not change because **IMEMode** for this control is 0. If you click CheckBox1, the IME changes to mode 1, because **IMEMode** for this control is 1. If you click again on TextBox1, the IME remains in mode 1 (**IMEMode** is 0, so the IME retains its last setting).

However, you can override **IMEMode**. For example, assume you click CheckBox1 and the IME enters mode 1, as defined by **IMEMode** for the **CheckBox**. If you then use the IME toolbar to put the IME in mode 3, then the IME will be set to mode 3 anytime you click the control. This does not change the value of the property, it overrides the property until the next time you run the form.

Index Property

Applies To

Page object, **Tab** object.

Description

The position of a **Tab** object within a **Tabs** collection or a **Page** object in a **Pages** collection.

Syntax

object.**Index** [= *Integer*]

The **Index** property syntax has these parts:

Part	Description
object	Required. A valid object.
Integer	Optional. The index of the currently selected **Tab** object.

Remarks

The **Index** property specifies the order in which tabs appear. Changing the value of **Index** visually changes the order of **Pages** in a **MultiPage** or **Tabs** on a **TabStrip**. The index value for the first page or tab is zero, the index value of the second page or tab is one, and so on.

In a **MultiPage**, **Index** refers to a **Page** as well as the page's **Tab**. In a **TabStrip**, **Index** refers to the tab only.

See Also

Pages collection, **Tabs** collection.

Example

The following example uses the **Index** property to change the order of the pages and tabs in a **MultiPage** and **TabStrip**. The user chooses CommandButton1 to move the third page and tab to the front of the **MultiPage** and **TabStrip.** The user chooses CommandButton2 to move the selected page and tab to the back of the **MultiPage** and **TabStrip**.

To use this example, copy this sample code to the Declarations portion of a form. Make sure that the form contains:

- Two **CommandButton** controls named CommandButton1 and CommandButton2.

- A **MultiPage** named MultiPage1.
- A **TabStrip** named TabStrip1.

```
Dim MyPageOrTab As Object

Private Sub CommandButton1_Click()
'Move third page and tab to front of control
   MultiPage1.page3.Index = 0
   TabStrip1.Tab3.Index = 0
End Sub

Private Sub CommandButton2_Click()
'Move selected page and tab to back of control
   Set MyPageOrObject = MultiPage1.SelectedItem
   MsgBox "MultiPage1.SelectedItem = " & MultiPage1.SelectedItem.Name
   MyPageOrObject.Index = 4

   Set MyPageOrObject = TabStrip1.SelectedItem
   MsgBox "TabStrip1.SelectedItem = " & TabStrip1.SelectedItem.Caption
   MyPageOrObject.Index = 4
End Sub

Private Sub UserForm_Initialize()
   MultiPage1.Width = 200
   MultiPage1.Pages.Add
   MultiPage1.Pages.Add
   MultiPage1.Pages.Add

   TabStrip1.Width = 200
   TabStrip1.Tabs.Add
   TabStrip1.Tabs.Add
   TabStrip1.Tabs.Add

   CommandButton1.Caption = "Move third page/tab to front"
   CommandButton1.Width = 120

   CommandButton2.Caption = "Move selected item to back"
   CommandButton2.Width = 120
End Sub
```

InsideHeight, InsideWidth Properties

Applies To

Frame control, **Page** object, **UserForm** object.

Description

InsideHeight returns the height, in points, of the client region inside a form.
InsideWidth returns the width, in points, of the client region inside a form.

Syntax

object.**InsideHeight**
object.**InsideWidth**

The **InsideHeight** and **InsideWidth** property syntaxes have these parts:

Part	Description
object	Required. A valid object.

Remarks

The **InsideHeight** and **InsideWidth** properties are read-only. If the region includes a scroll bar, the returned value does not include the height or width of the scroll bar.

See Also

Height, **Width** properties.

Example

The following example uses the **InsideHeight** and **InsideWidth** properties to resize a **CommandButton**. The user clicks the **CommandButton** to resize it.

Note **InsideHeight** and **InsideWidth** are read-only properties.

To use this example, copy this sample code to the Declarations portion of a form. Make sure that the form contains:

- A **CommandButton** named CommandButton1.

```
Dim Resize As Single

Private Sub UserForm_Initialize()
    Resize = 0.75
    CommandButton1.Caption = "Resize Button"

End Sub

Private Sub CommandButton1_Click()
    CommandButton1.Move 10, 10, UserForm1.InsideWidth * Resize, UserForm1 _
        .InsideHeight * Resize
    CommandButton1.Caption = "Button resized using InsideHeight and" _
        & " InsideWidth!"
End Sub
```

IntegralHeight Property

Applies To

ListBox control, **TextBox** control.

Description

Indicates whether a **ListBox** or **TextBox** displays full lines of text in a list or partial lines.

Syntax

object.**IntegralHeight** [= *Boolean*]

The **IntegralHeight** property syntax has these parts:

Part	Description
object	Required. A valid object.
Boolean	Optional. Whether the list displays partial lines of text.

Settings

The settings for *Boolean* are:

Value	Description
True	The list resizes itself to display only complete items (default).
False	The list does not resize itself even if the item is too tall to display completely.

Remarks

The **IntegralHeight** property relates to the height of the list, just as the **AutoSize** property relates to the width of the list.

If **IntegralHeight** is **True**, the list box automatically resizes when necessary to show full rows. If **False**, the list remains a fixed size; if items are taller than the available space in the list, the entire item is not shown.

See Also

AutoSize property.

Italic Property

See Bold, Italic, Size, StrikeThrough, Underline, Weight Properties.

Item Method

Applies To

Controls collection, **Pages** collection, **Tabs** collection.

Description

Returns a member of a collection, either by position or by name.

Syntax

Set *Object* = *object*.**Item**(*collectionindex*)

The **Item** method syntax has these parts:

Part	Description
object	Required. A valid object.
collectionindex	Required. A member's position, or index, within a collection.

Settings

The *collectionindex* can be either a string or an integer. If it is a string, it must be a valid member name. If it is an integer, the minimum value is 0 and the maximum value is one less than the number of items in the collection.

Remarks

If an invalid index or name is specified, an error occurs.

Example

The following example uses the **Item** method to access individual members of the **Controls** and **Pages** collections. The user chooses an option button for either the **Controls** collection or the **MultiPage**, and then clicks the **CommandButton**. The name of the appropriate control is returned in the **Label**.

To use this example, copy this sample code to the Declarations portion of a form. Make sure that the form contains:

- A **CommandButton** named CommandButton1.
- A **Label** named Label1.
- Two **OptionButton** controls named OptionButton1 and OptionButton2.
- A **MultiPage** named MultiPage1.

```
Dim MyControl As Object
Dim ControlsIndex As Integer

Private Sub CommandButton1_Click()
   If OptionButton1.Value = True Then
      'Process Controls collection for UserForm
      Set MyControl = Controls.Item(ControlsIndex)
      Label1.Caption = MyControl.Name
```

```
        'Prepare index for next control on Userform
        ControlsIndex = ControlsIndex + 1
        If ControlsIndex >= Controls.Count Then
            ControlsIndex = 0
        End If

    ElseIf OptionButton2.Value = True Then
        'Process Current Page of Pages collection
        Set MyControl = MultiPage1.Pages.Item(MultiPage1.Value)
        Label1.Caption = MyControl.Name
    End If
End Sub

Private Sub UserForm_Initialize()
    ControlsIndex = 0
    'TabsIndex = 0

    OptionButton1.Caption = "Controls Collection"
    OptionButton2.Caption = "Pages Collection"
    OptionButton1.Value = True

    CommandButton1.Caption = "Get Member Name"
End Sub
```

KeepScrollBarsVisible Property

Applies To

Frame control, **Page** object, **UserForm** object.

Description

Specifies whether scroll bars remain visible when not required.

Syntax

object.**KeepScrollBarsVisible** [= *fmScrollBars*]

The **KeepScrollBarsVisible** property syntax has these parts:

Part	Description
object	Required. A valid object.
fmScrollBars	Optional. Where scroll bars are displayed.

Settings

The settings for *fmScrollBars* are:

Constant	Value	Description
fmScrollBarsNone	0	Displays no scroll bars.
fmScrollBarsHorizontal	1	Displays a horizontal scroll bar.
fmScrollBarsVertical	2	Displays a vertical scroll bar.
fmScrollBarsBoth	3	Displays both a horizontal and a vertical scroll bar (default).

Remarks

If the visible region is large enough to display all the controls on an object such as a **Page** object or a form, scroll bars are not required. The **KeepScrollBarsVisible** property determines whether the scroll bars remain visible when they are not required.

If the scroll bars are visible when they are not required, they appear normal in size, and the scroll box fills the entire width or height of the scroll bar.

See Also

ScrollBars property.

Example

The following example uses the **ScrollBars** and the **KeepScrollBarsVisible** properties to add scroll bars to a page of a **MultiPage** and to a **Frame**. The user chooses an option button that, in turn, specifies a value for **KeepScrollBarsVisible**.

To use this example, copy this sample code to the Declarations portion of a form. Make sure that the form contains:

- A **MultiPage** named MultiPage1.
- A **Frame** named Frame1.
- Four **OptionButton** controls named OptionButton1 through OptionButton4.

```
Private Sub UserForm_Initialize()
   MultiPage1.Pages(0).ScrollBars = fmScrollBarsBoth
   MultiPage1.Pages(0).KeepScrollBarsVisible = fmScrollBarsNone

   Frame1.ScrollBars = fmScrollBarsBoth
   Frame1.KeepScrollBarsVisible = fmScrollBarsNone

   OptionButton1.Caption = "No scroll bars"
   OptionButton1.Value = True
   OptionButton2.Caption = "Horizontal scroll bars"
   OptionButton3.Caption = "Vertical scroll bars"
   OptionButton4.Caption = "Both scroll bars"
End Sub

Private Sub OptionButton1_Click()
   MultiPage1.Pages(0).KeepScrollBarsVisible = fmScrollBarsNone
   Frame1.KeepScrollBarsVisible = fmScrollBarsNone
End Sub

Private Sub OptionButton2_Click()
   MultiPage1.Pages(0).KeepScrollBarsVisible = fmScrollBarsHorizontal
   Frame1.KeepScrollBarsVisible = fmScrollBarsHorizontal
End Sub

Private Sub OptionButton3_Click()
   MultiPage1.Pages(0).KeepScrollBarsVisible = fmScrollBarsVertical
   Frame1.KeepScrollBarsVisible = fmScrollBarsVertical
End Sub
```

```
Private Sub OptionButton4_Click()
   MultiPage1.Pages(0).KeepScrollBarsVisible = fmScrollBarsBoth
   Frame1.KeepScrollBarsVisible = fmScrollBarsBoth
End Sub
```

KeyDown, KeyUp Events

Applies To

CheckBox control, **ComboBox** control, **CommandButton** control, **Frame** control, **ListBox** control, **MultiPage** control, **OptionButton** control, **ScrollBar** control, **SpinButton** control, **TabStrip** control, **TextBox** control, **ToggleButton** control, **UserForm** object.

Description

Occur in sequence when a user presses and releases a key. KeyDown occurs when the user presses a key. KeyUp occurs when the user releases a key.

Syntax

Private Sub *object*_**KeyDown(ByVal** *KeyCode* **As MSForms.ReturnInteger,**
➥ ByVal *Shift* **As fmShiftState)**
Private Sub *object*_**KeyUp(ByVal** *KeyCode* **As MSForms.ReturnInteger,**
➥ ByVal *Shift* **As fmShiftState)**

The KeyDown and KeyUp event syntaxes have these parts:

Part	Description
object	Required. A valid object name.
KeyCode	Required. An integer that represents the key code of the key that was pressed or released.
Shift	Required. The state of SHIFT, CTRL, and ALT.

Settings

The settings for *Shift* are:

Constant	Value	Description
fmShiftMask	1	SHIFT was pressed.
fmCtrlMask	2	CTRL was pressed.
fmAltMask	4	ALT was pressed.

Remarks

The KeyDown event occurs when the user presses a key on a running form while that form or a control on it has the focus. The KeyDown and KeyPress events alternate repeatedly until the user releases the key, at which time the KeyUp event occurs. The form or control with the focus receives all keystrokes. A form can have the focus only if it has no controls or all its visible controls are disabled.

These events also occur if you send a keystroke to a form or control using either the SendKeys action in a macro or the **SendKeys** statement in Visual Basic.

The KeyDown and KeyUp events are typically used to recognize or distinguish between:

- Extended character keys, such as function keys.
- Navigation keys, such as HOME, END, PAGEUP, PAGEDOWN, UP ARROW, DOWN ARROW, RIGHT ARROW, LEFT ARROW, and TAB.
- Combinations of keys and standard keyboard modifiers (SHIFT, CTRL, or ALT).
- The numeric keypad and keyboard number keys.

The KeyDown and KeyUp events do not occur under the following circumstances:

- The user presses ENTER on a form with a command button whose **Default** property is set to **True**.
- The user presses ESC on a form with a command button whose **Cancel** property is set to **True**.

The KeyDown and KeyPress events occur when you press or send an ANSI key. The KeyUp event occurs after any event for a control caused by pressing or sending the key. If a keystroke causes the focus to move from one control to another control, the KeyDown event occurs for the first control, while the KeyPress and KeyUp events occur for the second control.

The sequence of keyboard-related events is:

1. KeyDown
2. KeyPress
3. KeyUp

Note The KeyDown and KeyUp events apply only to forms and controls on a form. To interpret ANSI characters or to find out the ANSI character corresponding to the key pressed, use the KeyPress event.

See Also

Cancel property, **Default** property, KeyPress event.

Example

See the **CurLine** property example.

KeyPress Event

Applies To

CheckBox control, **ComboBox** control, **CommandButton** control, **Frame** control, **ListBox** control, **MultiPage** control, **OptionButton** control, **ScrollBar** control, **SpinButton** control, **TabStrip** control, **TextBox** control, **ToggleButton** control, **UserForm** object.

Description

Occurs when the user presses an ANSI key.

Syntax

Private Sub *object*_**KeyPress(ByVal** *KeyANSI* **As MSForms.ReturnInteger)**

The KeyPress event syntax has these parts:

Part	Description
object	Required. A valid object.
KeyANSI	Required. An integer value that represents a standard numeric ANSI key code.

Remarks

The KeyPress event occurs when the user presses a key that produces a typeable character (an ANSI key) on a running form while the form or a control on it has the focus. The event can occur either before or after the key is released. This event also occurs if you send an ANSI keystroke to a form or control using either the SendKeys action in a macro or the **SendKeys** statement in Visual Basic.

A KeyPress event can occur when any of the following keys are pressed:

- Any printable keyboard character.
- CTRL combined with a character from the standard alphabet.
- CTRL combined with any special character.
- BACKSPACE.
- ESC.

A KeyPress event does not occur under the following conditions:

- Pressing TAB.
- Pressing ENTER.
- Pressing an arrow key.
- When a keystroke causes the focus to move from one control to another.

Note BACKSPACE is part of the ANSI Character Set, but DELETE is not. Deleting a character in a control using BACKSPACE causes a KeyPress event; deleting a character using DELETE doesn't.

When a user holds down a key that produces an ANSI keycode, the KeyDown and KeyPress events alternate repeatedly. When the user releases the key, the KeyUp event occurs. The form or control with the focus receives all keystrokes. A form can have the focus only if it has no controls, or if all its visible controls are disabled.

The default action for the KeyPress event is to process the event code that corresponds to the key that was pressed. *KeyANSI* indicates the ANSI character that corresponds to the pressed key or key combination. The KeyPress event interprets the uppercase and lowercase of each character as separate key codes and, therefore, as two separate characters.

To respond to the physical state of the keyboard, or to handle keystrokes not recognized by the KeyPress event, such as function keys, navigation keys, and any combinations of these with keyboard modifiers (ALT, SHIFT, or CTRL), use the KeyDown and KeyUp event procedures.

The sequence of keyboard-related events is:

1. KeyDown
2. KeyPress
3. KeyUp

See Also

KeyDown, KeyUp events.

Example

The following example uses the KeyPress event to copy keystrokes from one **TextBox** to a second **TextBox**. The user types into the appropriately marked **TextBox**.

To use this example, copy this sample code to the Declarations portion of a form. Make sure that the form contains:

- Two **TextBox** controls named TextBox1 and TextBox2.

```
Private Sub TextBox1_KeyPress(ByVal KeyAscii As MSForms.ReturnInteger)
   TextBox2.Text = TextBox2.Text & Chr(KeyAscii)

   'To handle keyboard combinations (using SHIFT, CTRL, ALT, and another
   'key), or TAB or ENTER, use the KeyDown or KeyUp event.
End Sub

Private Sub UserForm_Initialize()
   Move 0, 0, 570, 380

   TextBox1.Move 30, 40, 220, 160
   TextBox1.MultiLine = True
   TextBox1.WordWrap = True
   TextBox1.Text = "Type text here."
   TextBox1.EnterKeyBehavior = True
```

```
    TextBox2.Move 298, 40, 220, 160
    TextBox2.MultiLine = True
    TextBox2.WordWrap = True
    TextBox2.Text = "Typed text copied here."
    TextBox2.Locked = True
End Sub
```

KeyUp Event

See KeyDown, KeyUp Events.

Label Control

Description

Displays descriptive text.

Remarks

A **Label** control on a form displays descriptive text such as titles, captions, pictures, or brief instructions. For example, labels for an address book might include a **Label** for a name, street, or city. A **Label** doesn't display values from data sources or expressions; it is always unbound and doesn't change as you move from record to record.

The default property for a **Label** is the **Caption** property.

The default event for a **Label** is the Click event.

Properties

Accelerator property, **AutoSize** property, **BackColor** property, **BackStyle** property, **BorderColor** property, **BorderStyle** property, **Caption** property, **ControlTipText** property, **Enabled** property, **Font** object, **ForeColor** property, **Height**, **Width** properties, **LayoutEffect** property, **Left**, **Top** properties, **MouseIcon** property, **MousePointer** property, **Name** property, **Object** property, **OldHeight**, **OldWidth** properties, **OldLeft**, **OldTop** properties, **Parent** property, **Picture** property, **PicturePosition** property, **SpecialEffect** property, **TabIndex** property, **Tag** property, **TextAlign** property, **Visible** property, **WordWrap** property.

Methods

Move method, **ZOrder** method.

Events

BeforeDragOver event, BeforeDropOrPaste event, Click event, DblClick event, Error event, MouseDown, MouseUp events, MouseMove event.

Example

The following example uses the **Zoom** event to evaluate the new value of the **Zoom** property and adds scroll bars to the form when appropriate. The example uses a **Label** to display the current value. The user specifies the size for the form by using the **SpinButton** and then clicks the **CommandButton** to set the value in the **Zoom** property.

To use this example, copy this sample code to the Declarations portion of a form. Make sure that the form contains:

- A **Label** named Label1.
- A **SpinButton** named SpinButton1.
- A **CommandButton** named CommandButton1.
- Other controls placed near the edges of the form.

```
Private Sub CommandButton1_Click()
   Zoom = SpinButton1.Value
End Sub

Private Sub SpinButton1_SpinDown()
   Label1.Caption = SpinButton1.Value
End Sub

Private Sub SpinButton1_SpinUp()
   Label1.Caption = SpinButton1.Value
End Sub

Private Sub UserForm_Initialize()
   SpinButton1.Min = 10
   SpinButton1.Max = 400
   SpinButton1.Value = 100
   Label1.Caption = SpinButton1.Value

   CommandButton1.Caption = "Zoom it!"
End Sub

Private Sub UserForm_Zoom(Percent As Integer)
   Dim MyResult As Double
```

```
    If Percent > 99 Then
        ScrollBars = fmScrollBarsBoth
        ScrollLeft = 0
        ScrollTop = 0

        MyResult = Width * Percent / 100
        ScrollWidth = MyResult

        MyResult = Height * Percent / 100
        ScrollHeight = MyResult
    Else
        ScrollBars = fmScrollBarsNone
        ScrollLeft = 0
        ScrollTop = 0
    End If
End Sub
```

LargeChange Property

Applies To

ScrollBar control.

Description

Specifies the amount of movement that occurs when the user clicks between the scroll box and scroll arrow.

Syntax

object.**LargeChange** [= *Long*]

The **LargeChange** property syntax has these parts:

Part	Description
object	Required. A valid object.
Long	Optional. An integer that specifies the amount of change to the **Value** property.

Remarks

The **LargeChange** property applies only to the **ScrollBar**. It does not apply to the scroll bars in other controls such as a **TextBox** or a drop-down **ComboBox**.

The value of **LargeChange** is the amount by which the **ScrollBar**'s **Value** property changes when the user clicks the area between the scroll box and scroll arrow. The direction of the movement is always toward the place where the user clicks. For example, in a horizontal **ScrollBar**, clicking to the left of the scroll box moves the scroll box to the left. In a vertical **ScrollBar**, clicking above the scroll box moves the scroll box up.

LargeChange does not have units. Any integer is a valid setting for **LargeChange**. The recommended range of values is from –32,767 to +32,767, and the value must be between the values of the **Max** and **Min** properties of the **ScrollBar**.

See Also

Max, **Min** properties, **SmallChange** property.

Example

The following example demonstrates the **LargeChange** and **SmallChange** properties when used with a stand-alone **ScrollBar**. The user can set the **LargeChange** and **SmallChange** values to any integer in the range of 0 to 100. This example also uses the **MaxLength** property to restrict the number of characters entered for the **LargeChange** and **SmallChange** values.

To use this example, copy this sample code to the Declarations portion of a form. Make sure that the form contains:

- A **Label** named Label1 and a **TextBox** named TextBox1.
- A **Label** named Label2 and a **TextBox** named TextBox2.
- A **ScrollBar** named ScrollBar1.
- A **Label** named Label3.

```
Dim TempNum As Integer

Private Sub ScrollBar1_Change()
   Label3.Caption = ScrollBar1.Value
End Sub

Private Sub TextBox1_Change()
   If IsNumeric(TextBox1.Text) Then
      TempNum = CInt(TextBox1.Text)
      If TempNum >= 0 And TempNum <= 100 Then
         ScrollBar1.SmallChange = TempNum
      Else
         TextBox1.Text = ScrollBar1.SmallChange
      End If
   Else
      TextBox1.Text = ScrollBar1.SmallChange
   End If
End Sub

Private Sub TextBox2_Change()
   If IsNumeric(TextBox2.Text) Then
      TempNum = CInt(TextBox2.Text)
      If TempNum >= 0 And TempNum <= 100 Then
         ScrollBar1.LargeChange = TempNum
      Else
         TextBox2.Text = ScrollBar1.LargeChange
      End If
   Else
      TextBox2.Text = ScrollBar1.LargeChange
   End If
End Sub
```

```
Private Sub UserForm_Initialize()
   ScrollBar1.Min = -1000
   ScrollBar1.Max = 1000

   Label1.Caption = "SmallChange 0 to 100"
   ScrollBar1.SmallChange = 1
   TextBox1.Text = ScrollBar1.SmallChange
   TextBox1.MaxLength = 3

   Label2.Caption = "LargeChange 0 to 100"
   ScrollBar1.LargeChange = 100
   TextBox2.Text = ScrollBar1.LargeChange
   TextBox2.MaxLength = 3

   ScrollBar1.Value = 0
   Label3.Caption = ScrollBar1.Value
End Sub
```

Layout Event

Applies To

Frame control, **MultiPage** control, **UserForm** object.

Description

Occurs when a form, **Frame**, or **MultiPage** changes size.

Syntax

For MultiPage

Private Sub *object*_**Layout(** *index* **As Long)**

For all other controls

Private Sub *object*_**Layout( )**

The Layout event syntax has these parts:

Part	Description
object	Required. A valid object.
index	Required. The index of the page in a **MultiPage** that changed size.

Remarks

The default action of the Layout event is to calculate new positions of controls and to repaint the screen.

A user can initiate the Layout event by changing the size of a control.

For controls that support the **AutoSize** property, the Layout event is initiated when **AutoSize** changes the size of the control. This occurs when the user changes the value of a property that affects the size of a control. For example, increasing the **Font** size of a **TextBox** or **Label** can significantly change the dimensions of the control and initiate a Layout event.

See Also

AutoSize property, **LayoutEffect** property, **OldHeight**, **OldWidth** properties, **OldLeft**, **OldTop** properties.

Example

The following example moves a selected control on a form with the **Move** method, and uses the Layout event and **LayoutEffect** property to identify the control that moved (and changed the layout of the **UserForm**). The user clicks a control to move and then clicks the **CommandButton**. A message box displays the name of the control that is moving.

To use this example, copy this sample code to the Declarations portion of a form. Make sure that the form contains:

- A **TextBox** named TextBox1.
- A **ComboBox** named ComboBox1.
- An **OptionButton** named OptionButton1.
- A **CommandButton** named CommandButton1.
- A **ToggleButton** named ToggleButton1.

```
Private Sub UserForm_Initialize()
    CommandButton1.Caption = "Move current control"
    CommandButton1.AutoSize = True
    CommandButton1.TakeFocusOnClick = False

    ToggleButton1.Caption = "Use Layout Event"
    ToggleButton1.Value = True
End Sub

Private Sub CommandButton1_Click()
    If ActiveControl.Name = "ToggleButton1" Then
        'Keep it stationary
    Else
        'Move the control, using Layout event when ToggleButton1.Value is True
        ActiveControl.Move 0, 0, , , ToggleButton1.Value
    End If
End Sub

Private Sub UserForm_Layout()
    Dim MyControl As Control

    MsgBox "In the Layout Event"
```

```
    'Find the control that is moving.
    For Each MyControl In Controls
       If MyControl.LayoutEffect = fmLayoutEffectInitiate Then
          MsgBox MyControl.Name & " is moving."
          Exit For
       End If
    Next
End Sub

Private Sub ToggleButton1_Click()
    If ToggleButton1.Value = True Then
       ToggleButton1.Caption = "Use Layout Event"
    Else
       ToggleButton1.Caption = "No Layout Event"
    End If
End Sub
```

LayoutEffect Property

Applies To

CheckBox control, **ComboBox** control, **CommandButton** control, **Image** control, **Label** control, **ListBox** control, **MultiPage** control, **OptionButton** control, **ScrollBar** control, **SpinButton** control, **TabStrip** control, **TextBox** control, **ToggleButton** control.

Description

Specifies whether a control was moved during a layout change.

Syntax

object.**LayoutEffect**

The **LayoutEffect** property syntax has these parts:

Part	Description
object	Required. A valid object.

Return Values

The **LayoutEffect** property return values are:

Constant	Value	Description
fmLayoutEffectNone	0	The control was not moved.
fmLayoutEffectInitiate	1	The control was moved.

Remarks

The **LayoutEffect** property is read-only and is available only in the Layout event. The Layout event is initiated by the **Move** method if the *Layout* argument is **True**.

The Layout event is not initiated when you change the settings of the **Left**, **Top**, **Height**, or **Width** properties of a control.

The Layout event sets **LayoutEffect** for any control that was involved in a move operation. For example, if you move a group of controls, **LayoutEffect** of each control is set.

See Also

Layout event, **Move** method, **OldHeight**, **OldWidth** properties, **OldLeft**, **OldTop** properties.

Example

See the Layout event example.

Left, Top Properties

Applies To

CheckBox control, **ComboBox** control, **CommandButton** control, **Image** control, **Label** control, **ListBox** control, **MultiPage** control, **OptionButton** control, **ScrollBar** control, **SpinButton** control, **TabStrip** control, **TextBox** control, **ToggleButton** control, **UserForm** object.

Description

The distance between a control and the left or top edge of the form that contains it.

Syntax

object.**Left** [= *Single*]
object.**Top** [= *Single*]

The **Left** and **Top** property syntaxes have these parts:

Part	Description
object	Required. A valid object.
Single	Optional. A numeric expression specifying the coordinates of an object.

Settings

Setting the **Left** or **Top** property to 0 places the control's edge at the left or top edge of its container.

Remarks

For most systems, the recommended range of values for **Left** and **Top** is from -32,767 to +32,767. Other values may also work depending on your system configuration. For a **ComboBox**, values of **Left** and **Top** apply to the text portion of the control, not to the list portion. When you move or size a control, its new **Left** setting is automatically entered in the property sheet. When you print a form, the control's horizontal or vertical location is determined by its **Left** or **Top** setting.

See Also

Height, **Width** properties.

Example

See the **ClientHeight**, **ClientLeft**, **ClientTop**, **ClientWidth** properties example.

LineCount Property

Applies To

ComboBox control, **TextBox** control.

Description

Returns the number of text lines in a **TextBox** or **ComboBox**.

Syntax

object.**LineCount**

The **LineCount** property syntax has these parts:

Part	Description
object	Required. A valid object.

Remarks

The **LineCount** property is read-only.

Note A **ComboBox** will only have one line.

Example

The following example counts the characters and the number of lines of text in a **TextBox** by using the **LineCount** and **TextLength** properties, and the **SetFocus** method. In this example, the user can type into a **TextBox**, and can retrieve current values of the **LineCount** and **TextLength** properties.

To use this example, copy this sample code to the Declarations portion of a form. Make sure that the form contains the following controls:

- A **TextBox** named TextBox1.
- A **CommandButton** named CommandButton1.
- Two **Label** controls named Label1 and Label2.

```
'Type SHIFT+ENTER to start a new line in the text box.

Private Sub CommandButton1_Click()
   'Must first give TextBox1 the focus to get line count
   TextBox1.SetFocus
   Label1.Caption = "LineCount = " & TextBox1.LineCount
   Label2.Caption = "TextLength = " & TextBox1.TextLength
End Sub
```

```
Private Sub UserForm_Initialize()
   CommandButton1.WordWrap = True
   CommandButton1.AutoSize = True
   CommandButton1.Caption = "Get Counts"

   Label1.Caption = "LineCount = "
   Label2.Caption = "TextLength = "

   TextBox1.MultiLine = True
   TextBox1.WordWrap = True
   TextBox1.Text = "Enter your text here."
End Sub
```

List Property

Applies To

ComboBox control, **ListBox** control.

Description

Returns or sets the list entries of a **ListBox** or **ComboBox**.

Syntax

object.**List(** *row, column* **)** [= *Variant*]

The **List** property syntax has these parts:

Part	Description
object	Required. A valid object.
row	Required. An integer with a range from 0 to one less than the number of entries in the list.
column	Required. An integer with a range from 0 to one less than the number of columns.
Variant	Optional. The contents of the specified entry in the **ListBox** or **ComboBox**.

Settings

Row and column numbering begins with zero. That is, the row number of the first row in the list is zero; the column number of the first column is zero. The number of the second row or column is 1, and so on.

Remarks

The **List** property works with the **ListCount** and **ListIndex** properties. Use **List** to access list items. A list is a variant array; each item in the list has a row number and a column number.

Initially, **ComboBox** and **ListBox** contain an empty list.

Note To specify items you want to display in a **ComboBox** or **ListBox**, use the **AddItem** method. To remove items, use the **RemoveItem** method.

Use **List** to copy an entire two-dimensional array of values to a control. Use **AddItem** to load a one-dimensional array or to load an individual element.

See Also

AddItem method, **Column** property, **ListCount** property, **ListIndex** property, **RemoveItem** method.

Example

The following example swaps columns of a multicolumn **ListBox**. The sample uses the **List** property in two ways:

1. To access and exchange individual values in the **ListBox**. In this usage, **List** has subscripts to designate the row and column of a specified value.
2. To initially load the **ListBox** with values from an array. In this usage, **List** has no subscripts.

To use this example, copy this sample code to the Declarations portion of a form. Make sure that the form contains a **ListBox** named ListBox1 and a **CommandButton** named CommandButton1.

```
Dim MyArray(6, 3)            'Array containing column values for ListBox.

Private Sub UserForm_Initialize()
   Dim i As Single

   ListBox1.ColumnCount = 3        'This list box contains 3 data columns

   'Load integer values MyArray
   For i = 0 To 5
      MyArray(i, 0) = i
      MyArray(i, 1) = Rnd
      MyArray(i, 2) = Rnd
   Next i

   'Load ListBox1
   ListBox1.List() = MyArray

End Sub

Private Sub CommandButton1_Click()
'Exchange contents of columns 1 and 3

   Dim i As Single
   Dim Temp As Single

   For i = 0 To 5
      Temp = ListBox1.List(i, 0)
      ListBox1.List(i, 0) = ListBox1.List(i, 2)
      ListBox1.List(i, 2) = Temp
   Next i
End Sub
```

ListBox Control

Description

Displays a list of values and lets you select one or more.

Remarks

If the **ListBox** is bound to a data source, then the **ListBox** stores the selected value in that data source.

The **ListBox** can either appear as a list or as a group of **OptionButton** controls or **CheckBox** controls.

The default property for a **ListBox** is the **Value** property.

The default event for a **ListBox** is the Click event.

Note You can't drop text into a drop-down **ListBox**.

Properties

BackColor property, **BorderColor** property, **BorderStyle** property, **BoundColumn** property, **BoundValue** property, **Column** property, **ColumnCount** property, **ColumnHeads** property, **ColumnWidths** property, **ControlSource** property, **ControlTipText** property, **Enabled** property, **Font** object, **ForeColor** property, **Height**, **Width** properties, **HelpContextID** property, **IMEMode** property, **IntegralHeight** property, **LayoutEffect** property, **Left**, **Top** properties, **List** property, **ListCount** property, **ListIndex** property, **ListStyle** property, **Locked** property, **MatchEntry** property, **MouseIcon** property, **MousePointer** property, **MultiSelect** property, **Name** property, **Object** property, **OldHeight**, **OldWidth** properties, **OldLeft**, **OldTop** properties, **Parent** property, **RowSource** property, **Selected** property, **SpecialEffect** property, **TabIndex** property, **TabStop** property, **Tag** property, **Text** property, **TextColumn** property, **TopIndex** property, **Value** property, **Visible** property.

Methods

AddItem method, **Clear** method, **Move** method, **RemoveItem** method, **SetFocus** method, **ZOrder** method.

Events

AfterUpdate event, BeforeDragOver event, BeforeDropOrPaste event, BeforeUpdate event, Change event, Click event, DblClick event, Enter, Exit events, Error event, KeyDown, KeyUp events, KeyPress event, MouseDown, MouseUp events, MouseMove event.

See Also

CheckBox control, **ComboBox** control, **OptionButton** control.

Example

The following example adds and deletes the contents of a **ListBox** using the **AddItem**, **RemoveItem**, and **SetFocus** methods, and the **ListIndex** and **ListCount** properties.

To use this example, copy this sample code to the Declarations portion of a form. Make sure that the form contains:

- A **ListBox** named ListBox1.
- Two **CommandButton** controls named CommandButton1 and CommandButton2.

```
Dim EntryCount As Single
Private Sub CommandButton1_Click()
   EntryCount = EntryCount + 1
   ListBox1.AddItem (EntryCount & " - Selection")
End Sub

Private Sub CommandButton2_Click()
   ListBox1.SetFocus

   'Ensure ListBox contains list items
   If ListBox1.ListCount >= 1 Then
      'If no selection, choose last list item.
      If ListBox1.ListIndex = -1 Then
         ListBox1.ListIndex = ListBox1.ListCount - 1
      End If
      ListBox1.RemoveItem (ListBox1.ListIndex)
   End If
End Sub

Private Sub UserForm_Initialize()
   EntryCount = 0
   CommandButton1.Caption = "Add Item"
   CommandButton2.Caption = "Remove Item"
End Sub
```

ListCount Property

Applies To

ComboBox control, **ListBox** control.

Description

Returns the number of list entries in a control.

Syntax

object.**ListCount**

The **ListCount** property syntax has these parts:

Part	Description
object	Required. A valid object.

Remarks

The **ListCount** property is read-only. **ListCount** is the number of rows over which you can scroll. **ListRows** is the maximum to display at once. **ListCount** is always one greater than the largest value for the **ListIndex** property, because index numbers begin with 0 and the count of items begins with 1. If no item is selected, **ListCount** is 0 and **ListIndex** is –1.

See Also

List property, **ListIndex** property, **Selected** property.

Example

See the **ListBox** control example.

ListIndex Property

Applies To

ComboBox control, **ListBox** control.

Description

Identifies the currently selected item in a **ListBox** or **ComboBox**.

Syntax

object.**ListIndex** [= *Variant*]

The **ListIndex** property syntax has these parts:

Part	Description
object	Required. A valid object.
Variant	Optional. The currently selected item in the control.

Remarks

The **ListIndex** property contains an index of the selected row in a list. Values of **ListIndex** range from –1 to one less than the total number of rows in a list (that is, **ListCount** – 1). When no rows are selected, **ListIndex** returns –1. When the user selects a row in a **ListBox** or **ComboBox**, the system sets the **ListIndex** value. The **ListIndex** value of the first row in a list is 0, the value of the second row is 1, and so on.

Note If you use the **MultiSelect** property to create a **ListBox** that allows multiple selections, the **Selected** property of the **ListBox** (rather than the **ListIndex** property) identifies the selected rows. The **Selected** property is an array with the same number of values as the number of rows in the **ListBox**. For each row in the list box, **Selected** is **True** if the row is selected and **False** if it is not. In a **ListBox** that allows multiple selections, **ListIndex** returns the index of the row that has focus, regardless of whether that row is currently selected.

The **ListIndex** value is also available by setting the **BoundColumn** property to 0 for a combo box or list box. If **BoundColumn** is 0, the underlying data source to which the combo box or list box is bound contains the same list index value as **ListIndex**.

See Also

BoundColumn property, **ListCount** property, **MultiSelect** property, **Selected** property.

Example

See the **ListBox** control example.

ListRows Property

Applies To

ComboBox control.

Description

Specifies the maximum number of rows to display in the list.

Syntax

object.**ListRows** [= *Long*]

The **ListRows** property syntax has these parts:

Part	Description
object	Required. A valid object.
Long	Optional. An integer indicating the maximum number of rows. The default value is 8.

Remarks

If the number of items in the list exceeds the value of the **ListRows** property, a scroll bar appears at the right edge of the list box portion of the combo box.

Example

The following example uses a **SpinButton** to control the number of rows in the drop-down list of a **ComboBox**. The user changes the value of the **SpinButton**, then clicks on the drop-down arrow of the **ComboBox** to display the list.

To use this example, copy this sample code to the Declarations portion of a form. Make sure that the form contains:

- A **ComboBox** named ComboBox1.
- A **SpinButton** named SpinButton1.
- A **Label** named Label1.

```
Private Sub UserForm_Initialize()
   Dim i As Integer

   For i = 1 To 20
      ComboBox1.AddItem "Choice " & (ComboBox1.ListCount + 1)
   Next i

   SpinButton1.Min = 0
   SpinButton1.Max = 12
   SpinButton1.Value = ComboBox1.ListRows
   Label1.Caption = "ListRows = " & SpinButton1.Value
End Sub

Private Sub SpinButton1_Change()
   ComboBox1.ListRows = SpinButton1.Value
   Label1.Caption = "ListRows = " & SpinButton1.Value
End Sub
```

ListStyle Property

Applies To

ComboBox control, **ListBox** control.

Description

Specifies the visual appearance of the list in a **ListBox** or **ComboBox**.

Syntax

object.**ListStyle** [= *fmListStyle*]

The **ListStyle** property syntax has these parts:

Part	Description
object	Required. A valid object.
fmListStyle	Optional. The visual style of the list.

Settings

The settings for *fmListStyle* are:

Constant	Value	Description
fmListStylePlain	0	Looks like a regular list box, with the background of items highlighted.
fmListStyleOption	1	Shows option buttons, or check boxes for a multi-select list (default). When the user selects an item from the group, the option button associated with that item is selected and the option buttons for the other items in the group are deselected.

Remarks

The **ListStyle** property lets you change the visual presentation of a **ListBox** or **ComboBox**. By specifying a setting other than **fmListStylePlain**, you can present the contents of either control as a group of individual items, with each item including a visual cue to indicate whether it is selected.

If the control supports a single selection (the **MultiSelect** property is set to **fmMultiSelectSingle**), the user can press one button in the group. If the control supports multiselect, the user can press two or more buttons in the group.

See Also

MultiSelect property.

Example

The following example uses the **ListStyle** and **MultiSelect** properties to control the appearance of a **ListBox**. The user chooses a value for **ListStyle** using the **ToggleButton** and chooses an **OptionButton** for one of the **MultiSelect** values. The appearance of the **ListBox** changes accordingly, as well as the selection behavior within the **ListBox**.

To use this example, copy this sample code to the Declarations portion of a form. Make sure that the form contains:

- A **ListBox** named ListBox1.
- A **Label** named Label1.
- Three **OptionButton** controls named OptionButton1 through OptionButton3.
- A **ToggleButton** named ToggleButton1.

```
Private Sub UserForm_Initialize()
   Dim i As Integer

   For i = 1 To 8
      ListBox1.AddItem "Choice" & (ListBox1.ListCount + 1)
   Next i

   Label1.Caption = "MultiSelect Choices"
   Label1.AutoSize = True
```

```
    ListBox1.MultiSelect = fmMultiSelectSingle
    OptionButton1.Caption = "Single entry"
    OptionButton1.Value = True
    OptionButton2.Caption = "Multiple entries"
    OptionButton3.Caption = "Extended entries"

    ToggleButton1.Caption = "ListStyle - Plain"
    ToggleButton1.Value = True
    ToggleButton1.Width = 90
    ToggleButton1.Height = 30
End Sub

Private Sub OptionButton1_Click()
    ListBox1.MultiSelect = fmMultiSelectSingle
End Sub

Private Sub OptionButton2_Click()
    ListBox1.MultiSelect = fmMultiSelectMulti
End Sub

Private Sub OptionButton3_Click()
    ListBox1.MultiSelect = fmMultiSelectExtended
End Sub

Private Sub ToggleButton1_Click()
    If ToggleButton1.Value = True Then
        ToggleButton1.Caption = "Plain ListStyle"
        ListBox1.ListStyle = fmListStylePlain
    Else
        ToggleButton1.Caption = "OptionButton or CheckBox"
        ListBox1.ListStyle = fmListStyleOption
    End If
End Sub
```

ListWidth Property

Applies To

ComboBox control.

Description

Specifies the width of the list in a **ComboBox**.

Syntax

object.**ListWidth** [= *Variant*]

The **ListWidth** property syntax has these parts:

Part	Description
object	Required. A valid object.
Variant	Optional. The width of the list. A value of zero makes the list as wide as the **ComboBox**. The default value is to make the list as wide as the text portion of the control.

Remarks

If you want to display a multicolumn list, enter a value that will make the list box wide enough to fit all the columns.

Tip When designing combo boxes, be sure to leave enough space to display your data and for a vertical scroll bar.

Example

The following example uses a **SpinButton** to control the width of the drop-down list of a **ComboBox**. The user changes the value of the **SpinButton**, then clicks on the drop-down arrow of the **ComboBox** to display the list.

To use this example, copy this sample code to the Declarations portion of a form. Make sure that the form contains:

- A **ComboBox** named ComboBox1.
- A **SpinButton** named SpinButton1.
- A **Label** named Label1.

```
Private Sub SpinButton1_Change()
   ComboBox1.ListWidth = SpinButton1.Value
   Label1.Caption = "ListWidth = " & SpinButton1.Value
End Sub

Private Sub UserForm_Initialize()
   Dim i As Integer

   For i = 1 To 20
      ComboBox1.AddItem "Choice " & (ComboBox1.ListCount + 1)
   Next i

   SpinButton1.Min = 0
   SpinButton1.Max = 130
   SpinButton1.Value = Val(ComboBox1.ListWidth)
   SpinButton1.SmallChange = 5
   Label1.Caption = "ListWidth = " & SpinButton1.Value
End Sub
```

Locked Property

Applies To

CheckBox control, **ComboBox** control, **CommandButton** control, **ListBox** control, **OptionButton** control, **TextBox** control, **ToggleButton** control.

Description

Specifies whether a control can be edited.

Syntax

object.**Locked** [= *Boolean*]

The **Locked** property syntax has these parts:

Part	Description
object	Required. A valid object.
Boolean	Optional. Whether the control can be edited.

Settings

The settings for *Boolean* are:

Value	Description
True	You can't edit the value.
False	You can edit the value (default).

Remarks

When a control is locked and enabled, it can still initiate events and can still receive the focus.

See Also

Enabled property.

Example

See the **Enabled** property example.

MatchEntry Property

Applies To

ComboBox control, **ListBox** control.

Description

Returns or sets a value indicating how a **ListBox** or **ComboBox** searches its list as the user types.

Syntax

object.**MatchEntry** [= *fmMatchEntry*]

The **MatchEntry** property syntax has these parts:

Part	Description
object	Required. A valid object.
fmMatchEntry	Optional. The rule used to match entries in the list.

Settings

The settings for *fmMatchEntry* are:

Constant	Value	Description
fmMatchEntryFirstLetter	0	Basic matching. The control searches for the next entry that starts with the character entered. Repeatedly typing the same letter cycles through all entries beginning with that letter.
FmMatchEntryComplete	1	Extended matching. As each character is typed, the control searches for an entry matching all characters entered (default).
FmMatchEntryNone	2	No matching.

Remarks

The **MatchEntry** property searches entries from the **TextColumn** property of a **ListBox** or **ComboBox**.

The control searches the column identified by **TextColumn** for an entry that matches the user's typed entry. Upon finding a match, the row containing the match is selected, the contents of the column are displayed, and the contents of its **BoundColumn** property become the value of the control. If the match is unambiguous, finding the match initiates the Click event.

The control initiates the Click event as soon as the user types a sequence of characters that match exactly one entry in the list. As the user types, the entry is compared with the current row in the list and with the next row in the list. When the entry matches only the current row, the match is unambiguous.

In Microsoft Forms, this is true regardless of whether the list is sorted. This means the control finds the first occurrence that matches the entry, based on the order of items in the list. For example, entering either "abc" or "bc" will initiate the Click event for the following list:

```
abcde
bcdef
abcxyz
bchij
```

Note that in either case, the matched entry is not unique; however, it is sufficiently different from the adjacent entry that the control interprets the match as unambiguous and initiates the Click event.

See Also

BoundColumn property, Click event, **MatchFound** property, **MatchRequired** property, **TextColumn** property.

Example

The following example uses the **MatchEntry** property to demonstrate character matching that is available for **ComboBox** and **ListBox**. In this example, the user can set the type of matching with the **OptionButton** controls and then type into the **ComboBox** to specify an item from its list.

To use this example, copy this sample code to the Declarations portion of a form. Make sure that the form contains:

- Three **OptionButton** controls named OptionButton1 through OptionButton3.
- A **ComboBox** named ComboBox1.

```
Private Sub OptionButton1_Click()
   ComboBox1.MatchEntry = fmMatchEntryNone
End Sub

Private Sub OptionButton2_Click()
   ComboBox1.MatchEntry = fmMatchEntryFirstLetter
End Sub

Private Sub OptionButton3_Click()
      ComboBox1.MatchEntry = fmMatchEntryComplete
End Sub

Private Sub UserForm_Initialize()
   Dim i As Integer

   For i = 1 To 9
      ComboBox1.AddItem "Choice " & i
   Next i
   ComboBox1.AddItem "Chocoholic"


   OptionButton1.Caption = "No matching"
   OptionButton1.Value = True

   OptionButton2.Caption = "Basic matching"
   OptionButton3.Caption = "Extended matching"
End Sub
```

MatchFound Property

Applies To

ComboBox control.

Description

Indicates whether the text that a user has typed into a combo box matches any of the entries in the list.

Syntax

object.**MatchFound**

The **MatchFound** property syntax has these parts:

Part	Description
object	Required. A valid object.

Return Values

The **MatchFound** property return values are:

Value	Description
True	The contents of the **Value** property matches one of the records in the list.
False	The contents of **Value** does not match any of the records in the list (default).

Remarks

The **MatchFound** property is read-only. It is not applicable when the **MatchEntry** property is set to **fmMatchEntryNone**.

See Also

MatchEntry property, **MatchRequired** property.

Example

The following example uses the **MatchFound** and **MatchRequired** properties to demonstrate additional character matching for **ComboBox**. The matching verification occurs in the Change event.

In this example, the user specifies whether the text portion of a **ComboBox** must match one of the listed items in the **ComboBox**. The user can specify whether matching is required by using a **CheckBox** and then type into the **ComboBox** to specify an item from its list.

To use this example, copy this sample code to the Declarations portion of a form. Make sure that the form contains:

- A **ComboBox** named ComboBox1.
- A **CheckBox** named CheckBox1.

```
Private Sub CheckBox1_Click()
   If CheckBox1.Value = True Then
      ComboBox1.MatchRequired = True
      MsgBox "To move the focus from the ComboBox, you must match an entry in the list
or press ESC."
   Else
      ComboBox1.MatchRequired = False
      MsgBox " To move the focus from the ComboBox, just tab to or click another
control. Matching is optional."
   End If
End Sub

Private Sub ComboBox1_Change()
   If ComboBox1.MatchRequired = True Then
   'MSForms handles this case automatically
   Else
      If ComboBox1.MatchFound = True Then
         MsgBox "Match Found; matching optional."
      Else
         MsgBox "Match not Found; matching optional."
      End If
   End If
End Sub

Private Sub UserForm_Initialize()
Dim i As Integer

For i = 1 To 9
   ComboBox1.AddItem "Choice " & i
Next i
ComboBox1.AddItem "Chocoholic"

CheckBox1.Caption = "MatchRequired"
CheckBox1.Value = True
End Sub
```

MatchRequired Property

Applies To

ComboBox control.

Description

Specifies whether a value entered in the text portion of a **ComboBox** must match an entry in the existing list portion of the control. The user can enter non-matching values, but may not leave the control until a matching value is entered.

Syntax

object.**MatchRequired** [= *Boolean*]

The **MatchRequired** property syntax has these parts:

Part	Description
object	Required. A valid object.
Boolean	Optional. Whether the text entered must match an existing item in the list.

Settings

The settings for *Boolean* are:

Value	Description
True	The text entered must match an existing list entry.
False	The text entered can be different from all existing list entries (default).

Remarks

If the **MatchRequired** property is **True**, the user cannot exit the **ComboBox** until the text entered matches an entry in the existing list. **MatchRequired** maintains the integrity of the list by requiring the user to select an existing entry.

Note Not all containers enforce this property.

See Also

MatchEntry property, **MatchFound** property, **Text** property.

Example

See the **MatchFound** property example.

Max, Min Properties

Applies To

ScrollBar control, **SpinButton** control.

Description

Specify the maximum and minimum acceptable values for the **Value** property of a **ScrollBar** or **SpinButton**.

Syntax

object.**Max** [= *Long*]
object.**Min** [= *Long*]

The **Max** and **Min** property syntaxes have these parts:

Part	Description
object	Required. A valid object.
Long	Optional. A numeric expression specifying the maximum or minimum **Value** property setting.

Remarks

Clicking a **SpinButton** or moving the scroll box in a **ScrollBar** changes the **Value** property of the control.

The value for the **Max** property corresponds to the lowest position of a vertical **ScrollBar** or the rightmost position of a horizontal **ScrollBar**. The value for the **Min** property corresponds to the highest position of a vertical **ScrollBar** or the leftmost position of a horizontal **ScrollBar**.

Any integer is an acceptable setting for this property. The recommended range of values is from –32,767 to +32,767. The default value is 1.

Note **Min** and **Max** refer to locations, not to relative values, on the **ScrollBar**. That is, the value of **Max** could be less than the value of **Min**. If this is the case, moving toward the **Max** (bottom) position means decreasing **Value**; moving toward the **Min** (top) position means increasing **Value**.

See Also

LargeChange property, **SmallChange** property, **Value** property.

Example

The following example demonstrates the **Max** and **Min** properties when used with a stand-alone **ScrollBar**. The user can set the **Max** and **Min** values to any integer in the range of –1000 to 1000. This example also uses the **MaxLength** property to restrict the number of characters entered for the **Max** and **Min** values.

To use this example, copy this sample code to the Declarations portion of a form. Make sure that the form contains:

- A **Label** named Label1 and a **TextBox** named TextBox1.
- A **Label** named Label2 and a **TextBox** named TextBox2.
- A **ScrollBar** named ScrollBar1.
- A **Label** named Label3.

```
Dim TempNum As Integer

Private Sub UserForm_Initialize()
   Label1.Caption = "Min -1000 to 1000"
   ScrollBar1.Min = -1000
   TextBox1.Text = ScrollBar1.Min
   TextBox1.MaxLength = 5

   Label2.Caption = "Max -1000 to 1000"
   ScrollBar1.Max = 1000
   TextBox2.Text = ScrollBar1.Max
   TextBox2.MaxLength = 5

   ScrollBar1.SmallChange = 1
   ScrollBar1.LargeChange = 100
   ScrollBar1.Value = 0
   Label3.Caption = ScrollBar1.Value
End Sub

Private Sub TextBox1_Change()
   If IsNumeric(TextBox1.Text) Then
      TempNum = CInt(TextBox1.Text)
      If TempNum >= -1000 And TempNum <= 1000 Then
         ScrollBar1.Min = TempNum
      Else
         TextBox1.Text = ScrollBar1.Min
      End If
   Else
      TextBox1.Text = ScrollBar1.Min
   End If
End Sub

Private Sub TextBox2_Change()
   If IsNumeric(TextBox2.Text) Then
      TempNum = CInt(TextBox2.Text)
      If TempNum >= -1000 And TempNum <= 1000 Then
         ScrollBar1.Max = TempNum
      Else
         TextBox2.Text = ScrollBar1.Max
      End If
   Else
      TextBox2.Text = ScrollBar1.Max
   End If
End Sub
```

```
Private Sub ScrollBar1_Change()
Label3.Caption = ScrollBar1.Value
End Sub
```

MaxLength Property

Applies To

ComboBox control, **TextBox** control.

Description

Specifies the maximum number of characters a user can enter in a **TextBox** or **ComboBox**.

Syntax

object.**MaxLength** [= *Long*]

The **MaxLength** property syntax has these parts:

Part	Description
object	Required. A valid object.
Long	Optional. An integer indicating the allowable number of characters.

Remarks

Setting the **MaxLength** property to 0 indicates there is no limit other than that created by memory constraints.

Example

See the **Max**, **Min** properties example.

Min Property

See Max, Min Properties.

MouseDown, MouseUp Events

Applies To

CheckBox control, **ComboBox** control, **CommandButton** control, **Frame** control, **Image** control, **Label** control, **ListBox** control, **MultiPage** control, **OptionButton** control, **TabStrip** control, **TextBox** control, **ToggleButton** control, **UserForm** object.

Description

Occur when the user clicks a mouse button. MouseDown occurs when the user presses the mouse button; MouseUp occurs when the user releases the mouse button.

Syntax

For MultiPage, TabStrip:

Private Sub *object*_**MouseDown(** *index* **As Long, ByVal** *Button* **As fmButton,**
➥ **ByVal** *Shift* **As fmShiftState, ByVal** *X* **As Single, ByVal** *Y* **As Single)**
Private Sub *object*_**MouseUp(** *index* **As Long, ByVal** *Button* **As fmButton,**
➥ **ByVal** *Shift* **As fmShiftState, ByVal** *X* **As Single, ByVal** *Y* **As Single)**

For other controls:

Private Sub *object*_**MouseDown(ByVal** *Button* **As fmButton, ByVal** *Shift*
➥ **As fmShiftState, ByVal** *X* **As Single, ByVal** *Y* **As Single)**
Private Sub *object*_**MouseUp(ByVal** *Button* **As fmButton, ByVal** *Shift*
➥ **As fmShiftState, ByVal** *X* **As Single, ByVal** *Y* **As Single)**

The MouseDown and MouseUp event syntaxes have these parts:

Part	Description
object	Required. A valid object.
index	Required. The index of the page or tab in a **MultiPage** or **TabStrip** with the specified event.
Button	Required. An integer value that identifies which mouse button caused the event.
Shift	Required. The state of SHIFT, CTRL, and ALT.
X, Y	Required. The horizontal or vertical position, in points, from the left or top edge of the form, **Frame**, or **Page**.

Settings

The settings for *Button* are:

Constant	Value	Description
fmButtonLeft	1	The left button was pressed.
fmButtonRight	2	The right button was pressed.
fmButtonMiddle	4	The middle button was pressed.

The settings for *Shift* are:

Value	Description
1	SHIFT was pressed.
2	CTRL was pressed.
3	SHIFT and CTRL were pressed.
4	ALT was pressed.
5	ALT and SHIFT were pressed.
6	ALT and CTRL were pressed.
7	ALT, SHIFT, and CTRL were pressed.

You can identify individual keyboard modifiers by using the following constants:

Constant	Value	Description
fmShiftMask	1	Mask to detect SHIFT.
fmCtrlMask	2	Mask to detect CTRL.
fmAltMask	4	Mask to detect ALT.

Remarks

For a **MultiPage**, the MouseDown event occurs when the user presses a mouse button over the control.

For a **TabStrip**, the index argument identifies the tab where the user clicked. An index of –1 indicates the user did not click a tab. For example, if there are no tabs in the upper right corner of the control, clicking in the upper right corner sets the index to –1.

For a form, the user can generate MouseDown and MouseUp events by pressing and releasing a mouse button in a blank area, record selector, or scroll bar on the form.

The sequence of mouse-related events is:

1. MouseDown
2. MouseUp
3. Click
4. DblClick
5. MouseUp

MouseDown or MouseUp event procedures specify actions that occur when a mouse button is pressed or released. MouseDown and MouseUp events enable you to distinguish between the left, right, and middle mouse buttons. You can also write code for mouse-keyboard combinations that use the SHIFT, CTRL, and ALT keyboard modifiers.

If a mouse button is pressed while the pointer is over a form or control, that object "captures" the mouse and receives all mouse events up to and including the last MouseUp event. This implies that the *X*, *Y* mouse-pointer coordinates returned by a mouse event may not always be within the boundaries of the object that receives them.

If mouse buttons are pressed in succession, the object that captures the mouse receives all successive mouse events until all buttons are released.

Use the *Shift* argument to identify the state of SHIFT, CTRL, and ALT when the MouseDown or MouseUp event occurred. For example, if both CTRL and ALT are pressed, the value of *Shift* is 6.

See Also

Click event, DblClick event, MouseMove event.

MouseIcon Property

Applies To

CheckBox control, **ComboBox** control, **CommandButton** control, **Frame** control, **Image** control, **Label** control, **ListBox** control, **OptionButton** control, **ScrollBar** control, **SpinButton** control, **TabStrip** control, **TextBox** control, **ToggleButton** control, **UserForm** object.

Description

Assigns a custom icon to an object.

Syntax

object.**MouseIcon = LoadPicture(** *pathname*)

The **MouseIcon** property syntax has these parts:

Part	Description
object	Required. A valid object.
pathname	Required. A string expression specifying the path and filename of the file containing the custom icon.

Remarks

The **MouseIcon** property is valid when the **MousePointer** property is set to 99. The mouse icon of an object is the image that appears when the user moves the mouse across that object.

To assign an image for the mouse pointer, you can either assign a picture to the **MouseIcon** property or load a picture from a file using the **LoadPicture** function.

See Also

MousePointer property.

Example

The following example demonstrates how to specify a mouse pointer that is appropriate for a specific control or situation. You can assign one of several available mouse pointers using the **MousePointer** property; or, you can assign a custom icon using the **MousePointer** and **MouseIcon** properties.

This example works in the following ways:

- Choose a mouse pointer from the **ListBox** to change the mouse pointer associated with the first **CommandButton**.
- Click the first **CommandButton** to associate its mouse pointer with the second **CommandButton**.
- Click the second **CommandButton** to load a custom icon for its mouse pointer.

To use this example, copy this sample code to the Declarations portion of a form. Make sure that the form contains:

- Two **CommandButton** controls named CommandButton1 and CommandButton2.
- A **ListBox** named ListBox1.

Note This example uses two icon files (identified by the ico file extension) that are loaded using the **LoadPicture** function. You should edit each **LoadPicture** function call to specify an icon file that resides on your system.

```
Private Sub ListBox1_Click()
   If IsNull(ListBox1.Value) = False Then
      CommandButton1.MousePointer = ListBox1.Value

      If CommandButton1.MousePointer = fmMousePointerCustom Then
         CommandButton1.MouseIcon = LoadPicture("c:\msvc20\cdk32\" _
         & "samples\circl\bix.ico")
      End If
   End If
End Sub

Private Sub CommandButton1_Click()
   CommandButton2.MousePointer = CommandButton1.MousePointer

   If CommandButton2.MousePointer = fmMousePointerCustom Then
      CommandButton2.MouseIcon = CommandButton1.MouseIcon
   End If
End Sub

Private Sub CommandButton2_Click()
   CommandButton2.MousePointer = fmMousePointerCustom
   CommandButton2.MouseIcon = LoadPicture("c:\msvc20\cdk32\samples\push" _
   & "\push.ico")
End Sub

Private Sub UserForm_Initialize()
   'Load ListBox with MousePointer choices
   ListBox1.ColumnCount = 2

   ListBox1.AddItem "fmMousePointerDefault"
   ListBox1.List(0, 1) = fmMousePointerDefault
   ListBox1.AddItem "fmMousePointerArrow"
   ListBox1.List(1, 1) = fmMousePointerArrow
   ListBox1.AddItem "fmMousePointerCross"
   ListBox1.List(2, 1) = fmMousePointerCross

   ListBox1.AddItem "fmMousePointerIBeam"
   ListBox1.List(3, 1) = fmMousePointerIBeam
   ListBox1.AddItem "fmMousePointerSizeNESW"
   ListBox1.List(4, 1) = fmMousePointerSizeNESW
   ListBox1.AddItem "fmMousePointerSizeNS"
   ListBox1.List(5, 1) = fmMousePointerSizeNS
```

```
    ListBox1.AddItem "fmMousePointerSizeNWSE"
    ListBox1.List(6, 1) = fmMousePointerSizeNWSE
    ListBox1.AddItem "fmMousePointerSizeWE"
    ListBox1.List(7, 1) = fmMousePointerSizeWE
    ListBox1.AddItem "fmMousePointerUpArrow"
    ListBox1.List(8, 1) = fmMousePointerUpArrow

    ListBox1.AddItem "fmMousePointerHourglass"
    ListBox1.List(9, 1) = fmMousePointerHourGlass
    ListBox1.AddItem "fmMousePointerNoDrop"
    ListBox1.List(10, 1) = fmMousePointerNoDrop
    ListBox1.AddItem "fmMousePointerAppStarting"
    ListBox1.List(11, 1) = fmMousePointerAppStarting

    ListBox1.AddItem "fmMousePointerHelp"
    ListBox1.List(12, 1) = fmMousePointerHelp
    ListBox1.AddItem "fmMousePointerSizeAll"
    ListBox1.List(13, 1) = fmMousePointerSizeAll
    ListBox1.AddItem "fmMousePointerCustom"
    ListBox1.List(14, 1) = fmMousePointerCustom

    ListBox1.BoundColumn = 2
    ListBox1.Value = fmMousePointerDefault

    MsgBox "ListBox1.Value =" & ListBox1.Value & "."
    CommandButton1.MousePointer = ListBox1.Value
End Sub
```

MouseMove Event

Applies To

CheckBox control, **ComboBox** control, **CommandButton** control, **Frame** control, **Image** control, **Label** control, **ListBox** control, **MultiPage** control, **OptionButton** control, **TabStrip** control, **TextBox** control, **ToggleButton** control, **UserForm** object.

Description

Occurs when the user moves the mouse.

Syntax

For MultiPage, TabStrip:

Private Sub *object*_**MouseMove(** *index* **As Long**, **ByVal** *Button* **As fmButton**, ➥ **ByVal** *Shift* **As fmShiftState**, **ByVal** *X* **As Single**, **ByVal** *Y* **As Single)**

For other controls:

Private Sub *object*_**MouseMove(** **ByVal** *Button* **As fmButton**, **ByVal** *Shift* **As** ➥ **fmShiftState**, **ByVal** *X* **As Single**, **ByVal** *Y* **As Single)**

The MouseMove event syntax has these parts:

Part	Description
object	Required. A valid object name.
index	Required. The index of the page or tab in a **MultiPage** or **TabStrip** associated with this event.
Button	Required. An integer value that identifies the state of the mouse buttons.
Shift	Required. Specifies the state of SHIFT, CTRL, and ALT.
X, Y	Required. The horizontal or vertical position, measured in points, from the left or top edge of the control.

Settings

The *index* argument specifies which page or tab was clicked over. A –1 designates that the user did not click on any of the pages or tabs.

The settings for *Button* are:

Value	Description
0	No button is pressed.
1	The left button is pressed.
2	The right button is pressed.
3	The right and left buttons are pressed.
4	The middle button is pressed.
5	The middle and left buttons are pressed.
6	The middle and right buttons are pressed.
7	All three buttons are pressed.

The settings for *Shift* are:

Value	Description
1	SHIFT was pressed.
2	CTRL was pressed.
3	SHIFT and CTRL were pressed.
4	ALT was pressed.
5	ALT and SHIFT were pressed.
6	ALT and CTRL were pressed.
7	ALT, SHIFT, and CTRL were pressed.

You can identify individual keyboard modifiers by using the following constants:

Constant	Value	Description
fmShiftMask	1	Mask to detect SHIFT.
fmCtrlMask	2	Mask to detect CTRL.
fmAltMask	4	Mask to detect ALT.

Remarks

The MouseMove event applies to forms, controls on a form, and labels.

MouseMove events are generated continually as the mouse pointer moves across objects. Unless another object has captured the mouse, an object recognizes a MouseMove event whenever the mouse position is within its borders.

Moving a form can also generate a MouseMove event even if the mouse is stationary. MouseMove events are generated when the form moves underneath the pointer. If a macro or event procedure moves a form in response to a MouseMove event, the event can continually generate (cascade) MouseMove events.

If two controls are very close together, and you move the mouse pointer quickly over the space between them, the MouseMove event might not occur for that space. In such cases, you might need to respond to the MouseMove event in both controls.

You can use the value returned in the *Button* argument to identify the state of the mouse buttons.

Use the *Shift* argument to identify the state of SHIFT, CTRL, and ALT when the MouseMove event occurred. For example, if both CTRL and ALT are pressed, the value of *Shift* is 6.

Note You can use MouseDown and MouseUp event procedures to respond to events caused by pressing and releasing mouse buttons.

See Also

MouseDown, MouseUp events.

Example

The following example demonstrates a drag-and-drop operation from one **ListBox** to another using a **DataObject** to contain the dragged text. This code sample uses the **SetText** and **StartDrag** methods in the MouseMove event to implement the drag-and-drop operation.

To use this example, copy this sample code to the Declarations portion of a form. Make sure that the form contains two **ListBox** controls named ListBox1 and ListBox2. You also need to add choices to the second **ListBox**.

```
Private Sub ListBox2_BeforeDragOver(ByVal Cancel As MSForms.ReturnBoolean, _
      ByVal Data As MSForms.DataObject, ByVal X As Single, ByVal Y As _
      Single, ByVal DragState As Long, ByVal Effect As MSForms.Return _
      Effect, ByVal Shift As Integer)
   Cancel = True
   Effect = 1
End Sub
```

```
Private Sub ListBox2_BeforeDropOrPaste(ByVal Cancel As MSForms.Return _
        Boolean, ByVal Action As Long, ByVal Data As MSForms.DataObject, _
        ByVal X As Single, ByVal Y As Single, ByVal Effect As MSForms. _
        ReturnEffect, ByVal Shift As Integer)
    Cancel = True
    Effect = 1
    ListBox2.AddItem Data.GetText
End Sub

Private Sub ListBox1_MouseMove(ByVal Button As Integer, ByVal Shift As _
        Integer, ByVal X As Single, ByVal Y As Single)
    Dim MyDataObject As DataObject
    If Button = 1 Then
        Set MyDataObject = New DataObject
        Dim Effect As Integer
        MyDataObject.SetText ListBox1.Value
        Effect = MyDataObject.StartDrag
    End If
End Sub

Private Sub UserForm_Initialize()
    For i = 1 To 10
        ListBox1.AddItem "Choice " & (ListBox1.ListCount + 1)
    Next i
End Sub
```

MousePointer Property

Applies To

CheckBox control, **ComboBox** control, **CommandButton** control, **Frame** control, **Image** control, **Label** control, **ListBox** control, **OptionButton** control, **ScrollBar** control, **SpinButton** control, **TabStrip** control, **TextBox** control, **ToggleButton** control, **UserForm** object.

Description

Specifies the type of pointer displayed when the user positions the mouse over a particular object.

Syntax

object.**MousePointer** [= *fmMousePointer*]

The **MousePointer** property syntax has these parts:

Part	Description
object	Required. A valid object.
fmMousePointer	Optional. The shape you want for the mouse pointer.

Settings

The settings for *fmMousePointer* are:

Constant	Value	Description
fmMousePointerDefault	0	Standard pointer. The image is determined by the object (default).
fmMousePointerArrow	1	Arrow.
fmMousePointerCross	2	Cross-hair pointer.
fmMousePointerIBeam	3	I-beam.
fmMousePointerSizeNESW	6	Double arrow pointing northeast and southwest.
fmMousePointerSizeNS	7	Double arrow pointing north and south.
fmMousePointerSizeNWSE	8	Double arrow pointing northwest and southeast.
fmMousePointerSizeWE	9	Double arrow pointing west and east.
fmMousePointerUpArrow	10	Up arrow.
fmMousePointerHourglass	11	Hourglass.
fmMousePointerNoDrop	12	"Not" symbol (circle with a diagonal line) on top of the object being dragged. Indicates an invalid drop target.
fmMousePointerAppStarting	13	Arrow with an hourglass.
fmMousePointerHelp	14	Arrow with a question mark.
fmMousePointerSizeAll	15	Size all cursor (arrows pointing north, south, east, and west).
fmMousePointerCustom	99	Uses the icon specified by the **MouseIcon** property.

Remarks

Use the **MousePointer** property when you want to indicate changes in functionality as the mouse pointer passes over controls on a form. For example, the hourglass setting (11) is useful to indicate that the user must wait for a process or operation to finish.

Some icons vary depending on system settings, such as the icons associated with desktop themes.

See Also

MouseIcon property.

Example

See the **MouseIcon** property example.

MouseUp Event

See MouseDown, MouseUp Events.

Move Method

Applies To

CheckBox control, **ComboBox** control, **CommandButton** control, **Controls** collection, **Frame** control, **Image** control, **Label** control, **ListBox** control, **MultiPage** control, **OptionButton** control, **ScrollBar** control, **SpinButton** control, **TabStrip** control, **TextBox** control, **ToggleButton** control, **UserForm** object.

Description

Moves a form or control, or moves all the controls in the **Controls** collection.

Syntax

For a form or control:

object.**Move(** [*Left* [, *Top* [, *Width* [, *Height* [, *Layout*]]]]])

For the Controls collection:

object.**Move(** X, Y)

The **Move** method syntax has these parts:

Part	Description
object	Required. A valid object name.
Left	Optional. Single-precision value, in points, indicating the horizontal coordinate for the left edge of the object.
Top	Optional. Single-precision value, in points, that specifies the vertical coordinate for the top edge of the object.
Width	Optional. Single-precision value, in points, indicating the width of the object.
Height	Optional. Single-precision value, in points, indicating the height of the object.
Layout	Optional. A Boolean value indicating whether the Layout event is initiated for the control's parent following this move. **False** is the default value.
X, Y	Required. Single-precision value, in points, that specifies the change from the current horizontal and vertical position for each control in the **Controls** collection.

Settings

The maximum and minimum values for the *Left*, *Top*, *Width*, *Height*, *X*, and *Y* arguments vary from one application to another.

Remarks

For a form or control, you can move a selection to a specific location relative to the edges of the form that contains the selection.

You can use named arguments, or you can enter the arguments by position. If you use named arguments, you can list the arguments in any order. If not, you must enter the arguments in the order shown, using commas to indicate the relative position of arguments you do not specify. Any unspecified arguments remain unchanged.

For the **Controls** collection, you can move all the controls in this collection a specific distance from their current positions on a form, **Frame**, or **Page**.

Example

The following example demonstrates moving all the controls on a form by using the **Move** method with the **Controls** collection. The user clicks on the **CommandButton** to move the controls.

To use this example, copy this sample code to the Declarations portion of a form. Make sure that the form contains a **CommandButton** named CommandButton1 and several other controls.

```
Private Sub CommandButton1_Click()
    'Move each control on the form right 25 points and up 25 points.
Controls.Move 25, -25
End Sub
```

Example

The following example moves a selected control on a form with the **Move** method, and uses the Layout event and **LayoutEffect** property to identify the control that moved (and changed the layout of the **UserForm**). The user clicks a control to move and then clicks the **CommandButton**. A message box displays the name of the control that is moving.

To use this example, copy this sample code to the Declarations portion of a form. Make sure that the form contains:

- A **TextBox** named TextBox1.
- A **ComboBox** named ComboBox1.
- An **OptionButton** named OptionButton1.
- A **CommandButton** named CommandButton1.
- A **ToggleButton** named ToggleButton1.

```
Private Sub UserForm_Initialize()
    CommandButton1.Caption = "Move current control"
    CommandButton1.AutoSize = True
    CommandButton1.TakeFocusOnClick = False

    ToggleButton1.Caption = "Use Layout Event"
    ToggleButton1.Value = True
End Sub
```

```
Private Sub CommandButton1_Click()
   If ActiveControl.Name = "ToggleButton1" Then
      'Keep it stationary
   Else
      'Move the control, using Layout event when ToggleButton1.Value is True
      ActiveControl.Move 0, 0, , , ToggleButton1.Value
   End If
End Sub

Private Sub UserForm_Layout()
   Dim MyControl As Control

   MsgBox "In the Layout Event"

   'Find the control that is moving.
   For Each MyControl In Controls
      If MyControl.LayoutEffect = fmLayoutEffectInitiate Then
         MsgBox MyControl.Name & " is moving."
         Exit For
      End If
   Next
End Sub

Private Sub ToggleButton1_Click()
   If ToggleButton1.Value = True Then
      ToggleButton1.Caption = "Use Layout Event"
   Else
      ToggleButton1.Caption = "No Layout Event"
   End If
End Sub
```

MultiLine Property

Applies To

TextBox control.

Description

Specifies whether a control can accept and display multiple lines of text.

Syntax

object.**MultiLine** [= *Boolean*]

The **MultiLine** property syntax has these parts:

Part	Description
object	Required. A valid object.
Boolean	Optional. Whether the control supports more than one line of text.

Settings

The settings for *Boolean* are:

Value	Description
True	The text is displayed across multiple lines (default).
False	The text is not displayed across multiple lines.

Remarks

A multiline **TextBox** allows absolute line breaks and adjusts its quantity of lines to accommodate the amount of text it holds. If needed, a multiline control can have vertical scroll bars.

A single-line **TextBox** doesn't allow absolute line breaks and doesn't use vertical scroll bars.

Single-line controls ignore the value of the **WordWrap** property.

Note If you change **MultiLine** to **False** in a multiline **TextBox**, all the characters in the **TextBox** will be combined into one line, including non-printing characters (such as carriage returns and new-lines).

See Also

AutoSize property, **EnterKeyBehavior** property, **ScrollBars** property, **WordWrap** property.

Example

The following example demonstrates the **MultiLine**, **WordWrap**, and **ScrollBars** properties on a **TextBox**.

To use this example, copy this sample code to the Declarations portion of a form. Make sure that the form contains:

- A **TextBox** named TextBox1.
- Four **ToggleButton** controls named ToggleButton1 through ToggleButton4.

To see the entire text placed in the **TextBox**, set **MultiLine** and **WordWrap** to **True** by clicking the **ToggleButton** controls.

When **MultiLine** is **True**, you can enter new lines of text by pressing SHIFT+ENTER.

ScrollBars appears when you manually change the content of the **TextBox**.

```
Private Sub UserForm_Initialize()
'Initialize TextBox properties and toggle buttons

   TextBox1.Text = "Type your text here. Enter SHIFT+ENTER to move " _
      & "to a new line."

   TextBox1.AutoSize = False
   ToggleButton1.Caption = "AutoSize Off"
   ToggleButton1.Value = False
   ToggleButton1.AutoSize = True
```

```
    TextBox1.WordWrap = False
    ToggleButton2.Caption = "WordWrap Off"
    ToggleButton2.Value = False
    ToggleButton2.AutoSize = True

    TextBox1.ScrollBars = 0
    ToggleButton3.Caption = "ScrollBars Off"
    ToggleButton3.Value = False
    ToggleButton3.AutoSize = True

    TextBox1.MultiLine = False
    ToggleButton4.Caption = "Single Line"
    ToggleButton4.Value = False
    ToggleButton4.AutoSize = True
 End Sub

Private Sub ToggleButton1_Click()
'Set AutoSize property and associated ToggleButton

    If ToggleButton1.Value = True Then
        TextBox1.AutoSize = True
        ToggleButton1.Caption = "AutoSize On"
    Else
        TextBox1.AutoSize = False
        ToggleButton1.Caption = "AutoSize Off"
    End If
End Sub

Private Sub ToggleButton2_Click()
'Set WordWrap property and associated ToggleButton

    If ToggleButton2.Value = True Then
        TextBox1.WordWrap = True
        ToggleButton2.Caption = "WordWrap On"
    Else
        TextBox1.WordWrap = False
        ToggleButton2.Caption = "WordWrap Off"
    End If
End Sub

Private Sub ToggleButton3_Click()
'Set ScrollBars property and associated ToggleButton

    If ToggleButton3.Value = True Then
        TextBox1.ScrollBars = 3
        ToggleButton3.Caption = "ScrollBars On"
    Else
        TextBox1.ScrollBars = 0
        ToggleButton3.Caption = "ScrollBars Off"
    End If
End Sub
```

```
Private Sub ToggleButton4_Click()
'Set MultiLine property and associated ToggleButton

   If ToggleButton4.Value = True Then
      TextBox1.MultiLine = True
      ToggleButton4.Caption = "Multiple Lines"
   Else
      TextBox1.MultiLine = False
      ToggleButton4.Caption = "Single Line"
   End If
End Sub
```

MultiPage Control

Description

Presents multiple screens of information as a single set.

Remarks

A **MultiPage** is useful when you work with a large amount of information that can be sorted into several categories. For example, use a **MultiPage** to display information from an employment application. One page might contain personal information such as name and address; another page might list previous employers; a third page might list references. The **MultiPage** lets you visually combine related information, while keeping the entire record readily accessible.

New pages are added to the right of the currently selected page rather than adjacent to it.

Note The **MultiPage** is a container of a **Pages** collection, each of which contains one or more **Page** objects.

The default property for a **MultiPage** is the **Value** property, which returns the index of the currently active **Page** in the **Pages** collection of the **MultiPage**.

The default event for a **MultiPage** is the Change event.

Properties

BackColor property, **BoundValue** property, **ControlTipText** property, **Enabled** property, **Font** object, **ForeColor** property, **Height**, **Width** properties, **HelpContextID** property, **LayoutEffect** property, **Left**, **Top** properties, **MultiRow** property, **Name** property, **Object** property, **OldHeight**, **OldWidth** properties, **OldLeft**, **OldTop** properties, **Parent** property, **SelectedItem** property, **Style** property, **TabFixedHeight**, **TabFixedWidth** properties, **TabIndex** property, **TabOrientation** property, **TabStop** property, **Tag** property, **Value** property, **Visible** property.

Methods

Move method, **SetFocus** method, **ZOrder** method.

Events

AddControl event, BeforeDragOver event, BeforeDropOrPaste event, Change event, Click event, DblClick event, Enter, Exit events, Error event, KeyDown, KeyUp events, KeyPress event, Layout event, MouseDown, MouseUp events, MouseMove event, RemoveControl event, Scroll event, Zoom event.

See Also

Controls collection, **Page** object, **Pages** collection.

Example

The following example accesses an individual page of a **MultiPage** in several ways:

- Using the **Pages** collection with a numeric index.
- Using the **Pages** collection with a string index.
- Using the **Pages** collection with the **Item** method.
- Using the name of the individual page in the **MultiPage**.
- Using the **SelectedItem** property.

To use this example, copy this sample code to the Declarations portion of a form. Make sure that the form contains a **MultiPage** named MultiPage1.

```
Private Sub UserForm_Initialize()
   Dim PageNAme As String

   For i = 0 To MultiPage1.Count - 1
      'Use index (numeric or string)
      MsgBox "MultiPage1.Pages(i).Caption = " & MultiPage1.Pages(i).Caption
      MsgBox "MultiPage1.Pages.Item(i).Caption = " & MultiPage1.Pages _
         .Item(i).Caption

      PageNAme = MultiPage1.Pages(i).Name
      MsgBox "PageName = " & PageNAme

      MsgBox "MultiPage1.Pages(PageName).Caption = " & MultiPage1. _
         Pages(PageNAme).Caption
      MsgBox "MultiPage1.Pages.Item(PageName).Caption = " & MultiPage1. _
         Pages.Item(PageNAme).Caption

      'Use Page object without referring to Pages collection
      If i = 0 Then
         MsgBox "MultiPage1.Page1.Caption= " & MultiPage1.Page1.Caption
      ElseIf i = 1 Then
         MsgBox "MultiPage1.Page2.Caption = " & MultiPage1.Page2.Caption
      End If

      'Use SelectedItem Property
      MultiPage1.Value = i
      MsgBox "MultiPage1.SelectedItem.Caption = " & MultiPage1.Selected _
         Item.Caption
   Next i
End Sub
```

MultiRow Property

Applies To

MultiPage control, **TabStrip** control.

Description

Specifies whether the control has more than one row of tabs.

Syntax

object.**MultiRow** [= *Boolean*]

The **MultiRow** property syntax has these parts:

Part	Description
object	Required. A valid object.
Boolean	Optional. Whether the control has more than one row of tabs.

Settings

The settings for *Boolean* are:

Value	Description
True	Allows more than one row of tabs.
False	Restricts tabs to a single row (default).

Remarks

The width and number of tabs determine the number of rows. Changing the control's size also changes the number of rows. This allows the developer to resize the control and ensure that tabs wrap to fit the control. If the **MultiRow** property is **False**, then truncation occurs if the width of the tabs exceeds the width of the control.

If **MultiRow** is **False** and tabs are truncated, there will be a small scroll bar on the **TabStrip** to allow scrolling to the other tabs or pages.

MultiSelect Property

Applies To

ListBox control.

Description

Indicates whether the object permits multiple selections.

Syntax

object.**MultiSelect** [= *fmMultiSelect*]

The **MultiSelect** property syntax has these parts:

Part	Description
object	Required. A valid object.
fmMultiSelect	Optional. The selection mode that the control uses.

Settings

The settings for *fmMultiSelect* are:

Constant	Value	Description
fmMultiSelectSingle	0	Only one item can be selected (default).
fmMultiSelectMulti	1	Pressing the SPACEBAR or clicking selects or deselects an item in the list.
fmMultiSelectExtended	2	Pressing SHIFT and clicking the mouse, or pressing SHIFT and one of the arrow keys, extends the selection from the previously selected item to the current item. Pressing CTRL and clicking the mouse selects or deselects an item.

Remarks

When the **MultiSelect** property is set to *Extended* or *Simple*, you must use the list box's **Selected** property to determine the selected items. Also, the **Value** property of the control is always **Null**.

The **ListIndex** property returns the index of the row with the keyboard focus.

See Also

ListIndex property, **Selected** property, **Value** property.

Example

The following example uses the **MultiSelect** and **Selected** properties to demonstrate how the user can select one or more items in a **ListBox**. The user specifies a selection method by choosing an option button and then selects an item(s) from the **ListBox**. The user can display the selected items in a second **ListBox** by clicking the **CommandButton**.

To use this example, copy this sample code to the Declarations portion of a form. Make sure that the form contains:

- Two **ListBox** controls named ListBox1 and ListBox2.
- A **CommandButton** named CommandButton1.
- Three **OptionButton** controls named OptionButton1 through OptionButton3.

```
Dim i As Integer

Private Sub CommandButton1_Click()
   ListBox2.Clear

   For i = 0 To 9
      If ListBox1.Selected(i) = True Then
         ListBox2.AddItem ListBox1.List(i)
      End If
   Next i

End Sub

Private Sub OptionButton1_Click()
   ListBox1.MultiSelect = fmMultiSelectSingle
End Sub

Private Sub OptionButton2_Click()
   ListBox1.MultiSelect = fmMultiSelectMulti
End Sub

Private Sub OptionButton3_Click()
   ListBox1.MultiSelect = fmMultiSelectExtended
End Sub

Private Sub UserForm_Initialize()
   For i = 0 To 9
      ListBox1.AddItem "Choice " & (ListBox1.ListCount + 1)
   Next i

   OptionButton1.Caption = "Single Selection"
   ListBox1.MultiSelect = fmMultiSelectSingle
   OptionButton1.Value = True

   OptionButton2.Caption = "Multiple Selection"
   OptionButton3.Caption = "Extended Selection"

   CommandButton1.Caption = "Show selections"
   CommandButton1.AutoSize = True
End Sub
```

Name Property

Applies To

CheckBox control, **ComboBox** control, **CommandButton** control, **Font** object, **Image** control, **Label** control, **ListBox** control, **MultiPage** control, **OptionButton** control, **Page** object, **ScrollBar** control, **SpinButton** control, **Tab** object, **TabStrip** control, **TextBox** control, **ToggleButton** control, **UserForm** object.

Description

Specifies the name of a control or an object, or the name of a font to associate with a **Font** object.

Syntax

For Font:

Font.**Name** [= *String*]

For all other controls and objects:

object.**Name** [= *String*]

The **Name** property syntax has these parts:

Part	Description
object	Required. A valid object.
String	Optional. The name you want to assign to the font or control.

Settings

Guidelines for assigning a string to **Name**, such as the maximum length of the name, vary from one application to another.

Remarks

For objects, the default value of **Name** consists of the object's class name followed by an integer. For example, the default name for the first **TextBox** you place on a form is TextBox1. The default name for the second **TextBox** is TextBox2.

You can set the **Name** property for a control from the control's property sheet or, for controls added at run time, by using program statements. If you add a control at design time, you cannot modify its **Name** property at run time.

Each control added to a form at design time must have a unique name.

For **Font** objects, **Name** identifies a particular typeface to use in the text portion of a control, object, or form. The font's appearance on screen and in print may differ, depending on your computer and printer. If you select a font that your system can't display or that isn't installed, Windows substitutes a similar font.

See Also

Bold, **Italic**, **Size**, **StrikeThrough**, **Underline**, **Weight** properties.

Example

The following example displays the **Name** property of each control on a form. This example uses the **Controls** collection to cycle through all the controls placed directly on the Userform.

To use this example, copy this sample code to the Declarations portion of a form. Make sure that the form contains a **CommandButton** named CommandButton1 and several other controls.

```
Private Sub CommandButton1_Click()
   Dim MyControl As Control

   For Each MyControl In Controls
      MsgBox "MyControl.Name = " & MyControl.Name
   Next
End Sub
```

Object Property

Applies To

CheckBox control, **ComboBox** control, **CommandButton** control, **Image** control, **Label** control, **ListBox** control, **MultiPage** control, **OptionButton** control, **ScrollBar** control, **SpinButton** control, **TabStrip** control, **TextBox** control, **ToggleButton** control.

Description

Overrides a standard property or method when a new control has a property or method of the same name.

Syntax

object.**Object**[.*property* |.*method*]

The **Object** property syntax has these parts:

Part	Description
object	Required. The name of an object you have added to the Microsoft Forms Toolbox.
property	Optional. A property that has the same name as a standard Microsoft Forms property.
method	Optional. A method that has the same name as a standard Microsoft Forms method.

Remarks

Object is read-only.

If you add a new control to the Microsoft Forms Toolbox, it is possible that the added control will have a property or method with the same name as a standard Microsoft Forms property or method. The **Object** property lets you use the property or method from the added control, rather than the standard property or method.

Example

Assume a new control has a **Top** property that is different from the standard **Top** property in Microsoft Forms. You can use either property, based on the syntax:

- `control.Top` uses the standard **Top** property.
- `control.Object.Top` uses the **Top** property from the added control.

OldHeight, OldWidth Properties

Applies To

CheckBox control, **ComboBox** control, **CommandButton** control, **Image** control, **Label** control, **ListBox** control, **MultiPage** control, **OptionButton** control, **ScrollBar** control, **SpinButton** control, **TabStrip** control, **TextBox** control, **ToggleButton** control.

Description

Returns the previous height or width, in points, of the control.

Syntax

object.**OldHeight**
object.**OldWidth**

The **OldHeight** and **OldWidth** property syntaxes have these parts:

Part	Description
object	Required. A valid object.

Remarks

OldHeight and **OldWidth** are read-only.

The **OldHeight** and **OldWidth** properties are automatically updated when you move or size a control. If you change the size of a control, the **Height** and **Width** properties store the new height and **OldHeight** and **OldWidth** store the previous height.

These properties are valid only in the Layout event.

See Also

Height, **Width** properties, Layout event, **LayoutEffect** property, **OldLeft**, **OldTop** properties.

Example

The following example uses the **OldLeft**, **OldTop**, **OldHeight**, and **OldWidth** properties within the Layout event to keep a control at its current position and size. The user clicks the **CommandButton** labeled **Move ComboBox** to move the control, and then responds to a message box. The user can click the **CommandButton** labeled **Reset ComboBox** to reset the control for another repetition.

To use this example, copy this sample code to the Declarations portion of a form. Make sure that the form contains:

- Two **CommandButton** controls named CommandButton1 and CommandButton2.
- A **ComboBox** named ComboBox1.

```
Dim Initialize As Integer
Dim ComboLeft, ComboTop, ComboWidth, ComboHeight As Integer

Private Sub UserForm_Initialize()
   Initialize = 0
   CommandButton1.Caption = "Move ComboBox"
   CommandButton2.Caption = "Reset ComboBox"

   'Information for resetting ComboBox
   ComboLeft = ComboBox1.Left
   ComboTop = ComboBox1.Top
   ComboWidth = ComboBox1.Width
   ComboHeight = ComboBox1.Height
End Sub

Private Sub CommandButton1_Click()
      ComboBox1.Move 0, 0, , , True
End Sub

Private Sub UserForm_Layout()
   Dim MyControl As Control
   Dim MsgBoxResult As Integer

   If Initialize = 0 Then   'Suppress MsgBox on initial layout event.
      Initialize = 1
      Exit Sub
   End If

   MsgBoxResult = MsgBox("In Layout event - Continue move?", vbYesNo)
   If MsgBoxResult = vbNo Then
      ComboBox1.Move ComboBox1.OldLeft, ComboBox1.OldTop, ComboBox1. _
         OldWidth, ComboBox1.OldHeight
   End If
End Sub
```

```
Private Sub CommandButton2_Click()
    ComboBox1.Move ComboLeft, ComboTop, ComboWidth, ComboHeight

    'OldLeft, OldTop, OldWidth, and OldHeight are not recognized here.
    'The following statement, if not commented, would produce an error
    'at run time.

    'ComboBox1.Move ComboBox1.OldLeft, ComboBox1.OldTop, ComboBox1.
    'OldWidth, ComboBox1.OldHeight
End Sub
```

OldLeft, OldTop Properties

Applies To

CheckBox control, **ComboBox** control, **CommandButton** control, **Image** control, **Label** control, **ListBox** control, **MultiPage** control, **OptionButton** control, **ScrollBar** control, **SpinButton** control, **TabStrip** control, **TextBox** control, **ToggleButton** control.

Description

Returns the distance, in points, between the previous position of a control and the left or top edge of the form that contains it.

Syntax

object.**OldLeft**
object.**OldTop**

The **OldLeft** and **OldTop** property syntaxes have these parts:

Part	Description
object	Required. A valid object.

Remarks

OldLeft and **OldTop** are read-only.

The **OldLeft** and **OldTop** properties are automatically updated when you move or size a control. If you move a control, the **Left** and **Top** properties store the new distance from the control to the left edge of its container and **OldLeft** and **OldTop** store the previous value of **Left**.

OldLeft and **OldTop** are valid only in the Layout event.

See Also

Layout event, **LayoutEffect** property, **Left**, **Top** properties, **OldHeight**, **OldWidth** properties.

Example

See the **OldHeight, OldWidth** properties example.

OldWidth Property

See OldHeight, OldWidth Properties.

OptionButton Control

Description

Shows the selection status of one item in a group of choices.

Remarks

Use an **OptionButton** to show whether a single item in a group is selected. Note that each **OptionButton** in a **Frame** is mutually exclusive.

If an **OptionButton** is bound to a data source, the **OptionButton** can show the value of that data source as either *Yes/No*, *True/False*, or *On/Off*. If the user selects the **OptionButton**, the current setting is *Yes*, *True*, or *On*; if the user does not select the **OptionButton**, the setting is *No*, *False*, or *Off*. For example, an **OptionButton** in an inventory-tracking application might show whether an item is discontinued. If the **OptionButton** is bound to a data source, then changing the settings changes the value of that data source. A disabled **OptionButton** is dimmed and does not show a value.

Depending on the value of the **TripleState** property, an **OptionButton** can also have a null value.

You can also use an **OptionButton** inside a group box to select one or more of a group of related items. For example, you can create an order form with a list of available items, with an **OptionButton** preceding each item. The user can select a particular item by checking the corresponding **OptionButton**.

The default property for an **OptionButton** is the **Value** property.

The default event for an **OptionButton** is the Click event.

Properties

Accelerator property, **Alignment** property, **AutoSize** property, **BackColor** property, **BackStyle** property, **BoundValue** property, **Caption** property, **ControlSource** property, **ControlTipText** property, **Enabled** property, **Font** object, **ForeColor** property, **GroupName** property, **Height**, **Width** properties, **HelpContextID** property, **LayoutEffect** property, **Left**, **Top** properties, **Locked** property, **MouseIcon** property, **MousePointer** property, **Name** property, **Object** property, **OldHeight**, **OldWidth** properties, **OldLeft**, **OldTop** properties, **Parent** property, **Picture** property, **PicturePosition** property, **SpecialEffect** property, **TabIndex** property, **TabStop** property, **Tag** property, **TripleState** property, **Value** property, **Visible** property, **WordWrap** property.

Methods

Move method, **SetFocus** method, **ZOrder** method.

Events

AfterUpdate event, BeforeDragOver event, BeforeDropOrPaste event, BeforeUpdate event, Change event, Click event, DblClick event, Enter, Exit events, Error event, KeyDown, KeyUp events, KeyPress event, MouseDown, MouseUp events, MouseMove event.

Example

See the **MatchEntry** property example.

Orientation Property

Applies To

ScrollBar control, **SpinButton** control.

Description

Specifies whether the **SpinButton** or **ScrollBar** is oriented vertically or horizontally.

Syntax

object.**Orientation** [= *fmOrientation*]

The **Orientation** property syntax has these parts:

Part	Description
object	Required. A valid object.
fmOrientation	Optional. Orientation of the control.

Settings

The settings for *fmOrientation* are:

Constant	Value	Description
fmOrientationAuto	–1	Automatically determines the orientation based upon the dimensions of the control (default).
FmOrientationVertical	0	Control is rendered vertically.
FmOrientationHorizontal	1	Control is rendered horizontally.

Remarks

If you specify automatic orientation, the height and width of the control determine whether it appears horizontally or vertically. For example, if the control is wider than it is tall, it appears horizontally; if it is taller than it is wide, the control appears vertically.

Page Object

Description

One page of a **MultiPage** and a single member of a **Pages** collection.

Remarks

Each **Page** object contains its own set of controls and does not necessarily rely on other pages in the collection for information. A **Page** inherits some properties from its container; the value of each inherited property is set by the container.

A **Page** has a unique name and index value within a **Pages** collection. You can reference a **Page** by either its name or its index value. The index of the first **Page** in a collection is 0; the index of the second **Page** is 1; and so on. When two **Page** objects have the same name, you must reference each **Page** by its index value. References to the name in code will access only the first **Page** that uses the name.

The default name for the first **Page** is Page1; the default name for the second **Page** is Page2.

Properties

Accelerator property, **ActiveControl** property, **CanPaste** property, **CanRedo** property, **CanUndo** property, **Caption** property, **ControlTipText** property, **Cycle** property, **Enabled** property, **HelpContextID** property, **Index** property, **InsideHeight**, **InsideWidth** properties, **KeepScrollBarsVisible** property, **Name** property, **Picture** property, **PictureAlignment** property, **PictureSizeMode** property, **PictureTiling** property, **ScrollBars** property, **ScrollHeight**, **ScrollWidth** properties, **ScrollLeft**, **ScrollTop** properties, **TabIndex** property, **TabStop** property, **Tag** property, **TransitionEffect** property, **TransitionPeriod** property, **VerticalScrollbarSide** property, **Visible** property, **Zoom** property.

Methods

Copy method, **Cut** method, **Paste** method, **RedoAction** method, **Repaint** method, **Scroll** method, **SetDefaultTabOrder** method, **UndoAction** method.

See Also

Controls collection, **MultiPage** control, **Pages** collection, **Tab** object.

Example

The following example uses the **Add**, **Clear**, and **Remove** methods to add and remove a control to a **Page** of a **MultiPage** at run time.

To use this example, copy this sample code to the Declarations portion of a form. Make sure that the form contains:

- A **MultiPage** named MultiPage1.
- Three **CommandButton** controls named CommandButton1 through CommandButton3.

```
Dim MyTextBox As Control

Private Sub CommandButton1_Click()
Set MyTextBox = MultiPage1.Pages(0).Controls.Add("Forms.TextBox.1", _
   "MyTextBox", Visible)
End Sub

Private Sub CommandButton2_Click()
   MultiPage1.Pages(0).Controls.Clear
End Sub

Private Sub CommandButton3_Click()
   If MultiPage1.Pages(0).Controls.Count > 0  Then
      MultiPage1.Pages(0).Controls.Remove "MyTextBox"
   End If
End Sub

Private Sub UserForm_Initialize()
   CommandButton1.Caption = "Add control"
   CommandButton2.Caption = "Clear controls"
   CommandButton3.Caption = "Remove control"
End Sub
```

Example

The following example uses the **Add**, **Cut**, and **Paste** methods to cut and paste a control from a **Page** of a **MultiPage**. The control involved in the cut and paste operations is dynamically added to the form.

This example assumes the user will add, then cut, then paste the new control.

To use this example, copy this sample code to the Declarations portion of a form. Make sure that the form contains:

- Three **CommandButton** controls named CommandButton1 through CommandButton3.
- A **MultiPage** named MultiPage1.

```
Dim MyTextBox As Control

Private Sub CommandButton1_Click()
   Set MyTextBox = MultiPage1.Pages(MultiPage1.Value).Controls.Add( _
      "Forms.TextBox.1", "MyTextBox", Visible)
   CommandButton2.Enabled = True
   CommandButton1.Enabled = False
End Sub
```

```
Private Sub CommandButton2_Click()
   MultiPage1.Pages(MultiPage1.Value).Controls.Cut
   CommandButton3.Enabled = True
   CommandButton2.Enabled = False
End Sub
Private Sub CommandButton3_Click()
   Dim MyPage As Object
   Set MyPage = MultiPage1.Pages.Item(MultiPage1.Value)

   MyPage.Paste
   CommandButton3.Enabled = False
End Sub
Private Sub UserForm_Initialize()
   CommandButton1.Caption = "Add"
   CommandButton2.Caption = "Cut"
   CommandButton3.Caption = "Paste"

   CommandButton1.Enabled = True
   CommandButton2.Enabled = False
   CommandButton3.Enabled = False
End Sub
```

Pages Collection

Applies To

MultiPage control.

Description

A **Pages** collection includes all the pages of a **MultiPage**.

Remarks

Each **Pages** collection provides the features to manage the number of pages in the collection and to identify the page that is currently in use.

A **Page** object has a unique name and index value within a **Pages** collection. You can reference a **Page** either by its name or its index value. The index of the first **Page** in a collection is 0; the index of the second **Page** is 1; and so on. The default name for the first page is Page1; the default name for the second page is Page2.

The default value of a **Pages** collection identifies the current **Page** of a collection.

Properties

Count property.

Methods

Add method, **Clear** method, **Item** method, **Remove** method.

See Also

Index property, **Page** object.

Example

See the **MultiPage** control example.

Parent Property

Applies To

CheckBox control, **ComboBox** control, **CommandButton** control, **Image** control, **Label** control, **ListBox** control, **MultiPage** control, **OptionButton** control, **ScrollBar** control, **SpinButton** control, **TabStrip** control, **TextBox** control, **ToggleButton** control.

Description

Returns the name of the form, object, or collection that contains a specific control, object, or collection.

Syntax

object.**Parent**

The **Parent** property syntax has these parts:

Part	Description
object	Required. A valid object.

Remarks

Parent is read-only.

Use the **Parent** property to access the properties, methods, or controls of an object's parent.

This property is useful in an application in which you pass objects as arguments. For example, you could pass a control variable to a general procedure in a module, and use **Parent** to access its parent form.

Example

The following example uses the **Parent** property to refer to the control or form that contains a specific control.

To use this example, copy this sample code to the Declarations portion of a form. Make sure that the form contains:

- Two **Label** controls named Label1 and Label2.
- A **CommandButton** named CommandButton1.
- One or more additional controls of your choice.

```
Dim MyControl As Object
Dim MyParent As Object
Dim ControlsIndex As Integer
```

```
Private Sub UserForm_Initialize()
   ControlsIndex = 0
   CommandButton1.Caption = "Get Control and Parent"
   CommandButton1.AutoSize = True
   CommandButton1.WordWrap = True
End Sub

Private Sub CommandButton1_Click()
   'Process Controls collection for UserForm
   Set MyControl = Controls.Item(ControlsIndex)
   Set MyParent = MyControl.Parent
   Label1.Caption = MyControl.Name
   Label2.Caption = MyParent.Name

   'Prepare index for next control on Userform
   ControlsIndex = ControlsIndex + 1
   If ControlsIndex >= Controls.Count Then
      ControlsIndex = 0
   End If
End Sub
```

PasswordChar Property

Applies To

TextBox control.

Description

Specifies whether placeholder characters are displayed instead of the characters actually entered in a **TextBox**.

Syntax

object.**PasswordChar** [= *String*]

The **PasswordChar** property syntax has these parts:

Part	Description
object	Required. A valid object.
String	Optional. A string expression specifying the placeholder character.

Remarks

You can use the **PasswordChar** property to protect sensitive information, such as passwords or security codes. The value of **PasswordChar** is the character that appears in a control instead of the actual characters that the user types. If you don't specify a character, the control displays the characters that the user types.

Paste Method

Applies To

ComboBox control, **Frame** control, **Page** object, **TextBox** control, **UserForm** object.

Description

Transfers the contents of the Clipboard to an object.

Syntax

object.**Paste**

The **Paste** method syntax has these parts:

Part	Description
object	Required. A valid object.

Remarks

Data pasted into a **ComboBox** or **TextBox** is treated as text.

When the **Paste** method is used with a form, you can paste any object onto the form.

See Also

CanPaste property, **Copy** method, **Cut** method.

Example

The following example uses the **CanPaste** property and the **Paste** method to paste a **ComboBox** from the Clipboard to a **Page** of a **MultiPage**. This sample also uses the **SetFocus** and **Copy** methods to copy a control from the form to the Clipboard.

The user clicks CommandButton1 to copy the **ComboBox** to the Clipboard. The user double-clicks (using the DblClick event) CommandButton1 to paste the **ComboBox** to the **MultiPage**.

To use this example, copy this sample code to the Declarations portion of a form. Make sure that the form contains:

- A **TextBox** named TextBox1.
- A **ComboBox** named ComboBox1.
- A **MultiPage** named MultiPage1.
- A **CommandButton** named CommandButton1.

Note This example also includes a subroutine to illustrate pasting text into a control.

```
Private Sub UserForm_Initialize()
   ComboBox1.AddItem "It's a beautiful day!"

   CommandButton1.Caption = "Copy ComboBox to Clipboard"
   CommandButton1.AutoSize = True
End Sub
```

```
Private Sub MultiPage1_DblClick(ByVal Index As Long, ByVal Cancel As _
      MSForms.ReturnBoolean)
   If MultiPage1.Pages(MultiPage1.Value).CanPaste = True Then
      MultiPage1.Pages(MultiPage1.Value).Paste
   Else
      TextBox1.Text = "Can't Paste"
   End If
End Sub

Private Sub CommandButton1_Click()
      UserForm1.ComboBox1.SetFocus
      UserForm1.Copy
End Sub

'Code for pasting text into a control
'Private Sub ComboBox1_DblClick(ByVal Cancel As MSForms.ReturnBoolean)
'    If ComboBox1.CanPaste = True Then
'         ComboBox1.Paste
'     Else
'         TextBox1.Text = "Can't Paste"
'     End If
'End Sub
```

Example

The following example uses the **Add**, **Cut**, and **Paste** methods to cut and paste a control from a **Page** of a **MultiPage**. The control involved in the cut and paste operations is dynamically added to the form.

This example assumes the user will add, then cut, then paste the new control.

To use this example, copy this sample code to the Declarations portion of a form. Make sure that the form contains:

- Three **CommandButton** controls named CommandButton1 through CommandButton3.
- A **MultiPage** named MultiPage1.

```
Dim MyTextBox As Control

Private Sub CommandButton1_Click()
   Set MyTextBox = MultiPage1.Pages(MultiPage1.Value).Controls.Add( _
      "Forms.TextBox.1", "MyTextBox", Visible)
   CommandButton2.Enabled = True
   CommandButton1.Enabled = False
End Sub
Private Sub CommandButton2_Click()
   MultiPage1.Pages(MultiPage1.Value).Controls.Cut
   CommandButton3.Enabled = True
   CommandButton2.Enabled = False
End Sub
```

```
Private Sub CommandButton3_Click()
   Dim MyPage As Object
   Set MyPage = MultiPage1.Pages.Item(MultiPage1.Value)

   MyPage.Paste
   CommandButton3.Enabled = False
End Sub
Private Sub UserForm_Initialize()
   CommandButton1.Caption = "Add"
   CommandButton2.Caption = "Cut"
   CommandButton3.Caption = "Paste"

   CommandButton1.Enabled = True
   CommandButton2.Enabled = False
   CommandButton3.Enabled = False
End Sub
```

Example

The following example uses the **Cut** and **Paste** methods to cut text from one **TextBox** and paste it into another **TextBox**.

To use this example, copy this sample code to the Declarations portion of a form. Make sure that the form contains:

- Two **TextBox** controls named TextBox1 and TextBox2.
- A **CommandButton** named CommandButton1.

```
Private Sub UserForm_Initialize()
   TextBox1.Text = "From TextBox1!"
   TextBox2.Text = "Hello "

   CommandButton1.Caption = "Cut and Paste"
   CommandButton1.AutoSize = True
End Sub

Private Sub CommandButton1_Click()
   TextBox2.SelStart = 0
   TextBox2.SelLength = TextBox2.TextLength
   TextBox2.Cut

   TextBox1.SetFocus
   TextBox1.SelStart = 0

   TextBox1.Paste
   TextBox2.SelStart = 0
End Sub
```

Picture Property

Applies To

CheckBox control, **CommandButton** control, **Frame** control, **Image** control, **Label** control, **OptionButton** control, **Page** object, **ToggleButton** control, **UserForm** object.

Description

Specifies the bitmap to display on an object.

Syntax

object.**Picture = LoadPicture(** *pathname***)**

The **Picture** property syntax has these parts:

Part	Description
object	Required. A valid object.
pathname	Required. The full path to a picture file.

Remarks

While designing a form, you can use the control's property page to assign a bitmap to the **Picture** property. While running a form, you must use the **LoadPicture** function to assign a bitmap to **Picture**.

To remove a picture that is assigned to a control, click the value of the **Picture** property in the property page and then press DELETE. Pressing BACKSPACE will not remove the picture.

Note For controls with captions, use the **PicturePosition** property to specify where to display the picture on the object. Use the **PictureSizeMode** property to determine how the picture fills the object.

Transparent pictures sometimes have a hazy appearance. If you do not like this appearance, display the picture on a control that supports opaque images. **Image** and **MultiPage** support opaque images.

See Also

PictureAlignment property, **PicturePosition** property, **PictureSizeMode** property, **PictureTiling** property.

Example

The following example uses a **ComboBox** to show the picture placement options for a control. Each time the user clicks a list choice, the picture and caption are updated on the **CommandButton**. This code sample also uses the **AddItem** method to populate the **ComboBox** choices.

To use this example, copy this sample code to the Declarations portion of a form. Make sure that the form contains:

- A **Label** named Label1.
- A **CommandButton** named CommandButton1.
- A **ComboBox** named ComboBox1.

```
Private Sub UserForm_Initialize()
   Label1.Left = 18
   Label1.Top = 12
   Label1.Height = 12
   Label1.Width = 190
   Label1.Caption = "Select picture placement relative to the caption."

   'Add list entries to combo box. The value of each entry matches the
   'corresponding ListIndex value in the combo box.
   ComboBox1.AddItem "Left Top"         'ListIndex = 0
   ComboBox1.AddItem "Left Center"      'ListIndex = 1
   ComboBox1.AddItem "Left Bottom"      'ListIndex = 2
   ComboBox1.AddItem "Right Top"        'ListIndex = 3
   ComboBox1.AddItem "Right Center"     'ListIndex = 4
   ComboBox1.AddItem "Right Bottom"     'ListIndex = 5

   ComboBox1.AddItem "Above Left"       'ListIndex = 6
   ComboBox1.AddItem "Above Center"     'ListIndex = 7
   ComboBox1.AddItem "Above Right"      'ListIndex = 8
   ComboBox1.AddItem "Below Left"       'ListIndex = 9
   ComboBox1.AddItem "Below Center"     'ListIndex = 10
   ComboBox1.AddItem "Below Right"      'ListIndex = 11

   ComboBox1.AddItem "Centered"         'ListIndex = 12

   ComboBox1.Style = fmStyleDropDownList  'Use drop-down list

   ComboBox1.BoundColumn = 0            'Combo box values are ListIndex values
   ComboBox1.ListIndex = 0              'Set combo box to first entry


   ComboBox1.Left = 18
   ComboBox1.Top = 36
   ComboBox1.Width = 90
   ComboBox1.ListWidth = 90

   'Initialize CommandButton1
   CommandButton1.Left = 230
   CommandButton1.Top = 36
   CommandButton1.Height = 120
   CommandButton1.Width = 120
```

```
    'Note: Be sure to refer to a bitmap file that is present on your
    'Note: system, and to include the path in the filename.
    CommandButton1.Picture = LoadPicture("c:\windows\argyle.bmp")
    CommandButton1.PicturePosition = ComboBox1.Value
End Sub

Private Sub ComboBox1_Click()
    Select Case ComboBox1.Value
    Case 0  'Left Top
        CommandButton1.Caption = "Left Top"
        CommandButton1.PicturePosition = fmPicturePositionLeftTop

    Case 1  'Left Center
        CommandButton1.Caption = "Left Center"
        CommandButton1.PicturePosition = fmPicturePositionLeftCenter

    Case 2  'Left Bottom
        CommandButton1.Caption = "Left Bottom"
        CommandButton1.PicturePosition = fmPicturePositionLeftBottom

    Case 3  'Right Top
        CommandButton1.Caption = "Right Top"
        CommandButton1.PicturePosition = fmPicturePositionRightTop

    Case 4  'Right Center
        CommandButton1.Caption = "Right Center"
        CommandButton1.PicturePosition = fmPicturePositionRightCenter

    Case 5  'Right Bottom
        CommandButton1.Caption = "Right Bottom"
        CommandButton1.PicturePosition = fmPicturePositionRightBottom

    Case 6  'Above Left
        CommandButton1.Caption = "Above Left"
        CommandButton1.PicturePosition = fmPicturePositionAboveLeft

    Case 7  'Above Center
        CommandButton1.Caption = "Above Center"
        CommandButton1.PicturePosition = fmPicturePositionAboveCenter

    Case 8  'Above Right
        CommandButton1.Caption = "Above Right"
        CommandButton1.PicturePosition = fmPicturePositionAboveRight

    Case 9  'Below Left
        CommandButton1.Caption = "Below Left"
        CommandButton1.PicturePosition = fmPicturePositionBelowLeft

    Case 10 'Below Center
        CommandButton1.Caption = "Below Center"
        CommandButton1.PicturePosition = fmPicturePositionBelowCenter
```

```
    Case 11 'Below Right
        CommandButton1.Caption = "Below Right"
        CommandButton1.PicturePosition = fmPicturePositionBelowRight

    Case 12 'Centered
        CommandButton1.Caption = "Centered"
        CommandButton1.PicturePosition = fmPicturePositionCenter

    End Select

End Sub
```

PictureAlignment Property

Applies To

Frame control, **Image** control, **Page** object, **UserForm** object.

Description

Specifies the location of a background picture.

Syntax

object.**PictureAlignment** [= *fmPictureAlignment*]

The **PictureAlignment** property syntax has these parts:

Part	Description
object	Required. A valid object.
fmPictureAlignment	Optional. The position where the picture aligns with the control.

Settings

The settings for *fmPictureAlignment* are:

Constant	Value	Description
fmPictureAlignmentTopLeft	0	The top left corner.
fmPictureAlignmentTopRight	1	The top right corner.
fmPictureAlignmentCenter	2	The center.
fmPictureAlignmentBottomLeft	3	The bottom left corner.
fmPictureAlignmentBottomRight	4	The bottom right corner.

Remarks

The **PictureAlignment** property identifies which corner of the picture is the same as the corresponding corner of the control or container where the picture is used.

For example, setting **PictureAlignment** to **fmPictureAlignmentTopLeft** means that the top left corner of the picture coincides with the top left corner of the control or container. Setting **PictureAlignment** to **fmPictureAlignmentCenter** positions the picture in the middle, relative to the height as well as the width of the control or container.

If you tile an image on a control or container, the setting of **PictureAlignment** affects the tiling pattern. For example, if **PictureAlignment** is set to **fmPictureAlignmentUpperLeft**, the first copy of the image is laid in the upper left corner of the control or container and additional copies are tiled from left to right across each row. If **PictureAlignment** is **fmPictureAlignmentCenter**, the first copy of the image is laid at the center of the control or container, additional copies are laid to the left and right to complete the row, and additional rows are added to fill the control or container.

Note Setting the **PictureSizeMode** property to **fmSizeModeStretch** overrides **PictureAlignment**. When **PictureSizeMode** is set to **fmSizeModeStretch**, the picture fills the entire control or container.

See Also

Picture property, **PicturePosition** property, **PictureSizeMode** property, **PictureTiling** property.

Example

The following example uses the **PictureAlignment** property to set up a background picture. The example also identifies the alignment options provided by **PictureAlignment**.

To use this example, copy this sample code to the Declarations portion of a form. Make sure that the form contains:

- A **Frame** named Frame1.
- A **SpinButton** named SpinButton1.
- A **TextBox** named TextBox1.

```
Dim Alignments(5) As String

Private Sub UserForm_Initialize()
   Alignments(0) = "0 - Top Left"
   Alignments(1) = "1 - Top Right"
   Alignments(2) = "2 - Center"
   Alignments(3) = "3 - Bottom Left"
   Alignments(4) = "4 - Bottom Right"

   'Specify a bitmap that exists on your system
   Frame1.Picture = LoadPicture("c:\winnt2\ball.bmp")

   SpinButton1.Min = 0
   SpinButton1.Max = 4
   SpinButton1.Value = 0
```

```
    TextBox1.Text = Alignments(0)
    Frame1.PictureAlignment = SpinButton1.Value
End Sub

Private Sub SpinButton1_Change()
    TextBox1.Text = Alignments(SpinButton1.Value)
    Frame1.PictureAlignment = SpinButton1.Value
End Sub

Private Sub TextBox1_Change()
    Select Case TextBox1.Text
    Case "0"
        TextBox1.Text = Alignments(0)
        Frame1.PictureAlignment = 0
    Case "1"
        TextBox1.Text = Alignments(1)
        Frame1.PictureAlignment = 1
    Case "2"
        TextBox1.Text = Alignments(2)
        Frame1.PictureAlignment = 2
    Case "3"
        TextBox1.Text = Alignments(3)
        Frame1.PictureAlignment = 3
    Case "4"
        TextBox1.Text = Alignments(4)
        Frame1.PictureAlignment = 4
    Case Else
        TextBox1.Text = Alignments(SpinButton1.Value)
        Frame1.PictureAlignment = SpinButton1.Value
    End Select
End Sub
```

PicturePosition Property

Applies To

CheckBox control, **CommandButton** control, **Label** control, **OptionButton** control, **ToggleButton** control.

Description

Specifies the location of the picture relative to its caption.

Syntax

object.**PicturePosition** [= *fmPicturePosition*]

The **PicturePosition** property syntax has these parts:

Part	Description
object	Required. A valid object.
fmPicturePosition	Optional. How the picture aligns with its container.

Settings

The settings for *fmPicturePosition* are:

Constant	Value	Description
fmPicturePositionLeftTop	0	The picture appears to the left of the caption. The caption is aligned with the top of the picture.
fmPicturePositionLeftCenter	1	The picture appears to the left of the caption. The caption is centered relative to the picture.
fmPicturePositionLeftBottom	2	The picture appears to the left of the caption. The caption is aligned with the bottom of the picture.
fmPicturePositionRightTop	3	The picture appears to the right of the caption. The caption is aligned with the top of the picture.
fmPicturePositionRightCenter	4	The picture appears to the right of the caption. The caption is centered relative to the picture.
fmPicturePositionRightBottom	5	The picture appears to the right of the caption. The caption is aligned with the bottom of the picture.
fmPicturePositionAboveLeft	6	The picture appears above the caption. The caption is aligned with the left edge of the picture.
fmPicturePositionAboveCenter	7	The picture appears above the caption. The caption is centered below the picture (default).
fmPicturePositionAboveRight	8	The picture appears above the caption. The caption is aligned with the right edge of the picture.
fmPicturePositionBelowLeft	9	The picture appears below the caption. The caption is aligned with the left edge of the picture.
fmPicturePositionBelowCenter	10	The picture appears below the caption. The caption is centered above the picture.
fmPicturePositionBelowRight	11	The picture appears below the caption. The caption is aligned with the right edge of the picture.
fmPicturePositionCenter	12	The picture appears in the center of the control. The caption is centered horizontally and vertically on top of the picture.

Remarks

The picture and the caption, as a unit, are centered on the control. If no caption exists, the picture's location is relative to the center of the control.

This property is ignored if the **Picture** property does not specify a picture.

See Also

Picture property, **PictureAlignment** property, **PictureSizeMode** property, **PictureTiling** property.

Example

See the **Picture** property example.

PictureSizeMode Property

Applies To

Frame control, **Image** control, **Page** object, **UserForm** object.

Description

Specifies how to display the background picture on a control, form, or page.

Syntax

object.**PictureSizeMode** [= *fmPictureSizeMode*]

The **PictureSizeMode** property syntax has these parts:

Part	Description
object	Required. A valid object.
fmPictureSizeMode	Optional. The action to take if the picture and the form or page that contains it are not the same size.

Settings

The settings for *fmPictureSizeMode* are:

Constant	Value	Description
fmPictureSizeModeClip	0	Crops any part of the picture that is larger than the form or page (default).
fmPictureSizeModeStretch	1	Stretches the picture to fill the form or page. This setting distorts the picture in either the horizontal or vertical direction.
fmPictureSizeModeZoom	3	Enlarges the picture, but does not distort the picture in either the horizontal or vertical direction.

Remarks

The **fmPictureSizeModeClip** setting indicates you want to show the picture in its original size and scale. If the form or page is smaller than the picture, this setting only shows the part of the picture that fits within the form or page.

The **fmPictureSizeModeStretch** and **fmPictureSizeModeZoom** settings both enlarge the image, but **fmPictureSizeModeStretch** causes distortion. The **fmPictureSizeModeStretch** setting enlarges the image horizontally and vertically until the image reaches the corresponding edges of the container or control. The **fmPictureSizeModeZoom** setting enlarges the image until it reaches either the horizontal or vertical edges of the container or control. If the image reaches the horizontal edges first, any remaining distance to the vertical edges remains blank. If it reaches the vertical edges first, any remaining distance to the horizontal edges remains blank.

See Also

Picture property, **PictureAlignment** property, **PicturePosition** property, **PictureTiling** property.

Example

The following example uses the **PictureSizeMode** property to demonstrate three display options for a picture: showing the picture as is, changing the size of the picture while maintaining its original proportions, and stretching the picture to fill a space.

To use this example, copy this sample code to the Declarations portion of a form. Make sure that the form contains:

- A **Frame** named Frame1.
- A **SpinButton** named SpinButton1.
- A **TextBox** named TextBox1.
- Three **OptionButton** controls named OptionButton1 through OptionButton3.

Note This example is an enhanced version of the **PictureAlignment** property example, as the two properties complement each other. The enhancements are three **OptionButton** event subroutines that control whether the image is cropped, zoomed, or stretched.

```
Dim Alignments(5) As String

Private Sub UserForm_Initialize()
   Alignments(0) = "0 - Top Left"
   Alignments(1) = "1 - Top Right"
   Alignments(2) = "2 - Center"
   Alignments(3) = "3 - Bottom Left"
   Alignments(4) = "4 - Bottom Right"

   'Specify a bitmap that exists on your system
   Frame1.Picture = LoadPicture("c:\winnt2\ball.bmp")

   SpinButton1.Min = 0
   SpinButton1.Max = 4
   SpinButton1.Value = 0

   TextBox1.Text = Alignments(0)
   Frame1.PictureAlignment = SpinButton1.Value
```

```
    OptionButton1.Caption = "Crop"
    OptionButton1.Value = True
    OptionButton2.Caption = "Stretch"
    OptionButton3.Caption = "Zoom"
End Sub

Private Sub OptionButton1_Click()
    If OptionButton1.Value = True Then
        Frame1.PictureSizeMode = fmPictureSizeModeClip
    End If
End Sub

Private Sub OptionButton2_Click()
    If OptionButton2.Value = True Then
        Frame1.PictureSizeMode = fmPictureSizeModeStretch
    End If
End Sub

Private Sub OptionButton3_Click()
    If OptionButton3.Value = True Then
        Frame1.PictureSizeMode = fmPictureSizeModeZoom
    End If
End Sub

Private Sub SpinButton1_Change()
    TextBox1.Text = Alignments(SpinButton1.Value)
    Frame1.PictureAlignment = SpinButton1.Value
End Sub

Private Sub TextBox1_Change()
    Select Case TextBox1.Text
    Case "0"
        TextBox1.Text = Alignments(0)
        Frame1.PictureAlignment = 0
    Case "1"
        TextBox1.Text = Alignments(1)
        Frame1.PictureAlignment = 1
    Case "2"
        TextBox1.Text = Alignments(2)
        Frame1.PictureAlignment = 2
    Case "3"
        TextBox1.Text = Alignments(3)
        Frame1.PictureAlignment = 3
    Case "4"
        TextBox1.Text = Alignments(4)
        Frame1.PictureAlignment = 4
    Case Else
        TextBox1.Text = Alignments(SpinButton1.Value)
        Frame1.PictureAlignment = SpinButton1.Value
    End Select
End Sub
```

PictureTiling Property

Applies To

Frame control, **Image** control, **Page** object, **UserForm** object.

Description

Lets you tile a picture in a form or page.

Syntax

object.**PictureTiling** [= *Boolean*]

The **PictureTiling** property syntax has these parts:

Part	Description
object	Required. A valid object.
Boolean	Optional. Whether a picture is repeated across a background.

Settings

The settings for *Boolean* are:

Value	Description
True	The picture is tiled across the background.
False	The picture is not tiled across the background (default).

Remarks

If a picture is smaller than the form or page that contains it, you can tile the picture on the form or page.

The tiling pattern depends on the current setting of the **PictureAlignment** and **PictureSizeMode** properties. For example, if **PictureAlignment** is set to **fmPictureAlignmentTopLeft**, the tiling pattern starts at the upper left and repeats the picture across the form or page and down the height of the form or page. If **PictureSizeMode** is set to **fmPictureSizeModeClip**, the tiling pattern crops the last tile if it doesn't completely fit on the form or page.

See Also

Picture property, **PictureAlignment** property, **PicturePosition** property, **PictureSizeMode** property.

ProportionalThumb Property

Applies To

ScrollBar control.

Description

Specifies whether the size of the scroll box is proportional to the scrolling region or fixed.

Syntax

object.**ProportionalThumb** [= *Boolean*]

The **ProportionalThumb** property syntax has these parts:

Part	Description
object	Required. A valid object.
Boolean	Optional. Whether the scroll box is proportional or fixed.

Settings

The settings for *Boolean* are:

Value	Description
True	The scroll box is proportional in size to the scrolling region (default).
False	The scroll box is a fixed size.

Remarks

The size of a proportional scroll box graphically represents the percentage of the object that is visible in the window. For example, if 75 percent of an object is visible, the scroll box covers three-fourths of the scrolling region in the scroll bar.

If the scroll box is a fixed size, the system determines its size based on the height and width of the scroll bar.

PutInClipboard Method

Applies To

DataObject object.

Description

Moves data from a **DataObject** to the Clipboard.

Syntax

object.**PutInClipboard**

The **PutInClipboard** method syntax has these parts:

Part	Description
object	Required. A valid object.

Remarks

The **PutInClipboard** method replaces the contents of the Clipboard with the contents of the **DataObject** that is in Text format.

See Also

GetFromClipboard method, **GetText** method, **SetText** method.

Example

The following example demonstrates data movement from a **TextBox** to a **DataObject**, from a **DataObject** to the Clipboard, and from the Clipboard to another **TextBox**. The **PutInClipboard** method transfers the data from a **DataObject** to the Clipboard. The **SetText** and **Paste** methods are also used.

To use this example, copy this sample code to the Declarations portion of a form. Make sure that the form contains:

- Two **TextBox** controls named TextBox1 and TextBox2.
- A **CommandButton** named CommandButton1.

```
Dim MyData As DataObject

Private Sub CommandButton1_Click()
   Set MyData = New DataObject

   MyData.SetText TextBox1.Text
   MyData.PutInClipboard

   TextBox2.Paste
End Sub

Private Sub UserForm_Initialize()
   TextBox1.Text = "Move this data to a DataObject, to the Clipboard," _
   & " then to TextBox2!"
End Sub
```

RedoAction Method

Applies To

Frame control, **Page** object, **UserForm** object.

Description

Reverses the effect of the most recent Undo action.

Syntax

Boolean = *object*.**RedoAction**

The **RedoAction** method syntax has these parts:

Part	Description
object	Required. A valid object.

Remarks

Redo reverses the last Undo, which is not necessarily the last action taken. Not all actions can be undone.

For example, after pasting text into a **TextBox** and then choosing the **Undo** command to remove the text, you can choose the **Redo** command to put the text back in.

Note If the **CanRedo** property is **False**, the **Redo** command is not available in the user interface, and the **RedoAction** method is not valid in code.

RedoAction returns **True** if it was successful.

See Also

CanRedo property, **CanUndo** property, **UndoAction** method.

Example

See the **CanRedo** property example.

Remove Method

Applies To

Controls collection, **Pages** collection, **Tabs** collection.

Description

Removes a member from a collection; or, removes a control from a **Frame**, **Page**, or form.

Syntax

object.**Remove**(*collectionindex*)

The **Remove** method syntax has these parts:

Part	Description
object	Required. A valid object.
collectionindex	Required. A member's position, or index, within a collection. Numeric as well as string values are acceptable. If the value is a number, the minimum value is zero, and the maximum value is one less than the number of members in the collection. If the value is a string, it must correspond to a valid member name.

Remarks

This method deletes any control that was added at run time. However, attempting to delete a control that was added at design time will result in an error.

See Also

Add method, **Clear** method.

Example

The following example uses the **Add**, **Clear**, and **Remove** methods to add and remove a control to a **Page** of a **MultiPage** at run time.

To use this example, copy this sample code to the Declarations portion of a form. Make sure that the form contains:

- A **MultiPage** named MultiPage1.
- Three **CommandButton** controls named CommandButton1 through CommandButton3.

```
Dim MyTextBox As Control

Private Sub CommandButton1_Click()
Set MyTextBox = MultiPage1.Pages(0).Controls.Add("Forms.TextBox.1", _
   "MyTextBox", Visible)
End Sub

Private Sub CommandButton2_Click()
   MultiPage1.Pages(0).Controls.Clear
End Sub

Private Sub CommandButton3_Click()
   If MultiPage1.Pages(0).Controls.Count > 0  Then
      MultiPage1.Pages(0).Controls.Remove "MyTextBox"
   End If
End Sub

Private Sub UserForm_Initialize()
   CommandButton1.Caption = "Add control"
   CommandButton2.Caption = "Clear controls"
   CommandButton3.Caption = "Remove control"
End Sub
```

RemoveControl Event

Applies To

Frame control, **MultiPage** control, **UserForm** object.

Description

Occurs when a control is deleted from the container.

Syntax

For MultiPage:

Private Sub *object*_**RemoveControl(** *index* **As Long**, *ctrl* **As Control)**

For all other controls:

Private Sub *object*_**RemoveControl(** *ctrl* **As Control)**

The **RemoveControl** event syntax has these parts:

Part	Description
object	Required. A valid object name.
index	Required. The index of the page in a **MultiPage** that contained the deleted control.
ctrl	Required. The deleted control.

Remarks

This event occurs when a control is deleted from the form, not when a control is unloaded due to a form being closed.

RemoveItem Method

Applies To

ComboBox control, **ListBox** control.

Description

Removes a row from the list in a list box or combo box.

Syntax

Boolean = *object*.**RemoveItem(** *index***)**

The **RemoveItem** method syntax has these parts:

Part	Description
object	Required. A valid object.
index	Required. Specifies the row to delete. The number of the first row is 0; the number of the second row is 1, and so on.

This method will not remove a row from the list if the **ListBox** is data bound (that is, when the **RowSource** property specifies a data source for the **ListBox**).

See Also

RowSource property.

Example

The following example adds and deletes the contents of a **ListBox** using the **AddItem**, **RemoveItem**, and **SetFocus** methods, and the **ListIndex** and **ListCount** properties.

To use this example, copy this sample code to the Declarations portion of a form. Make sure that the form contains:

- A **ListBox** named ListBox1.
- Two **CommandButton** controls named CommandButton1 and CommandButton2.

```
Dim EntryCount As Single
Private Sub CommandButton1_Click()
   EntryCount = EntryCount + 1
   ListBox1.AddItem (EntryCount & " - Selection")
End Sub

Private Sub CommandButton2_Click()
   ListBox1.SetFocus

   'Ensure ListBox contains list items
   If ListBox1.ListCount >= 1 Then
      'If no selection, choose last list item.
      If ListBox1.ListIndex = -1 Then
         ListBox1.ListIndex = ListBox1.ListCount - 1
      End If
      ListBox1.RemoveItem (ListBox1.ListIndex)
   End If
End Sub

Private Sub UserForm_Initialize()
   EntryCount = 0
   CommandButton1.Caption = "Add Item"
   CommandButton2.Caption = "Remove Item"
End Sub
```

Repaint Method

Applies To

Frame control, **Page** object, **UserForm** object.

Description

Updates the display by redrawing the form or page.

Syntax

Boolean = *object*.**Repaint**

The **Repaint** method syntax has these parts:

Part	Description
object	Required. A valid object.

Remarks

The **Repaint** method is useful if the contents or appearance of an object changes significantly, and you don't want to wait until the system automatically repaints the area.

See Also

DrawBuffer property.

RowSource Property

Applies To

ComboBox control, **ListBox** control.

Description

Specifies the source providing a list for a **ComboBox** or **ListBox**.

Syntax

object.**RowSource** [= *String*]

The **RowSource** property syntax has these parts:

Part	Description
object	Required. A valid object.
String	Optional. The source of the list for the **ComboBox** or **ListBox**.

Remarks

The **RowSource** property accepts worksheet ranges from Microsoft Excel.

Example

The following example uses a range of worksheet cells in a **ListBox** and, when the user selects a row from the list, displays the row index in another worksheet cell. This code sample uses the **RowSource**, **BoundColumn**, and **ControlSource** properties.

To use this example, copy this sample code to the Declarations portion of a form. Make sure that the form contains a **ListBox** named ListBox1. In the worksheet, enter data in cells A1:E4. You also need to make sure cell A6 contains no data.

```
Private Sub UserForm_Initialize()

ListBox1.ColumnCount = 5
ListBox1.RowSource = "a1:e4"

ListBox1.ControlSource = "a6"
ListBox1.BoundColumn = 0          'Place the ListIndex into cell a6
End Sub
```

Scroll Event

Applies To

Frame control, **MultiPage** control, **ScrollBar** control, **UserForm** object.

Description

Occurs when the scroll box is repositioned.

Syntax

For ScrollBar:

Private Sub *object*_**Scroll( )**

For MultiPage:

Private Sub *object*_**Scroll(** *index* **As Long**, *ActionX* **As fmScrollAction**, *ActionY* **As**
↪ **fmScrollAction**, **ByVal** *RequestDx* **As Single**, **ByVal** *RequestDy* **As Single**, **ByVal**
↪ *ActualDx* **As MSForms.ReturnSingle**, **ByVal** *ActualDy* **As MSForms.ReturnSingle)**

For Frame:

Private Sub *object*_**Scroll(** *ActionX* **As fmScrollAction**, *ActionY* **As fmScrollAction**,
↪ **ByVal** *RequestDx* **As Single**, **ByVal** *RequestDy* **As Single**, **ByVal** *ActualDx* **As**
↪ **MSForms.ReturnSingle**, **ByVal** *ActualDy* **As MSForms.ReturnSingle)**

The Scroll event syntax has these parts:

Part	Description
object	Required. A valid object name.
index	Required. The index of the page in a **MultiPage** associated with this event.
ActionX	Required. The action that occurred in the horizontal direction.
ActionY	Required. The action that occurred in the vertical direction.
RequestDx	Required. The distance, in points, you want the scroll bar to move in the horizontal direction.
RequestDy	Required. The distance, in points, you want the scroll bar to move in the vertical direction.
ActualDx	Required. The distance, in points, the scroll bar traveled in the horizontal direction.
ActualDy	Required. The distance, in points, the scroll bar traveled in the vertical direction.

Settings

The settings for *ActionX* and *ActionY* are:

Constant	Value	Description
fmScrollActionNoChange	0	No change occurred.
FmScrollActionLineUp	1	A small distance up on a vertical scroll bar; a small distance to the left on a horizontal scroll bar. Movement is equivalent to pressing the up or left arrow keys on the keyboard to move the scroll bar.
fmScrollActionLineDown	2	A small distance down on a vertical scroll bar; a small distance to the right on a horizontal scroll bar. Movement is equivalent to pressing the down or right arrow keys on the keyboard to move the scroll bar.
fmScrollActionPageUp	3	One page up on a vertical scroll bar; one page to the left on a horizontal scroll bar. Movement is equivalent to pressing PAGE UP on the keyboard to move the scroll bar.
fmScrollActionPageDown	4	One page down on a vertical scroll bar; one page to the right on a horizontal scroll bar. Movement is equivalent to pressing PAGE DOWN on the keyboard to move the scroll bar.
fmScrollActionBegin	5	The top of a vertical scroll bar; the left end of a horizontal scroll bar.
fmScrollActionEnd	6	The bottom of a vertical scroll bar; the right end of a horizontal scroll bar.
fmScrollActionPropertyChange	8	The value of either the **ScrollTop** or the **ScrollLeft** property changed. The direction and amount of movement depend on which property was changed and on the new property value.
fmScrollActionControlRequest	9	A control asked its container to scroll. The amount of movement depends on the specific control and container involved.
fmScrollActionFocusRequest	10	The user moved to a different control. The amount of movement depends on the placement of the selected control, and generally has the effect of moving the selected control so it is completely visible to the user.

Remarks

The Scroll events associated with a form, **Frame**, or **Page** return the following arguments: *ActionX*, *ActionY*, *ActualX*, and *ActualY*. *ActionX* and *ActionY* identify the action that occurred. *ActualX* and *ActualY* identify the distance that the scroll box traveled.

The default action is to calculate the new position of the scroll box and then scroll to that position.

You can initiate a Scroll event by issuing a **Scroll** method for a form, **Frame**, or **Page**. Users can generate Scroll events by moving the scroll box.

The Scroll event associated with the stand-alone **ScrollBar** indicates that the user moved the scroll box in either direction. This event is not initiated when the value of the **ScrollBar** changes by code or by the user clicking on parts of the **ScrollBar** other than the scroll box.

See Also

Scroll method.

Example

The following example demonstrates the stand-alone **ScrollBar** and reports the change in its value as the user moves the scroll box. The user can move the scroll box by clicking on either arrow at the ends of the control, by clicking in the region between scroll box and either arrow, or by dragging the scroll box. When the user drags the scroll box, the Scroll event displays a message indicating that the user scrolled to obtain the new value.

To use this example, copy this sample code to the Declarations portion of a form. Make sure that the form contains:

- A **ScrollBar** named ScrollBar1.
- Two **Label** controls named Label1 and Label2. Label1 contains scaling information for the user. Label2 reports the delta value.

```
Dim ScrollSaved As Integer        'Previous ScrollBar setting

Private Sub UserForm_Initialize()
   ScrollBar1.Min = -225
   ScrollBar1.Max = 289
   ScrollBar1.Value = 0

   Label1.Caption = "-225  -----Widgets-----   289"
   Label1.AutoSize = True

   Label2.Caption = ""
End Sub

Private Sub ScrollBar1_Change()
   Label2.Caption = " Widget Changes " & (ScrollSaved - ScrollBar1.Value)
End Sub
```

```
Private Sub ScrollBar1_Exit(ByVal Cancel as MSForms.ReturnBoolean)
   Label2.Caption = " Widget Changes " & (ScrollSaved - ScrollBar1.Value)
   ScrollSaved = ScrollBar1.Value
End Sub

Private Sub ScrollBar1_Scroll()
   Label2.Caption = (ScrollSaved - ScrollBar1.Value) & " Widget Changes" _
   & " by Scrolling"
End Sub
```

Scroll Method

Applies To

Frame control, **Page** object, **UserForm** object.

Description

Moves the scroll bar on an object.

Syntax

object.**Scroll(** [*ActionX* [, *ActionY*]])

The **Scroll** method syntax has these parts:

Part	Description
object	Required. A valid object name.
ActionX	Optional. Identifies the action to occur in the horizontal direction.
ActionY	Optional. Identifies the action to occur in the vertical direction.

Settings

The settings for *ActionX* and *ActionY* are:

Constant	Value	Description
fmScrollActionNoChange	0	Do not scroll in the specified direction.
fmScrollActionLineUp	1	Move up on a vertical scroll bar or left on a horizontal scroll bar. Movement is equivalent to pressing the up or left arrow key on the keyboard to move the scroll bar.
fmScrollActionLineDown	2	Move down on a vertical scroll bar or right on a horizontal scroll bar. Movement is equivalent to pressing the right or down arrow key on the keyboard to move the scroll bar.

(continued)

fmScrollActionPageUp	3	Move one page up on a vertical scroll bar or one page left on a horizontal scroll bar. Movement is equivalent to pressing PAGE UP on the keyboard to move the scroll bar.
fmScrollActionPageDown	4	Move one page down on a vertical scroll bar or one page right on a horizontal scroll bar. Movement is equivalent to pressing PAGE DOWN on the keyboard to move the scroll bar.
fmScrollActionBegin	5	Move to the top of a vertical scroll bar or to the left end of a horizontal scroll bar.
fmScrollActionEnd	6	Move to the bottom of a vertical scroll bar or to the right end of a horizontal scroll bar.

Remarks

The **Scroll** method applies scroll bars that appear on a form, **Frame**, or **Page** that is larger than its display area. This method does not apply to the stand-alone **ScrollBar** or to scroll bars that appear on a **TextBox**.

See Also

Scroll event, **ScrollLeft**, **ScrollTop** properties.

ScrollBar Control

Description

Returns or sets the value of another control based on the position of the scroll box.

Remarks

A **ScrollBar** is a stand-alone control you can place on a form. It is visually like the scroll bar you see in certain objects such as a **ListBox** or the drop-down portion of a **ComboBox**. However, unlike the scroll bars in these examples, the stand-alone **ScrollBar** is not an integral part of any other control.

To use the **ScrollBar** to set or read the value of another control, you must write code for the **ScrollBar**'s events and methods. For example, to use the **ScrollBar** to update the value of a **TextBox**, you can write code that reads the **Value** property of the **ScrollBar** and then sets the **Value** property of the **TextBox**.

The default property for a **ScrollBar** is the **Value** property.

The default event for a **ScrollBar** is the Change event.

Note To create a horizontal or vertical **ScrollBar**, drag the sizing handles of the **ScrollBar** horizontally or vertically on the form.

Properties

BackColor property, **BoundValue** property, **ControlSource** property, **ControlTipText** property, **Delay** property, **Enabled** property, **ForeColor** property, **Height**, **Width** properties, **HelpContextID** property, **LargeChange** property, **LayoutEffect** property, **Left**, **Top** properties, **Max**, **Min** properties, **MouseIcon** property, **MousePointer** property, **Name** property, **Object** property, **OldHeight**, **OldWidth** properties, **OldLeft**, **OldTop** properties, **Orientation** property, **Parent** property, **ProportionalThumb** property, **SmallChange** property, **TabIndex** property, **TabStop** property, **Tag** property, **Value** property, **Visible** property.

Methods

Move method, **SetFocus** method, **ZOrder** method.

Events

AfterUpdate event, BeforeDragOver event, BeforeUpdate event, Change event, Enter, Exit events, Error event, KeyDown, KeyUp events, KeyPress event, Scroll event.

See Also

SpinButton control.

Example

See the Scroll event example.

ScrollBars Property

Applies To

Frame control, **Page** object, **TextBox** control, **UserForm** object.

Description

Specifies whether a control, form, or page has vertical scroll bars, horizontal scroll bars, or both.

Syntax

object.**ScrollBars** [= *fmScrollBars*]

The **ScrollBars** property syntax has these parts:

Part	Description
object	Required. A valid object.
fmScrollBars	Optional. Where scroll bars should be displayed.

Settings

The settings for *fmScrollBars* are:

Constant	Value	Description
fmScrollBarsNone	0	Displays no scroll bars (default).
fmScrollBarsHorizontal	1	Displays a horizontal scroll bar.

(continued)

fmScrollBarsVertical	2	Displays a vertical scroll bar.
fmScrollBarsBoth	3	Displays both a horizontal and a vertical scroll bar.

Remarks

If the **KeepScrollBarsVisible** property is **True**, any scroll bar on a form or page is always visible, regardless of whether the object's contents fit within the object's borders.

If visible, a scroll bar constrains its scroll box to the visible region of the scroll bar. It also modifies the scroll position as needed to keep the entire scroll bar visible. The range of a scroll bar changes when the value of the **ScrollBars** property changes, the scroll size changes, or the visible size changes.

If a scroll bar is not visible, then you can set its scroll position to any value. Negative values and values greater than the scroll size are both valid.

For a single-line control, you can display a horizontal scroll bar by using the **ScrollBars** and **AutoSize** properties. Scroll bars are hidden or displayed according to the following rules:

1. When **ScrollBars** is set to **fmScrollBarsNone**, no scroll bar is displayed.
2. When **ScrollBars** is set to **fmScrollBarsHorizontal** or **fmScrollBarsBoth**, the control displays a horizontal scroll bar if the text is longer than the edit region and if the control has enough room to include the scroll bar underneath its edit region.
3. When **AutoSize** is **True**, the control enlarges itself to accommodate the addition of a scroll bar unless the control is at or near its maximum size.

For a multiline **TextBox**, you can display scroll bars by using the **ScrollBars**, **WordWrap**, and **AutoSize** properties. Scroll bars are hidden or displayed according to the following rules:

1. When **ScrollBars** is set to **fmScrollBarsNone**, no scroll bar is displayed.
2. When **ScrollBars** is set to **fmScrollBarsVertical** or **fmScrollBarsBoth**, the control displays a vertical scroll bar if the text is longer than the edit region and if the control has enough room to include the scroll bar at the right edge of its edit region.
3. When **WordWrap** is **True**, the multiline control will not display a horizontal scroll bar. Most multiline controls do not use a horizontal scroll bar.
4. A multiline control can display a horizontal scroll bar if the following conditions occur simultaneously:
   - The edit region contains a word that is longer than the edit region's width.
   - The control has enabled horizontal scroll bars.
   - The control has enough room to include the scroll bar under the edit region.

- The **WordWrap** property is set to **False**.

See Also

AutoSize property, **KeepScrollBarsVisible** property, **MultiLine** property, **ScrollHeight**, **ScrollWidth** properties, **ScrollLeft**, **ScrollTop** properties, **VerticalScrollbarSide** property, **WordWrap** property.

Example

See the **KeepScrollBarsVisible** property example.

ScrollHeight, ScrollWidth Properties

Applies To

Frame control, **Page** object, **UserForm** object.

Description

Specify the height, in points, of the total area that can be viewed by moving the scroll bars on the control, form, or page.

Syntax

object.**ScrollHeight** [= *Single*]
object.**ScrollWidth** [= *Single*]

The **ScrollHeight** and **ScrollWidth** property syntaxes have these parts:

Part	Description
object	Required. A valid object.
Single	Optional. The height or width of the scrollable region.

See Also

ScrollBars property, **ScrollLeft**, **ScrollTop** properties.

Example

The following example uses a page of a **MultiPage** as a scrolling region. The user can use the scroll bars on Page2 of the **MultiPage** to gain access to parts of the page that are not initially displayed.

To use this example, copy this sample code to the Declarations portion of a form. Make sure that the form contains a **MultiPage** named MultiPage1, and that each page of the **MultiPage** contains one or more controls.

Note Each page of a **MultiPage** is unique. Page1 has no scroll bars. Page2 has horizontal and vertical scroll bars.

```
Private Sub UserForm_Initialize()
    MultiPage1.Pages(1).ScrollBars = fmScrollBarsBoth
    MultiPage1.Pages(1).KeepScrollBarsVisible = fmScrollBarsNone
```

```
    MultiPage1.Pages(1).ScrollHeight = 2 * MultiPage1.Height
    MultiPage1.Pages(1).ScrollWidth = 2 * MultiPage1.Width

    'Set ScrollHeight, ScrollWidth before setting ScrollLeft, ScrollTop
    MultiPage1.Pages(1).ScrollLeft = MultiPage1.Width / 2
    MultiPage1.Pages(1).ScrollTop = MultiPage1.Height / 2
End Sub
```

ScrollLeft, ScrollTop Properties

Applies To

Frame control, **Page** object, **UserForm** object.

Description

Specify the distance, in points, of the left or top edge of the visible form from the left or top edge of the logical form, page, or control.

Syntax

object.**ScrollLeft** [= *Single*]
object.**ScrollTop** [= *Single*]

The **ScrollLeft** and **ScrollTop** property syntaxes have these parts:

Part	Description
object	Required. A valid object.
Single	Optional. The distance from the edge of the form.

Remarks

The minimum value is zero; the maximum value is the difference between the value of the **ScrollWidth** property and the value of the **Width** property for the form or page.

See Also

Height, **Width** properties, **ScrollBars** property, **ScrollHeight**, **ScrollWidth** properties.

Example

See the **ScrollHeight**, **ScrollWidth** properties example.

ScrollWidth Property

See ScrollHeight, ScrollWidth Properties.

Selected Property

Applies To

ListBox control.

Description

Returns or sets the selection state of items in a **ListBox**.

Syntax

object.**Selected(** *index*) [= *Boolean*]

The **Selected** property syntax has these parts:

Part	Description
object	Required. A valid object.
index	Required. An integer with a range from 0 to one less than the number of items in the list.
Boolean	Optional. Whether an item is selected.

Settings

The settings for *Boolean* are:

Value	Description
True	The item is selected.
False	The item is not selected.

Remarks

The **Selected** property is useful when users can make multiple selections. You can use this property to determine the selected rows in a multi-select list box. You can also use this property to select or deselect rows in a list from code.

The default value of this property is based on the current selection state of the **ListBox**.

For single-selection list boxes, the **Value** or **ListIndex** properties are recommended for getting and setting the selection. In this case, **ListIndex** returns the index of the selected item. However, in a multiple selection, **ListIndex** returns the index of the row contained within the focus rectangle, regardless of whether the row is actually selected.

When a list box control's **MultiSelect** property is set to *None*, only one row can have its **Selected** property set to **True**.

Entering a value that is out of range for the index does not generate an error message, but does not set a property for any item in the list.

See Also

ListCount property, **ListIndex** property, **MultiSelect** property, **Value** property.

Example

See the **MultiSelect** property example.

SelectedItem Property

Applies To

MultiPage control, **TabStrip** control.

Description

Returns the currently selected **Tab** or **Page** object.

Syntax

object.**SelectedItem**

The **SelectedItem** property syntax has these parts:

Part	Description
object	Required. A valid **TabStrip** or **MultiPage**.

Remarks

The **SelectedItem** property is read-only. Use **SelectedItem** to programmatically control the currently selected **Tab** or **Page** object. For example, you can use **SelectedItem** to assign values to properties of a **Tab** or **Page** object.

See Also

Caption property, **Page** object, **Tab** object.

Example

See the **MultiPage** control example.

SelectionMargin Property

Applies To

ComboBox control, **TextBox** control.

Description

Specifies whether the user can select a line of text by clicking in the region to the left of the text.

Syntax

object.**SelectionMargin** [= *Boolean*]

The **SelectionMargin** property syntax has these parts:

Part	Description
object	Required. A valid object.
Boolean	Optional. Whether clicking in the margin selects a line of text.

Settings

The settings for *Boolean* are:

Value	Description
True	Clicking in margin causes selection of text (default).
False	Clicking in margin does not cause selection of text.

Remarks

When the **SelectionMargin** property is **True**, the selection margin occupies a thin strip along the left edge of a control's edit region. When set to **False**, the entire edit region can store text.

If the **SelectionMargin** property is set to **True** when a control is printed, the selection margin also prints.

SelLength Property

Applies To

ComboBox control, **TextBox** control.

Description

The number of characters selected in a text box or the text portion of a combo box.

Syntax

object.**SelLength** [= *Long*]

The **SelLength** property syntax has these parts:

Part	Description
object	Required. A valid object.
Long	Optional. A numeric expression specifying the number of characters selected. For **SelLength** and **SelStart**, the valid range of settings is 0 to the total number of characters in the edit area of a **ComboBox** or **TextBox**.

Remarks

The **SelLength** property is always valid, even when the control does not have focus. Setting **SelLength** to a value less than zero creates an error. Attempting to set **SelLength** to a value greater than the number of characters available in a control results in a value equal to the number of characters in the control.

Note Changing the value of the **SelStart** property cancels any existing selection in the control, places an insertion point in the text, and sets **SelLength** to zero.

The default value, zero, means that no text is currently selected.

See Also

SelStart property, **SelText** property.

Example

The following example tracks the selection-related properties (**SelLength**, **SelStart**, and **SelText**) that change as the user moves the insertion point and extends the selection using the keyboard. This example also uses the **Enabled** and **EnterFieldBehavior** properties.

To use this example, copy this sample code to the Declarations portion of a form. Make sure that the form contains:

- One large **TextBox** named TextBox1.
- Three **TextBox** controls in a column named TextBox2 through TextBox4.

```
Private Sub TextBox1_KeyUp(ByVal KeyCode As MSForms.ReturnInteger, _
      ByVal Shift As Integer)
   TextBox2.Text = TextBox1.SelStart
   TextBox3.Text = TextBox1.SelLength
   TextBox4.Text = TextBox1.SelText
End Sub

Private Sub UserForm_Initialize()
   TextBox1.MultiLine = True
   TextBox1.EnterFieldBehavior = fmEnterFieldBehaviorRecallSelection

   TextBox1.Text = "Type your text here. Use CTRL+ENTER to start a new line."
End Sub
```

SelStart Property

Applies To

ComboBox control, **TextBox** control.

Description

Indicates the starting point of selected text, or the insertion point if no text is selected.

Syntax

object.**SelStart** [= *Long*]

The **SelStart** property syntax has these parts:

Part	Description
object	Required. A valid object.
Long	Optional. A numeric expression specifying the starting point of text selected. For **SelLength** and **SelStart**, the valid range of settings is 0 to the total number of characters in the edit area of a **ComboBox** or **TextBox**. The default value is zero.

Remarks

The **SelStart** property is always valid, even when the control does not have focus. Setting **SelStart** to a value less than zero creates an error. Attempting to set **SelStart** to a value greater than the number of characters available in a control results in a value equal to the number of characters in the control.

Changing the value of **SelStart** cancels any existing selection in the control, places an insertion point in the text, and sets the **SelLength** property to zero.

See Also

SelLength property, **SelText** property.

Example

See the **SelLength** property example.

SelText Property

Applies To

ComboBox control, **TextBox** control.

Description

Returns or sets the selected text of a control.

Syntax

object.**SelText** [= *String*]

The **SelText** property syntax has these parts:

Part	Description
object	Required. A valid object.
String	Optional. A string expression containing the selected text.

Remarks

If no characters are selected in the edit region of the control, the **SelText** property returns a zero length string. This property is valid regardless of whether the control has the focus.

See Also

SelLength property, **SelStart** property.

Example

See the **SelLength** property example.

SetDefaultTabOrder Method

Applies To

Frame control, **Page** object, **UserForm** object.

Description

Sets the **TabIndex** property of each control on a form, using a default top-to-bottom, left-to-right tab order.

Syntax

object.**SetDefaultTabOrder**

The **SetDefaultTabOrder** method syntax has these parts:

Part	Description
object	Required. A valid object.

Remarks

Microsoft Forms sets the tab order beginning with controls in the upper left corner of the form and moving to the right. It places controls closest to the left edge of the form earlier in the tab order. If more than one control is the same distance from the left edge of the form, tab order values are assigned from top to bottom.

See Also

TabIndex property.

SetFocus Method

Applies To

CheckBox control, **ComboBox** control, **CommandButton** control, **ListBox** control, **MultiPage** control, **OptionButton** control, **ScrollBar** control, **SpinButton** control, **TabStrip** control, **TextBox** control, **ToggleButton** control.

Description

Moves the focus to this instance of an object.

Syntax

object.**SetFocus**

The **SetFocus** method syntax has these parts:

Part	Description
object	Required. A valid object.

Remarks

If setting the focus fails, the focus reverts to the previous object and an error is generated.

By default, setting the focus to a control does not activate the control's window or place it on top of other controls.

The **SetFocus** method is valid for an empty **Frame** as well as a **Frame** that contains other controls. An empty **Frame** will take the focus itself, and any subsequent keyboard events apply to the **Frame**. In a **Frame** that contains other controls, the focus moves to the first control in the **Frame**, and subsequent keyboard events apply to the control that has the focus.

See Also

Frame control, **ZOrder** method.

Example

The following example adds and deletes the contents of a **ListBox** using the **AddItem**, **RemoveItem**, and **SetFocus** methods, and the **ListIndex** and **ListCount** properties.

To use this example, copy this sample code to the Declarations portion of a form. Make sure that the form contains:

- A **ListBox** named ListBox1.
- Two **CommandButton** controls named CommandButton1 and CommandButton2.

```
Dim EntryCount As Single
Private Sub CommandButton1_Click()
   EntryCount = EntryCount + 1
   ListBox1.AddItem (EntryCount & " - Selection")
End Sub

Private Sub CommandButton2_Click()
   ListBox1.SetFocus

   'Ensure ListBox contains list items
   If ListBox1.ListCount >= 1 Then
      'If no selection, choose last list item.
      If ListBox1.ListIndex = -1 Then
         ListBox1.ListIndex = ListBox1.ListCount - 1
      End If
      ListBox1.RemoveItem (ListBox1.ListIndex)
   End If
End Sub
```

```
Private Sub UserForm_Initialize()
    EntryCount = 0
    CommandButton1.Caption = "Add Item"
    CommandButton2.Caption = "Remove Item"
End Sub
```

Example

The following example counts the characters and the number of lines of text in a **TextBox** by using the **LineCount** and **TextLength** properties, and the **SetFocus** method. In this example, the user can type into a **TextBox**, and can retrieve current values of the **LineCount** and **TextLength** properties.

To use this example, copy this sample code to the Declarations portion of a form. Make sure that the form contains the following controls:

- A **TextBox** named TextBox1.
- A **CommandButton** named CommandButton1.
- Two **Label** controls named Label1 and Label2.

```
'Type SHIFT+ENTER to start a new line in the text box.

Private Sub CommandButton1_Click()
    'Must first give TextBox1 the focus to get line count
    TextBox1.SetFocus
    Label1.Caption = "LineCount = " & TextBox1.LineCount
    Label2.Caption = "TextLength = " & TextBox1.TextLength
End Sub

Private Sub UserForm_Initialize()
    CommandButton1.WordWrap = True
    CommandButton1.AutoSize = True
    CommandButton1.Caption = "Get Counts"

    Label1.Caption = "LineCount = "
    Label2.Caption = "TextLength = "

    TextBox1.MultiLine = True
    TextBox1.WordWrap = True
    TextBox1.Text = "Enter your text here."
End Sub
```

SetText Method

Applies To

DataObject object.

Description

Copies a text string to the **DataObject** using a specified format.

Syntax

object.**SetText(** *StoreData* [, *format*])

The **SetText** method syntax has these parts:

Part	Description
object	Required. A valid object.
StoreData	Required. Defines the data to store on the **DataObject**.
format	Optional. An integer or string specifying the format of *StoreData*. When retrieving data from the **DataObject**, the format identifies the piece of data to retrieve.

Settings

The settings for *format* are:

Value	Description
1	Text format.
A string or integer value other than 1	A user-defined **DataObject** format.

Remarks

The **DataObject** stores data according to its format. When the user supplies a string, the **DataObject** saves the text under the specified format.

If the **DataObject** contains data in the same format as new data, the new data replaces the existing data in the **DataObject**. If the new data is in a new format, the new data and the new format are both added to the **DataObject**, and the previously existing data is there as well.

If no format is specified, the **SetText** method assigns the Text format to the text string. If a new format is specified, the **DataObject** registers the new format with the system.

See Also

GetFormat method, **GetFromClipboard** method, **GetText** method, **PutInClipboard** method.

Example

See the **GetFormat** method example.

ShowDropButtonWhen Property

Applies To

ComboBox control, **TextBox** control.

Description

Specifies when to show the drop-down button for a **ComboBox** or **TextBox**.

Syntax

object.**ShowDropButtonWhen** [= *fmShowDropButtonWhen*]

The **ShowDropButtonWhen** property syntax has these parts:

Part	Description
object	Required. A valid object.
fmShowDropButtonWhen	Optional. The circumstances under which the drop-down button will be visible.

Settings

The settings for *fmShowDropButtonWhen* are:

Constant	Value	Description
fmShowDropButtonWhenNever	0	Do not show the drop-down button under any circumstances.
fmShowDropButtonWhenFocus	1	Show the drop-down button when the control has the focus.
fmShowDropButtonWhenAlways	2	Always show the drop-down button.

For a **ComboBox**, the default value is *fmShowDropButtonWhenAlways*; for a **TextBox**, the default value is *fmShowDropButtonWhenNever*.

See Also

DropButtonClick event, **DropButtonStyle** property, **DropDown** method.

Example

See the **DropButtonStyle** property example.

Size Property

See Bold, Italic, Size, StrikeThrough, Underline, Weight Properties.

SmallChange Property

Applies To

ScrollBar control, **SpinButton** control.

Description

Specifies the amount of movement that occurs when the user clicks either scroll arrow in a **ScrollBar** or **SpinButton**.

Syntax

object.**SmallChange** [= *Long*]

The **SmallChange** property syntax has these parts:

Part	Description
object	Required. A valid object.
Long	Optional. An integer that specifies the amount of change to the **Value** property.

Remarks

The **SmallChange** property does not have units.

Any integer is an acceptable setting for this property. The recommended range of values is from –32,767 to +32,767. The default value is 1.

See Also

LargeChange property, **Max**, **Min** properties.

Example

See the **LargeChange** property example.

SpecialEffect Property

Applies To

CheckBox control, **ComboBox** control, **Frame** control, **Image** control, **Label** control, **ListBox** control, **OptionButton** control, **TextBox** control, **ToggleButton** control, **UserForm** object.

Description

Specifies the visual appearance of an object.

Syntax

For CheckBox, OptionButton, ToggleButton:

object.**SpecialEffect** [= *fmButtonEffect*]

For other controls:

object.**SpecialEffect** [= *fmSpecialEffect*]

The **SpecialEffect** property syntax has these parts:

Part	Description
object	Required. A valid object.
fmButtonEffect	Optional. The desired visual appearance for a **CheckBox**, **OptionButton**, or **ToggleButton**.
fmSpecialEffect	Optional. The desired visual appearance of an object other than a **CheckBox**, **OptionButton**, or **ToggleButton**.

Settings

The settings for *fmSpecialEffect* are:

Constant	Value	Description
fmSpecialEffectFlat	0	Object appears flat, distinguished from the surrounding form by a border, a change of color, or both. Default for **Image** and **Label**, valid for all controls.
fmSpecialEffectRaised	1	Object has a highlight on the top and left and a shadow on the bottom and right. Not valid for check boxes or option buttons.
fmSpecialEffectSunken	2	Object has a shadow on the top and left and a highlight on the bottom and right. The control and its border appear to be carved into the form that contains them. Default for **CheckBox** and **OptionButton**, valid for all controls (default).
fmSpecialEffectEtched	3	Border appears to be carved around the edge of the control. Not valid for check boxes or option buttons.
fmSpecialEffectBump	6	Object has a ridge on the bottom and right and appears flat on the top and left. Not valid for check boxes or option buttons.

For a **Frame**, the default value is *Sunken*.

Note that only *Flat* and *Sunken* (0 and 2) are acceptable values for **CheckBox**, **OptionButton**, and **ToggleButton**. All values listed are acceptable for other controls.

Remarks

You can use either the **SpecialEffect** or the **BorderStyle** property to specify the edging for a control, but not both. If you specify a nonzero value for one of these properties, the system sets the value of the other property to zero. For example, if you set **SpecialEffect** to **fmSpecialEffectRaised**, the system sets **BorderStyle** to zero (**fmBorderStyleNone**).

For a **Frame**, **BorderStyle** is ignored if **SpecialEffect** is **fmSpecialEffectFlat**.

SpecialEffect uses the system colors to define its borders.

Note Although the **SpecialEffect** property exists on the **ToggleButton**, the property is disabled. You cannot set or return a value for this property on the **ToggleButton**.

See Also

BorderStyle property.

Example

The following example demonstrates the **BorderStyle** and **SpecialEffect** properties, showing each border available through these properties. The example also demonstrates how to control color settings by using the **BackColor**, **BackStyle**, **BorderColor**, and **ForeColor** properties.

To use this example, copy this sample code to the Declarations portion of a form. Make sure that the form contains:

- Six **TextBox** controls named TextBox1 through TextBox6.
- Two **ToggleButton** controls named ToggleButton1 and ToggleButton2.

```
Private Sub UserForm_Initialize()
'Initialize each TextBox with a border style or special effect,
'and foreground and background colors

'TextBox1 initially uses a borderstyle
TextBox1.Text = "BorderStyle-Single"
TextBox1.BorderStyle = fmBorderStyleSingle
TextBox1.BorderColor = RGB(255, 128, 128)   'Color - Salmon
TextBox1.ForeColor = RGB(255, 255, 0)       'Color - Yellow
TextBox1.BackColor = RGB(0, 128, 64)        'Color - Green #2

'TextBoxes 2 through 6 initially use special effects
TextBox2.Text = "Flat"
TextBox2.SpecialEffect = fmSpecialEffectFlat
TextBox2.ForeColor = RGB(64, 0, 0)          'Color - Brown
TextBox2.BackColor = RGB(0, 0, 255)         'Color - Blue

'Ensure the background style for TextBox2 is initially opaque.
TextBox2.BackStyle = fmBackStyleOpaque

TextBox3.Text = "Etched"
TextBox3.SpecialEffect = fmSpecialEffectEtched
TextBox3.ForeColor = RGB(128, 0, 255)       'Color - Purple
TextBox3.BackColor = RGB(0, 255, 255)       'Color - Cyan

'Define BorderColor for later use (when borderstyle=fmBorderStyleSingle)
TextBox3.BorderColor = RGB(0, 0, 0)         'Color - Black

TextBox4.Text = "Bump"
TextBox4.SpecialEffect = fmSpecialEffectBump
TextBox4.ForeColor = RGB(255, 0, 255)       'Color - Magenta
TextBox4.BackColor = RGB(0, 0, 100)         'Color - Navy blue

TextBox5.Text = "Raised"
TextBox5.SpecialEffect = fmSpecialEffectRaised
TextBox5.ForeColor = RGB(255, 0, 0)         'Color - Red
TextBox5.BackColor = RGB(128, 128, 128)     'Color - Gray

TextBox6.Text = "Sunken"
TextBox6.SpecialEffect = fmSpecialEffectSunken
TextBox6.ForeColor = RGB(0, 64, 0)          'Color - Olive
TextBox6.BackColor = RGB(0, 255, 0)         'Color - Green #1
```

```
ToggleButton1.Caption = "Swap styles"
ToggleButton2.Caption = "Transparent/Opaque background"
End Sub

Private Sub ToggleButton1_Click()

'Swap borders between TextBox1 and TextBox3
If ToggleButton1.Value = True Then
   'Change TextBox1 from BorderStyle to Etched
   TextBox1.Text = "Etched"
   TextBox1.SpecialEffect = fmSpecialEffectEtched

   'Change TextBox3 from Etched to BorderStyle
   TextBox3.Text = "BorderStyle-Single"
   TextBox3.BorderStyle = fmBorderStyleSingle
Else
   'Change TextBox1 back to BorderStyle
   TextBox1.Text = "BorderStyle-Single"
   TextBox1.BorderStyle = fmBorderStyleSingle

   'Change TextBox3 back to Etched
   TextBox3.Text = "Etched"
   TextBox3.SpecialEffect = fmSpecialEffectEtched
End If
End Sub

Private Sub ToggleButton2_Click()

'Set background to Opaque or Transparent
If ToggleButton2.Value = True Then
   'Change TextBox2 to a transparent background
   TextBox2.BackStyle = fmBackStyleTransparent
Else
   'Change TextBox2 back to opaque background
   TextBox2.BackStyle = fmBackStyleOpaque
End If

End Sub
```

SpinButton Control

Description

Increments and decrements numbers.

Remarks

Clicking a **SpinButton** changes only the value of the **SpinButton**. You can write code that uses the **SpinButton** to update the displayed value of another control. For example, you can use a **SpinButton** to change the month, the day, or the year shown on a date. You can also use a **SpinButton** to scroll through a range of values or a list of items, or to change the value displayed in a text box.

To display a value updated by a **SpinButton**, you must assign the value of the **SpinButton** to the displayed portion of a control, such as the **Caption** property of a **Label** or the **Text** property of a **TextBox**. To create a horizontal or vertical **SpinButton**, drag the sizing handles of the **SpinButton** horizontally or vertically on the form.

The default property for a **SpinButton** is the **Value** property.

The default event for a **SpinButton** is the Change event.

Properties

BackColor property, **BoundValue** property, **ControlSource** property, **ControlTipText** property, **Delay** property, **Enabled** property, **ForeColor** property, **Height**, **Width** properties, **HelpContextID** property, **LayoutEffect** property, **Left**, **Top** properties, **Max**, **Min** properties, **MouseIcon** property, **MousePointer** property, **Name** property, **Object** property, **OldHeight**, **OldWidth** properties, **OldLeft**, **OldTop** properties, **Orientation** property, **Parent** property, **SmallChange** property, **TabIndex** property, **TabStop** property, **Tag** property, **Value** property, **Visible** property.

Methods

Move method, **SetFocus** method, **ZOrder** method.

Events

AfterUpdate event, BeforeDragOver event, BeforeUpdate event, Change event, Enter, Exit events, Error event, KeyDown, KeyUp events, KeyPress event, SpinDown, SpinUp events.

See Also

ScrollBar control.

Example

The following example uses the **PictureSizeMode** property to demonstrate three display options for a picture: showing the picture as is, changing the size of the picture while maintaining its original proportions, and stretching the picture to fill a space.

To use this example, copy this sample code to the Declarations portion of a form. Make sure that the form contains:

- A **Frame** named Frame1.
- A **SpinButton** named SpinButton1.
- A **TextBox** named TextBox1.
- Three **OptionButton** controls named OptionButton1 through OptionButton3.

Note This example is an enhanced version of the **PictureAlignment** property example, as the two properties complement each other. The enhancements are three **OptionButton** event subroutines that control whether the image is cropped, zoomed, or stretched.

```
Dim Alignments(5) As String

Private Sub UserForm_Initialize()
   Alignments(0) = "0 - Top Left"
   Alignments(1) = "1 - Top Right"
   Alignments(2) = "2 - Center"
   Alignments(3) = "3 - Bottom Left"
   Alignments(4) = "4 - Bottom Right"

   'Specify a bitmap that exists on your system
   Frame1.Picture = LoadPicture("c:\winnt2\ball.bmp")

   SpinButton1.Min = 0
   SpinButton1.Max = 4
   SpinButton1.Value = 0

   TextBox1.Text = Alignments(0)
   Frame1.PictureAlignment = SpinButton1.Value

   OptionButton1.Caption = "Crop"
   OptionButton1.Value = True
   OptionButton2.Caption = "Stretch"
   OptionButton3.Caption = "Zoom"
End Sub

Private Sub OptionButton1_Click()
   If OptionButton1.Value = True Then
      Frame1.PictureSizeMode = fmPictureSizeModeClip
   End If
End Sub

Private Sub OptionButton2_Click()
   If OptionButton2.Value = True Then
      Frame1.PictureSizeMode = fmPictureSizeModeStretch
   End If
End Sub

Private Sub OptionButton3_Click()
   If OptionButton3.Value = True Then
      Frame1.PictureSizeMode = fmPictureSizeModeZoom
   End If
End Sub

Private Sub SpinButton1_Change()
   TextBox1.Text = Alignments(SpinButton1.Value)
   Frame1.PictureAlignment = SpinButton1.Value
End Sub

Private Sub TextBox1_Change()
   Select Case TextBox1.Text
   Case "0"
      TextBox1.Text = Alignments(0)
      Frame1.PictureAlignment = 0
```

```
        Case "1"
            TextBox1.Text = Alignments(1)
            Frame1.PictureAlignment = 1
        Case "2"
            TextBox1.Text = Alignments(2)
            Frame1.PictureAlignment = 2
        Case "3"
            TextBox1.Text = Alignments(3)
            Frame1.PictureAlignment = 3
        Case "4"
            TextBox1.Text = Alignments(4)
            Frame1.PictureAlignment = 4
        Case Else
            TextBox1.Text = Alignments(SpinButton1.Value)
            Frame1.PictureAlignment = SpinButton1.Value
    End Select
End Sub
```

SpinDown, SpinUp Events

Applies To

SpinButton control.

Description

SpinDown occurs when the user clicks the lower or left spin-button arrow. SpinUp occurs when the user clicks the upper or right spin-button arrow.

Syntax

Private Sub *object*_**SpinDown( )**
Private Sub *object*_**SpinUp( )**

The SpinDown and SpinUp event syntaxes have these parts:

Part	Description
object	Required. A valid object.

Remarks

The SpinDown event decreases the **Value** property. The SpinUp event increases **Value**.

See Also

Value property.

Example

See the **Delay** property example.

StartDrag Method

Applies To

DataObject object.

Description

Initiates a drag-and-drop operation for a **DataObject**.

Syntax

fmDropEffect=Object.**StartDrag**(*[Effect as fmDropEffect]*)

The **StartDrag** method syntax has these parts:

Part	Description
Object	Required. A valid object.
Effect	Optional. Effect of the drop operation on the target control.

Settings

The settings for *Effect* are:

Constant	Value	Description
fmDropEffectNone	0	Does not copy or move the drop source to the drop target.
fmDropEffectCopy	1	Copies the drop source to the drop target.
fmDropEffectMove	2	Moves the drop source to the drop target.
fmDropEffectCopyOrMove	3	Copies or moves the drop source to the drop target.

Remarks

The drag action starts at the current mouse pointer position with the current keyboard state and ends when the user releases the mouse. The effect of the drag-and-drop operation depends on the effect chosen for the drop target.

For example, a control's MouseMove event might include the **StartDrag** method. When the user clicks the control and moves the mouse, the mouse pointer changes to indicate whether *Effect* is valid for the drop target.

See Also

BeforeDragOver event, BeforeDropOrPaste event.

Example

The following example demonstrates a drag-and-drop operation from one **ListBox** to another using a **DataObject** to contain the dragged text. This code sample uses the **SetText** and **StartDrag** methods in the MouseMove event to implement the drag-and-drop operation.

To use this example, copy this sample code to the Declarations portion of a form. Make sure that the form contains two **ListBox** controls named ListBox1 and ListBox2. You also need to add choices to the second **ListBox**.

```
Private Sub ListBox2_BeforeDragOver(ByVal Cancel As MSForms.ReturnBoolean, _
      ByVal Data As MSForms.DataObject, ByVal X As Single, ByVal Y _
      As Single, ByVal DragState As Long, ByVal Effect As MSForms. _
      ReturnEffect, ByVal Shift As Integer)
   Cancel = True
   Effect = 1
End Sub

Private Sub ListBox2_BeforeDropOrPaste(ByVal Cancel As MSForms.ReturnBoolean, _
      ByVal Action As Long, ByVal Data As MSForms.DataObject, ByVal _
      X As Single, ByVal Y As Single, ByVal Effect As MSForms. _
      ReturnEffect, ByVal Shift As Integer)
   Cancel = True
   Effect = 1
   ListBox2.AddItem Data.GetText
End Sub

Private Sub ListBox1_MouseMove(ByVal Button As Integer, ByVal Shift _
      As Integer, ByVal X As Single, ByVal Y As Single)
   Dim MyDataObject As DataObject
   If Button = 1 Then
      Set MyDataObject = New DataObject
      Dim Effect As Integer
      MyDataObject.SetText ListBox1.Value
      Effect = MyDataObject.StartDrag
   End If
End Sub

Private Sub UserForm_Initialize()
   For i = 1 To 10
      ListBox1.AddItem "Choice " & (ListBox1.ListCount + 1)
   Next i
End Sub
```

StrikeThrough Property

See Bold, Italic, Size, StrikeThrough, Underline, Weight Properties.

Style Property

Applies To

ComboBox control, **MultiPage** control, **TabStrip** control.

Description

For **ComboBox**, specifies how the user can choose or set the control's value. For **MultiPage** and **TabStrip**, identifies the style of the tabs on the control.

Syntax

For ComboBox:

object.**Style** [= *fmStyle*]

For MultiPage and TabStrip:

object.**Style** [= *fmTabStyle*]

The **Style** property syntax has these parts:

Part	Description
object	Required. A valid object.
fmStyle	Optional. Specifies how a user sets the value of a **ComboBox**.
fmTabStyle	Optional. Specifies the tab style in a **MultiPage** or **TabStrip**.

Settings

The settings for *fmStyle* are:

Constant	Value	Description
fmStyleDropDownCombo	0	The **ComboBox** behaves as a drop-down combo box. The user can type a value in the edit region or select a value from the drop-down list (default).
fmStyleDropDownList	2	The **ComboBox** behaves as a list box. The user must choose a value from the list.

The settings for *fmTabStyle* are:

Constant	Value	Description
fmTabStyleTabs	0	Displays tabs on the tab bar (default).
fmTabStyleButtons	1	Displays buttons on the tab bar.
fmTabStyleNone	2	Does not display the tab bar.

Example

The following example uses the **Style** property to change the effect of typing in the text area of a **ComboBox**. The user chooses a style by selecting an **OptionButton** control and then types into the **ComboBox** to select an item. When **Style** is *fmStyleDropDownList*, the user must choose an item from the drop-down list. When **Style** is *fmStyleDropDownCombo*, the user can type into the text area to specify an item in the drop-down list.

To use this example, copy this sample code to the Declarations portion of a form. Make sure that the form contains:

- Two **OptionButton** controls named OptionButton1 and OptionButton2.
- A **ComboBox** named ComboBox1.

```
Private Sub OptionButton1_Click()
   ComboBox1.Style = fmStyleDropDownCombo
End Sub

Private Sub OptionButton2_Click()
   ComboBox1.Style = fmStyleDropDownList
End Sub

Private Sub UserForm_Initialize()
   Dim i As Integer

   For i = 1 To 10
      ComboBox1.AddItem "Choice " & i
   Next i

   OptionButton1.Caption = "Select like ComboBox"
   OptionButton1.Value = True
   ComboBox1.Style = fmStyleDropDownCombo

   OptionButton2.Caption = "Select like ListBox"
End Sub
```

Example

The following example uses the **Style** property to specify the appearance of the tabs in **MultiPage** and **TabStrip**. This example also demonstrates using a **Label**. The user chooses a style by selecting an **OptionButton**.

To use this example, copy this sample code to the Declarations portion of a form. Make sure that the form contains:

- A **Label** named Label1.
- Three **OptionButton** controls named OptionButton1 through OptionButton3.
- A **MultiPage** named MultiPage1.
- A **TabStrip** named TabStrip1.
- Any control inside the **TabStrip**.
- Any control in each page of the **MultiPage**.

```
Private Sub OptionButton1_Click()
   MultiPage1.Style = fmTabStyleTabs
   TabStrip1.Style = fmTabStyleTabs
End Sub
```

```
Private Sub OptionButton2_Click()
   'Note that the page borders are invisible
   MultiPage1.Style = fmTabStyleButtons
   TabStrip1.Style = fmTabStyleButtons
End Sub

Private Sub OptionButton3_Click()
   'Note that the page borders are invisible and
   'the page body begins where the tabs normally appear.
   MultiPage1.Style = fmTabStyleNone
   TabStrip1.Style = fmTabStyleNone
End Sub

Private Sub UserForm_Initialize()
   Label1.Caption = "Page/Tab Style"
   OptionButton1.Caption = "Tabs"
   OptionButton1.Value = True
   MultiPage1.Style = fmTabStyleTabs
   TabStrip1.Style = fmTabStyleTabs

   OptionButton2.Caption = "Buttons"
   OptionButton3.Caption = "No Tabs or Buttons"
End Sub
```

Tab Object

Description

A **Tab** is an individual member of a **Tabs** collection.

Remarks

Visually, a **Tab** object appears as a rectangle protruding from a larger rectangular area or as a button adjacent to a rectangular area.

In contrast to a **Page**, a **Tab** does not contain any controls. Controls that appear within the region bounded by a **TabStrip** are contained on the form, as is the **TabStrip**.

Each **Tab** has its own set of properties, but has no methods or events. You must use events from the appropriate **TabStrip** to initiate processing of an individual **Tab**.

Each **Tab** has a unique name and index value within the collection. You can reference a **Tab** by either its name or its index value. The index of the first **Tab** is 0; the index of the second **Tab** is 1; and so on. When two **Tab** objects have the same name, you must reference each **Tab** by its index value. References to the name in code will access only the first **Tab** that uses the name.

Properties

Accelerator property, **Caption** property, **ControlTipText** property, **Enabled** property, **Index** property, **Name** property, **Tag** property, **Visible** property.

See Also

Page object, **Tabs** collection, **TabStrip** control.

Example

The following example accesses an individual tab of a **TabStrip** in several ways:

- Using the **Tabs** collection with a numeric index.
- Using the **Tabs** collection with a string index.
- Using the **Tabs** collection with the **Item** method.
- Using the name of the individual **Tab**.
- Using the **SelectedItem** property.

To use this example, copy this sample code to the Declarations portion of a form. Make sure that the form contains a **TabStrip** named TabStrip1.

```
Private Sub UserForm_Initialize()
    Dim TabName As String

    For i = 0 To TabStrip1.Count - 1
        'Using index (numeric or string)
        MsgBox "TabStrip1.Tabs(i).Caption = " & TabStrip1.Tabs(i). _
            Caption
        MsgBox "TabStrip1.Tabs.Item(i).Caption = " & TabStrip1.Tabs _
            .Item(i).Caption

        TabName = TabStrip1.Tabs(i).Name
        MsgBox "TabName = " & TabName

        MsgBox "TabStrip1.Tabs(TabName).Caption = " & TabStrip1.Tabs _
            (TabName).Caption
        MsgBox "TabStrip1.Tabs.Item(TabName).Caption = " & TabStrip1. _
            Tabs.Item(TabName).Caption

        'Use Tab object without referring to Tabs collection
        If i = 0 Then
            MsgBox "TabStrip1.Tab1. Caption = " & TabStrip1.Tab1.Caption
        ElseIf i = 1 Then
            MsgBox "TabStrip1.Tab2. Caption = " & TabStrip1.Tab2.Caption
        EndIf

        'Use SelectedItem Property
        TabStrip1.Value = i
        MsgBox " TabStrip1.SelectedItem.Caption = " & TabStrip1. _
            SelectedItem.Caption
    Next i
End Sub
```

TabFixedHeight, TabFixedWidth Properties

Applies To

MultiPage control, **TabStrip** control.

Description

Sets or returns the fixed height or width of the tabs in points.

Syntax

object.**TabFixedHeight** [= *Single*]
object.**TabFixedWidth** [= *Single*]

The **TabFixedHeight** and **TabFixedWidth** property syntaxes have these parts:

Part	Description
object	Required. A valid object.
Single	Optional. The number of points of the height or width of the tabs on a **TabStrip** or **MultiPage**.

Settings

If the value is 0, tab widths are automatically adjusted so that each tab is wide enough to accommodate its contents and each row of tabs spans the width of the control.

If the value is greater than 0, all tabs have an identical width as specified by this property.

Remarks

The minimum size is 4 points.

Example

The following example uses the **TabFixedHeight** and **TabFixedWidth** properties to set the size of the tabs used in **MultiPage** and **TabStrip**. The user clicks the **SpinButton** controls to adjust the height and width of the tabs within the **MultiPage** and **TabStrip**.

To use this example, copy this sample code to the Declarations portion of a form. Make sure that the form contains:

- A **MultiPage** named MultiPage1.
- A **TabStrip** named TabStrip1.
- A **Label** named Label1 for the width control.
- A **SpinButton** named SpinButton1 for the width control.
- A **TextBox** named TextBox1 for the width control.
- A **Label** named Label2 for the height control.
- A **SpinButton** named SpinButton2 for the height control.
- A **TextBox** named TextBox2 for the height control.

```
Private Sub UpdateTabWidth()
   TextBox1.Text = SpinButton1.Value
   TabStrip1.TabFixedWidth = SpinButton1.Value
   MultiPage1.TabFixedWidth = SpinButton1.Value
End Sub

Private Sub UpdateTabHeight()
   TextBox2.Text = SpinButton2.Value
   TabStrip1.TabFixedHeight = SpinButton2.Value
   MultiPage1.TabFixedHeight = SpinButton2.Value
End Sub

Private Sub UserForm_Initialize()
   MultiPage1.Style = fmTabStyleButtons

   Label1.Caption = "Tab Width"
   SpinButton1.Min = 0
   SpinButton1.Max = TabStrip1.Width / TabStrip1.Tabs.Count
   SpinButton1.Value = 0
   TextBox1.Locked = True

   UpdateTabWidth

   Label2.Caption = "Tab Height"
   SpinButton2.Min = 0
   SpinButton2.Max = TabStrip1.Height
   SpinButton2.Value = 0
   TextBox2.Locked = True

   UpdateTabHeight
End Sub

Private Sub SpinButton1_SpinDown()
   UpdateTabWidth
End Sub

Private Sub SpinButton1_SpinUp()
   UpdateTabWidth
End Sub

Private Sub SpinButton2_SpinDown()
   UpdateTabHeight
End Sub

Private Sub SpinButton2_SpinUp()
   UpdateTabHeight
End Sub
```

TabIndex Property

Applies To

CheckBox control, **ComboBox** control, **CommandButton** control, **Label** control, **ListBox** control, **MultiPage** control, **OptionButton** control, **Page** object, **ScrollBar** control, **SpinButton** control, **TabStrip** control, **TextBox** control, **ToggleButton** control.

Description

Specifies the position of a single object in the form's tab order.

Syntax

object.**TabIndex** [= *Integer*]

The **TabIndex** property syntax has these parts:

Part	Description
object	Required. A valid object.
Integer	Optional. An integer from 0 to one less than the number of controls on the form that have a **TabIndex** property. Assigning a **TabIndex** value of less than 0 generates an error. If you assign a **TabIndex** value greater than the largest index value, the system resets the value to the maximum allowable value.

Remarks

The index value of the first object in the tab order is zero.

See Also

SetDefaultTabOrder method, **TabStop** property.

Example

The following example uses the **TabIndex** property to display and set the tab order for individual controls. The user can press TAB to reach the next control in the tab order and to display the **TabIndex** of that control. The user can also click on a control to display its **TabIndex**. The user can change the **TabIndex** of a control by specifying a new index value in the **TextBox** and clicking CommandButton3. Changing the **TabIndex** for one control also updates the **TabIndex** for other controls in the **Frame**.

To use this example, copy this sample code to the Declarations portion of a form. Make sure that the form contains:

- A **Label** named Label1.
- A **TextBox** named TextBox1.
- A **Frame** named Frame1.
- A **TextBox** in the **Frame** named TextBox2.
- Two **CommandButton** controls in the **Frame** named CommandButton1 and CommandButton2.
- A **ScrollBar** in the **Frame** named ScrollBar1.

- A **CommandButton** (not in the **Frame**) named CommandButton3.

```
Private Sub MoveToFront()
   Dim i, Temp As Integer

   Temp = Frame1.ActiveControl.TabIndex
   For i = 0 To Temp - 1
      Frame1.Controls.Item(i).TabIndex = i + 1
   Next i

   Frame1.ActiveControl.TabIndex = 0
   TextBox1.Text = Frame1.ActiveControl.TabIndex
End Sub

Private Sub CommandButton3_Click()
   Dim i, Temp As Integer

   If IsNumeric(TextBox1.Text) Then
      Temp = Val(TextBox1.Text)

      If Temp >= Frame1.Controls.Count Or Temp < 0 Then
         'Entry out of range; move control to front of tab order
         MoveToFront
      ElseIf Temp > Frame1.ActiveControl.TabIndex Then
         'Move entry down the list
         For i = Frame1.ActiveControl.TabIndex + 1 To Temp
            Frame1.Controls.Item(i).TabIndex = i - 1
         Next i
         Frame1.ActiveControl.TabIndex = Temp
         TextBox1.Text = Frame1.ActiveControl.TabIndex
      Else
         'Move Entry up the list
         For i = Frame1.ActiveControl.TabIndex - 1 To Temp
            Frame1.Controls.Item(i).TabIndex = i + 1
         Next i
         Frame1.ActiveControl.TabIndex = Temp
         TextBox1.Text = Frame1.ActiveControl.TabIndex
      End If
   Else
      'Text entry; move control to front of tab order
      MoveToFront
   End If
End Sub

Private Sub UserForm_Initialize()
   Label1.Caption = "TabIndex"

   Frame1.Controls(0).SetFocus
   TextBox1.Text = Frame1.ActiveControl.TabIndex

   Frame1.Cycle = fmCycleCurrentForm
```

```
    CommandButton3.Caption = "Set TabIndex"
    CommandButton3.TakeFocusOnClick = False
End Sub

Private Sub TextBox2_Enter()
    TextBox1.Text = Frame1.ActiveControl.TabIndex
End Sub

Private Sub CommandButton1_Enter()
    TextBox1.Text = Frame1.ActiveControl.TabIndex
End Sub

Private Sub CommandButton2_Enter()
    TextBox1.Text = Frame1.ActiveControl.TabIndex
End Sub

Private Sub ScrollBar1_Enter()
    TextBox1.Text = Frame1.ActiveControl.TabIndex
End Sub
```

TabKeyBehavior Property

Applies To

TextBox control.

Description

Determines whether tabs are allowed in the edit region.

Syntax

object.**TabKeyBehavior** [= *Boolean*]

The **TabKeyBehavior** property syntax has these parts:

Part	Description
object	Required. A valid object.
Boolean	Optional. The effect of pressing TAB.

Settings

The settings for *Boolean* are:

Value	Description
True	Pressing TAB inserts a tab character in the edit region.
False	Pressing TAB moves the focus to the next object in the tab order (default).

Remarks

The **TabKeyBehavior** and **MultiLine** properties are closely related. The values described above only apply if **MultiLine** is **True**. If **MultiLine** is **False**, pressing TAB always moves the focus to the next control in the tab order regardless of the value of **TabKeyBehavior**.

The effect of pressing CTRL+TAB also depends on the value of **MultiLine**. If **MultiLine** is **True**, pressing CTRL+TAB creates a new line regardless of the value of **TabKeyBehavior**. If **MultiLine** is **False**, pressing CTRL+TAB has no effect.

See Also

EnterKeyBehavior property, **MultiLine** property.

TabOrientation Property

Applies To

MultiPage control, **TabStrip** control.

Description

Specifies the location of the tabs on a **MultiPage** or **TabStrip**.

Syntax

object.**TabOrientation** [= *fmTabOrientation*]

The **TabOrientation** property syntax has these parts:

Part	Description
object	Required. A valid object.
fmTabOrientation	Optional. Where the tabs will appear.

Settings

The settings for *fmTabOrientation* are:

Constant	Value	Description
fmTabOrientationTop	0	The tabs appear at the top of the control (default).
fmTabOrientationBottom	1	The tabs appear at the bottom of the control.
fmTabOrientationLeft	2	The tabs appear at the left side of the control.
fmTabOrientationRight	3	The tabs appear at the right side of the control.

Remarks

If you use TrueType fonts, the text rotates when the **TabOrientation** property is set to **fmTabOrientationLeft** or **fmTabOrientationRight**. If you use bitmapped fonts, the text does not rotate.

Tabs Collection

Applies To

TabStrip control.

Description

A **Tabs** collection includes all **Tabs** of a **TabStrip**.

Remarks

Each **Tabs** collection provides the features to manage the number of tabs in the collection and to identify the tab that is currently in use.

The default value of the **Tabs** collection identifies the current **Tab** of a collection.

A **Tab** object has a unique name and index value within a **Tabs** collection. You can reference a **Tab** either by its name or its index value. The index value reflects the ordinal position of the **Tab** within the collection. The index of the first **Tab** in a collection is 0; the index of the second **Tab** is 1; and so on.

Properties

Count property.

Methods

Add method, **Clear** method, **Item** method, **Remove** method.

See Also

Index property, **Tab** object.

Example

See the **Tab** object example.

TabStop Property

Applies To

CheckBox control, **ComboBox** control, **CommandButton** control, **ListBox** control, **MultiPage** control, **OptionButton** control, **Page** object, **ScrollBar** control, **SpinButton** control, **TabStrip** control, **TextBox** control, **ToggleButton** control.

Description

Indicates whether an object can receive focus when the user tabs to it.

Syntax

object.**TabStop** [= *Boolean*]

The **TabStop** property syntax has these parts:

Part	Description
object	Required. A valid object.
Boolean	Optional. Whether the object is a tab stop.

Settings

The settings for *Boolean* are:

Value	Description
True	Designates the object as a tab stop (default).
False	Bypasses the object when the user is tabbing, although the object still holds its place in the actual tab order, as determined by the **TabIndex** property.

See Also

TabIndex property, **TakeFocusOnClick** property.

Example

The following example uses the **TabStop** property to control whether a user can press TAB to move the focus to a particular control. The user presses TAB to move the focus among the controls on the form, and then clicks the **ToggleButton** to change **TabStop** for CommandButton1. When **TabStop** is **False**, CommandButton1 will not receive the focus by using TAB.

To use this example, copy this sample code to the Declarations portion of a form. Make sure that the form contains:

- A **CommandButton** named CommandButton1.
- A **ToggleButton** named ToggleButton1.
- One or two other controls, such as an **OptionButton** or **ListBox**.

```
Private Sub CommandButton1_Click()
   MsgBox "Clicked CommandButton1."
End Sub

Private Sub ToggleButton1_Click()
   If ToggleButton1 = True Then
      CommandButton1.TabStop = True
      ToggleButton1.Caption = "TabStop On"
   Else
      CommandButton1.TabStop = False
      ToggleButton1.Caption = "TabStop Off"
   End If
End Sub

Private Sub UserForm_Initialize()
   CommandButton1.Caption = "Show Message"

   ToggleButton1.Caption = "TabStop On"
   ToggleButton1.Value = True
   ToggleButton1.Width = 90
End Sub
```

TabStrip Control

Description

Presents a set of related controls as a visual group.

Remarks

You can use a **TabStrip** to view different sets of information for related controls.

For example, the controls might represent information about a daily schedule for a group of individuals, with each set of information corresponding to a different individual in the group. Set the title of each tab to show one individual's name. Then, you can write code that, when you click a tab, updates the controls to show information about the person identified on the tab.

Note The **TabStrip** is implemented as a container of a **Tabs** collection, which in turn contains a group of **Tab** objects.

The default property for a **TabStrip** is the **SelectedItem** property.

The default event for a **TabStrip** is the Change event.

Properties

BackColor property, **BoundValue** property, **ClientHeight**, **ClientLeft**, **ClientTop**, **ClientWidth** properties, **ControlTipText** property, **Enabled** property, **Font** object, **ForeColor** property, **Height**, **Width** properties, **HelpContextID** property, **LayoutEffect** property, **Left**, **Top** properties, **MouseIcon** property, **MousePointer** property, **MultiRow** property, **Name** property, **Object** property, **OldHeight**, **OldWidth** properties, **OldLeft**, **OldTop** properties, **Parent** property, **SelectedItem** property, **Style** property, **TabFixedHeight**, **TabFixedWidth** properties, **TabIndex** property, **TabOrientation** property, **TabStop** property, **Tag** property, **Value** property, **Visible** property.

Methods

Move method, **SetFocus** method, **ZOrder** method.

Events

BeforeDragOver event, BeforeDropOrPaste event, Change event, Click event, DblClick event, Enter, Exit events, Error event, KeyDown, KeyUp events, KeyPress event, MouseDown, MouseUp events, MouseMove event.

See Also

Tab object, **Tabs** collection.

Example

See the **Tab** object example.

Tag Property

Applies To

CheckBox control, **ComboBox** control, **CommandButton** control, **Image** control, **Label** control, **ListBox** control, **MultiPage** control, **OptionButton** control, **Page** object, **ScrollBar** control, **SpinButton** control, **Tab** object, **TabStrip** control, **TextBox** control, **ToggleButton** control, **UserForm** object.

Description

Stores additional information about an object.

Syntax

object.**Tag** [= *String*]

The **Tag** property syntax has these parts:

Part	Description
object	Required. A valid object.
String	Optional. A string expression identifying the object. The default is a zero-length string (" ").

Remarks

Use the **Tag** property to assign an identification string to an object without affecting other property settings or attributes.

For example, you can use **Tag** to check the identity of a form or control that is passed as a variable to a procedure.

Example

The following example uses the **Tag** property to store additional information about each control on the **UserForm**. The user clicks a control and then clicks the **CommandButton**. The contents of **Tag** for the appropriate control are returned in the **TextBox**.

To use this example, copy this sample code to the Declarations portion of a form. Make sure that the form contains:

- A **TextBox** named TextBox1.
- A **CommandButton** named CommandButton1.
- A **ScrollBar** named ScrollBar1.
- A **ComboBox** named ComboBox1.
- A **MultiPage** named MultiPage1.

```
Private Sub CommandButton1_Click()
   TextBox1.Text = ActiveControl.Tag
End Sub
```

```
Private Sub UserForm_Initialize()
    TextBox1.Locked = True
    TextBox1.Tag = "Display area for Tag properties."
    TextBox1.AutoSize = True

    CommandButton1.Caption = "Show Tag of Current Control."
    CommandButton1.AutoSize = True
    CommandButton1.WordWrap = True
    CommandButton1.TakeFocusOnClick = False
    CommandButton1.Tag = "Shows tag of control that has the focus."

    ComboBox1.Style = fmStyleDropDownList
    ComboBox1.Tag = "ComboBox Style is that of a ListBox."

    ScrollBar1.Max = 100
    ScrollBar1.Min = -273
    ScrollBar1.Tag = "Max = " & ScrollBar1.Max & " , Min = " & _
        ScrollBar1.Min

    MultiPage1.Pages.Add
    MultiPage1.Pages.Add
    MultiPage1.Tag = "This MultiPage has " & MultiPage1.Pages.Count _
        & " pages."
End Sub
```

TakeFocusOnClick Property

Applies To

CommandButton control.

Description

Specifies whether a control takes the focus when clicked.

Syntax

object.**TakeFocusOnClick** [= *Boolean*]

The **TakeFocusOnClick** property syntax has these parts:

Part	Description
object	Required. A valid object.
Boolean	Optional. Specifies whether a control takes the focus when clicked.

Settings

The settings for *Boolean* are:

Value	Description
True	The button takes the focus when clicked (default).
False	The button does not take the focus when clicked.

Remarks

The **TakeFocusOnClick** property defines only what happens when the user clicks a control. If the user tabs to the control, the control takes the focus regardless of the value of **TakeFocusOnClick**.

Use this property to complete actions that affect a control without requiring that control to give up focus. For example, assume your form includes a **TextBox** and a **CommandButton** that checks for correct spelling of text. You would like to be able to select text in the **TextBox**, then click the **CommandButton** and run the spelling checker without taking focus away from the **TextBox**. You can do this by setting the **TakeFocusOnClick** property of the **CommandButton** to **False**.

See Also

TabStop property.

Example

The following example uses the **TakeFocusOnClick** property to control whether a **CommandButton** receives the focus when the user clicks on it. The user clicks a control other than CommandButton1 and then clicks CommandButton1. If **TakeFocusOnClick** is **True**, CommandButton1 receives the focus after it is clicked. The user can change the value of **TakeFocusOnClick** by clicking the **ToggleButton**.

To use this example, copy this sample code to the Declarations portion of a form. Make sure that the form contains:

- A **CommandButton** named CommandButton1.
- A **ToggleButton** named ToggleButton1.
- One or two other controls, such as an **OptionButton** or **ListBox**.

```
Private Sub CommandButton1_Click()
   MsgBox "Watch CommandButton1 to see if it takes the focus."
End Sub

Private Sub ToggleButton1_Click()
   If ToggleButton1 = True Then
      CommandButton1.TakeFocusOnClick = True
      ToggleButton1.Caption = "TakeFocusOnClick On"
   Else
      CommandButton1.TakeFocusOnClick = False
      ToggleButton1.Caption = "TakeFocusOnClick Off"
   End If
End Sub

Private Sub UserForm_Initialize()
   CommandButton1.Caption = "Show Message"

   ToggleButton1.Caption = "TakeFocusOnClick On"
   ToggleButton1.Value = True
   ToggleButton1.Width = 90
End Sub
```

Text Property

Applies To

ComboBox control, **ListBox** control, **TextBox** control.

Description

Returns or sets the text in a **TextBox**. Changes the selected row in a **ComboBox** or **ListBox**.

Syntax

object.**Text** [= *String*]

The **Text** property syntax has these parts:

Part	Description
object	Required. A valid object.
String	Optional. A string expression specifying text. The default value is a zero-length string (" ").

Remarks

For a **TextBox**, any value you assign to the **Text** property is also assigned to the **Value** property.

For a **ComboBox**, you can use **Text** to update the value of the control. If the value of **Text** matches an existing list entry, the value of the **ListIndex** property (the index of the current row) is set to the row that matches **Text**. If the value of **Text** does not match a row, **ListIndex** is set to –1.

For a **ListBox**, the value of **Text** must match an existing list entry. Specifying a value that does not match an existing list entry causes an error.

You cannot use **Text** to change the value of an entry in a **ComboBox** or **ListBox**; use the **Column** or **List** property for this purpose.

The **ForeColor** property determines the color of the text.

See Also

ForeColor property, **ListIndex** property, **MatchRequired** property, **Value** property.

Example

See the **CurLine** property example.

TextAlign Property

Applies To

ComboBox control, **Label** control, **TextBox** control.

Description

Specifies how text is aligned in a control.

Syntax

object.**TextAlign** [= *fmTextAlign*]

The **TextAlign** property syntax has these parts:

Part	Description
object	Required. A valid object.
fmTextAlign	Optional. How text is aligned in the control.

Settings

The settings for *fmTextAlign* are:

Constant	Value	Description
fmTextAlignLeft	1	Aligns the first character of displayed text with the left edge of the control's display or edit area (default).
fmTextAlignCenter	2	Centers the text in the control's display or edit area.
fmTextAlignRight	3	Aligns the last character of displayed text with the right edge of the control's display or edit area.

Remarks

For a **ComboBox**, the **TextAlign** property only affects the edit region; this property has no effect on the alignment of text in the list. For stand-alone labels, **TextAlign** determines the alignment of the label's caption.

TextBox Control

Description

Displays information from a user or from an organized set of data.

Remarks

A **TextBox** is the control most commonly used to display information entered by a user. Also, it can display a set of data, such as a table, query, worksheet, or a calculation result. If a **TextBox** is bound to a data source, then changing the contents of the **TextBox** also changes the value of the bound data source.

Formatting applied to any piece of text in a **TextBox** will affect all text in the control. For example, if you change the font or point size of any character in the control, the change will affect all characters in the control.

The default property for a **TextBox** is the **Value** property.

The default event for a **TextBox** is the Change event.

Properties

AutoSize property, **AutoTab** property, **AutoWordSelect** property, **BackColor** property, **BackStyle** property, **BorderColor** property, **BorderStyle** property, **BoundValue** property, **CanPaste** property, **ControlSource** property, **ControlTipText** property, **CurLine** property, **CurTargetX** property, **CurX** property, **DragBehavior** property, **DropButtonStyle** property, **Enabled** property, **EnterFieldBehavior** property, **EnterKeyBehavior** property, **Font** object, **ForeColor** property, **Height**, **Width** properties, **HelpContextID** property, **HideSelection** property, **IMEMode** property, **IntegralHeight** property, **LayoutEffect** property, **Left**, **Top** properties, **LineCount** property, **Locked** property, **MaxLength** property, **MouseIcon** property, **MousePointer** property, **MultiLine** property, **Name** property, **Object** property, **OldHeight**, **OldWidth** properties, **OldLeft**, **OldTop** properties, **Parent** property, **PasswordChar** property, **ScrollBars** property, **SelectionMargin** property, **SelLength** property, **SelStart** property, **SelText** property, **ShowDropButtonWhen** property, **SpecialEffect** property, **TabIndex** property, **TabKeyBehavior** property, **TabStop** property, **Tag** property, **Text** property, **TextAlign** property, **TextLength** property, **Value** property, **Visible** property, **WordWrap** property.

Methods

Copy method, **Cut** method, **Move** method, **Paste** method, **SetFocus** method, **ZOrder** method.

Events

AfterUpdate event, BeforeDragOver event, BeforeDropOrPaste event, BeforeUpdate event, Change event, DblClick event, DropButtonClick event, Enter, Exit events, Error event, KeyDown, KeyUp events, KeyPress event, MouseDown, MouseUp events, MouseMove event,

See Also

ComboBox control.

Example

The following example demonstrates the **MultiLine**, **WordWrap**, and **ScrollBars** properties on a **TextBox**.

To use this example, copy this sample code to the Declarations portion of a form. Make sure that the form contains:

- A **TextBox** named TextBox1.
- Four **ToggleButton** controls named ToggleButton1 through ToggleButton4.

To see the entire text placed in the **TextBox**, set **MultiLine** and **WordWrap** to **True** by clicking the **ToggleButton** controls.

When **MultiLine** is **True**, you can enter new lines of text by pressing SHIFT+ENTER.

ScrollBars appears when you manually change the content of the **TextBox**.

```
Private Sub UserForm_Initialize()
'Initialize TextBox properties and toggle buttons

   TextBox1.Text = "Type your text here. Enter SHIFT+ENTER to move to" _
      & " a new line."

   TextBox1.AutoSize = False
   ToggleButton1.Caption = "AutoSize Off"
   ToggleButton1.Value = False
   ToggleButton1.AutoSize = True

   TextBox1.WordWrap = False
   ToggleButton2.Caption = "WordWrap Off"
   ToggleButton2.Value = False
   ToggleButton2.AutoSize = True

   TextBox1.ScrollBars = 0
   ToggleButton3.Caption = "ScrollBars Off"
   ToggleButton3.Value = False
   ToggleButton3.AutoSize = True

   TextBox1.MultiLine = False
   ToggleButton4.Caption = "Single Line"
   ToggleButton4.Value = False
   ToggleButton4.AutoSize = True
 End Sub

Private Sub ToggleButton1_Click()
'Set AutoSize property and associated ToggleButton

   If ToggleButton1.Value = True Then
      TextBox1.AutoSize = True
      ToggleButton1.Caption = "AutoSize On"
   Else
      TextBox1.AutoSize = False
      ToggleButton1.Caption = "AutoSize Off"
   End If
End Sub

Private Sub ToggleButton2_Click()
'Set WordWrap property and associated ToggleButton
```

```
    If ToggleButton2.Value = True Then
        TextBox1.WordWrap = True
        ToggleButton2.Caption = "WordWrap On"
    Else
        TextBox1.WordWrap = False
        ToggleButton2.Caption = "WordWrap Off"
    End If
End Sub

Private Sub ToggleButton3_Click()
'Set ScrollBars property and associated ToggleButton

    If ToggleButton3.Value = True Then
        TextBox1.ScrollBars = 3
        ToggleButton3.Caption = "ScrollBars On"
    Else
        TextBox1.ScrollBars = 0
        ToggleButton3.Caption = "ScrollBars Off"
    End If
End Sub

Private Sub ToggleButton4_Click()
'Set MultiLine property and associated ToggleButton

    If ToggleButton4.Value = True Then
        TextBox1.MultiLine = True
        ToggleButton4.Caption = "Multiple Lines"
    Else
        TextBox1.MultiLine = False
        ToggleButton4.Caption = "Single Line"
    End If
End Sub
```

Example

The following example sets the z-order of a **TextBox**, so the user can display the entire **TextBox** (by bringing it to the front of the z-order) or can place the **TextBox** behind other controls (by sending it to the back of the z-order).

To use this example, copy this sample code to the Declarations portion of a form. Make sure that the form contains:

- Three **TextBox** controls named TextBox1 through TextBox3.
- A **ToggleButton** named ToggleButton1.

```
Private Sub ToggleButton1_Click()
If ToggleButton1.Value = True Then
    TextBox2.ZOrder (fmTop)          'Place TextBox2 on Top of z-order

    'Update ToggleButton caption to identify next state
    ToggleButton1.Caption = "Send TextBox2 to back"
Else
    TextBox2.ZOrder (1)              'Place TextBox2 on Bottom of z-order
```

```
        'Update ToggleButton caption to identify next state
        ToggleButton1.Caption = "Bring TextBox2 to front"
    End If
    End Sub

    Private Sub UserForm_Initialize()
    'Set up text boxes to show z-order in the form
    TextBox1.Text = "TextBox 1"
    TextBox2.Text = "TextBox 2"
    TextBox3.Text = "TextBox 3"

    TextBox1.Height = 40
    TextBox2.Height = 40
    TextBox3.Height = 40

    TextBox1.Width = 60
    TextBox2.Width = 60
    TextBox3.Width = 60

    TextBox1.Left = 10
    TextBox1.Top = 10

    TextBox2.Left = 25      'Overlap TextBox2 on TextBox1
    TextBox2.Top = 25

    TextBox3.Left = 40      'Overlap TextBox3 on TextBox2, TextBox1
    TextBox3.Top = 40

    ToggleButton1.Value = False
    ToggleButton1.Caption = "Bring TextBox2 to Front"
    ToggleButton1.Left = 10
    ToggleButton1.Top = 90
    ToggleButton1.Width = 50
    ToggleButton1.Height = 50

    End Sub
```

Example

The following example demonstrates the effects of the **AutoSize** property with a single-line **TextBox** and a multiline **TextBox**. The user can enter text into either **TextBox** and turn **AutoSize** on or off independently of the contents of the **TextBox**. This code sample also uses the **Text** property.

To use this example, copy this sample code to the Declarations portion of a form. Make sure that the form contains:

- Two **TextBox** controls named TextBox1 and TextBox2.
- A **ToggleButton** named ToggleButton1.

```
Private Sub UserForm_Initialize()
   TextBox1.Text = "Single-line TextBox. Type your text here."

   TextBox2.MultiLine = True
   TextBox2.Text = "Multi-line TextBox. Type your text here. Use CTRL+ENTER to start a
new line."

   ToggleButton1.Value = True
   ToggleButton1.Caption = "AutoSize On"
   TextBox1.AutoSize = True
   TextBox2.AutoSize = True
End Sub

Private Sub ToggleButton1_Click()
   If ToggleButton1.Value = True Then
      ToggleButton1.Caption = "AutoSize On"
      TextBox1.AutoSize = True
      TextBox2.AutoSize = True
   Else
      ToggleButton1.Caption = "AutoSize Off"
      TextBox1.AutoSize = False
      TextBox2.AutoSize = False
   End If
End Sub
```

Example

The following example tracks the **CurLine**, **CurTargetX**, and **CurX** property settings in a multiline **TextBox**. These settings change in the KeyUp event as the user types into the **Text** property, moves the insertion point, and extends the selection using the keyboard.

To use this example, follow these steps:

1. Copy this sample code to the Declarations portion of a form.
2. Add one large **TextBox** named TextBox1 to the form.
3. Add three **TextBox** controls named TextBox2, TextBox3, and TextBox4 in a column.

```
Private Sub TextBox1_KeyUp(ByVal KeyCode As MSForms.ReturnInteger, _
      ByVal Shift As Integer)
   TextBox2.Text = TextBox1.CurLine
   TextBox3.Text = TextBox1.CurX
   TextBox4.Text = TextBox1.CurTargetX
End Sub
```

```
Private Sub UserForm_Initialize()
   TextBox1.MultiLine = True

   TextBox1.Text = "Type your text here. User CTRL + ENTER to start" _
   & " a new line."
End Sub
```

Example

The following example uses the **Cut** and **Paste** methods to cut text from one **TextBox** and paste it into another **TextBox**.

To use this example, copy this sample code to the Declarations portion of a form. Make sure that the form contains:

- Two **TextBox** controls named TextBox1 and TextBox2.
- A **CommandButton** named CommandButton1.

```
Private Sub UserForm_Initialize()
   TextBox1.Text = "From TextBox1!"
   TextBox2.Text = "Hello "

   CommandButton1.Caption = "Cut and Paste"
   CommandButton1.AutoSize = True
End Sub

Private Sub CommandButton1_Click()
   TextBox2.SelStart = 0
   TextBox2.SelLength = TextBox2.TextLength
   TextBox2.Cut

   TextBox1.SetFocus
   TextBox1.SelStart = 0

   TextBox1.Paste
   TextBox2.SelStart = 0
End Sub
```

TextColumn Property

Applies To

ComboBox control, **ListBox** control.

Description

Identifies the column in a **ComboBox** or **ListBox** to display to the user.

Syntax

object.**TextColumn** [= *Variant*]

The **TextColumn** property syntax has these parts:

Part	Description
object	Required. A valid object.
Variant	Optional. The column to be displayed.

Settings

Values for the **TextColumn** property range from –1 to the number of columns in the list. The **TextColumn** value for the first column is 1, the value of the second column is 2, and so on. Setting **TextColumn** to 0 displays the **ListIndex** values. Setting **TextColumn** to –1 displays the first column that has a **ColumnWidths** value greater than 0.

Remarks

When the user selects a row from a **ComboBox** or **ListBox**, the column referenced by **TextColumn** is stored in the **Text** property. For example, you could set up a multicolumn **ListBox** that contains the names of holidays in one column and dates for the holidays in a second column. To present the holiday names to users, specify the first column as the **TextColumn**. To store the dates of the holidays, specify the second column as the **BoundColumn**.

When the **Text** property of a **ComboBox** changes (such as when a user types an entry into the control), the new text is compared to the column of data specified by **TextColumn**.

See Also

BoundColumn property, **ColumnWidths** property, **ListIndex** property, **Text** property.

Example

The following example uses the **TextColumn** property to identify the column of data in a **ListBox** that supplies data for its **Text** property. This example sets the third column of the **ListBox** as the text column. As you select an entry from the **ListBox**, the value from the **TextColumn** will be displayed in the **Label**.

This example also demonstrates how to load a multicolumn **ListBox** using the **AddItem** method and the **List** property.

To use this example, copy this sample code to the Declarations portion of a form. Make sure that the form contains:

- A **ListBox** named ListBox1.
- A **TextBox** named TextBox1.

```
Private Sub UserForm_Initialize()
ListBox1.ColumnCount = 3

ListBox1.AddItem "Row 1, Col 1"
ListBox1.List(0, 1) = "Row 1, Col 2"
ListBox1.List(0, 2) = "Row 1, Col 3"
```

```
ListBox1.AddItem "Row 2, Col 1"
ListBox1.List(1, 1) = "Row 2, Col 2"
ListBox1.List(1, 2) = "Row 2, Col 3"

ListBox1.AddItem "Row 3, Col 1"
ListBox1.List(2, 1) = "Row 3, Col 2"
ListBox1.List(2, 2) = "Row 3, Col 3"

ListBox1.TextColumn = 3
End Sub

Private Sub ListBox1_Change()
TextBox1.Text = ListBox1.Text
End Sub
```

TextLength Property

Applies To

ComboBox control, **TextBox** control.

Description

Returns the length, in characters, of text in the edit region of a **TextBox** or **ComboBox**.

Syntax

object.**TextLength**

The **TextLength** property syntax has these parts:

Part	Description
object	Required. A valid object.

Remarks

The **TextLength** property is read-only. For a multiline **TextBox**, **TextLength** includes LF (line feed) and CR (carriage return) characters.

Example

See the **LineCount** property example.

ToggleButton Control

Description

Shows the selection state of an item.

Remarks

Use a **ToggleButton** to show whether an item is selected. If a **ToggleButton** is bound to a data source, the **ToggleButton** shows the current value of that data source as either *Yes/No*, *True/False*, *On/Off*, or some other choice of two settings. If the user selects the **ToggleButton**, the current setting is *Yes*, *True*, or *On*; if the user does not select the **ToggleButton**, the setting is *No*, *False*, or *Off*. If the **ToggleButton** is bound to a data source, changing the setting changes the value of that data source. A disabled **ToggleButton** shows a value, but is dimmed and does not allow changes from the user interface.

You can also use a **ToggleButton** inside a **Frame** to select one or more of a group of related items. For example, you can create an order form with a list of available items, with a **ToggleButton** preceding each item. The user can select a particular item by selecting the appropriate **ToggleButton**.

The default property of a **ToggleButton** is the **Value** property.

The default event of a **ToggleButton** is the Click event.

Properties

Accelerator property, **Alignment** property, **AutoSize** property, **BackColor** property, **BackStyle** property, **BoundValue** property, **Caption** property, **ControlSource** property, **ControlTipText** property, **Enabled** property, **Font** object, **ForeColor** property, **Height**, **Width** properties, **HelpContextID** property, **LayoutEffect** property, **Left**, **Top** properties, **Locked** property, **MouseIcon** property, **MousePointer** property, **Name** property, **Object** property, **OldHeight**, **OldWidth** properties, **OldLeft**, **OldTop** properties, **Parent** property, **Picture** property, **PicturePosition** property, **SpecialEffect** property, **TabIndex** property, **TabStop** property, **Tag** property, **TripleState** property, **Value** property, **Visible** property, **WordWrap** property.

Methods

Move method, **SetFocus** method, **ZOrder** method.

Events

AfterUpdate event, BeforeDragOver event, BeforeDropOrPaste event, BeforeUpdate event, Change event, Click event, DblClick event, Enter, Exit events, Error event, KeyDown, KeyUp events, KeyPress event, MouseDown, MouseUp events, MouseMove event.

Example

The following example uses the **TripleState** property to allow **Null** as a legal value of a **CheckBox** and a **ToggleButton**. The user controls the value of **TripleState** through ToggleButton2. The user can set the value of a **CheckBox** or **ToggleButton** based on the value of **TripleState**.

To use this example, copy this sample code to the Declarations portion of a form. Make sure that the form contains:

- A **CheckBox** named CheckBox1.
- A **ToggleButton** named ToggleButton1.
- A **ToggleButton** named ToggleButton2.

```
Private Sub UserForm_Initialize()
   CheckBox1.Caption = "Value is True"
   CheckBox1.Value = True
   CheckBox1.TripleState = False

   ToggleButton1.Caption = "Value is True"
   ToggleButton1.Value = True
   ToggleButton1.TripleState = False

   ToggleButton2.Value = False
   ToggleButton2.Caption = "Triple State Off"
End Sub

Private Sub ToggleButton2_Click()
   If ToggleButton2.Value = True Then
      ToggleButton2.Caption = "Triple State On"
      CheckBox1.TripleState = True
      ToggleButton1.TripleState = True
   Else
      ToggleButton2.Caption = "Triple State Off"
      CheckBox1.TripleState = False
      ToggleButton1.TripleState = False
   End If
End Sub

Private Sub CheckBox1_Change()
   If IsNull(CheckBox1.Value) Then
      CheckBox1.Caption = "Value is Null"
   ElseIf CheckBox1.Value = False Then
      CheckBox1.Caption = "Value is False"
   ElseIf CheckBox1.Value = True Then
      CheckBox1.Caption = "Value is True"
   End If
End Sub
```

```
Private Sub ToggleButton1_Change()
    If IsNull(ToggleButton1.Value) Then
        ToggleButton1.Caption = "Value is Null"
    ElseIf ToggleButton1.Value = False Then
        ToggleButton1.Caption = "Value is False"
    ElseIf ToggleButton1.Value = True Then
        ToggleButton1.Caption = "Value is True"
    End If
End Sub
```

Top Property

See Left, Top Properties.

TopIndex Property

Applies To

ComboBox control, **ListBox** control.

Description

Sets and returns the item that appears in the topmost position in the list.

Syntax

object.**TopIndex** [= *Variant*]

The **TopIndex** property syntax has these parts:

Part	Description
object	Required. A valid object.
Variant	Optional. The number of the list item that is displayed in the topmost position. The default is 0, or the first item in the list.

Settings

Returns the value –1 if the list is empty or not displayed.

Example

The following example identifies the top item displayed in a **ListBox** and the item that has the focus within the **ListBox**. This example uses the **TopIndex** property to identify the item displayed at the top of the **ListBox** and the **ListIndex** property to identify the item that has the focus. The user selects an item in the **ListBox**. The displayed values of **TopIndex** and **ListIndex** are updated when the user selects an item or when the user clicks the **CommandButton**.

To use this example, copy this sample code to the Declarations portion of a form. Make sure that the form contains:

- A **Label** named Label1.
- A **TextBox** named TextBox1.
- A **Label** named Label2.
- A **TextBox** named TextBox2.
- A **CommandButton** named CommandButton1.
- A **ListBox** named ListBox1.

```
Private Sub CommandButton1_Click()
   ListBox1.TopIndex = ListBox1.ListIndex
   TextBox1.Text = ListBox1.TopIndex
   TextBox2.Text = ListBox1.ListIndex
End Sub

Private Sub ListBox1_Change()
   TextBox1.Text = ListBox1.TopIndex
   TextBox2.Text = ListBox1.ListIndex
End Sub

Private Sub UserForm_Initialize()
   Dim i As Integer

   For i = 0 To 24
      ListBox1.AddItem "Choice " & (i + 1)
   Next i
   ListBox1.Height = 66
   CommandButton1.Caption = "Move to top of list"
   CommandButton1.AutoSize = True
   CommandButton1.TakeFocusOnClick = False

   Label1.Caption = "Index of top item"
   TextBox1.Text = ListBox1.TopIndex

   Label2. Caption = "Index of current item"
   Label2.AutoSize = True
   Label2.WordWrap = False
   TextBox2.Text = ListBox1.ListIndex
End Sub
```

TransitionEffect Property

Applies To

Page object.

Description

Specifies the visual effect to use when changing from one page to another.

Syntax

object.**TransitionEffect** [= *fmTransitionEffect*]

The **TransitionEffect** property syntax has these parts:

Part	Description
object	Required. A valid object.
fmTransitionEffect	Optional. The transition effect you want between pages.

Settings

The settings for *fmTransitionEffect* are:

Constant	Value	Description
fmTransitionEffectNone	0	No special effect (default).
fmTransitionEffectCoverUp	1	The new page covers the old page, moving from the bottom to the top.
fmTransitionEffectCoverRightUp	2	The new page covers the old page, moving from the bottom left corner to the top right corner.
fmTransitionEffectCoverRight	3	The new page covers the old page, moving from the left edge to the right.
fmTransitionEffectCoverRightDown	4	The new page covers the old page, moving from the top left corner to the bottom right corner.
fmTransitionEffectCoverDown	5	The new page covers the old page, moving from the top to the bottom.
fmTransitionEffectCoverLeftDown	6	The new page covers the old page, moving from the top right corner to the bottom left corner.
fmTransitionEffectCoverLeft	7	The new page covers the old page, moving from the right to the left.
fmTransitionEffectCoverLeftUp	8	The new page covers the old page, moving from the bottom right corner to the top left corner.

(continued)

Constant	Value	Description
fmTransitionEffectPushUp	9	The new page pushes the old page out of view, moving from the bottom to the top.
fmTransitionEffectPushRight	10	The new page pushes the old page out of view, moving from the left to the right.
fmTransitionEffectPushDown	11	The new page pushes the old page out of view, moving from the top to the bottom.
fmTransitionEffectPushLeft	12	The new page pushes the old page out of view, moving from the right to the left.

Remarks

Use the **TransitionPeriod** property to specify the duration of a transition effect.

See Also

TransitionPeriod property.

TransitionPeriod Property

Applies To

Page object.

Description

Specifies the duration, in milliseconds, of a transition effect.

Syntax

object.**TransitionPeriod** [= *Long*]

The **TransitionPeriod** property syntax has these parts:

Part	Description
object	Required. A valid object.
Long	Optional. How long it takes to complete the transition from one page to another.

Remarks

Any integer from zero to 10000 is a valid setting for this property. Setting the **TransitionPeriod** property to zero disables the transition effect; setting **TransitionPeriod** to 10000 creates a 10-second transition.

See Also

TransitionEffect property.

TripleState Property

Applies To

CheckBox control, **OptionButton** control, **ToggleButton** control.

Description

Determines whether a user can specify, from the user interface, the Null state for a **CheckBox** or **ToggleButton**.

Syntax

object.**TripleState** [= *Boolean*]

The **TripleState** property syntax has these parts:

Part	Description
object	Required. A valid object.
Boolean	Optional. Whether the control supports the Null state.

Settings

The settings for *Boolean* are:

Value	Description
True	The button clicks through three states.
False	The button only supports True and False (default).

Remarks

Although the **TripleState** property exists on the **OptionButton**, the property is disabled. Regardless of the value of **TripleState**, you cannot set the control to **Null** through the user interface.

When the **TripleState** property is **True**, a user can choose from the values of **Null**, **True**, and **False**. The **Null** value is displayed as a shaded button.

When **TripleState** is **False**, the user can choose either **True** or **False**.

A control set to **Null** does not initiate the Click event.

Regardless of the property setting, the **Null** value can always be assigned programmatically to a **CheckBox** or **ToggleButton**, causing that control to appear shaded.

See Also

Click event.

Example

See the **ToggleButton** control example.

Underline Property

See Bold, Italic, Size, StrikeThrough, Underline, Weight Properties.

UndoAction Method

Applies To

Frame control, **Page** object, **UserForm** object.

Description

Reverses the most recent action that supports the Undo command.

Syntax

Boolean = *object*.**UndoAction**

The **UndoAction** method syntax has these parts:

Part	Description
object	Required. A valid object.

Remarks

The Undo command in the user interface uses the **UndoAction** method. For example, if you paste text into a **TextBox**, you can use **UndoAction** to remove that text and restore the previous contents of the **TextBox**.

Not all user actions can be undone. If an action cannot be undone, the Undo command is unavailable following the action.

Note If the **CanUndo** property is **False**, the Undo command is not available in the user interface, and **UndoAction** is not valid in code.

If **UndoAction** is applied to a form, all changes to the current record are lost. If **UndoAction** is applied to a control, only the control itself is affected.

You must apply this method before the form or control is updated. You may want to include this method in a form's BeforeUpdate event or a control's Change event.

UndoAction is an alternative to using the **SendKeys** statement to send the value of ESC in an event procedure.

See Also

BeforeUpdate event, **CanRedo** property, **CanUndo** property, Change event, **RedoAction** method, **TextBox** control.

Example

See the **CanRedo** property example.

Value Property

Applies To

CheckBox control, **ComboBox** control, **CommandButton** control, **ListBox** control, **MultiPage** control, **OptionButton** control, **ScrollBar** control, **SpinButton** control, **TabStrip** control, **TextBox** control, **ToggleButton** control.

Description

Specifies the state or content of a given control.

Syntax

object.**Value** [= *Variant*]

The **Value** property syntax has these parts:

Part	Description
object	Required. A valid object.
Variant	Optional. The state or content of the control.

Settings

Control	Description
CheckBox	An integer value indicating whether the item is selected: Null Indicates the item is in a null state, neither selected nor cleared. –1 True. Indicates the item is selected. 0 False. Indicates the item is cleared.
OptionButton	Same as **CheckBox**.
ToggleButton	Same as **CheckBox**.
ScrollBar	An integer between the values specified for the **Max** and **Min** properties.
SpinButton	Same as **ScrollBar**.
ComboBox, ListBox	The value in the **BoundColumn** of the currently selected rows.
CommandButton	Always **False**.
MultiPage	An integer indicating the currently active page. Zero (0) indicates the first page. The maximum value is one less than the number of pages.
TextBox	The text in the edit region.

Remarks

For a **CommandButton**, setting the **Value** property to **True** in a macro or procedure initiates the button's Click event.

For a **ComboBox**, changing the contents of **Value** does not change the value of **BoundColumn**. To add or delete entries in a **ComboBox**, you can use the **AddItem** or **RemoveItem** method.

Value cannot be used with a multi-select list box.

See Also

AddItem method, **BoundColumn** property, **BoundValue** property, **Max**, **Min** properties, **RemoveItem** method.

Example

The following example demonstrates the values that the different types of controls can have by displaying the **Value** property of a selected control. The user chooses a control by pressing TAB or by clicking on the control. Depending on the type of control, the user can also specify a value for the control by typing in the text area of the control, by clicking one or more times on the control, or by selecting an item, page, or tab within the control. The user can display the value of the selected control by clicking the appropriately labeled **CommandButton**.

To use this example, copy this sample code to the Declarations portion of a form. Make sure that the form contains:

- A **CommandButton** named CommandButton1.
- A **TextBox** named TextBox1.
- A **CheckBox** named CheckBox1.
- A **ComboBox** named ComboBox1.
- A **CommandButton** named CommandButton2.
- A **ListBox** named ListBox1.
- A **MultiPage** named MultiPage1.
- Two **OptionButton** controls named OptionButton1 and OptionButton2.
- A **ScrollBar** named ScrollBar1.
- A **SpinButton** named SpinButton1.
- A **TabStrip** named TabStrip1.
- A **TextBox** named TextBox2.
- A **ToggleButton** named ToggleButton1.

```
Dim i As Integer

Private Sub CommandButton1_Click()
   TextBox1.Text = "Value of " & ActiveControl.Name & " is " & _
   ActiveControl.Value
End Sub
```

```
Private Sub UserForm_Initialize()
   CommandButton1.Caption = "Get value of current control"
   CommandButton1.AutoSize = True
   CommandButton1.TakeFocusOnClick = False
   CommandButton1.TabStop = False

   TextBox1.AutoSize = True

   For i = 0 To 10
      ComboBox1.AddItem "Choice " & (i + 1)
      ListBox1.AddItem "Selection " & (100 - i)
   Next i

   CheckBox1.TripleState = True
   ToggleButton1.TripleState = True

   TextBox2.Text = "Enter text here."
End Sub
```

VerticalScrollbarSide Property

Applies To

Frame control, **Page** object, **UserForm** object.

Description

Specifies whether a vertical scroll bar appears on the right or left side of a form or page.

Syntax

object.**VerticalScrollbarSide** [= *fmVerticalScrollbarSide*]

The **VerticalScrollbarSide** property syntax has these parts:

Part	Description
object	Required. A valid object.
fmVerticalScrollbarSide	Optional. Where the scroll bar should appear.

Settings

The settings for *fmVerticalScrollbarSide* are:

Constant	Value	Description
fmVerticalScrollbarSideRight	0	Puts the scroll bar on the right side (default).
fmVerticalScrollbarSideLeft	1	Puts the scroll bar on the left side.

Remarks

The **VerticalScrollBarSide** property is particularly useful if the form will be used in an environment where reading occurs from right to left.

See Also

IMEMode property, **ScrollBars** property.

Visible Property

Applies To

CheckBox control, **ComboBox** control, **CommandButton** control, **Image** control, **Label** control, **ListBox** control, **MultiPage** control, **OptionButton** control, **Page** object, **ScrollBar** control, **SpinButton** control, **Tab** object, **TabStrip** control, **TextBox** control, **ToggleButton** control, **UserForm** object.

Description

Specifies whether an object is visible or hidden.

Syntax

object.**Visible** [= *Boolean*]

The **Visible** property syntax has these parts:

Part	Description
object	Required. A valid object.
Boolean	Optional. Whether the object is visible or hidden.

Settings

The settings for *Boolean* are:

Value	Description
True	Object is visible (default).
False	Object is hidden.

Remarks

Use the **Visible** property to control access to information without displaying it. For example, you could use the value of a control on a hidden form as the criteria for a query.

All controls are visible at design time.

Weight Property

See Bold, Italic, Size, StrikeThrough, Underline, Weight Properties.

Width Property

See Height, Width Properties.

WordWrap Property

Applies To

CheckBox control, **CommandButton** control, **Label** control, **OptionButton** control, **TextBox** control, **ToggleButton** control.

Description

Indicates whether the contents of a control automatically wrap at the end of a line.

Syntax

object.**WordWrap** [= *Boolean*]

The **WordWrap** property syntax has these parts:

Part	Description
object	Required. A valid object.
Boolean	Optional. Whether the control expands to fit the text.

Settings

The settings for *Boolean* are:

Value	Description
True	The text wraps (default).
False	The text does not wrap.

Remarks

For controls that support the **MultiLine** property as well as the **WordWrap** property, **WordWrap** is ignored when **MultiLine** is **False**.

See Also

AutoSize property, **MultiLine** property, **ScrollBars** property.

Example

See the **MultiLine** property example.

Zoom Event

Applies To

Frame control, **MultiPage** control, **UserForm** object.

Description

Occurs when the value of the **Zoom** property changes.

Syntax

For Frame:

Private Sub *object*_**Zoom(** *Percent* **As Integer)**

For MultiPage:

Private Sub *object*_**Zoom(** *index* **As Long**, *Percent* **As Integer)**

The Zoom event syntax has these parts:

Part	Description
object	Required. A valid object name.
index	Required. The index of the page in a **MultiPage** associated with this event.
Percent	Required. The percentage the form is to be zoomed. Valid values range from 10 percent to 400 percent.

Remarks

The value of the **Zoom** property identifies how the size of the form or **Page** changes. The value of the property indicates how the size of the control should change relative to its current size. Values less than 100 reduce the displayed size of the form; values greater than 100 increase the displayed size of the form.

You can set this property to any integer from 10 to 400.

See Also

Zoom property.

Example

See the **Label** control example.

Zoom Property

Applies To

Frame control, **Page** object, **UserForm** object.

Description

Specifies how much to change the size of a displayed object.

Syntax

object.**Zoom** [= *Integer*]

The **Zoom** property syntax has these parts:

Part	Description
object	Required. A valid object.
Integer	Optional. The percentage to increase or decrease the displayed image.

Remarks

The value of the **Zoom** property specifies a percentage of image enlargement or reduction by which an image display should change. Values from 10 to 400 are valid. The value specified is a percentage of the object's original size; thus, a setting of 400 means you want to enlarge the image to four times its original size (or 400 percent), while a setting of 10 means you want to reduce the image to one-tenth of its original size (or 10 percent).

Example

See the **Frame** control example.

ZOrder Method

Applies To

CheckBox control, **ComboBox** control, **CommandButton** control, **Image** control, **Label** control, **ListBox** control, **MultiPage** control, **OptionButton** control, **ScrollBar** control, **SpinButton** control, **TabStrip** control, **TextBox** control, **ToggleButton** control.

Description

Places the object at the front or back of the z-order.

Syntax

object.**ZOrder**([*zPosition*])

The **ZOrder** method syntax has these parts:

Part	Description
object	Required. A valid object.
zPosition	Optional. A control's position, front or back, in the container's z-order.

Settings

The settings for *zPosition* are:

Constant	Value	Description
fmTop	0	Places the control at the front of the z-order. The control appears on top of other controls (default).
fmBottom	1	Places the control at the back of the z-order. The control appears underneath other controls.

Remarks

The z-order determines how windows and controls are stacked when they are presented to the user. Items at the back of the z-order are overlaid by closer items; items at the front of the z-order appear to be on top of items at the back. When the *zPosition* argument is omitted, the object is brought to the front.

In design mode, the **Bring to Front** or **Send To Back** commands set the z-order. **Bring to Front** is equivalent to using the **ZOrder** method and putting the object at the front of the z-order. **Send to Back** is equivalent to using **ZOrder** and putting the object at the back of the z-order.

This method does not affect content or sequence of the controls in the **Controls** collection.

Note You can't Undo or Redo layering commands, such as **Send to Back** or **Bring to Front**. For example, if you select an object and click **Move Backward** on the shortcut menu, you won't be able to Undo or Redo that action.

See Also

SetFocus method.

Example

The following example sets the z-order of a **TextBox**, so the user can display the entire **TextBox** (by bringing it to the front of the z-order) or can place the **TextBox** behind other controls (by sending it to the back of the z-order).

To use this example, copy this sample code to the Declarations portion of a form. Make sure that the form contains:

- Three **TextBox** controls named TextBox1 through TextBox3.
- A **ToggleButton** named ToggleButton1.

```
Private Sub ToggleButton1_Click()
If ToggleButton1.Value = True Then
   TextBox2.ZOrder (fmTop)           'Place TextBox2 on Top of z-order

   'Update ToggleButton caption to identify next state
   ToggleButton1.Caption = "Send TextBox2 to back"
Else
   TextBox2.ZOrder (1)               'Place TextBox2 on Bottom of z-order

   'Update ToggleButton caption to identify next state
   ToggleButton1.Caption = "Bring TextBox2 to front"
End If
End Sub

Private Sub UserForm_Initialize()
'Set up text boxes to show z-order in the form
TextBox1.Text = "TextBox 1"
TextBox2.Text = "TextBox 2"
TextBox3.Text = "TextBox 3"

TextBox1.Height = 40
TextBox2.Height = 40
TextBox3.Height = 40
```

```
TextBox1.Width = 60
TextBox2.Width = 60
TextBox3.Width = 60

TextBox1.Left = 10
TextBox1.Top = 10

TextBox2.Left = 25       'Overlap TextBox2 on TextBox1
TextBox2.Top = 25

TextBox3.Left = 40       'Overlap TextBox3 on TextBox2, TextBox1
TextBox3.Top = 40

ToggleButton1.Value = False
ToggleButton1.Caption = "Bring TextBox2 to Front"
ToggleButton1.Left = 10
ToggleButton1.Top = 90
ToggleButton1.Width = 50
ToggleButton1.Height = 50

End Sub
```

Extensibility Object Model Language Reference

Visual Basic Editor

Default location: \Program Files\Common Files\Microsoft Shared\VBA

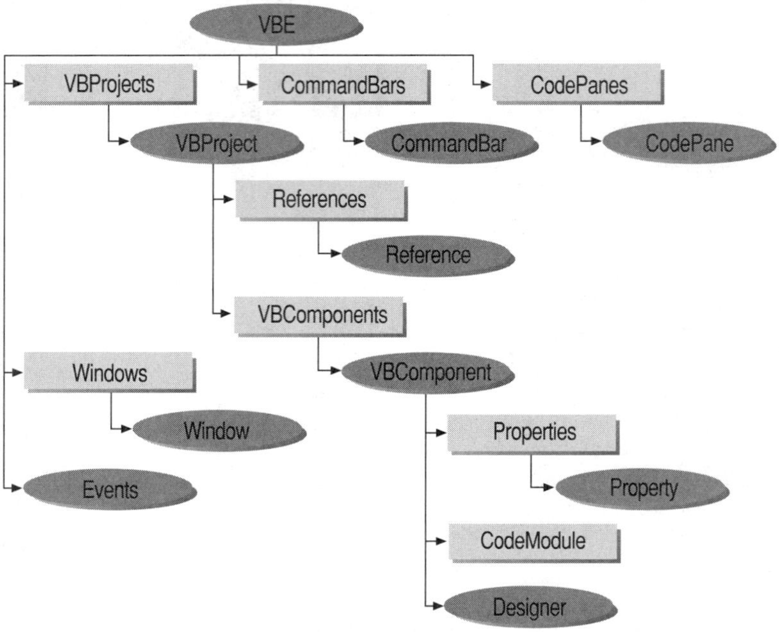

Source (Type Library)

The Visual Basic Editor object model is provided by VBEEXT1.OLB, which is included when you install Microsoft Office 97, Microsoft Excel 97, Microsoft Outlook 97, Microsoft PowerPoint 97, or Microsoft Word 97.

ActiveCodePane Property

Applies To

VBE object.

Description

Returns the active or last active **CodePane** object or sets the active **CodePane** object. Read/write.

Remarks

You can set the **ActiveCodePane** property to any valid **CodePane** object, as shown in the following example:

```
Set MyApp.VBE.ActiveCodePane = MyApp.VBE.CodePanes(1)
```

The preceding example sets the first code pane in a collection of code panes to be the active code pane. You can also activate a code pane using the **Set** method.

See Also

ActiveWindow property, **CodePane** object, **CodePanes** collection, **CodePaneView** property.

Example

The following example uses the **ActiveCodePane** property and **TopLine** properties to obtain the number of the top line in the active code pane.

```
Debug.Print Application.VBE.ActiveCodePane.TopLine
```

ActiveVBProject Property

Applies To

VBE object.

Description

Returns the active project in the **Project** window. Read-only.

Remarks

The **ActiveVBProject** property returns the project that is selected in the **Project** window or the project in which the components are selected. In the latter case, the project itself isn't necessarily selected. Whether or not the project is explicitly selected, there is always an active project.

See Also

VBProject object, **VBProjects** collection.

Example

The following example uses the **ActiveVBProject** property to return the name of the active project.

```
Debug.Print Application.VBE.ActiveVBProject.Name
```

ActiveWindow Property

Applies To

VBE object.

Description

Returns the active window in the development environment. Read-only.

Remarks

When more than one window is open in the development environment, the **ActiveWindow** property setting is the window with the focus. If the main window has the focus, the **ActiveWindow** property returns **Nothing**.

See Also

ActiveCodePane property, **MainWindow** property, **SetFocus** method, **Window** object.

Example

The following example uses the **ActiveWindow** property to return the caption of the active window.

```
Debug.Print Application.VBE.ActiveWindow.Caption
```

Add Method

Applies To

LinkedWindows collection, **VBComponents** collection.

Description

Adds an object to a collection.

Syntax

object.**Add**(*component*)

The **Add** syntax has these parts:

Part	Description
object	Required. An object expression that evaluates to an object in the Applies To list.
component	Required. For the **LinkedWindows** collection, an object. For the **VBComponents** collection, an enumerated constant representing a class module, a form, or a standard module.

You can use one of the following constants for the *component* argument:

Constant	Description
vbext_ct_ClassModule	Adds a class module to the collection.
vbext_ct_MSForm	Adds a form to the collection.
vbext_ct_StdModule	Adds a standard module to the collection.

Remarks

For the **LinkedWindows** collection, the **Add** method adds a window to the collection of currently linked windows.

Note You can add a window that is a pane in one linked window frame to another linked window frame; the window is simply moved from one pane to the other. If the linked window frame that the window was moved from no longer contains any panes, it's destroyed.

For the **VBComponents** collection, the **Add** method creates a new standard component and adds it to the project.

For the **VBComponents** collection, the **Add** method returns a **VBComponent** object. For the **LinkedWindows** collection, the **Add** method returns **Nothing**.

See Also

AddFromFile method, **AddFromGuid** method, **AddFromString** method, **Remove** method.

AddFromFile Method

Applies To

CodeModule object, **References** collection.

Description

For the **References** collection, adds a reference to a project from a file. For the **CodeModule** object, adds the contents of a file to a module.

Syntax

object.**AddFromFile**(*filename*)

The **AddFromFile** syntax has these parts:

Part	Description
object	Required. An object expression that evaluates to an object in the Applies To list.
filename	Required. A string expression specifying the name of the file you want to add to the project or module. If the file name isn't found and a path name isn't specified, the directories searched by the **Windows OpenFile** function are searched.

Remarks

For the **CodeModule** object, the **AddFromFile** method inserts the contents of the file starting on the line preceding the first procedure in the code module. If the module doesn't contain procedures, **AddFromFile** places the contents of the file at the end of the module.

See Also

Add method, **AddFromGuid** method, **AddFromString** method, ItemAdded event, ItemRemoved event, **Remove** method.

Example

The following example uses the **AddFromFile** method to add the contents of a file to a specified code pane.

```
Application.VBE.CodePanes(3).CodeModule.AddFromFile "c:\Code Files\book2.frm"
```

AddFromGuid Method

Applies To

References collection.

Description

Adds a reference to the **References** collection using the globally unique identifier (GUID) of the reference.

Syntax

object.**AddFromGuid**(*guid*, *major*, *minor*) **As Reference**

The **AddFromGuid** syntax has these parts:

Part	Description
object	Required. An object expression that evaluates to an object in the Applies To list.
guid	Required. A string expression representing the GUID of the reference.
major	Required. A **Long** specifying the major version number of the reference.
minor	Required. A **Long** specifying the minor version number of the reference.

Remarks

The **AddFromGuid** method searches the registry to find the reference you want to add. The GUID can be a type library, control, class identifier, and so on.

See Also

Add method, **AddFromString** method, ItemAdded event, ItemRemoved event, **Remove** method.

Example

The following example uses the **AddFromGuid** method to add a reference to the current project, identifying the reference using the globally unique ID value of the **Reference** object.

```
Application.VBE.ActiveVBProject.References.AddFromGuid( _
    "{000204EF-0000-0000-C000-000000000046}", 5, 0)
```

AddFromString Method

Applies To

CodeModule object.

Description

Adds text to a module.

Syntax

object.**AddFromString**

The *object* placeholder is an object expression that evaluates to an object in the Applies To list.

Remarks

The **AddFromString** method inserts the text starting on the line preceding the first procedure in the module. If the module doesn't contain procedures, **AddFromString** places the text at the end of the module.

See Also

CreateEventProc method, **DeleteLines** method, **InsertLines** method, **Lines** method, **ProcBodyLine** method, **ProcCountLines** method, **ProcOfLine** method, **ProcStartLine** method, **ReplaceLine** method.

Example

The following example uses the **AddFromString** method to add a line, "Dim intJack As Integer," to the specified code pane.

```
Application.VBE.CodePanes(3).CodeModule.AddFromString "Dim intJack As Integer"
```

BuiltIn Property

Applies To

Reference object.

Description

Returns a **Boolean** value indicating whether or not the reference is a default reference that can't be removed. Read-only.

Return Values

The **BuiltIn** property returns these values:

Value	Description
True	The reference is a default reference that can't be removed.
False	The reference isn't a default reference; it can be removed.

See Also

Description property, **FullPath** property, **GUID** property, **IsBroken** property, **References** collection, **Remove** method.

Example

The following example uses the **BuiltIn** property to return a **Boolean** indicating whether or not a particular reference in the active project is built-in.

```
Debug.Print Application.VBE.ActiveVBProject.References(1).BuiltIn
```

Caption Property

Applies To

Window object.

Description

Returns a **String** containing the title of the active window. Read-only.

Remarks

The title of the active window is the text displayed in the window's title bar.

See Also

SetFocus method.

Example

The following example uses the **Caption** property to display the caption of the active window.

```
Debug.Print Application.VBE.ActiveWindow.Caption
```

Click Event

Description

Occurs when the **OnAction** property of a corresponding command bar control is set.

Syntax

Sub *object*_**Click (ByVal** *ctrl* **As Object, ByRef** *handled* **As Boolean, ByRef** *canceldefault* **As ↳ Boolean)**

The Click event syntax has these ***named arguments***:

Part	Description
ctrl	Required; **Object**. Specifies the object that is the source of the Click event.
handled	Required; **Boolean**. If **True**, other add-ins should handle the event. If **False**, the action of the command bar item has not been handled.
canceldefault	Required; **Boolean**. If **True**, default behavior is performed unless canceled by a downstream add-in. If **False**, default behavior is not performed unless restored by a downstream add-in.

Remarks

The Click event is specific to the **CommandBarEvents** object. Use a variable declared using the **WithEvents** keyword to receive the Click event for a **CommandBar** control. This variable should be set to the return value of the **CommandBarEvents** property of the **Events** object. The **CommandBarEvents** property takes the **CommandBar** control as an argument. When the **CommandBar** control is clicked (for the variable you declared using the **WithEvents** keyword), the code is executed.

Example

The following example illustrates how you can set up code for a Click event procedure using **WithEvents** and **Set**. Note that the object reference `ce` is used in place of the menu name **Tools** in the name of the Click event.

```
Private WithEvents ce As CommandBarEvents

Sub Test()
   Dim c As CommandBarControl
   Set c = Application.VBE.CommandBars("Tools").Controls(1)
   Set ce = Application.VBE.Events.CommandBarEvents(c)
End Sub

Private Sub ce_Click(ByVal CommandBarControl As Object, Handled As Boolean,
CancelDefault As Boolean)
   ' Put event-handling code here
End Sub
```

Close Method

Applies To

Window object.

Description

Closes and destroys a window.

Syntax

object.**Close**

The *object* placeholder is an object expression that evaluates to an object in the Applies To list.

Remarks

The following types of windows respond to the **Close** method in different ways:

- For a window that is a code pane, **Close** destroys the code pane.
- For a window that is a designer, **Close** destroys the contained designer.
- For windows that are always available on the **View** menu, **Close** hides the window.

See Also

Add method, **Remove** method.

Example

The following example uses the **Close** method to close a specified member of the **Windows** collection.

```
Application.VBE.Windows(9).Close
```

CodeModule Object

Description

Represents the code behind a component, such as a form, class, or document.

Remarks

You use the **CodeModule** object to modify (add, delete, or edit) the code associated with a component.

Each component is associated with one **CodeModule** object. However, a **CodeModule** object can be associated with multiple code panes.

The methods associated with the **CodeModule** object enable you to manipulate and return information about the code text on a line-by-line basis. For example, you can use the **AddFromString** method to add text to the module. **AddFromString** places the text just above the first procedure in the module or places the text at the end of the module if there are no procedures.

Use the **Parent** property to return the **VBComponent** object associated with a code module.

Properties

CountOfDeclarationLines property, **CountOfLines** property, **Parent** property, **VBE** property.

Methods

AddFromFile method, **AddFromString** method, **CreateEventProc** method, **DeleteLines** method, **Find** method, **InsertLines** method, **Lines** method, **ProcBodyLine** method, **ProcCountLines** method, **ProcOfLine** method, **ProcStartLine** method, **ReplaceLine** method.

See Also

CodePane object, **CodePanes** collection, **VBComponent** object, **VBComponents** collection.

CodeModule Property

Applies To

CodePane object, **VBComponent** object.

Description

Returns an object representing the code behind the component. Read-only.

Remarks

The **CodeModule** property returns **Nothing** if the component doesn't have a code module associated with it.

Note The **CodePane** object represents a visible code window. A given component can have several **CodePane** objects. The **CodeModule** object represents the code within a component. A component can only have one **CodeModule** object.

See Also

CodeModule object.

Example

The following example uses the **CodeModule** and **CountOfLines** properties to return the number of lines in a particular code module.

```
Debug.Print Application.VBE.ActiveVBProject.VBComponents(6).CodeModule. _
   CountOfLines
```

CodePane Object

Description

Represents a code pane.

Remarks

Use the **CodePane** object to manipulate the position of visible text or the text selection displayed in the code pane.

You can use the **Show** method to make the code pane you specify visible. Use the **SetSelection** method to set the selection in a code pane and the **GetSelection** method to return the location of the selection in a code pane.

Properties

CodeModule property, **CodePaneView** property**, Collection** property, **CountOfVisibleLines** property, **TopLine** property, **VBE** property, **Window** property.

Methods

GetSelection method, **SetSelection** method, **Show** method.

See Also

CodeModule object, **CodePanes** collection.

CodePane Property

Applies To

CodeModule object.

Description

Returns a **CodePane** object. Read-only.

Remarks

If a code pane exists, it becomes the active code pane, and the window that contains it becomes the active window. If a code pane doesn't exist for the module, the **CodePane** property creates one.

See Also

ActiveCodePane property, **CodePane** object, **CodePanes** collection, **CodePanes** property.

CodePanes Collection

Description

Contains the active code panes in the **VBE** object.

Remarks

Use the **CodePanes** collection to access the open code panes in a project.

You can use the **Count** property to return the number of active code panes in a collection.

Properties

Count property, **Parent** property, **VBE** property.

Methods

Item method.

See Also

CodeModule object, **CodePane** object, **VBE** object.

CodePanes Property

Applies To

VBE object.

Description

Returns the collection of active **CodePane** objects. Read-only.

See Also

ActiveCodePane property, **CodePanes** collection.

Example

The following example uses the **CodePanes** and **TopLine** properties to display the line number of the top line in the specified code pane.

```
Debug.Print Application.VBE.CodePanes(3).TopLine
```

CodePaneView Property

Applies To

CodePane object.

Description

Returns a value indicating whether the code pane is in Procedure view or Full Module view. Read-only.

Return Values

The **CodePaneView** property return values are:

Constant	Description
vbext_cv_ProcedureView	The specified code pane is in Procedure view.
vbext_cv_FullModuleView	The specified project is in Full Module view.

Example

The following example uses the **CodePaneView** property to return a value indicating whether the specified code pane is in Procedure view or Full Module view.

```
Debug.Print Application.VBE.CodePanes(3).CodePaneView
```

Collection Property

Applies To

CodePane object, **Property** object, **Reference** object, **VBComponent** object, **VBProject** object, **Window** object.

Description

Returns the collection that contains the object you are working with. Read-only.

Remarks

Most objects in this object model have either a **Parent** property or a **Collection** property that points to the object's parent object.

Use the **Collection** property to access the properties, methods, and controls of the collection to which the object belongs.

See Also

Parent property.

Example

The following example uses the **Collection** and **Count** properties to return the number of objects the active project contains, when viewed as a collection of objects.

```
Debug.Print Application.VBE.ActiveVBProject.Collection.Count
```

CommandBarEvents Object

Description

Returned by the **CommandBarEvents** property. The **CommandBarEvents** object triggers an event when a control on the command bar is clicked.

Remarks

The **CommandBarEvents** object is returned by the **CommandBarEvents** property of the **Events** object. The object that is returned has one event in its interface, the Click event. You can handle this event using the **WithEvents** object declaration.

Events

Click event.

See Also

CommandBars collection, **Events** object.

CommandBarEvents Property

Applies To

Events object.

Description

Returns the **CommandBarEvents** object. Read-only.

Settings

The setting for the argument you pass to the **CommandBarEvents** property is:

Argument	Description
vbcontrol	Must be an object of type **CommandBarControl**.

Remarks

Use the **CommandBarEvents** property to return an event source object that triggers an event when a command bar button is clicked. The argument passed to the **CommandBarEvents** property is the command bar control for which the Click event will be triggered.

See Also

Click event, **CommandBarEvents** object, **CommandBars** collection, **ReferencesEvents** property.

Example

The following example uses code including the **CommandBarEvents** property to support any code to handle a mouse click on a command bar.

```
Private WithEvents ce As CommandBarEvents

Sub Test()
   Dim c As CommandBarControl
   Set c = Application.VBE.CommandBars("Tools").Controls(1)
   Set ce = Application.VBE.Events.CommandBarEvents(c)
End Sub

Private Sub ce_Click(ByVal CommandBarControl As Object, Handled As Boolean,
CancelDefault As Boolean)
   ' Put event-handling code here.
End Sub
```

CommandBars Collection

Description

Contains all of the command bars in a project, including command bars that support shortcut menus.

Remarks

Use the **CommandBars** collection to enable add-ins to add command bars and controls or to add controls to existing, built-in, command bars.

See Also

CommandBarEvents object, **CommandBarEvents** property, **Events** object.

Count Property

Applies To

CodePanes collection, **Properties** collection, **References** collection, **VBComponents** collection, **VBProjects** collection.

Description

Returns a **Long** containing the number of items in a collection. Read-only.

Example

The following example uses the **Count** property to return the number of **VBComponent** objects in a particular project.

```
Debug.Print Application.VBE.VBProjects(1).VBComponents.Count
```

CountOfDeclarationLines Property

Applies To

CodeModule object.

Description

Returns a **Long** containing the number of lines of code in the Declarations section of a code module. Read-only.

See Also

CountOfLines property, **CountOfVisibleLines** property, **DeleteLines** method, **InsertLines** method, **Lines** method, **ReplaceLine** method.

Example

The following example uses the **CountOfDeclarationLines** property to return the number of declaration lines in a particular code pane.

```
Debug.Print Application.VBE.CodePanes(2).CodeModule.CountOfDeclarationLines
```

CountOfLines Property

Applies To

CodeModule object.

Description

Returns a **Long** containing the number of lines of code in a code module. Read-only.

See Also

CountOfDeclarationLines property, **CountOfVisibleLines** property, **DeleteLines** method, **InsertLines** method, **Lines** method, **ReplaceLine** method.

Example

The following example uses the **CountOfLines** property to return the total number of lines in a particular code pane.

```
Application.VBE.CodePanes(2).CodeModule.CountOfLines
```

CountOfVisibleLines Property

Applies To

CodePane object.

Description

Returns a **Long** containing the number of lines visible in a code pane. Read-only.

See Also

CountOfDeclarationLines property, **CountOfLines** property, **DeleteLines** method, **InsertLines** method, **Lines** method, **ReplaceLine** method.

Example

The following example uses the **CountOfVisibleLines** property to return the number of lines visible at one time in a particular code pane, based on the height of the pane.

```
Debug.Print Application.VBE.Codepanes(3).CountOfVisibleLines
```

CreateEventProc Method

Applies To

CodeModule object.

Description

Creates an event procedure.

Syntax

object.**CreateEventProc(***eventname*, *objectname***) As Long**

The **CreateEventProc** syntax has these parts:

Part	Description
object	Required. An object expression that evaluates to an object in the Applies To list.
eventname	Required. A string expression specifying the name of the event you want to add to the module.
objectname	Required. A string expression specifying the name of the object that is the source of the event.

Remarks

Use the **CreateEventProc** method to create an event procedure. For example, to create an event procedure for the Click event of a **Command Button** control named `Command1` you would use the following code, where `CM` represents a object of type **CodeModule**:

```
TextLocation = CM.CreateEventProc("Click", "Command1")
```

The **CreateEventProc** method returns the line at which the body of the event procedure starts. **CreateEventProc** fails if the arguments refer to a nonexistent event.

See Also

AddFromString method, **DeleteLines** method, **InsertLines** method, **ProcBodyLine** method, **ProcCountLines** method, **ProcOfLine** method, **ProcStartLine** method, **ReplaceLine** method.

Example

The following example uses the **CreateEventProc** method to create the Button_Click procedure.

```
Debug.Print Application.VBE.SelectVBComponents.CodeModule.CreateEventProc( _
    "Click", "Button")
```

DeleteLines Method

Applies To

CodeModule object.

Description

Deletes a single line or a specified range of lines.

Syntax

object.**DeleteLines** (*startline* [, *count*])

The **DeleteLines** syntax has these parts.

Part	Description
object	Required. An object expression that evaluates to an object in the Applies To list.
startline	Required. A **Long** specifying the first line you want to delete.
count	Optional. A **Long** specifying the number of lines you want to delete.

Remarks

If you don't specify how many lines you want to delete, the **DeleteLines** method deletes one line.

See Also

InsertLines method, **Lines** method.

Example

The following example has two steps. The first **For...Next** loop uses the **InsertLines** method to insert into `CodePanes(1)` 26 ever-longer initial segments of the alphabet, starting with "a". The last line inserted is the entire alphabet.

The second **For...Next** loop uses the **DeleteLines** method to delete the odd-numbered lines. Although it seems that the second loop should simply delete every other line, note that after each deletion the lines get renumbered. Therefore the deletion is advancing by two lines at each step, one line because *I* is increasing by one and another line because the larger line numbers are each decreasing by one.

```
For I = 1 to 26
   Application.VBE.SelectedVBComponent.CodeModule.InsertLines i, _
      Mid$("abcdefghijklmnopqrstuvwxyz", 1, I)
Next
For I = 1 to 13
   Application.VBE.SelectedVBComponent.CodeModule.DeleteLines I
Next
```

Description Property

Applies To

VBProject object.

Description

Returns or sets a string expression containing a descriptive string associated with an object. For the **VBProject** object, read/write; for the **Reference** object, read-only.

Remarks

For the **VBProject** object, the **Description** property returns or sets a descriptive string associated with the active project.

For the **Reference** object, the **Description** property returns the descriptive name of the reference.

See Also

GUID property, **HelpContextID** property, **Major** property, **Minor** property, **Name** property, **Version** property.

Example

The first of the following examples uses the **Description** property to assign a description to a particular project; the example also prints the description to verify that the assignment was successful.

The second example uses the **Description** property to return the descriptive names of the specified **Reference** objects in a particular project.

```
Application.VBE.VBProjects(1).Description = "Hot Sauce"
Debug.Print Application.VBE.VBProjects(1).Description

Debug.Print Application.VBE.VBProjects(1).References(1).Description

Debug.Print Application.VBE.VBProjects(1).References(2).Description
```

Designer Property

Applies To

VBComponent object.

Description

Returns the object that enables you to access the design characteristics of a component.

Remarks

If the object has an open designer, the **Designer** property returns the open designer; otherwise a new designer is created. The designer is a characteristic of certain **VBComponent** objects. For example, when you create certain types of **VBComponent** object, a designer is created along with the object. A component can have only one designer, and it's always the same designer. The **Designer** property enables you to access a component-specific object. In some cases, such as in standard modules and class modules, a designer isn't created because that type of **VBComponent** object doesn't support a designer.

The **Designer** property returns **Nothing** if the **VBComponent** object doesn't have a designer.

See Also

DesignerWindow property, **HasOpenDesigner** property.

Example

The following example uses the **Designer** and **Count** properties to return the number of controls on a form. Note that the window containing the form must be selected. The **Designer** object is the form itself.

```
Debug.Print Application.VBE.SelectVBComponent.Designer.Controls.Count
```

DesignerWindow Property

Applies To

VBComponent object.

Description

Returns the **Window** object that represents the component's designer.

Remarks

If the component supports a designer but doesn't have an open designer, accessing the **DesignerWindow** property creates the designer, but it isn't visible. To make the window visible, set the **Window** object's **Visible** property to **True**.

See Also

Designer property, **HasOpenDesigner** property, **Visible** property, **Window** object.

Example

The following example uses the **DesignerWindow** and **Visible** properties to find out whether or not a particular designer is visible. Note that the **VBComponent** object must be a form.

```
Debug.Print Application.VBE.VBProjects(1).VBComponents(1). _
   DesignerWindow.Visible
```

Events Object

Description

Supplies properties that enable add-ins to connect to all events in Visual Basic for Applications.

Remarks

The **Events** object provides properties that return event source objects. Use the properties to return event source objects that notify you of changes in the Visual Basic for Applications environment.

The properties of the **Events** object return objects of the same type as the property name. For example, the **CommandBarEvents** property returns the **CommandBarEvents** object.

Properties

CommandBarEvents property, **ReferencesEvents** property.

See Also

Click event, **CommandBarEvents** object, **ReferencesEvents** object.

Export Method

Applies To

VBComponent object.

Description

Saves a component as a separate file or files.

Syntax

object.**Export**(*filename*)

The **Export** syntax has these parts.

Part	Description
object	Required. An object expression that evaluates to an object in the Applies To list.
filename	Required. A **String** specifying the name of the file that you want to export the component to.

Remarks

When you use the **Export** method to save a component as a separate file or files, use a file name that doesn't already exist; otherwise, an error occurs.

See Also

Import method.

Example

The following example creates a file named test.bas and uses the **Export** method to copy the contents of the `VBComponents(1)` code module into the file.

```
Application.VBE.ActiveVBProject.VBComponents(1).Export("test.bas")
```

Find Method

Applies To

CodeModule object.

Description

Searches the active module for a specified string.

Syntax

object.**Find**(*target*, *startline*, *startcol*, *endline*, *endcol* [, *wholeword*] [, *matchcase*] [, *patternsearch*])
➥**As Boolean**

The **Find** syntax has these parts.

Part	Description
object	Required. An object expression that evaluates to an object in the Applies To list.
target	Required. A **String** containing the text or pattern you want to find.
startline	Required. A **Long** specifying the line at which you want to start the search; will be set to the line of the match if one is found.
startcol	Required. A **Long** specifying the column at which you want to start the search; will be set to the column containing the match if one is found.
endline	Required. A **Long** specifying the last line of the match if one is found.
endcol	Required. A **Long** specifying the last line of the match if one is found.

(continued)

Part	Description
wholeword	Optional. A **Boolean** value specifying whether to only match whole words. If **True**, only matches whole words. **False** is the default.
matchcase	Optional. A **Boolean** value specifying whether to match case. If **True**, the search is case sensitive. **False** is the default.
patternsearch	Optional. A **Boolean** value specifying whether or not the target string is a regular expression pattern. If **True**, the target string is a regular expression pattern. **False** is the default.

Remarks

Find returns **True** if a match is found and **False** if a match isn't found.

The *matchcase* and *patternsearch* arguments are mutually exclusive; if both arguments are passed as **True**, an error occurs.

The content of the **Find** dialog box isn't affected by the **Find** method.

See Also

CodePane object, **GetSelection** method, **Lines** method, **ProcBodyLine** method, **ProcCountLines** method, **ProcOfLine** method, **ProcStartLine** method.

Example

The following example uses the **Find** method to verify that the specified block of lines, lines 1261 through 1279, of a particular code pane does contain the string "Tabs.Clear."

```
Application.VBE.CodePanes(2).CodeModule.Find ("Tabs.Clear", 1261, _
    1, 1280, 1, False, False)
```

FullPath Property

Applies To

Reference object.

Description

Returns a **String** containing the path and file name of the referenced type library. Read-only.

See Also

AddFromFile method, **AddFromGuid** method, **BuiltIn** property, **GUID** property, **IsBroken** property.

Example

The following example uses the **FullPath** property to return the full path of the object library for the specified reference.

```
Debug.Print Application.VBE.ActiveVBProject.References(1).FullPath
```

GetSelection Method

Applies To

CodePane object.

Description

Returns the selection in a code pane.

Syntax

object.**GetSelection(***startline*, *startcol*, *endline*, *endcol***)**

The **GetSelection** syntax has these parts.

Part	Description
object	Required. An object expression that evaluates to an object in the Applies To list.
startline	Required. A **Long** that returns a value specifying the first line of the selection in the code pane.
startcol	Required. A **Long** that returns a value specifying the first column of the selection in the code pane.
endline	Required. A **Long** that returns a value specifying the last line of the selection in the code pane.
endcol	Required. A **Long** that returns a value specifying the last column of the selection in the code pane.

Remarks

When you use the **GetSelection** method, information is returned in output arguments. As a result, you must pass in variables because the variables will be modified to contain the information when returned.

See Also

CodeModule object, **DeleteLines** method, **Find** method, **InsertLines** method, **Lines** method, **ProcBodyLine** method, **ProcCountLines** method, **ProcOfLine** method, **ProcStartLine** method.

Example

The following example returns the locations of the starting and ending points of the current selection in `CodePanes(1)`. The last line in the example uses the **GetSelection** method to place the four values in the four variables.

```
Dim m As Long
Dim n As Long
Dim x As Long
Dim y As Long
Application.VBE.CodePanes(1).GetSelection m, n, x, y
```

GUID Property

Applies To

Reference object.

Description

Returns a **String** containing the class identifier of an object. Read-only.

See Also

AddFromGuid method, **FullPath** property.

Example

The following example uses the **GUID** property to return the globally unique ID number for the specified **Reference** object in the specified project.

```
Debug.Print Application.VBE.VBProjects(1).References(1).GUID
```

HasOpenDesigner Property

Applies To

VBComponent object.

Description

Returns a **Boolean** value indicating whether or not the **VBComponent** object has an open designer. Read-only.

Return Values

The **HasOpenDesigner** property returns these values.

Value	Description
True	The **VBComponent** object has an open **Design** window.
False	The **VBComponent** object doesn't have an open **Design** window.

See Also

Designer property, **DesignerWindow** property.

Example

The following example uses the **HasOpenDesigner** property to return whether or not the specified component, in this case a form, of a particular project has an open designer.

```
Debug.Print Application.VBE.VBProjects(1).VBComponents(1).HasOpenDesigner
```

Height Property

Applies To

Window object.

Description

Returns or sets a **Single** containing the height of the window in twips. Read/write.

Remarks

Changing the **Height** property setting of a linked window or docked window has no effect as long as the window remains linked or docked.

See Also

Left property, **Top** property, **Width** property.

Example

The following example uses the **Height** and **Width** properties to return the height and width of the specified window, in twips. These property settings change after a window is linked or docked because then they refer to the **Window** object to which the original window is linked or docked.

```
Debug.Print Application.VBE.Windows(9).Height
Debug.Print Application.VBE.Windows(9).Width
```

HelpContextID Property

Applies To

VBProject object.

Description

Returns or sets a **String** containing the context ID for a topic in a Microsoft Windows Help file. Read/write.

See Also

HelpFile property.

Example

The following example uses the **HelpContextID** property to return the context ID for the Help file corresponding to a project.

```
Debug.Print Application.VBE.VBProjects(1).HelpContextID
```

HelpFile Property

Applies To

VBProject object.

Description

Returns or sets a **String** specifying the Microsoft Windows Help file for a project. Read/write.

See Also

HelpContextID property.

Example

The following example uses the **HelpFile** property to assign a Help file to a project; the example verifies that the assignment was successful by printing the full path of the Help file.

```
Application.VBE.VBProjects(1).HelpFile = "C:\HelpStuff\veenob3.hlp"
Debug.Print Application.VBE.VBProjects(1).HelpFile
```

Import Method

Applies To

VBComponents collection.

Description

Adds a component to a project from a file; returns the newly added component.

Syntax

object.**Import**(*filename*) **As VBComponent**

The **Import** syntax has these parts.

Part	Description
object	Required. An object expression that evaluates to an object in the Applies To list.
filename	Required. A **String** specifying path and file name of the component that you want to import the component from.

Remarks

You can use the **Import** method to add a component, form, module, class, and so on, to your project.

See Also

Export method.

Example

The following example uses the **Import** method on the **VBComponents** collection to copy the contents of the test.bas file into the a code module.

```
Application.VBE.ActiveVBProject.VBComponents.Import("test.bas")
```

IndexedValue Property

Applies To

Property object.

Description

Returns or sets a value for a member of a property that is an indexed list or an array.

Remarks

The value returned or set by the **IndexedValue** property is an expression that evaluates to a type that is accepted by the object. For a property that is an indexed list or array, you must use the **IndexedValue** property instead of the **Value** property. An indexed list is a numeric expression specifying index position.

IndexedValue accepts up to 4 indices. The number of indices accepted by **IndexedValue** is the value returned by the **NumIndices** property.

The **IndexedValue** property is used only if the value of the **NumIndices** property is greater than zero. Values in indexed lists are set or returned with a single index.

See Also

Item method, **NumIndices** property, **Value** property.

InsertLines Method

Applies To

CodeModule object.

Description

Inserts a line or lines of code at a specified location in a block of code.

Syntax

object.**InsertLines(***line*, *code***)**

The **InsertLines** syntax has these parts

Part	Description
object	Required. An object expression that evaluates to an object in the Applies To list.
line	Required. A **Long** specifying the location at which you want to insert the code.
code	Required. A **String** containing the code you want to insert.

Remarks

If the text you insert using the **InsertLines** method is carriage return–linefeed delimited, it will be inserted as consecutive lines.

See Also

DeleteLines method, **Lines** method.

Example

The following example uses the **InsertLines** method to insert a line, "Option Explicit," in the specified code pane.

```
Application.VBE.CodePanes(1).CodeModule.InsertLines 1, "Option Explicit"
```

IsBroken Property

Applies To

Reference object.

Description

Returns a **Boolean** value indicating whether or not the **Reference** object points to a valid reference in the registry. Read-only.

Return Values

The **IsBroken** property returns these values.

Value	Description
True	The **Reference** object no longer points to a valid reference in the registry.
False	The **Reference** object points to a valid reference in the registry.

See Also

BuiltIn property, **FullPath** property.

Example

The following example uses the **IsBroken** property to return a value indicating whether or not the specified **Reference** object in a particular project is broken.

```
Debug.Print Application.VBE.vbprojects(1).References(1).IsBroken
```

Item Method

Applies To

CodePanes collection, **LinkedWindows** collection, **Properties** collection, **References** collection, **VBComponents** collection, **VBProjects** collection, **Windows** collection.

Description

Returns the indexed member of a collection.

Syntax

object.**Item**(*index*)

The **Item** method syntax has these parts.

Part	Description
object	Required. An object expression that evaluates to an object in the Applies To list.
index	Required. An expression that specifies the position of a member of the collection. If a numeric expression, *index* must be a number from 1 to the value of the collection's **Count** property. If a string expression, *index* must correspond to the ***key*** argument specified when the member was added to the collection.

The following table lists the collections and their corresponding ***key*** arguments for use with the **Item** method. The string you pass to the **Item** method must match the collection's ***key*** argument.

Collection	Key argument
Windows	**Caption** property setting.
LinkedWindows	**Caption** property setting.
CodePanes	No unique string is associated with this collection.
VBProjects	**Name** property setting.
VBComponents	**Name** property setting.
References	**Name** property setting.
Properties	**Name** property setting.

Remarks

The *index* argument can be a numeric value or a string containing the title of the object.

ItemAdded Event

Description

Occurs after a reference is added.

Syntax

Sub *object*_**ItemAdded(ByVal** *item* **As Reference)**

The required *item* argument specifies the item that was added.

Remarks

The ItemAdded event occurs when a **Reference** is added to the **References** collection.

ItemRemoved Event

Description

Occurs after a reference is removed from a project.

Syntax

Sub *object*_**ItemRemoved(ByVal** *item* **As Reference)**

The required item argument specifies the Reference that was removed.

Left Property

Applies To

Window object.

Description

Returns or sets a **Single** containing the location of the left edge of the window on the screen in twips. Read/write.

Remarks

The value returned by the **Left** property depends on whether or not the window is linked or docked.

Note Changing the **Left** property setting of a linked or docked window has no effect as long as the window remains linked or docked.

See Also

Height property, **Top** property, **Width** property.

Example

The following example uses the **Left** and **Top** properties to return the coordinates of the upper-left corner of a particular window, in twips. These property settings change after a window is linked or docked because then they refer to the **Window** object to which the original window is linked or docked.

```
Debug.Print Application.VBE.Windows(9).Left
Debug.Print Application.VBE.Windows(9).Top
```

Lines Method

Applies To

CodeModule object.

Description

Returns a specified line of code.

Syntax

object.**Lines**(*startline*, *count*) **As String**

The **Lines** syntax has these parts:

Part	Description
object	Required. An object expression that evaluates to an object in the Applies To list.
startline	Required. A **Long** specifying the first line of the code you want to return.
count	Required. A **Long** specifying the number of lines you want to return.

Remarks

The line numbers in a code module begin at 1.

See Also

CodePane object, **DeleteLines** method, **Find** method, **GetSelection** method, **InsertLines** method, **ProcBodyLine** method, **ProcCountLines** method, **ProcOfLine** method, **ProcStartLine** method.

Example

The following example uses the **Lines** method to return a specific block of code, lines 1 through 4, in a particular code pane.

```
Debug.Print Application.VBE.CodePanes(1).CodeModule.Lines(1, 4)
```

LinkedWindowFrame Property

Applies To

Window object.

Description

Returns the **Window** object representing the frame that contains the window. Read-only.

Remarks

The **LinkedWindowFrame** property enables you to access the object representing the linked window frame, which has properties distinct from the window or windows it contains. If the window isn't linked, the **LinkedWindowFrame** property returns **Nothing**.

See Also

Add method, **DesignerWindow** property, **LinkedWindows** collection, **Remove** method, **SetFocus** method, **Visible** property, **WindowState** property.

LinkedWindows Collection

Description

Contains all linked windows in a linked window frame.

Remarks

Use the **LinkedWindows** collection to modify the docked and linked state of windows in the development environment.

The **LinkedWindowFrame** property of the **Window** object returns a **Window** object that has a valid **LinkedWindows** collection.

Linked window frames contain all windows that can be linked or docked. This includes all windows except code windows, designers, the **Object Browser** window, and the **Search and Replace** window.

If all the panes from one linked window frame are moved to another window, the linked window frame with no panes is destroyed. However, if all the panes are removed from the main window, it isn't destroyed.

Use the **Visible** property to check or set the visibility of a window.

You can use the **Add** method to add a window to the collection of currently linked windows. A window that is a pane in one linked window frame can be added to another linked window frame. Use the **Remove** method to remove a window from the collection of currently linked windows; this results in the window being unlinked or undocked.

The **LinkedWindows** collection is used to dock and undock windows from the main window frame.

Properties

Count property, **Parent** property, **VBE** property.

Methods

Add method, **Item** method, **Remove** method.

See Also

LinkedWindowFrame property, **Visible** property, **Window** object, **Windows** collection.

MainWindow Property

Applies To

VBE object.

Description

Returns a **Window** object representing the main window of the Visual Basic development environment. Read-only.

Remarks

You can use the **Window** object returned by the **MainWindow** property to add or remove docked windows. You can also use the **Window** object returned by the **MainWindow** property to maximize, minimize, hide, or restore the main window of the Visual Basic development environment.

See Also

ActiveWindow property, **Add** method, **Caption** property, **Close** method, **Remove** method, **SetFocus** method, **Visible** property, **Window** object, **Windows** collection.

Example

The following example uses the **MainWindow** property to return the **Window** object representing the main window, and then prints the caption of the main window.

```
Debug.Print Application.VBE.MainWindow.Caption
```

Major Property

Applies To

Reference object.

Description

Returns a **Long** containing the major version number of the referenced type library. Read-only.

Remarks

The number returned by the **Major** property corresponds to the major version number stored in the type library to which you have set the reference.

See Also

Minor property, **Version** property.

Example

The following example uses the **Major** property to return the major version number of the specified **Reference** object in a particular project.

```
Debug.Print Application.VBE.VBProjects(1).References(1).Major
```

Minor Property

Applies To

Reference object.

Description

Returns a **Long** indicating the minor version number of the referenced type library. Read-only.

Remarks

The number returned by the **Minor** property corresponds to the minor version number stored in the type library to which you have set the reference.

See Also

Major property, **Version** property.

Example

The following example uses the **Minor** property to return the minor version number of the specified **Reference** object in a particular project.

```
Debug.Print Application.VBE.VBProjects(1).References(1).Minor
```

Mode Property

Applies To

VBProject object.

Description

Returns a value containing the mode of the specified project. Read-only.

Return Values

The **Mode** property return values are:

Constant	Description
vbext_vm_RunMode	The specified project is in run mode.
vbext_vm_BreakMode	The specified project is in break mode.
vbext_vm_DesignMode	The specified project is in design mode.

See Also

ActiveVBProject property, **Protection** property.

Example

The following example uses the **Mode** property to return the mode of the active project. The value returned is a predefined constant representing the project's mode.

```
Debug.Print Application.VBE.ActiveVBProject.Mode
```

Name Property

Applies To

Property object, **Reference** object, **VBComponent** object, **VBProject** object.

Description

Returns or sets a **String** containing the name used in code to identify an object. For the **VBProject** object and the **VBComponent** object, read/write; for the **Property** object and the **Reference** object, read-only.

Remarks

The following table describes how the **Name** property setting applies to different objects.

Object	Result of using Name property setting
VBProject	Returns or sets the name of the active project.
VBComponent	Returns or sets the name of the component. An error occurs if you try to set the **Name** property to a name already being used or an invalid name.
Property	Returns the name of the property as it appears in the **Property Browser**. This is the value used to index the **Properties** collection. The name can't be set.
Reference	Returns the name of the reference in code. The name can't be set.

The default name for new objects is the type of object plus a unique integer. For example, the first new **Form** object is Form1, a new **Form** object is Form1, and the third text box control you create on a form is TextBox3.

An object's **Name** property must start with a letter and can be a maximum of 40 characters. It can include numbers and underline (_) characters but can't include punctuation or spaces. Forms and modules can't have the same name as another public object such as **Clipboard**, **Screen**, or **App**. Although the **Name** property setting can be a keyword, property name, or the name of another object, this can create conflicts in your code.

See Also

Description property, **Type** property.

Example

The following example uses the **Name** property to return the name of the specified member of the **VBComponents** collection in a particular project.

```
Debug.Print Application.VBE.VBProjects(1).VBComponents(1).Name
```

NumIndices Property

Applies To

Property object.

Description

Returns the number of indices on the property returned by the **Property** object.

Remarks

The value of the **NumIndices** property can be an integer from 0 to 4. For most properties, **NumIndices** returns 0. Conventionally indexed properties return 1. Property arrays might return 2.

See Also

IndexedValue property, **Item** method, **Object** property, **Value** property.

Example

The following example uses the **NumIndices** property to return the number of indexes belonging to the specified property of a particular **VBComponent** object

```
Debug.Print Application.VBE.VBProjects(1).VBComponents(1).Properties(40). _
   NumIndices
```

Object Property

Applies To

Property object.

Description

Returns or sets the value of an object returned by a property. Read/write.

Remarks

If a property returns an object, you must use the **Object** property to return or set the value of that object.

See Also

IndexedValue property, **NumIndices** property, **Value** property.

Example

The following example loads the name of an icon into the icon list for the specified object, which must be a form.

```
Set Application.VBE.ActiveVBProject.VBComponents(1).Properties("Icon"). _
   Object = LoadPicture("Baseball.ico")
```

Parent Property

Applies To

CodeModule object, **CodePanes** collection, **LinkedWindows** collection, **Properties** collection, **References** collection, **VBComponents** collection, **VBE** object, **VBProjects** collection, **Windows** collection.

Description

Returns the object or collection that contains another object or collection. Read-only.

Remarks

Most objects have either a **Parent** property or a **Collection** property that points to the object's parent object in this object model. The **Collection** property is used if the parent object is a collection.

Use the **Parent** property to access the properties, methods, and controls of an object's parent object.

See Also

Collection property.

Example

The following example uses the **Parent** property to return the name of an object's parent in the object hierarchy.

```
Debug.Print Application.VBE.ActiveVBProject.VBComponents.Parent.Name
```

ProcBodyLine Method

Applies To

CodeModule object.

Description

Returns the first line of a procedure.

Syntax

object.**ProcBodyLine(***procname*, *prockind***)** **As Long**

The **ProcBodyLine** syntax has these parts:

Part	Description
object	Required. An object expression that evaluates to an object in the Applies To list.
procname	Required. A **String** containing the name of the procedure.
prockind	Required. Specifies the kind of procedure to locate. Because property procedures can have multiple representations in the module, you must specify the kind of procedure you want to locate. All procedures other than property procedures (that is, **Sub** and **Function** procedures) use **vbext_pk_Proc**.

You can use one of the following constants for the *prockind* argument:

Constant	Description
vbext_pk_Get	Specifies a procedure that returns the value of a property.
vbext_pk_Let	Specifies a procedure that assigns a value to a property.
vbext_pk_Set	Specifies a procedure that sets a reference to an object.
vbext_pk_Proc	Specifies all procedures other than property procedures.

Remarks

The first line of a procedure is the line on which the **Sub**, **Function**, or **Property** statement appears.

See Also

CodePane object, **DeleteLines** method, **Find** method, **GetSelection** method, **InsertLines** method, **ProcCountLines** method, **ProcOfLine** method, **ProcStartLine** method.

Example

The following example uses the **ProcBodyLine** method to return the line number of the first line of code in the specified procedure, SetupTabs, in a particular code pane.

```
Debug.Print Application.VBE.CodePanes(3).CodeModule.ProcBodyLine _
    ("SetupTabs", vbext_pk_Proc)
```

ProcCountLines Method

Applies To

CodeModule object.

Description

Returns the number of lines in the specified procedure.

Syntax

object.**ProcCountLines(***procname*, *prockind***) As Long**

The **ProcCountLines** syntax has these parts:

Part	Description
object	Required. An object expression that evaluates to an object in the Applies To list.
procname	Required. A **String** containing the name of the procedure.
prockind	Required. Specifies the kind of procedure to locate. Because property procedures can have multiple representations in the module, you must specify the kind of procedure you want to locate. All procedures other than property procedures (that is, **Sub** and **Function** procedures) use **vbext_pk_Proc**.

You can use one of the following constants for the *prockind* argument:

Constant	Description
vbext_pk_Get	Specifies a procedure that returns the value of a property.
vbext_pk_Let	Specifies a procedure that assigns a value to a property.
vbext_pk_Set	Specifies a procedure that sets a reference to an object.
vbext_pk_Proc	Specifies all procedures other than property procedures.

Remarks

The **ProcCountLines** method returns the count of all blank or comment lines preceding the procedure declaration and, if the procedure is the last procedure in a code module, any blank lines following the procedure.

See Also

CodePane object, **DeleteLines** method, **Find** method, **GetSelection** method, **InsertLines** method, **ProcBodyLine** method, **ProcOfLine** method, **ProcStartLine** method.

Example

The following example uses the **ProcCountLines** method to return the number of lines of code in the specified procedure, SetupTabs, in a particular code pane.

```
Debug.Print Application.VBE.CodePanes(3).CodeModule.ProcCountLines _
   ("SetupTabs", vbext_pk_Proc)
```

ProcOfLine Method

Applies To

CodeModule object.

Description

Returns the name of the procedure that the specified line is in.

Syntax

object.**ProcOfLine(***line*, *prockind*) **As String**

The **ProcOfLine** syntax has these parts:

Part	Description
object	Required. An object expression that evaluates to an object in the Applies To list.
line	Required. A **Long** specifying the line to check.
prockind	Required. Specifies the kind of procedure to locate. Because property procedures can have multiple representations in the module, you must specify the kind of procedure you want to locate. All procedures other than property procedures (that is, **Sub** and **Function** procedures) use **vbext_pk_Proc**.

You can use one of the following constants for the *prockind* argument:

Constant	Description
vbext_pk_Get	Specifies a procedure that returns the value of a property.
vbext_pk_Let	Specifies a procedure that assigns a value to a property.
vbext_pk_Set	Specifies a procedure that sets a reference to an object.
vbext_pk_Proc	Specifies all procedures other than property procedures.

Remarks

A line is within a procedure if it's a blank line or comment line preceding the procedure declaration and, if the procedure is the last procedure in a code module, a blank line or lines following the procedure.

See Also

CodePane object, **DeleteLines** method, **Find** method, **GetSelection** method, **InsertLines** method, **ProcBodyLine** method, **ProcCountLines** method, **ProcStartLine** method.

Example

The following example uses the **ProcOfLine** method to return the name of the procedure containing the specified line number in a particular code pane.

```
Debug.Print Application.VBE.CodePanes(3).CodeModule.ProcOfLine (1270, _
   vbext_pk_Proc)
```

ProcStartLine Method

Applies To

CodeModule object.

Description

Returns the line at which the specified procedure begins.

Syntax

object.**ProcStartLine**(*procname*, *prockind*) **As Long**

The **ProcStartLine** syntax has these parts:

Part	Description
object	Required. An object expression that evaluates to an object in the Applies To list.
procname	Required. A **String** containing the name of the procedure.
prockind	Required. Specifies the kind of procedure to locate. Because property procedures can have multiple representations in the module, you must specify the kind of procedure you want to locate. All procedures other than property procedures (that is, **Sub** and **Function** procedures) use **vbext_pk_Proc**.

You can use one of the following constants for the *prockind* argument:

Constant	Description
vbext_pk_Get	Specifies a procedure that returns the value of a property.
vbext_pk_Let	Specifies a procedure that assigns a value to a property.
vbext_pk_Set	Specifies a procedure that sets a reference to an object.
vbext_pk_Proc	Specifies all procedures other than property procedures.

Remarks

A procedure starts at the first line below the **End Sub** statement of the preceding procedure. If the procedure is the first procedure, it starts at the end of the general Declarations section.

See Also

CodePane object, **DeleteLines** method, **Find** method, **GetSelection** method, **InsertLines** method, **ProcBodyLine** method, **ProcCountLines** method, **ProcOfLine** method.

Example

The following example uses the **ProcStartLine** method to return the line at which the specified procedure begins in a particular code pane.

```
Debug.Print Application.VBE.CodePanes(3).CodeModule.ProcStartLine _
   ("SetupTabs", vbext_pk_Proc)
```

Properties Collection

Description

Represents the properties of an object.

Remarks

Use the **Properties** collection to access the properties displayed in the **Properties** window. For every property listed in the **Properties** window, there is an object in the **Properties** collection.

Properties

Count property, **Parent** property, **VBE** property.

Methods

Item method.

See Also

Object property, **Property** object.

Property Object

Description

Represents the properties of an object that are visible in the **Properties** window for any given component.

Remarks

Use **Value** property of the **Property** object to return or set the value of a property of a component.

At a minimum, all components have a **Name** property. Use the **Value** property of the **Property** object to return or set the value of a property. The **Value** property returns a **Variant** of the appropriate type. If the value returned is an object, the **Value** property returns the **Properties** collection that contains **Property** objects representing the individual properties of the object. You can access each of the **Property** objects by using the **Item** method on the returned **Properties** collection.

If the value returned by the **Property** object is an object, you can use the **Object** property to set the **Property** object to a new object.

Properties

Collection property, **IndexedValue** property, **Name** property, **NumIndices** property, **Object** property, **Value** property, **VBE** property.

See Also

Item method, **Properties** collection.

Protection Property

Applies To

VBProject object.

Description

Returns a value indicating the state of protection of a project. Read-only.

Return Values

The **Protection** property return values are:

Constant	Description
vbext_pp_locked	The specified project is locked.
vbext_pp_none	The specified project isn't protected.

See Also

Mode property, **Saved** property.

Example

The following example uses the **Protection** property to return a value indicating whether or not a project is protected. The value returned is a number that corresponds to a predefined constant representing the project's status.

```
Debug.Print Application.VBE.ActiveVBProject.Protection
```

Reference Object

Description

Represents a reference to a type library or a project.

Remarks

Use the **Reference** object to verify whether a reference is still valid.

The **IsBroken** property returns **True** if the reference no longer points to a valid reference. The **BuiltIn** property returns **True** if the reference is a default reference that can't be moved or removed. Use the **Name** property to determine if the reference you want to add or remove is the correct one.

Properties

BuiltIn property**, Collection** property, **Description** property, **FullPath** property, **GUID** property, **IsBroken** property, **Major** property, **Minor** property, **Name** property, **Type** property, **VBE** property.

See Also

AddFromFile method, **AddFromGuid** method, **References** collection.

References Collection

Description

Represents the set of references in the project.

Remarks

Use the **References** collection to add or remove references. The **References** collection is the same as the set of references selected in the **References** dialog box.

Properties

Count property, **Parent** property, **VBE** property.

Methods

AddFromFile method, **AddFromGuid** method, **Item** method, **Remove** method.

Events

ItemAdded event, ItemRemoved event.

See Also

AddFromFile method, **AddFromGuid** method, **Item** method, **Reference** object, **ReferencesEvents** object, **Remove** method, **VBProject** object.

ReferencesEvents Object

Description

Returned by the **ReferencesEvents** property.

Remarks

The **ReferencesEvents** object is the source of events that occur when a reference is added to or removed from a project. The ItemAdded event is triggered after a reference is added to a project. The ItemRemoved event is triggered after a reference is removed from a project.

See Also

Events object, **References** collection, **ReferencesEvents** property.

ReferencesEvents Property

Applies To

Events object.

Description

Returns the **ReferencesEvents** object. Read-only.

Settings

The setting for the argument you pass to the **ReferencesEvents** property is:

Argument	Description
vbproject	If *vbproject* points to **Nothing**, the object that is returned will supply events for the **References** collections of all **VBProject** objects in the **VBProjects** collection. If *vbproject* points to a valid **VBProject** object, the object that is returned will supply events for only the **References** collection for that project.

Remarks

The **ReferencesEvents** property takes an argument and returns an event source object. The **ReferencesEvents** object is the source for events that are triggered when references are added or removed.

See Also

Add method, **CommandBarEvents** property, **ReferencesEvents** object, **Remove** method, **VBProject** object, **VBProjects** collection.

Example

The following example uses code including the **ReferencesEvents** property to support event-handling code for adding or removing references.

```
Private WithEvents X As ReferencesEvents

Sub Test()
   Set X = Application.VBE.Events.ReferencesEvents
End Sub

Private Sub X_ItemAdded(ByVal Reference As VBIDE.Reference)
   ' Put code to support item addition here
End Sub

Private Sub X_ItemRemoved(ByVal Reference As VBIDE.Reference)
   ' Put code to support item removal here
End Sub
```

Remove Method

Applies To

LinkedWindows collection, **References** collection, **VBComponents** collection.

Description

Removes an item from a collection.

Syntax

object.**Remove**(*component*)

The **Remove** syntax has these parts:

Part	Description
object	Required. An object expression that evaluates to an object in the Applies To list.
component	Required. For the **LinkedWindows** collection, an object. For the **References** collection, a reference to a type library or a project. For the **VBComponents** collection, an enumerated constant representing a class module, a form, or a standard module.

Remarks

When used on the **LinkedWindows** collection, the **Remove** method removes a window from the collection of currently linked windows. The removed window becomes a floating window that has its own linked window frame.

ReplaceLine Method

Applies To

CodeModule object.

Description

Replaces an existing line of code with a specified line of code.

Syntax

object.**ReplaceLine(***line***,** *code***)**

The **ReplaceLine** syntax has these parts:

Part	Description
object	Required. An object expression that evaluates to an object in the Applies To list.
line	Required. A **Long** specifying the location of the line you want to replace.
code	Required. A **String** containing the code you want to insert.

See Also

CountOfDeclarationLines property, **CountOfLines** property, **CountOfVisibleLines** property, **CreateEventProc** method, **DeleteLines** method, **InsertLines** method.

Example

The following example has two steps. The first **For...Next** loop uses the **InsertLines** method to insert into `CodePanes(1)` 26 ever-longer initial segments of the alphabet, starting with "a." The last line inserted is the entire alphabet.

The second **For...Next** loop uses the **ReplaceLine** method to replace each even-numbered line with the last letter in the string that previously occupied that line. Odd-numbered lines are unchanged.

```
For I = 1 to 26
   Application.VBE.CodePanes(1).CodeModule.InsertLines I,
Mid$("abcdefghijklmnopqrstuvwxyz", 1, I)
Next I
For I = 1 to 13
   Application.VBE.CodePanes(1).CodeModule.ReplaceLine 2*I,
Mid$("abcdefghijklmnopqrstuvwxyz", 1, I)
Next I
```

Saved Property

Applies To

VBProject object.

Description

Returns a **Boolean** value indicating whether or not the object was edited since the last time it was saved. Read/write.

Return Values

The **Saved** property returns these values:

Value	Description
True	The object has not been edited since the last time it was saved.
False	The object has been edited since the last time it was saved.

Remarks

The **SaveAs** method sets the **Saved** property to **True**.

Note If you set the **Saved** property to **False** in code, it returns **False**, and the object is marked as if it were edited since the last time it was saved.

See Also

Protection property.

Example

The following example uses the **Saved** property to return a **Boolean** value indicating whether or not the specified project has been saved in its current state.

```
Debug.Print Application.VBE.VBProjects(1).Saved
```

SelectedVBComponent Property

Applies To

VBE object.

Description

Returns the selected component. Read-only.

Remarks

The **SelectedVBComponent** property returns the selected component in the **Project** window. If the selected item in the **Project** window isn't a component, **SelectedVBComponent** returns **Nothing**.

See Also

ActiveVBProject property, **VBComponent** object, **VBComponents** collection.

Example

The following example uses the **SelectedVBComponent** property to return the selected component.

```
Debug.Print Application.VBE.SelectedVBComponent.Name
```

SetFocus Method

Applies To

Window object.

Description

Moves the focus to the specified window.

Syntax

object.**SetFocus**

The *object* placeholder is an object expression that evaluates to an object in the Applies To list.

Remarks

Use the **SetFocus** method on windows that are already visible.

See Also

CodePane object, **SetSelection** method, **Show** method, **Visible** property.

Example

The following example uses the **SetFocus** method to move the focus to a particular member of the **Windows** collection; that is, it makes that window behave as if you had clicked its title bar with your mouse.

```
Application.VBE.Windows(9).SetFocus
```

SetSelection Method

Applies To

CodePane object.

Description

Sets the selection in the code pane.

Syntax

object.**SetSelection**(*startline*, *startcol*, *endline*, *endcol*)

The **SetSelection** syntax has these parts:

Part	Description
object	Required. An object expression that evaluates to an object in the Applies To list.
startline	Required. A **Long** specifying the first line of the selection.
startcol	Required. A **Long** specifying the first column of the selection.
endline	Required. A **Long** specifying the last line of the selection.
endcol	Required. A **Long** specifying the last column of the selection.

See Also

GetSelection method, **SetFocus** method, **Window** object.

Example

The following example uses the **SetSelection** method to select the text whose first character is the one immediately after the fourth character on the second line of `CodePanes(1)` and whose last character is the fifteenth character on the third line.

```
Application.VBE.CodePanes(1).SetSelection 2,4,3,15
```

Show Method

Applies To

CodePane object, **UserForm** object.

Description

Makes the specified code pane the visible code pane in its window.

Syntax

object.**Show**

The *object* placeholder is an object expression that evaluates to an object in the Applies To list.

Remarks

The **Show** method makes the specified code pane the pane with the focus in its window.

See Also

Hide method ("Microsoft Visual Basic for Applications Language Reference"), **Load** statement ("Microsoft Visual Basic for Applications Language Reference"), **SetFocus** method, **Unload** statement ("Microsoft Visual Basic for Applications Language Reference").

Example

The following example uses the **Show** method to move the specified code pane to the foreground.

```
Application.VBE.CodePanes(2).Show
```

Top Property

Applies To

Window object.

Description

Returns or sets a **Single** specifying the location of the top of the window on the screen in twips. Read/write.

Remarks

The value returned by the **Top** property depends on whether or not the window is docked, linked, or in docking view.

Note Changing the **Top** property setting of a linked or docked window has no effect as long as the window remains linked or docked.

See Also

Height property, **Left** property, **Width** property.

Example

See the **Left** property example.

TopLine Property

Applies To

CodePane object.

Description

Returns a **Long** specifying the line number of the line at the top of the code pane or sets the line showing at the top of the code pane. Read/write.

Remarks

Use the **TopLine** property to return or set the line showing at the top of the code pane. For example, if you want line 25 to be the first line showing in a code pane, set the **TopLine** property to 25.

The **TopLine** property setting must be a positive number. If the **TopLine** property setting is greater than the actual number of lines in the code pane, the setting will be the last line in the code pane.

See Also

CountOfVisibleLines property, **GetSelection** method, **SetSelection** method.

Example

The following example uses the **TopLine** property to return the line number of the top line in the specified code pane.

```
Debug.Print Application.VBE.CodePanes(3).TopLine
```

Type Property

Applies To

Reference object, **VBComponent** object, **Window** object.

Description

Returns a numeric or string value containing the type of object. Read-only.

Return Values

The **Type** property settings for the **Window** object are described in the following table:

Constant	Value	Description
vbext_wt_CodeWindow	0	**Code** window
vbext_wt_Designer	1	Designer
vbext_wt_Browser	2	**Object Browser**
vbext_wt_Watch	3	Watch pane
vbext_wt_Locals	4	Locals
vbext_wt_Immediate	5	**Immediate** window
vbext_wt_ProjectWindow	6	**Project** window
vbext_wt_PropertyWindow	7	**Properties** window
vbext_wt_Find	8	**Find** dialog box
vbext_wt_FindReplace	9	**Search and Replace** dialog box
vbext_wt_LinkedWindowFrame	11	Linked window frame
vbext_wt_MainWindow	12	Main window

The **Type** property settings for the **VBComponent** object are described in the following table:

Constant	Description
vbext_ct_ClassModule	Class module
vbext_ct_MSForm	Microsoft Form
vbext_ct_StdModule	Standard module
vbext_ct_Document	Document module

The **Type** property settings for the **Reference** object are described in the following table:

Constant	Description
vbext_rk_TypeLib	Type library
vbext_rk_Project	Project

See Also

IndexedValue property, **Name** property, **Value** property.

Example

The following example uses the **Type** property to return a value indicating the type of the specified member of the **VBComponents** collection in a particular project. The value returned is a number that corresponds to a predefined constant for one of the component object types.

```
Debug.Print Application.VBE.VBProjects(1).VBComponents(1).Type
```

Value Property

Applies To

Property object.

Description

Returns or sets a **Variant** specifying the value of the property. Read/write.

Remarks

Because the **Value** property returns a **Variant**, you can access any property. To access a list, use the **IndexedValue** property.

If the property that the **Property** object represents is read/write, the **Value** property is read/write. If the property is read-only, attempting to set the **Value** property causes an error. If the property is write-only, attempting to return the **Value** property causes an error.

The **Value** property is the default property for the **Property** object.

See Also

IndexedValue property, **Name** property, **Object** property, **Type** property.

Example

The following example uses the **Value** property to return the value of the specified property of a member of the **VBComponents** collection.

```
Debug.Print Application.VBE.ActiveVBProject.VBComponents(1).Properties( _
    "AcceptLabelsInFormulas").Value
```

VBComponent Object

Description

Represents a component, such as a class module or standard module, contained in a project.

Remarks

Use the **VBComponent** object to access the code module associated with a component or to change a component's property settings.

You can use the **Type** property to find out what type of component the **VBComponent** object refers to. Use the **Collection** property to find out what collection the component is in.

Properties

CodeModule property**, Collection** property, **Designer** property, **DesignerWindow** property, **HasOpenDesigner** property, **Name** property, **Saved** property, **Type** property, **VBE** property.

Methods

Export method.

See Also

CodeModule object, **VBComponents** collection, **VBProject** object.

VBComponents Collection

Description

Represents the components contained in a project.

Remarks

Use the **VBComponents** collection to access, add, or remove components in a project. A component can be a form, module, or class. The **VBComponents** collection is a standard collection that can be used in a **For Each** block.

You can use the **Parent** property to return the project the **VBComponents** collection is in.

In Visual Basic for Applications, you can use **Import** method to add a component to a project from a file.

Properties

Count property, **Parent** property, **VBE** property.

Methods

Add method, **Import** method, **Item** method, **Remove** method.

Events

ItemAdded event, ItemRemoved event.

See Also

CodeModule object, **VBComponent** object, **VBProject** object.

VBE Object

Description

The root object that contains all other objects and collections represented in Visual Basic for Applications.

Remarks

You can use the following collections to access the objects contained in the **VBE** object

- Use the **VBProjects** collection to access the collection of projects.
- Use the **Windows** collection to access the collection of windows.
- Use the **CodePanes** collection to access the collection of code panes.
- Use the **CommandBars** collection to access the collection of command bars.

Use the **Events** object to access properties that enable add-ins to connect to all events in Visual Basic for Applications. The properties of the **Events** object return objects of the same type as the property name. For example, the **CommandBarEvents** property returns the **CommandBarEvents** object.

You can use the **SelectedVBComponent** property to return the active component. The active component is the component that is being tracked in the **Project** window. If the selected item in the **Project** window isn't a component, **SelectedVBComponent** returns **Nothing**.

Note All objects in this object model have a **VBE** property that points to the **VBE** object.

Properties

ActiveCodePane property, **ActiveVBProject** property, **ActiveWindow** property, **MainWindow** property, **Parent** property, **SelectedVBComponent** property, **Version** property.

See Also

CodePanes collection, **CommandBars** collection, **Events** object, **VBE** property, **VBProjects** collection, **Windows** collection.

VBE Property

Applies To

CodeModule object, **CodePane** object, **CodePanes** collection, **LinkedWindows** collection, **Properties** collection, **Property** object, **Reference** object, **References** collection, **VBComponent** object, **VBComponents** collection, **VBProject** object, **VBProjects** collection, **Window** object, **Windows** collection.

Description

Returns the root of the **VBE** object. Read-only.

Remarks

All objects have a **VBE** property that points to the root of the **VBE** object.

See Also

Collection property, **Parent** property.

Example

The following example uses the **VBE** and **Name** properties to return the name of the active project.

```
Debug.Print Application.VBE.ActiveVBProject.Name
```

VBProject Object

Description

Represents a project.

Remarks

Use the **VBProject** object to set properties for the project, to access the **VBComponents** collection, and to access the **References** collection.

Properties

Collection property, **Description** property, **HelpContextID** property, **HelpFile** property, **Mode** property, **Name** property, **Protection** property, **Saved** property, **VBE** property.

See Also

References collection, **VBComponents** collection.

VBProjects Collection

Description

Represents all the projects that are open in the development environment.

Remarks

Use the **VBProjects** collection to access specific projects in an instance of the development environment. **VBProjects** is a standard collection that can be used in a **For Each** block.

Properties

Count property, **Parent** property, **VBE** property.

Methods

Item method.

Events

ItemAdded event, ItemRemoved event.

See Also

VBProject object.

Version Property

Applies To

VBE object.

Description

Returns a **String** containing the version of Visual Basic for Applications that the application is using. Read-only.

Remarks

The **Version** property value is a string beginning with one or two digits, a period, and two digits; the rest of the string is undefined and may contain text or numbers.

See Also

Major property, **Minor** property.

Example

The following example uses the **Version** property to return the version number of the host application.

```
Debug.Print Application.VBE.Version
```

Visible Property

Applies To

Window object.

Description

For the **Window** object, returns or sets a **Boolean** value that specifies the visibility of a window. Read/write. For the **CodePane** object, returns a **Boolean** value that indicates whether or not the code pane is visible in the window. Read-only.

Return Values

The **Visible** property returns the following values:

Value	Description
True	(Default) Object is visible.
False	Object is hidden.

See Also

ActiveWindow property, **Caption** property, **MainWindow** property, **SetFocus** method, **Show** method, **WindowState** property.

Example

The following example uses the **Visible** property to return a **Boolean** value indicating whether or not the specified window is visible.

```
Debug.Print Application.VBE.Windows(9).Visible
```

Width Property

Applies To

Window object.

Description

Returns or sets a **Single** containing the width of the window in twips. Read/write.

Remarks

Changing the **Width** property setting of a linked window or docked window has no effect as long as the window remains linked or docked.

See Also

Height property, **Left** property, **Top** property.

Example

See the **Height** property example.

Window Object

Description

Represents a window in the development environment.

Remarks

Use the **Window** object to show, hide, or position windows.

You can use the **Close** method to close a window in the **Windows** collection. The **Close** method affects different types of windows as follows:

Window	Result of using Close method
Code window	Removes the window from the **Windows** collection.
Designer	Removes the window from the **Windows** collection.
Window objects of type linked window frame	Windows become unlinked separate windows.

Note Using the **Close** method with code windows and designers actually closes the window. Setting the **Visible** property to **False** hides the window but doesn't close the window. Using the **Close** method with development environment windows, such as the **Project** window or **Properties** window, is the same as setting the **Visible** property to **False**.

You can use the **SetFocus** method to move the focus to a window.

You can use the **Visible** property to return or set the visibility of a window.

To find out what type of window you are working with, you can use the **Type** property. If you have more than one window of a type, for example, multiple designers, you can use the **Caption** property to determine the window you're working with. You can also find the window you want to work with using the **DesignerWindow** property of the **VBComponent** object or the **Window** property of the **CodePane** object.

Properties

Caption property, **Collection** property, **Height** property, **Left** property, **LinkedWindowFrame** property, **Top** property, **Type** property, **VBE** property, **Visible** property, **Width** property, **WindowState** property.

Methods

Close method, **SetFocus** method.

See Also

CodePane object, **DesignerWindow** property, **VBComponent** object, **Window** property, **Windows** collection.

Window Property

Applies To

CodePane object.

Description

Returns the window in which the code pane is displayed. Read-only.

See Also

CodePaneView property, **LinkedWindowFrame** property, **SetFocus** method, **SetSelection** method, **Show** method, **TopLine** property, **Visible** property.

Example

The following example uses the **Window** and **Caption** properties to return the caption of the specified code pane.

```
Debug.Print Application.VBE.CodePanes(1).Window.Caption
```

Windows Collection

Description

Contains all open or permanent windows.

Remarks

Use the **Windows** collection to access **Window** objects.

The **Windows** collection has a fixed set of windows that are always available in the collection, such as the **Project** window, the **Properties** window, and a set of windows that represent all open code windows and designer windows. Opening a code or designer window adds a new member to the **Windows** collection. Closing a code or designer window removes a member from the **Windows** collection. Closing a permanent development environment window doesn't remove the corresponding object from this collection, but results in the window not being visible.

Properties

Count property, **Parent** property, **VBE** property.

Methods

Item method.

See Also

CodePane object, **CodePanes** collection, **Window** object.

WindowState Property

Applies To

Window object.

Description

Returns or sets a numeric value specifying the visual state of the window. Read/write.

Settings

The **WindowState** property returns or sets the following values:

Constant	Value	Description
vbext_ws_Normal	0	(Default) Normal
vbext_ws_Min	1	Minimized (minimized to an icon)
vbext_ws_Max	2	Maximized (enlarged to maximum size)

See Also

ActiveWindow property, **MainWindow** property, **SetFocus** method, **Visible** property.

Example

The following example uses the **WindowState** property to return the visual state of the specified window. The value returned is a number that corresponds to a predefined constant that specifies the visual state of a window.

```
Debug.Print Application.VBE.Windows(9).WindowState
```

Microsoft Binder Language Reference

Microsoft Binder

Default location: \Program Files\Microsoft Office\Office

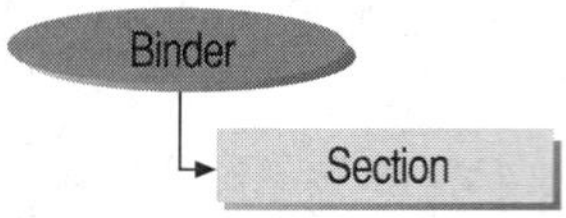

Source (Type Library)

The Microsoft Office Binder object model is provided by MSBDR8.OLB, which is included when you install Microsoft Office 97.

Activate Method

Applies To

Section object.

Description

Activates a specified section in the binder.

Syntax

expression.**Activate**

expression Required. An expression that returns a **Section** object.

Remarks

You can select several sections at the same time, but only one of them can be the active section. If you activate a hidden section, it becomes visible.

Use the **SelectedSectionNames** property to return or set the array of selected section names.

See Also

ActiveSection property.

Example

This example creates a new binder, adds a Microsoft Excel workbook and a Word document, and then activates the first section in the binder.

```
Set myBinder = CreateObject("Binder1.Binder")
myBinder.Visible = True
myBinder.Sections.Add Type:="Excel.Sheet"
myBinder.Sections.Add Type:="Word.Document"
myBinder.Sections(1).Activate
```

ActiveSection Property

Applies To

Binder object.

Description

Returns a **Section** object that represents the active section in the binder. If the binder doesn't contain any visible sections, an error occurs. Read-only.

Remarks

To make a section the active section, use the **Activate** method.

See Also

Activate method.

Example

This example opens Binder2.obd, activates the first section, and creates a copy of the active section, if the active section is an Excel chart. The new section is renamed "Copy of Section 1."

```
Set newBinder = GetObject("C:\Binder2.obd", "Office.Binder")
With newBinder
   .Visible = True
   .Sections(1).Activate
   If .ActiveSection.Type = "Excel.Chart.8" Then
      .ActiveSection.Copy
   .ActiveSection.Name = "Copy of Section 1"
   End If
End With
```

Add Method

Applies To

Sections collection object.

Description

Creates a new section in the specified binder and returns a **Section** object that represents the new section. You can add a section by either creating a new object or inserting a section based on an existing file.

Syntax

expression.**Add**(***Type, FileName, Before, After***)

expression Required. An expression that returns a **Sections** object.

Type Optional **Variant**. The type of section to be created. Can be one of the following classes: **Excel.Chart**, **Excel.Sheet**, **Word.Document**, **PowerPoint.Show**, or **PowerPoint.Slide**. If this argument is omitted, ***FileName*** is required.

FileName Optional **Variant**. The full path and file name of the file on which to base the section you want to add. If this argument is omitted, ***Type*** is required.

Before Optional **Variant**. The section that the new section will be added before. You cannot specify ***Before*** if you've specified ***After***.

After Optional **Variant**. The section that the new section will be added after. You cannot specify ***After*** if you've specified ***Before***.

Remarks

You must specify either ***Type*** or ***FileName***. The name specified for ***Type*** doesn't need to include the version number included in the value returned by the **Type** property.

If you omit both ***Before*** and ***After***, the section is added after the last section in the binder.

Example

This example adds a Word document to Binder1.obd and names the resulting document "Totals."

```
Set myBinder = GetObject("C:\Binder1.obd", "OfficeBinder.Binder")
Set newSection = mybinder.Sections _
    .Add(Type:="Word.Document", Before:=1)
newSection.Name = "Totals"
```

Binder Object

Description

Represents a Microsoft Office binder. A binder is created or opened in Visual Basic as an Automation object (formerly OLE Automation object).

Using the Binder Object

Use the **CreateObject** function to create a new binder. The following example creates a new binder, makes it visible, and then saves it as Mybind.obd.

```
Set myBinder = CreateObject("OfficeBinder.Binder")
myBinder.Visible = True
myBinder.SaveAs Filename := "Mybind.obd"
```

Use the **GetObject** function to open an existing binder. The following example opens the previously created binder and makes it visible.

```
Set myBinder = GetObject("Mybind.obd", "OfficeBinder.Binder")
myBinder.Visible = True
```

Remarks

When a binder is created or opened, it's hidden by default. Set the **Visible** property for the specified binder to **True** to display the binder.

Properties

ActiveSection property, **BuiltinDocumentProperties** property, **CustomDocumentProperties** property, **DefaultFilePath** property, **DisplayAlerts** property, **DisplayLeftPaneAndButton** property, **DisplayStatusBar** property, **LeftPane** property, **Name** property, **PageSetup** property, **Path** property, **Sections** property, **SelectedSectionNames** property, **SinglePrintJob** property, **Visible** property.

Methods

Close method, **ExitOpenMode** method, **Open** method, **PrintOut** method, **Save** method, **SaveAs** method, **ViewOpenMode** method.

BuiltinDocumentProperties Property

Applies To

Binder object.

Description

Returns a **DocumentProperties** collection that represents all the built-in document properties for the specified binder. Read-only.

Remarks

Use the **CustomDocumentProperties** property to return the **DocumentProperties** collection that represents all the custom document properties for the specified binder.

See Also

CustomDocumentProperties property.

Example

This example displays the name of the author of Binder1.obd.

```
Set nb = GetObject("C:\Binder1.obd", "OfficeBinder.Binder")
MsgBox nb.BuiltinDocumentProperties("Author").Value
Set nb = Nothing
```

CenterFooter Property

Applies To

PageSetup object.

Description

Returns or sets the center part of the footer in sections that support headers or footers (or both) and that are included in the binder at the time the footer is set. Read/write **String**.

Remarks

You can use special format codes in the footer text.

See Also

HasBinderHeaderFooter property, **LeftFooter** property, **RightFooter** property.

Example

This example prints the page number—in bold, italic type—in the center of every page in each section of Binder1.obd that supports headers or footers (or both).

```
Set myBinder = GetObject("C:\Binder1.obd", "OfficeBinder.Binder")
With myBinder
For Each s In .Sections
   If s.SupportsBinderHeaderFooter Then
      .PageSetup.CenterFooter = "&B &I &P &B"
      s.HasBinderHeaderFooter = True
   End If
Next
.Close SaveChanges:=True
End With
```

CenterHeader Property

Applies To

PageSetup object.

Description

Returns or sets the center part of the header in sections that support headers or footers (or both) and that are included in the binder at the time the header is set. Read/write **String**.

Remarks

You can use special format codes in the header text.

See Also

HasBinderHeaderFooter property, **LeftHeader** property, **RightHeader** property.

Example

This example prints the date and the time, in bold type, at the center of each page in every section of Binder1.obd that supports headers or footers (or both).

```
Set myBinder = GetObject("c:\Binder1.obd", "OfficeBinder.Binder")
With myBinder
For Each s In .Sections
   If s.SupportsBinderHeaderFooter Then
      .PageSetup.CenterHeader = "&B &D &T &B"
      s.HasBinderHeaderFooter = True
   End If
Next
.Close SaveChanges:=True
End With
```

Close Method

Applies To

Binder object.

Description

Closes the specified binder.

Syntax

expression.**Close**(***SaveChanges, FileName***)

expression Required. An expression that returns a **Binder** object.

SaveChanges Optional **Variant**. **True** to save changes to the binder. **False** to save the binder without saving changes. If this argument is omitted and there are changes to the binder, a dialog box is displayed asking the user whether to save changes. If there are no changes, this argument is ignored.

FileName Optional **Variant**. The name you want to give the binder when you save it, if it hasn't been previously saved. If this argument is omitted and the binder hasn't been saved at least once, the **Save As** dialog is displayed. If the binder has already been saved, this argument is ignored.

Example

This example closes the binder represented by `newBinder` and saves it as NewBinder2.obd.

```
newBinder.Close _
    SaveChanges:=True,FileName:="NewBinder2.obd"
```

Copy Method

Applies To

Section object.

Description

Copies the specified section to another location in the binder, and returns the copy as a **Section** object. The new copy will automatically be given the name of the original section, with a number in parentheses appended; the original section won't be moved or altered.

Syntax

expression.**Copy**(***Before, After***)

expression Required. An expression that returns a **Section** object.

Before Optional **Variant**. The name or number of the section that the object will be copied before. You cannot specify ***Before*** if you've specified ***After***.

After Optional **Variant**. The name or number of the section that the object will be copied after. You cannot specify ***After*** if you've specified ***Before***.

Example

This example determines whether the second section in Binder1.obd is a Microsoft Excel worksheet. If so, it will be copied after the section named "Totals."

```
Set myBinder = GetObject("C:\Binder1.obd", "OfficeBinder.Binder")
myBinder.Sections(2).Activate
With myBinder.ActiveSection
If .Type = "Excel.Sheet.8" Then
   .Copy After:="Totals"
End If
End With
```

Count Property

Applies To

Sections collection object.

Description

Returns the number of items in the **Sections** collection. Read-only **Long**.

Remarks

All sections, whether visible or hidden, are included in the count.

Example

This example displays the number of sections in Binder1.obd.

```
Set myBinder = GetObject("C:\Binder1.obd", "OfficeBinder.Binder")
MsgBox "There are " & myBinder.Sections.Count & _
   " sections in the binder named: " & myBinder.Name
```

CustomDocumentProperties Property

Applies To

Binder object.

Description

Returns a **DocumentProperties** collection that represents all the custom document properties for the specified binder. Read-only.

Remarks

Use the **BuiltinDocumentProperties** property to return the **DocumentProperties** collection that represents all the built-in document properties for the specified binder.

See Also

BuiltinDocumentProperties property.

Example

This example adds a custom document property to Binder1.obd and then saves the binder.

```
Set nb = GetObject("C:\Binder1.obd", "OfficeBinder.Binder")
nb.CustomDocumentProperties.Add Name:="complete", _
   LinkToContent:=False, Type:=offPropertyTypeBoolean, Value:=False
nb.Save
Set nb = Nothing
```

DefaultFilePath Property

Applies To

Binder object.

Description

Returns or sets the default path that Microsoft Office Binder uses when it either opens files or saves them. Read/write **String**.

Remarks

The default path after installation of Microsoft Office is C:\My Documents.

Example

This example displays the current default file path.

```
MsgBox "The current default file path is " & _
   newBinder.DefaultFilePath
```

Delete Method

Applies To

Section object.

Description

Deletes the specified **Section** object.

Syntax

expression.**Delete**

expression   Required. An expression that returns a **Section** object.

Example

This example deletes the section named "Sums" in Binder1.obd. The example references the section by name, but you can also reference the section by number. You can permanently delete the section only after you've saved the binder.

```
Set myBinder = GetObject("C:\Binder1.obd", "OfficeBinder.Binder")
With myBinder
    .Sections("Sums").Delete
    .Save
End With
```

DisplayAlerts Property

Applies To

Binder object.

Description

True if Microsoft Office Binder displays certain alerts and messages when the specified binder is active. Read/write **Boolean**.

Example

This example closes the binder represented by `newBinder`, without prompting the user to save changes. Changes to the binder aren't saved.

```
newBinder.DisplayAlerts = False
newBinder.Close
```

DisplayLeftPaneAndButton Property

Applies To

Binder object.

Description

True if the left pane (also known as the Binder pane) of the specified binder and the button that allows the user to display this pane are visible. Read/write **Boolean**.

See Also

DisplayStatusBar property.

Example

This example displays the binder represented by `newBinder` but doesn't display the Binder pane. The button that allows the user to display this pane isn't available.

```
newBinder.DisplayLeftPaneAndButton = False
newBinder.Visible = True
```

DisplayStatusBar Property

Applies To

Binder object.

Description

True if Microsoft Office Binder displays a status bar at the bottom of the application window. Read/write **Boolean**.

See Also

DisplayLeftPaneAndButton property.

Example

This example opens Binder2.obd, displays the status bar, and makes the binder visible.

```
Set newb = GetObject("C:\Binder2.obd", "Office.Binder")
newb.DisplayStatusBar = True
newb.Visible = True
```

ExitOpenMode Method

Applies To

Binder object.

Description

Closes the host application and returns to Microsoft Office Binder.

Syntax

expression.**ExitOpenMode**

expression Required. An expression that returns a **Binder** object.

See Also

ViewOpenMode method.

Example

This example adds a new Microsoft Excel workbook to the binder and opens the new section in the host application (Microsoft Excel). It adds the number 45 to a range in a worksheet and then closes the host application and saves the new binder file.

```
Set newbinder = GetObject("C:\Binder2.obd", _
   "Office.Binder")
newbinder.ViewOpenMode
Set newSection = newbinder.Sections.Add(Type:="Excel.Sheet")
With newSection
   .Object.Worksheets(1).Range("a1").Value = 45
End With
```

```
newbinder.ExitOpenMode
newbinder.Close _
   savechanges:=True, FileName:="changed.obd"
```

FirstPage Property

Applies To

PageSetup object.

Description

Returns or sets the number of the first page in a section that supports headers or footers (or both). Read/write **Long**.

Remarks

When a binder is first created, this property is set to 1. Use this property if you want to set the number of the first page to something other than 1.

See Also

PrintOut method.

Example

This example prints the first section of Binder1.obd, and it starts the page numbering at 100. The page number will be printed as a right-aligned footer in the first section, if it supports headers or footers (or both).

```
Set myBinder = GetObject("C:\Binder1.obd", "OfficeBinder.Binder")
With myBinder
If .Sections(1).SupportsBinderHeaderFooter Then
   With .PageSetup
      .FirstPage = 100
      .RightFooter = "&P"
      .PrintWhat = bindPageSetupSelectedSections
   End With
End If
.Close SaveChanges:=True
End With
```

HasBinderHeaderFooter Property

Applies To

Section object.

Description

True if the specified binder section contains a printable header or footer. Read/write **Boolean**.

See Also

SupportsBinderHeaderFooter Property

Example

This example prints the page number ¾ in bold, italic type ¾ in the center of every page in each section of Binder1.obd that supports headers or footers (or both).

```
Set myBinder = GetObject("C:\Binder1.obd", _
   "OfficeBinder.Binder")
With myBinder
For Each s In .Sections
   If s.SupportsBinderHeaderFooter Then
      .PageSetup.CenterFooter = "&B &I &P &B"
      s.HasBinderHeaderFooter = True
   End If
Next
.Close SaveChanges:=True
End With
```

Index Property

Applies To

Section object.

Description

Returns the index number of the **Section** object within the **Sections** collection. Read-only **Long**.

Remarks

All sections, whether visible or hidden, are included in the index count.

To change the order of sections, use the **Move** method.

Example

This example determines whether the active section is the first section in Binder1.obd. If it is, the example moves the first section and places it after the third section.

```
Set myBinder = GetObject("C:\Binder1.obd", "OfficeBinder.Binder")
myBinder.Visible = True
If myBinder.ActiveSection.Index = 1 Then
   myBinder.ActiveSection.Move after:=3
End If
```

Item Property

Applies To

Sections collection object.

Description

Returns a **Section** object from the **Sections** collection. Read-only.

Syntax

expression.**Item(*Index*)**

expression Required. An expression that returns a **Sections** object.

Index Required **Variant**. The name or number of the section.

Remarks

The **Item** property is the default property of the **Sections** collection. You can use **Sections(***index***)**, where *index* represents the name or index number of the section, to return a single **Section** object. The index number represents the order in which the section is listed in the Binder pane. `Sections(1)` is the first document, and `Sections(Sections.Count)` is the last document.

Example

This example displays the name of the third section in Binder1.obd.

```
Set myBinder = GetObject("C:\Binder1.obd", "OfficeBinder.Binder")
sectionName = myBinder.Sections.Item(3).Name
Set myBinder = Nothing
MsgBox sectionName
```

LeftFooter Property

Applies To

PageSetup object.

Description

Returns or sets the left-aligned part of the footer in sections that support headers or footers (or both) and that are included in the binder at the time the footer is set. Read/write String.

Remarks

You can use special format codes in the footer text.

See Also

CenterFooter property, **HasBinderHeaderFooter** property, **RightFooter** property, **SupportsBinderHeaderFooter** property.

Example

This example prints the page number ¾ in bold, italic type ¾ in the lower-left corner of each page in every section of Binder1.obd that supports headers or footers (or both).

```
Set myBinder = GetObject("C:\Binder1.obd", "OfficeBinder.Binder")
With myBinder
```

```
For Each s In .Sections
   If s.SupportsBinderHeaderFooter Then
      s.PageSetup.LeftFooter = "&B &I &P &B"
      s.HasBinderHeaderFooter = True
   End If
Next
.Close SaveChanges:=True
End With
```

LeftHeader Property

Applies To

PageSetup object.

Description

Returns or sets the left-aligned part of the header in sections that support headers or footers (or both) and that are included in the binder at the time the header is set. Read/write **String**.

Remarks

You can use special format codes in the header text.

See Also

CenterHeader property, **HasBinderHeaderFooter** property, **RightHeader** property, **SupportsBinderHeaderFooter** property.

Example

This example prints the date and the time, in bold type, in the upper-left corner of each page in every section of Binder1.obd that supports headers or footers (or both).

```
Set myBinder = GetObject("C:\Binder1.obd", "OfficeBinder.Binder")
With myBinder
For Each s In .Sections
   If s.SupportsBinderHeaderFooter Then
      .PageSetup.LeftHeader = "&B &D &T &B"
      s.HasBinderHeaderFooter = True
   End If
Next
.Close SaveChanges:=True
End With
```

LeftPane Property

Applies To

Binder object.

Description

True if the left pane of the Binder window is visible. The left pane, also called the Binder pane, includes the icons for all the sections in the binder. Read/write **Boolean**.

Remarks

If this property is **False**, the Binder pane of the binder isn't visible, but a button that you can use to display the Binder pane is available.

See Also

DisplayLeftPaneAndButton property.

Example

This example uses the **Open** method to open the binder Binder2.obd. The example adds a new Word document to the binder, and it makes Binder pane visible.

```
Set myBinder = CreateObject("Binder1.Binder")
With myBinder
    .Open "binder2.obd"
    .Visible = True
    .Sections.Add Type:="Word.Document"
    .LeftPane = False
End With
```

Move Method

Applies To

Section object.

Description

Moves the specified section to another location in the binder.

Syntax

expression.**Move(*Before, After*)**

expression Required. An expression that returns a **Section** object.

Before Optional **Variant**. The name or index number of the section that the object will be moved before. You cannot specify **Before** if you've specified **After**.

After Optional **Variant**. The name or index number of the section that the object will be moved after. You cannot specify **After** if you've specified **Before**.

Example

This example moves all Microsoft Excel workbooks in Binder1.obd to the last sections in the binder.

```
Set myBinder = GetObject("C:\Binder1.obd", "OfficeBinder.Binder")
lastOne = myBinder.Sections.Count
For Each thing In myBinder.Sections
   If thing.Type = "Excel.Sheet.8" Then
      thing.Move after:=lastOne
   End If
Next
```

Name Property

Applies To

Binder object, **Section** object.

Description

Binder object: Returns the file name of the binder, not including its path. Read-only **String**.

Section object: Returns or sets the name of the section, as displayed on the icon in the Binder pane. Read/write **String**.

Remarks

Use the **Path** property to return the location and the file name of the binder.

Example

This example sets the name of the second section in Binder1.obd to "Budget 95" and then saves the changes to the binder.

```
Set myBinder = GetObject("C:\Binder1.obd", "OfficeBinder.Binder")
If myBinder.Sections(2).Type = "Excel.Sheet.8" Then
   myBinder.Sections(2).Name = "Budget 95"
   MsgBox "Binder contents have changed."
End If
myBinder.Save
```

Numbering Property

Applies To

PageSetup object.

Description

Returns or sets the type of numbering that the sections of the specified binder will contain. Can be either of the following **BindPrintNumbering** constants: **bindConsecutivePages** or **bindRestartEachSection**. Read/write **Variant**.

Example

This example places the page number in the lower-left corner of each page in Binder1.obd, and it restarts the page numbering at the beginning of each section in the binder.

```
Set myBinder = GetObject("C:\Binder1.obd", "OfficeBinder.Binder")
With myBinder.PageSetup
    .LeftFooter = "&P"
    .Numbering = bindRestartEachSection
End With
```

Object Property

Applies To

Section object.

Description

Returns the OLE object associated with the specified section. Read-only.

Remarks

Use this property to access the contents of the specified section (for example, the value of cell A1 on a Microsoft Excel worksheet) and all the objects, methods, and properties of the application that created the section.

Example

This example displays the value of the cell named "GrandTotal" on worksheet one in the section named "Revenue 96" in Binder1.obd.

```
Set myBinder = GetObject("C:\Binder1.obd", "OfficeBinder.Binder")
myBinder.Visible = True
total = myBinder.Sections("Revenue 96").Object.Range("GrandTotal")
MsgBox "The grand total for 1996 is " & total
```

Open Method

Applies To

Binder object.

Description

Opens either an existing binder or a new binder based on an existing binder template.

Note The preferred method for opening an existing binder is to use the **GetObject** function, and then to use the **Visible** method if you want to display the binder to the user. If you use the **Open** method instead of the **GetObject** function, use the **Open** method immediately after using **CreateObject**; otherwise, an error will occur.

Syntax

expression.**Open**(***FileName, OpenAsTemplate***)

expression Required. An expression that returns a **Binder** object.

FileName Required **String**. The name of the file to be opened.

OpenAsTemplate Optional **Variant**. **True** to open the file as a new binder based on the specified binder template. **False** (or omitted) to open the file as a binder file.

Example

This example opens Binder2.obd. The example adds a new Word document to the binder and then makes the binder visible.

```
Set myBinder = CreateObject("OfficeBinder.Binder")
With myBinder
    .Open "binder2.obd"
    .Sections.Add Type:="Word.Document"
    .Visible = True
End With
```

PageSetup Object

Description

Represents the page setup description. The PageSetup object contains all the page setup attributes (left footer, center header, numbering, and so on) as properties.

Using the PageSetup Object

Use the PageSetup property to return the PageSetup object. This example prints the visible sections of the binder, and it starts the page numbering at 100. The page numbers are printed as right-aligned footers.

```
Set myBinder = GetObject("C:\Binder1.obd", "OfficeBinder.Binder")
With myBinder.PageSetup
    .FirstPage = 100
    .RightFooter = "&P"
    .PrintWhat = bindPrintVisibleSections
End With
```

Remarks

To print a header or footer in a section, the section must first be capable of supporting printed headers or footers (or both), and it must contain a printable header or footer. Use the SupportsBinderHeaderFooter property to determine whether the section supports headers or footers. Use the HasBinderHeaderFooter to determine whether the section contains a printable header or footer.

Example

The following example sets the page number, in bold type, in the center of each page in every section of MyBinder.doc that supports headers or footers, and then it prints all visible sections of the binder.

```
Set myBinder = GetObject("c:\Binder1.obd", "OfficeBinder.Binder")
With myBinder
For Each s In .Sections
   If s.SupportsBinderHeaderFooter Then
      .PageSetup.CenterFooter = "&B &P &B"
      s.HasBinderHeaderFooter = True
   End If
Next
myBinder.PrintOut What:=bindPrintVisibleSections
.Close SaveChanges:=True
End With
```

PageSetup Property

Applies To

Binder object.

Description

Returns a **PageSetup** object that represents the page setup description. Read-only.

See Also

PrintOut method.

Example

This example prints the page number—in bold, italic print—in the center of each page in the binder represented by `myBinder`.

```
Set myBinder = GetObject("C:\Binder1.obd", "OfficeBinder.Binder")
myBinder.PageSetup.CenterFooter = "&B &I &P &B"
```

Parent Property

Applies To

PageSetup object, **Section** object, **Sections** collection object.

Description

Returns the parent object for the specified object. Read-only.

Example

This example adds a new section to the front of Binder1.obd and sets the name of the section.

```
Set myBinder = GetObject("C:\Binder1.obd", "OfficeBinder.Binder")
Set newSection = myBinder.Sections.Add(Type:="Word.Document", _
   Before:=1)
newSection.Name = "Intro to " & newSection.Parent.Name
```

Path Property

Applies To

Binder object.

Description

Returns the complete path and file name of the specified binder. Read-only **String**.

See Also

DefaultFilePath property.

Example

This example prompts the user for the name of a binder to open, and then it confirms the choice by displaying the path of the specified binder.

```
myBinder = InputBox("Type the name of the binder you want to open")
Set myBinder = GetObject(myBinder, "OfficeBinder.Binder")
MsgBox "The binder you specified is located in " _
   & myBinder.Path
```

PrintOut Method

Applies To

Binder object, **Section** object.

Description

Prints every section, a subset of sections, or a single section in the binder.

Syntax 1

expression.**PrintOut(*What, Numbering, FirstPage, Sections, FileName, PrinterName,* ➥*DriverName, NoPrinting*)**

Syntax 2

expression.**PrintOut**

expression Required. An expression that returns a **Binder** object (Syntax 1) or a **Section** object (Syntax 2).

What Required **Variant**. The section or sections to be printed. Can be one of the following **BindPrintWhat** constants: **bindPrintActiveSection**, **bindPrintVisibleSections**, **bindPrintSelectedSections**, or **bindPrintSectionSubset**.

Numbering Optional **Variant**. The page numbering scheme. Can be either of the following **BindPrintNumbering** constants: **bindConsecutivePages** or **bindRestartEachSection**. The default value is **bindConsecutivePages**.

FirstPage Optional **Variant**. The first page number. If this argument is omitted, page numbering starts at 1.

Sections Optional **Variant**. If ***What*** is **bindPrintSectionSubset**, this argument is a one-dimensional array of the indexes of the sections to be printed. You can specify the index number to print one section or a one-dimensional array of indexes to print multiple sections.

FileName Optional **Variant**. The name of the file to which the printing will be redirected.

PrinterName Optional **Variant**. The name of the printer to be used. If this argument is omitted, the default printer is used.

DriverName Optional **Variant**. The name of the printer driver to be used. If this argument is omitted, the default driver is used.

NoPrinting Optional **Variant**. **True** to set ***PrinterName*** and ***DriverName*** but not print anything. **False** (or omitted) to print the specified section or sections.

Remarks

You can print a single section by using Syntax 1 and specifying the index number of the section for the ***Sections*** argument, or by using one of the printing methods that the section type provides in its object model (accessed through the **Object** property).

See Also

PrintWhat property, **SelectedSectionNames** property, **SinglePrintJob** property.

Example

This example prints all visible sections in Binder1.obd. The first page is numbered 10.

```
Set myBinder = GetObject("C:\Binder1.obd", "OfficeBinder.Binder")
myBinder.PrintOut what:=bindPrintVisibleSections, _
   numbering:=bindConsecutivePages, firstPage:=10
Set myBinder = Nothing
```

This example prints the first and second sections and the section named “Expense Report” in Binder4.obd.

```
Set myBinder = GetObject("Binder4.obd", "OfficeBinder.Binder")
myBinder.PrintOut what:=bindPrintSectionSubset, _
   sections:=Array(1, 2, "Expense Report")
Set myBinder = Nothing
```

PrintWhat Property

Applies To

PageSetup object.

Description

Returns or sets the sections of the specified binder that will be printed. Can be either of the following **BindPageSetupPrintWhat** constants: **bindPageSetupSelectedSections** or **bindPageSetupVisibleSections**. Read/write **Variant**.

See Also

PrintOut method, **SelectedSectionNames** property, **SinglePrintJob** property.

Example

This example places the date and the time in the upper-left corner of each page in Binder1.obd, and it sets all the visible sections of the binder that support headers or footers (or both) to print.

```
Set myBinder = GetObject("C:\Binder1.obd", "OfficeBinder.Binder")
With myBinder
For Each s In .Sections
   If s.SupportsBinderHeaderFooter Then
      .PageSetup.LeftHeader = "&D &T"
      .PageSetup.PrintWhat = bindPageSetupVisibleSections
      s.HasBinderHeaderFooter = True
   End If
Next
.Close SaveChanges:=True
End With
```

RightFooter Property

Applies To

PageSetup object.

Description

Returns or sets the right-aligned part of the footer in sections that support headers or footers (or both) and that are included in the binder at the time the footer is set. Read/write **String**.

Remarks

You can use special format codes in the footer text.

See Also

CenterFooter property, **HasBinderHeaderFooter** property, **LeftFooter** property, **SupportsBinderHeaderFooter** property.

Example

This example prints the page number—in bold, italic type—in the lower-right corner of each page in every section of Binder1.obd that supports headers or footers (or both).

```
Set myBinder = GetObject("C:\Binder1.obd", "OfficeBinder.Binder")
With myBinder
For Each s In .Sections
   If s.SupportsBinderHeaderFooter Then
      .PageSetup.RightFooter = "&B &I &P &B"
      s.HasBinderHeaderFooter = True
   End If
Next
.Close SaveChanges:=True
End With
```

RightHeader Property

Applies To

PageSetup object.

Description

Returns or sets the right-aligned part of the header in sections of the specified binder that support headers or footers (or both) and that are included in the binder at the time the header is set. Read/write **String**.

Remarks

You can use special format codes in the header text.

See Also

CenterHeader property, **HasBinderHeaderFooter** property, **LeftHeader** property, **SupportsBinderHeaderFooter** property.

Example

This example prints the date and the time, in bold type, in the upper-right corner of each page in every section of Binder1.obd that support headers or footers (or both).

```
Set myBinder = GetObject("C:\Binder1.obd", "OfficeBinder.Binder")
With myBinder
For Each s In .Sections
   If s.SupportsBinderHeaderFooter Then
      .PageSetup.LeftHeader = "&B &D &T &B"
      s.HasBinderHeaderFooter = True
   End If
Next
.Close SaveChanges:=True
End With
```

Save Method

Applies To

Binder object.

Description

Saves changes to the specified binder. Use this method only for binders that have been previously saved.

Syntax

expression.**Save**

expression Required. An expression that returns a **Binder** object.

Remarks

If you use the **Save** method to save a new binder, an error occurs. The first time you save a new binder, use the **SaveAs** method.

See Also

SaveAs Method

Example

This example sets the name of the second section in Binder1.obd to "Budget 95" and then saves the changes to the binder.

```
Set myBinder = GetObject("C:\Binder1.obd", "OfficeBinder.Binder")
If myBinder.Sections(2).Type = "Excel.Sheet.8" Then
   myBinder.Sections(2).Name = "Budget 95"
   MsgBox "Binder contents have changed."
End If
myBinder.Save
```

SaveAs Method

Applies To

Binder object, **Section** object.

Description

Saves changes to the specified binder or section to a different file. Use this method only for visible binders, or for newly created binders that haven't yet been saved. Returns **True** if the binder is saved or **False** if an error occurs and the binder cannot be saved.

Syntax 1

expression.**SaveAs(*FileName, SaveOption*)**

expression.**SaveAs(*FileName*)**

expression Required. An expression that returns a **Binder** object (Syntax 1) or a **Section** object (Syntax 2).

FileName Required for **Section**, optional for **Binder**. A string that indicates the name of the file to be saved. You can include a full path; if you don't, the file is saved in the current folder.

SaveOption Optional **Variant**. Specifies the way the specified binder is saved. Can be one of the following **BindSaveOption** constants.

Constant	Description
bindFailIfFileExists	If ***FileName*** exists, an error occurs (***FileName*** must be specified). This constant is the default value.
bindOverwriteExisting	If ***FileName*** exists, **SaveAs** overwrites it (***FileName*** must be specified).
bindDisplayDialog	Displays the **Save As** dialog box (***FileName*** is optional). If the user closes the **Save As** dialog box without saving, **SaveAs** returns **False**.

Remarks

The **SaveAs** method saves sections as unique files without deleting the corresponding sections in the binder. If you want to delete a section from the binder, use the **Delete** method.

See Also

Save method.

Example

This example determines whether the first section in Binder1.obd is of type Excel.Sheet.8. If it is, the example saves it as the workbook Book1.xls.

```
Set myBinder = GetObject("C:\Binder1.obd", "OfficeBinder.Binder")
If myBinder.Sections(1).Type = "Excel.Sheet.8" Then
   myBinder.Sections(1).SaveAs "MyBook1.xls"
End If
Set myBinder = Nothing
```

This example creates a new binder, makes it visible, and then prompts the user to save it as Binder1.obd.

```
Set newBinder = CreateObject("OfficeBinder.Binder")
newBinder.Visible = True
newBinder.SaveAs fileName:="Binder1.obd", _
   saveOption:=bindDisplayDialog
```

Section Object

Description

Represents a section (a specific document) in a binder. For example, if a binder contains a Microsoft Excel spreadsheet, two Word documents, and a PowerPoint presentation, the binder contains four sections. The **Section** object is a member of the **Sections** collection.

Using the Section Object

Use **Sections**(*index*), where *index* is the number of the section you want to return, to return a single **Section** object. The index number represents the order in which the sections are listed in the Binder pane. `Sections(1)` is the first document, and `Sections(Sections.Count)` is the last document.

Activating a section opens the document in place; it doesn't change the document's index number. All sections are included in the index count, even sections that are hidden. The following example activates the first document in the binder represented by `myBinder`.

```
myBinder.Sections(1).Activate
```

Remarks

The **Name** property returns or sets the name of the specified section. The following example displays the name of the first section in Binder1.obd.

```
Set myBinder = GetObject("Binder1.obd", "OfficeBinder.Binder")
theName = myBinder.Sections(1).Name
Set myBinder = Nothing
MsgBox theName
```

Use the **SaveAs** method to save a copy of the specified section to a different file. The following example saves section one in Binder1.obd to a new Microsoft Excel workbook.

```
Set myBinder = GetObject("C:\Binder1.obd", "OfficeBinder.Binder")
If myBinder.Sections(1).Type = "Excel.Sheet.8" Then
   myBinder.Sections(1).SaveAs "MyBook3.xls"
End If
```

The following example activates the section named "Sumsales" in Annual Report.obd.

```
Set myBinder = GetObject("C:\reports\Annual Report.obd", _
   "OfficeBinder.Binder")
myBinder.Visible = True
myBinder.Sections("Sumsales").Activate
```

Properties

HasBinderHeaderFooter property, **Index** property, **Name** property, **Object** property, **Parent** property, **SupportsBinderHeaderFooter** property, **Type** property, **Visible** property.

Methods

Activate method, **Copy** method, **Delete** method, **Move** method, **PrintOut** method, **SaveAs** method, **Update** method.

Sections Collection Object

Description

A collection of all the **Section** objects in a binder, whether they're visible or hidden.

Using the Sections Collection

Use the **Sections** property to return the **Sections** collection. The following example displays the number of sections in Binder1.obd.

```
Set myBinder = GetObject("C:\Binder1.obd", "OfficeBinder.Binder")
MsgBox "there are " & myBinder.Sections.Count & _
    " sections in this binder"
```

Use the **Add** method to create a new section or to add an existing file as a section. The following example adds a blank Microsoft Excel workbook section to the newly created binder.

```
Set myBinder = CreateObject("OfficeBinder.Binder")
myBinder.Sections.Add Type:="Excel.Sheet"
```

The following example opens an existing binder and adds the Word file Samples.doc as the last section in the binder.

```
Set myBinder = GetObject("C:\Binder1.obd", "OfficeBinder.Binder")
myBinder.Sections.Add _
    FileName:="C:\Program Files\Microsoft Office\Winword\Samples.doc"
```

Use **Sections**(*index*), where *index* is the number of the section you want to return, to return a single **Section** object. The following example sets the name of the second section in Binder1.obd to "Budget 95," and then it saves the changes.

```
Set myBinder = GetObject("C:\Binder1.obd", "OfficeBinder.Binder")
If myBinder.Sections(2).Type = "Excel.Sheet.8" Then
    myBinder.Sections(2).Name = "Budget 95"
    MsgBox "Binder contents have changed."
End If
myBinder.Save
```

Properties

Count property, **Item** property, **Parent** property.

Methods

Add method.

Sections Property

Applies To

Binder object.

Description

Returns a **Sections** collection that represents all the sections in the specified binder. Read-only.

See Also

Activate method, **ActiveSection** property.

Example

This example displays the number of Microsoft Excel sections in Binder1.obd.

```
Set myBinder = GetObject("C:\Binder1.obd", "OfficeBinder.Binder")
wk = 0
For Each s In myBinder.Sections
   If s.Type = "Excel.Sheet.8" Then
      wk = wk + 1
   End If
Next
MsgBox "There are " & wk & " Microsoft Excel sections in this binder."
Set myBinder = Nothing
```

This example displays the name of the third section in Binder1.obd.

```
Set myBinder = GetObject("C:\Binder1.obd", "OfficeBinder.Binder")
MsgBox myBinder.Sections(3).Name
Set myBinder = Nothing
```

SelectedSectionNames Property

Applies To

Binder object.

Description

Returns or sets the array that contains the names of the selected sections. Read/write **Variant**.

Remarks

When you set the **SelectedSectionNames** property, the first section named in the array becomes the active section. If the array contains the name of a section that doesn't exist, an error occurs.

Example

This example displays the names of the selected sections in Binder1.obd.

```
Set myBinder = GetObject("C:\Binder1.obd", "OfficeBinder.Binder")
With myBinder
myarray = .SelectedSectionNames
MsgBox UBound(myarray) & " section is selected."
For x = 1 To UBound(myarray)
   MsgBox "The section name is " & myarray(x)
Next
End With
```

SinglePrintJob Property

Applies To

Binder object.

Description

True if all the sections in the binder are printed together, as a unit. **False** if each section in the binder will be printed as a separate job. Read/write **Boolean**.

See Also

PrintOut method.

Example

This example opens a Binder file and prints it as a single print job.

```
Set newbinder = GetObject("C:\Binder2.obd", _
   "Office.Binder")
With newbinder
   .SinglePrintJob = True
   .PrintOut what:=bindPrintVisibleSections, _
      Numbering:=bindConsecutivePages
   .Close SaveChanges:=True, FileName:="changed.obd"
End With
```

SupportsBinderHeaderFooter Property

Applies To

Section object.

Description

True if the specified binder section supports headers or footers. Read-only **Boolean**.

See Also

HasBinderHeaderFooter property.

Example

This example prints the page number—in bold, italic type—in the center of every page in each section of Binder1.obd that supports headers or footers (or both).

```
Set myBinder = GetObject("C:\Binder1.obd", _
   "OfficeBinder.Binder")
With myBinder
For Each s In .Sections
   If s.SupportsBinderHeaderFooter Then
      .PageSetup.CenterFooter = "&B &I &P &B"
      s.HasBinderHeaderFooter = True
   End If
Next
.Close SaveChanges:=True
End With
```

Type Property

Applies To

Section object.

Description

Returns a string that contains the OLE long class name for the **Section** object. Read-only **String**.

Remarks

OLE long class names are specified as *appName.objectType.versionNumber* (for example, "Word.Document.8"). For more information about available binder section types, see the **Add** method.

Example

This example moves all Microsoft Excel workbooks in the binder Binder1.obd to the last sections in the binder.

```
Set myBinder = GetObject("C:\Binder1.obd", "OfficeBinder.Binder")
lastOne = myBinder.Sections.Count
For Each thing In myBinder.Sections
   If thing.Type = "Excel.Sheet.8" Then
      thing.Move after:=lastOne
   End If
Next
```

Update Method

Applies To

Section object.

Description

Updates the specified section, but doesn't save changes made to the binder. Use the **Save** method to save changes to the binder.

Syntax

expression.**Update**

expression Required. An expression that returns a **Section** object.

Remarks

The **Update** method is useful if several sections need to be updated before the binder is saved.

Example

This example adds a Microsoft Excel worksheet to an existing binder, inserts a value in the worksheet, and updates the new section. Without the **Update** method, the change would be lost when the new **Section** object is set to **Nothing**. (Use the **Save** method to permanently save these changes to the binder.)

```
Set newBinder = GetObject("C:\Binder1.obd", "OfficeBinder.Binder")
Set newSection = newBinder.Sections.Add(Type:="Excel.Sheet")
With newSection
   .Object.Worksheets(1).Range("a1").Value = 3.14159
   .Update
End With
Set newSection = Nothing
```

ViewOpenMode Method

Applies To

Binder object.

Description

Displays the active section of the specified binder within the section's host application.

Syntax

expression.**ViewOpenMode**

expression Required. An expression that returns a **Binder** object.

Remarks

If the host application isn't available or isn't installed, an error will occur.

See Also

ExitOpenMode Method

Example

This example adds a new Microsoft Excel workbook to the binder and opens the new section in the host application (Microsoft Excel). It adds the number 45 to a range in a worksheet and then closes the host application and saves the new binder file.

```
Set newbinder = GetObject("C:\Binder2.obd", _
   "Office.Binder")
newbinder.ViewOpenMode
Set newSection = newbinder.Sections.Add(Type:="Excel.Sheet")
With newSection
   .Object.Worksheets(1).Range("a1").Value = 45
End With
newbinder.ExitOpenMode
newbinder.Close _
   savechanges:=True, FileName:="changed.obd"
```

Visible Property

Applies To

Binder object, **Section** object.

Description

True if the specified binder or section is visible. Read/write **Boolean**.

Remarks

When a **Binder** object is created by the **CreateObject** function or opened by the **GetObject** function, the **Visible** property is **False**. To make the binder visible, set the **Visible** property to **True**.

Hidden sections are included in the count for the **Sections** collection.

Example

This example opens Binder1.obd and makes it visible.

```
Set myBinder = GetObject("C:\Binder1.obd", "OfficeBinder.Binder")
myBinder.Visible = True
```

Microsoft Graph Language Reference

Microsoft Graph 97

Default location: \Program Files\Common Files\Microsoft Shared\MSGraph

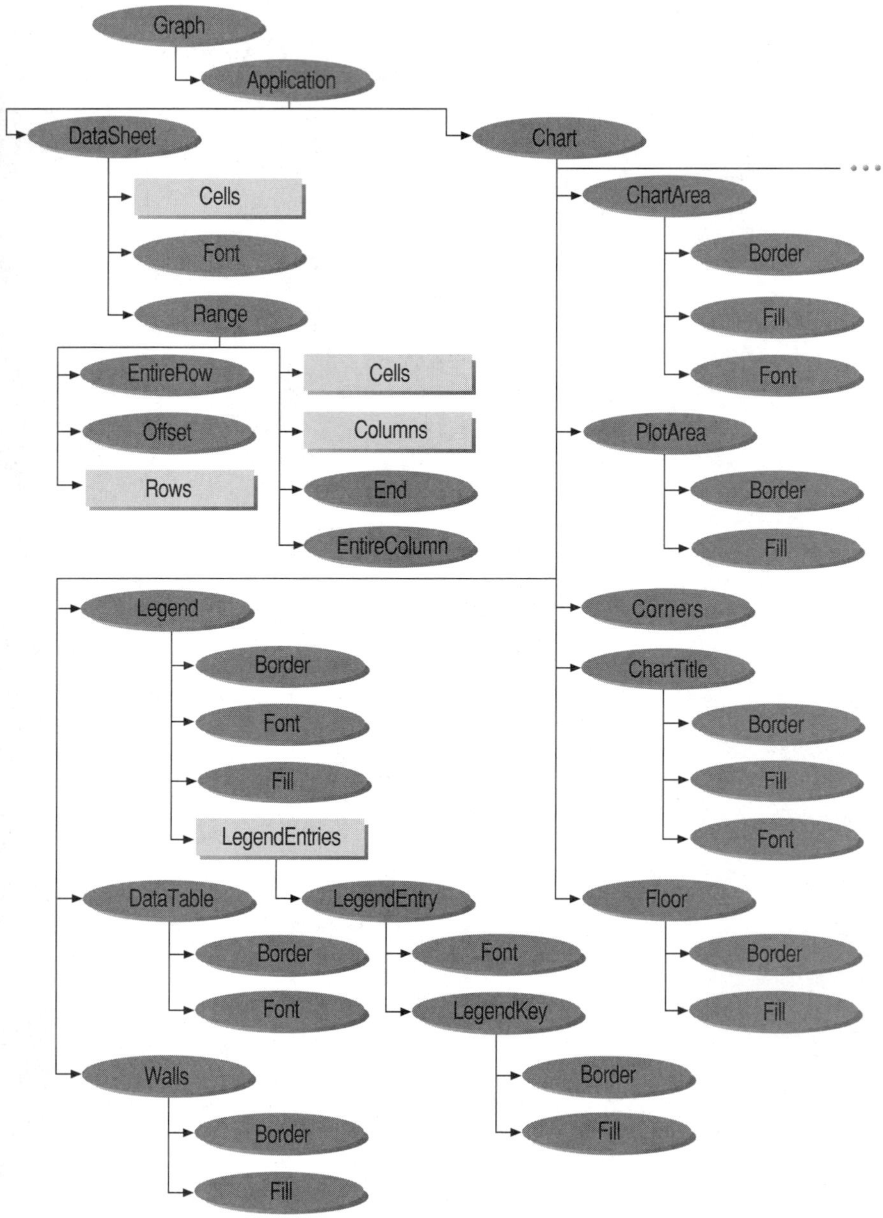

Source (Type Library)

The Microsoft Graph 97 object model is provided by GRAPH8.OLB, which is included when you install Microsoft Graph 97.

The dotted line (...) indicates that the diagram continues across pages.

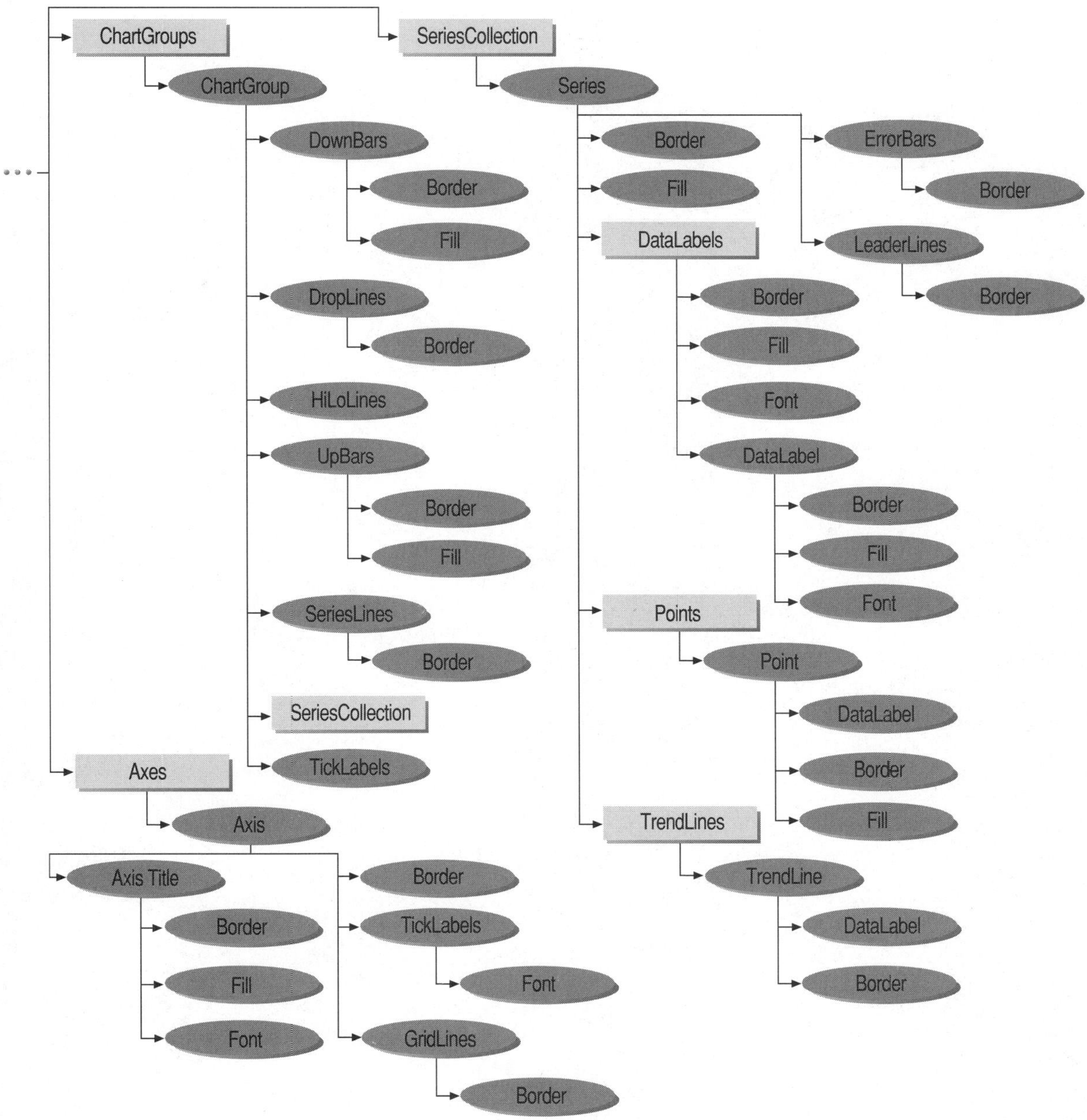

The dotted line (…) indicates that the diagram continues across pages.

Activate Method

Applies To

Chart object, **DataSheet** object.

Description

Activates the object.

Syntax

expression.**Activate**

expression Required. An expression that returns an object in the Applies To list.

Example

This example activates the datasheet.

```
myChart.Application.DataSheet.Activate
```

Add Method

Applies To

Trendlines Collection object.

Description

Creates a new trendline. Returns a **Trendline** object.

Syntax

expression.**Add(*Type, Order, Period, Forward, Backward, Intercept, DisplayEquation,* ↪ *DisplayRSquared, Name*)**

expression Required. An expression that returns a **Trendlines** object.

Type Optional **Variant**. The trendline type. Can be one of the following **XlTrendlineType** constants: **xlLinear**, **xlLogarithmic**, **xlExponential**, **xlPolynomial**, **xlMovingAvg**, or **xlPower**. The default value is **xlLinear**.

Order Optional **Variant**. Required if ***Type*** is **xlPolynomial**. The trendline order. Must be an integer from 2 through 6.

Period Optional **Variant**. Required if ***Type*** is **xlMovingAvg**. The trendline period. Must be an integer greater than 1 and less than the number of data points in the series you're adding a trendline to.

Forward Optional **Variant**. The number of periods (or units on a scatter chart) that the trendline extends forward.

Backward Optional **Variant**. The number of periods (or units on a scatter chart) that the trendline extends backward.

Intercept Optional **Variant**. The trendline intercept. If this argument is omitted, the intercept is automatically set by the regression.

DisplayEquation Optional **Variant**. **True** to display the equation of the trendline on the chart (in the same data label as the R-squared value). The default value is **False**.

DisplayRSquared Optional **Variant**. **True** to display the R-squared value of the trendline on the chart (in the same data label as the equation). The default value is **False**.

Name Optional **Variant**. The name of the trendline, as text. If this argument is omitted, Microsoft Graph generates a name.

Example

This example creates a new linear trendline on the chart.

```
myChart.SeriesCollection(1).Trendlines.Add
```

AddChartAutoFormat Method

Applies To

Application object.

Description

Adds a custom chart autoformat to the list of available chart autoformats.

Syntax

expression.**AddChartAutoFormat**(***Name, Description***)

expression Required. An expression that returns an **Application** object.

Name Required **String**. The name of the autoformat.

Description Optional **String**. A description of the custom autoformat.

See Also

DeleteChartAutoFormat method, **SetDefaultChart** method.

Example

This example adds a new autoformat.

```
myChart.Application.AddChartAutoFormat _
    Name:="Presentation Chart"
```

AddReplacement Method

Applies To

AutoCorrect object.

Description

Adds an entry to the array of AutoCorrect replacements.

Syntax

expression.**AddReplacement(*What, Replacement*)**

expression Required. An expression that returns an **AutoCorrect** object.

What Required **String**. The text to be replaced. If this string already exists in the array of AutoCorrect replacements, the existing substitute text is replaced by the new text.

Replacement Required **String**. The replacement text.

See Also

DeleteReplacement method, **ReplacementList** method.

Example

This example substitutes the word "Temp." for the word "Temperature" in the array of AutoCorrect replacements.

```
With myChart.Application.AutoCorrect
    .AddReplacement "Temperature", "Temp."
End With
```

Application Object

Description

Represents the entire Microsoft Graph application. The **Application** object represents the top level of the object hierarchy and contains all of the objects, properties, and methods for the application.

Using the Application Object

Use the **Application** property to return the **Application** object. The following example applies the **DataSheet** property to the **Application** object.

```
myChart.Application.DataSheet.Range("A1").Value = 32
```

Properties

Application property, **AutoCorrect** property, **CellDragAndDrop** property, **CommandBars** property, **Creator** property, **DataSheet** property, **DisplayAlerts** property, **HasLinks** property, **Height** property, **Left** property, **MoveAfterReturn** property, **Name** property, **Parent** property, **PlotBy** property, **ShowChartTipNames**

property, **ShowChartTipValues** property, **Top** property, **Version** property, **Visible** property, **Width** property, **WindowState** property.

Methods

AddChartAutoFormat method, **Chart** method, **DeleteChartAutoFormat** method, **Evaluate** method, **FileImport** method, **Quit** method, **SaveAsOldFileFormat** method, **SetDefaultChart** method, **Update** method.

Application Property

Applies To

Application object, **AutoCorrect** object, **Axes** Collection object, **Axis** object, **AxisTitle** object, **Border** object, **Chart** object, **ChartArea** object, **ChartColorFormat** object, **ChartFillFormat** object, **ChartGroup** object, **ChartGroups** Collection object, **ChartTitle** object, **Corners** object, **DataLabel** object, **DataLabels** Collection object, **DataSheet** object, **DataTable** object, **DownBars** object, **DropLines** object, **ErrorBars** object, **Floor** object, **Font** object, **Gridlines** object, **HiLoLines** object, **Interior** object, **LeaderLines** object, **Legend** object, **LegendEntries** Collection object, **LegendEntry** object, **LegendKey** object, **PlotArea** object, **Point** object, **Points** Collection object, **Range** object, **Series** object, **SeriesCollection** Collection object, **SeriesLines** object, **TickLabels** object, **Trendline** object, **Trendlines** Collection object, **UpBars** object, **Walls** object.

Description

Returns an **Application** object that represents the Microsoft Graph application.

See Also

Creator property.

Example

This example substitutes the word "Temp." for the word "Temperature" in the array of AutoCorrect replacements.

```
With myChart.Application.AutoCorrect
   .AddReplacement "Temperature", "Temp."
End With
```

ApplyCustomType Method

Applies To

Chart object, **Series** object.

Description

Applies a standard or custom chart type to a chart or series.

Syntax

expression.**ApplyCustomType**(***ChartType***, ***TypeName***)

expression An expression that returns a **Chart** or **Series** object.

ChartType Required **Long**. A standard chart type (see the **ChartType** property for the list of available constants). For **Chart** objects, this can also be one of the following **XlChartGallery** constants: **xlBuiltIn**, **xlUserDefined**, or **xlAnyGallery**.

TypeName Optional **Variant** (used only with **Chart** objects). A **String** naming the custom chart type when ***ChartType*** specifies a custom chart gallery.

Example

This example applies the "Line with Data Markers" chart type to Chart1.

```
Charts(1).ApplyCustomType xlLineMarkers
```

ApplyDataLabels Method

Applies To

Chart object, **Point** object, **Series** object.

Description

Applies data labels to a point, a series, or all the series in a chart.

Syntax

expression.**ApplyDataLabels(*Type, LegendKey*)**

expression Required. An expression that returns a **Chart**, **Point**, or **Series** object.

Type Optional **Variant**. The data label type. Can be one of the following **XlDataLabelsType** constants.

Constant	Description
xlDataLabelsShowNone	No data labels.
xlDataLabelsShowValue	Value for the point (assumed if this argument isn't specified).
xlDataLabelsShowPercent	Percentage of the total. Available only for pie charts and doughnut charts.
xlDataLabelsShowLabel	Category for the point. This is the default value.
xlDataLabelsShowLabelAndPercent	Percentage of the total, and category for the point. Available only for pie charts and doughnut charts.

LegendKey Optional **Variant**. **True** to show the legend key next to the point. The default value is **False**.

See Also

DataLabel property, **HasDataLabel** property, **HasDataLabels** property.

Example

This example applies category labels to series one.

```
myChart.SeriesCollection(1). _
    ApplyDataLabels Type:=xlDataLabelsShowLabel
```

ApplyPictToEnd Property

Applies To

Point object, **Series** object.

Description

True if a picture is applied to the end of the point or all points in the series. Read/write **Boolean**.

See Also

ApplyPictToFront property, **ApplyPictToSides** property.

Example

This example applies pictures to the end of all points in series one. The series must already have pictures applied to it (setting this property changes the picture orientation).

```
myChart.SeriesCollection(1).ApplyPictToEnd = True
```

ApplyPictToFront Property

Applies To

Point object, **Series** object.

Description

True if a picture is applied to the front of the point or all points in the series. Read/write **Boolean**.

See Also

ApplyPictToEnd property, **ApplyPictToSides** property.

Example

This example applies pictures to the front of all points in series one. The series must already have pictures applied to it (setting this property changes the picture orientation).

```
myChart.SeriesCollection(1).ApplyPictToFront = True
```

ApplyPictToSides Property

Applies To

Point object, **Series** object.

Description

True if a picture is applied to the sides of the point or all points in the series. Read/write **Boolean**.

See Also

ApplyPictToEnd property, **ApplyPictToFront** property.

Example

This example applies pictures to the sides of all points in series one. The series must already have pictures applied to it (setting this property changes the picture orientation).

```
myChart.SeriesCollection(1).ApplyPictToSides = True
```

Area3DGroup Property

Applies To

Chart object.

Description

Returns a **ChartGroup** object that represents the specified area chart group on a 3-D chart. Read-only.

See Also

AreaGroups method.

Example

This example turns on drop lines for the 3-D area chart group.

```
myChart.Area3DGroup.HasDropLines = True
```

AreaGroups Method

Applies To

Chart object.

Description

On a 2-D chart, this method returns an object that represents either a single area chart group (a **ChartGroup** object, Syntax 1) or a collection of all the area chart groups (a **ChartGroups** collection, Syntax 2).

Syntax 1

expression.**AreaGroups**(***Index***)

Syntax 2

expression.**AreaGroups**

expression Required. An expression that returns a **Chart** object.

Index Optional **Variant**. The index number of the specified chart group.

See Also

Area3DGroup property, **BarGroups** method, **ChartGroups** method, **ColumnGroups** method, **DoughnutGroups** method, **LineGroups** method, **PieGroups** method.

Example

This example turns on drop lines for the 2-D area chart group.

```
myChart.AreaGroups(1).HasDropLines = True
```

AutoCorrect Object

Description

Contains Microsoft Graph AutoCorrect attributes (capitalization of names of days, correction of two initial capital letters, automatic correction list, and so on).

Using the AutoCorrect Object

Use the **AutoCorrect** property to return the **AutoCorrect** object. The following example sets Microsoft Graph to correct words that begin with two initial capital letters.

```
With myChart.Application.AutoCorrect
    .TwoInitialCapitals = True
    .ReplaceText = True
End With
```

Properties

Application property, **CapitalizeNamesOfDays** property, **CorrectCapsLock** property, **CorrectSentenceCap** property, **Creator** property, **Parent** property, **ReplaceText** property, **TwoInitialCapitals** property.

Methods

AddReplacement method, **DeleteReplacement** method, **ReplacementList** method.

AutoCorrect Property

Applies To

Application object.

Description

Returns an **AutoCorrect** object that represents the Microsoft Graph AutoCorrect attributes. Read-only.

See Also

AddReplacement method, **CapitalizeNamesOfDays** property, **DeleteReplacement** method, **ReplacementList** method, **ReplaceText** property, **TwoInitialCapitals** property.

Example

This example substitutes the word “Temp.” for the word “Temperature” in the array of AutoCorrect replacements.

```
With myChart.Application.AutoCorrect
    .AddReplacement "Temperature", "Temp."
End With
```

AutoFit Method

Applies To

Range object.

Description

Changes the width of the columns in the specified range to achieve the best fit.

Syntax

expression.**AutoFit**

expression Required. An expression that returns a **Range** object. Must be a row or a range of rows, or a column or a range of columns. Otherwise, this method causes an error.

Remarks

One unit of column width is equal to the width of one character in the Normal style.

See Also

ColumnWidth property.

Example

This example changes the width of columns A through I on the datasheet to achieve the best fit.

```
myChart.Application.DataSheet.Columns("A:I").AutoFit
```

This example changes the width of columns A through E on the datasheet to achieve the best fit, based only on the contents of cells A1:E1.

```
myChart.Application.DataSheet.Range("A1:E1").Columns.AutoFit
```

AutoScaleFont Property

Applies To

AxisTitle object, **ChartArea** object, **ChartTitle** object, **DataLabel** object, **DataLabels** Collection object, **DataTable** object, **Legend** object, **LegendEntry** object, **TickLabels** object.

Description

True if the text in the object changes font size when the object size changes. The default value is **True**. Read/write **Variant**.

Example

This example adds a title to the chart, and it causes the title font to remain the same size whenever the chart size changes.

```
With myChart
    .HasTitle = True
    .ChartTitle.Text = "1996 sales"
    .ChartTitle.AutoScaleFont = False
End With
```

AutoScaling Property

Applies To

Chart object.

Description

True if Microsoft Graph scales a 3-D chart so that it's closer in size to the equivalent 2-D chart. The **RightAngleAxes** property must be **True**. Read/write **Boolean**.

Example

This example automatically scales the chart. The example should be run on a 3-D chart.

```
With myChart
    .RightAngleAxes = True
    .AutoScaling = True
End With
```

AutoText Property

Applies To

DataLabel object, **DataLabels** Collection object.

Description

True if the object automatically generates appropriate text based on context. Read/write **Boolean**.

Example

This example sets the data labels for series one to automatically generate appropriate text.

```
myChart.SeriesCollection(1).DataLabels.AutoText = True
```

Axes Collection Object

Description

A collection of all the **Axis** objects in the specified chart.

Using the Axes Collection

Use the **Axes** method to return the **Axes** collection. The following example displays the number of axes in the chart.

```
With myChart
   MsgBox .Axes.Count
End With
```

Use **Axes(***type*, *group***)**, where *type* is the axis type and *group* is the axis group, to return a single **Axis** object. *Type* can be one of the following **XlAxisType** constants: **xlCategory**, **xlSeries**, or **xlValue**. *Group* can be either of the following **XlAxisGroup** constants: **xlPrimary** or **xlSecondary**. For more information, see the **Axes** method.

The following example sets the title text for the category axis.

```
With myChart.Axes(xlCategory)
   .HasTitle = True
   .AxisTitle.Caption = "1994"
End With
```

Properties

Application property, **Count** property, **Creator** property, **Parent** property.

Methods

Item method.

Axes Method

Applies To

Chart object.

Description

Returns an object that represents either a single axis (an **Axis** object, Syntax 1) or a collection of the axes on the chart (an **Axes** collection, Syntax 2).

Syntax 1

expression.**Axes(*Type, AxisGroup*)**

Syntax 2

expression.**Axes**

expression   Required. An expression that returns a **Chart** object.

Type   Optional **Variant**. Specifies the axis to return. Can be one of the following **XlAxisType** constants: **xlValue**, **xlCategory**, or **xlSeriesAxis** (**xlSeriesAxis** is valid only for 3-D charts).

AxisGroup   Optional **Variant**. Specifies the axis group. Can be one of the following **XlAxisGroup** constants: **xlPrimary** or **xlSecondary**. If this argument is omitted, the primary group is used. 3-D charts have only one axis group.

Example

This example adds an axis label to the category axis.

```
With myChart.Axes(xlCategory)
   .HasTitle = True
   .AxisTitle.Text = "July Sales"
End With
```

This example turns off major gridlines for the category axis.

```
myChart.Axes(xlCategory).HasMajorGridlines = False
```

This example turns off all gridlines for all axes.

```
For Each a In myChart.Axes
   a.HasMajorGridlines = False
   a.HasMinorGridlines = False
Next a
```

Axis Object

Description

Represents a single axis in a chart. The **Axis** object is a member of the **Axes** collection.

Using the Axis Object

Use **Axes(***type*, *group***)**, where *type* is the axis type and *group* is the axis group, to return a single **Axis** object. *Type* can be one of the following **XlAxisType** constants: **xlCategory**, **xlSeries**, or **xlValue**. *Group* can be either of the following **XlAxisGroup** constants: **xlPrimary** or **xlSecondary**. For more information, see the **Axes** method.

The following example sets the text of the category axis title in the chart.

```
With myChart.Axes(xlCategory)
    .HasTitle = True
    .AxisTitle.Caption = "1994"
End With
```

Properties

Application property, **AxisBetweenCategories** property, **AxisGroup** property, **AxisTitle** property, **BaseUnit** property, **BaseUnitIsAuto** property, **Border** property, **CategoryType** property, **Creator** property, **Crosses** property, **CrossesAt** property, **HasMajorGridlines** property, **HasMinorGridlines** property, **HasTitle** property, **Height** property, **Left** property, **MajorGridlines** property, **MajorTickMark** property, **MajorUnit** property, **MajorUnitIsAuto** property, **MajorUnitScale** property, **MaximumScale** property, **MaximumScaleIsAuto** property, **MinimumScale** property, **MinimumScaleIsAuto** property, **MinorGridlines** property, **MinorTickMark** property, **MinorUnit** property, **MinorUnitIsAuto** property, **MinorUnitScale** property, **Parent** property, **ReversePlotOrder** property, **ScaleType** property, **TickLabelPosition** property, **TickLabels** property, **TickLabelSpacing** property, **TickMarkSpacing** property, **Top** property, **Type** property, **Width** property.

Methods

Delete method.

AxisBetweenCategories Property

Applies To

Axis object.

Description

True if the value axis crosses the category axis between categories. Read/write **Boolean**.

Remarks

This property applies only to category axes, and it doesn't apply to 3-D charts.

Example

This example causes the value axis to cross the category axis between categories.

```
myChart.Axes(xlCategory).AxisBetweenCategories = True
```

AxisGroup Property

Applies To

Axis object, **ChartGroup** object, **Series** object.

Description

Returns the group for the specified axis, chart group, or series. Can be one of the following **XlAxisGroup** constants: **xlPrimary** or **xlSecondary**. Read/write **Long** for **Series**; read-only **Long** for **Axis** and **ChartGroup**.

Remarks

For 3-D charts, only **xlPrimary** is valid.

Example

This example deletes the value axis if it's in the secondary group.

```
With myChart.Axes(xlValue)
   If .AxisGroup = xlSecondary Then .Delete
End With
```

AxisTitle Object

Description

Represents the title of an axis in a chart.

Using the AxisTitle Object

Use the **AxisTitle** property to return an **AxisTitle** object. The following example sets the text of the value axis title, sets the font to 10-point Bookman, and formats the word "millions" as italic.

```
With myChart.Axes(xlValue)
   .HasTitle = True
   With .AxisTitle
      .Caption = "Revenue (millions)"
      .Font.Name = "bookman"
      .Font.Size = 10
      .Characters(10, 8).Font.Italic = True
   End With
End With
```

Remarks

The **AxisTitle** object doesn't exist and cannot be used unless the **HasTitle** property for the specified axis is **True**.

Properties

Application property, **AutoScaleFont** property, **Border** property, **Caption** property, **Creator** property, **Fill** property, **Font** property, **HorizontalAlignment** property, **Interior** property, **Left** property, **Name** property, **Orientation** property, **Parent** property, **ReadingOrder** property, **Shadow** property, **Text** property, **Top** property, **VerticalAlignment** property.

Methods

Delete method.

AxisTitle Property

Applies To

Axis object.

Description

Returns an **AxisTitle** object that represents the title of the specified axis. Read-only.

See Also

ChartTitle property, **HasTitle** property.

Example

This example adds an axis label to the category axis in `myChart`.

```
With myChart.Axes(xlCategory)
    .HasTitle = True
    .AxisTitle.Text = "July Sales"
End With
```

BackColor Property

Applies To

ChartFillFormat object.

Description

Returns a **ChartColorFormat** object that represents the fill background color.

Example

This example sets the gradient, background color, and foreground color for the chart area fill.

```
With myChart.ChartArea.Fill
    .Visible = True
    .ForeColor.SchemeColor = 15
    .BackColor.SchemeColor = 17
    .TwoColorGradient msoGradientHorizontal, 1
End With
```

Background Property

Applies To

Font object.

Description

Returns or sets the text background type. Can be one of the following **XlBackground** constants: **xlBackgroundAutomatic**, **xlBackgroundOpaque**, or **xlBackgroundTransparent**. This property is used only for text on charts. Read/write **Long**.

Example

This example adds a chart title and then sets the font size and background type for the title.

```
With myChart
    .HasTitle = True
    .ChartTitle.Text = "1995 Rainfall Totals by Month"
    With .ChartTitle.Font
        .Size = 10
        .Background = xlBackgroundTransparent
    End With
End With
```

Backward Property

Applies To

Trendline object.

Description

Returns or sets the number of periods (or units on a scatter chart) that the trendline extends backward. Read/write **Long**

See Also

Forward property.

Example

This example sets the number of units that the trendline extends forward and backward. The example should be run on a 2-D column chart that contains a single series with a trendline.

```
With myChart.SeriesCollection(1).Trendlines(1)
   .Forward = 5
   .Backward = .5
End With
```

Bar3DGroup Property

Applies To

Chart object.

Description

Returns a **ChartGroup** object that represents the specified bar chart group on a 3-D chart. Read-only.

See Also

BarGroups method.

Example

This example sets the space between bar clusters in the 3-D bar chart group to be 50 percent of the bar width.

```
myChart.BarGroup3DGroup.GapWidth = 50
```

BarGroups Method

Applies To

Chart object.

Description

On a 2-D chart, this method returns an object that represents either a single bar chart group (a **ChartGroup** object, Syntax 1) or a collection of all the bar chart groups (a **ChartGroups** collection, Syntax 2).

Syntax 1

expression.**BarGroups(*Index*)**

Syntax 2

expression.**BarGroups**

expression Required. An expression that returns a **Chart** object.

Index Optional **Variant**. The index number of the specified bar chart group.

See Also

AreaGroups method, **Bar3DGroup** property, **ChartGroups** method, **ColumnGroups** method, **DoughnutGroups** method, **LineGroups** method, **PieGroups** method.

Example

This example sets the space between bar clusters in the 2-D bar chart group to be 50 percent of the bar width.

```
myChart.BarGroups(1).GapWidth = 50
```

BarShape Property

Applies To

Chart object, **Series** object.

Description

Returns or sets the shape used with the specified 3-D bar or column chart. Can be one of the following **XlBarShape** constants: **xlBox**, **xlConeToMax**, **xlConeToPoint**, **xlCylinder**, **xlPyramidToMax**, or **xlPyramidToPoint**. Read/write **Long**.

Example

This example sets the shape used with series one on the chart.

```
myChart.SeriesCollection(1).Barshape = xlConeToPoint
```

BaseUnit Property

Applies To

Axis object.

Description

Returns or sets the base unit for the specified category axis. Can be one of the following **XlTimeUnit** constants: **xlDays**, **xlMonths**, or **xlYears**. Read/write **Long**.

Remarks

Setting this property has no visible effect if the **CategoryType** property for the specified axis is set to **xlCategoryScale**. The set value is retained, however, and takes effect when the **CategoryType** property is set to **xlTimeScale**.

You cannot set this property for a value axis.

See Also

BaseUnitIsAuto property, **CategoryType** property, **MajorUnitScale** property, **MinorUnitScale** property.

Example

This example sets the category axis on the chart to use a time scale, with months as the base unit.

```
With myChart
    With .Axes(xlCategory)
        .CategoryType = xlTimeScale
        .BaseUnit = xlMonths
    End With
End With
```

BaseUnitIsAuto Property

Applies To

Axis object.

Description

True if Microsoft Graph chooses appropriate base units for the specified category axis. The default value is **True**. Read/write **Boolean**.

Remarks

You cannot set this property for a value axis.

See Also

BaseUnit property, **CategoryType** property.

Example

This example sets the category axis on the chart to use a time scale with automatic base units.

```
With myChart
    With .Axes(xlCategory)
        .CategoryType = xlTimeScale
        .BaseUnitIsAuto = True
    End With
End With
```

Bold Property

Applies To

Font object.

Description

True if the font style is bold. Read/write **Variant**.

Example

This example sets the font style to bold for the chart title.

```
myChart.ChartTitle.Font.Bold = True
```

Border Object

Description

Represents the border of the specified object.

Using the Border Object

An object's border is treated as a single entity and is always returned as a unit (in its entirety), regardless of how many sides it has. Use the **Border** property to return the **Border** object. The following example places a dashed border around the chart area and places a dotted border around the plot area.

```
With myChart
    .ChartArea.Border.LineStyle = xlDash
    .PlotArea.Border.LineStyle = xlDot
End With
```

Properties

Application property, **Color** property, **ColorIndex** property, **Creator** property, **LineStyle** property, **Parent** property, **Weight** property.

Border Property

Applies To

Axis object, **AxisTitle** object, **ChartArea** object, **ChartTitle** object, **DataLabel** object, **DataLabels** Collection object, **DataTable** object, **DownBars** object, **DropLines** object, **ErrorBars** object, **Floor** object, **Gridlines** object, **HiLoLines** object, **LeaderLines** object, **Legend** object, **LegendKey** object, **PlotArea** object, **Point** object, **Series** object, **SeriesLines** object, **Trendline** object, **UpBars** object, **Walls** object.

Description

Returns a **Border** object that represents the border of the object. Read-only.

Example

This example sets the color of the chart area border to red.

```
myChart.ChartArea.Border.ColorIndex = 3
```

BubbleScale Property

Applies To

ChartGroup object.

Description

Returns or sets the scale factor for bubbles in the specified chart group. Can be an integer value from 0 (zero) to 300, corresponding to a percentage of the default size. Applies only to bubble charts. Read/write **Long**.

Example

This example sets the bubble size in chart group one to 200 percent of the default size.

```
With myChart
    .ChartGroups(1).BubbleScale = 200
End With
```

CapitalizeNamesOfDays Property

Applies To

AutoCorrect object.

Description

True if the first letter of day names is capitalized automatically. Read/write **Boolean**.

Example

This example sets Microsoft Graph to capitalize the first letter of the names of days.

```
With myChart.Application.AutoCorrect
    .CapitalizeNamesOfDays = True
    .ReplaceText = True
End With
```

Caption Property

Applies To

AxisTitle object, **ChartTitle** object, **DataLabel** object.

Description

Returns text with one of several different meanings, depending on the object type to which **Caption** is applied. Read/write **String**.

Object type	Meaning
AxisTitle	The axis title text
ChartTitle	The chart title text
DataLabel	The data label text

See Also

Text property.

Example

This example adds the title "Annual Salary Figures" to the chart.

```
myChart.HasTitle = True
myChart.ChartTitle.Caption = "Annual Salary Figures"
```

CategoryType Property

Applies To

Axis object.

Description

Returns or sets the category axis type. Can be one of the following **XlCategoryType** constants: **xlCategoryScale**, **xlTimeScale**, or **xlAutomaticScale**. Read/write **Long**.

Remarks

You cannot set this property for a value axis.

See Also

BaseUnit property, **BaseUnitIsAuto** property, **MajorUnitScale** property, **MinorUnitScale** property, **Type** property.

Example

This example sets the category axis on the chart to use a time scale, with months as the base unit.

```
With myChart
    With .Axes(xlCategory)
        .CategoryType = xlTimeScale
        .BaseUnit = xlMonths
    End With
End With
```

CellDragAndDrop Property

Applies To

Application object.

Description

True if dragging and dropping cells is enabled. Read/write **Boolean**.

Example

This example enables dragging and dropping cells.

```
myChart.Application.CellDragAndDrop = True
```

Cells Property

Applies To

DataSheet object, **Range** object.

Description

Range object: Returns a **Range** object that represents the cells in the specified range. Read-only.

DataSheet object: Returns a **Range** object that represents all the cells on the datasheet (not just the cells that are currently in use). Read-only.

See Also

Range property.

Example

This example clears the formula in cell A1 on the datasheet. Note that on the datasheet, column A is the second column and row 1 is the second row.

```
myChart.Application.DataSheet.Cells(2,2).ClearContents
```

This example loops through cells A1:I3 on the datasheet. If any of these cells contains a value less than 0.001, the example replaces that value with 0 (zero).

```
Set mySheet = myChart.Application.DataSheet
For rwIndex = 2 to 4
    For colIndex = 2 to 10
        If mySheet.Cells(rwIndex, colIndex) < .001 Then
            mySheet.Cells(rwIndex, colIndex).Value = 0
        End If
    Next colIndex
Next rwIndex
```

Chart Method

Applies To

Application object.

Description

Returns a **Chart** object that represents the Microsoft Graph chart.

Chart Object

Description

Represents the specified Microsoft Graph chart.

Using the Chart Object

Use the **Chart** property to return a **Chart** object. Most of the time, you'll create a reference to a Microsoft Graph chart and then use the reference in your code.

Properties

Application property, **Area3DGroup** property, **AutoScaling** property, **Bar3DGroup** property, **BarShape** property, **ChartArea** property, **ChartTitle** property, **ChartType** property, **Column3DGroup** property, **CommandBars** property, **Corners** property, **Creator** property, **DataTable** property, **DepthPercent** property, **DisplayBlanksAs** property, **Elevation** property, **Floor** property, **GapDepth** property, **HasAxis** property, **HasDataTable** property, **HasLegend** property, **HasTitle** property, **Height** property, **HeightPercent** property, **Left** property, **Legend** property, **Line3DGroup** property, **Name** property, **Parent** property, **Perspective** property, **Pie3DGroup** property, **PlotArea** property, **RightAngleAxes** property, **Rotation** property, **SurfaceGroup** property, **Top** property, **Walls** property, **WallsAndGridlines2D** property, **Width** property.

Methods

Activate method, **ApplyCustomType** method, **ApplyDataLabels** method, **AreaGroups** method, **Axes** method, **BarGroups** method, **ChartGroups** method, **ColumnGroups** method, **Deselect** method, **DoughnutGroups** method, **Export** method, **LineGroups** method, **PieGroups** method, **RadarGroups** method, **Refresh** method, **SeriesCollection** method, **XYGroups** method.

ChartArea Object

Description

Represents the chart area of the specified chart. The chart area in a 2-D chart contains the axes, the chart title, the axis titles, and the legend. The chart area in a 3-D chart contains the chart title and the legend; it doesn't include the plot area (the area within the chart area where the data is plotted). For information about formatting the plot area, see the **PlotArea** object.

Using the ChartArea Object

Use the **ChartArea** property to return the **ChartArea** object. The following example sets the pattern for the chart area.

```
myChart.ChartArea.Interior.Pattern = xlLightDown
```

Properties

Application property, **AutoScaleFont** property, **Border** property, **Creator** property, **Fill** property, **Font** property, **Height** property, **Interior** property, **Left** property, **Name** property, **Parent** property, **Shadow** property, **Top** property, **Width** property.

Methods

Clear method, **ClearContents** method, **ClearFormats** method, **Copy** method.

ChartArea Property

Applies To

Chart object.

Description

Returns a **ChartArea** object that represents the complete chart area for the chart. Read-only.

Example

This example sets the chart area interior color of `myChart` to red and sets the border color to blue.

```
With myChart.ChartArea
    .Interior.ColorIndex = 3
    .Border.ColorIndex = 5
End With
```

ChartColorFormat Object

Description

Represents a foreground or background color.

Using the ChartColorFormat Object

Use the **ForeColor** property to return a **ChartColorFormat** object that represents the foreground fill color. Use the **BackColor** property to return the background fill color. Use the **RGB** property to return the color as an explicit red-green-blue value, and use the **SchemeColor** property to return or set the color as one of the colors in the current color scheme. The following example sets the foreground color, background color, and gradient for the chart area fill in `myChart`.

```
With myChart.ChartArea.Fill
    .Visible = True
    .ForeColor.SchemeColor = 15
    .BackColor.SchemeColor = 17
    .TwoColorGradient msoGradientHorizontal, 1
End With
```

Properties

Application property, **Creator** property, **Parent** property, **RGB** property, **SchemeColor** property, **Type** property.

ChartFillFormat Object

Description

Represents fill formatting.

Using the ChartFillFormat Object

Use the **Fill** property to return the **ChartFillFormat** object. The following example sets the foreground color, background color, and gradient for the chart area fill in myChart.

```
With myChart.ChartArea.Fill
    .Visible = True
    .ForeColor.SchemeColor = 15
    .BackColor.SchemeColor = 17
    .TwoColorGradient msoGradientHorizontal, 1
End With
```

Properties

Application property, **BackColor** property, **Creator** property, **ForeColor** property, **GradientColorType** property, **GradientDegree** property, **GradientStyle** property, **GradientVariant** property, **Parent** property, **Pattern** property, **PresetGradientType** property, **PresetTexture** property, **TextureName** property, **TextureType** property, **Type** property, **Visible** property.

Methods

OneColorGradient method, **Patterned** method, **PresetGradient** method, **PresetTextured** method, **Solid** method, **TwoColorGradient** method, **UserPicture** method, **UserTextured** method.

ChartGroup Object

Description

Represents one or more series of points plotted in a chart with the same format. A chart contains one or more chart groups, each chart group contains one or more series, and each series contains one or more points. For example, a single chart might contain both a line chart group, which contains all the series plotted with the line chart format, and a bar chart group, which contains all the series plotted with the bar chart format. The **ChartGroup** object is a member of the **ChartGroups** collection.

Using the ChartGroup Object

Use **ChartGroups**(*index*), where *index* is the chart group's index number, to return a single **ChartGroup** object. The following example adds drop lines to chart group one in the chart.

```
myChart.ChartGroups(1).HasDropLines = True
```

Because the index number for a particular chart group can change if the chart format used for that group is changed, it may be easier to use one of the named shortcut methods for chart groups to return a particular chart group. The **PieGroups** method returns the collection of pie chart groups in a chart, the **LineGroups** method returns the collection of all the line chart groups, and so on. You can use each of these methods with an index number to return a single **ChartGroup** object, or you can use each one without an index number to return a **ChartGroups** collection. The following methods are available for chart groups:

- **AreaGroups** method
- **BarGroups** method
- **ColumnGroups** method
- **DoughnutGroups** method
- **LineGroups** method
- **PieGroups** method

Properties

Application property, **AxisGroup** property, **BubbleScale** property, **Creator** property, **DoughnutHoleSize** property, **DownBars** property, **DropLines** property, **FirstSliceAngle** property, **GapWidth** property, **Has3DShading** property, **HasDropLines** property, **HasHiLoLines** property, **HasRadarAxisLabels** property, **HasSeriesLines** property, **HasUpDownBars** property, **HiLoLines** property, **Index** property, **Overlap** property, **Parent** property, **RadarAxisLabels** property, **SecondPlotSize** property, **SeriesLines** property, **ShowNegativeBubbles** property, **SizeRepresents** property, **SplitType** property, **SplitValue** property, **UpBars** property, **VaryByCategories** property.

Methods

SeriesCollection method.

ChartGroups Collection Object

Description

A collection of all the **ChartGroup** objects in the specified chart. Each **ChartGroup** object represents one or more series plotted with the same format in a chart. A chart contains one or more chart groups, each chart group contains one or more series, and each series contains one or more points. For example, a single chart might contain both a line chart group, containing all the series plotted with the line chart format, and a bar chart group, containing all the series plotted with the bar chart format.

Using the ChartGroups Collection

Use the **ChartGroups** method to return the **ChartGroups** collection. The following example displays the number of chart groups in the chart.

```
MsgBox myChart.ChartGroups.Count
```

Use **ChartGroups**(*index*), where *index* is the chart group's index number, to return a single **ChartGroup** object. The following example adds drop lines to chart group one in the chart.

```
myChart.ChartGroups(1).HasDropLines = True
```

Because the index number for a particular chart group can change if the chart format used for that group is changed, it may be easier to use one of the named chart-group shortcut methods to return a particular chart group. The **PieGroups** method returns the collection of pie chart groups in the specified chart, the **LineGroups** method returns the collection of line chart groups, and so on. Each of these methods can be used with an index number to return a single **ChartGroup** object, or used without an index number to return a **ChartGroups** collection. The following methods are available for chart groups:

- **AreaGroups** method
- **BarGroups** method
- **ColumnGroups** method
- **DoughnutGroups** method
- **LineGroups** method
- **PieGroups** method

Properties

Application property, **Count** property, **Creator** property, **Parent** property.

Methods

Item method.

ChartGroups Method

Applies To

Chart object.

Description

Returns an object that represents either a single chart group (a **ChartGroup** object, Syntax 1) or a collection of all the chart groups in the chart (a **ChartGroups** object, Syntax 2). The returned collection includes every type of group.

Syntax 1

expression.**ChartGroups(*Index*)**

Syntax 2

expression.**ChartGroups**

expression   Required. An expression that returns a **Chart** object.

Index   Optional **Variant**. The chart group number.

See Also

AreaGroups method, **BarGroups** method, **ColumnGroups** method, **DoughnutGroups** method, **LineGroups** method, **PieGroups** method.

Example

This example turns on up and down bars for chart group one and then sets their colors. The example should be run on a 2-D line chart containing two series that intersect at one or more data points.

```
With myChart.ChartGroups(1)
    .HasUpDownBars = True
    .DownBars.Interior.ColorIndex = 3
    .UpBars.Interior.ColorIndex = 5
End With
```

ChartTitle Object

Description

Represents the title of the specified chart.

Using the ChartTitle Object

Use the **ChartTitle** property to return the **ChartTitle** object. The following example adds a title to the chart.

```
With myChart
    .HasTitle = True
    .ChartTitle.Text = "February Sales"
End With
```

Remarks

The **ChartTitle** object doesn't exist and cannot be used unless the **HasTitle** property for the chart is **True**.

Properties

Application property, **AutoScaleFont** property, **Border** property, **Caption** property, **Creator** property, **Fill** property, **Font** property, **HorizontalAlignment** property, **Interior** property, **Left** property, **Name** property, **Orientation** property, **Parent** property, **ReadingOrder** property, **Shadow** property, **Text** property, **Top** property, **VerticalAlignment** property.

Methods

Delete method.

ChartTitle Property

Applies To

Chart object.

Description

Returns a **ChartTitle** object that represents the title of the specified chart. Read-only.

See Also

AxisTitle property, **HasTitle** property.

Example

This example sets the text for the title of the chart.

```
With myChart
   .HasTitle = True
   .ChartTitle.Text = "First Quarter Sales"
End With
```

ChartType Property

Applies To

Chart object, **Series** object.

Description

Returns or sets the chart type. Read/write **Long**.

Can be one of the following **XlChartType** constants.

Chart type	Description	Constant
Column	Clustered Column	**xlColumnClustered**
	3-D Clustered Column	**xl3DColumnClustered**
	Stacked Column	**xlColumnStacked**
	3-D Stacked Column	**xl3DColumnStacked**
	100% Stacked Column	**xlColumnStacked100**
	3-D 100% Stacked Column	**xl3DColumnStacked100**
	3-D Column	**xl3DColumn**
Bar	Clustered Bar	**xlBarClustered**
	3-D Clustered Bar	**xl3DBarClustered**
	Stacked Bar	**xlBarStacked**
	3-D Stacked Bar	**xl3DBarStacked**
	100% Stacked Bar	**xlBarStacked100**
	3-D 100% Stacked Bar	**xl3DBarStacked100**

(continue)

Line	Line	**xlLine**
	Line with Data Markers	**xlLineMarkers**
	Stacked Line	**xlLineStacked**
	Stacked Line with Data Markers	**xlLineMarkersStacked**
	100% Stacked Line	**xlLineStacked100**
	100% Stacked Line with Data Markers	**xlLineMarkersStacked100**
	3-D Line	**xl3DLine**
Pie	Pie	**xlPie**
	Exploded Pie	**xlPieExploded**
	3-D Pie	**xl3DPie**
	Exploded 3-D Pie	**xl3DPieExploded**
	Pie of Pie	**xlPieOfPie**
	Bar of Pie	**xlBarOfPie**
XY (Scatter)	Scatter	**xlXYScatter**
	Scatter with Smoothed Lines	**xlXYScatterSmooth**
	Scatter with Smoothed Lines and No Data Markers	**xlXYScatterSmoothNoMarkers**
	Scatter with Lines	**xlXYScatterLines**
	Scatter with Lines and No Data Markers	**xlXYScatterLinesNoMarkers**
Bubble	Bubble	**xlBubble**
	Bubble with 3-D Effects	**xlBubble3DEffect**
Area	Area	**xlArea**
	3-D Area	**xl3DArea**
	Stacked Area	**xlAreaStacked**
	3-D Stacked Area	**xl3DAreaStacked**
	100% Stacked Area	**xlAreaStacked100**
	3-D 100% Stacked Area	**xl3DAreaStacked100**
Doughnut	Doughnut	**xlDoughnut**
	Exploded Doughnut	**xlDoughnutExploded**
Radar	Radar	**xlRadar**
	Radar with Data Markers	**xlRadarMarkers**
	Filled Radar	**xlRadarFilled**
Surface	3-D Surface	**xlSurface**
	Surface (Top View)	**xlSurfaceTopView**
	3-D Surface (wire-frame)	**xlSurfaceWireframe**
	Surface (Top View wire-frame)	**xlSurfaceTopViewWireframe**

(continue)

Chart type	Description	Constant
Stock Quotes	High-Low-Close	**xlStockHLC**
	Volume-High-Low-Close	**xlStockVHLC**
	Open-High-Low-Close	**xlStockOHLC**
	Volume-Open-High-Low-Close	**xlStockVOHLC**
Cylinder	Clustered Cylinder Column	**xlCylinderColClustered**
	Clustered Cylinder Bar	**xlCylinderBarClustered**
	Stacked Cylinder Column	**xlCylinderColStacked**
	Stacked Cylinder Bar	**xlCylinderBarStacked**
	100% Stacked Cylinder Column	**xlCylinderColStacked100**
	100% Stacked Cylinder Bar	**xlCylinderBarStacked100**
	3-D Cylinder Column	**xlCylinderCol**
Cone	Clustered Cone Column	**xlConeColClustered**
	Clustered Cone Bar	**xlConeBarClustered**
	Stacked Cone Column	**xlConeColStacked**
	Stacked Cone Bar	**xlConeBarStacked**
	100% Stacked Cone Column	**xlConeColStacked100**
	100% Stacked Cone Bar	**xlConeBarStacked100**
	3-D Cone Column	**xlConeCol**
Pyramid	Clustered Pyramid Column	**xlPyramidColClustered**
	Clustered Pyramid Bar	**xlPyramidBarClustered**
	Stacked Pyramid Column	**xlPyramidColStacked**
	Stacked Pyramid Bar	**xlPyramidBarStacked**
	100% Stacked Pyramid Column	**xlPyramidColStacked100**
	100% Stacked Pyramid Bar	**xlPyramidBarStacked100**
	3-D Pyramid Column	**xlPyramidCol**

See Also

Type property.

Example

This example sets the bubble size in chart group one to 200 percent of the default size if the chart is a 2-D bubble chart.

```
With myChart
   If .ChartType = xlBubble Then
      .ChartGroups(1).BubbleScale = 200
   End If
End With
```

Clear Method

Applies To

ChartArea object, **Legend** object, **Range** object.

Description

Clears the entire range or chart area.

Syntax

expression.**Clear**

expression Required. An expression that returns a **ChartArea** or **Range** object.

See Also

ClearContents method, **ClearFormats** method.

Example

This example clears the formulas and formatting in cells A1:G37 on the datasheet.

```
myChart.Application.DataSheet.Range("A1:G37").Clear
```

This example clears the chart area (the chart data and formatting) of `myChart`.

```
myChart.ChartArea.Clear
```

ClearContents Method

Applies To

ChartArea object, **Range** object.

Description

Clears the formulas from the range. Clears the data from a chart but leaves the formatting.

Syntax

expression.**ClearContents**

expression Required. An expression that returns a **ChartArea** or **Range** object.

Example

This example clears the formulas from cells A1:G37 on the datasheet but leaves the formatting intact.

```
myChart.Application.DataSheet.Range("A1:G37").ClearContents
```

This example clears the chart data from a chart but leaves the formatting intact.

```
myChart.ChartArea.ClearContents
```

ClearFormats Method

Applies To

ChartArea object, **ErrorBars** object, **Floor** object, **LegendKey** object, **PlotArea** object, **Point** object, **Range** object, **Series** object, **Trendline** object, **Walls** object.

Description

Clears the formatting of the object.

Syntax

expression.**ClearFormats**

expression Required. An expression that returns an object in the Applies To list.

See Also

Clear method, **ClearContents** method.

Example

This example clears all formatting from cells A1:G37 on the datasheet.

```
myChart.Application.DataSheet.Range("A1:G37").ClearFormats
```

This example clears the formatting from the chart.

```
myChart.ChartArea.ClearFormats
```

Color Property

Applies To

Border object, **Font** object, **Interior** object.

Description

Returns or sets the primary color of the object, as shown in the following table. Use the **RGB** function to create a color value. Read/write **Long**.

Object	Color
Border	The color of the border.
Font	The color of the font.
Interior	The cell shading color or the drawing object fill color.

Example

This example sets the color of the tick-mark labels on the value axis.

```
myChart.Axes(xlValue).TickLabels.Font.Color = RGB(0, 255, 0)
```

ColorIndex Property

Applies To

Border object, **Font** object, **Interior** object.

Description

Returns or sets the color of the border or interior, as shown in the following table. The color is specified as an index value into the current color palette, or as one of the following **XlColorIndex** constants: **xlColorIndexAutomatic** or **xlColorIndexNone**. Read/write **Variant**.

Object	Description
Border	The color of the border.
Interior	The color of the interior fill. Set **ColorIndex** to **xlColorIndexNone** to specify that you don't want an interior fill. Set **ColorIndex** to **xlColorIndexAutomatic** to specify the automatic fill (for drawing objects).

Remarks

This property specifies a color as an index into the color palette. The following table shows the color-index values in the default color palette.

Color	Index value
Aqua	8, 28, 33, 34, 42
Black	1, 51, 52
Blue	5, 32, 41, 49
Fuchsia	7, 26
Gray	16, 46, 47, 48, 56
Green	10, 43
Lime	4
Maroon	9, 30, 53
Navy	11, 25, 55
Olive	12, 44, 45
Purple	13, 18, 21, 29, 54
Red	3
Silver	15, 17, 20, 22, 24, 35, 36, 37, 38, 39
Teal	14, 23, 31, 50
White	2, 19, 40
Yellow	6, 27

See Also

Color property, **PatternColor** property.

Example

The following examples assume that you're using the default color palette.

This example sets the color of the major gridlines for the value axis.

```
With myChart.Axes(xlValue)
   If .HasMajorGridlines Then
      .MajorGridlines.Border.ColorIndex = 5   ' Set color to blue.
   End If
End With
```

This example sets the color of the chart area interior to red and sets the border color to blue.

```
With myChart.ChartArea
   .Interior.ColorIndex = 3
   .Border.ColorIndex = 5
End With
```

Column3DGroup Property

Applies To

Chart object.

Description

Returns a **ChartGroup** object that represents the specified column chart group on a 3-D chart. Read-only.

See Also

ColumnGroups method.

Example

This example sets the space between column clusters in the 3-D column chart group to be 50 percent of the column width.

```
myChart.Column3DGroup.GapWidth = 50
```

ColumnGroups Method

Applies To

Chart object.

Description

On a 2-D chart, returns an object that represents either a single column chart group (a **ChartGroup** object, Syntax 1) or a collection of the column chart groups (a **ChartGroups** collection, Syntax 2).

Syntax 1

expression.**ColumnGroups(*Index*)**

Syntax 2

expression.**ColumnGroups**

expression Required. An expression that returns a **Chart** object.

Index Optional **Variant**. The index number of the specified column chart group.

See Also

AreaGroups method, **BarGroups** method, **ChartGroups** method, **Column3DGroup** property, **DoughnutGroups** method, **LineGroups** method, **PieGroups** method.

Example

This example sets the space between column clusters in the 2-D column chart group to be 50 percent of the column width.

```
myChart.ColumnGroups(1).GapWidth = 50
```

Columns Property

Applies To

DataSheet object, **Range** object.

Description

Range object: Returns a **Range** object that represents the columns in the specified range. Read-only.

DataSheet object: Returns a **Range** object that represents all the columns on the datasheet. Read-only.

See Also

Range property, **Rows** property.

Example

This example clears column A of the datasheet.

```
myChart.Application.DataSheet.Columns(2).ClearContents
```

ColumnWidth Property

Applies To

Range object.

Description

Returns or sets the width of all columns in the specified range. Read/write **Variant**.

Remarks

One unit of column width is equal to the width of one character in the Normal style. For proportional fonts, the width of the character 0 (zero) is used.

If all columns in the range have the same width, the **ColumnWidth** property returns the width. If columns in the range have different widths, this property returns **Null**.

Example

This example doubles the width of column A on the datasheet.

```
With myChart.Application.DataSheet.Columns("A")
   .ColumnWidth = .ColumnWidth * 2
End With
```

CommandBars Property

Applies To

Application object, **Chart** object.

Description

Returns a **CommandBars** object that represents the Microsoft Graph command bars. Read-only.

Example

This example deletes all custom command bars that aren't visible.

```
For Each bar In myChart.Application.CommandBars
   If Not bar.BuiltIn And Not bar.Visible Then bar.Delete
Next
```

Copy Method

Applies To

ChartArea object, **Range** object.

Description

Syntax 1: Copies the object to the Clipboard. Copies a picture of the point or series to the Clipboard.

Syntax 2: Copies the **Range** to the specified range or to the Clipboard.

Syntax 1

expression.**Copy**

Syntax 2

expression.**Copy(*Destination*)**

expression   Required. An expression that returns an object in the Applies To list.

Destination   Optional **Variant**. Specifies the new range to which the specified range will be copied. If this argument is omitted, Microsoft Graph copies the range to the Clipboard.

See Also

Paste method.

Example

This example copies the formulas in cells A1:D4 on the datasheet into cells E5:H8.

```
Set mySheet = myChart.Application.DataSheet
mySheet.Range("A1:D4").Copy _
   Destination:= mySheet.Range("E5")
```

Corners Object

Description

Represents the corners of the specified 3-D chart. This object isn't a collection.

Using the Corners Object

Use the **Corners** property to return the **Corners** object. The following example selects the corners of the chart.

```
myChart.Corners.Select
```

If the chart isn't a 3-D chart, the **Corners** property fails.

Properties

Application property, **Creator** property, **Name** property, **Parent** property.

Corners Property

Applies To

Chart object.

Description

Returns a **Corners** object that represents the corners of the specified 3-D chart. Read-only.

CorrectCapsLock Property

Applies To

AutoCorrect object.

Description

True if Microsoft Graph automatically corrects accidental use of the CAPS LOCK key. Read/write **Boolean**.

Example

This example enables Microsoft Graph to automatically correct accidental use of the CAPS LOCK key.

```
myChart.Application.AutoCorrect.CorrectCapsLock = True
```

CorrectSentenceCap Property

Applies To

AutoCorrect object.

Description

True if Microsoft Graph automatically corrects sentence (first word) capitalization. Read/write **Boolean**.

Example

This example enables Microsoft Graph to automatically correct sentence capitalization.

```
myChart.Application.AutoCorrect.CorrectSentenceCap = True
```

Count Property

Applies To

Axes Collection object, **ChartGroups** Collection object, **DataLabels** Collection object, **LegendEntries** Collection object, **Points** Collection object, **SeriesCollection** Collection object, **Trendlines** Collection object.

Description

Returns the number of objects in the specified collection. Read-only **Long**.

Example

This example displays the number of chart groups in the chart.

```
MsgBox "The chart contains " & myChart.ChartGroups.Count & " chart groups."
```

Creator Property

Applies To

Application object, **AutoCorrect** object, **Axes** Collection object, **Axis** object, **AxisTitle** object, **Border** object, **Chart** object, **ChartArea** object, **ChartColorFormat** object, **ChartFillFormat** object, **ChartGroup** object, **ChartGroups** Collection object, **ChartTitle** object, **Corners** object, **DataLabel** object, **DataLabels** Collection object, **DataSheet** object, **DataTable** object, **DownBars** object, **DropLines** object, **ErrorBars** object, **Floor** object, **Font** object,

Gridlines object, **HiLoLines** object, **Interior** object, **LeaderLines** object, **Legend** object, **LegendEntries** Collection object, **LegendEntry** object, **LegendKey** object, **PlotArea** object, **Point** object, **Points** Collection object, **Range** object, **Series** object, **SeriesCollection** Collection object, **SeriesLines** object, **TickLabels** object, **Trendline** object, **Trendlines** Collection object, **UpBars** object, **Walls** object.

Description

Returns a 32-bit integer that indicates the application in which this object was created. If the object was created in Microsoft Graph, this property returns the string MSGR, which is equivalent to the hexadecimal number 4D534752. Read-only **Long**.

Remarks

The **Creator** property is designed to be used in Microsoft Graph for the Macintosh, where each application has a four-character creator code.

See Also

Application property.

Example

This example displays a message about the creator of `myChart`.

```
If myChart.Creator = &h4D534752 Then
   MsgBox "This is a Microsoft Graph object"
Else
   MsgBox "This is not a Microsoft Graph object"
End If
```

Crosses Property

Applies To

Axis object.

Description

Returns or sets the point on the specified axis where the other axis crosses. Read/write **Long**.

Can be one of the following **XlAxisCrosses** constants.

Constant	Meaning
xlAxisCrossesAutomatic	Microsoft Graph sets the axis crossing point.
xlMinimum	The axis crosses at the minimum value.
xlMaximum	The axis crosses at the maximum value.
xlAxisCrossesCustom	The **CrossesAt** property specifies the axis crossing point.

Remarks

This property isn't available for 3-D charts or radar charts.

This property can be used for both category and value axes. On the category axis, **xlMinimum** sets the value axis to cross at the first category, and **xlMaximum** sets the value axis to cross at the last category.

Note that **xlMinimum** and **xlMaximum** can have different meanings, depending on the axis.

See Also

CrossesAt property.

Example

This example sets the value axis to cross the category axis at the maximum x value.

```
myChart.Axes(xlCategory).Crosses = xlMaximum
```

CrossesAt Property

Applies To

Axis object.

Description

Returns or sets the point on the value axis where the category axis crosses it. Applies only to the value axis. Read/write **Double**.

Remarks

Setting this property causes the **Crosses** property to change to **xlAxisCrossesCustom**.

This property cannot be used on 3-D charts or radar charts.

See Also

Crosses property.

Example

This example sets the category axis to cross the value axis at value 3.

```
With myChart.Axes(xlValue)
    .Crosses = xlAxisCrossesCustom
    .CrossesAt = 3
End With
```

Cut Method

Applies To

Range object.

Description

Cuts the specified range to the Clipboard or pastes it into a specified destination.

Syntax

expression.**Cut**(***Destination***)

expression Required. An expression that returns a **Range** object.

Destination Optional **Variant**. The range where the object should be pasted. If this argument is omitted, the object is cut to the Clipboard.

See Also

Copy method, **Paste** method.

Example

This example cuts the range A1:G37 on the datasheet and places it on the Clipboard.

```
Set mySheet = myChart.Application.DataSheet
mySheet.Range("A1:G37").Cut
```

DataLabel Object

Description

Represents the data label for the specified point or trendline in a chart. For a series, the **DataLabel** object is a member of the **DataLabels** collection, which contains a **DataLabel** object for each point. For a series without definable points (such as an area series), the **DataLabels** collection contains a single **DataLabel** object.

Using the DataLabel Object

Use **DataLabels**(*index*), where *index* is the data label's index number, to return a single **DataLabel** object. The following example sets the number format for the fifth data label in series one in the chart.

```
myChart.SeriesCollection(1).DataLabels(5).NumberFormat = "0.000"
```

Use the **DataLabel** property to return the **DataLabel** object for a single point. The following example turns on the data label for the second point in series one in the chart, and sets the data label text to "Saturday."

```
With myChart
   With .SeriesCollection(1).Points(2)
      .HasDataLabel = True
      .DataLabel.Text = "Saturday"
   End With
End With
```

For a trendline, the **DataLabel** property returns the text shown with the trendline. This can be the equation, the R-squared value, or both (if both are showing). The following example sets the trendline text to show only the equation and then places the data label text in cell A1 on the datasheet.

```
With myChart.SeriesCollection(1).Trendlines(1)
   .DisplayRSquared = False
   .DisplayEquation = True
```

```
    x = .DataLabel.Text
End With
With myChart.Application.DataSheet
    .Range("A1").Value = x
End With
```

Properties

Application property, **AutoScaleFont** property, **AutoText** property, **Border** property, **Caption** property, **Creator** property, **Fill** property, **Font** property, **HorizontalAlignment** property, **Interior** property, **Left** property, **Name** property, **NumberFormat** property, **Orientation** property, **Parent** property, **Position** property, **ReadingOrder** property, **Shadow** property, **ShowLegendKey** property, **Text** property, **Top** property, **Type** property, **VerticalAlignment** property.

Methods

Delete method.

DataLabel Property

Applies To

Point object, **Trendline** object.

Description

Returns a **DataLabel** object that represents the data label associated with the specified point or trendline. Read-only.

See Also

ApplyDataLabels method, **HasDataLabel** property.

Example

This example turns on the data label for point seven in series three, and then it sets the data label color to blue.

```
With myChart.SeriesCollection(3).Points(7)
    .HasDataLabel = True
    .ApplyDataLabels type:=xlValue
    .DataLabel.Font.ColorIndex = 5
End With
```

DataLabels Collection Object

Description

A collection of all the **DataLabel** objects for the specified series. Each **DataLabel** object represents a data label for a point or trendline. For a series without definable points (such as an area series), the **DataLabels** collection contains a single data label.

Using the DataLabels Collection

Use the **DataLabels** method to return the **DataLabels** collection. The following example sets the number format for data labels in series one in the chart.

```
With myChart.SeriesCollection(1)
    .HasDataLabels = True
    .DataLabels.NumberFormat = "##.##"
End With
```

Use **DataLabels(***index***)**, where *index* is the data label's index number, to return a single **DataLabel** object. The following example sets the number format for the fifth data label in series one in the chart.

```
myChart.SeriesCollection(1).DataLabels(5).NumberFormat = "0.000"
```

Properties

Application property, **AutoScaleFont** property, **AutoText** property, **Border** property, **Count** property, **Creator** property, **Fill** property, **Font** property, **HorizontalAlignment** property, **Interior** property, **Name** property, **NumberFormat** property, **Orientation** property, **Parent** property, **Position** property, **ReadingOrder** property, **Shadow** property, **ShowLegendKey** property, **Type** property, **VerticalAlignment** property.

Methods

Delete method, **Item** method.

DataLabels Method

Applies To

Series object.

Description

Returns an object that represents either a single data label (a **DataLabel** object, Syntax 1) or a collection of all the data labels for the series (a **DataLabels** collection, Syntax 2).

Syntax 1

*expression***.DataLabels(*****Index*****)**

Syntax 2

expression.**DataLabels**

expression Required. An expression that returns a **Series** object.

Index Optional **Variant**. The number of the data label.

See Also

DataLabel property.

Example

This example sets the data labels for series one to show their key, assuming that their values are visible when the example runs.

```
With myChart.SeriesCollection(1)
   .HasDataLabels = True
   With .DataLabels
      .ShowLegendKey = True
      .Type = xlValue
   End With
End With
```

DataSheet Object

Description

Represents the Microsoft Graph datasheet.

Using the DataSheet Object

After you've established a reference to a chart, you can use the **Application** property of the chart to retrieve the datasheet. The following example applies the **DataSheet** property to the **Application** object, and then it applies the **Range** property to the datasheet to set the value of cell A1 to 32.

```
myChart.Application.DataSheet.Range("A1").Value = 32
```

Remarks

On the datasheet, the first column heading (starting on the left) is A, followed by B, C, D, and so on. The first row heading (starting on the left) is 1, followed by 2, 3, 4, and so on. Neither the leftmost column nor the top row has a heading. In other words, column A is actually the second column from the left; likewise, row 1 is the second row from the top. The leftmost column and the top row, which are commonly used for legend text or axis labels, are referred to as column 0 (zero) and row 0 (zero). Thus, the following example inserts the text "Annual Sales" in the top cell in column A (the second column).

```
myChart.Application.DataSheet.Range("A0").Value = "Annual Sales"
```

And the following example inserts the text "District 1" in the leftmost cell in row 2 (the third row).

```
myChart.Application.DataSheet.Range("02").Value = "District 1"
```

Properties

Application property, **Cells** property, **Columns** property, **Creator** property, **Font** property, **Height** property, **Left** property, **Parent** property, **Range** property, **Rows** property, **Top** property, **Width** property.

Methods

Activate method.

DataSheet Property

Applies To

Application object.

Description

Returns the **DataSheet** object. Read-only.

Example

This example sets the value of cell A1 on the datasheet to 3.14159.

```
With myChart.Application
    .DataSheet.Range("A1").Value = 3.14159
End With
```

DataTable Object

Description

Represents a data table in the specified chart.

Using the DataTable Object

Use the **DataTable** property to return a **DataTable** object. The following example adds a data table with an outline border to the embedded chart.

```
With myChart
    .HasDataTable = True
    .DataTable.HasBorderOutline = True
End With
```

Properties

Application property, **AutoScaleFont** property, **Border** property, **Creator** property, **Font** property, **HasBorderHorizontal** property, **HasBorderOutline** property, **HasBorderVertical** property, **Parent** property, **ShowLegendKey** property.

Methods

Delete method.

DataTable Property

Applies To

Chart object.

Description

Returns a **DataTable** object that represents the chart data table. Read-only.

Example

This example adds a data table with an outline border to the chart.

```
With myChart
    .HasDataTable = True
    .DataTable.HasBorderOutline = True
End With
```

Delete Method

Applies To

Axis object, **AxisTitle** object, **ChartTitle** object, **DataLabel** object, **DataLabels** collection object, **DataTable** object, **DownBars** object, **DropLines** object, **ErrorBars** object, **Gridlines** object, **HiLoLines** object, **LeaderLines** object, **Legend** object, **LegendEntry** object, **LegendKey** object, **Point** object, **Range** object, **Series** object, **SeriesLines** object, **TickLabels** object, **Trendline** object, **UpBars** object.

Description

Deletes the specified object. Syntax 2 applies only to **Range** objects.

Syntax 1

expression.**Delete**

Syntax 2

expression.**Delete(*Shift*)**

expression Required. An expression that returns an object in the Applies To list.

Shift Optional **Variant**. Used only with **Range** objects. Specifies how to shift cells to replace deleted cells. Can be one of the following **XlDeleteShiftDirection** constants: **xlShiftToLeft** or **xlShiftUp**. If this argument is omitted, Microsoft Graph decides based on the shape of the range.

Remarks

Deleting a **Point** or **LegendKey** object deletes the entire series.

Example

This example deletes cells A1:D10 on the datasheet and shifts the remaining cells to the left.

```
Set mySheet = myChart.Application.DataSheet
mySheet.Range("A1:D10").Delete Shift:=xlShiftToLeft
```

This example deletes the chart title.

```
myChart.ChartTitle.Delete
```

DeleteChartAutoFormat Method

Applies To

Application object.

Description

Removes a custom chart autoformat from the list of available chart autoformats.

Syntax

expression.**DeleteChartAutoFormat(*Name*)**

expression Required. An expression that returns an **Application** object.

Name Required **String**. The name of the custom autoformat to be removed.

See Also

AddChartAutoFormat method, **SetDefaultChart** method.

Example

This example deletes the custom autoformat named "Presentation Chart."

```
myChart.Application.DeleteChartAutoFormat Name:="Presentation Chart"
```

DeleteReplacement Method

Applies To

AutoCorrect object.

Description

Deletes an entry from the array of AutoCorrect replacements.

Syntax

expression.**DeleteReplacement(*What*)**

expression Required. An expression that returns an **AutoCorrect** object.

What Required **String**. The text to be replaced, as it appears in the row to be deleted from the array of AutoCorrect replacements. If this string doesn't exist in the array of AutoCorrect replacements, this method fails.

See Also

AddReplacement method, **ReplacementList** method.

Example

This example removes the word "Temperature" from the array of AutoCorrect replacements.

```
With myChart.Application.AutoCorrect
    .DeleteReplacement "Temperature"
End With
```

DepthPercent Property

Applies To

Chart object.

Description

Returns or sets the depth of a 3-D chart as a percentage of the chart width (between 20 and 2000 percent). Read/write **Long**.

See Also

HeightPercent property.

Example

This example sets the depth of the chart to be 50 percent of its width. The example should be run on a 3-D chart (the **DepthPercent** property fails on 2-D charts).

```
myChart.DepthPercent = 50
```

Deselect Method

Applies To

Chart object.

Description

Cancels the selection for the chart.

Syntax

expression.**Deselect**

expression Required. An expression that returns a **Chart** object.

Example

This example is equivalent to pressing ESC while working on the chart. The example should be run on a chart that has a component (such as an axis) selected.

```
myChart.Deselect
```

DisplayAlerts Property

Applies To

Application object.

Description

True if Microsoft Graph displays certain alerts and messages while a macro is running. Read/write **Boolean**.

Remarks

The default value is **True**. Set this property to **False** if you don't want to be disturbed by prompts and alert messages while a macro is running; any time a message requires a response, Microsoft Graph chooses the default response.

If you set this property to **False**, Microsoft Graph doesn't automatically set it back to **True** when your macro stops running. Write your macro such that it always sets this property back to **True** when it stops running.

DisplayBlanksAs Property

Applies To

Chart object.

Description

Returns or sets the way that blank cells are plotted on a chart. Can be one of the following **XlDisplayBlanksAs** constants: **xlNotPlotted**, **xlInterpolated**, or **xlZero**. Read/write **Long**.

Example

This example sets Microsoft Graph to not plot blank cells.

```
myChart.DisplayBlanksAs = xlNotPlotted
```

DisplayEquation Property

Applies To

Trendline object.

Description

True if the equation for the trendline is displayed on the chart (in the same data label as the R-squared value). Setting this property to **True** automatically turns on data labels. Read/write **Boolean**.

See Also

Add method, **DisplayRSquared** property.

Example

This example displays the R-squared value and equation for trendline one. The example should be run on a 2-D column chart that has a trendline for the first series.

```
With myChart.SeriesCollection(1).Trendlines(1)
   .DisplayRSquared = True
   .DisplayEquation = True
End With
```

DisplayRSquared Property

Applies To

Trendline object.

Description

True if the R-squared value of the trendline is displayed on the chart (in the same data label as the equation). Setting this property to **True** automatically turns on data labels. Read/write **Boolean**.

See Also

Add method, **DisplayEquation** property.

Example

This example displays the R-squared value and equation for trendline one. The example should be run on a 2-D column chart that has a trendline for the first series.

```
With myChart.SeriesCollection(1).Trendlines(1)
   .DisplayRSquared = True
   .DisplayEquation = True
End With
```

DoughnutGroups Method

Applies To

Chart object.

Description

On a 2-D chart, returns an object that represents either a single doughnut chart group (a **ChartGroup** object, Syntax 1) or a collection of the doughnut chart groups (a **ChartGroups** collection, Syntax 2).

Syntax 1

expression.**DoughnutGroups(*Index*)**

Syntax 2

expression.**DoughnutGroups**

expression Required. An expression that returns a **Chart** object.

Index Optional **Variant**. Specifies the chart group.

See Also

AreaGroups method, **BarGroups** method, **ChartGroups** method, **ColumnGroups** method, **LineGroups** method, **PieGroups** method.

Example

This example sets the starting angle for doughnut group one.

```
myChart.DoughnutGroups(1).FirstSliceAngle = 45
```

DoughnutHoleSize Property

Applies To

ChartGroup object.

Description

Returns or sets the size of the hole in a doughnut chart group. The hole size is expressed as a percentage of the chart size, between 10 and 90 percent. Read/write **Long**.

Example

This example sets the hole size for doughnut group one. The example should be run on a 2-D doughnut chart.

```
myChart.DoughnutGroups(1).DoughnutHoleSize = 10
```

DownBars Object

Description

Represents the down bars in the specified chart group. Down bars connect points in the first series in the chart group with lower values in the last series (the lines go down from the first series). Only 2-D line groups that contain at least two series can have down bars. This object isn't a collection. There's no object that represents a single down bar; either you have up bars and down bars turned on for all points in a chart group or you have them turned off.

Using the DownBars Object

Use the **DownBars** property to return the **DownBars** object. The following example turns on up and down bars for chart group one in the chart. The example then sets the up-bar color to blue and the down-bar color to red.

```
With myChart.ChartGroups(1)
    .HasUpDownBars = True
    .UpBars.Interior.Color = RGB(0, 0, 255)
    .DownBars.Interior.Color = RGB(255, 0, 0)
End With
```

Remarks

If the **HasUpDownBars** property is **False**, most properties of the **DownBars** object are disabled.

Properties

Application property, **Border** property, **Creator** property, **Fill** property, **Interior** property, **Name** property, **Parent** property.

Methods

Delete method.

See Also

UpBars object.

DownBars Property

Applies To

ChartGroup object.

Description

Returns a **DownBars** object that represents the down bars on a line chart. Applies only to line charts. Read-only.

See Also

HasUpDownBars property, **UpBars** property.

Example

This example turns on up bars and down bars for chart group one and then sets their colors. The example should be run on a 2-D line chart that has two series that cross each other at one or more data points.

```
With myChart.ChartGroups(1)
    .HasUpDownBars = True
    .DownBars.Interior.ColorIndex = 3
    .UpBars.Interior.ColorIndex = 5
End With
```

DropLines Object

Description

Represents the drop lines in the specified chart group. Drop lines connect the points in the chart with the x-axis. Only line and area chart groups can have drop lines. This object isn't a collection. There's no object that represents a single drop line; either you have drop lines turned on for all points in a chart group or you have them turned off.

Using the DropLines Object

Use the **DropLines** property to return the **DropLines** object. The following example turns on drop lines for chart group one in the chart and then sets the drop-line color to red.

```
myChart.ChartGroups(1).HasDropLines = True
myChart.ChartGroups(1).DropLines.Border.ColorIndex = 3
```

Remarks

If the **HasDropLines** property is **False**, most properties of the **DropLines** object are disabled.

Properties

Application property, **Border** property, **Creator** property, **Name** property, **Parent** property.

Methods

Delete method.

DropLines Property

Applies To

ChartGroup object.

Description

Returns a **DropLines** object that represents the drop lines for a series on a line chart or area chart. Applies only to line charts or area charts. Read-only.

See Also

HasDropLines property.

Example

This example turns on drop lines for chart group one and then sets their line style, weight, and color. The example should be run on a 2-D line chart that has one series.

```
With myChart.ChartGroups(1)
   .HasDropLines = True
   With .DropLines.Border
      .LineStyle = xlThin
      .Weight = xlMedium
      .ColorIndex = 3
   End With
End With
```

Elevation Property

Applies To

Chart object.

Description

Returns or sets the elevation of the 3-D chart view, in degrees. Read/write **Long**.

Remarks

The chart elevation is the height at which you view the chart, in degrees. The default is 15 for most chart types. The value of this property must be between -90 and 90, except for 3-D bar charts, where it must be between 0 and 44.

See Also

Perspective property, **Rotation** property.

Example

This example sets the chart elevation to 34 degrees. The example should be run on a 3-D chart (the **Elevation** property fails on 2-D charts).

```
myChart.Elevation = 34
```

EndStyle Property

Applies To

ErrorBars object.

Description

Returns or sets the end style for the error bars. Can be one of the following **XlEndStyleCap** constants: **xlCap** or **xlNoCap**. Read/write **Long**.

Example

This example sets the end style for the error bars for series one. The example should be run on a 2-D line chart that has Y error bars for the first series.

```
myChart.SeriesCollection(1).ErrorBars.EndStyle = xlCap
```

ErrorBar Method

Applies To

Series object.

Description

Applies error bars to the specified series.

Syntax

expression.**ErrorBar(*Direction, Include, Type, Amount, MinusValues*)**

expression Required. An expression that returns a **Series** object.

Direction Optional **Variant**. The error bar direction. Can be one of the following **XlErrorBarDirection** constants: **xlX** or **xlY**. **xlX** can only be used with scatter charts. The default value is **xlY**.

Include Optional **Variant**. The error bar parts to be included. Can be one of the following **XlErrorBarInclude** constants: **xlErrorBarIncludePlusValues**, **xlErrorBarIncludeMinusValues**, **xlErrorBarIncludeNone**, or **xlErrorBarIncludeBoth**. The default value is **xlErrorBarIncludeBoth**.

Type Optional **Variant**. The error bar type. Can be one of the following **XlErrorBarType** constants: **xlErrorBarTypeFixedValue**, **xlErrorBarTypePercent**, **xlErrorBarTypeStDev**, **xlErrorBarTypeStError**, or **xlErrorBarTypeCustom**.

Amount Optional **Variant**. The error amount. Used for only the positive error amount when ***Type*** is **xlErrorBarTypeCustom**.

MinusValues Optional **Variant**. The negative error amount when ***Type*** is **xlErrorBarTypeCustom**.

See Also

ErrorBars property, **HasErrorBars** property.

Example

This example applies standard error bars in the Y direction for series one. The error bars are applied in the positive and negative directions. The example should be run on a 2-D line chart.

```
myChart.SeriesCollection(1).ErrorBar _
    Direction:=xlY, Include:=xlErrorBarIncludeBoth, _
    Type:=xlErrorBarTypeStError
```

ErrorBars Object

Description

Represents the error bars for the specified chart series. Error bars indicate the degree of uncertainty for chart data. Only series in area, bar, column, line, and scatter groups in a 2-D chart can have error bars. Only series in scatter groups can have x and y error bars.

This object isn't a collection. There's no object that represents a single error bar; either you have x error bars or y error bars turned on for all points in a series or you have them turned off.

Using the ErrorBars Object

Use the **ErrorBars** property to return the **ErrorBars** object. The following example turns on error bars for series one in `myChart` and then sets the end style for the error bars.

```
myChart.SeriesCollection(1).HasErrorBars = True
myChart.SeriesCollection(1).ErrorBars.EndStyle = xlNoCap
```

Remarks

The **ErrorBar** method changes the format and type of error bars.

Properties

Application property, **Border** property, **Creator** property, **EndStyle** property, **Name** property, **Parent** property.

Methods

ClearFormats method, **Delete** method.

ErrorBars Property

Applies To

Series object.

Description

Returns an **ErrorBars** object that represents the error bars for the series. Read-only.

See Also

ErrorBar method, **HasErrorBars** property.

Example

This example sets the error bar color for series one. The example should be run on a 2-D line chart that has error bars for series one.

```
With myChart.SeriesCollection(1)
    .ErrorBars.Border.ColorIndex = 8
End With
```

Evaluate Method

Applies To

Application object.

Description

Converts a Microsoft Graph name to an object or a value.

Syntax

expression.**Evaluate**(*Name*)

expression Required. An expression that returns a Microsoft Graph **Application** object.

Name Required **String**. The name of the specified object, using the Microsoft Graph naming convention.

Remarks

You can use the following types of names in Microsoft Graph with this method:

- A1-style references. You can use any reference to a single cell in A1-style notation. All references are considered to be absolute references.
- Ranges. You can use the range, intersect, and union operators (colon, space, and comma, respectively) with references.

- Defined names. You can specify any name in the language of the macro.

Note Using square brackets (for example, "[A1:C5]") is identical to calling the **Evaluate** method with a string argument. For example, the following expressions are equivalent:

```
myChart.Application.[a1].Value = 25
myChart.Application.Evaluate("A1").Value = 25
```

The advantage of using square brackets is that the code is shorter. The advantage of using **Evaluate** is that the argument is a string, so you can either construct the string in your code or use a Visual Basic variable.

Example

This example clears cell A1 on the datasheet.

```
clearCell = "A1"
myChart.Application.Evaluate(clearCell).Clear
```

Explosion Property

Applies To

Point object, **Series** object.

Description

Returns or sets the explosion value for a pie-chart or doughnut-chart slice. Returns 0 (zero) if there's no explosion (the tip of the slice is in the center of the pie). Read/write **Long**.

Example

This example sets the explosion value for point two. The example should be run on a pie chart.

```
myChart.SeriesCollection(1).Points(2).Explosion = 20
```

Export Method

Applies To

Chart object.

Description

Exports the chart in a graphic format.

Syntax

expression.**Export**(***FileName, FilterName, Interactive***)

expression Required. An expression that returns a **Chart** object.

FileName Required **String**. The name of the exported file.

FilterName Optional **Variant**. The language-independent name of the graphic filter as it appears in the registry.

Interactive Optional **Variant**. **True** to display the dialog box that contains the filter-specific options. If this argument is **False**, Microsoft Graph uses the default values for the filter. The default value is **False**.

Example

This example exports the chart as a GIF file.

```
myChart.Export _
   FileName:="current_sales.gif", FilterName:="GIF"
```

FileImport Method

Applies To

Application object.

Description

Imports a specified file or range, or an entire sheet of data.

Syntax

expression.**FileImport(*FileName, Password, ImportRange, WorksheetName, OverwriteCells*)**

expression Required. An expression that returns an **Application** object.

FileName Required **String**. The file that contains the data to be imported.

Password Optional **Variant**. The password for the file to be imported, if the file is password protected.

ImportRange Optional **Variant**. The range of cells to be imported, if the file to be imported is a Microsoft Excel worksheet or workbook. If this argument is omitted, the complete contents of the worksheet are imported.

WorksheetName Optional **Variant**. The name of the worksheet to be imported, if the file to be imported is a Microsoft Excel workbook.

OverwriteCells Optional **Variant**. **True** to specify that the user be notified before imported data overwrites existing data on the specified datasheet. The default value is **True**.

Example

This example imports data from the range A2:D5 on the worksheet named "MySheet" in the Microsoft Excel workbook named "mynums.xls."

```
With myChart.Application
   .FileImport FileName:="C:\mynums.xls" _
      ImportRange:="A2:D5" WorksheetName:="MySheet" _
      OverwriteCells:=False
End With
```

Fill Property

Applies To

AxisTitle object, **ChartArea** object, **ChartTitle** object, **DataLabel** object, **DataLabels** collection object, **DownBars** object, **Floor** object, **Legend** object, **LegendKey** object, **PlotArea** object, **Point** object, **Series** object, **UpBars** object, **Walls** object.

Description

Returns a **ChartFillFormat** object that contains fill formatting properties for the specified chart. Read-only.

Example

This example sets the fill format for the chart to the preset brass color.

```
With myChart.ChartArea.Fill
    .Visible = True
    .PresetGradient msoGradientDiagonalDown, 3, msoGradientBrass
End With
```

FirstSliceAngle Property

Applies To

ChartGroup object.

Description

Returns or sets the angle of the first pie-chart or doughnut-chart slice, in degrees (clockwise from vertical). Applies only to pie, 3-D pie, and doughnut charts. Read/write **Long**.

Example

This example sets the angle for the first slice in chart group one. The example should be run on a 2-D pie chart.

```
myChart.ChartGroups(1).FirstSliceAngle = 15
```

Floor Object

Description

Represents the floor of the specified 3-D chart.

Using the Floor Object

Use the **Floor** property to return the **Floor** object. The following example sets the floor color for the chart to cyan. If the chart isn't a 3-D chart, this example will fail.

```
myChart.Floor.Interior.Color = RGB(0, 255, 255)
```

Properties

Application property, **Border** property, **Creator** property, **Fill** property, **Interior** property, **Name** property, **Parent** property, **PictureType** property.

Methods

ClearFormats method.

Floor Property

Applies To

Chart object.

Description

Returns a **Floor** object that represents the floor of the 3-D chart. Read-only.

Example

This example sets the floor color to blue. The example should be run on a 3-D chart (the **Floor** property fails on 2-D charts).

```
myChart.Floor.Interior.ColorIndex = 5
```

Font Object

Description

Contains the font attributes (font name, font size, color, and so on) for the specified object.

Using the Font Object

Use the **Font** property to return the **Font** object. The following example sets the title text for the value axis, sets the font to 10-point Bookman, and formats the word "millions" as italic.

```
With myChart.Axes(xlValue)
   .HasTitle = True
   With .AxisTitle
      .Caption = "Revenue (millions)"
      .Font.Name = "bookman"
      .Font.Size = 10
      .Characters(10, 8).Font.Italic = True
   End With
End With
```

Properties

Application property, **Background** property, **Bold** property, **Color** property, **ColorIndex** property, **Creator** property, **FontStyle** property, **Italic** property, **Name** property, **OutlineFont** property, **Parent** property, **Shadow** property, **Size** property, **Strikethrough** property, **Subscript** property, **Superscript** property, **Underline** property.

Font Property

Applies To

AxisTitle object, **ChartArea** object, **ChartTitle** object, **DataLabel** object, **DataLabels** collection object, **DataSheet** object, **DataTable** object, **Legend** object, **LegendEntry** object, **TickLabels** object.

Description

Returns a **Font** object that represents the font of the specified object. Read-only.

See Also

Font object.

Example

This example sets the font in the chart title to 14-point bold italic.

```
With myChart.ChartTitle.Font
   .Size = 14
   .Bold = True
   .Italic = True
End With
```

FontStyle Property

Applies To

Font object.

Description

Returns or sets the font style. Read/write **String**.

Remarks

Changing this property may affect other **Font** properties (such as **Bold** and **Italic**).

See Also

Background property, **Bold** property, **Color** property, **ColorIndex** property, **Font** object, **Italic** property, **Name** property, **OutlineFont** property, **Shadow** property, **Size** property, **Strikethrough** property, **Subscript** property, **Superscript** property, **Underline** property.

Example

This example sets the font style for the chart title to bold and italic.

```
myChart.ChartTitle.Font.FontStyle = "Bold Italic"
```

ForeColor Property

Applies To

ChartFillFormat object.

Description

Returns a **ChartColorFormat** object that represents the foreground fill color.

Example

This example sets the gradient, background color, and foreground color for the chart area fill.

```
With myChart.ChartArea.Fill
   .Visible = True
   .ForeColor.SchemeColor = 15
   .BackColor.SchemeColor = 17
   .TwoColorGradient msoGradientHorizontal, 1
End With
```

Forward Property

Applies To

Trendline object.

Description

Returns or sets the number of periods (or units on a scatter chart) that the trendline extends forward. Read/write **Long**.

See Also

Backward property.

Example

This example sets the number of units that the trendline extends forward and backward. The example should be run on a 2-D column chart that contains a single series with a trendline.

```
With myChart.SeriesCollection(1).Trendlines(1)
   .Forward = 5
   .Backward = .5
End With
```

GapDepth Property

Applies To

Chart object.

Description

Returns or sets the distance between the data series on a 3-D chart, as a percentage of the marker width. The value of this property must be between 0 and 500. Read/write **Long**.

Example

This example sets the distance between the data series to 200 percent of the marker width. The example should be run on a 3-D chart (the **GapDepth** property fails on 2-D charts).

```
myChart.GapDepth = 200
```

GapWidth Property

Applies To

ChartGroup object.

Description

Bar and Column charts: Returns or sets the space between bar or column clusters, as a percentage of the bar or column width. The value of this property must be between 0 and 500. Read/write **Long**.

Pie of Pie and Bar of Pie charts: Returns or sets the space between the primary and secondary sections of the specified chart. The value of this property must be between 5 and 200. Read/write **Long**.

See Also

Overlap property.

Example

This example sets the space between column clusters to be 50 percent of the column width.

```
myChart.ChartGroups(1).GapWidth = 50
```

GradientColorType Property

Applies To

ChartFillFormat object.

Description

Returns the gradient color type for the specified fill. Can be one of the following **MsoGradientColorType** constants: **msoGradientColorMixed**, **msoGradientOneColor**, **msoGradientPresetColors**, or **msoGradientTwoColors**. Read-only **Long**.

Example

This example sets the fill format for the chart if its chart area has a one-color gradient fill.

```
With myChart.ChartArea.Fill
   If .Type = msoFillGradient Then
      If .GradientColorType = msoGradientOneColor Then
         .OneColorGradient Style:= msoGradientFromCorner, _
            Variant:= 1, Degree := 0.3
      End If
   End If
End With
```

GradientDegree Property

Applies To

ChartFillFormat object.

Description

Returns the gradient degree of the specified one-color shaded fill as a floating-point value from 0.0 (dark) through 1.0 (light). Read-only **Single**.

This property is read-only. Use the **OneColorGradient** method to set the gradient degree for the fill.

Example

This example sets the chart's fill format so that its gradient degree is at least 0.3.

```
With myChart.ChartArea.Fill
   If .Type = msoFillGradient Then
      If .GradientColorType = msoGradientOneColor Then
         If .GradientDegree < 0.3 Then
            .OneColorGradient .GradientStyle, .GradientVariant, 0.3
         End If
      End If
   End If
End With
```

GradientStyle Property

Applies To

ChartFillFormat object.

Description

Returns the gradient style for the specified fill. Can be one of the following **MsoGradientStyle** constants: **msoGradientDiagonalDown**, **msoGradientDiagonalUp**, **msoGradientFromCenter**, **msoGradientFromCorner**, **msoGradientFromTitle**, **msoGradientHorizontal**, **msoGradientMixed**, or **msoGradientVertical**. Read-only **Long**.

This property is read-only. Use the **OneColorGradient** or **TwoColorGradient** method to set the gradient style for the fill.

Example

This example sets the chart's fill format so that its gradient style is changed to **msoGradientDiagonalUp** if it was originally **msoGradientDiagonalDown**.

```
With myChart.ChartArea.Fill
   If .Type = msoFillGradient Then
      If .GradientColorType = msoGradientOneColor Then
         If .GradientStyle = msoGradientDiagonalDown Then
            .OneColorGradient msoGradientDiagonalUp, _
               .GradientVariant, .GradientDegree
         End If
      End If
   End If
End With
```

GradientVariant Property

Applies To

ChartFillFormat object.

Description

Returns the shade variant for the specified fill as an integer value from 1 through 4. The values for this property correspond to the gradient variants (numbered from left to right and from top to bottom) listed on the **Gradient** tab in the **Fill Effects** dialog box. Read-only **Long**.

This property is read-only. Use the **OneColorGradient** or **TwoColorGradient** method to set the gradient variant for the fill.

Example

This example sets the chart's fill format so that it's displayed using the second shade variant if it's currently using the first shade variant.

```
With myChart.ChartArea.Fill
   If .Type = msoFillGradient Then
      If .GradientColorType = msoGradientOneColor Then
         If .GradientVariant = 1 Then
            .OneColorGradient .GradientStyle, 2, _
               .GradientDegree
         End If
      End If
   End If
End With
```

Gridlines Object

Description

Represents major or minor gridlines on the specified chart axis. Gridlines extend the tick marks on a chart axis to make it easier to see the values associated with the data markers. This object isn't a collection. There's no object that represents a single gridline; either you have all gridlines for an axis turned on or you have them all turned off.

Using the Gridlines Object

Use the **MajorGridlines** property to return the **GridLines** object that represents the major gridlines for the axis. Use the **MinorGridlines** property to return the **GridLines** object that represents the minor gridlines for the axis. It's possible to return both major and minor gridlines at the same time.

The following example turns on major gridlines for the category axis on the chart and then formats the gridlines to be blue dashed lines.

```
With myChart.Axes(xlCategory)
    .HasMajorGridlines = True
    .MajorGridlines.Border.Color = RGB(0, 0, 255)
    .MajorGridlines.Border.LineStyle = xlDash
End With
```

Properties

Application property, **Border** property, **Creator** property, **Name** property, **Parent** property.

Methods

Delete method.

Has3DEffect Property

Applies To

Series object.

Description

True if the series has a three-dimensional appearance. Applies only to bubble charts. Read/write **Boolean**.

Example

This example gives series one on the bubble chart a three-dimensional appearance.

```
With myChart
    .SeriesCollection(1).Has3DEffect = True
End With
```

Has3DShading Property

Applies To

ChartGroup object.

Description

True if the chart group has three-dimensional shading. Read/write **Boolean**.

Example

This example adds three-dimensional shading to chart group one on the chart.

```
Charts(1).ChartGroups(1).Has3DShading = True
```

HasAxis Property

Applies To

Chart object.

Description

Returns or sets which axes exist on the chart. Read/write **Variant**.

Syntax

expression.**HasAxis(*Index1, Index2*)**

expression   Required. An expression that returns a **Chart** object.

Index1   Optional **Variant**. The axis type. Can be one of the following **XlAxisType** constants: **xlCategory**, **xlValue**, or **xlSeriesAxis**. Series axes apply only to 3-D charts.

Index2   Optional **Variant**. The axis group. Can be either of the following **XlAxisGroup** constants: **xlPrimary** or **xlSecondary**. 3-D charts have only one set of axes.

Remarks

Microsoft Graph may create or delete axes if you change the chart type or change the **AxisGroup** property.

See Also

Axes collection object.

Example

This example turns on the primary value axis.

```
myChart.HasAxis(xlValue, xlPrimary) = True
```

HasBorderHorizontal Property

Applies To

DataTable object.

Description

True if the chart data table has horizontal cell borders. Read/write **Boolean**.

See Also

HasBorderOutline property, **HasBorderVertical** property.

Example

This example causes the chart data table to be displayed with an outline border and no cell borders.

```
With myChart
    .HasDataTable = True
    With .DataTable
        .HasBorderHorizontal = False
        .HasBorderVertical = False
        .HasBorderOutline = True
    End With
End With
```

HasBorderOutline Property

Applies To

DataTable object.

Description

True if the chart data table has outline borders. Read/write **Boolean**.

See Also

HasBorderHorizontal property, **HasBorderVertical** property.

Example

This example causes the chart data table to be displayed with an outline border and no cell borders.

```
With myChart
    .HasDataTable = True
    With .DataTable
        .HasBorderHorizontal = False
        .HasBorderVertical = False
        .HasBorderOutline = True
    End With
End With
```

HasBorderVertical Property

Applies To

DataTable object.

Description

True if the chart data table has vertical cell borders. Read/write **Boolean**.

See Also

HasBorderHorizontal property, **HasBorderOutline** property.

Example

This example causes the chart data table to be displayed with an outline border and no cell borders.

```
With myChart
   .HasDataTable = True
   With .DataTable
      .HasBorderHorizontal = False
      .HasBorderVertical = False
      .HasBorderOutline = True
   End With
End With
```

HasDataLabel Property

Applies To

Point object.

Description

True if the point has a data label. Read/write **Boolean**.

See Also

ApplyDataLabels method, **DataLabel** property, **HasDataLabels** property.

Example

This example turns on the data label for point seven in series three, and then it sets the data label color to blue.

```
With myChart.SeriesCollection(3).Points(7)
   .HasDataLabel = True
   .ApplyDataLabels Type:=xlValue
   .DataLabel.Font.ColorIndex = 5
End With
```

HasDataLabels Property

Applies To

Series object.

Description

True if the series has data labels. Read/write **Boolean**.

See Also

ApplyDataLabels method, **DataLabel** property, **HasDataLabel** property.

Example

This example turns on data labels for series three.

```
With myChart.SeriesCollection(3)
    .HasDataLabels = True
    .ApplyDataLabels Type:=xlValue
End With
```

HasDataTable Property

Applies To

Chart object.

Description

True if the chart has a data table. Read/write **Boolean**.

Example

This example causes the chart data table to be displayed with an outline border and no cell borders.

```
With myChart
    .HasDataTable = True
    With .DataTable
        .HasBorderHorizontal = False
        .HasBorderVertical = False
        .HasBorderOutline = True
    End With
End With
```

HasDropLines Property

Applies To

ChartGroup object.

Description

True if the line chart or area chart has drop lines. Applies only to line and area charts. Read/write **Boolean**.

See Also

DropLines property.

Example

This example turns on drop lines for chart group one and then sets their line style, weight, and color. The example should be run on a 2-D line chart that has one series.

```
With myChart.ChartGroups(1)
   .HasDropLines = True
   With .DropLines.Border
      .LineStyle = xlThin
      .Weight = xlMedium
      .ColorIndex = 3
   End With
End With
```

HasErrorBars Property

Applies To

Series object.

Description

True if the series has error bars. This property isn't available for 3-D charts. Read/write **Boolean**.

See Also

ErrorBar method, **ErrorBars** property.

Example

This example removes error bars from series one. The example should be run on a 2-D line chart that has error bars for series one.

```
myChart.SeriesCollection(1).HasErrorBars = False
```

HasHiLoLines Property

Applies To

ChartGroup object.

Description

True if the line chart has high-low lines. Applies only to line charts. Read/write **Boolean**.

See Also

HiLoLines property.

Example

This example turns on high-low lines for chart group one and then sets line style, weight, and color. The example should be run on a 2-D line chart that has three series of stock-quote-like data (high-low-close).

```
With myChart.ChartGroups(1)
   .HasHiLoLines = True
   With .HiLoLines.Border
      .LineStyle = xlThin
      .Weight = xlMedium
      .ColorIndex = 3
   End With
End With
```

HasLeaderLines Property

Applies To

Series object.

Description

True if the series has leader lines. Read/write **Boolean**.

Example

This example adds data labels and blue leader lines to series one on the pie chart.

```
With myChart.SeriesCollection(1)
   .HasDataLabels = True
   .DataLabels.Position = xlLabelPositionBestFit
   .HasLeaderLines = True
   .LeaderLines.Border.ColorIndex = 5
End With
```

HasLegend Property

Applies To

Chart object.

Description

True if the chart has a legend. Read/write **Boolean**.

See Also

Legend property.

Example

This example turns on the legend for the chart and then sets the legend font color to blue.

```
With myChart
    .HasLegend = True
    .Legend.Font.ColorIndex = 5
End With
```

HasLinks Property

Applies To

Application object.

Description

True if the specified chart has links to an external data source. Read-only **Boolean**.

Example

This example clears cells A1:D4 on the datasheet if the chart has no links.

```
With myChart.Application
    If .HasLinks = False Then
        .DataSheet.Range("A1:D4").Clear
    End If
End With
```

HasMajorGridlines Property

Applies To

Axis object.

Description

True if the axis has major gridlines. Only axes in the primary axis group can have gridlines. Read/write **Boolean**.

See Also

AxisGroup property, **HasMinorGridlines** property, **MajorGridlines** property, **MinorGridlines** property.

Example

This example sets the color of the major gridlines for the value axis.

```
With myChart.Axes(xlValue)
    If .HasMajorGridlines Then
        .MajorGridlines.Border.ColorIndex = 3    ' Set color to red.
    End If
End With
```

HasMinorGridlines Property

Applies To

Axis object.

Description

True if the axis has minor gridlines. Only axes in the primary axis group can have gridlines. Read/write **Boolean**.

See Also

AxisGroup property, **HasMajorGridlines** property, **MajorGridlines** property, **MinorGridlines** property.

Example

This example sets the color of the minor gridlines for the value axis.

```
With myChart.Axes(xlValue)
    If .HasMinorGridlines Then
        .MinorGridlines.Border.ColorIndex = 4    ' Set color to green.
    End If
End With
```

HasRadarAxisLabels Property

Applies To

ChartGroup object.

Description

True if a radar chart has axis labels. Applies only to radar charts. Read/write **Boolean**.

See Also

RadarAxisLabels property.

Example

This example turns on radar axis labels for chart group one and sets their color. The example should be run on a radar chart.

```
With myChart.ChartGroups(1)
    .HasRadarAxisLabels = True
    .RadarAxisLabels.Font.ColorIndex = 3
End With
```

HasSeriesLines Property

Applies To

ChartGroup object.

Description

True if a stacked column chart or bar chart has series lines or if a Pie of Pie chart or Bar of Pie chart has connector lines between the two sections. Applies only to stacked column charts, bar charts, Pie of Pie charts, or Bar of Pie charts. Read/write **Boolean**.

See Also

SeriesLines property.

Example

This example turns on series lines for chart group one and then sets their line style, weight, and color. The example should be run on a 2-D stacked column chart that has two or more series.

```
With myChart.ChartGroups(1)
    .HasSeriesLines = True
    With .SeriesLines.Border
        .LineStyle = xlThin
        .Weight = xlMedium
        .ColorIndex = 3
    End With
End With
```

HasTitle Property

Applies To

Axis object, **Chart** object.

Description

True if the axis or chart has a visible title. Read/write **Boolean**.

Remarks

An axis title is represented by an **AxisTitle** object.

A chart title is represented by a **ChartTitle** object.

Example

This example adds an axis label to the category axis.

```
With myChart.Axes(xlCategory)
    .HasTitle = True
    .AxisTitle.Text = "July Sales"
End With
```

HasUpDownBars Property

Applies To

ChartGroup object.

Description

True if the specified line chart has up and down bars. Applies only to line charts. Read/write **Boolean.**

See Also

DownBars property, **UpBars** property.

Example

This example turns on up and down bars for chart group one and then sets their colors. The example should be run on a 2-D line chart containing two series that cross each other at one or more data points.

```
With myChart.ChartGroups(1)
    .HasUpDownBars = True
    .DownBars.Interior.ColorIndex = 3
    .UpBars.Interior.ColorIndex = 5
End With
```

Height Property

Applies To

Application object, **Axis** object, **Chart** object, **ChartArea** object, **DataSheet** object, **Legend** object, **LegendEntry** object, **LegendKey** object, **PlotArea** object.

Description

Returns or sets the height of an object, in points. Read/write **Long**, except as shown in the following table.

Remarks

The meaning of the **Height** property depends on the specified object.

Object type	Height
Application	The height of the main application window. On the Macintosh, this is always equal to the total height of the screen, in points. Setting this value to something else on the Macintosh will have no effect. In Windows, if the window is minimized, this property is read-only and refers to the height of the icon. If the window is maximized, this property cannot be set. Use the **WindowState** property to determine the window state.
Axis, **LegendEntry**, **LegendKey**	The height of the object. Read-only.
ChartArea, **Chart**, **DataSheet**, **Legend**, **PlotArea**	The height of the object.

See Also

Left property, **Top** property, **Width** property.

Example

This example sets the height of the chart legend to 1 inch (72 points).

```
myChart.Legend.Height = 72
```

HeightPercent Property

Applies To

Chart object.

Description

Returns or sets the height of a 3-D chart as a percentage of the chart width (between 5 and 500 percent). Read/write **Long**.

See Also

DepthPercent property.

Example

This example sets the height of the chart to 80 percent of its width. The example should be run on a 3-D chart.

```
myChart.HeightPercent = 80
```

HiLoLines Object

Description

Represents the high-low lines in the specified chart group. High-low lines connect the highest point with the lowest point in every category in the chart group. Only 2-D line groups can have high-low lines. This object isn't a collection. There's no object that represents a single high-low line; either you have high-low lines turned on for all points in a chart group or you have them turned off.

Using the HiLoLines Object

Use the **HiLoLines** property to return the **HiLoLines** object. The following example makes the high-low lines in chart group one in the chart blue.

```
myChart.ChartGroups(1).HiLoLines.Border.Color = RGB(0, 0, 255)
```

Remarks

If the **HasHiLoLines** property is **False**, most properties of the **HiLoLines** object are disabled.

Properties

Application property, **Border** property, **Creator** property, **Name** property, **Parent** property.

Methods

Delete method.

HiLoLines Property

Applies To

ChartGroup object.

Description

Returns a **HiLoLines** object that represents the high-low lines for the specified series on a line chart. Applies only to line charts. Read-only.

See Also

HasHiLoLines property.

Example

This example turns on high-low lines for chart group one on the chart and then sets their line style, weight, and color. The example should be run on a 2-D line chart that has three series of stock-quote-like data (high-low-close).

```
With myChart.ChartGroups(1)
    .HasHiLoLines = True
    With .HiLoLines.Border
        .LineStyle = xlThin
        .Weight = xlMedium
        .ColorIndex = 3
    End With
End With
```

HorizontalAlignment Property

Applies To

AxisTitle object, **ChartTitle** object, **DataLabel** object, **DataLabels** collection object.

Description

Returns or sets the horizontal alignment for the object. For all objects, this can be one of the following **XlHAlign** constants: **xlHAlignCenter**, **xlHAlignDistributed**, **xlHAlignJustify**, **xlHAlignLeft**, or **xlHAlignRight**. Read/write **Long**.

Remarks

The **xlHAlignDistributed** alignment style works only in Far East versions of Microsoft Graph.

See Also

VerticalAlignment property.

Example

This example centers the chart title.

```
myChart.ChartTitle.HorizontalAlignment = xlCenter
```

Include Property

Applies To

Range object.

Description

True if the data in the specified row or column is included in the chart. Read/write **Boolean.**

Example

This example causes the data in the second row on the datasheet to be excluded from the chart.

```
With myChart.Application.DataSheet
    .Rows(2).Include = False
End With
```

Index Property

Applies To

ChartGroup object, **LegendEntry** object, **Trendline** object.

Description

Returns the index number of the object within the collection of similar objects. Read-only **Long**.

Example

This example displays the index number of an object passed to this procedure.

```
MsgBox "The index number of this object is " & obj.Index
```

Insert Method

Applies To

Range object.

Description

Inserts a cell or a range of cells into the datasheet and shifts other cells away to make space.

Syntax

expression.**Insert**(***Shift***)

expression   Required. An expression that returns a **Range** object.

Shift   Optional **Variant**. Specifies which way to shift the cells. Can be one of the following **XlInsertShiftDirection** constants: **xlShiftToRight** or **xlShiftDown**. If this argument is omitted, Microsoft Graph decides based on the shape of the range.

Example

This example inserts a new row before row four on the datasheet.

```
myChart.Application.DataSheet.Rows(4).Insert
```

This example inserts new cells at the range A1:C5 on the datasheet and shifts cells downward.

```
Set mySheet = myChart.Application.DataSheet
mySheet.Range("A1:C5").Insert Shift:=xlShiftDown
```

InsideHeight Property

Applies To

PlotArea object.

Description

Returns the inside height of the plot area, in points. Read-only **Double**.

Remarks

The plot area used for this measurement doesn't include the axis labels. The **Height** property for the plot area uses the bounding rectangle that includes the axis labels.

InsideLeft Property

Applies To

PlotArea object.

Description

Returns the distance from the chart edge to the inside left edge of the plot area, in points. Read-only **Double**.

Remarks

The plot area used for this measurement doesn't include the axis labels. The **Left** property for the plot area uses the bounding rectangle that includes the axis labels.

InsideTop Property

Applies To

PlotArea object.

Description

Returns the distance from the chart edge to the inside top edge of the plot area, in points. Read-only **Double**.

Remarks

The plot area used for this measurement doesn't include the axis labels. The **Top** property for the plot area uses the bounding rectangle that includes the axis labels.

InsideWidth Property

Applies To

PlotArea object.

Description

Returns the inside width of the plot area, in points. Read-only **Double**.

Remarks

The plot area used for this measurement doesn't include the axis labels. The **Width** property for the plot area uses the bounding rectangle that includes the axis labels.

Intercept Property

Applies To

Trendline object.

Description

Returns or sets the point where the trendline crosses the value axis. Read/write **Double**.

Remarks

Setting this property sets the **InterceptIsAuto** property to **False**.

See Also

InterceptIsAuto property.

Example

This example sets trendline one to cross the value axis at 5. The example should be run on a 2-D column chart that contains a single series with a trendline.

```
myChart.SeriesCollection(1).Trendlines(1).Intercept = 5
```

InterceptIsAuto Property

Applies To

Trendline object.

Description

True if the point where the trendline crosses the value axis is automatically determined by the regression. Read/write **Boolean**.

Remarks

Setting the **Intercept** property sets this property to **False**.

See Also

Intercept property.

Example

This example sets Microsoft Graph to automatically determine the trendline intercept point. The example should be run on a 2-D column chart that contains a single series with a trendline.

```
myChart.SeriesCollection(1).Trendlines(1) _
    .InterceptIsAuto = True
```

Interior Object

Description

Represents the interior of the specified object.

Using the Interior Object

Use the **Interior** property to return the **Interior** object. The following example sets the chart area color to gray and the plot area color to green.

```
With myChart
    .PlotArea.Interior.Color = RGB(0, 100, 150)
    .ChartArea.Interior.Color = RGB(50, 10, 50)
End With
```

Properties

Application property, **Color** property, **ColorIndex** property, **Creator** property, **InvertIfNegative** property, **Parent** property, **Pattern** property, **PatternColor** property, **PatternColorIndex** property.

Interior Property

Applies To

AxisTitle object, **ChartArea** object, **ChartTitle** object, **DataLabel** object, **DataLabels** collection object, **DownBars** object, **Floor** object, **Legend** object, **LegendKey** object, **PlotArea** object, **Point** object, **Series** object, **UpBars** object, **Walls** object.

Description

Returns an **Interior** object that represents the interior of the specified object. Read-only.

Example

This example sets the interior color of the chart title.

```
myChart.ChartTitle.Interior.ColorIndex = 8
```

InvertIfNegative Property

Applies To

Interior object, **LegendKey** object, **Point** object, **Series** object.

Description

True if Microsoft Graph inverts the pattern in the item when it corresponds to a negative number. Read/write **Variant** for the **Interior** object; read/write **Boolean** for all other objects.

Example

This example inverts the pattern for negative values in series one. The example should be run on a 2-D column chart.

```
myChart.SeriesCollection(1).InvertIfNegative = True
```

Italic Property

Applies To

Font object.

Description

True if the font style is italic. Read/write **Boolean**.

Example

This example sets the font style to italic for the chart title.

```
myChart.ChartTitle.Font.Italic = True
```

Item Method

Applies To

Axes collection object, **ChartGroups** collection object, **DataLabels** collection object, **LegendEntries** collection object, **Points** collection object, **SeriesCollection** collection object, **Trendlines** collection object.

Description

Returns part of the specified collection. The **Item** method is the default method for collections. For example, the following two lines of code are equivalent:

```
myChart.SeriesCollection.Item(1)
myChart.SeriesCollection(1)
```

Item Property

Applies To

Chart object.

Description

Returns a **Range** object that represents a range that's offset from the specified range. Read-only.

Syntax 1

expression.**Item(*RowIndex, ColumnIndex*)**

Syntax 2

expression.**Item(*RowIndex*)**

expression Required. An expression that returns a **Range** object.

RowIndex Syntax 1: Required **Variant**. The row number of the cell you want to work with (the first row in the range is 1).

Syntax 2: Required **Variant**. The index number of the cell you want to work with, counting from left to right and from top to bottom. `Range.Item(1)` returns the cell in the upper-left corner of the range; `Range.Item(2)` returns the cell immediately to the right of this cell.

ColumnIndex Optional **Variant**. A number or string that indicates the column number of the cell you want to work with (the first column in the range is either 1 or A).

Remarks

Syntax 1 uses a row number and either a column number or a letter as index arguments. For more information about this syntax, see the **Range** object. The ***RowIndex*** and ***ColumnIndex*** arguments are relative offsets. In other words, specifying 1 for ***RowIndex*** returns cells in the first row in the range, not the first row on the datasheet.

Example

This example clears cell B2 on the datasheet.

```
myChart.Application.DataSheet.Range("A1").Item(2, 2).Clear
```

LeaderLines Object

Description

Represents leader lines in the specified chart. Leader lines connect data labels to data points. This object isn't a collection; there's no object that represents a single leader line.

Using the LeaderLines Object

Use the **LeaderLines** property to return the **LeaderLines** object. The following example adds data labels and blue leader lines to series one in the chart.

```
With myChart.SeriesCollection(1)
    .HasDataLabels = True
    .DataLabels.Position = xlLabelPositionBestFit
    .HasLeaderLines = True
    .LeaderLines.Border.ColorIndex = 5
End With
```

Properties

Application property, **Border** property, **Creator** property, **Parent** property.

Methods

Delete method.

LeaderLines Property

Applies To

Series object.

Description

Returns a **LeaderLines** object that represents the leader lines for the specified series. Read-only.

Example

This example adds data labels and blue leader lines to series one on the pie chart.

```
With myChart.SeriesCollection(1)
    .HasDataLabels = True
    .DataLabels.Position = xlLabelPositionBestFit
    .HasLeaderLines = True
    .LeaderLines.Border.ColorIndex = 5
End With
```

Left Property

Applies To

Application object, **Axis** object, **AxisTitle** object, **Chart** object, **ChartArea** object, **ChartTitle** object, **DataLabel** object, **DataSheet** object, **Legend** object, **LegendEntry** object, **LegendKey** object, **PlotArea** object.

Description

Returns or sets the position of the specified object, in points. Read/write **Long**, except as shown in the following table.

Remarks

The meaning of the **Left** property depends on the specified object.

Object	Meaning
Application	The distance from the left edge of the screen to the left edge of the main Microsoft Graph window.
Chart, **DataSheet**	The distance from the left edge of the object to the left edge of the Microsoft Graph window.
Axis, **LegendEntry**, **LegendKey**	The distance from the left edge of the object to the left edge of the chart area. Read-only.
AxisTitle, **ChartArea**, **ChartTitle**, **DataLabel**, **Legend**, **PlotArea**	The distance from the left edge of the object to the left edge of the chart area.

If the window is maximized, `Application.Left` returns a negative number that varies based on the width of the window border. Setting `Application.Left` to 0 (zero) will make the window a tiny bit smaller than it would be if the application window were maximized. In other words, if `Application.Left` is 0 (zero), the left border of the main Microsoft Graph window will just barely be visible on the screen.

On the Macintosh, `Application.Left` is always 0 (zero). Setting this value to something else on the Macintosh will have no effect.

In Windows, if the Microsoft Graph window is minimized, `Application.Left` controls the position of the window icon.

See Also

Height property, **Top** property, **Width** property.

Example

This example aligns the left edge of the chart title with the left edge of the chart area.

```
myChart.ChartTitle.Left = 0
```

Legend Object

Description

Represents the legend in the specified chart. Each chart can have only one legend. The **Legend** object contains one or more **LegendEntry** objects; each **LegendEntry** object contains a **LegendKey** object.

Using the Legend Object

Use the **Legend** property to return the **Legend** object. The following example sets the font style for the legend to bold.

```
myChart.Legend.Font.Bold = True
```

Remarks

The chart legend isn't visible unless the **HasLegend** property is **True**. If this property is **False**, properties and methods of the **Legend** object will fail.

Properties

Application property, **AutoScaleFont** property, **Border** property, **Creator** property, **Fill** property, **Font** property, **Height** property, **Interior** property, **Left** property, **Name** property, **Parent** property, **Position** property, **Shadow** property, **Top** property, **Width** property.

Methods

Clear method, **Delete** method, **LegendEntries** method.

Legend Property

Applies To

Chart object.

Description

Returns a **Legend** object that represents the legend for the specified chart. Read-only.

See Also

HasLegend property.

Example

This example turns on the legend for the chart and then sets the font color for the legend to blue.

```
myChart.HasLegend = True
myChart.Legend.Font.ColorIndex = 5
```

LegendEntries Collection Object

Description

A collection of all the **LegendEntry** objects in the specified chart legend. Each legend entry has two parts: the text of the entry, which is the name of the series or trendline associated with the entry; and the entry marker, which visually links the legend entry with its associated series or trendline in the chart. The formatting properties for the entry marker and its associated series or trendline are contained in the **LegendKey** object.

Using the LegendEntries Collection

Use the **LegendEntries** method to return the **LegendEntries** collection. The following example loops through the collection of legend entries in the chart and changes their font color to blue.

```
With myChart.Legend
   For i = 1 To .LegendEntries.Count
      .LegendEntries(i).Font.ColorIndex = 5
   Next
End With
```

Use **LegendEntries**(*index*), where *index* is the legend entry's index number, to return a single **LegendEntry** object. You cannot return legend entries by name.

The index number represents the position of the legend entry in the legend. `LegendEntries(1)` is at the top of the legend; `LegendEntries(LegendEntries.Count)` is at the bottom. The following example changes the font style to italic for the text of the legend entry at the top of the legend (this is usually the legend for series one) in `myChart`.

```
myChart.Legend.LegendEntries(1).Font.Italic = True
```

Properties

Application property, **Count** property, **Creator** property, **Parent** property.

Methods

Item method.

LegendEntries Method

Applies To

Legend object.

Description

Returns an object that represents either a single legend entry (a **LegendEntry** object, Syntax 1) or a collection of legend entries (a **LegendEntries** object, Syntax 2) for the legend.

Syntax 1

expression.**LegendEntries(*Index*)**

Syntax 2

expression.**LegendEntries**

expression   Required. An expression that returns a **Legend** object.

Index   Optional **Variant**. The number of the legend entry.

Example

This example sets the font for legend entry one.

```
myChart.Legend.LegendEntries(1).Font.Name = "Arial"
```

LegendEntry Object

Description

Represents a legend entry in the specified chart legend. The **LegendEntry** object is a member of the **LegendEntries** collection, which contains all the **LegendEntry** objects in the legend.

Each legend entry has two parts: the text of the entry, which is the name of the series associated with the entry; and an entry marker, which visually links the legend entry with its associated series or trendline in the chart. Formatting properties for the entry marker and its associated series or trendline are contained in the **LegendKey** object.

You cannot change the text of a legend entry. **LegendEntry** objects support font formatting, and they can be deleted. No pattern formatting is supported for legend entries. The position and size of entries is fixed.

Using the LegendEntry Object

Use **LegendEntries**(*index*), where *index* is the legend entry's index number, to return a single **LegendEntry** object. You cannot return legend entries by name.

The index number represents the position of the legend entry in the legend. `LegendEntries(1)` is at the top of the legend, and `LegendEntries(LegendEntries.Count)` is at the bottom. The following example changes the font style for the text of the legend entry at the top of the legend (this is usually the legend for series one).

```
myChart.Legend.LegendEntries(1).Font.Italic = True
```

Remarks

There's no direct way to return the series or trendline that corresponds to a particular legend entry.

After legend entries have been deleted, the only way to restore them is to remove and then recreate the legend that contained them by setting the **HasLegend** property for the chart to **False** and then back to **True**.

Properties

Application property, **AutoScaleFont** property, **Creator** property, **Font** property, **Height** property, **Index** property, **Left** property, **LegendKey** property, **Parent** property, **Top** property, **Width** property.

Methods

Delete method.

LegendKey Object

Description

Represents a legend key in the specified chart legend. Each legend key is a graphic that visually links a legend entry with its associated series or trendline in the chart. The legend key is linked to its associated series or trendline in such a way that changing the formatting of one simultaneously changes the formatting of the other.

Using the LegendKey Object

Use the **LegendKey** property to return the **LegendKey** object. The following example changes the marker background color to blue for the legend entry at the top of the legend in the chart. This simultaneously changes the formatting of every point in the series associated with this legend entry (if, that is, the associated series supports data markers).

```
myChart.Legend.LegendEntries(1).LegendKey.MarkerBackgroundColorIndex = 5
```

Properties

Application property, **Border** property, **Creator** property, **Fill** property, **Height** property, **Interior** property, **InvertIfNegative** property, **Left** property, **MarkerBackgroundColor** property, **MarkerBackgroundColorIndex** property, **MarkerForegroundColor** property, **MarkerForegroundColorIndex** property, **MarkerSize** property, **MarkerStyle** property, **Parent** property, **PictureType** property, **PictureUnit** property, **Shadow** property, **Smooth** property, **Top** property, **Width** property.

Methods

ClearFormats method, **Delete** method.

LegendKey Property

Applies To

LegendEntry object.

Description

Returns a **LegendKey** object that represents the legend key associated with the entry.

Example

This example sets the legend key for legend entry one to be a triangle. The example should be run on a 2-D line chart.

```
myChart.Legend.LegendEntries(1).LegendKey _
    .MarkerStyle = xlMarkerStyleTriangle
```

Line3DGroup Property

Applies To

Chart object.

Description

Returns a **ChartGroup** object that represents the line chart group on a 3-D chart. Read-only.

See Also

LineGroups method.

Example

This example sets the 3-D line group to use a different color for each data marker.

```
myChart.Line3DGroup.VaryByCategories = True
```

LineGroups Method

Applies To

Chart object.

Description

On a 2-D chart, returns an object that represents either a single line chart group (a **ChartGroup** object, Syntax 1) or a collection of the line chart groups (a **ChartGroups** collection, Syntax 2).

Syntax 1

expression.**LineGroups(*Index*)**

Syntax 2

expression.**LineGroups**

expression   Required. An expression that returns a **Chart** object.

Index   Optional **Variant**. Specifies the chart group.

See Also

AreaGroups method, **BarGroups** method, **ChartGroups** method, **ColumnGroups** method, **DoughnutGroups** method, **Line3DGroup** property, **PieGroups** method.

Example

This example sets line group one to use a different color for each data marker. The example should be run on a 2-D chart.

```
myChart.LineGroups(1).VaryByCategories = True
```

LineStyle Property

Applies To

Border object.

Description

Returns or sets the line style for the border. Can be one of the following **XlLineStyle** constants: **xlContinuous**, **xlDash**, **xlDashDot**, **xlDashDotDot**, **xlDot**, **xlDouble**, **xlSlantDashDot**, or **xlLineStyleNone**. Read/write **Long**.

Example

This example puts a border around the chart area and the plot area.

```
With myChart
    .ChartArea.Border.LineStyle = xlDashDot
    With .PlotArea.Border
        .LineStyle = xlDashDotDot
        .Weight = xlThick
    End With
End With
```

MajorGridlines Property

Applies To

Axis object.

Description

Returns a **Gridlines** object that represents the major gridlines for the specified axis. Only axes in the primary axis group can have gridlines. Read-only.

See Also

AxisGroup property, **HasMajorGridlines** property, **HasMinorGridlines** property, **MinorGridlines** property.

Example

This example sets the color of the major gridlines for the value axis in the chart.

```
With myChart.Axes(xlValue)
    If .HasMajorGridlines Then
        .MajorGridlines.Border.ColorIndex = 5
    End If
End With
```

MajorTickMark Property

Applies To

Axis object.

Description

Returns or sets the type of major tick mark for the specified axis. Can be one of the following **XlTickMark** constants: **xlTickMarkNone**, **xlTickMarkInside**, **xlTickMarkOutside**, or **xlTickMarkCross**. Read/write **Long**.

See Also

MinorTickMark property.

Example

This example sets the major tick marks for the value axis to be outside the axis.

```
myChart.Axes(xlValue).MajorTickMark = xlTickMarkOutside
```

MajorUnit Property

Applies To

Axis object.

Description

Returns or sets the major units for the axis. Read/write **Double**.

Remarks

Setting this property sets the **MajorUnitIsAuto** property to **False**.

Use the **TickMarkSpacing** property to set tick-mark spacing on the category axis.

See Also

MajorUnitIsAuto property, **MajorUnitScale** property, **MinorUnit** property, **MinorUnitIsAuto** property, **MinorUnitScale** property, **TickMarkSpacing** property.

Example

This example sets the major and minor units for the value axis.

```
With myChart.Axes(xlValue)
   .MajorUnit = 100
   .MinorUnit = 20
End With
```

MajorUnitIsAuto Property

Applies To

Axis object.

Description

True if Microsoft Graph calculates the major units for the axis. Read/write **Boolean**.

Remarks

Setting the **MajorUnit** property sets this property to **False**.

See Also

MajorUnit property, **MajorUnitScale** property, **MinorUnit** property, **MinorUnitIsAuto** property, **MinorUnitScale** property.

Example

This example automatically sets the major and minor units for the value axis.

```
With myChart.Axes(xlValue)
    .MajorUnitIsAuto = True
    .MinorUnitIsAuto = True
End With
```

MajorUnitScale Property

Applies To

Axis object.

Description

Returns or sets the major unit scale value for the category axis when the **CategoryType** property is set to **xlTimeScale**. Can be one of the following **XlTimeUnit** constants: **xlDays**, **xlMonths**, or **xlYears**. Read/write **Long**.

See Also

BaseUnit property, **MajorUnit** property, **MajorUnitIsAuto** property, **MinorUnit** property, **MinorUnitIsAuto** property, **MinorUnitScale** property.

Example

This example sets the category axis to use a time scale and sets the major and minor units.

```
With myChart.Axes(xlCategory)
    .CategoryType = xlTimeScale
    .MajorUnit = 5
    .MajorUnitScale = xlDays
    .MinorUnit = 1
    .MinorUnitScale = xlDays
End With
```

MarkerBackgroundColor Property

Applies To

LegendKey object, **Point** object, **Series** object.

Description

Returns or sets the marker background color as an RGB value. Applies only to line, scatter, and radar charts. Read/write **Long**.

See Also

MarkerBackgroundColorIndex property, **MarkerForegroundColor** property, **MarkerStyle** property.

Example

This example sets the marker background and foreground colors for the second point in series one.

```
With myChart.SeriesCollection(1).Points(2)
    .MarkerBackgroundColor = RGB(0,255,0)      ' green
    .MarkerForegroundColor = RGB(255,0,0)      ' red
End With
```

MarkerBackgroundColorIndex Property

Applies To

LegendKey object, **Point** object, **Series** object.

Description

Returns or sets the marker background color as an index into the current color palette, or as one of the following **XlColorIndex** constants: **xlColorIndexAutomatic** or **xlColorIndexNone**. Applies only to line, scatter, and radar charts. Read/write **Long**.

Remarks

The following table shows the color-index values in the default color palette.

Color	Index value
Aqua	8, 28, 33, 34, 42
Black	1, 51, 52
Blue	5, 32, 41, 49
Fuchsia	7, 26
Gray	16, 46, 47, 48, 56
Green	10, 43
Lime	4
Maroon	9, 30, 53

(continued)

Navy	11, 25, 55
Olive	12, 44, 45
Purple	13, 18, 21, 29, 54
Red	3
Silver	15, 17, 20, 22, 24, 35, 36, 37, 38, 39
Teal	14, 23, 31, 50
White	2, 19, 40
Yellow	6, 27

See Also

MarkerBackgroundColor property, **MarkerForegroundColorIndex** property, **MarkerStyle** property.

Example

This example sets the marker background and foreground colors for the second point in series one.

```
With myChart.SeriesCollection(1).Points(2)
    .MarkerBackgroundColorIndex = 4    ' green
    .MarkerForegroundColorIndex = 3    ' red
End With
```

MarkerForegroundColor Property

Applies To

LegendKey object, **Point** object, **Series** object.

Description

Returns or sets the foreground color of the marker as an RGB value. Applies only to line, scatter, and radar charts. Read/write **Long**.

See Also

MarkerBackgroundColor property, **MarkerForegroundColorIndex** property, **MarkerStyle** property.

Example

This example sets the marker background and foreground colors for the second point in series one.

```
With myChart.SeriesCollection(1).Points(2)
    .MarkerBackgroundColor = RGB(0,255,0)      ' green
    .MarkerForegroundColor = RGB(255,0,0)      ' red
End With
```

MarkerForegroundColorIndex Property

Applies To

LegendKey object, **Point** object, **Series** object.

Description

Returns or sets the marker foreground color as an index into the current color palette, or as one of the following **XlColorIndex** constants: **xlColorIndexAutomatic** or **xlColorIndexNone**. Applies only to line, scatter, and radar charts. Read/write **Long**.

Remarks

The following table shows the color-index values in the default color palette.

Color	Index value
Aqua	8, 28, 33, 34, 42
Black	1, 51, 52
Blue	5, 32, 41, 49
Fuchsia	7, 26
Gray	16, 46, 47, 48, 56
Green	10, 43
Lime	4
Maroon	9, 30, 53
Navy	11, 25, 55
Olive	12, 44, 45
Purple	13, 18, 21, 29, 54
Red	3
Silver	15, 17, 20, 22, 24, 35, 36, 37, 38, 39
Teal	14, 23, 31, 50
White	2, 19, 40
Yellow	6, 27

See Also

MarkerBackgroundColorIndex property, **MarkerForegroundColor** property, **MarkerStyle** property.

Example

This example sets the marker background and foreground colors for the second point in series one.

```
With myChart.SeriesCollection(1).Points(2)
    .MarkerBackgroundColorIndex = 4    ' green
    .MarkerForegroundColorIndex = 3    ' red
End With
```

MarkerSize Property

Applies To

LegendKey object, **Point** object, **Series** object.

Description

Returns or sets the data-marker size, in points. Read/write **Long**.

Example

This example sets the data-marker size for all data markers in series one.

```
MyChart.SeriesCollection(1).MarkerSize = 10
```

MarkerStyle Property

Applies To

LegendKey object, **Point** object, **Series** object.

Description

Returns or sets the marker style for a point or series in a line chart, scatter chart, or radar chart. Read/write **Long**.

Can be one of the following **XlMarkerStyle** constants.

Constant	Description
xlMarkerStyleNone	No markers
xlMarkerStyleAutomatic	Automatic markers
xlMarkerStyleSquare	Square markers
xlMarkerStyleDiamond	Diamond-shaped markers
xlMarkerStyleTriangle	Triangular markers
xlMarkerStyleX	Square markers with an X
xlMarkerStyleStar	Square markers with an asterisk
xlMarkerStyleDot	Short bar markers
xlMarkerStyleDash	Long bar markers
xlMarkerStyleCircle	Circular markers
xlMarkerStylePlus	Square markers with a plus sign
xlMarkerStylePicture	Picture markers

Example

This example sets the marker style for series one. The example should be run on a 2-D line chart.

```
myChart.SeriesCollection(1).MarkerStyle = xlMarkerStyleCircle
```

MaximumScale Property

Applies To

Axis object.

Description

Returns or sets the maximum value on the axis. Read/write **Double**.

Remarks

Setting this property sets the **MaximumScaleIsAuto** property to **False**.

See Also

MaximumScaleIsAuto property, **MinimumScale** property, **MinimumScaleIsAuto** property.

Example

This example sets the minimum and maximum values for the value axis.

```
With myChart.Axes(xlValue)
    .MinimumScale = 10
    .MaximumScale = 120
End With
```

MaximumScaleIsAuto Property

Applies To

Axis object.

Description

True if Microsoft Graph calculates the maximum value for the axis. Read/write **Boolean**.

Remarks

Setting the **MaximumScale** property sets this property to **False**.

See Also

MaximumScale property, **MinimumScale** property, **MinimumScaleIsAuto** property.

Example

This example automatically calculates the minimum scale and the maximum scale for the value axis.

```
With myChart.Axes(xlValue)
    .MinimumScaleIsAuto = True
    .MaximumScaleIsAuto = True
End With
```

MinimumScale Property

Applies To

Axis object.

Description

Returns or sets the minimum value on the axis. Read/write **Double**.

Remarks

Setting this property sets the **MinimumScaleIsAuto** property to **False**.

See Also

MaximumScale property, **MaximumScaleIsAuto** property, **MinimumScaleIsAuto** property.

Example

This example sets the minimum and maximum values for the value axis.

```
With myChart.Axes(xlValue)
    .MinimumScale = 10
    .MaximumScale = 120
End With
```

MinimumScaleIsAuto Property

Applies To

Axis object.

Description

True if Microsoft Graph calculates the minimum value for the axis. Read/write **Boolean**.

Remarks

Setting the **MinimumScale** property sets this property to **False**.

See Also

MaximumScale property, **MaximumScaleIsAuto** property, **MinimumScale** property.

Example

This example automatically calculates the minimum scale and the maximum scale for the value axis.

```
With myChart.Axes(xlValue)
    .MinimumScaleIsAuto = True
    .MaximumScaleIsAuto = True
End With
```

MinorGridlines Property

Applies To

Axis object.

Description

Returns a **Gridlines** object that represents the minor gridlines for the specified axis. Only axes in the primary axis group can have gridlines. Read-only.

See Also

AxisGroup property, **HasMajorGridlines** property, **HasMinorGridlines** property, **MajorGridlines** property.

Example

This example sets the color of the minor gridlines for the value axis in the chart to blue.

```
With myChart.Axes(xlValue)
    If .HasMinorGridlines Then
        .MinorGridlines.Border.ColorIndex = 5
    End If
End With
```

MinorTickMark Property

Applies To

Axis object.

Description

Returns or sets the type of minor tick mark for the specified axis. Can be one of the following **XlTickMark** constants: **xlTickMarkNone**, **xlTickMarkInside**, **xlTickMarkOutside**, or **xlTickMarkCross**. Read/write **Long**.

See Also

MajorTickMark property.

Example

This example sets the minor tick marks for the value axis to be inside the axis.

```
myChart.Axes(xlValue).MinorTickMark = xlTickMarkInside
```

MinorUnit Property

Applies To

Axis object.

Description

Returns or sets the minor units on the axis. Read/write **Double**.

Remarks

Setting this property sets the **MinorUnitIsAuto** property to **False**.

Use the **TickMarkSpacing** property to set tick-mark spacing on the category axis.

See Also

MajorUnit property, **MajorUnitIsAuto** property, **MajorUnitScale** property, **MinorUnitIsAuto** property, **MinorUnitScale** property, **TickMarkSpacing** property.

Example

This example sets the major and minor units for the value axis.

```
With myChart.Axes(xlValue)
    .MajorUnit = 100
    .MinorUnit = 20
End With
```

MinorUnitIsAuto Property

Applies To

Axis object.

Description

True if Microsoft Graph calculates minor units for the axis. Read/write **Boolean**.

Remarks

Setting the **MinorUnit** property sets this property to **False**.

See Also

MajorUnit property, **MajorUnitIsAuto** property, **MajorUnitScale** property, **MinorUnit** property, **MinorUnitScale** property.

Example

This example automatically calculates major and minor units for the value axis.

```
With myChart.Axes(xlValue)
    .MajorUnitIsAuto = True
    .MinorUnitIsAuto = True
End With
```

MinorUnitScale Property

Applies To

Axis object.

Description

Returns or sets the minor unit scale value for the category axis when the **CategoryType** property is set to **xlTimeScale**. Can be one of the following **XlTimeUnit** constants: **xlDays**, **xlMonths**, or **xlYears**. Read/write **Long**.

See Also

BaseUnit property, **MajorUnit** property, **MajorUnitIsAuto** property, **MajorUnitScale** property, **MinorUnit** property, **MinorUnitIsAuto** property.

Example

This example sets the category axis to use a time scale and sets the major and minor units.

```
With myChart.Axes(xlCategory)
    .CategoryType = xlTimeScale
    .MajorUnit = 5
    .MajorUnitScale = xlDays
    .MinorUnit = 1
    .MinorUnitScale = xlDays
End With
```

MoveAfterReturn Property

Applies To

Application object.

Description

True if the active cell will be moved as soon as the ENTER (RETURN) key is pressed. Read/write **Boolean**.

Example

This example sets the **MoveAfterReturn** property to **True**.

```
myChart.Application.MoveAfterReturn = True
```

Name Property

Applies To

Application object, **AxisTitle** object, **Chart** object, **ChartArea** object, **ChartTitle** object, **Corners** object, **DataLabel** object, **DataLabels** collection object, **DownBars**

object, **DropLines** object, **ErrorBars** object, **Floor** object, **Font** object, **Gridlines** object, **HiLoLines** object, **Legend** object, **PlotArea** object, **SeriesLines** object, **TickLabels** object, **Trendline** object, **UpBars** object, **Walls** object.

Description

Returns or sets the name of the object. Read/write **String**.

Example

This example assigns the name of the first trendline to the variable `myTrendname`.

```
myTrendname = myChart.SeriesCollection(1).Trendlines(1).Name
```

NameIsAuto Property

Applies To

Trendline object.

Description

True if Microsoft Graph automatically determines the name of the trendline. Read/write **Boolean**.

Example

This example sets Microsoft Graph to automatically determine the name for trendline one. The example should be run on a 2-D column chart that contains a single series with a trendline.

```
myChart.SeriesCollection(1).Trendlines(1).NameIsAuto = True
```

NumberFormat Property

Applies To

DataLabel object, **DataLabels** collection object, **Range** object, **TickLabels** object.

Description

Returns or sets the format code for the object. Returns **Null** if the cells in the specified range don't all have the same number format. Read/write **Variant** for the **Range** object; read/write **String** for all other objects.

Example

This example sets the number format for the data labels for series one.

```
myChart.SeriesCollection(1).DataLabels.NumberFormat = "General"
```

OneColorGradient Method

Applies To

ChartFillFormat object.

Description

Sets the specified fill to a one-color gradient.

Syntax

expression.**OneColorGradient**(***Style***, ***Variant***, ***Degree***)

expression Required. An expression that returns a **ChartFillFormat** object.

Style Required **Long**. The gradient style for the specified fill. Can be one of the following **MsoGradientStyle** constants: **msoGradientDiagonalDown**, **msoGradientDiagonalUp**, **msoGradientFromCenter**, **msoGradientFromCorner**, **msoGradientHorizontal**, or **msoGradientVertical**.

Variant Required **Long**. The gradient variant for the specified fill. Can be a value from 1 through 4, corresponding to the four variants listed on the **Gradient** tab in the **Fill Effects** dialog box. If ***Style*** is **msoGradientFromCenter**, the ***Variant*** argument can only be 1 or 2.

Degree Required **Single**. The gradient degree for the specified fill. Can be a value from 0.0 (dark) through 1.0 (light).

Example

This example sets the chart's fill format.

```
With myChart.ChartArea.Fill
    If .Type = msoFillGradient Then
        If .GradientColorType = msoGradientOneColor Then
            .OneColorGradient Style:=msoGradientFromCorner, _
                Variant:=1, Degree:=0.3
        End If
    End If
End With
```

Order Property

Applies To

Trendline object.

Description

Returns or sets the trendline order (an integer greater than 1) when the trendline type is **xlPolynomial**. Read/write **Long**.

Example

This example sets the order of the first trendline for series one if it's polynomial.

```
With myChart.SeriesCollection(1).Trendlines(1)
   If .Type = xlPolynomial Then .Order = 3
End With
```

Orientation Property

Applies To

AxisTitle object, **ChartTitle** object, **DataLabel** object, **DataLabels** collection object, **TickLabels** object.

Description

Returns or sets the object's orientation, as shown in the following table. Read/write **Long**.

Object	Orientation
AxisTitle, **ChartTitle**, **DataLabel**, **Range**, **Style**, **TextFrame**	The text orientation. Can be an integer value from –90 to 90 degrees or one of the following **XlOrientation** constants: **xlDownward**, **xlHorizontal**, **xlUpward**, or **xlVertical**.
TickLabels	The text orientation. Can be an integer value from –90 to 90 degrees or one of the following **XlTickLabelOrientation** constants: **xlTickLabelOrientationAutomatic**, **xlTickLabelOrientationDownward**, **xlTickLabelOrientationHorizontal**, **xlTickLabelOrientationUpward**, or **xlTickLabelOrientationVertical**.

Example

This example sets the orientation for the chart title.

```
myChart.ChartTitle.Orientation = xlHorizontal
```

OutlineFont Property

Applies To

Font object.

Description

True if the font is an outline font. Read/write **Boolean**.

Remarks

This property has no effect in Windows, but its value is retained (it can be set and returned).

Example

This example sets the font for the chart title to an outline font.

```
myChart.ChartTitle.Font.OutlineFont = True
```

Overlap Property

Applies To

ChartGroup object.

Description

Specifies how bars and columns are positioned. Can be a value between –100 and 100. Applies only to 2-D bar and 2-D column charts. Read/write **Long**.

Remarks

If this property is set to –100, bars are positioned so that there's one bar width between them. If the overlap is 0 (zero), there's no space between bars (one bar starts immediately after the preceding bar). If the overlap is 100, bars are positioned on top of each other.

See Also

GapWidth property.

Example

This example sets the overlap for chart group one to –50. The example should be run on a 2-D column chart that has two or more series.

```
myChart.ChartGroups(1).Overlap = -50
```

Parent Property

Applies To

Application object, **AutoCorrect** object, **Axes** collection object, **Axis** object, **AxisTitle** object, **Border** object, **Chart** object, **ChartArea** object, **ChartColorFormat** object, **ChartFillFormat** object, **ChartGroup** object, **ChartGroups** collection object, **ChartTitle** object, **Corners** object, **DataLabel** object, **DataLabels** collection object, **DataSheet** object, **DataTable** object, **DownBars** object, **DropLines** object, **ErrorBars** object, **Floor** object, **Font** object, **Gridlines** object, **HiLoLines** object, **Interior** object, **LeaderLines** object, **Legend** object, **LegendEntries** collection object, **LegendEntry** object, **LegendKey** object, **PlotArea** object, **Point** object, **Points** collection object, **Range** object, **Series** object, **SeriesCollection** collection object, **SeriesLines** object, **TickLabels** object, **Trendline** object, **Trendlines** collection object, **UpBars** object, **Walls** object.

Description

Returns the parent object for the specified object. Read-only.

Paste Method

Applies To

Range object.

Description

Pastes the contents of the Clipboard into the specified range on the datasheet.

Syntax

expression.**Paste**(***Link***)

expression Required. An expression that returns a **Range** object.

Link Optional **Variant**. **True** to establish a link to the source of the pasted data. The default value is **False**.

Example

This example pastes the contents of the Clipboard into cell A1 on the datasheet.

```
myChart.Application.DataSheet.Range("A1").Paste
```

Pattern Property

Applies To

ChartFillFormat object, **Interior** object.

Description

Interior object: Returns or sets the interior pattern. Read/write **Long**.

Can be one of the following **XlPattern** constants:

xlPatternAutomatic	**xlPatternChecker**
xlPatternCrissCross	**xlPatternDown**
xlPatternGray8	**xlPatternGray16**
xlPatternGray25	**xlPatternGray50**
xlPatternGray75	**xlPatternGrid**
xlPatternHorizontal	**xlPatternLightDown**
xlPatternLightHorizontal	**xlPatternLightUp**
xlPatternLightVertical	**xlPatternNone**
xlPatternSemiGray75	**xlPatternSolid**
xlPatternUp	**xlPatternVertical**

ChartFillFormat object: Returns or sets the fill pattern. Read-only **Long**.

Can be one of the following **MsoPatternType** constants:

msoPattern5Percent	**msoPattern10Percent**
msoPattern20Percent	**msoPattern25Percent**
msoPattern30Percent	**msoPattern40Percent**
msoPattern50Percent	**msoPattern60Percent**
msoPattern70Percent	**msoPattern75Percent**
msoPattern80Percent	**msoPattern90Percent**
msoPatternDarkDownwardDiagonal	**msoPatternDarkHorizontal**
msoPatternDarkUpwardDiagonal	**msoPatternDarkVertical**
msoPatternDashedDownwardDiagonal	**msoPatternDashedHorizontal**
msoPatternDashedUpwardDiagonal	**msoPatternDashedVertical**
msoPatternDiagonalBrick	**msoPatternDivot**
msoPatternDottedGrid	**msoPatternHorizontalBrick**
msoPatternLargeCheckerBoard	**msoPatternLargeConfetti**
msoPatternLargeGrid	**msoPatternLightDownwardDiagonal**
msoPatternLightHorizontal	**msoPatternLightUpwardDiagonal**
msoPatternLightVertical	**msoPatternMixed**
msoPatternNarrowHorizontal	**msoPatternNarrowVertical**
msoPatternOutlinedDiamond	**msoPatternPlaid**
msoPatternShingle	**msoPatternSmallCheckerBoard**
msoPatternSmallConfetti	**msoPatternSmallGrid**
msoPatternSolidDiamond	**msoPatternSphere**
msoPatternTrellis	**msoPatternWave**
msoPatternWeave	**msoPatternWideDownwardDiagonal**
msoPatternWideUpwardDiagonal	**msoPatternZigZag**

See Also

PatternColor property.

Example

This example adds a crisscross pattern to the interior of the plot area.

```
myChart.PlotArea.Interior.Pattern = xlPatternCrissCross
```

PatternColor Property

Applies To

Interior object.

Description

Returns or sets the color of the interior pattern as an RGB value. Read/write **Variant**.

See Also

Color property, **Pattern** property, **PatternColorIndex** property.

Example

This example sets the color of the interior pattern for the chart area.

```
myChart.ChartArea.Interior.PatternColor = RGB(255,0,0)
```

PatternColorIndex Property

Applies To

Interior object.

Description

Returns or sets the color of the interior pattern as an index into the current color palette, or as one of the following **XlColorIndex** constants: **xlColorIndexAutomatic** or **xlColorIndexNone**. Read/write **Long**.

Remarks

Set this property to **xlColorIndexAutomatic** to specify the automatic pattern for cells or the automatic fill style for drawing objects. Set this property to **xlColorIndexNone** to specify that you don't want a pattern (this is the same as setting the **Pattern** property of the **Interior** object to **xlPatternNone**).

The following table shows the color-index values in the default color palette.

Color	Index value
Aqua	8, 28, 33, 34, 42
Black	1, 51, 52
Blue	5, 32, 41, 49
Fuchsia	7, 26
Gray	16, 46, 47, 48, 56
Green	10, 43
Lime	4
Maroon	9, 30, 53

(continued)

Navy	11, 25, 55
Olive	12, 44, 45
Purple	13, 18, 21, 29, 54
Red	3
Silver	15, 17, 20, 22, 24, 35, 36, 37, 38, 39
Teal	14, 23, 31, 50
White	2, 19, 40
Yellow	6, 27

See Also

Color property, **Pattern** property, **PatternColor** property.

Example

This example sets the color of the interior pattern for the chart area.

```
myChart.ChartArea.Interior.PatternColorIndex = 5
```

Patterned Method

Applies To

ChartFillFormat object.

Description

Sets a pattern for the specified fill.

Syntax

expression.**Patterned(*Pattern*)**

expression Required. An expression that returns a **ChartFillFormat** object.

Pattern Required **Long**. The pattern type. Can be one of the following **MsoPatternType** constants.

msoPattern5Percent	**msoPattern10Percent**
msoPattern20Percent	**msoPattern25Percent**
msoPattern30Percent	**msoPattern40Percent**
msoPattern50Percent	**msoPattern60Percent**
msoPattern70Percent	**msoPattern75Percent**
msoPattern80Percent	**msoPattern90Percent**
msoPatternDarkDownwardDiagonal	**msoPatternDarkHorizontal**
msoPatternDarkUpwardDiagonal	**msoPatternDarkVertical**
msoPatternDashedDownwardDiagonal	**msoPatternDashedHorizontal**
msoPatternDashedUpwardDiagonal	**msoPatternDashedVertical**

(continued)

msoPatternDiagonalBrick
msoPatternDivot
msoPatternDottedGrid
msoPatternHorizontalBrick
msoPatternLargeCheckerBoard
msoPatternLargeConfetti
msoPatternLargeGrid
msoPatternLightDownwardDiagonal
msoPatternLightHorizontal
msoPatternLightUpwardDiagonal
msoPatternLightVertical
msoPatternMixed
msoPatternNarrowHorizontal
msoPatternNarrowVertical
msoPatternOutlinedDiamond
msoPatternPlaid
msoPatternShingle
msoPatternSmallCheckerBoard
msoPatternSmallConfetti
msoPatternSmallGrid
msoPatternSolidDiamond
msoPatternSphere
msoPatternTrellis
msoPatternWave
msoPatternWeave
msoPatternWideDownwardDiagonal
msoPatternWideUpwardDiagonal
msoPatternZigZag

Example

This example sets the fill pattern.

```
With myChart.ChartArea.Fill
    .Patterned msoPatternDiagonalBrick
    .Visible = True
End With
```

Period Property

Applies To

Trendline object.

Description

Returns or sets the period for the moving-average trendline. Read/write **Long**.

See Also

Type property.

Example

This example sets the period for the moving-average trendline. The example should be run on a 2-D column chart with a single series that contains 10 data points and a moving-average trendline.

```
With myChart.SeriesCollection(1).Trendlines(1)
    If .Type = xlMovingAvg Then .Period = 5
End With
```

Perspective Property

Applies To

Chart object.

Description

Returns or sets the perspective for the 3-D chart view. Must be from 0 through 100. This property is ignored if the **RightAngleAxes** property is **True**. Read/write **Long**.

See Also

Elevation property, **RightAngleAxes** property, **Rotation** property.

Example

This example sets the perspective of `myChart` to 70. The example should be run on a 3-D chart.

```
myChart.RightAngleAxes = False
myChart.Perspective = 70
```

PictureType Property

Applies To

Floor object, **LegendKey** object, **Point** object, **Series** object, **Walls** object.

Description

Returns or sets the way pictures are displayed on a column or bar picture chart or on the walls and faces of a 3-D chart. Read/write **Variant**.

Can be one of the following **XlPictureType** constants.

Value	Description
xlStretch	Stretches the picture to reach the necessary value.
xlStack	Stacks the pictures to reach the necessary value.
xlScale	Stacks the pictures; use the **PictureUnit** property to determine what unit each picture represents.
xlTile	Tiles the pictures.

See Also

PictureUnit property.

Example

This example sets series one to stretch pictures. The example should be run on a 2-D column chart with picture data markers.

```
myChart.SeriesCollection(1).PictureType = xlStretch
```

PictureUnit Property

Applies To

LegendKey object, **Point** object, **Series** object, **Walls** object.

Description

Returns or sets the unit for each picture on the chart if the **PictureType** property is set to **xlScale** (otherwise, this property is ignored). Read/write **Long**.

See Also

PictureType property.

Example

This example sets series one to stack pictures and uses each picture to represent five units. The example should be run on a 2-D column chart with picture data markers.

```
With myChart.SeriesCollection(1)
    .PictureType = xlScale
    .PictureUnit = 5
End With
```

Pie3DGroup Property

Applies To

Chart object.

Description

Returns a **ChartGroup** object that represents the pie chart group on a 3-D chart. Read-only.

See Also

PieGroups method.

Example

This example sets the 3-D pie group to use a different color for each data marker.

```
myChart.Pie3DGroup.VaryByCategories = True
```

PieGroups Method

Applies To

Chart object.

Description

On a 2-D chart, returns an object that represents either a single pie chart group (a **ChartGroup** object, Syntax 1) or a collection of the pie chart groups (a **ChartGroups** collection, Syntax 2).

Syntax 1

expression.**PieGroups(*Index*)**

Syntax 2

expression.**PieGroups**

expression Required. An expression that returns a **Chart** object.

Index Optional **Variant**. Specifies the chart group.

See Also

AreaGroups method, **BarGroups** method, **ChartGroups** method, **ColumnGroups** method, **DoughnutGroups** method, **LineGroups** method, **Pie3DGroup** property.

Example

This example sets pie group one to use a different color for each data marker. The example should be run on a 2-D chart.

```
myChart.PieGroups(1).VaryByCategories = True
```

PlotArea Object

Description

Represents the plot area of the specified chart. This is the area where your chart data is plotted. The plot area in a 2-D chart contains the data markers, gridlines, data labels, trendlines, and optional chart items placed in the chart area. The plot area in a 3-D chart contains all the above items plus the walls, floor, axes, axis titles, and tick-mark labels in the chart.

The plot area is surrounded by the chart area. The chart area in a 2-D chart contains the axes, the chart title, the axis titles, and the legend. The chart area in a 3-D chart contains the chart title and the legend. For information about formatting the chart area, see the **ChartArea** object.

Using the PlotArea Object

Use the **PlotArea** property to return the **PlotArea** object. The following example places a dashed border around the chart area and places a dotted border around the plot area.

```
With myChart
    .ChartArea.Border.LineStyle = xlDash
    .PlotArea.Border.LineStyle = xlDot
End With
```

Properties

Application property, **Border** property, **Creator** property, **Fill** property, **Height** property, **InsideHeight** property, **InsideLeft** property, **InsideTop** property, **InsideWidth** property, **Interior** property, **Left** property, **Name** property, **Parent** property, **Top** property, **Width** property.

Methods

ClearFormats method.

PlotArea Property

Applies To

Chart object.

Description

Returns a **PlotArea** object that represents the plot area of a chart. Read-only.

Example

This example sets the color of the plot area interior of `myChart` to cyan.

```
myChart.PlotArea.Interior.ColorIndex = 8
```

PlotBy Property

Applies To

Application object.

Description

Returns or sets the way columns or rows are used as data series on the chart. Can be one of the following **XlRowCol** constants: **xlColumns** or **xlRows**. Read/write **Long**.

Example

This example causes the embedded chart to plot data by columns.

```
myChart.PlotBy = xlColumns
```

Point Object

Description

Represents a single point in a series on the specified chart. The **Point** object is a member of the **Points** collection, which contains all the points in the specified series.

Using the Point Object

Use **Points(***index***)**, where *index* is the point's index number, to return a single **Point** object. Points are numbered from left to right in the series. `Points(1)` is the leftmost point, and `Points(Points.Count)` is the rightmost point. The following example sets the marker style for the third point in series one. For this example to work, series one must be a 2-D line, scatter, or radar series.

```
myChart.SeriesCollection(1).Points(3).MarkerStyle = xlDiamond
```

Properties

Application property, **ApplyPictToEnd** property, **ApplyPictToFront** property, **ApplyPictToSides** property, **Border** property, **Creator** property, **DataLabel** property, **Explosion** property, **Fill** property, **HasDataLabel** property, **Interior** property, **InvertIfNegative** property, **MarkerBackgroundColor** property, **MarkerBackgroundColorIndex** property, **MarkerForegroundColor** property, **MarkerForegroundColorIndex** property, **MarkerSize** property, **MarkerStyle** property, **Parent** property, **PictureType** property, **PictureUnit** property, **SecondaryPlot** property, **Shadow** property.

Methods

ApplyDataLabels method, **ClearFormats** method, **Delete** method.

Points Collection Object

Description

A collection of all the **Point** objects in the specified series in a chart.

Using the Points Collection

Use the **Points** method to return the **Points** collection. The following example adds a data label to the last point in series one in the chart.

```
Dim pts As Points

Set pts = myChart.SeriesCollection(1).Points
pts(pts.Count).ApplyDataLabels Type:=xlShowValue
```

Use **Points**(*index*), where *index* is the point's index number, to return a single **Point** object. Points are numbered from left to right in the series. `Points(1)` is the leftmost point, and `Points(Points.Count)` is the rightmost point. The following example sets the marker style for the third point in series one in the chart. The specified series must be a 2-D line, scatter, or radar series.

```
myChart.SeriesCollection(1).Points(3).MarkerStyle = xlDiamond
```

Properties

Application property, **Count** property, **Creator** property, **Parent** property.

Methods

Item method.

Points Method

Applies To

Series object.

Description

Returns an object that represents a single point (a **Point** object, Syntax 1) or a collection of all the points (a **Points** collection, Syntax 2) in the series. Read-only.

Syntax 1

expression.**Points(*Index*)**

Syntax 2

expression.**Points**

expression Required. An expression that returns a **Series** object.

Index Optional **Variant**. The name or number of the point.

Example

This example applies a data label to point one in series one.

```
myChart.SeriesCollection(1).Points(1).ApplyDataLabels
```

Position Property

Applies To

DataLabel object, **DataLabels** collection object, **Legend** object.

Description

Returns or sets the position of the specified object, as shown in the following table. Read/write **Long**.

Object	Position
DataLabel, **DataLabels**	The position of the data label. Can be one of the following **XlDataLabelPosition** constants: **xlLabelPositionAbove**, **xlLabelPositionBelow**, **xlLabelPositionBestFit**, **xlLabelPositionCenter**, **xlLabelPositionCustom**, **xlLabelPositionInsideBase**, **xlLabelPositionInsideEnd**, **xlLabelPositionLeft**, **xlLabelPositionMixed**, **xlLabelPositionOutsideEnd**, or **xlLabelPositionRight**.
Legend	The position of the legend on the chart. Can be one of the following **XlLegendPosition** constants: **xlLegendPositionBottom**, **xlLegendPositionCorner**, **xlLegendPositionLeft**, **xlLegendPositionRight**, or **xlLegendPositionTop**.

Example

This example sets the position of the legend to the top of the chart.

```
myChart.Legend.Position = xlLegendPositionTop
```

PresetGradient Method

Applies To

ChartFillFormat object.

Description

Sets the specified fill to a preset gradient.

Syntax

expression.**PresetGradient(*Style*, *Variant*, *PresetGradientType*)**

expression Required. An expression that returns a **ChartFillFormat** object.

Style Required **Long**. The gradient style for the specified fill. Can be one of the following **MsoGradientStyle** constants: **msoGradientDiagonalDown**, **msoGradientDiagonalUp**, **msoGradientFromCenter**, **msoGradientFromCorner**, **msoGradientHorizontal**, or **msoGradientVertical**.

Variant Required **Long**. The gradient variant for the specified fill. Can be a value from 1 through 4, corresponding to the four variants listed on the **Gradient** tab in the **Fill Effects** dialog box. If ***Style*** is **msoGradientFromCenter**, the ***Variant*** argument can only be 1 or 2.

PresetGradientType Required **Long**. The gradient type for the specified fill. Can be one of the following **MsoPresetGradientType** constants: **msoGradientBrass**, **msoGradientCalmWater**, **msoGradientChrome**, **msoGradientChromeII**, **msoGradientDaybreak**, **msoGradientDesert**, **msoGradientEarlySunset**, **msoGradientFire**, **msoGradientFog**, **msoGradientGold**, **msoGradientGoldII**, **msoGradientHorizon**, **msoGradientLateSunset**, **msoGradientMahogany**, **msoGradientMoss**, **msoGradientNightfall**, **msoGradientOcean**, **msoGradientParchment**, **msoGradientPeacock**, **msoGradientRainbow**, **msoGradientRainbowII**, **msoGradientSapphire**, **msoGradientSilver**, **msoGradientWheat**, or **msoPresetGradientMixed**.

Example

This example sets the chart's fill format to the preset brass color.

```
With myChart.ChartArea.Fill
    .Visible = True
    .PresetGradient msoGradientDiagonalDown, 3, msoGradientBrass
End With
```

PresetGradientType Property

Applies To

ChartFillFormat object.

Description

Returns the preset gradient type for the specified fill. Can be one of the following **MsoPresetGradientType** constants: **msoGradientBrass**, **msoGradientCalmWater**, **msoGradientChrome**, **msoGradientChromeII**, **msoGradientDaybreak**, **msoGradientDesert**, **msoGradientEarlySunset**, **msoGradientFire**, **msoGradientFog**, **msoGradientGold**, **msoGradientGoldII**, **msoGradientHorizon**, **msoGradientLateSunset**, **msoGradientMahogany**, **msoGradientMoss**, **msoGradientNightfall**, **msoGradientOcean**, **msoGradientParchment**, **msoGradientPeacock**, **msoGradientRainbow**, **msoGradientRainbowII**, **msoGradientSapphire**, **msoGradientSilver**, **msoGradientWheat**, or **msoPresetGradientMixed**. Read-only **Long**.

This property is read-only. Use the **PresetGradient** method to set the preset gradient type for the fill.

Example

This example changes the chart's preset gradient fill format from silver to gold.

```
With myChart.ChartArea.Fill
   If .Type = msoFillGradient Then
      If .GradientColorType = msoGradientPresetColors Then
         If .PresetGradientType = msoGradientSilver Then
            .PresetGradient .GradientStyle, _
               .GradientVariant, msoGradientGold
         End If
      End If
   End If
End With
```

PresetTexture Property

Applies To

ChartFillFormat object.

Description

Returns the preset texture for the specified fill. Can be one of the following **MsoPresetTexture** constants: **msoPresetTextureMixed**, **msoTextureBlueTissuePaper**, **msoTextureBouquet**, **msoTextureBrownMarble**, **msoTextureCanvas**, **msoTextureCork**, **msoTextureDenim**, **msoTextureFishFossil**, **msoTextureGranite**, **msoTextureGreenMarble**, **msoTextureMediumWood**, **msoTextureNewsprint**, **msoTextureOak**, **msoTexturePaperBag**, **msoTexturePapyrus**, **msoTextureParchment**, **msoTexturePinkTissuePaper**, **msoTexturePurpleMesh**, **msoTextureRecycledPaper**, **msoTextureSand**, **msoTextureStationery**, **msoTextureWalnut**, **msoTextureWaterDroplets**, **msoTextureWhiteMarble**, or **msoTextureWovenMat**. Read-only **Long**.

This property is read-only. Use the **PresetTextured** method to set the preset texture for the fill.

Example

This example changes the chart's textured fill format from oak to walnut.

```
With myChart.ChartArea.Fill
   If .Type = msoFillTextured Then
      If .TextureType = msoTexturePreset Then
         If .PresetTexture = msoTextureOak Then
            .PresetTextured msoTextureWalnut
         End If
      End If
   End If
End With
```

PresetTextured Method

Applies To

ChartFillFormat object.

Description

Sets the format of the specified fill to a preset texture.

Syntax

expression.**PresetTextured**(***PresetTexture***)

expression An expression that returns a **ChartFillFormat** object.

PresetTexture Required **Long**. The preset texture for the specified fill. Can be one of the following **MsoPresetTexture** constants: **msoPresetTextureMixed**, **msoTextureBlueTissuePaper**, **msoTextureBouquet**, **msoTextureBrownMarble**, **msoTextureCanvas**, **msoTextureCork**, **msoTextureDenim**, **msoTextureFishFossil**, **msoTextureGranite**, **msoTextureGreenMarble**, **msoTextureMediumWood**, **msoTextureNewsprint**, **msoTextureOak**, **msoTexturePaperBag**, **msoTexturePapyrus**, **msoTextureParchment**, **msoTexturePinkTissuePaper**, **msoTexturePurpleMesh**, **msoTextureRecycledPaper**, **msoTextureSand**, **msoTextureStationery**, **msoTextureWalnut**, **msoTextureWaterDroplets**, **msoTextureWhiteMarble**, or **msoTextureWovenMat**.

Example

This example changes the chart's textured fill format from oak to walnut.

```
With myChart.ChartArea.Fill
    If .Type = msoFillTextured Then
        If .TextureType = msoTexturePreset Then
            If .PresetTexture = msoTextureOak Then
                .PresetTextured msoTextureWalnut
            End If
        End If
    End If
End With
```

Quit Method

Applies To

Application object.

Description

Quits Microsoft Graph.

Syntax

expression.**Quit**

expression Required. An expression that returns an **Application** object.

Example

This example quits Microsoft Graph.

```
myChart.Application.Quit
```

RadarAxisLabels Property

Applies To

ChartGroup object.

Description

Returns a **TickLabels** object that represents the radar axis labels for the specified chart group. Read-only.

See Also

HasRadarAxisLabels property.

Example

This example turns on radar axis labels for chart group one on the chart and then sets the color for the labels. The example should be run on a radar chart.

```
With myChart.ChartGroups(1)
    .HasRadarAxisLabels = True
    .RadarAxisLabels.Font.ColorIndex = 3
End With
```

RadarGroups Method

Applies To

Chart object.

Description

On a 2-D chart, returns an object that represents either a single radar chart group (a **ChartGroup** object, Syntax 1) or a collection of the radar chart groups (a **ChartGroups** collection, Syntax 2).

Syntax 1

expression.**RadarGroups(*Index*)**

Syntax 2

expression.**RadarGroups**

expression Required. An expression that returns a **Chart** object.

Index Optional **Variant**. Specifies the chart group.

Example

This example sets radar group one to use a different color for each data marker. The example should be run on a 2-D chart.

```
myChart.RadarGroups(1).VaryByCategories = True
```

Range Object

Description

Represents a cell, a row, a column, or a selection of cells that contains one or more contiguous blocks of cells.

Using the Range Object

The following properties for returning a **Range** object are described in this section:

- **Range** property
- **Cells** property

Range Property

Use **Range**(*arg*), where *arg* is the name of the range, to return a **Range** object that represents a single cell or a range of cells. The following example places the value of cell A1 in cell A5.

```
myChart.Application.DataSheet.Range("A5").Value = _
    myChart.Application.DataSheet.Range("A1").Value
```

The following example fills the range A1:H8 with the value 20.

```
myChart.Application.DataSheet.Range("A1:H8").Value = 20
```

Cells Property

Use **Cells**(*row*, *column*), where *row* is the row's index number and *column* is the column's index number, to return a single cell. The following example sets the value of cell A1 to 24 (column A is the second column on the datasheet, and row 1 is the second row on the datasheet).

```
myChart.Application.DataSheet.Cells(2, 2).Value = 24
```

Although you can also use `Range("A1")` to return cell A1, there may be times when the **Cells** property is more convenient because you can use a variable for the row or column. The following example creates column and row headings on the datasheet.

```
Sub SetUpTable()
With myChart.Application.DataSheet
   For theYear = 1 To 5
      .Cells(1, theYear + 1).Value = 1990 + theYear
   Next theYear
   For theQuarter = 1 To 4
      .Cells(theQuarter + 1, 1).Value = "Q" & theQuarter
   Next theQuarter
End With
End Sub
```

Although you can use Visual Basic string functions to alter A1-style references, it's much easier (and much better programming practice) to use the `Cells(1, 1)` notation.

Use *expression*.**Cells**(*row*, *column*), where *expression* is an expression that returns a **Range** object, and *row* and *column* are relative to the upper-left corner of the range, to return part of a range. The following example sets the value for cell C5.

```
myChart.Application.Range("C5:C10").Cells(1, 1).Value = 35
```

Properties

Application property, **Cells** property, **Columns** property, **ColumnWidth** property, **Creator** property, **Include** property, **Item** property, **NumberFormat** property, **Parent** property, **Rows** property, **Value** property.

Methods

AutoFit method, **Clear** method, **ClearContents** method, **ClearFormats** method, **Copy** method, **Cut** method, **Delete** method, **Insert** method, **Paste** method.

Range Property

Applies To

DataSheet object.

Description

Returns a **Range** object that represents the specified cell or range of cells.

Syntax 1

expression.**Range**(*Cell1*)

Syntax 2

expression.**Range(*Cell1, Cell2*)**

expression Required. An expression that returns a **DataSheet** object.

Cell1 Required for Syntax 1. The name of the specified range. This must be an A1-style reference in the language the macro is written in. It can include the range operator (a colon), the intersection operator (a space), or the union operator (a comma). It can also include dollar signs, but they're ignored.

Cell1, ***Cell2*** Required for Syntax 2. The cells in the upper-left and lower-right corners of the specified range. Each argument can be a **Range** object that contains a single cell (or an entire column or entire row), or the argument can be a string that names a single cell in the language the macro is written in.

Remarks

On the datasheet, the first column heading (starting on the left) is A, followed by B, C, D, and so on. The first row heading (starting at the top) is 1, followed by 2, 3, 4, and so on. Neither the leftmost column nor the top row has a heading. In other words, column A is actually the second column from the left; likewise, row 1 is the second row from the top. The leftmost column and the top row, which are commonly used for legend text or axis labels, are referred to as column 0 (zero) and row 0 (zero). Thus, the following example inserts the text "Annual Sales" in the top cell in column A (the second column).

```
myChart.Application.DataSheet.Range("A0").Value = "Annual Sales"
```

And the following example inserts the text "District 1" in the leftmost cell in row 2 (the third row).

```
myChart.Application.DataSheet.Range("02").Value = "District 1"
```

See Also

Cells property.

Example

This example sets the value of cell A1 on the datasheet to 3.14159.

```
myChart.DataSheet.Range("A1").Value = 3.14159
```

This example loops on cells A1:C3 on the datasheet. If one of the cells has a value less than 0.001, the example replaces that value with 0 (zero).

```
With myChart.Application.DataSheet
    For Each c in .Range("A1:C3")
        If c.Value < .001 Then
            c.Value = 0
        End If
    Next c
End With
```

ReadingOrder Property

Applies To

AxisTitle object, **ChartTitle** object, **DataLabel** object, **DataLabels** collection object, **TickLabels** object.

Description

This property isn't used in the U.S. English version of Microsoft Graph.

Refresh Method

Applies To

Chart object.

Description

Causes the specified chart to be redrawn immediately.

Syntax

expression.**Refresh**

expression Required. An expression that returns a **Chart** object.

ReplacementList Method

Applies To

AutoCorrect object.

Description

Returns the array of AutoCorrect replacements.

Syntax

expression.**ReplacementList(*Index*)**

expression Required. An expression that returns an **AutoCorrect** object.

Index Optional **Variant**. The row of the array of AutoCorrect replacements to be returned. The row is returned as a one-dimensional array with two elements: The first element is the text in column 1, and the second element is the text in column 2. If ***Index*** is out of range, this method fails.

If ***Index*** is omitted, this method returns a two-dimensional array. Each row in the array contains one replacement, as shown in the following table.

Column	Contents
1	The text to be replaced
2	The replacement text

Remarks

Use the **AddReplacement** method to add an entry to the replacement list.

See Also

AddReplacement method, **DeleteReplacement** method.

Example

This example searches the replacement list for "Temperature" and displays the replacement entry if it exists.

```
repl = myChart.Application.AutoCorrect.ReplacementList
For x = 1 To UBound(repl)
      If repl(x, 1) = "Temperature" Then MsgBox repl(x, 2)
Next
```

ReplaceText Property

Applies To

AutoCorrect object.

Description

True if text in the list of AutoCorrect replacements is replaced automatically. Read/write **Boolean**.

See Also

ReplacementList method.

Example

This example turns off automatic text replacement for the chart.

```
With myChart.Application.AutoCorrect
   .CapitalizeNamesOfDays = True
   .ReplaceText = False
End With
```

ReversePlotOrder Property

Applies To

Axis object.

Description

True if Microsoft Graph plots data points from last to first. Read/write **Boolean**.

Remarks

This property cannot be used on radar charts.

Example

This example plots data points from last to first on the value axis.

```
myChart.Axes(xlValue).ReversePlotOrder = True
```

RGB Property

Applies To

ChartColorFormat object.

Description

Returns the red-green-blue value of the specified color. Read-only **Long**.

Example

This example sets the color of the legend font to the foreground fill color of the plot area.

```
myChart.Legend.Font.Color = _
    myChart.PlotArea.Fill.ForeColor.RGB
```

RightAngleAxes Property

Applies To

Chart object.

Description

True if the chart axes are at right angles, independent of chart rotation or elevation. Applies only to 3-D line, column, and bar charts. Read/write **Boolean**.

Remarks

If this property is **True**, the **Perspective** property is ignored.

See Also

Elevation property, **Perspective** property, **Rotation** property.

Example

This example sets the axes to intersect at right angles. The example should be run on a 3-D chart.

```
myChart.RightAngleAxes = True
```

Rotation Property

Applies To

Chart object.

Description

Returns or sets the rotation of the 3-D chart view (the rotation of the plot area around the z-axis, in degrees). The value of this property must be from 0 to 360, except for 3-D bar charts, where the value must be from 0 to 44. The default value is 20. Applies only to 3-D charts. Read/write **Variant**.

See Also

Elevation property, **Perspective** property, **RightAngleAxes** property.

Example

This example sets the rotation of `myChart` to 30 degrees. The example should be run on a 3-D chart.

```
myChart.Rotation = 30
```

Rows Property

Applies To

DataSheet object, **Range** object.

Description

Range object: Returns a **Range** object that represents the rows in the specified range. Read-only.

DataSheet object: Returns a **Range** object that represents all the rows on the datasheet. Read-only.

See Also

Columns property, **Range** property.

Example

This example deletes row three on the datasheet.

```
myChart.Application.DataSheet.Rows(3).Delete
```

SaveAsOldFileFormat Method

Applies To

Application object.

Description

In a host application such as Microsoft PowerPoint, saves a chart in the specified older file format.

Syntax

expression.**FileImport(*MajorVersion, MinorVersion*)**

expression Required. An expression that returns an **Application** object.

MajorVersion Optional **Variant**. Specifies the major version number of the file format you want to use.

MinorVersion Optional **Variant**. Specifies the minor version number of the file format you want to use.

Example

This example saves the chart in Microsoft Graph version 5.0 file format.

```
myChart.Application.SaveAsOldFileFormat MajorVersion:=5
```

ScaleType Property

Applies To

Axis object.

Description

Returns or sets the value axis scale type. Can be one of the following **XlScaleType** constants: **xlScaleLinear** or **xlScaleLogarithmic**. Applies only to the value axis. Read/write **Long**.

Remarks

A logarithmic scale uses base 10 logarithms.

Example

This example sets the value axis to use a logarithmic scale.

```
myChart.Axes(xlValue).ScaleType = xlScaleLogarithmic
```

SchemeColor Property

Applies To

ChartColorFormat object.

Description

Returns or sets the color of the specified **ChartColorFormat** object as an index in the current color scheme. Read/write **Long**.

Example

This example sets the foreground color, background color, and gradient for the chart area fill on the chart.

```
With myChart.ChartArea.Fill
    .Visible = True
    .ForeColor.SchemeColor = 15
    .BackColor.SchemeColor = 17
    .TwoColorGradient msoGradientHorizontal, 1
End With
```

SecondaryPlot Property

Applies To

Point object.

Description

True if the point is in the secondary section of either a pie of pie chart or a bar of pie chart. Applies only to points on pie of pie charts or bar of pie charts. Read/write **Boolean**.

Example

This example must be run on either a pie of pie chart or a bar of pie chart. The example moves point four to the secondary section of the chart.

```
With myChart.SeriesCollection(1)
    .Points(4).SecondaryPlot = True
End With
```

SecondPlotSize Property

Applies To

ChartGroup object.

Description

Returns or sets the size of the secondary section of either a pie of pie chart or a bar of pie chart, as a percentage of the size of the primary pie. Can be a value from 5 through 200. Read/write **Long**.

Example

This example must be run on either a pie of pie chart or a bar of pie chart. The example splits the two sections of the chart by value, combining all values under 10 in the primary pie and displaying them in the secondary section. The secondary section is 50 **percent** of the size of the primary pie.

```
With myChart.ChartGroups(1)
   .SplitType = xlSplitByValue
   .SplitValue = 10
   .VaryByCategories = True
   .SecondPlotSize = 50
End With
```

Series Object

Description

Represents a series in the specified chart. The **Series** object is a member of the **SeriesCollection** collection.

Using the Series Object

Use **SeriesCollection**(*index*), where *index* is the series' index number or name, to return a single **Series** object. The following example sets the color of the interior for series one in the chart.

```
myChart.SeriesCollection(1).Interior.Color = RGB(255, 0, 0)
```

The series index number indicates the order in which the series are added to the chart. `SeriesCollection(1)` is the first series added to the chart, and `SeriesCollection(SeriesCollection.Count)` is the last one added.

Properties

Application property, **ApplyPictToEnd** property, **ApplyPictToFront** property, **ApplyPictToSides** property, **AxisGroup** property, **BarShape** property, **Border** property, **ChartType** property, **Creator** property, **ErrorBars** property, **Explosion** property, **Fill** property, **Has3DEffect** property, **HasDataLabels** property, **HasErrorBars** property, **HasLeaderLines** property, **Interior** property,

InvertIfNegative property, **LeaderLines** property, **MarkerBackgroundColor** property, **MarkerBackgroundColorIndex** property, **MarkerForegroundColor** property, **MarkerForegroundColorIndex** property, **MarkerSize** property, **MarkerStyle** property, **Parent** property, **PictureType** property, **PictureUnit** property, **Shadow** property, **Smooth** property, **Type** property.

Methods

ApplyCustomType method, **ApplyDataLabels** method, **ClearFormats** method, **DataLabels** method, **Delete** method, **ErrorBar** method, **Points** method, **Trendlines** method.

SeriesCollection Collection Object

Description

A collection of all the **Series** objects in the specified chart or chart group.

Using the SeriesCollection Collection

Use the **SeriesCollection** method to return the **SeriesCollection** collection. The following example adjusts the interior color for each series in the collection:

```
For X = 1 To myChart.SeriesCollection.Count
   With myChart.SeriesCollection(X)
      .Interior.Color = RGB(X * 75, 50, X * 50)
   End With
Next X
```

Use **SeriesCollection**(*index*), where *index* is the series' index number or name, to return a single **Series** object. The following example sets the color of the interior for series one in the chart to red.

```
myChart.SeriesCollection(1).Interior.Color = RGB(255, 0, 0)
```

Properties

Application property, **Count** property, **Creator** property, **Parent** property.

Methods

Item method.

SeriesCollection Method

Applies To

Chart object, **ChartGroup** object.

Description

Returns an object that represents either a single series (a **Series** object, Syntax 1) or a collection of all the series (a **SeriesCollection** collection, Syntax 2) in the chart or chart group.

Syntax 1

expression.**SeriesCollection(*Index*)**

Syntax 2

expression.**SeriesCollection**

expression   Required. An expression that returns a **Chart** or **ChartGroup** object.

Index   Optional **Variant**. The name or number of the series.

Example

This example turns on data labels for series one.

```
myChart.SeriesCollection(1).HasDataLabels = True
```

SeriesLines Object

Description

Represents series lines in the specified chart group. Series lines connect the data values in each series. Only 2-D stacked-bar or column chart groups can have series lines. This object isn't a collection. There's no object that represents a single series line; either you have series lines turned on for all points in a chart group or you have them turned off.

Using the SeriesLines Object

Use the **SeriesLines** property to return the **SeriesLines** object. The following example adds series lines to chart group one in the chart. The chart must be a 2-D stacked-bar or column chart.

```
With myChart.ChartGroups(1)
    .HasSeriesLines = True
    .SeriesLines.Border.Color = RGB(0, 0, 255)
End With
```

Remarks

If the **HasSeriesLines** property is **False**, most properties of the **SeriesLines** object are disabled.

Properties

Application property, **Border** property, **Creator** property, **Name** property, **Parent** property.

Methods

Delete method.

SeriesLines Property

Applies To

ChartGroup object.

Description

Returns a **SeriesLines** object that represents the series lines for the specified stacked bar chart or stacked column chart. Applies only to stacked bar and stacked column charts. Read-only.

See Also

HasSeriesLines property.

Example

This example turns on series lines for chart group one on the chart and then sets their line style, weight, and color. The example should be run on a 2-D stacked column chart that has two or more series.

```
With myChart.ChartGroups(1)
   .HasSeriesLines = True
   With .SeriesLines.Border
      .LineStyle = xlThin
      .Weight = xlMedium
      .ColorIndex = 3
   End With
End With
```

SetDefaultChart Method

Applies To

Application object.

Description

Specifies the name of the chart template that Microsoft Graph will use when creating new charts.

Syntax

expression.**SetDefaultChart(*FormatName*)**

expression Required. An expression that returns an **Application** object.

FormatName Optional **Variant**. The name of the specified custom autoformat. This name can be a string that denotes the custom autoformat, or it can be the special constant **xlBuiltIn** to specify the built-in chart template.

Example

This example sets the default chart template to the custom autoformat named "Monthly Sales."

```
myChart.Application.SetDefaultChart FormatName:="Monthly Sales"
```

Shadow Property

Applies To

AxisTitle object, **ChartArea** object, **ChartTitle** object, **DataLabel** object, **DataLabels** collection object, **Font** object, **Legend** object, **LegendKey** object, **Point** object, **Series** object.

Description

True if the font is a shadow font or if the specified object has a shadow. Read/write **Boolean**.

Remarks

For the **Font** object, this property has no effect in Microsoft Windows, but its value is retained (it can be set and returned).

Example

This example adds a shadow to the title of `myChart`.

```
myChart.ChartTitle.Shadow = True
```

ShowChartTipNames Property

Applies To

Application object.

Description

True if charts show chart tip names. The default value is **True**. Read/write **Boolean**.

Example

This example turns off chart tip names and values.

```
With myChart.Application
    .ShowChartTipNames = False
    .ShowChartTipValues = False
End With
```

ShowChartTipValues Property

Applies To

Application object.

Description

True if charts show chart tip values. The default value is **True**. Read/write **Boolean**.

Example

This example turns off chart tip names and values.

```
With myChart.Application
    .ShowChartTipNames = False
    .ShowChartTipValues = False
End With
```

ShowLegendKey Property

Applies To

DataLabel object, **DataLabels** collection object, **DataTable** object.

Description

True if the data label legend key is visible. Read/write **Boolean**.

Example

This example sets the data labels for series one to show values and the legend key.

```
With myChart.SeriesCollection(1).DataLabels
    .ShowLegendKey = True
    .Type = xlShowValue
End With
```

ShowNegativeBubbles Property

Applies To

ChartGroup object.

Description

True if negative bubbles are shown for the chart group. Valid only for bubble charts. Read/write **Boolean**.

Example

This example makes negative bubbles visible for chart group one.

```
myChart.ChartGroups(1).ShowNegativeBubbles = True
```

Size Property

Applies To

Font object.

Description

Returns or sets the size of the font. Read/write **Variant**.

Example

This example sets the font size for the chart title.

```
myChart.ChartTitle.Font.Size = 12
```

SizeRepresents Property

Applies To

ChartGroup object.

Description

Returns or sets what the bubble size represents on a bubble chart. Can be either of the following **XlSizeRepresents** constants: **xlSizeIsArea** or **xlSizeIsWidth**. Read/write **Long**.

Example

This example sets what the bubble size represents for the chart. (The example assumes that the chart is a bubble chart.)

```
myChart.ChartGroups(1).SizeRepresents = xlSizeIsWidth
```

Smooth Property

Applies To

LegendKey object, **Series** object.

Description

True if curve smoothing is turned on for the line chart or scatter chart. Applies only to line and scatter charts. Read/write.

Example

This example turns on curve smoothing for series one. The example should be run on a 2-D line chart.

```
myChart.SeriesCollection(1).Smooth = True
```

Solid Method

Applies To

ChartFillFormat object.

Description

Sets the specified fill to a uniform color. Use this method to convert a gradient, textured, patterned, or background fill back to a solid fill.

Example

This example converts the chart area fill to a solid color.

```
myChart.ChartArea.Fill.Solid
```

SplitType Property

Applies To

ChartGroup object.

Description

Returns or sets the way the two sections of either a pie of pie chart or a bar of pie chart are split. Can be one of the following **XlChartSplitType** constants: **xlSplitByPosition**, **xlSplitByPercentValue**, **xlSplitByCustomSplit**, or **xlSplitByValue**. Read/write **Long**.

See Also

SplitValue property.

Example

This example must be run on either a pie of pie chart or a bar of pie chart. The example splits the two sections of the chart by value, combining all values under 10 in the primary pie and displaying them in the secondary section.

```
With myChart.ChartGroups(1)
    .SplitType = xlSplitByValue
    .SplitValue = 10
    .VaryByCategories = True
End With
```

SplitValue Property

Applies To

ChartGroup object.

Description

Returns or sets the threshold value separating the two sections of either a pie of pie chart or a bar of pie chart. Read/write **Variant**.

See Also

SplitType property.

Example

This example must be run on either a pie of pie chart or a bar of pie chart. The example splits the two sections of the chart by value, combining all values under 10 in the primary pie and displaying them in the secondary section.

```
With myChart.ChartGroups(1)
    .SplitType = xlSplitByValue
    .SplitValue = 10
    .VaryByCategories = True
End With
```

Strikethrough Property

Applies To

Font object.

Description

True if the font is struck through with a horizontal line. Read/write **Boolean**.

Example

This example sets the font in the chart title to strikethrough.

```
myChart.ChartTitle.Font.Strikethrough = True
```

Subscript Property

Applies To

Font object.

Description

True if the specified font is formatted as subscript. The default value is **False**. Read/write **Variant**.

See Also

Superscript property.

Superscript Property

Applies To

Font object.

Description

True if the specified font is formatted as superscript. The default value is **False**. Read/write **Variant**.

See Also

Subscript property.

SurfaceGroup Property

Applies To

Chart object.

Description

Returns a **ChartGroup** object that represents the surface chart group of a 3-D chart. Read-only.

Example

This example sets the 3-D surface group to use a different color for each data marker. The example should be run on a 3-D chart.

```
myChart.SurfaceGroup.VaryByCategories = True
```

Text Property

Applies To

AxisTitle object, **ChartTitle** object, **DataLabel** object.

Description

Returns or sets the text for the specified object. Read/write **String**.

Example

This example sets the text for the title of the chart.

```
With myChart
    .HasTitle = True
    .ChartTitle.Text = "First Quarter Sales"
End With
```

This example sets the axis title text for the category axis.

```
With myChart.Axes(xlCategory)
    .HasTitle = True
    .AxisTitle.Text = "Month"
End With
```

TextureName Property

Applies To

ChartFillFormat object.

Description

Returns the name of the custom texture file for the specified fill. Read-only **String**.

This property is read-only. Use the **UserPicture** or **UserTextured** method to set the texture file for the fill.

Example

This example changes the user-defined texture type for the chart's fill format.

```
With myChart.ChartArea.Fill
   If .Type = msoFillTextured Then
      If .TextureType = msoTextureUserDefined Then
         If .TextureName = "brick.bmp" Then
            .UserTextured "stone.bmp"
         End If
      End If
   End If
End With
```

TextureType Property

Applies To

ChartFillFormat object.

Description

Returns the texture type for the specified fill. Can be one of the following **MsoTextureType** constants: **msoTexturePreset**, **msoTextureTypeMixed**, or **msoTextureUserDefined**. Read-only **Long**.

This property is read-only. Use the **UserTextured** method to set the texture type for the fill.

Example

This example changes the user-defined texture type for the chart's fill format.

```
With myChart.ChartArea.Fill
   If .Type = msoFillTextured Then
      If .TextureType = msoTextureUserDefined Then
         If .TextureName = "C:\brick.bmp" Then
            .UserTextured "C:\stone.bmp"
         End If
      End If
   End If
End With
```

TickLabelPosition Property

Applies To

Axis object.

Description

Describes the position of tick-mark labels on the specified axis. Can be one of the following **XlTickLabelPosition** constants: **xlTickLabelPositionNone**, **xlTickLabelPositionLow**, **xlTickLabelPositionHigh**, or **xlTickLabelPositionNextToAxis**. Read/write **Long**.

See Also

MajorTickMark property, **MinorTickMark** property, **TickLabels** property, **TickLabelSpacing** property, **TickMarkSpacing** property.

Example

This example sets tick-mark labels on the category axis to the high position (above the chart).

```
myChart.Axes(xlCategory) _
   .TickLabelPosition = xlTickLabelPositionHigh
```

TickLabels Object

Description

Represents the tick-mark labels associated with tick marks on the specified chart axis. This object isn't a collection. There's no object that represents a single tick-mark label; you must return all the tick-mark labels as a unit.

Tick-mark label text for the category axis comes from the name of the associated category in the chart. The default tick-mark label text for the category axis is the number that indicates the position of the category relative to the left end of this axis. To change the number of unlabeled tick marks between tick-mark labels, you must change the **TickLabelSpacing** property for the category axis.

Tick-mark label text for the value axis is calculated based on the **MajorUnit**, **MinimumScale**, and **MaximumScale** properties of the value axis. To change the tick-mark label text for the value axis, you must change the values of these properties.

Using the TickLabels Object

Use the **TickLabels** property to return the **TickLabels** object. The following example sets the number format for the tick-mark labels on the value axis in the chart.

```
myChart.Axes(xlValue).TickLabels.NumberFormat = "0.00"
```

Properties

Application property, **AutoScaleFont** property, **Creator** property, **Font** property, **Name** property, **NumberFormat** property, **Orientation** property, **Parent** property, **ReadingOrder** property.

Methods

Delete method.

TickLabels Property

Applies To

Axis object.

Description

Returns a **TickLabels** collection that represents the tick-mark labels for the specified axis. Read-only.

See Also

MajorTickMark property, **MinorTickMark** property, **TickLabelPosition** property, **TickLabelSpacing** property, **TickMarkSpacing** property.

Example

This example sets the color of the tick-mark label font for the value axis.

```
myChart.Axes(xlValue).TickLabels.Font.ColorIndex = 3
```

TickLabelSpacing Property

Applies To

Axis object.

Description

Returns or sets the number of categories or series between tick-mark labels. Applies only to category and series axes. Read/write **Long**.

Remarks

Tick-mark label spacing on the value axis is always calculated by Microsoft Graph.

See Also

MajorTickMark property, **MinorTickMark** property, **TickLabelPosition** property, **TickLabels** property, **TickMarkSpacing** property.

Example

This example sets the number of categories between tick-mark labels on the category axis.

```
myChart.Axes(xlCategory).TickLabelSpacing = 10
```

TickMarkSpacing Property

Applies To

Axis object.

Description

Returns or sets the number of categories or series between tick marks. Applies only to category and series axes. Read/write **Long**.

Remarks

Use the **MajorUnit** and **MinorUnit** properties to set tick-mark spacing on the value axis.

See Also

MajorTickMark property, **MajorUnit** property, **MinorTickMark** property, **MinorUnit** property, **TickLabelPosition** property, **TickLabels** property, **TickLabelSpacing** property.

Example

This example sets the number of categories between tick marks on the category axis.

```
myChart.Axes(xlCategory).TickMarkSpacing = 10
```

Top Property

Applies To

Application object, **Axis** object, **AxisTitle** object, **Chart** object, **ChartArea** object, **ChartTitle** object, **DataLabel** object, **DataSheet** object, **Legend** object, **LegendEntry** object, **LegendKey** object, **PlotArea** object.

Description

Returns or sets the position of the specified object, in points. Read/write **Long**, except as shown in the following table.

Remarks

The meaning of the **Top** property depends on the specified object.

Object	Meaning
Application	The distance from the top edge of the screen to the top edge of the main Microsoft Graph window. In Windows, if the application window is minimized, this property controls the position of the window icon (anywhere on the screen). On the Macintosh, the value is always 0 (zero); setting the value to something else will have no effect.
Axis, **AxisTitle**, **ChartArea**, **Chart**, **ChartTitle**, **DataLabel**, **DataSheet**, **Legend**, **LegendEntry**, **LegendKey**, **PlotArea**	The distance from the top edge of the object to the top of row 1 (on a datasheet) or the top of the chart area (on a chart). Read-only for **Axis**, **LegendEntry**, and **LegendKey**.

See Also

Height property, **Left** property, **Width** property.

Example

This example sets the position of the top of the chart title.

```
myChart.ChartTitle.Top = 10
```

Trendline Object

Description

Represents a trendline in the specified chart. A trendline shows the trend, or direction, of data in a series. The **Trendline** object is a member of the **Trendlines** collection, which contains all the **Trendline** objects for a single series.

Using the Trendline Object

Use **Trendlines**(*index*), where *index* is the trendline's index number, to return a single **Trendline** object. The following example changes the trendline type for series one in the chart. If the series has no trendline, this example will fail.

```
myChart.SeriesCollection(1).Trendlines(1).Type = xlMovingAvg
```

The index number denotes the order in which the trendlines are added to the series. `Trendlines(1)` is the first trendline added to the series, and `Trendlines(Trendlines.Count)` is the last one added.

Properties

Application property, **Backward** property, **Border** property, **Creator** property, **DataLabel** property, **DisplayEquation** property, **DisplayRSquared** property, **Forward** property, **Index** property, **Intercept** property, **InterceptIsAuto** property, **Name** property, **NameIsAuto** property, **Order** property, **Parent** property, **Period** property, **Type** property.

Methods

ClearFormats method, **Delete** method.

Trendlines Collection Object

Description

A collection of all the **Trendline** objects for the specified series. Each **Trendline** object represents a trendline in a chart. A trendline shows the trend, or direction, of data in a series.

Using the Trendlines Collection

Use the **Trendlines** method to return the **Trendlines** collection. The following example displays the number of trendlines for series one in the chart.

```
MsgBox myChart.SeriesCollection(1).Trendlines.Count
```

Use the **Add** method to create a new trendline and add it to the series. The following example adds a linear trendline to series one in the chart.

```
With myChart.SeriesCollection(1).Trendlines
    .Add Type:=xlLinear, Name:="Linear Trend"
End With
```

Use **Trendlines**(*index*), where *index* is the trendline's index number, to return a single **TrendLine** object. The following example changes the trendline type for series one in the chart. If the series has no trendline, this example will fail.

```
myChart.SeriesCollection(1).Trendlines(1).Type = xlMovingAvg
```

The index number denotes the order in which the trendlines are added to the series. `Trendlines(1)` is the first trendline added to the series, and `Trendlines(Trendlines.Count)` is the last one added.

Properties

Application property, **Count** property, **Creator** property, **Parent** property.

Methods

Add method, **Item** method.

Trendlines Method

Applies To

Series object.

Description

Returns an object that represents a single trendline (a **Trendline** object, Syntax 1) or a collection of all the trendlines (a **Trendlines** collection, Syntax 2) for the series.

Syntax 1

object.**Trendlines(*Index*)**

Syntax 2

object.**Trendlines**

object Required. The **Series** object.

Index Optional **Variant**. The name or number of the trendline.

Example

This example adds a linear trendline to series one.

```
myChart.SeriesCollection(1).Trendlines.Add Type:=xlLinear
```

TwoColorGradient Method

Applies To

ChartFillFormat object.

Description

Sets the specified fill to a two-color gradient.

Syntax

expression.**TwoColorGradient(*Style, Variant*)**

expression Required. An expression that returns a **ChartFillFormat** object.

Style Required **Long**. Specifies the gradient style. Can be one of the following **MsoGradientStyle** constants: **msoGradientDiagonalDown**, **msoGradientDiagonalUp**, **msoGradientFromCenter**, **msoGradientFromCorner**, **msoGradientHorizontal**, or **msoGradientVertical**.

Variant Required **Long**. Specifies the gradient variant. Can be a value from 1 through 4, corresponding to the four variants on the **Gradient** tab in the **Fill Effects** dialog box. If ***Style*** is **msoGradientFromCenter**, the ***Variant*** argument can only be either 1 or 2.

Example

This example sets the gradient, background color, and foreground color for the chart area fill on the chart.

```
With myChart.ChartArea.Fill
    .Visible = True
    .ForeColor.SchemeColor = 15
    .BackColor.SchemeColor = 17
    .TwoColorGradient msoGradientHorizontal, 1
End With
```

TwoInitialCapitals Property

Applies To

AutoCorrect object.

Description

True if words that begin with two capital letters are corrected automatically. Read/write **Boolean**.

Example

This example sets Microsoft Graph to automatically correct words that begin with two capital letters.

```
With myChart.Application.AutoCorrect
   .TwoInitialCapitals = True
   .ReplaceText = True
End With
```

Type Property

Applies To

Axis object, **ChartColorFormat** object, **ChartFillFormat** object, **DataLabel** object, **DataLabels** collection object, **Series** object, **Trendline** object.

Description

Returns or sets the type of the specified object, as shown in the following table.

Object	Type
Axis	Axis type. Can be one of the following **XlAxisType** constants: **xlCategory**, **xlSeriesAxis**, or **xlValue**. Read/write **Long**.
ChartColorFormat	Color type. Can be one of the following **MsoColorType** constants: **msoColorTypeMixed**, **msoColorTypeRGB**, or **msoColorTypeScheme**. Read-only **Long**.
DataLabel, DataLabels	Data label type. Can be one of the following **XlDataLabelsType** constants: **xlDataLabelsShowBubbleSizes**, **xlDataLabelsShowLabel**, **xlDataLabelsShowLabelAndPercent**, **xlDataLabelsShowNone**, **xlDataLabelsShowPercent**, or **xlDataLabelsShowValue**. Read/write **Long**.
ChartFillFormat	Fill type. Can be one of the following **MsoFillType** constants: **msoFillBackground**, **msoFillGradient**, **msoFillMixed**, **msoFillPatterned**, **msoFillPicture**, **msoFillSolid**, or **msoFillTextured**. Read-only **Long**.
Trendline	Trendline type. Can be one of the following **XlTrendlineType** constants: **xlExponential**, **xlLinear**, **xlLogarithmic**, **xlMovingAvg**, **xlPolynomial**, or **xlPower**. Read/write **Long**.

See Also

ChartType property.

Example

This example changes the trendline type for the first series in the chart. If the series has no trendline, this example fails.

```
myChart.SeriesCollection(1).Trendlines(1).Type = xlMovingAvg
```

Underline Property

Applies To

Font object.

Description

Returns or sets the type of underline applied to the font. Can be one of the following **XlUnderlineStyle** constants: **xlUnderlineStyleNone**, **xlUnderlineStyleSingle**, **xlUnderlineStyleDouble**, **xlUnderlineStyleSingleAccounting**, or **xlUnderlineStyleDoubleAccounting**. Read/write **Long**.

Example

This example sets the font in the chart title to single underline.

```
myChart.ChartTitle.Font.Underline = xlUnderlineStyleSingle
```

UpBars Object

Description

Represents the up bars in a chart group. Up bars connect points in series one with higher values in the last series in the chart group (the lines go up from series one). Only 2-D line groups that contain at least two series can have up bars. This object isn't a collection. There's no object that represents a single up bar; either you have up bars turned on for all points in a chart group or you have them turned off.

Using the UpBars Object

Use the **UpBars** property to return the **UpBars** object. The following example turns on up and down bars for chart group one in the chart. The example then sets the up-bar color to blue and sets the down-bar color to red.

```
With myChart.ChartGroups(1)
    .HasUpDownBars = True
    .UpBars.Interior.Color = RGB(0, 0, 255)
    .DownBars.Interior.Color = RGB(255, 0, 0)
End With
```

Remarks

If the **HasUpDownBars** property is **False**, most properties of the **UpBars** object are disabled.

Properties

Application property, **Border** property, **Creator** property, **Fill** property, **Interior** property, **Name** property, **Parent** property.

Methods

Delete method.

See Also

DownBars object.

UpBars Property

Applies To

ChartGroup object.

Description

Returns an **UpBars** object that represents the up bars on a line chart. Applies only to line charts. Read-only.

See Also

DownBars property, **HasUpDownBars** property.

Example

This example turns on up and down bars for chart group one and then sets their colors. The example should be run on a 2-D line chart containing two series that cross each other at one or more data points.

```
With myChart.ChartGroups(1)
    .HasUpDownBars = True
    .DownBars.Interior.ColorIndex = 3
    .UpBars.Interior.ColorIndex = 5
End With
```

Update Method

Applies To

Application object.

Description

Updates the specified embedded object in the host file.

Syntax

expression.**Update**

expression Required. An expression that returns an **Application** object.

UserPicture Method

Applies To

ChartFillFormat object.

Description

Fills the specified shape with an image.

Syntax

expression.**UserPicture**(***PictureFile***, ***PictureFormat***, ***PictureStackUnit***, ***PicturePlacement***)

expression An expression that returns a **ChartFillFormat** object.

PictureFile Required **String**. The name of the specified picture file.

PictureFormat Optional **Long**. The format of the specified picture. Can be one of the following **XlChartPictureType** constants: **xlScale**, **xlStackScale**, **xlStack**, or **xlStretch**.

PictureStackUnit Optional **Long**. The stack or scale unit for the specified picture (depends on the ***PictureFormat*** argument).

PicturePlacement Optional **Long**. The placement of the specified picture. Can be one of the following **XlChartPicturePlacement** constants: **xlSides**, **xlEnd**, **xlEndSides**, **xlFront**, **xlFrontSides**, **xlFrontEnd**, or **xlAllFaces**.

Example

This example sets the chart's fill format so that it's based on a user-supplied picture.

```
With myChart.ChartArea.Fill
    .UserPicture PictureFile:="C:\My Documents\brick.bmp"
    .Visible = True
End With
```

UserTextured Method

Applies To

ChartFillFormat object.

Description

Fills the specified shape with small tiles of an image. If you want to fill the shape with one large image, use the **UserPicture** method.

Syntax

expression.**UserTextured**(***TextureFile***)

expression Required. An expression that returns a **ChartFillFormat** object.

TextureFile Required **String**. The name of the specified picture file.

Example

This example changes the user-defined texture type for the chart's fill format.

```
With myChart.ChartArea.Fill
   If .Type = msoFillTextured Then
      If .TextureType = msoTextureUserDefined Then
         If .TextureName = "C:\brick.bmp" Then
            .UserTextured "C:\stone.bmp"
         End If
      End If
   End If
End With
```

Value Property

Applies To

Range object.

Description

Returns the value of the specified cell. If the cell is empty, **Value** returns the value **Empty** (use the **IsEmpty** function to test for this case). If the **Range** object contains more than one cell, this property returns an array of values (use the **IsArray** function to test for this case). Read/write.

See Also

LineStyle property.

Example

This example sets the value of cell A1 on the datasheet to 3.14159.

```
myChart.Application.DataSheet.Range("A1").Value = 3.14159
```

VaryByCategories Property

Applies To

ChartGroup object.

Description

True if Microsoft Graph assigns a different color or pattern to each data marker. The chart must contain only one series. Read/write **Boolean**.

Example

This example assigns a different color or pattern to each data marker in chart group one. The example should be run on a 2-D line chart that has data markers on a series.

```
myChart.ChartGroups(1).VaryByCategories = True
```

Version Property

Applies To

Application object.

Description

Returns the Microsoft Graph version number. Read-only **String**.

Example

This example displays a message box that contains the Microsoft Graph version number and the name of the operating system.

```
MsgBox "Welcome to Microsoft Graph version " & _
   myChart.Application.Version
```

VerticalAlignment Property

Applies To

AxisTitle object, **ChartTitle** object, **DataLabel** object, **DataLabels** collection object.

Description

Returns or sets the vertical alignment of the object. Can be one of the following **XlVAlign** constants: **xlVAlignBottom**, **xlVAlignCenter**, **xlVAlignDistributed**, **xlVAlignJustify**, or **xlVAlignTop**. Read/write **Long**.

Remarks

The **xlVAlignDistributed** alignment style works only in Far East versions of Microsoft Graph.

See Also

HorizontalAlignment property.

Example

This example sets the vertical alignment of the chart title.

```
myChart.ChartTitle.VerticalAlignment = xlCenter
```

Visible Property

Applies To

Application object, **ChartFillFormat** object.

Description

True if the specified object is visible. Read/write **Boolean** or **Long**.

Example

This example formats the chart's fill with a preset gradient and then makes the fill visible.

```
With myChart.ChartArea.Fill
    .Visible = True
    .PresetGradient msoGradientDiagonalDown, _
        3, msoGradientBrass
End With
```

Walls Object

Description

Represents the walls of the specified 3-D chart. This object isn't a collection. There's no object that represents a single wall; you must return all the walls as a unit.

Using the Walls Object

Use the **Walls** property to return the **Walls** object. The following example sets the pattern on the walls for the chart. If the chart isn't a 3-D chart, this example will fail.

```
myChart.Walls.Interior.Pattern = xlGray75
```

Properties

Application property, **Border** property, **Creator** property, **Fill** property, **Interior** property, **Name** property, **Parent** property, **PictureType** property, **PictureUnit** property.

Methods

ClearFormats method.

Walls Property

Applies To

Chart object.

Description

Returns a **Walls** collection that represents the walls of the 3-D chart. Read-only.

Remarks

This property doesn't apply to 3-D pie charts.

Example

This example sets the color of the wall border of the chart to red. The example should be run on a 3-D chart.

```
myChart.Walls.Border.ColorIndex = 3
```

WallsAndGridlines2D Property

Applies To

Chart object.

Description

True if gridlines are drawn two-dimensionally on a 3-D chart. Read/write **Boolean**.

Example

This example causes Microsoft Graph to draw 2-D gridlines for the chart.

```
myChart.WallsAndGridlines2D = True
```

Weight Property

Applies To

Border object.

Description

Returns or sets the weight of the border. Can be one of the following **XlBorderWeight** constants: **xlHairline**, **xlThin**, **xlMedium**, or **xlThick**. Read/write **Long**.

Example

This example sets the border weight for the chart area.

```
myChart.ChartArea.Border.Weight = xlMedium
```

Width Property

Applies To

Application object, **Axis** object, **Chart** object, **ChartArea** object, **DataSheet** object, **Legend** object, **LegendEntry** object, **LegendKey** object, **PlotArea** object.

Description

Returns or sets an object's width, in points. Read/write **Long**, except as shown in the following table.

Remarks

The meaning of the **Width** property depends on the specified object.

Object	Description
Application	The distance from the left edge of the application window to the right edge of the application window.
Axis, **LegendEntry**, **LegendKey**	The width of the object. Read-only.
ChartArea, **Chart**, **DataSheet**, **Legend**, **PlotArea**	The width of the object.

On the Macintosh, `Application.Width` is always equal to the total width of the screen, in points. Setting this value to any other value has no effect.

In Windows, if the window is minimized, `Application.Width` is read-only and returns the width of the window icon.

See Also

Height property, **Left** property, **Top** property.

Example

This example sets the width of the chart.

```
myChart.Width = 360
```

WindowState Property

Applies To

Application object.

Description

Returns or sets the state of the window. Can be one of the following **XlWindowState** constants: **xlMaximized**, **xlMinimized**, or **xlNormal**. Read/write **Long**.

Example

This example maximizes the application window in Microsoft Graph for Windows. (This property cannot be set on the Macintosh.)

```
myChart.Application.WindowState = xlMaximized
```

XYGroups Method

Applies To

Chart object.

Description

On a 2-D chart, returns an object that represents either a single scatter chart group (a **ChartGroup** object, Syntax 1) or a collection of the scatter chart groups (a **ChartGroups** collection, Syntax 2).

Syntax 1

expression.**XYGroups(*Index*)**

Syntax 2

expression.**XYGroups**

expression Required. An expression that returns a **Chart** object.

Index Optional **Variant**. Specifies the chart group.

Example

This example sets X-Y group (scatter group) one to use a different color for each data marker. The example should be run on a 2-D chart.

```
myChart.XYGroups(1).VaryByCategories = True
```

Finish faster.

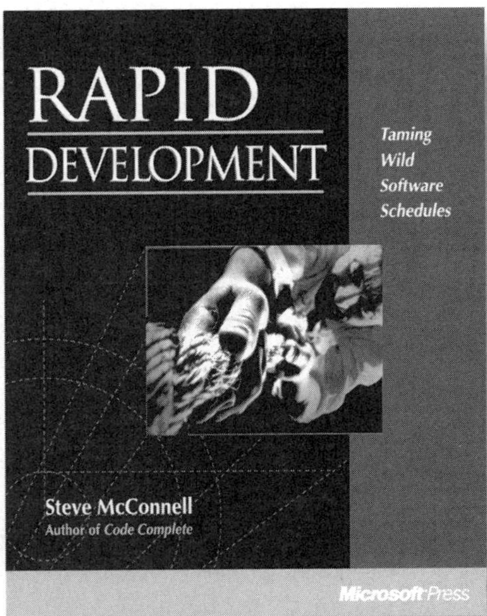

U.S.A.	**$35.00**
U.K.	£32.49
Canada	$46.95

ISBN 1-55615-900-5

"An indispensable road map for those who wish to write code as fast as humanly possible..."

— *G. Pascal Zachary, author of SHOWSTOPPER!: The Breakneck Race to Create Windows NT and the Next Generation at Microsoft*

In RAPID DEVELOPMENT, award-winning author Steve McConnell reveals the secrets to taming wild software schedules. He analyzes the development-speed implications of many traditional development practices, pointing out which are effective and which are harmful. The book alerts you to 36 classic mistakes—practices intended to shorten the development process that lengthen it instead. McConnell counters with 27 proven ways to shorten schedules and reduce the risk of schedule overruns. RAPID DEVELOPMENT has a hard-headed, practical focus—with the emphasis on suggestions you can use right away to finish your next development project faster.

Microsoft Press® products are available worldwide wherever quality computer books are sold. For more information, contact your book retailer, computer reseller, or local Microsoft Sales Office.

To locate your nearest source for Microsoft Press products, reach us at www.microsoft.com/mspress/, or call 1-800-MSPRESS in the U.S. (in Canada: 1-800-667-1115 or 416-293-8464).

To order Microsoft Press products, call 1-800-MSPRESS in the U.S. (in Canada: 1-800-667-1115 or 416-293-8464).

Microsoft® Press

Prices and availability dates are subject to change.